New Labour's Pasts

New Labour's Pasts

THE LABOUR PARTY AND ITS DISCONTENTS

James E. Cronin

Harlow, England • London • New York • Boston • San Francisco • Toronto
Sydney • Tokyo • Singapore • Hong Kong • Seoul • Taipei • New Delhi
Cape Town • Madrid • Mexico City • Amsterdam • Munich • Paris • Milan

PEARSON EDUCATION LIMITED

Edinburgh Gate
Harlow CM20 2JE
United Kingdom
Tel: +44 (0)1279 623623
Fax: +44 (0)1279 431059
Website: www.pearsoned.co.uk

_____

First edition published in Great Britain in 2004

© Pearson Education Limited 2004

ISBN 0 582 43827 6

British Library Cataloguing-in-Publication Data
A CIP catalogue record for this book can be obtained from the British Library

Library of Congress Cataloging-in-Publication Data
Cronin, James E.
    New Labour's pasts: the Labour Party and its discontents / James E. Cronin. – 1st ed.
        p. cm.
    Includes bibliographical references and index.
    ISBN 0–582–43827–6 (hardback)
    1. Labour Party (Great Britan) – History – 20th Century.   I. Title.

JN1129.L32C76 2004
324.24107–dc22

                                                           2003070662

10   9   8   7   6   5   4   3   2   1

Set by 35 in 9.5/14pt Melior
Printed in China
PPLC/01

The Publishers' policy is to use paper manufactured from sustainable forests.

Contents

Acknowledgements

Writing feels like a lonely pursuit, but it is in fact a very collaborative process. It involves a recurring dialogue with those who have written before, an active engagement with the sources, and a running argument with real or imagined critics. The product has an owner, responsible for its insights and its mistakes, but it is nonetheless a creation that emerges from recurring interactions and constant borrowings in the course of which considerable debts are incurred. The scale of my indebtedness, and to whom the debts are owed, should be clear from the notes that accompany this book.

But some debts require more explicit acknowledgement. It would have been impossible, for instance, to write this book without access to archival materials at the Public Record Office, now the National Archives. Equally essential for this project have been the records of the Labour Party's National Executive Committee and Research Department, which are reproduced in microfiche up through 1979 but available only at the Labour History Archive and Study Centre at Manchester for the years after. I am also in debt to the Bodleian Library at Oxford, where the papers of George Brown and Harold Wilson are available; to the Modern Records Centre at the University of Warwick, where the TUC General Council papers are kept; to the LSE Archive, home to the Crosland Papers and the Diaries of Samuel Brittan; and to Churchill College, Cambridge, where I consulted Neil Kinnock's papers. The material in Neil Kinnock's papers was especially valuable and I am particularly grateful to him for permission to consult and quote from this uniquely important source. Not all sources, of course, come from institutions: John Rentoul, for example, provided me with a copy of Blair's revealing Australia lecture of 1982. I have also profited immensely from interviews with selected leaders and activists whose experience in the Labour Party spanned the years of Labour's decline as well as the period of its renewal. These include

Stuart Holland, Tom (now Lord) Sawyer, Larry (now Lord) Whitty, Giles (now Lord) Radice, Martin Jacques, Anna Coote and Tony Benn. These more formal interviews were augmented by a wide range of conversations – with journalists like Polly Toynbee, with former officials like Liz Atkins, and with a wide sampling of party members and delegates whom I encountered at the Labour Party Annual Conference in Bournemouth in 2003. Special thanks to the friends and party officials who made that experience possible and so enjoyable.

There is nothing quite so helpful in clarifying one's thinking as being forced to make it intelligible to an informed audience. I am therefore particularly grateful for several opportunities to present the arguments developed in this book. Kay Lawson and Thomas Poguntke provided the first, with an invitation to participate in a workshop on parties sponsored by the European Consortium for Political Research (ECPR) held in Copenhagen in April 2000. The reactions of Patrick Seyd, Paul Webb and Paul Whiteley to what I had written were unusually helpful. Wm. Roger Louis kindly followed up with an invitation to talk to the Faculty Seminar on British Studies at the University of Texas. Mark Wickham-Jones deserves a very special thanks for arranging for me to discuss my ideas with colleagues and students at the University of Bristol in July 2002, first as Benjamin Meaker Professor and then at a meeting of the Labour Movements Group of the Political Studies Association. I found particularly helpful comments in these venues by Robert Taylor, Eric Shaw, Steve Ludlam, Rodney Lowe, Diane Hayter, Lawrence Black and, of course, Mark Wickham-Jones. John Davis and Michael Dintenfass performed a similar service at a seminar they organised at the University of Connecticut in November 2003. Two conferences in North Carolina – one at Chapel Hill in 2001, the other at Wake Forest in 2002 – were also important in the evolution of this book. The meetings were not devoted to New Labour or to British politics, but were focused on the 'varieties of capitalism' and the perhaps related varieties of welfare states, but they raised critical issues about the global economic context in which New Labour took shape and about the problems it was meant to address. I very much want to thank John Stephens and his colleagues at the University of North Carolina and Duke University and David Coates of Wake Forest for the opportunity to participate and to learn in these settings.

We work best, of course, in congenial institutions and when surrounded by helpful, but critical, colleagues. The Department of History at Boston College, ably chaired during this book's gestation by my friends Peter Weiler and Alan Rogers, was a constantly stimulating and often entertaining environment. A fellowship from the College of Arts and Sciences allowed precious time for research; and a series of small grants from the Graduate School facilitated research trips to archives in the UK. At Harvard University the Minda de Gunzburg Center for European Studies was host to a steady flow of seminars, conferences and visitors that never failed to educate and provoke. The Center sponsored two meetings that were especially important in getting this project going. On the day New Labour won its first general election, Alice Kelikian arranged a panel on which several of us debated the many merits of Donald Sassoon's important book, *A Hundred Years of Socialism*. The conjuncture was critical: we were discussing the long-term crisis of social democracy at a rare moment of triumph; and the effect was to stimulate arguments and hypotheses about the continuing possibilities of democratic socialism. The Center, urged on mainly by Stuart White, also organised a uniquely informative conference in November, 1998 on 'Labour in Government: the "Third Way" and the Future of Social Democracy,' bringing together scholars and policy-makers from Europe and the United States to discuss what seemed at the time the most exciting political phenomenon of the post-Cold War era. Again, the debate provoked all sorts of questions and a decision on my part that answering them would be extremely worthwhile. Serving as one of the organisers of the British Study Group at the Center was also unusually helpful, for it brought me into regular contact with scholars of British history and politics whose work has been consistently enlightening. I want to thank my successive co-chairs – Susan Pedersen, Robert Travers and Pippa Norris – and the Center's directors – Charles Maier, Peter Hall, George Ross and David Blackbourn — for helping to make this possible.

Individual colleagues were also extremely important in helping me along with this project. Larry Wolff was an inspiration throughout; so, too, if in a different way, was Paul Breines. Jim Shoch, Lou Ferleger and George Ross were great companions who taught me a great deal; and Richard Price gave the sage advice and encouragement that I have come to expect and need. Leads and suggestions came from a wide variety of colleagues, but I remember that John Thane, Ross McKibbin, Ewen Green, Desmond King, Joel Krieger, Jon Lawrence and Jon Schneer were unusually helpful. My editor, Heather McCallum, was a firm supporter and a thoughtful critic. A few dedicated souls read all or at least large parts of the book manuscript and made comments that proved essential to later revisions. I want to thank in particular David Coates, Lou Ferleger, Jim Obelkevich, Richard Price, Pat Thane, Mark Wickham-Jones and George Ross. Two other readers, equally helpful, must remain anonymous.

Personal debts are sometimes harder to specify, but we know how much they matter. Rebecca and Johanna expressed great faith in this project and cheered it on, if from a safe distance. My partner, Laura Frader, was less able to distance herself and so was compelled to listen to my earliest speculations and then to bear what I am sure were endless repetitions, disguised as refinements, with great patience. Nevertheless, she persisted and made extremely useful comments on what I had written; and she was a wonderful companion on this fairly protracted venture. I would like to be equally helpful to her, though her example will be difficult to match. But I shall try.

New Labour and its pasts

The very phrase 'New Labour' announces a dual ambition: to distance the present Labour Party from the record and image of its predecessors and simultaneously to capture what is useful in its legacy. The party clearly hopes that the label will allow it to inherit what remains of the constituencies of 'old Labour' by laying claim to Labour's achievements while also garnering the votes of those who do not identify either with the party's heritage or with the interests that it has aspired to represent. The ambition is not unique to New Labour. Parties rejected by voters have been forced repeatedly to reinvent themselves, to readjust their policies, programmes and appeals, and are regularly confronted with the difficult question of how much to innovate and how much of their party's inheritance to embrace. What makes the story of New Labour distinctive are the depths to which the party's fortunes sank before it began to rebuild; the initial response to its gathering crisis – a move to the left rather than a more predictable tacking towards the political centre; the intensity of the subsequent battle over the party's future; and the enormous success of the transformation from the 'old' to the new party. The renewal and rebranding of parties is a routine phenomenon in the advanced democracies; and the tendency for social-democratic parties to traverse a path from the left to the centre, or centre-left, is common as well. But Labour in Britain did it differently, with unusual twists and turns and an uncommon degree of internal conflict and bloodletting.[1] And this atypical process produced a party, and in short order a government, in which the balance was sharply skewed towards innovation and away from the past.

This break with the past is central to any understanding of New Labour. Its programme, for example, is at the very least a departure from the commitments of the party in the past and might even be regarded, at crucial points, as a direct repudiation; and it is consciously so. New Labour's style and structure – how it makes policy, how it deliberates, how it relates to its members, to the trade unions and to the public, how it deals with the press – have likewise been fashioned as the very antithesis of what had for so long been the norm. The party as an organisation has been restructured precisely in order to distinguish itself from the historic Labour Party and to ensure that the party operates in a fundamentally different manner both in office and in opposition. The rejection of old Labour is not just a matter of policy, but of what the party has become, of what it now stands for, how it works and who, quite literally, it is.

Why this stark contrast, this thorough rejection not only of past policies and governing styles, but also of the party's traditional political philosophy and rhetoric, its internal structure, ethos and procedures? Very simply, the rejection of the past has been so total and so comprehensive because those who remade the party had come to believe that no mere programmatic adjustment would suffice. Labour as a party has been defined as much by its culture as by its specific programme and as much by the unique institutional connections that structured its relationship to its key supporters as by the social location of that base. The policies and practices that characterised Labour, both when it was successful and when it was not, were not the products of tactics, whether clever or misguided, or of good or bad leadership, but of the party's identity as a political organisation. It was therefore inevitable that the effort to reshape the party would bump up against the very nature of the party. Those who undertook that effort, the self-defined 'modernisers', would thus discover very quickly that if they were to win the argument about policy and presentation, they would have to prevail within the organisation and alter the institutions and the culture of the party.

The first steps in 'modernising' Labour were not of course informed by such a grand ambition, but by rather more limited and mundane electoral concerns. Indeed, the simplest and most economical explanation for New Labour's antithetical relationship to its past is that the party's new leaders had come to believe that if the party were ever again to become 'electable', it needed to separate itself from the disastrously negative perceptions of the performance of previous Labour governments and of the controversial policies adopted in the 1970s and early 1980s. There can be no doubt, for example, that the desire to get elected was what set the entire process of 'modernising' Labour decisively in motion during Neil Kinnock's tenure as leader. Kinnock had vowed upon taking the reins of the party in 1983 to make it electable once again, and from that determination flowed efforts first to reshape the party's, and Kinnock's own, image and presentation, and to face down the left; later, after the defeat in 1987, a sustained campaign was undertaken to bring the party's programme more closely into line with what was perceived to be public opinion. Even after the ensuing Policy Review was completed, electoral considerations continued to inspire additional shifts, including the leadership's sustained effort to court business opinion and further to moderate its economic policies, and finally required Kinnock's own resignation after his efforts failed to produce victory in 1992. The desire to shed unwelcome past associations in order to reassure potential voters was equally at work in convincing Kinnock's successor, John Smith, to abolish the block vote and to diminish the unions' representation at conference and in the electoral college that selected the party leadership. A similar rationale attended the party's parallel efforts to limit its commitments on spending and taxation. The desperate need to recover the possibility of winning office was thus transparently the spur to the protracted process that gave birth to New Labour. It was also what brought together and sustained the shifting coalition of trade union leaders and politicians of the so-called 'soft left' that provided Kinnock with the support needed for the reshaping of the party.

Electoral calculations cannot fully explain the extent of Labour's transformation, however, nor the thoroughness, even ruthlessness, with which the task was pressed in the end. It was thus only in the later stages of refashioning the party, after Tony Blair's accession to the leadership in 1994, that the modernisers took to calling the party by a new name: New Labour. They decided as well to revise Clause IV, the historic commitment to nationalisation, and thereby to confront the most sacred icon and the central doctrine in the system of beliefs held dear by party members. And it was in this final act of updating that Blair, Gordon Brown and their allies began explicitly to confront and to recast the party's history and philosophy in a kind of *Kulturkampf* aimed at displacing the party's inherited political culture.

Why was it necessary to take on so directly the party's traditions, its doctrines and ethos, and also its organisational structure? There were alternatives. John Smith's supporters, for example, had proceeded on the very different assumption that, with a new leader in place and with the Tories beset by perceived failures, 'one more heave' might well have brought Labour into power, perhaps in coalition, and a second heave would mean a solid electoral victory. It would also have been possible, at least in theory, to couch a demand for novelty and reform in the more neutral language of social and economic change. So much had in fact changed since the party last held power in 1979 that Labour's leaders could have justified almost any revision, any deviation from prior belief, as merely responding to the evolving needs of Britain in a new, technologically advanced and increasingly globalised world. Instead, New Labour mounted a frontal assault on the party's traditions. In so doing the modernisers took considerable risks, for the decision to challenge the party's past would provide ammunition for its critics and enemies. New Labour's opponents on the left could easily use their critique of the party's legacy and outlook to claim that the party's leaders had abandoned its past and its principles in the vain pursuit of short-term electoral advantage.[2] On the Tory right, the criticism of Labour's past could be portrayed as confirmation of their long-standing attacks and afforded an opportunity to question the sincerity of Labour's supposed rethinking. Electoral success might, of course, blunt such charges, or delay their effectiveness, and success in government might render them ineffective over the long term, but it was a gamble to bet on achieving both. Nevertheless, that is precisely the gamble New Labour's leaders chose to take. Why? What had they to gain?

At a minimum they gained a rhetorical edge over their opponents within the party by portraying themselves as modern, their critics as backward-looking. To 'modernise' is transparently a good thing; to resist a sign of a stubborn and irrational attachment to tradition or an unhealthy reluctance to face reality.[3] To the extent that the modernisers could define the internal party battle in this way, they controlled the terms of the discussion about how Labour should respond to its deepening crisis. The definition was not uncontested, but on the whole it worked, in large

part because the alternatives to 'modernisation' were in fact either a continuation of the failed policies of the recent past, embodied most clearly
in the Callaghan government of the late 1970s, or the more vigorous prosecution of the programme of the left. But the Callaghan government had
been decisively repudiated in 1979 while the alternative proposed by the
left had been presented to voters in 1983 and forcefully rejected as well.
In recasting the recent history of the Labour Party as a struggle between
'modernisation' and the resistance to it, moreover, the advocates of the
new acquired a past of their own, in which their small band heroically,
and against great opposition, rescued the party from its self-destructive
impulses and from likely electoral oblivion. As New Labour supporters
like Philip Gould told the story, the party had begun a 'long death march'
sometime in the late 1960s and 1970s and the descent continued until the
mid-1980s, when the modernisers stepped in to save it.[4] Setting themselves up as prescient and lonely voices battling established orthodoxy
thus afforded New Labour a 'foundation myth' of its own.

Equally important, it would seem, was the security and the freedom of
action New Labour thought it would gain by banishing from the party
beliefs, commitments and expectations that could very well haunt them
while in office. Neil Kinnock had joked at one point about getting his
'betrayals in early'. Blair was far more aggressive in lecturing the party
against the tendency to charge betrayal on the part of its leaders. What
Kinnock and Blair – and perhaps Gordon Brown more than either –
understood was that Labour's ability to govern would be seriously constrained if it assumed power bound by an elaborate set of commitments
or by the need to answer quickly and directly to an army of followers
demanding more than the party could easily and rapidly deliver. The
Callaghan government, it was commonly agreed, had been largely
undone by its close friends and allies in the trade unions and the party,
and Labour's new leaders were desperate to avoid a repeat of that performance. The desire to escape the constraints of party on their behaviour
in government seems to have been especially attractive to the generation
represented by Blair and Brown, for while Kinnock seems mainly to have
wanted to taste victory, they wanted to win, to govern and then to win
again and again. Almost from the beginning the cohort that would
become New Labour aspired to be 'the natural party of government', as
Harold Wilson had once envisioned, and Blair and Brown at least were

bold enough to imagine that future at a moment when Labour had lost four successive general elections. Remaking the political culture of the Labour Party would in this view make it far easier to rule and therefore possible to be re-elected, because the party itself, inside and outside Parliament, would remain more loyal and supportive. The decision to fight a battle for the soul of the Labour Party, and to reject so much of its history, would also facilitate the restructuring of the party's organisation, with its over-representation of the trade union interest, with its recurring tendency to privilege the input of local activists whose left-wing views might embarrass the leadership, and with its belief that the 'movement' was bigger and more important than the party's representatives in Parliament, who were merely its agents, or even a Labour government.[5] Redefining the party's culture and institutions would make it possible to win power and, more important, to achieve long-term political ascendancy.

New Labour's leaders seem to have been encouraged to take on the party's past so directly by their formative experiences in the late 1970s and early 1980s and how they came to interpret these events. Politicians who came of age in that era, even those with origins and initial sympathies on the left, had witnessed a destructive clash between the left and the right of the party that left the whole much reduced and that discredited both sides in the debate. The rising generation also confronted in the Thatcher government a regime that sought utter political domination and whose practice gave meaning to increasingly fashionable notions of 'hegemony' and of 'hegemonic projects'. These terms first entered discussions of British politics from the left, as New Left thinkers sought to make use of the ideas of the Italian Marxist, Antonio Gramsci, to diagnose the problems of Labour in Britain and its inability to become truly 'hegemonic'. The usage took on new life with the rise of Margaret Thatcher, for she was the politician who came to embody, in her person and her highly ideological politics, a genuinely hegemonic project. The debate about Thatcherism made it obvious that ideas mattered and were essential to the establishment of political dominance; while the Thatcher governments provided a practical example of an unfolding project held together by certain broad goals and beliefs but informed at particular moments by a tactically sophisticated sense of the shifting structure of political opportunity that provided a unique purchase on what policies to emphasise, which battles to fight, and how gradually to remake the political terrain so as to win power over the long term. The phenomenon of Thatcherism could be, and undoubtedly was, an inspiration and a model, but it was presumably much harder for Labour Party veterans, whose hopes were shattered by her domination of British politics after 1979, fully to appreciate its lessons than it was for the generation that included Blair, Brown, Mandelson, Mowlam, Straw and the rest. If nothing else, New Labour would learn from Thatcher that for a government to make a difference it needed considerably longer than a single full term in office, something that had eluded all previous Labour governments.

New Labour, and others who studied the impact of Thatcher, also learned from her to think about politics differently and more broadly and to see politics in terms of ideas, assumptions and paradigms rather than merely policies and elections. Whether or not this sense of politics as a totality of goals, values and programmatic commitments is best labelled and understood as a 'project', it was nevertheless obvious from the late 1970s that parties did have encompassing beliefs and cultures within which specific policies and strategic emphases took shape and which provided the overall framework for policy and strategy. This understanding led to a more thorough examination and critique of Labour as a 'project'. For those trying to make sense of Labour and its history, the term 'Labourism' has proved particularly useful as a description of the 'project' and the package of ideas, attitudes and predispositions that has held it all together.[6] The word is perhaps a bit too vague, its meaning too broad; it also lacks sociological specificity and so misses the unique complex of social groupings that have at various moments coalesced behind Labour. More important, the term might well do Labour a disservice in depriving its vision of any greater ideological precision. That is also part of its attraction and usefulness, however, for it describes an ethos, a culture that to some extent transcends and conceptually precedes doctrines.[7] More specifically, the term 'Labourism' connotes a largely defensive posture, not only on the part of the party but also on the part of the working class that Labour seeks to represent; and such a posture has been manifestly a defining feature of Labour's long history.

What Labour is supposed to defend is not a diffuse working-class interest that the party itself gets to define, but rather a very concrete set of institutions, the most important of which are the trade unions.[8] The desire to defend and protect the role of the trade unions as institutions was what has made Labour instinctively 'corporatist' in orientation, if not always effectively so, and imparted a corporatist bias to its policies and approach to governance. 'Corporatism' in this context implies a view of politics in which organised – i.e. 'corporate' – interests are the key actors and in which effective governance means working with and through these organised interests and securing their input, if possible their acquiescence, in the making and implementation of policy. The close link to the trade unions, which is a precondition for corporatist policy-making, has of course also been the foundation of Labour's peculiar constitutional structure as a party. The unions have largely funded the party; union members have accounted for the bulk of the party membership – dwarfing the ranks of individual members; and trade union block votes have determined programme at the party's annual conference. Labour has therefore been constitutionally predisposed to practise such a politics. It seems not unreasonable to label the resulting political stance as 'Labourism' and to regard it as both genuinely distinctive and potentially valuable.[9]

Where the term Labourism is less useful is in its implication that the project it refers to was merely defensive and corporatist. It was in reality more than defensive: the party's political project was also socialist, at least from 1918 and the adoption of Clause IV. Arguments about the nature of the Labour Party have often counterposed Labourism to socialism as if they were distinct and rival perspectives, but the actual record of the party demonstrates instead a coexistence, an interaction, a compatibility that the debates about their theoretical incompatibility would simply not predict. For generations of Labour activists, and for key supporters, socialism was the end of Labourism, the distant goal whose achievement would be the ultimate defence of the working class.[10] There was no necessary and fundamental contradiction – at least in theory – between defending working-class institutions and the positions to which the working class had advanced to date, and proceeding to conquer new territory and ultimately to run society as a whole. Socialism, symbolised by Clause IV, was the big idea and also the 'organisational glue' that kept Labour together as an institution, uniting its competing interests, informing its appeal to solidarity and providing the party with an identity uniquely its own. Labourism as an outlook might begin as defence but its logic leads left, even if the party's leaders and managers have seldom allowed it to move very far or for very long in that direction.

Understanding Labour as a project, as simultaneously a Labourist and socialist project, has several implications. The first is that the factions and divisions within the party nevertheless shared a common set of assumptions and goals. They operated within the same broad intellectual framework that was basically hostile to capitalism and sceptical of its ability to generate sustained economic growth and social justice; they shared the same fundamental preference for collective solutions over market mechanisms and the same belief in collective provision over privately organised welfare.[11] They all believed as well in the sense of moral superiority and the inherent virtue that attached to the Labour Party because of the wide and deep interpenetration of the party and the institutions, and also the subculture, of the working class, or at least of the organised working class. Treasuring that linkage, even while occasionally acknowledging its costs and limitations, meant that left, right and centre in the party all bought into the idea that 'this great movement of ours' clearly went beyond the normal definition of a political party and gave to Labour a different imperative and a special *raison d'être*. It was not supposed to behave as other parties did and alter its policy in response to voter preferences, but was instead expected to remain true to its essential political identity. The left would take this logic still further during the 1970s and early 1980s and argue that the party in Parliament should defer to the party outside, whether in the form of unions or local activists, that it should mobilise and defend movements of direct action against the decisions of the government of the day, and that in its electoral behaviour it should seek to shape voter preferences rather than accommodate to the whims of a volatile and often ill-informed electorate. The Labour right was, of course, traditionally much more deferential to Parliament, but could never truly contemplate the abandonment of what was seen as special about the Labour Party. More practically, the right not only long depended on the block votes of moderate union leaders in order to keep control of the party, but its strategy for successive Labour governments was premised on the party's close relationship with the unions. Harold Wilson – an enigmatic politician who was neither firmly on the left nor the right wing of the party – made Labour's supposed ability to secure union cooperation in tripartite bargaining central to the government's programme for growth and industrial modernisation, and when inflation, inertia and incompetence threatened to wreck the strategy, he chose to lean on the unions in the effort to control strikes and wage increases. Even after the spectacular failure of that approach with the rejection of *In Place of Strife*, the party leadership reaffirmed its dependence on the unions by concluding the 'social contract' while in opposition. The very legitimacy of the Wilson/Callaghan governments of 1974–79 was based on the claim that Labour would govern in a partnership with the unions and thus avoid the conflict, and the impasse over economic policy, that marked the failed regime of Edward Heath.

But if left and right shared so much, if their existence was so symbiotic and mutually reinforcing, if they were a messy package that nevertheless hung together, then that very same interconnectedness dictated a similar fate when the project ran aground. Specifically, if the cumulative failures that overcame 'old Labour' were to be overcome in a New Labour project, the package needed to be rejected as a whole, not merely in parts. That belief would seem to be the basic inspiration behind the New Labour effort to confront, reject and to reimagine the party's past and, with it, the party's possible future. The essential premise of New Labour's break with the past is thus a particular take on the coherence and embeddedness of that past: a view that the left, the right and the centre within the Labour Party were more or less equally implicated in its failures, that the dilemmas of the party were insoluble in the terms of the left-right discourse within which party business was routinely conducted, and that the party as an institution – its political culture and its constitutional arrangements especially – was ultimately responsible for its failures in government and in opposition.

These assumptions have seldom been spelled out quite so explicitly, but they are not hard to discern within and beneath the rhetoric and the practice of New Labour. Tony Blair himself gave an early indication of this perspective in a lecture delivered in Australia in 1982, even before he was elected to Parliament.[12] His speech focused on the hard choices facing Labour and it was particularly notable for its refusal to align itself with either the right or the left of the party. However closely his later policies might suggest that Blair was the true and proper heir to the early Gaitskellite revisionists, in 1982 he spoke as if coming from the left or new left. He was particularly scathing in his critique of those of

Gaitskell's followers who had become the centre-right establishment of the party and who were now leaving to found a new party. He not only rejected the treachery of those who deserted Labour to form the Social Democrats, but also attacked their past role in the party and ridiculed their claim to be 'mould-breakers'. 'They are strange mould-breakers: Roy Jenkins, Shirley Williams, David Owen, Bill Rodgers. If anything,' Blair argued, 'they are the failed representatives of the old mould. They all held office in the last Labour government; and not merely did they hold office in it, they were, in a very real sense, its ideological lieutenants.' In the very next breath, however, Blair also separated himself from the left, speaking of the 'mixed economy' as if it were a viable compromise with a promising future and criticising the left for deluding itself over the meaning of the party's recent defeat at the hands of the Tories. The arguments of Tony Benn and his supporters to the effect 'that Labour lost the [1979] election by alienating its working-class support' and that it should therefore respond by more forthright support of industrial militancy and more left-wing policies simply 'cannot be sustained'. Blair also complained of the left's attitude to the party: 'The left's position is often inconsistent. It will advocate party democracy, yet refuse one member, one vote . . .' The left were particularly wrong in imagining that 'there is anything to be gained from capturing control of the Labour Party machine and leaving the voters behind'.

The Blair view was even at this point self-consciously 'modern'. Society had changed and so too had the Labour Party, but neither the left nor the right had come to terms with these new realities. Over the past half-century there had been 'an enormous sociological shift in the class composition of Britain', with growing affluence, increasing home owner-ship, a decline in old industries and manufacturing and a massive increase in the numbers working 'in service industries or the public sector'. As Blair saw it, Tony Crosland had been 'right in 1956 when he identified, in *The Future of Socialism*, major alterations in British society . . .'. Labour as a party had evolved as well: 'The party has changed irreversibly.' Its 'rank and file' had become increasingly white collar and university educated and more often employed in the public sector. They tended to belong not to the old industrial unions that had previously dominated the Trades Union Congress and the Labour Party, but to public sector unions with different political agendas. Many more were women, some were minorities. And they were also more left wing and carried into the party concerns for new 'social issues: nuclear disarmament, ecology, race relations, feminism'. It was with this 'new left' of largely middle-class origin that Blair seemed instinctively to identify; to him it was 'a genuine, if limited social movement' that might well be 'open to many criticisms' but that should not be dismissed. The main weakness, and it was not trivial, was that both this new party of local activists and the more established party of industrial unions, block votes and MPs centred at Westminster lacked a serious connection with the voters. 'The party must have a democratic relationship with the electorate . . .', Blair argued, and it did not yet have one. It had to listen to voters, who were not well represented in or by the party or in any of its institutions and for whom no major political faction spoke effectively. But it was unwilling or unprepared to do so.

This need to reconnect with voters therefore posed enormous challenges to both the left and the right of the party, for 'The Labour Party, left and right, is a prisoner of its history' and so unable to respond effectively to a changing society or a changing electorate. 'Both sides', Blair wrote, 'feel a need to represent themselves as the "true" Labour Party in an historical sense. In doing so, instead of using history to explain the present and point to the future, they chain themselves to the past.' Neither faction would be able to forge a lasting connection with the electorate unless it gave up cherished illusions and habits of thought. The right needed a whole new set of policies, and it had to recognise the new shape of the party. To refuse to reckon with the New Left and the new sociology of Labour as a party would be 'an error of enormous proportions' and it would preclude a proper reckoning with social change in the electorate. For its part, the left had to recognise the limits of its appeal and the necessity of broadening Labour's base of support and, as a prerequisite, it had to accept that voters largely did not share its outlook. It had in particular 'to correct the impression of the voters that it is indifferent, if not hostile, to their feelings'. That in turn demanded a greater degree of pragmatism and a greater willingness to compromise; and it would also require a new 'political philosophy', 'something more sensitive, more visionary, in a word more modern, than Marxism . . .'.

To the young Blair, then, neither of the two dominant traditions within the Labour Party had bequeathed a legacy that could be claimed without major excisions. Neither the Labour left nor the revisionist right had left a usable past, let alone a map to a better future. Blair's views were perhaps atypical. Although Blair might have shared a vaguely 'new left' background with many of his generation, his attachment to the left was obviously less firm and more fleeting than that of others who would join up with the New Labour project.[13] He was also unusually clear and unsentimental about his party's past, present and future at a very early date; and he was oddly both an obvious product of his time and at the same time more or less immune to many of its most powerful intellectual currents – e.g. the revival of Marxism. Blair's ally and rival Gordon Brown, for example, had a more radical youth, was more comfortable in the traditional Labour Party, and was more deeply influenced by Marxism. Yet Blair's response to the dire realities of the early 1980s was also paradigmatic: watching his party – in which he was beginning to carve out a career – decline precipitously, then consume itself in a civil war, he was moved to reject all of the major antagonists and insist on a new beginning, a new outlook, and a new strategy designed to win a new majority.

More than a decade later, Blair as party leader would repeatedly reiterate his sceptical stance towards the party's past and towards the myths of both the left and the right. Characteristically, he remained decidedly un-willing to embrace fully even the most celebrated moment in the party's mythic history. In a lecture commemorating the fiftieth anniversary of the Labour victory in 1945, for example, Blair began by offering ritual praise for the achievements of the Attlee government but proceeded to interpret its successes not as a triumph of Labour on its own but rather as the fulfilment of the potential of the radical, progressive coalition first adumbrated in the alliance between the nascent Labour Party and the 'New Liberalism' before 1914. By 1945, Blair argued, Labour's support had grown beyond its working-class roots and had come to embody 'the hopes of war-torn Britain better than the Tories'. Its 'vision chimed with the vision for which the British people had been fighting . . .' and not merely with the interests of workers and trade unions. Indeed, 'In 1945 Labour was the patriotic party . . .' And the ideas behind the Labour victory were not theirs alone. On the contrary, 'The ideas of Keynes and Beveridge were the cornerstone of reform . . .' and, as T.H. Marshall ex-plained, Labour was best understood as the latest instalment in the long march of citizenship and democracy. 'Democratic socialism', Blair claimed, was truly 'the political heir of the radical Liberal tradition: distinctive for its own roots, principles, priorities and practices, but with recognisable affinities when put next to its progressive Liberal cousin.'[14]

What was usable in Labour's past, then – according to Blair, Brown and the growing camp of modernisers they led – were not its programmes and policies and economic strategies but rather the party's enduring values and aspirations. Blair would argue, for example, that the party needed to be liberated 'from the terrible tyranny of confusing means and ends . . .' and should refocus on its goals.[15] The formulation is instructive: Labour's heritage is not just outdated, in need of refurbishing; it is rather a 'terrible tyranny'. 'Forget the past', he would tell the 1996 annual conference.[16] Equally significant in this new rhetoric was the way in which the embrace of Labour's rather vague ends – social justice, freedom, community – but none of the means by which previous generations tried to achieve them, had the effect, no doubt intended, of relegating virtually all of Labour's previous thinking and arguing and understanding of the world to the graveyard of failed programmes from which little or nothing can be salvaged. Labourism as a set of loyalties and a source of identity and socialism as a vision of a new social order were both spectres to be exorcised from the new Labour Party. The rejection of the past was thus central to New Labour's emerging identity. And the basic reason was the modernisers' firm belief that 'old Labour's' failures were endemic: they pervaded the entire party and its seemingly diverse and competing tendencies. Most important, the shared political culture that produced such failed policies and options was structurally rooted in the party's institutions and in its political identity.

How New Labour came to view the party it sought to lead so critically is the central question running through the story told here. The aim is neither to endorse nor to refute the insight upon which the Labour Party has been rebuilt and rethought, but to explain how its present came to be so antithetical to its past. What was it, for example, about the record of the Labour governments of the 1960s and 1970s that led the New Labour leadership to repudiate it with what seemed more passion than they attacked the record of the Tory governments of the 1980s and early 1990s? What convinced those who came to lead Labour as it entered the new millennium that the party's history – though marked by a steady rise, by numerous election victories and by lasting achievements in government – was so poisoned a legacy? What inspired the modernisers' determination to restructure the party itself so thoroughly that the organisation's role in making policy and programme would virtually disappear? If the effort to make Labour electable did not at first envision such dramatic transformation, then what was it about the task of making Labour 'modern' that rendered the process ultimately so complete? The progress recorded and reviewed in this study will show, in fact, that New Labour had become so new, so radically different from Labour's past, only in confrontation with that past and with the party that its history had left in place. It was in this sense itself a historical product, neither a choice nor an inevitability, but a result of the clash between what the Labour Party's past had made it and what its new leaders believed the party would have to become if it were to have a present and a future.

Notes and references

1 The Labour Party in Britain seems not to conform especially well to various theories of parties and party competition and would seem to occupy a rather unique place within the history of political parties, even of the left. Its practice has certainly not followed a Downsian model. For the classic argument, see Anthony Downs, *An Economic Theory of Democracy* (New York: Harper, 1957); and for recent reformulations, see Bernard Gronfman, ed., *Information, Participation and Choice: An Economic Theory of Democracy in Perspective* (Ann Arbor: University of Michigan, 1993); and also Hans-Dieter Klingemann, Richard Hofferbert and Ian Budge, *Parties, Policies and Democracies* (Boulder: Westview Press, 1994). Even theories crafted to explain the somewhat distinctive pattern of socialist or social-democratic parties – pioneered by Robert Michels but elaborated much further – do not seem especially apposite. The classic formulation is probably Otto Kirchheimer, 'The Transformation of the Western European Party Systems', in Joseph La Palombara and Myron Weiner, eds, *Political Parties and Political Development* (Princeton: Princeton University Press, 1966), 177–200. For a more formal version, see Adam Przeworski and John Sprague, *Paper Stones: A History of Electoral Socialism* (Chicago: University of Chicago Press, 1988). Still, the recent history of European social-democratic parties has in fact been marked by moves in roughly the same direction as that taken by New Labour. This suggests that all centre-left parties confront conditions that require a certain updating and adaptation, especially since 1989. See, for example, Herbert Kitschelt, *The*

Transformation of European Social Democracy (Cambridge: Cambridge University Press, 1994); Thomas Koelble, *The Left Unravelled: Social Democracy and the New Left Challenge in Britain and West Germany* (Durham, NC: Duke University Press, 1991); Donald Sassoon, *One Hundred Years of Socialism* (New York: The New Press, 1997); Geoffrey Garrett, *Partisan Politics in the Global Economy* (Cambridge: Cambridge University Press, 1998); and Gerassimos Moschonas, *In the Name of Social Democracy: The Great Transformation: 1945 to the Present*, translated by Gregory Elliott (London: Verso, 2002) and Ilaria Favretto, *The Long Search for the Third Way: The British Labour Party and the Italian Left since 1950* (London: Palgrave, 2003). For divergent perspectives that are less convinced of the imperative of adaptation, see Colin Hay, 'Globalization, social democracy, and the persistence of partisan politics: A commentary on Garrett', *Review of International Political Economy*, VII, 1 (2000), 138–52; and also Joel Krieger, *British Politics in the Global Age: Can Social Democracy Survive?* (New York: Oxford University Press, 1999). Steven Fielding and David Coates have each made useful efforts to relate some of these broader frameworks to the history and current politics of the British Labour Party. See Fielding, *The Labour Party: Continuity and Change in the Making of 'New' Labour* (New York: Palgrave, 2003), esp. chapter 5; and Coates, 'Capitalist models and social democracy: the case of New Labour', *British Journal of Politics and International Relations*, III, 3 (2001).

2 See Jon Lawrence, 'Labour – The Myths It Has Lived By', 340–66, and Steven Fielding, 'New Labour and the Past', 367–92, in Duncan Tanner, Pat Thane and Nick Tiratsoo, eds, *Labour's First Century* (Cambridge: Cambridge University Press, 2000).

3 The term 'moderniser' – and related terms like modernising, modernisation and simply modern – will recur throughout this book, sometimes with and often without quotation marks. Of course, the term is loaded and its use tendentious and it is obvious that those who declared themselves 'modernisers' wanted not merely change, but change in a particular direction. Deploying these terms with or without quotes should not be taken to denote acceptance of the modernisers' claims about themselves or their opponents. It is a style choice, not an interpretive point.

4 Philip Gould, *The Unfinished Revolution: How the Modernisers Saved the Labour Party* (London: Little, Brown, 1998), 35. See also Peter Mandelson and Roger Liddle, *The Blair Revolution* (London: Faber & Faber, 1996).

5 See Peter Mair, 'Partyless democracy: Solving the paradox of New Labour', *New Left Review*, 2 (March–April 2000), and Ross McKibbin's response, 'Treading water?', *New Left Review*, 4 (July–August 2000), 69–74, who disagree about the coherence of New Labour's constitutional reforms but

agree that a central objective of the leadership is to prevent the party from behaving as it did in the 1970s and 1980s; see also Patrick Seyd and Paul Whiteley, *New Labour's Grass Roots: The Transformation of the Labour Party Membership* (New York: Palgrave, 2002).

6 See John Saville, 'The Ideology of Labourism', in Robert Benewick, R.N. Berki and Bhiku Parekh, eds, *Knowledge and Belief in Politics – The Problem of Ideology* (London: Allen & Unwin, 1973). See also Andrew Thorpe, *A History of the Labour Party*, 2nd edition (London: Palgrave, 2001), especially 11–12; and, more generally, Andrew Davies, *To Build a New Jerusalem: The British Labour Party from Keir Hardie to Tony Blair* (London: Abacus, 1996).

7 H.M. Drucker, *Doctrine and Ethos in the Labour Party* (London: Allen & Unwin, 1979). It is perhaps worth noting Drucker's connection with the young Gordon Brown. Drucker was his mentor, Brown his spectacularly eager student. Brown apparently commented on Drucker's manuscript and would seem to have learned a great deal from it.

8 However fluid the language of class and of 'Labour' over the long sweep of modern British history, it would seem that by the post-war era Labour as a concept and as a political force was deeply embedded and firmly rooted in institutions and in distinctive patterns of social life. For a rendering of Labour's past that stresses the distance between language and its social referents, see Gareth Stedman Jones, *Languages of Class: Studies in English working class history, 1832–1982* (Cambridge: Cambridge University Press, 1983).

9 David Marquand suggests, in fact, that 'In world terms Labourism is the exception . . . not the rule'. See Marquand, *The Progressive Dilemma: From Lloyd George to Blair*, 2nd edn (London: Phoenix, 1999), 17.

10 Drucker, *Doctrine and Ethos in the Labour Party*, 41.

11 On Labour's historic antipathy to markets, see Jim Tomlinson, 'The limits of Tawney's Ethical Socialism: A historical perspective on the Labour Party and the market', *Contemporary British History*, XVI, 4 (Winter 2002), 1–16.

12 Tony Blair's Australian lecture was written up at the end of 1982. It was first delivered in August at Murdoch University in Perth. I want to thank John Rentoul for providing me with a copy of this important text. The most useful discussion to date is, appropriately enough, contained in John Rentoul, *Tony Blair: Prime Minister* (London: Little, Brown, 2001), 69–78.

13 See Ross McKibbin, 'How to put the politics back into New Labour', *London Review of Books*, 7 August 2003, on the 'soft left' origins of New Labour. Rentoul (70–5) would disagree about Blair himself, whom he would locate on the 'soft right'. There was real confusion about where Blair belonged in the early 1980s, surely an accurate reflection of the man and his politics.

14 Tony Blair, 'The Radical Coalition' (1995), in Blair, *New Britain: My Vision of a Young Country* (London: Fourth Estate, 1996), 8–13.

15 Blair, *New Britain*, xii.

16 The phrase was typically used in tandem with the notion of the Labour Party serving as 'the political arm' of the labour movement. Quoted in Steve Ludlam, 'Norms and Blocks: Trade Unions and the Labour Party since 1964', in Brian Brivati and Richard Heffernan, eds, *The Labour Party: A Centenary History* (London: Macmillan, 2000), 236.

CHAPTER 1

· · · · · · · · · · · · · · · · ·

The burden of
Labour's legacy

Labour was never just a political party. It was a movement, a way of thinking and feeling, and an intense set of loyalties and antipathies. Its evolution therefore refused to obey the logic of a mere political party and the party acted, at least on occasion, as if the winning and holding of office was a distinctly secondary, perhaps even unworthy, objective. Again and again it did not behave as other parties, which typically renew themselves in response to shifting social and economic realities, to electoral defeats or to the regular succession of one generation of leaders by another. For much of its history, by contrast, the British Labour Party proved fiercely resistant to critique and renewal. This has been particularly the case when criticism was deemed to come from those hostile to the unions and when new policies were regarded as pulling the party towards the centre, away from socialism and away from its roots and attachments in the working class. Its inertia was especially marked in the post-war period: during its 13 years of opposition from 1951 to 1964, for example, the party responded with very little in the way of new thinking, new policy or even new rhetoric. This prolonged era of stasis would establish a pattern that ensured that future innovation, if and when it came, would have to be drastic and thoroughgoing, and that it would necessarily entail a decisive break with the party's past. The 'new' in 'New Labour' was to this extent an inevitable product of what went before, or rather, of what did not happen before.

The party's reluctance to embrace the new during the 1950s and early 1960s was deeply embedded in its unique past and anchored in its unusual structure, but it was reinforced by the circumstances in which Labour found itself in opposition. Most important was the powerful legacy of achievement bequeathed to the party by the governments of 1945–51. By almost any standard, the Attlee governments were a resounding success. Labour had been elected in 1945 on a series of pledges that were fulfilled almost to the letter. The party promised to create a genuine welfare state by reorganising existing social services, by adding programmes for those previously left out, and by the establishment of the National Health Service. All this they did. The party also promised to implement policies that would maintain a 'high and stable' level of employment. This, too, came to pass, even if it is difficult to know precisely whom, or what, to credit for the achievement. The party also committed itself to keeping in place a variety of policies – in terms of taxation, price controls, controls over land and rents, regional policy – aimed at making Britain a fairer and more egalitarian society. These promises were also kept, even at the cost of some popular resentment and loud opposition from the Tories, from business and from the self-appointed spokesmen of the middle classes.

Not only did Labour deliver on its promises. The Labour governments of 1945–51 also presided successfully over a difficult transition from war to peace and proved beyond doubt the party's capacity to govern. There were bad moments, of course: the fuel and exchange crises of 1947 were the worst; and the devaluation of the pound in 1949 was a wise move that nonetheless was often portrayed as a failure. And there were divisions and unseemly squabbles as well: over NHS charges, over foreign policy and over rearmament. But for the most part, Labour governed in a reasonably unified fashion over a recovering Britain in which things were steadily and visibly improving. The Attlee governments thus left a record of which the party could be justly proud and around which there quickly grew up a memory that undoubtedly exaggerated the successes, minimised the weaknesses, and put a retrospective shine on activities whose lustre might well not have elicited praise from contemporary observers. Historians have understandably sought to right the balance and to restore the nuances to the picture of Labour's achievement, but it remains the case that at the core of the heroic memory was a solid set of accomplishments.[1]

Electoral defeat of 1951 was thus not interpreted as a sign of any fundamental problem in Labour's programme or practice. After all, the party won the popular vote and there was no evidence that the Tory victory augured a prolonged absence from government. That victory itself was won on terms that seemed to confirm the beliefs of many in the Labour Party that their victories had a permanent, or semi-permanent, status. The Conservatives did not question the commitment to full employment or the need to maintain the welfare state. They promised to relax controls and to free up the market, to push back the frontier of nationalisation, and to build more houses. But they did not campaign on a plan to reverse what Labour had done or to return to the policies of the 1930s. 'Consensus' is clearly too strong a word to describe the convergence of opinion in the early 1950s, but there was sufficient common ground for Labour to think that its legacy was not in any way in jeopardy.

Labour not only won the popular vote in 1951, but in doing so consolidated its base of support within the working class. The Labour Party was never merely a class party. It always needed middle-class votes to win. Nor, conversely, could the Conservatives prevail at the polls without significant working-class support. But over the life of the Labour governments of 1945–51, class loyalties had actually become firmer and more unambiguous; in the elections of 1951, therefore, Labour relied largely upon working-class support and probably received a higher share of working-class votes than ever before or since in its history. The Conservatives had likewise by 1951 recaptured many of those middle-class voters who had been moved to vote Labour in 1945 by an enthusiasm for reconstruction but who became increasingly restive in the later years of Labour rule. Class and party therefore fitted together especially closely in the early 1950s and Labour had little reason to doubt that it could rely on continued electoral support from workers and their families.

The prospect of enduring class loyalty meant that Labour's base was secure and that the party could contemplate a period in opposition confident in the assumption that the electoral tide would turn and, in the not too distant future, carry the party back into office. In power once more, it was assumed that Labour would press on with its agenda of social transformation with renewed enthusiasm and with a leadership tested, and now also rested, and ready to get on with the business of running the country. There were worries, of course: the factional strife that marked the last years of the Labour government needed to be overcome, the party would have to confront the problem of succession as an older generation left the scene, and there were genuine questions of policy that had to be resolved. But the problems were all manageable, or so it seemed, and the party itself seemed to stand on very solid foundations.

What were those foundations? Put very simply, Labour was the party of the working class and had as its aim the representation of working-class interests in British politics. But behind this clear formula and simple identity was much complexity: the working class itself was a historical construct, not a fact of nature or a sociological given; and the connections that linked the party and its supporters were forged over time out of particular experiences, needs and understandings. Both the nature of the class Labour sought to serve and the character of the linkages require interrogation.

The very phrase, 'working class', implies a common condition and shared interests among people who may in fact not see themselves as part of anything larger than their family or community. Nevertheless, a distinctive feature of social life in modern Britain has been the way in which all sorts of institutions – from the schools to the churches to the factory to the pub – and all variety of customs have conspired to create a sense of class and to reproduce it over generations. Despite the raw facts of social mobility and the evident diversity of local, working-class cultures, the replication of inequities from one setting to another, from one place to another, and in various spheres of life, regularly convinced most people in Britain that they lived in a class society. And thinking so, they acted so; and thus routinely defined their interests as distinct, and also as opposed. A signal consequence was a powerful tendency to organise: to establish institutions that informally reflected, and further embedded, social divisions while formally serving all sorts of more specific and practical purposes. Among working people these would include clubs and churches, friendly societies and, most important, trade unions. Reinforcing, perhaps also underpinning, this rich but class-infused, associational life were distinctive working-class cultures, ways of talking and playing and courting and saving and spending, with styles that varied locally and regionally but that were consistently different from the styles and behaviours of their 'betters'.[2]

The working class that Labour sought to represent was thus neither incoherent nor homogeneous. It was structured and organised internally, prior to and independent of its affiliation to any party. The connection to Labour, then, was mediated and indirect. The most visible linkage was through the trade unions, whose rights the original Labour Representation Committee was founded explicitly to defend. Indeed, prior to 1914 the party's growth was registered more accurately by the increasing affiliation of trade unions than by the rise in its voting strength. When the party's constitution was drafted in 1918, the unions were accorded a privileged position and it was subsequently the preferences of union leaders that largely determined party policy. The unions were not the only institutions formally represented in the party: there was also a place for the cooperative societies and, more significantly, for socialist societies like the Fabians, the Independent Labour Party and the Social Democratic Federation – organisations that often served as training grounds for future leaders and as sources of ideas and policies. And it was possible to belong to the party directly by joining a local, constituency party. But effective control was in the hands of the leaders of the largest unions, whose views were magnified many times over by their ability to cast 'block votes' on behalf of their membership.

The role accorded to the unions was for obvious reasons not given to the less formal social organisations that so marked working-class life in Britain, but it would seem that a diffuse class awareness and allegiance to the Labour Party permeated this dense network. The effect was often to naturalise support for Labour, to make it reflexive and customary rather than a matter for debate and choice. The attachment, though by no means universal, was nevertheless largely a matter of culture and disposition rather than ideology, a reflection of sentiment more than conviction, and it was wrapped in a rhetoric meant to inspire, to reassure and when necessary to obscure rather than to convince.[3]

Labour attached itself therefore to a working class that was already structured and organised within itself and the party became thoroughly imbricated with those pre-existing patterns. The associations that filled up and structured the more public spheres of working-class life were largely the preserve of adult men, with women engaged in more informal networks and young people consorting with each other before settling into the routines of the community. But the boundaries were often blurred, divisions more a matter of taste, temperament and locale than of exclusion, and the ethos largely collective. No doubt a facilitating factor was the absence of sharp and enduring cleavages of religion or ethnicity, but even where these existed and mattered, the highly local character of working-class cultures dampened the broader and poten-tially fragmenting impact for Labour on a national basis. Although Labour as a party would inevitably conform to the shapes, divisions, prejudices and exclusions embodied in the class it sought to represent, the net effect was nonetheless a broad sense of class awareness and political loyalty.

Both the unions and the party, for example, were more eager and effective spokesmen for the skilled than the unskilled and for those in powerfully organised industries than for those in unskilled, unorganised employment. They tended likewise to identify spontaneously and intuit-ively with the interests of male workers and to regard the interests of female workers, or working-class women more generally, as less pressing, or to subsume them under the needs of the family headed by a male breadwinner. Nevertheless, the differences that fragmented working-class existence in Britain were fluid and inconsistent and they were often overcome by the recognition that ordinary men and women shared a common fate, a common exclusion from the world of the middle and upper classes, and a common set of vulnerabilities. Perhaps more important, the predisposition to organise was pervasive and it was never regarded as the province of a distinct and privileged section of the working class. Indeed, the assumption within the world of labour was that trade unions were good for all workers and that, if possible, all workers should join. Unions were active, therefore, throughout the eco-nomy and enrolled the unskilled as well as the skilled and semi-skilled, and rather large numbers of women were also organised. The preference for organisation was so widely accepted, among working people but also on the part of the state, that it was considered the natural condition of relations at work. Thus when and where it proved difficult to establish stable unions and employers' associations, as in the so-called sweated trades, the government stepped in with formal, legal provision for setting wages and conditions through the Trade Boards. But such action was always considered a departure from the norm and less effective than setting wages and conditions through collective bargaining.

Even if employers were frequently reluctant to acquiesce to the role of trade unions and to abandon what they saw as their rightful managerial prerogatives, and even if it took a very long time for the reach of union organisation to approximate the aspirations of its advocates, the principle that everyone should be represented by a trade union became deeply entrenched in working-class life, in industrial relations and ultimately in politics as well. In its uneven progress, the growth of the unions paralleled, and was reinforced by, the waxing and waning of the Labour Party as an electoral force. The weakness of the unions during the inter-war era, especially after the defeat of the General Strike in 1926, was matched by the inability of the party even to come close to winning a parliamentary majority. Labour's participation in the wartime coalition inevitably marked a decisive breakthrough on both fronts. The party was finally brought within the political mainstream and it was rewarded with a pre-eminent role in running the home front, a position Labour used to encourage unionisation. The power of the state was now deployed to sponsor organisation both by workers and employers and to insist that employers bargain in good faith. The process was taken further after the war: with the coming to power of the first majority Labour government in 1945, the unions became virtual partners in government and used their new-found access to insert themselves widely into the apparatus of policy-making and consultation. In turn, the unions used their clout with ordinary workers to secure support for the party's aims in government, particularly the effort to control prices and wages. The link between Labour and the unions was thus very firmly established, and understood as a critical resource for a Labour government, by the early 1950s.

The working class upon which Labour relied was thus a very solid, rooted and well-organised social force whose political preferences, once registered, would be diffused, replicated and passed down through generations. Resting on such a stable foundation, however, Labour as a party was not very amenable to change, and a tendency to stasis was a corollary of the party's very strength and identity. And the fact that the stability of working-class life and organisation was achieved in opposition to the insecurities of daily existence meant that it was highly prized and vigorously defended, and what might be criticised from without or in hindsight as stasis or complacency appeared from within and at the moment as loyalty and pride.

Loyalty was indeed central to the ethos of the Labour Party at mid-century and had served the party especially well during difficult moments between the wars. The lore of the party was replete with stories of manifest disloyalty that were regularly held up as examplars of what not to do and of how not to behave. The most compelling case was the defection of the leadership in 1931, when Ramsay MacDonald, Philip Snowden and J.H. Thomas broke with the rest of the Cabinet to join with the opposition in the 'National Government'. Whatever the circumstances behind the split, it was a history that could easily be told using the familiar class-inflected discourse of the labour movement. The former leaders were guilty of political treason and of disloyalty to their class. They were 'class traitors' whose desertion followed a familiar trajectory and confirmed a reading of British politics and society as a story of class allegiances, antagonisms, triumphs, defeats and (worst of all) betrayals.[4]

Attachments, loyalties, customary allegiances, cultures and values shared and passed on, a collectivist ethos – these are the terms that seem best to describe the connection between Labour and its working-class base. What, then, the role of ideas, of formal beliefs or ideology?[5] Labour's big idea was of course socialism, but socialism as interpreted through 'a marked anti-doctrinal and anti-theoretical bias'.[6] The key statement was Clause IV in the party constitution of 1918 in which Labour committed itself:

> To secure for the workers by hand or by brain the full fruits of their
> industry, and the most equitable distribution thereof that may be
> possible, upon the basis of the common ownership of the means of
> production, distribution and exchange, and the best obtainable system
> of popular administration and control of each industry and service.

Almost inevitably, socialism merged with planning in a vision of state ownership and direction over the economy, although interminable debate attended the discussion of what both would mean in practice.

But both socialism and planning also would be defined in a manner consistent with the party's institutional character and its unique connection to its constituents. The settled and stable nature of the working-class base from which Labour drew its strength imposed as a first duty on the party the defence of that class, its organisations and way of life. The party's defensive, Labourist stance ensured that the party's objectives combined distinct and different goals – some linked to a Labourist perspective and others derived from a more distinctly socialist view; and there have been inevitable tensions, choices and shifts of emphasis. What is not clear is whether this has been a productive combination or whether it has been a distraction, a constraint, and hence a source of weakness and incoherence. It is often implied that Labourism is a less lofty vision than socialism and that the party's Labourist orientation diminished the commitment to socialism. But the implication should perhaps be queried as a matter of strategy and as a matter of history: is the struggle to get working-class interests recognised and legitimised in a hostile society somehow lacking and unworthy? Is a commitment to doctrine superior to what might be called a 'preferential option' for the workers? Or is the projection of a working-class presence into the polity and the battle to protect working-class institutions such as trade unions a necessary function for any party that seeks the support of working people? Do Labourism and socialism have to be in competition, or can they be mutually reinforcing? More important, does the commitment to what might be considered the more modest programme of Labourism weaken the commitment to a grander design for remaking society or provide an important grounding for the more ambitious socialist project?

In practice, Labour in power did undoubtedly give the protection of existing working-class interests top priority. Nevertheless, the very same leaders and governments also undertook quite ambitious schemes of structural change. The Labour governments of 1945–51, for example, were eager to put in place a whole series of measures to make the lives of ordinary people more stable and secure – basically, the package of reforms known as the welfare state – but they also took large chunks of British industry into public ownership and were prepared, if returned to office, to do more. Critics have often taken note of the moderation of Labour's leaders and the resolve to move forward by constitutional or parliamentary means and suggested that their caution indicated a lack of commitment to the goal of socialism.[7] If by socialism is understood only a revolutionary break with capitalism and the rapid assertion of state control over the economy, then few Labour leaders would qualify as proper adherents. Cautious tactics, however, may mean very little about ultimate objectives, and those criticised for moving too slowly would undoubtedly counter, as they often did, that theirs was the only effective strategy that could transform a democratic capitalist state into a democratic socialist society.

The most regular source of such criticism in the post-war era was the so-called 'Labour Left', who repeatedly suggested that the party's leaders were lukewarm about socialism and too ready to compromise. But the Labour Left was itself a curious phenomenon, ever ready to criticise but unwilling or unable to offer a compelling and genuinely alternative vision for achieving socialism.[8] The very name they chose to mark their movement in the 1940s, 'Keep Left', was indicative of their symbiotic relation to the supposed 'right' within the party: the aim was to put pressure on the leaders, to exert a counterweight to the pull towards the centre that the exercise of power exerted, and to act as the conscience of the party and remind it of first principles. But a genuine break, a fundamental alternative, was seldom contemplated; and hence, too, the recurring phenomenon of spokesmen of the Labour Left moving in and out of the leadership and the Shadow Cabinet, tacking to the centre and then back again, but seldom constituting a consistent dissenting pole around which to organise a distinct and compelling strategy.

The Labour Left confronted three more specific problems and liabilities that limited its effectiveness. First, for much of the party's history the left was largely the preserve of middle-class intellectuals and enjoyed little support from the trade unions or their leaders, whose class resentments allied with their accustomed sense of loyalty to deprive the left of significant working-class support. In fact, it was the reassertion of union control of the party in the aftermath of the 1931 debacle that began the institutional marginalisation of the left; and it was the trade unions' continued control that prevented any move towards a 'popular front' during the 1930s and ensured the expulsion of Stafford Cripps and Aneurin Bevan in 1939.[9] During the 1940s and 1950s it was the block vote of the big trade unions that consistently overwhelmed the more left-wing preferences of constituency activists and kept the right in power in the party and allowed the leadership to prevail at conference.[10] Nye Bevan would denounce this arrangement as a 'travesty of democracy': as he explained to *Tribune* readers in October 1955, 'The concentration of power in a few hands is always bad, and even if the political policies of the general unions were progressive, their ascendancy within the Labour Party would not be justified.'[11] Bevan would in fact base his 1954 and 1955 campaigns for party treasurer on a pledge to undo Labour's constitutional settlement in order to break the 'stranglehold of bureaucracy' on the party and free it to resume progress towards socialism.[12]

Not only was the Labour Left often at odds with the unions, however. It was also, perhaps inevitably given the shortage of trade union allies, regularly seen to be allied with the wrong people and so smeared for associating with real or alleged communists. The charge seemed confirmed on a different level, if again unfairly, by the left's inclination towards pacifism and later, in the Cold War era, neutralism, a stance not shared by a party leadership keen to demonstrate that the nation's fate was secure in its hands. Even more important, however, was the difficulty that the Labour Left faced in making its principal charge against the leadership – that it was not seriously interested in socialism – actually stick to its opponents. Again and again the party's moderate leaders reaffirmed their commitments to socialism, to nationalisation, to social spending and to high taxation, even at the cost of electoral viability. Whatever the failings of the party's leadership, whatever their practical omissions and compromises while in office and however pronounced their tactical moderation, they did not lack for real commitment to the party's goals. Socialism was in this sense a genuine part of the culture of the Labour Party rather than a mere graft onto a movement better understood as 'Labourist'. It was, of course, a variety of socialism that privileged the institutions of the organised working class in its detailed programmes and policies. The content of the socialist commitment thus precluded initiatives that would threaten what existed and what had already been achieved in favour of what might become. But the embedded character of Labour's vision did not vitiate the commitment to achieving it.

The nature and meaning of Labour's socialism also, and necessarily, developed over time and in response to shifting contexts and the challenges faced by the party and its supporters. When Labour first proclaimed itself a socialist party in 1918, its socialist identity was compatible with a wide variety of beliefs about what shape the new society would take and about what policies should be pursued in the short and the long run. For many, the concept of socialism was understood as a particular ethic more than as a model of economy and society; and for very few was it linked to the notion of a revolutionary break. Socialism did, or would, entail a necessary departure from, and a repudiation of, the norms of capitalist society, however, and with its characteristic values of competition and individual advance. The Labour Party thus consistently manifested an antipathy to business and business culture and exhibited a concern for community over the firm or the entrepreneur.

The broader ambivalence about business and industry within British culture was to this extent fully shared by Labour and might well have reinforced the party's partisan preferences.[13] It also meant that the party would participate in a genuine dialogue with other 'progressives' and reformers who shared its antipathy towards business and the market.[14] Labour's programme before 1918, for example, was not easily distinguished from the goals of the more advanced of the 'New Liberals'. Even after 1918 the Liberal Party, or sections of it, offered what could be regarded as more radical proposals than Labour, which tended between the wars to combine a distinctly alternative vision of a new society with a set of very modest and practical policy proposals. The Liberals, for example, were much more daring in their advocacy of government measures to combat unemployment and they were less afraid to break with the fiscal orthodoxies that dominated the thinking of Treasury officials and of most economists. The Liberal rejection of laissez-faire and its replacement with a more communitarian rhetoric was yet another indication that Labour and the Liberals shared a common philosophical grounding upon which they built their separate programmes and appeals. But however much was shared, what made Labour genuinely distinctive was the character of its link with the institutional life of the working class. The party's Labourist inclinations, then, were a reflection of what made Labour different and what in the long run allowed it to emerge as the dominant opposition to Conservatism in British politics.

Labour's socialism also gradually took on a more defined shape and became embodied in a distinctive set of preferred policies. Of particular importance was the role of the state.[15] In its early years Labour was far from being enamoured of the state or of collectivist solutions to economic and social problems. Within the party there was significant support for local, municipal initiatives and for models of production and distribution based on cooperation rather than state ownership and control. And there was widespread distrust of the existing state. The very founding of the party was a response to the infringement by the state, the courts in particular, of what were seen as the essential rights of trade unions; and that infringement confirmed a long-standing resentment of the state's intrusion into the affairs of the unions. Working people were also attached to a variety of institutions, like friendly societies, that zealously guarded their independence from the state and feared entanglement with government and the dependent status that might produce. This early ambivalence was further complicated by the experience of labour during the First World War. To some, the tremendous feats of organisation undertaken by the state during wartime provided a convincing demonstration of the state's ability to control the economy and to reshape society along more egalitarian lines. But to others the wartime state was a fearsome thing that elicited strong resistance: government control of the labour market was particularly threatening to the independence of trade unions and understandably the unions insisted at war's end on the restoration of pre-war practices. Antipathy to the enlarged state also spurred interest in theories of workers' control and guild socialism. Even as Labour formally chose to opt for socialism and public ownership, therefore, questions about the state remained unresolved.

Labour slowly came around to a more statist vision between the wars, though the conversion was largely indirect. The state did little to endear itself to working people, to the unions or to Labour supporters and more often appeared as alien, indifferent or even hostile. It was run, most often, by Conservatives ruling directly or, for much of the 1930s, through the National Government. Dominated by Labour's political enemies, the British state generally followed economic policies that favoured capital over labour and fiscal responsibility over the maintenance of employment and that tolerated the emergence of mass unemployment. Aided by a labour marked skewed in favour of employers, the state presided over a decisive weakening in the influence of trade unions between the wars and it directly confronted and defeated union power in the General Strike of 1926. During the Depression, moreover, the state strongly resisted efforts to reflate and chose to preside over a gradual, to some imperceptible, recovery rather than to jeopardise the finances of the state or the stability of the pound. Keynes may have won the debate about the need to stimulate demand with the publication of *The General Theory* in 1935, but the Conservatives who dominated the government and the Treasury which oversaw policy-making ruled out measures that might have generated an economic revival. The feeling that civil servants conspired with the bankers to bring down the Labour government in 1931 served further to increase Labour's antipathy to the existing state. In its aftermath, moreover, there was a brief, and perhaps inevitable, flirtation with notions of extra-parliamentary action and an outburst of quasi-insurrectionary rhetoric about the need to overcome and utterly transform, rather than merely to lay hold of, the institutions of the British state.

Despite – and perhaps also because of – these negative experiences with the state, Labour slowly reoriented its programme in a collectivist and statist direction. The First World War was decisive in beginning this shift, but the party's reflection on the experience of the Depression led even more forcefully in that direction. Seeing the state firmly in the hands of one's opponents after 1931 had driven home to Labour the importance of controlling the levers of power. Witnessing the impotence of reform efforts that did not have the backing of the state further helped to convince party and trade union leaders that only central government had the capacity to implement the party's vision. The fiscal constraints on local government, for example, illustrated how little could be accomplished at that level and how much more important it was to control the centre. The inability of trade unions to maintain, let alone increase, membership in an adverse labour market likewise underscored the need for a supportive state. The scope of the unemployment problem between the wars also made it obvious that revival would probably require the intervention of the central state and the adoption of economic planning. Planning, of course, would mean augmenting the power of the state, rearranging its priorities and internal organisation, and increasing its ability to intervene in the market and to overrule its outcomes.

The precise definition of planning and of what mechanisms would be required for its effectiveness continued to be debated throughout the 1930s, both within the Labour Party and outside of it.[16] By 1939 a consensus had begun to emerge around a rather modest Keynesian middle ground, but the Second World War ushered in yet another phase of debate about the state and its role in society and economy. Once again, the mobilisation for war vastly expanded the state and demonstrated even more forcefully and convincingly its capacity to steer the economy, to guarantee the equitable distribution of essential goods and services, and to fight and win a war. Labour, its leaders installed at the centre of domestic policy-making, became more confident of their ability to manage the state and of the state's ability to manage the economy and bring about social change. When Labour took office on its own after the election victory of 1945, therefore, the party put in place a programme more statist, more dirigiste and less Keynesian than would have been likely prior to the war. The party, the unions and Labour voters had become reconciled to the state and looked almost exclusively to collectivist solutions to the problems they confronted.

By 1945–51, therefore, Labour's socialism had become closely identified with nationalisation, planning and the state. When the party moved into opposition in the 1950s, its leaders and thinkers retained their faith in the state, in state control and in collectivist policies. A curious but indirect reflection of just how thoroughly the party's qualms about the state had been dissipated was the discussion in *New Fabian Essays* (1952) of how to understand and to label the new society that Labour had created. The issue was taken up forcefully and unabashedly by the young and 'brilliant' Tony Crosland, who was sure that 'capitalism is undergoing a metamorphosis into a quite different system' and that this new 'post-capitalist society' was 'quite different in kind from the capitalism which it succeeds'. 'What should the new society be called?' Crosland asked. A series of terms had been suggested – 'the Welfare State, the Mixed Economy, the Managerial State . . .' and so on, but 'the best that I can suggest', Crosland concluded, 'was Statism'.[17] Conceding the ugliness of the term, Crosland nevertheless argued that it was the most accurate term on offer, for it captured the most salient feature of the new society – 'state control' – and conjured up a broader vision in which the path out of the chaos of capitalism ran through the state.

Two critical assumptions – about capitalism and about the state – underpinned this assertion and it is difficult to know which was the more remarkable. Crosland apparently had no doubts that capitalism had been superseded by a qualitatively different society: the issue was how to describe it. Labour Party revisionists, of whom Crosland was surely the most eminent, have been typically criticised for lacking a firm commitment to socialism and socialist transformation. Here at least the problem is very different: a prematurely triumphalist view that capitalism had already been replaced and a remarkably confident claim that, although the features of the post-capitalist society might still need further definition, the fundamental battle had been won. What Crosland also obviously assumed was that the state could be relied upon as an agent both to manage the economy and to oversee social provision in the short term and as a mechanism for effecting further transformation towards socialism. The suspicion of the state so often found among earlier generations of socialists and of trade unionists was largely forgotten, its effectiveness and neutrality now simply taken for granted. Most important, there was little doubt in Crosland's mind – nor, it seems, in the minds of other Labour leaders – that government in the proper hands was a far superior instrument for directing the economy than the decisions of capitalists themselves. The idea that capitalism was a progressive force, that unleashing the forces of entrepreneurship was a reasonable path to progress, was simply unthinkable. Capitalists as a class and capital as an instrument were understood essentially to have failed the nation in the past and were not expected to do better in the future. What success business achieved was understood to result from the efforts not of owners or investors, but from the work of managers chosen on a professional and meritocratic basis. Labour Party thinkers were especially taken with the thesis that a 'managerial revolution' had occurred within capitalism, that ownership had therefore been severed from control, and that profit was no longer the overriding goal of business.[18] To this extent the 'revisionists' did not disagree with the 'left' over the relative merits of capitalism versus socialism. Socialism was a shared inheritance. The difference was over how far the transition to socialism had progressed. Both sides held to a largely common set of goals and values, even if their immediate political strategies varied a great deal.

By mid-century, Labour's political identity as the party of the state, of nationalisation and planning, of a socialism inflected with the particularities that derived from Labourism, was thus firmly established. With a very solid base of support among the working class and the trade unions and the prospect of building on that core of support to regain office, moreover, there was little incentive to alter its identity, its image or its most cherished policies. The defeat of 1951 was almost a welcome respite, and even a second loss in 1955 elicited no great anguish. That 'result', Crosland argued shortly after, '. . . does not justify angry inquests' and it indicated the need for but a modest set of adjustments.[19] This insouciance was neither arrogant nor foolish, for the party's foundations were probably stronger in the 1950s than they had been at any previous moment. The unions that supported it were larger than ever and had secured for themselves a decisive presence in industry and in the counsels of the state. The working class whose votes the party relied upon continued to dominate the social landscape and its way of life was as yet relatively untouched by the supposedly corrosive effects of affluence and mass consumption, upward social mobility and the destruction of compact communities by new trends in housing and transportation. The industries in which those workers toiled, and where trade unionism was most deeply entrenched, had waxed prosperous during the war and still offered stable employment and good prospects. Labour had shown itself fit to govern in trying circumstances and its policies continued to command respect and even, on occasion, enthusiasm. Major changes might lie ahead, but they were scarcely visible and not at all compelling in the early post-war era.

The effect was a certain complacency about the party's programme and practice that was disturbed only by the factional antagonism surrounding Bevanism. It was reinforced, of course, by the very structure of the party. The central authority within the Labour Party was the annual conference, which made policy and elected the National Executive Committee.[20] Within the party conference effective power resided with the trade unions, whose block votes easily overwhelmed the opinions of constituency activists. The culture of the party was nevertheless highly democratic, anti-elitist, as well as vaguely anti-intellectual. Both activists and trade unionists were suspicious of party leaders, who were often more educated and more middle class than the rank and file and who were assumed to be especially vulnerable to the temptations of office-holding and to the corrupting effects of regular mingling with the wealthy and powerful. Again, the memory of Ramsay MacDonald was a potent reminder of the risks involved in giving too much deference to party leaders. Leaders were in turn very wary of running foul of party opinion, even if their own views differed significantly.

The resulting inhibition did not prevent debate and discussion and Labour remained during the 1950s a more open and diverse political formation than did the Conservatives. But it did constrain the range of policy options that could get a genuine hearing within the party. In particular, the priority accorded to the defence of trade union interests and perquisites operated as a de facto veto over policies that might be seen as threatening those rights and practices. It was only recently, after all, that the unions had secured a place at the bargaining table in many industries and a recognised role in policy-making. Their leaders were not about to give these up. Their success in securing representation in the workplace and within the state, moreover, confirmed the unions in their historic preference for 'voluntarism' and their antipathy to formal state regulation. The framework of formal legal regulation that surrounded industrial relations in other countries – in the United States, for example – was explicitly rejected; as was the more activist pattern of government involvement in the setting of wages and economic policy-making more commonly found on the continent, especially in the Scandinavian countries. So unions worked assiduously to ensure that they maintained all of their existing rights to negotiate and to be consulted as well as complete independence in running their own internal affairs, and they firmly resisted policies that might jeopardise this status, whether these emanated from the left or the right.

The unions' fundamentally defensive stance had implications for industrial strategy as well. Throughout the early post-war years the labour market was characterised by an exceptionally high level of demand and resulted in a state of 'over-full' employment. Employers, officials, economists and politicians of both major parties fretted about the likely consequences for inflation. They reasoned that unions would use their collective strength and the exceedingly tight labour market to push wages up faster than prices and productivity, in the process jeopardising the strategy of export-led growth on which Britain's economic prospects ultimately depended. Remarkably, however, unions seldom utilised their clout to that end and overall put forth relatively modest wage demands. The reason was a very deeply ingrained preference for security and stability over growth, for jobs over wages. That preference had roots in the bitter memories of the Depression but it was also a reflection of the fact that Britain remained very much a class society, in which working-class horizons and reference groups were restricted and in which the culture of mass consumption had as yet made very little impact. Again and again, of course, Labour spokesmen lamented the negative effects of affluence upon working-class culture, but until the late 1950s there was in fact very little to complain about.[21] Living standards did rise and workers enjoyed the fruits of steady work and dependable wages, but improvements came slowly; and until the 1960s a wide range of consumer goods was beyond the reach of working-class households.

The predisposition to moderate wage claims but to fight vigorously against initiatives that might cause job loss caused trouble within the union ranks, of course, as workers in the more prosperous industries sought to use their power at the workplace to extract more from employers despite a lack of support from their own leaders. The effect was a rise in the number of unofficial strikes, especially in growing industries like motor cars, in the mid- to late-1950s, and a growth in the number and role of shop stewards who were more responsive to the needs and wishes of the rank and file. This de facto devolution of authority to the shop floor further accentuated tensions within the trade union movement, which was already divided into competing and overlapping organisations. The fragmented character of British trade unionism would prevent the unions from exercising the control over their membership that a functioning corporatism would require. Corporatism in Britain would thus come to mean that the unions had multiple vetoes over new policies but little capacity for coordinated action on behalf of a more positive and forward-looking agenda. Without a potentially unifying vision, however, union leaders were pulled in several directions in the 1950s: their better-off members wanted greater wage militancy; others, particularly in declining industries, were more concerned with protecting jobs – a concern shared widely in the unions, in the Labour Party and, it seems, among the public at large. The mix of pressures varied from one union to another, based in part on the mix of membership but also on the tradition of the union itself. But all unions experienced the tension between fighting aggressively for the interests of their members and protecting their rights as organisations to represent workers in dealings with employers and the state. Increasingly, moreover, businessmen and government became convinced that the key to economic growth was wage stability and so pressure began to build for union leaders to hold back the claims of their members. Efforts were made as well to involve the unions in formal rules and agreements to moderate wage claims – precisely the sort of arrangement that British unions were predisposed to oppose.

The impact on the Labour Party was not particularly deleterious in the short run. The heritage of Labourism and the continued practical

importance of the unions in the party's affairs produced a determination
to protect the unions at all costs, but the costs were not great while
Labour remained in opposition. Economists associated with Labour
clearly recognised the need for control of wages in an expanding economy, but couched their recommendations in phrases about a planned
growth of incomes and prices, about 'fair shares' and social justice; and
they scrupulously avoided proposals that might seem to place the burden
mainly upon the unions.[22] To this extent Labour eschewed policies that
might provoke worry among the unions. But the party did not suffer
seriously from this fudging, this lacuna in its policy proposals, for the
electoral and institutional incentives for a radical reworking of policy
remained minimal until at least 1959. And throughout the 1950s and
early 1960s the party's leadership profited from the fact that, most often,
the block votes of the unions were cast for policies approved by the leaders. Nor was public opinion especially alarmed at the visible dependence
of the party upon the goodwill of the trade unions, for there was a
substantial reservoir of public support for the unions. Memories of an
earlier era, when unions were weak and workers badly treated, faded
slowly and continued to inspire a sympathy with unions and their claims.
The alternative vision of unions as selfish, sectional, undemocratic and
impervious to the public interest was not as yet widespread, at least
outside the most right-wing Tory circles. The balance of gains and losses
stemming from Labour's links to the unions, and the policy stances it
produced, was decidedly positive prior to 1960, but the connection
nonetheless did serve to reinforce the tendency to stasis and immobilism
that was becoming so characteristic of the party.

The party's unresponsiveness was manifest repeatedly during the
years of opposition, but it was most thoroughly on display in the
aftermath of the defeat in the general election of 1959. Labour had good
reason to expect a better result in that contest, particularly because it
was widely agreed that the party machine functioned well during the
campaign and that Gaitskell performed better than expected. The party
had hoped to profit, too, from the fact that the often bitter rivalry between
Bevan and Gaitskell, and their supporters, had diminished and been
replaced by a reasonably smooth pattern of cooperation. But the Tory
government led by Macmillan won an unexpectedly solid victory and
Labour's third loss in a row prompted a determination finally to discuss

rethinking and updating the party's image and programme. Part of the discussion was sociological: had affluence so transformed Britain's social structure that Labour's appeal had lost effective purchase over the electorate, or at least over 'swing voters'?[23] But even before the sociological arguments were engaged, politicians in Gaitskell's orbit began to draw conclusions about the need to change the party's programme and policies, its image, its links with the trade unions and even, some thought, its very name. These heretical thoughts might have begun to crystallise into a thorough revisionist agenda, but they were uncoordinated and merely inchoate; and well before the proposals could be made coherent they were leaked to the press and their proponents placed on the defensive.

The first effect was to rekindle internal dissension. The result was a series of battles that have become legendary in the party's history: debates over the revision of Clause IV and the place of public ownership in the party's vision of socialism; over nuclear disarmament; and over the Common Market. Though the outcome of the debates varied – with the leadership backing down over the question of public ownership, ultimately prevailing over disarmament, and at one with its key constituencies over the party's sceptical stance toward Europe – the net effect on the party's programme and outlook was to keep both in place and to avoid change. The emerging 'modernising' project was blocked and progress in that direction delayed for a full quarter-century. The process illustrated painfully the institutional resistance within the party to efforts to move towards the political centre. It put on display the party's peculiar culture, the dominant influence of the trade unions, the relative impotence of the party's parliamentary leadership, and the remarkable insularity of the party's core supporters.

The arguments over nationalisation, defence and Europe had a long prehistory in the policy discourse of Labour stretching far back into the party's past. The commitment to nationalise industry had come to symbolise Labour's socialist vision both to its supporters and, as often, to its opponents. The party's leaders had therefore paid careful attention to the issue: they had taken care to restate regularly their faith in common ownership, but they had also been at pains to describe the preference in pragmatic terms and to avoid giving the impression that they regarded nationalised industry as the only model for economic organisation. They tried to avoid, for example, producing a 'shopping list' of industries that would be brought under public control; and in the most extensive policy statement on the issue, *Industry and Society* (1957), Labour promised only 'to extend public ownership in any industry or part of industry which, after thorough enquiry, is found to be seriously failing the nation'. Much of industry, the document acknowledged, was '. . . serving the nation well' and since Labour had 'no intention of intervening in the management of any firm which is doing a good job', the implication was that nationalisation would be limited. The statement was ambiguous, of course, and could be interpreted variously by those wanting more or less nationalisation. Within the Labour Party, that was its fundamental attraction; outside, it allowed the Conservatives to claim that despite the reasonable tone, Labour had secret plans to nationalise 500 companies that were supposedly 'failing the nation'.[24]

Though a few might fantasise about such things, the party leadership had no such plans. Not only was there a reluctance to commit to extensive further nationalisation, there was also a reasonably widespread recognition – encompassing leaders as different as Gaitskell, Bevan and Roy Jenkins – that the existing nationalised industries, while not exactly 'failing the nation', had nevertheless failed to produce socialism. They had not become the centres of innovation, cooperation and social harmony that their creators had envisioned. They were criticised as bureaucratic in their structure and ethos, unresponsive to consumers, and not much better places to work than private firms. In addition, the 'Morrisonian' model of political independence and the commitment to run the industries as businesses made it impossible to integrate the nationalised industries into an overall plan to run the economy.[25]

The caution displayed in the advocacy of public ownership could be, and often was, interpreted as evidence of a lack of commitment to socialism, a recognition of the virtues of capitalism and an acceptance of the inevitability of 'the mixed economy'. 'Revisionism' of this sort had necessarily to be resisted by committed socialists and it was this determination that underpinned the opposition to any further moves in that direction – such as replacing or modifying Clause IV. Gaitskell and his revisionist allies repeatedly contended that they were misinterpreted, however, and that they remained committed to the party's goals. To them, the debate was about means, not ends, and thus ought not to provoke such passionate defence and antagonism. The leadership were genuinely moved by reports from the field that nationalisation was an electoral liability and that, whatever their own views, the public needed to be educated and brought along on a case-by-case basis. The party organiser, Morgan Philips, reported the results of a questionnaire sent to over 100 Labour parliamentary candidates in which just six reported that support for public ownership helped their cause, while 97 felt that it had hurt their chances in the 1959 election.[26] It was hard to ignore such unambiguous evidence and it would have been irresponsible for a party leader to do so.

Gaitskell was not afraid to argue for unpopular causes and had earlier made it clear that the party could not run away from its past, its pledges or its identity. He accepted, for example, that the attacks on Labour were unfair but not without a basis in reality, and he would not run away from what the party was: 'Labour is a high taxation party,' he had explained in 1958, 'Labour is a trade union party, Labour is a nationalisation party, and Labour is not as sound as the Tories on the foreign issue . . . there was little one could do. He himself would play down the nationalisation of steel, but after all we are a trade union party with these views . . .'[27] In 1959 this willingness to defend principle was deployed to argue for a break – for a shift in party policy, for an updating of its image and also for a reform of its structure. Inevitably, the debate was also about power and personalities: Gaitskell's leadership, the battle over who might come to replace Gaitskell if he should fail, the role of the trade unions in the party structure.

Gaitskell, by all accounts, did a poor job of handling the specific issues and in that way weakened the broader effort to begin transforming the party.[28] In particular, he did not effectively orchestrate the actions of his supporters. Many of his allies on the right, for example, were dubious about joining the battle over Clause IV and believed it a tactical mistake to open up that front. Crosland felt it was simply not worth it since nobody paid much attention to the issue. But others, like Douglas Jay, were more forceful than the leader and took it upon themselves to float a series of quite radical proposals for eliminating Clause IV, for restructuring the party and for changing its name. In short, Gaitskell prepared very poorly for what, if successful, would have been a major struggle for the soul of the party and he did not even bring his core supporters properly into line. It is clear that he also miscalculated how resistant the party, especially the unions, would be to these initiatives and also that he underestimated his opponents, the wily Harold Wilson in particular. He failed most notably to reckon on the emotional attachment to nationalisation as a symbol of socialism. Bevan, in a strange but well-received speech at the party conference at Blackpool in 1959, gave an indication of just how deep feeling ran. He actually went so far as to assert that the Soviets had got it right in terms of the economy and they were ready now 'to reap the material fruits of economic planning and public ownership'. Labour must therefore insist that 'in a modern complex society it is impossible to get rational order by leaving things to private economic adventure. Therefore I am a socialist. I believe in public ownership.'[29] Bevan was not alone in believing that the planned economy, whether in the Soviet Union or in more democratic states, would ultimately prevail, and such faith precluded the abandonment of the promise of nationalisation.

But what really doomed the effort to eliminate Clause IV – and, in effect, the broader effort to modernise the party's structure – were the political culture and institutions of 'the Labour Movement: that mysterious collectivity beyond MPs, officers, trade unions, and constituency parties, which gave the party its identity'.[30] The decisive actors were in this case, as so often, the unions. Though the unions had been largely in the hands of moderate or right-wing leaders during the 1950s, and for many years before, the trade unions refused to be mobilised by the revisionist agenda of 'modernising' the party. They grasped instinctively that a restructuring would diminish their influence and they were determined instead that it should increase. By 1959–60, as Ralph Miliband noted, the unions had 'behind them two decades of increased confidence in their own strength – of increased confidence generated by the experience of war, by the achievements of Labour's New Deal after the war, and by full employment after 1951'. The consequence was both 'a far less defensive attitude towards employers' and 'the rejection of that grand reconciliation between the Labour movement and contemporary capitalism which is the essence of revisionism'.[31] Eliminating or modifying the commitment to nationalisation would signal precisely that reconciliation; sticking to it therefore became a sign of the unions' strength and independence. Thus for miners and transport workers the demand for public ownership was a matter of recognition and respect for the position they had secured in their respective industries. For others, it represented an aspiration to a status co-equal with management as well as a mechanism for transforming society. Jettisoning Clause IV would in the context be 'felt by many loyal trade unionists' to be the political equivalent of 'taking down the signpost to the promised land'.[32] Thus even after Gaitskell had compromised and produced a proposal that retained Clause IV but modified it with further elaboration – the so-called 'New Testament' – it was the large unions that refused to back the effort. They approved the text as a statement of current policy but were unwilling to include it in the party constitution.

If the Clause IV disaster illustrated the strength of the institutional resistance to innovation, it also showed how forcefully that resistance had registered in the minds of many party leaders. Even Gaitskell held back from declaring his intentions early on in large part out of deference to the tradition of letting conference lead and decide policy. Among his erstwhile revisionist allies, a few might have rushed ahead precipitously, but even more held back for fear of running afoul of party and trade union sentiment. They preferred revisionism achieved in small increments and by stealth. Members of Gaitskell's Shadow Cabinet, though privately agreeing with Gaitskell, remained mostly silent throughout the contest. And while Harold Wilson, whose machinations effectively stymied the leader, spoke publicly about Labour as 'an ethical Movement' which Clause IV helped to sustain, rather than 'a technocratic alternative to the Conservatives' – an ironic comment, given his own subsequent position on technology – he did so in the name of the party, its institutions and procedures.[33] In sum, Gaitskell's colleagues at the top of the party made clear their collective unwillingness to move the party from its anchorage in the political philosophy and programme they had inherited from an earlier era.

The debate over defence told much the same lesson, though the outcome was in fact a solid victory for the leadership. The question of Britain's nuclear deterrent had long troubled the Labour Party, whose pacifist inheritance was hard to reconcile with the possession, and possible use, of nuclear weapons. But Labour's past was also a liability: the party's attachment to disarmament and belated conversion to rearmament in the 1930s left Labour's leaders eager to prove that they could be trusted with the nation's security. The party's record in office from 1940 to 1951 made the party's claim credible, but at the price of complicity in the decision to become an atomic power. Inevitably, the question of nuclear weapons was also bound up with ambivalence over the alliance with the United States. Leaders of both powers knew that Britain could continue to play a major role in world affairs only in partnership with the United States, but there was tangible resentment that the latter was always the senior partner. More specifically, British leaders were never as resolutely hostile to the Soviet Union as the Americans and the prospect of finding a 'third way' and becoming a 'third force' was a constant attraction, especially within the Labour Party.

The question of Britain's continuing role as a nuclear power became increasingly contentious as existing weapons systems became obsolete and decisions loomed about their replacement. With the decision to cancel Blue Streak in 1960, the burden of Britain maintaining an independent deterrent was increased, while the prospect of relying more fully on the Americans became more likely. That these decisions would be made at a time when the intensity of the early Cold War had begun to lessen ensured that the political battle would be more intense. The lessening of Cold War tensions also lent more credibility to the unilateralist argument that Britain could renounce nuclear weapons without facing serious consequences in international relations. But it was an argument with few supporters among the party leadership. Gaitskell and the right were clearly opposed; Bevan had early on broken with the unilateralists, and Wilson was not eager for their embrace. Factional rivalry in the party's inner circles might still be a factor, of course, but the central challenge came from without, from the Campaign for Nuclear Disarmament founded in 1957, and from their supporters within the party.[34]

CND's annual Easter marches at Aldermaston had begun to attract growing support from the public and within the unions and led regularly to Labour Party conference resolutions and to demands for a revision of policy. The leadership was eager to avoid controversy and the charge that it was soft on issues of defence and foreign policy, but it became increasingly difficult to compromise the basic issues at stake. Uncharacteristically, unilateralist sentiment had also taken hold within the two large general unions, the NUGM and TGWU, and came near to provoking a split in the run-up to the election of 1959. After the election, the pressure for unity evaporated and the pressure for altering the party's position increased. By March 1960 a sizeable bloc of MPs were willing to sign on to a unilateralist statement; at the end of April 1960 the Engineering Union (AEU) passed a unilateralist proposal and they were joined soon after by the Yorkshire miners. Over the summer George Brown and Richard Crossman tried to strike a compromise among Labour Party and TUC leaders, but the effort failed because of the anti-nuclear views of Frank Cousins, the new and powerful leader of the Transport and General Workers' Union (TGWU), the nation's largest union. Cousins had strong and clear-cut views on the issue of nuclear weapons, but he was also determined to use the debate to force the leadership 'to take more notice of where power lies in the Party'.[35]

It was fitting that once again the question of whether Labour would persist in its defence policies or opt for unilateralism would ultimately be decided by the machinations of trade union leaders wielding the block votes of their memberships. Gaitskell had been defeated on the issue at the conference in Scarborough in October 1960, but by a lesser margin than feared. Emboldened because the worst had not transpired, he vowed to 'fight and fight again' and at the next year's conference in Blackpool secured a reversal of policy. The triumph was preceded by furious manoeuvring within the party but it was truly won within and through the trade unions. It required concretely that three of the six largest trade unions cast their block votes differently. The outcome confirmed both the reluctance of the party's leaders to stray very far from previous policy and the predominant influence of the trade unions and their leaders in the determination of party policy.

The third issue that troubled Labour between its defeat in the general election of 1959 and its victory in 1964 was Europe. Even more clearly than on defence or on the debate about whether to abandon or modify Clause IV, the question of Europe presented party leaders with an opportunity to look to the future relatively unburdened by past commitments and policy legacies. The Labour governments of 1945–51 had been lukewarm towards efforts at European unity and took no steps towards joining the European Coal and Steel Community, but the question had not been very prominent in party discussions. Overall, Labour was mildly Euro-sceptic during the 1950s and early 1960s, with the left more thoroughly 'anti' – fearful that in joining, Britain would be 'sucked up in a kind of giant capitalist, Catholic conspiracy' – and a pro-Market right worried that Britain would miss out on the economic dynamism of a reborn and revitalised Europe.[36] Gaitskell's position was perhaps typically insular in that he was simply not much interested: he regarded the issue as 'a bore and a nuisance and it had always been so'.[37] Among the unions it was assumed that the members would be sceptical at best, though the leaders were willing to work with the party leadership to marginalise anti-Market sentiments. So, if the balance of party opinion leaned slightly against the membership, it was not firmly so; and a modest investment of political energy by a committed leadership could probably have produced a consensus either for or against.

But that was precisely what Gaitskell, so recently traumatized by his defeat over Clause IV and his difficulties over the bomb, refused to do. He chose to do nothing that might generate a further split. Gaitskell could have decided differently, for in his sustained effort to reverse the conference decision on nuclear weapons he had much strengthened his relationship with what Barbara Castle called the 'Praetorian Guard of the General Council' of the TUC.[38] He also now had at his disposal a formidable group of supporters armed with a vision of changing the party and willing to follow his lead. After his initial setback on Clause IV and anticipating defeat on nuclear weapons, his allies on the centre-right of the party had rallied and mobilised under the leadership of the Campaign for Democratic Socialism, whose Oxford Manifesto garnered surprisingly widespread support. The young Bill Rodgers – formerly general secretary of the Fabians – took on a leading role in organising the movement; Roy Jenkins, Patrick Gordon Walker, Douglas Jay, Dick Taverne, Michael Shanks, Brian Walden, Denis Howell and Philip Williams were also involved from early on.[39] At the very centre was Tony Crosland, who was often seen as too aloof and frivolous to engage in factional struggle but who now decided it was time to cease being mere intellectuals and to act, at least for the moment, as 'apparatchiks'.[40] Crosland appointed himself as the revisionists' key strategist and outlined very clearly where his leader ought to lead. In May 1960 he told Gaitskell pointedly that his recent defeats proved 'that your leadership still lacks a proper system of intelligence and forward planning . . .' and indicated 'our total lack of *any overall plan* for changing the party'.[41]

When the tide began to turn after Gaitskell's surprisingly good showing at the 1960 party conference at Scarborough, Crosland proceeded to lay out for Gaitskell's benefit what ought to be their next objectives. They would first have to defeat Harold Wilson's challenge to Gaitskell, of course, but then move on to win more support on the NEC in order to reverse the recent conference decision. That done, they should seek 'to establish absolute control over the P.L.P. . . .'. They should then make use of that control by 'expelling a section of the extreme left . . .', for in general 'the Left is too strong . . . it constantly pulls us towards the Left when the electorate is moving Right'. 'Then back to revisionism and modernisation.'[42] It was also essential to make sure the right people were selected to stand for Parliament, for this would secure the revisionists' long-term domination. Eventually, however, the revisionists would have to wage a fight for 'a *change in the Constitution*. The present position', Crosland argued in 1961, 'is obviously appalling, with the annual night-mare of Conference, the terrifying unpredictability of the block votes, and the unfitness of the NEC to govern the Party.'[43]

Gaitskell listened to Crosland and made effective use of his support and of the broader effort to give organisational substance to the revision-ist cause. But he backed away from provoking the sort of 'paroxysmic crisis in the party' that Tony Benn accused Crosland of secretly trying to engineer.[44] The leader's decision to defer rather than to fight was made painfully clear in his handling of the issue of Europe. Gaitskell insisted that the party wait upon events and not take the initiative, and when forced to take a position, he carefully crafted a stance that was at the same time non-committal and resolutely backward-looking. In this manner the party's right-wing leader delighted the left and effectively 'healed the breach between him and conference', as Castle noted, but at the cost of disappointing his newly energised and organised supporters on the right-wing of the party and among trade union leaders.[45] More important, Gaitskell's choice over Europe meant that whatever opportunity for beginning the transformation of the party his new-found authority might have created was not seized. The task of 'modernising' Labour was put off for a quarter-century. The effect was to reinforce the party's penchant for stasis and its resistance to change.[46]

The details of the compromise were in themselves neither unreason-able nor unworthy. Gaitskell argued that entry was not impossible but would have to be based on a series of conditions affecting agriculture and relations with the Commonwealth and Britain's other European trading partners. The Conservatives, he argued, were willing to enter on any terms and it was this that was held to be unacceptable. The official position articulated under Gaitskell, then, was to avoid a firm commitment either way and to reserve judgement. It was a convenient stance, since it avoided alienating militants on either side of the issue. But Gaitskell surrounded this careful and limited message with a grander rhetoric of patriotism and national independence and conjured up fears that entry might mean 'the end of Britain as an independent state . . . the end of a thousand years of history . . .', the nation reduced to being a mere 'province of Europe'.[47] His most widely-praised conference speech was thus a repudiation of what he, and his supporters, claimed to be his most distinctive traits: a willingness to lead, to educate and if necessary to confront opponents; a determination to eschew the luxury of pure opposition and instead to think as if he were in office and responsible for the decision; and a predisposition to think anew and not rely upon accepted truths, myths and prejudices. The outcome is explicable only in terms of the enormous constraints that bore down upon the party leader and hemmed him in on matters of vital importance.

These constraints were a product of the party's distinctive structure, ethos and outlook. Labour's identity as the embodiment of the working class and its institutions, whose defence not only preceded the commitment to socialism but helped to shape it, ensured that the party would be slow to innovate and reluctant to abandon the goals and the rhetoric bequeathed by its past. It was a party long on loyalty, rich in traditional lore, weak on theory and determined to achieve and maintain a recognition not only of its claims to represent 'the people' but of the inherent social worth of the particular interests, and values, it sought to represent. It was not simply a projection into politics of the narrow interests of trade unions or of the self-interest of their members, but rather a political vehicle much like the trade unions that demanded recognition as a sign that its constituencies mattered to the nation. Labour was in this sense a political movement that was much more closely bound up with its identity than other parties typically were and to this extent also trapped within that identity and unable to veer very far from the views, habits and policies held dear by those who inhabited its political space and on whose loyalty the party depended.

It had not always been such. Prior to the Second World War, Labour was not especially integrated into the mainstream of national life or governance; it was very much in opposition. The unions were likewise kept at some distance from the levers of power in industry and the state and they were numerically much weaker. The transformations wrought by war and the success of the Labour governments of 1945–51 changed that and created the conditions for Labour to become a party of the status quo, resistant to innovation, jealous of its privileges and those of the unions with which it was affiliated, and unwilling to be led very far in any direction. This was the political formation that came to be labelled, after its passing, as 'old Labour'. It was not really very old, however. Rather, it was a fairly recent product of the achievements of the 1940s and only it took on solid institutional form in the 13 years of opposition that followed the defeat of 1951. But once established – and then sustained by the organisational ballast provided by the block vote and kept in line with inhibitions instilled by a rhetoric and culture of loyalty – the Labour Party of the post-war era was hard to inspire and to motivate, almost impossible to argue with, inured to criticism, and so very difficult to lead. It was a political entity that drove its leaders to despair and that routinely tempted its best supporters to give it up. But, as if in response to the frustrations it regularly engendered, it was extremely solid and resilient and would again and again prove its ability to endure.

Notes and references

1 Steven Fielding, Peter Thompson and Nick Tiratsoo, *England Arise! The Labour Party and Popular Politics in 1940s Britain* (Manchester: Manchester University Press, 1995).

2 The most recent and comprehensive discussion is Ross McKibbin, *Classes and Cultures: England, 1918–1951* (Oxford: Oxford University Press, 1998).

3 It is obvious that the development of a language of class – and of 'socialism' and the 'labour movement' – had to accompany the political development of a party claiming to represent the class. But the class itself was no mere discursive creation. This argument is made more fully in James Cronin, *Labour and Society, 1918–1979* (London: Batsford, 1984).

4 See Jon Lawrence, 'Labour – The Myths It Has Lived By', in Duncan Tanner, Pat Thane and Nick Tiratsoo, eds, *Labour's First Century* (Cambridge: Cambridge University Press, 2000), 341–66.

5 The distinction between the vague if powerful political culture of the party and its more explicit ideological outlook was made very effectively in H.M. Drucker, *Doctrine and Ethos in the Labour Party* (London: Allen & Unwin, 1979).

6 C.A.R. Crosland, *The Future of Socialism* (London: Jonathan Cape, 1956), 80.

7 Ralph Miliband, *Parliamentary Socialism* (London: Allen & Unwin, 1961).

8 See Jonathan Schneer, *Labour's Conscience: The Labour Left, 1945–51* (London: Allen & Unwin, 1988); and Patrick Seyd, *The Rise and Fall of the Labour Left* (New York: St Martin's, 1987).

9 John Campbell, *Nye Bevan: A Biography* (London: Richard Cohen Books, 1997), 82–3.

10 The obvious effect was to turn the Labour Left against the block vote. Barbara Castle, who would later take it upon herself to restructure the unions themselves in 1968–69, was typical. See Anne Perkins, *Red Queen: The Authorised Biography of Barbara Castle* (London: Macmillan, 2003).

11 Campbell, *Nye Bevan*, 305–6.

12 Michael Foot, *Aneurin Bevan: A Biography*, Volume II: *1945–1960* (London: David-Poynter, 1973), 491, 514.

13 The by-now classic statement – much debated and perhaps overstated in its original form – is Martin Weiner, *English Culture and the Decline of the Industrial Spirit, 1850–1980* (Cambridge: Cambridge University Press, 1981).

14 The point has been made forcefully, if contentiously, by David Marquand, *The Progressive Dilemma: From Lloyd George to Blair* (London: Phoenix, 1999).

15 See James Cronin, *The Politics of State Expansion* (London: Routledge, 1991), chapters 3 and 7.

16 Daniel Ritschel, *The Politics of Planning: The Debate on Economic Planning in Britain during the 1930s* (Oxford: Clarendon, 1997).

17 C.A.R. Crosland, 'The Transition from Capitalism', in R.H.S. Crossman, ed., *New Fabian Essays* (London: Turnstile, 1952), 35, 38, 42–3. For the origins and reception of the volume and its particular essays, see Kevin Jefferys, *Anthony Crosland: A New Biography* (London: Politico's, 2000), 44–7.

18 The fascination with the notion of a 'managerial revolution' and with what it meant for the understanding of capitalism and socialism was not confined to revisionists like Crosland. On the left, Richard Crossman was

equally interested but drew rather different conclusions. See Martin Francis, 'Mr Gaitskell's "Ganymede"? Re-assessing Crosland's *The Future of Socialism*', *Contemporary British History*, XI, 2 (Summer 1997), 56. See, for example, Crossman's Fabian Tract, *Socialism and the New Despotism* (London: Fabian Society, 1956).

19 C.A.R. Crosland, 'The future of the Labour Party', *The National and English Review*, CXLV, 869 (July 1955), 13–17.

20 The definitive study is Lewis Minkin, *The Labour Party Conference: A Study in the Politics of Intra-party Democracy* (Manchester: Manchester University Press, 1980).

21 Steven Fielding, 'Activists against "affluence": Labour Party culture during the "Golden age", c. 1950–1970', *Journal of British Studies*, XL, 2 (2001); Lawrence Black, *The Political Culture of the Left in Britain, 1951–64: Old Labour, New Britain* (New York: Palgrave, 2002).

22 The discussion about the need to control prices and wages was thus recurrent but typically inconclusive. For aspects of it, see Noel Thompson, *Political Economy and the Labour Party* (London: UCL Press, 1996), 159–60, 182.

23 The key text was Mark Abrams and R. Rose, *Must Labour Lose?* (London: Penguin, 1960). See also Anthony Crosland, *Can Labour Win?* (London: Fabian Society, 1960).

24 See Philip Williams, *Hugh Gaitskell: A Political Biography* (London: Jonathan Cape, 1979), 546ff; and Brian Brivati, *Hugh Gaitskell* (London: Metro, 1997).

25 Labour Party, *Industry and Society, Labour's policy on future public ownership* (London: Labour Party, 1957), 48 and *passim*. On the debates surrounding the document, see Williams, *Gaitskell*, 446–52; on the document itself, see Thompson, *Political Economy*, 179–81.

26 Williams, *Gaitskell*, 531.

27 Gaitskell's views recorded in Crossman's diaries, 18 February 1958, and cited in Williams, *Gaitskell*, 472.

28 For a judicious assessment, see Tudor Jones, ' "Taking Genesis out of the Bible": Hugh Gaitskell, Clause IV and the Socialist Myth', *Contemporary British History*, XI, 2 (Summer 1997), 1–23.

29 Aneurin Bevan, quoted in Ben Pimlott, *Harold Wilson* (London: HarperCollins, 1992), 230.

30 Pimlott, *Harold Wilson*, 235.

31 The quotes are taken from selections from Miliband, *Parliamentary Socialism*, reprinted in David Coates, ed., *Paving the Third Way: The Critique*

of Parliamentary Socialism (London: Merlin, 2003), 69. This collection – with articles and excerpts from work by Miliband, Coates, Leo Panitch, John Saville, Colin Leys and Hilary Wainwright – represents probably the most sustained and effective argument from the left against New Labour and 'modernisation'.

32 Williams, *Gaitskell*, 570.

33 Wilson quoted in *The Observer*, 8 November 1959.

34 On the history of CND, see Meredith Veldman, *Fantasy, the Bomb and the Greening of Britain* (Cambridge: Cambridge University Press, 1994).

35 Williams, *Gaitskell*, 509.

36 Richard Heffernan, 'Beyond Euro-Scepticism? Labour and the European Union since 1945', in Brian Brivati and Richard Heffernan, eds, *The Labour Party: A Centenary History* (London: Macmillan, 2000), 384–6.

37 Williams, *Gaitskell*, 702–4.

38 Barbara Castle, 7 October 1962, in Williams, *Gaitskell*, 739.

39 See Giles Radice, *Friends and Rivals: Crosland, Jenkins and Healey* (London: Little, Brown, 2002), 116–17; and Bill Rodgers, *Fourth among Equals* (London: Politico's, 2000), 51–70.

40 Crosland to Taverne, cited in Brivati, *Hugh Gaitskell*, 362–3.

41 Crosland to Gaitskell, 4 May 1960, Anthony Crosland Papers, LSE Archive, File 6/1.

42 Crosland to Gaitskell, November 1960, Crosland Papers 6/1. Crosland even gave Gaitskell his estimate that approximately 20 MPs would have to be expelled, mostly Tribune supporters. The list did not include Crossman and Wilson, 'intolerable and neurotic people' who nevertheless 'belong in the party', nor Tony Benn, who was also 'a hopeless neurotic, but he could be won back'.

43 Crosland to Gaitskell, October 1961, Crosland Papers 6/1.

44 Benn to Crosland, 31 October 1960, Crosland Papers 6/1.

45 Barbara Castle, 5 October 1962, in Williams, *Gaitskell*, 739; Jefferys, *Anthony Crosland*, 80–1.

46 Quoted in Williams, *Gaitskell*, 739.

47 Gaitskell, 3 October 1962, in *Report of the Labour Party Annual Conference 1962*.

CHAPTER 2

The Labour Party, planning and growth

The internal party battles of the early 1960s produced a highly anomalous outcome: a clear winner but no mandate. The defeat of 1959 had seemed to call out for some adaptation in the party's outlook, programme or organisation – perhaps in all three – informed by a strategy to put together a broader electoral coalition. Gaitskell's allies proposed an alternative, but their efforts were completely inadequate. Gaitskell himself emerged in a very strong personal position by late 1962, having vanquished the left over unilateralism and putting the right in its place over Europe, but his victories and his status provided no licence to move the party in any particular direction. Had he lived and gone on to lead a Labour government after the election of 1964, he might well have used his position more creatively, though it is perhaps more likely that the press of governing would have precluded any fundamental rethinking and reorientation.

But Gaitskell would not have that opportunity; and his untimely death in 1963 allowed the enigmatic but highly talented Harold Wilson to become leader of the Labour Party. It was a signal triumph for a man whose career had taken many turns and whose instincts for survival, for reinvention and for repositioning himself were to become legendary. Wilson would stake his claim to leadership on a commitment to unleashing the transforming powers of science and technology and to a programme of modernising both the Labour Party and the nation it sought to govern. Wilson's strategy was neither revisionist nor a mere continuation of previous Labour Party policy. It was a novel and distinct amalgam that was as much a product of the rethinking of the late 1950s and early 1960s as the competing revisionist alternative; and it was more consistent with the most fundamental aspirations of the Labour Party. Wilson's programme of state-led planning, growth and economic 'modernisation' would dominate the Labour Party's political agenda for at least the next decade; and coping with its legacy would preoccupy Labour for another ten years. It would eclipse the rival agenda of the revisionists and ensure that when the project of 'modernising' Labour re-emerged in the 1980s, the party itself – the object to be defended, transformed or recast in the process – was nothing like the party inherited by Harold Wilson. Wilson's approach had successfully created a framework that linked 'modernisation' with Labour's socialist and collectivist beliefs and that facilitated a subtle turn to the left, even if that was not quite understood at the time.

Wilson's vision was in large measure a response to, and grew out of, the debate about the rapid changes that were said to be remaking Britain and represented an answer of sorts to the questions raised in the aftermath of the 1959 electoral defeat: had prosperity so muted or altered class structures and sentiments as to make Labour's appeal fundamentally outdated? Was the working class itself becoming a social relic? Did it still make sense to counterpose capitalism and socialism and to choose between them? Wilson's accession to power in fact coincided with the emergence and confrontation of three competing discourses about social change and politics – Wilson's, the revisionists' and the roughly parallel debates among social scientists. Charting the course of politics during the Wilson years thus means assessing the fate and the usefulness of these distinct visions. Was society in fact changing in the manner anticipated by the revisionists or by social scientists? Were they even asking the right questions? And was Wilson's formula for addressing the problem of modernising Britain a genuine response to the evolution of society and economy or an electoral ploy? Or was it merely a sophisticated compromise designed to fudge the differences between the left and the right within the Labour Party?[1] Definitive answers may be elusive even in hindsight, but a first step would be to separate the rhetoric of social change and the uses made of it politically from the empirical analysis of shifting economic and social structures.

It is, after all, unlikely that the pace of social and economic change was registered directly in politics, if only because of the lag that ordinarily exists between shifts in the character of society and the public's awareness of those shifts. The stimulus for the debate about the impact of social change on political allegiance and party fortunes presumably came therefore from the realm of politics proper. Labour's third successive general election defeat in 1959 surely constituted a compelling reason to look at the fit between Labour's identity and programme and its social bases of support. But the examination was not conducted by neutral observers. On the contrary, the argument about the nature of social change and Labour's appropriate response to it was an occasion on which politicians, activists and researchers pronounced not only on the nature of social change but also on whether they approved of how Britain was evolving and on what the course of future change should be. What passed for social science in the discourse in and around the party was anything but neutral. Nor was there anything surprising about this. Labour was a party with a distinct social base and with an equally distinctive vision of how society should be reformed. To expect the party to defer to mere data on the issues dearest to its identity would be to expect, or demand, that Labour be something other than it was.

Labour's identity as a socialist party has been much debated, but there can be little debate about the party's core antipathy to capitalism. To many within the party, even those moderates willing to concede the viability of the mixed economy, capitalism was not merely unjust and inefficient, it was also immoral and ugly. The elevation of private pleasures over the public good, the competitive individualism it spawned, the sacrifice of aesthetic principle for commercial gain and the culture of consumption all made capitalism unworthy. Socialism, by contrast, promised not merely equity and efficiency but a restoration of collective virtue, an ethic of use over display and of public over private, and a standard of judgement that privileged the community over the individual or the firm. The liberation promised by socialism was not, in most cases, seen as a matter of increased consumption and freedom from constraint but rather participation in what Labour thinkers talked about as a cooperative or socialist commonwealth. Security and a shared fate were prized over risk and opportunity.

This rather austere vision testifies eloquently to Labour's rootedness in British society and on the reforming wing of British political culture, with its emphasis on community and morality and its aversion to markets and the 'cash nexus'. It speaks as well to the fact that so many of its leading thinkers were drawn either from the middle class or from the respectable, self-improving section of the working class, both of which distrusted the unfettered workings of the market and the untutored preferences of the mass of workers. To them workers, especially working-class women, needed to be protected from the lures and swindles typical of capitalism and literally instructed on what to buy. Douglas Jay had put the case most famously and in the most blatantly paternalist language: 'housewives as a whole cannot be trusted to buy the right things . . . for, in the case of nutrition and health, just as in the case of education, the gentleman in Whitehall really does know better what is good for the people than the people themselves'.[2] Labour's fears over mass consumption during the 1950s and early 1960s were also eloquent testimony to the limited horizons of most British workers and the narrow social comparisons they tended to make.[3] The Labourist character of the Labour party guaranteed that the party's outlook would reflect this restricted framework and these modest aspirations. The ethical and cultural critique of capitalism and the resistance to the materialism and individualism supposedly characteristic of capitalism thus predisposed Labour to look with disfavour upon the growth of affluence and its spread among the working class.

As early as 1950 Labour had argued that 'the moral basis of the new society' would build on 'what is good in people, not what is bad' and 'rely on friendship and friendliness not on fear and greed'.[4] They urged a rejection of the Tories' 'crude materialist appeal to the purely self-regarding interests of the electors' and denounced both advertising, for creating insatiable and unnecessary wants, and buying on credit or 'hire-purchase'.[5] A delegate to the 1960 Labour Women's Conference believed not only that 'women were being hoodwinked when they bought things on hire-purchase' but that in so doing 'they were playing the Tory game'.[6] The Tories, by contrast, played a different game in which they identified Labour with controls and rationing. The link was not fanciful, for Labour was unwilling to give up the idea that controls were necessary to ensure stable prices and 'fair shares' and there is reason to believe that Labour's stance against rising prices and rents resonated with a working-class constituency that craved security and stability and did not yet aspire to much more. There were, of course, Labour politicians and thinkers who sought to distance the party from policies of controls and shared poverty. Crosland, for example, wanted Labour to shed its vaguely puritan image and embrace not merely increased consumption but more social freedom and more 'liberty and gaiety in private life'. Britain should become, he argued, a 'more colourful and civilised country . . .' with

> more open-air cafés, brighter and gayer streets at night, later closing-hours for public houses, more local repertory theatres, better and more hospitable hoteliers, brighter and cleaner eating-houses [to ask for better food would presumably have made him a utopian], more riverside cafés, more pleasure gardens on the Battersea model, more murals and pictures in public places, better designs for furniture and pottery and women's clothes [an interesting ordering of preferences], statues in the centre of new housing-estates, better-designed street-lamps and telephone kiosks and so on *ad infinitum*.

But Crosland was in a very small and distinct minority and, as his writing made clear, he was self-consciously iconoclastic and knew well the icons that needed to be smashed: 'The enemy in all this', he asserted, 'will often be in unexpected disguise; it is not only dark Satanic things and people that now bar the road to the new Jerusalem, but also, if not mainly, hygienic, respectable, virtuous things and people, lacking only in grace and gaiety.'[7]

The bulk of the Labour party was prepared to resist the spread of affluence and its political implications even before most working people tasted its benefits. Their response to the argument over social and economic change was thus hardly unrehearsed. But how affluent was Britain? And how much had life changed for ordinary working men and women, the historic base of the Labour Party, by the early 1960s? Tory claims about the extent of prosperity were presumably somewhat exaggerated, but the fact that Labour largely accepted them suggests that things were definitely improving. But again, how much? The most impressive indicator was, of course, the low rate of unemployment, that great scourge of working-class life between the wars. Unemployment had been eliminated during the war and the wartime labour shortages, but it rose a bit to an average of 3.1 per cent in 1947. After the passing difficulties associated with post-war readjustment, however, it fell back to less than 2 per cent by 1950–51. There it stayed; and between 1951 and 1960 it averaged under 2 per cent. The extremely tight labour market made it possible for workers to bargain for higher wages, but these unprecedentedly low rates of unemployment translated into only modest gains in real wages. The late 1940s were genuinely a period of austerity and the unions and the government managed to keep wage demands in check with the result that real wages were actually slightly lower in 1951–52 than they had been just after the war. From that moment real wages began a steady, but by no means spectacular, rise: between 1953 and 1959, the year of the third consecutive Conservative general election victory, real wages had increased by just about 12 per cent. Given the low levels from which they started, this meant that working people were able to spend more on food and rent and to begin acquiring a very few, and very modest, home furnishings, but that for most working-class consumers expensive items like refrigerators, washing machines and cars still remained quite out of reach.[8] The early and wide spread of television might well bring the possibility of greater consumption into view, but the prospect and meaning of genuine affluence remained obscure and unattainable for most.

While the average standard of living and consumption rose modestly, but steadily, changes were taking place in the industrial and occupational structure of the working class and also in the 'sexual division of labour'. Again, however, the shifts were modest and incremental. In the decade after 1949, for example, the proportion of employees working in manufacturing and mining actually rose slightly from 42 per cent to 43.2 per cent, while employment in coal mining – an industry destined ultimately to shrink massively – actually increased marginally from 779,000 to 786,000 over the period 1950–58. From 1959, the moment when discussions of affluence and the decline of the working class became rampant, until 1964 the number of workers in mining and manufacturing continued to expand slightly in absolute terms – by just under 200,000 – though it declined as a proportion of total employment by roughly 1 per cent.[9] Indeed, manufacturing employment alone grew by 350,000 during the early 1960s (1959–64), while the losses were heavily concentrated in the mining industry, which shed almost precisely that number. The traditional strongholds of the British working class therefore remained well populated into the mid-1960s.

The demography of the working class changed apace, but again only modestly. The proportion of UK employees who were female rose only marginally in the 1950s (1949–58), from 32.3 per cent to 33.7 per cent and by roughly the same rate over the next half-decade (1959–64), from 33.8 per cent to 34.7 per cent. That did mean that the labour force participation rate for British women rose from 37.1 per cent in 1951 to 40.6 per cent ten years later and to 42.3 per cent in 1966, an increase due primarily to a sharp jump in the percentage of married women working – from 26.1 per cent in 1951 to 38.5 per cent in 1966.[10] It is clear that a very large share of the increase in women's work was concentrated in services: in the distributive trades, which added over 800,000 jobs over the period 1949–64 and in other services which increased by about 1.6 million. Growth on this scale would require both more men and more women, but the net effect would be to increase the share of women in total paid employment.

The data would seem to suggest, then, that the picture of the working class as decreasing in size and increasing in affluence was very much exaggerated, if not actually wrong. A better description would focus on the fact that the industrial working class, where Labour support was strongest, was fully employed and even growing in absolute terms while it was also becoming gradually better off. Within the industrial working class some industries were indeed beginning to shrink: textiles, which employed just over a million workers in 1949, had begun to decline in the late 1950s and had decreased by about 150,000 by 1964; mining followed a similar pattern, holding steady at over 850,000 employees throughout the 1950s but also dropping by about 160,000 to 1964. These losses were largely offset by increases in engineering and motor cars, although the precise timing meant that some workers faced difficult transitions. Rather more extensive, but still incremental, change was occurring around the edges of the class in that more and more men and women were finding work in services and relatively more women were working. Overall, however, the argument that the working class had been substantially transformed in the period leading up to the election of 1959 was hard to sustain in the face of what was in fact a very solid social formation. The structures of employment and working-class life did begin to shift more noticeably after that, but again only relatively slowly.

This impression that on balance the changes adumbrated in the affluent worker discussion were much less substantial in reality than in public debate was basically confirmed in a series of sophisticated sociological studies that began appearing in the mid-1960s.[11] The rather scant evidence of social change turned up in these studies reinforced the preconceptions of many within the Labour Party as well as their reluctance to accept its implications for party policy and programme. The effect was to reduce the appeal of revisionist pleas to update the party's programme and to refashion its appeal accordingly. The institutional structures and intellectual traditions of the party worked in much the same direction. Undoubtedly, the tactical mistakes of the revisionists, especially Gaitskell, and their rivalries and disunity after 1963, contributed mightily to their failure to make much of an impact, but in a more fundamental sense the social conditions were not yet ripe for their triumph. The very same conditions were, however, much more conducive to the agenda proposed by Harold Wilson.

Still, the sense of unease that gripped the very top of the party after 1959 was nonetheless real; and it had been underlined by the verdict of three successive elections. The more thoughtful among party leaders and activists knew intuitively that Labour's appeal had not been updated; they understood, as did the public at large, that Britain was beginning to change and that there was a growing impatience with the status quo. The problem was to figure out what direction social and economic change would take and what to make of it politically. Perhaps the clearest evidence of change and dissatisfaction was the novel interest in growth that pervaded the discussion of politics and economics in the late 1950s and early 1960s. The fascination with growth was in a curious way a perfect reflection of a society and an economy poised on the brink of transformation but not as yet experiencing it. The full employment of the 1950s had gone some way towards easing the fear of depression and of a return to unemployment and had begun, but only just barely, to raise the prospect of increased material consumption. Economic performance nevertheless seemed precarious, as recurring balance of payments problems forced governments alternately to pump up and then dampen down demand. The mechanisms by which demand was regulated tended further to reinforce ordinary people's sense of vulnerability: the impact of the tightening and loosening of hire-purchase terms, for example, fell directly on working-class and lower middle-class consumption. So while expectations and promises began gradually to increase, faith in the ability of the economy to deliver did not. In response, attention turned to how to raise the level of growth of the economy.

The concern for growth led to a convergence on the aims of economic policy but a marked divergence on how to get there. Labour and the Tories agreed on the necessity of raising the rate of growth and they seemed to share an interest in planning as a means of getting there. But there the agreement ended, and on matters of detail the two parties actually came to differ more; and as the debate over growth and planning progressed, Labour could be seen reverting to a more aggressively 'socialist' policy. Planning, after all, had been central to the history of the Labour Party and integrally linked to public ownership and control. By contrast, the Conservatives' interest in planning was an aberration, and quite short-lived at that. As the need to plan in order to secure growth became more deeply embedded in Labour's perspective, the party's plans and programmes became more imbued with Labour's traditional hostility to business and markets, its predisposition for state control and for state-sponsored solutions. As planning came to be defined in the 1960s, moreover, it became as well a vehicle for modernising both society and the party, a programme that gave Labour a more persuasive claim to national leadership and that linked the party's fortunes with the waxing influence of science and technology. It was an intoxicating brew and it was to be the key to the peculiar politics of Harold Wilson, a politics that did not so much respond to the imperatives of social change as to tap into the aspiration for it.

Labour did not need to be converted to planning in the early 1960s. The notion had been part of the party's policy repertoire going back at least to the 1930s. More important still was the practical legacy of planning during 1945–51, when Labour was able to utilise the wartime inheritance of economic controls to make its preferences into reality. Not only did the Labour government nationalise large sections of industry, it also exercised direct 'physical controls' over manpower, prices and rents, imports and the allocation of scarce raw materials, building and the location of industry. Labour also oversaw the process by which Keynesian techniques of demand management became accepted practice within the Treasury and in its decision-making over budgets and macro-economic policy.

The experience of 1945–51 did not, however, result in a clear sense of how Labour would plan in the future. The legacy of planning in the 1940s was extremely mixed: in terms of theory, policy, technique and administration. As James Meade, the head of the Economic Section and a leading advocate of planning, argued, Labour planners were split between 'liberal-socialists' and 'Gosplanites'. 'Liberal-socialists' were content to use Keynesian techniques of demand management and selective intervention to steer the economy; 'Gosplanites' wanted to set prices and quotas and exert detailed control. The practice of the Labour governments of 1945–51 made use of both types of control and although there was a growing recognition that 'physical controls' were onerous and unpopular, they continued to enjoy support from those eager to ensure 'fair shares'. The argument was not resolved in the 1940s because the government did not need actually to impose detailed controls, they inherited them from wartime; and so controls could be gradually relaxed without abandoning the belief that they might occasionally be necessary. Likewise, the wisdom of Keynesian policy went largely unchallenged because in the 1940s the big economic problem was not a lack of demand, to which Keynesians would respond with borrowing and tax reductions that could be labelled irresponsible, but rather excess demand and the consequent need to control prices. So the turn to Keynes was also accomplished without major controversy. In consequence, however, the tough choices that would confront a peacetime Labour government coming to power after an extended period of Tory rule were neither anticipated nor discussed.

Nor were the Labour governments of 1945–51 able to leave behind institutions that could be used or plans that could be implemented by a future Labour administration eager to build on past achievements. For example, a variety of expedients were used in the 1940s to bypass the traditional 'Treasury control' over policy: interdepartmental committees, the creation of the Economic Section and the Central Economic Planning Staff, and so on. By the early 1950s, the Treasury had managed to eliminate, tame or absorb these innovations and to reassert its control over economic policy. As for specific programmes, Labour planners sought to put in place a set of plans that could be deployed in case of a downturn. They wanted commitments to use investment in nationalised industries to offset shortfalls in private investment during periods of slack demand; and they devised schemes to create a backlog of feasible and desirable public works projects that could be pushed forward countercyclically to provide jobs and an economic stimulus. Neither set of plans won approval within the government, especially the Treasury, and so would not survive the subsequent era of Tory government. And finally, the Labour government had begun to realise in the late 1940s that it needed to get inside industry, and even specific firms, in order to pressure management to adopt new techniques and processes. To that end they gave support to the Anglo-American Productivity Council, aimed in importing more efficient American methods into British industry, and to a series of regional interventions by the Board of Trade. Neither policy proved notably effective, however, and British firms remained relatively immune to the need for the updating of technique or managerial style.[12] When Labour left office in 1951, therefore, the party was as committed as ever to the virtues of planning and public ownership, but questions about how to plan were quite unresolved. So, too, was the issue of how to utilise the nationalised industries in the interests either of the workers they employed or of the wider economy of which they were a key part. While in opposition Labour could safely ignore the details of planning and economic management and content themselves with platitudes, criticism of the Tories, and the memories of successful economic policy-making during 1945–51.

The Tories were no more interested in how to run a regime of planning during the early 1950s, but the concern with economic growth that marked the late 1950s began to effect a transformation of attitudes among the public at large and among Conservatives. The intense focus on growth stemmed not merely from impatience with the 'stop-go' pattern of industrial development, but from an expanded vision of what might be possible if it were overcome. Britain's erratic growth rate contrasted particularly unfavourably with the steadier and more robust rates of growth experienced by the major European economies – France, Germany and Italy – and by Japan, and the proximity of the former somehow made it reasonable to think that their achievements could be emulated by Britain. By the late 1950s there was thus a sense that, even if people in Britain had 'never had it so good', the performance of the economy was still not good enough. More specifically, the concern with the apparent success of Britain's European competitors produced a particular and growing interest in the 'indicative planning' that seemed to be work-ing so well in France. The effect was a 'remarkable conversion' among businessmen, politicians and journalists.[13] Specifically, the discussion about growth and planning prompted the Federation of British Industries (FBI) at its meeting in Brighton in 1960 to publish a report on 'The Next Five Years' that urged something like planning upon the government. The Macmillan government responded by setting up in 1962 the National Economic Development Council ('Neddy'), designed to bring together the FBI, the Trades Union Congress (TUC) and representatives of the state in an effort to work out a plan for growth.[14]

The new respectability of planning offered Labour an unprecedented opportunity, for it shifted the terms of the debate about national economic policy onto a new terrain – a terrain on which Labour was not only comfortable ideologically, but where they could claim superior expertise. It was an issue, moreover, that allowed Labour to come together after the bitter splits of the last years of Gaitskell's leadership. It meant that when Harold Wilson led the party to victory in the election of 1964, there was widespread support for a truly serious effort to plan the economy. This support encompassed both sides of industry and infected state officials as well; it also crossed party lines. It was a circumstance unlikely ever to recur and it would be a decisive test of whether planning was genuinely feasible in an advanced economy in peacetime.

If the context was uniquely promising, the administrative and policy legacy and the intellectual framework which would inspire it neverthe-less remained much less so. The theoretical debate of the 1940s over styles of planning might have been won by the 'liberal-socialists' rather than the 'Gosplanites', but there was a lingering attachment to controls. And, more important, contemporary advocates of the mixed economy had done little to fashion the tools with which to make their vision into reality. Because Labour had left office in 1951 without putting in place a set of mechanisms to intervene effectively in the economy and nothing substantial had been done to remedy that gap in the interim, they cast around for mechanisms that might be put to use in the task. They turned first to Neddy, which offered at least a forum for the two sides of industry to meet, but soon it was criticised for lacking the power to translate its goals into policy. Despite this supposed institutional inadequacy, Labour grasped at its possibilities and argued that by taking direct control of Neddy and hence of planning, a new government could give more substance and direction to the planning process. Party leaders went on to convince themselves that their sincere commitment and drive would overcome all political obstacles and administrative resistances.

This rather naive faith had many sources: among them, the party's traditional belief in the superiority of public enterprise and of collective ownership; excessive optimism about the nation's economic prospects in general; a simplistic tendency to assume that what was socially just, or what was in the immediate economic interest of the organised workers – as articulated by the trade unions – would also be efficient; and a faulty memory of the post-war Labour government that tended to exaggerate its achievements, to minimise its difficulties and conveniently to forget the growing resentment of physical controls.[15] Added to these historic inheritances were two curious features of the political climate of the late 1950s and early 1960s which together made it possible for Labour to overestimate its chances of stimulating growth through planning. The first was a fascination with science and technology and its potential for stimulating economic growth. Wilson, whose background and career strongly predisposed him to stress scientific training and research, was utterly smitten with the notion that technology could transform Britain, and his vision for Labour's future was premised upon exploiting 'the link between planning, technological development and growth'.[16] Closely related to the hopes newly invested in science and technology was an almost tangible impatience with the backwardness of the British Establishment. Labour's appeal was based in Wilson's words on an 'attack on the complacency, on the stagnation, on the Edwardian nostalgia' of the Macmillan government and its offer of a leadership that was 'modern . . . [and] relevant'.[17] In this view political conservatism was merely a manifestation of a broader social retardation that marked industry, the professions and the civil service. It was Wilson's friend and future special economic adviser, Thomas Balogh, who so effectively accused the civil service and the Treasury of 'dilettantism' and lack of professionalism in a famous essay of 1959.[18] Business, it was widely assumed, was afflicted with the same curse: as Wilson explained, 'British business – with honourable exceptions – has been too hide bound, backward-looking and restrictionist; too ready to believe, in a setting where ancestor worship and hereditary succession are still prevalent, that "what was good enough in father's (or grand-father's) day is good enough for me".'[19]

The emphasis on removing the fetters imposed by social conservatism upon the forces of science and technology and thereby liberating the nation's productive capacities and entrepreneurial spirit provided a novel inflection to Labour's traditional class outlook.[20] Long the friend of the working man, Labour could now also present itself as the representative of the new, educated, professional and scientific classes whose creativity was allegedly constrained by the outmoded structures of British society and the narrow class biases of management.[21] The indictment of management was a familiar one by the early 1960s. It had been articulated earlier during and after the war and then again very forcefully by Labour during the 1940s. It was now updated by adding a new charge: British capitalists were constitutionally incapable of grasping the benefits of the emerging scientific revolution. Under Wilson, the fascination with technology and its possibilities took on a mystical, almost utopian, quality and served indirectly to deflect attention from the more mundane question of how the government would make its plans into reality.[22] The effect was to allow Labour and its economic planners to ignore the obvious fact that in their repertoire of policies they had no effective mechanisms for getting inside industry and making it more productive and efficient.

Labour's planning effort reflected both these legacies from past experience and the intellectual fashions of the moment. The combination imparted to the process a breadth and a dynamism that distinguished the 1960s from earlier periods, but it did not solve the practical problems of making planning work. While the joint consultation implied in the existence of Neddy was at the core of the government's strategy, it was to be augmented by a major institutional innovation: the Department of Economic Affairs.[23] The new ministry was to be a sort of cheerleader for planning: it was meant to rival the Treasury in matters of economic policy-making and was charged directly with the task of making and issuing *The National Plan*.[24] The department's sorry fate – it was dissolved in 1969, but had lost influence much earlier – and the abandonment of the *Plan* within less than a year of its unveiling betrayed the deep flaws in Labour's conception of how and why to plan and indicated the extent to which its policies and programme were by now in need of revision. Even then, however, the party's intellectual heritage and its institutional

rigidities would prevent Labour from drawing the lessons that many outside the party drew from the experience.

Though the failure of the Department of Economic Affairs (DEA) and
of the *Plan* were predictable enough in 1964, and highly visible when
they came to pass just a couple of years later, the process repays
examination still. The very first days of the DEA would set the tone, as
the Treasury baulked at its requests for space and furniture. But because
the creation of the new ministry was a top priority of the government,
Treasury resistance was overcome and a talented staff – headed by
Donald MacDougall as director, who was assisted by Fred Catherwood
from industry and who managed to recruit Eric Roll to run the office –
was assembled very quickly. At the very top was the second most important person in the government – George Brown, equally famous for
his abilities and for his willingness to let a taste for alcohol and the good
life interfere with the exercise of those capabilities.[25] Just under him the
Economic Secretary was Tony Crosland, who brought genuine expertise
to the job; and just below him was the capable and experienced Douglas
Allen, later Lord Croham. Bill Rodgers was Parliamentary Secretary to
Brown with responsibility for regional organisation.[26] So long as Brown
and his impressive team remained intact and in charge, the department
would have clout within the Cabinet and could successfully defend itself
from the Treasury's unflagging hostility.[27] The 'concordat' agreed with
the Treasury in late 1964 therefore granted to the DEA the primary
responsibility for economic growth and long-term economic policy-
making and mandated cooperation between the two departments.[28]
More specifically, it allocated to the Treasury responsibility for short-
term economic issues and gave the DEA the job of looking to the future
and grappling with the big issues. The obvious flaw in the arrangement –
i.e. the way in which the short term can constrain or even overwhelm
the long term – is clear, but the division of labour seemed at first not
unreasonable. Nevertheless, very quickly DEA officials realised that by
virtue of the Treasury's role as the key co-ordinating department and its
privileged access to the flow of financial data, the agreed-upon 'division
leaves both information and powers effectively in the hands of the
Treasury'.[29] There was a feeling as well, expressed privately by Samuel
Brittan – then at the DEA – that, freed of its responsibility for the long
term, the 'Treasury now had no role but to be restrictive' and thus 'was

becoming more balanced-budget conscious and financially conservative because of DEA . . .'.[30]

The more immediate challenge confronting the department was how actually to devise *The National Plan*, which was to be produced rapidly and which was to serve simultaneously to lay out the government's economic strategy and to begin to make it happen. Previous experience in economic planning and policy-making offered two models that were almost by definition inapplicable. Keynesian techniques of demand management had been tried under the Tories and, however valuable in smoothing out fluctuations and maintaining stability, they had not produced growth rates comparable to those achieved by Britain's competitors. So while Keynesian approaches would be incorporated into whatever plans Labour made, they were deemed insufficient for the task Labour had set itself. Labour had also had considerable experience of physical planning in the war and immediate post-war years, but direct controls were cumbersome, unpopular with consumers, and unattractive to the economists responsible for carrying out the planning exercise. So both of these models were deemed inappropriate. In the absence of an agreed technique for effective planning, the DEA would fall back upon process and seek to make use of the existing tripartite structure embodied in Neddy. They would confer with businessmen and seek jointly to determine the maximum rate of growth and the measures needed to achieve it.

The problem was that the dialogue with business proceeded within a set of very narrow constraints. The government had no power to tell business what to do, it could only suggest. Even then, what could it suggest? More important, what was the basis on which the consultation would take place? In practice, the department chose to survey business and ask businessmen what they would do on the assumption that growth would be in the range of 4 per cent per annum. That figure itself was 'more or less clutched out of the air', as Allen later explained.[31] It did not derive from any economic calculation of what was possible given rates of investment and resource utilisation; rather, it was more or less carried over from the projections of Neddy operating under the previous Tory government. Labour ministers felt it would be a political mistake to set a growth target lower than the Tories and so simply took over the 4 per cent. In practice, they would reduce this to 3.8 per cent, but then projected it forward where it compounded to 25 per cent for the entire period 1964–70.

The information gathered from business was thus premised upon the principle that growth would be high and that the relevant questions for specific firms would involve how they would respond successfully to such a booming economy: how much money, for example, would they invest to meet rising demand; how much labour would they require; what new facilities would they foresee building; what supply problems could they anticipate? In this peculiar mode of operation, what begins as 'entirely hypothetical figuring . . . really becomes the key to the whole Plan'.[32] Inevitably, then, the data the process elicited had little or nothing to do with what business actually intended to do. The dialogue was circular and self-reproducing, an exercise in imaginary economics with minimal purchase on reality.

The planners understood full well, of course, that in specifying the rate of growth prior to collecting the data from businesses they were not going to get reliable information. But they rationalised the process by claiming that once the *Plan* was worked out and had been made public, it would be to some extent self-fulfilling. In fact, Labour Party strategists believed that 'Up to a point the plan will carry itself out. The knowledge that the Government is going to give growth priority and have a national plan for expansion will itself go far to create an optimistic mood in industry so that industrialists are eager to invest to supply the buoyant markets they foresee.' Beyond that, 'confronting firms with the national plan' would produce the desired result because businessmen would be 'anxious to avoid being branded as inefficient and unpatriotic'.[33] So the *Plan* would exercise a sort of moral suasion, bordering on blackmail, that would alter business behaviour and produce growth. The logic behind such a strategy would seem forced and feeble, but can perhaps be understood in terms of the broader attitudes of the government towards business. Business in Britain was elitist, hidebound and complacent, and its leaders needed to be shaken out of their lethargy. Once liberated from these artificial social and cultural constraints, industry would move forward rapidly, propelled by the energy of new men with professional training and scientific expertise and eager to deploy the latest technologies.

This rather unusual strategy, in which exhortation substitutes for incentives and the *Plan* is utilised to shame businessmen into action, made the relationship between business and the government critical to the success of planning. Hence the sustained effort to make the tripartite structure embodied in Neddy work; and hence, too, the frantic bargaining that Brown and MacDougall would be forced to undertake in order to secure support for the *Plan* from the Confederation of British Industry.[34] The need to produce the proper response on the part of business also lay behind the consistent interest shown by the DEA – and by the NEDC and later also the new Ministry of Technology – in encouraging firms to modernise and the department's rather curious desire to have businesses employ management consultants to that end.[35]

Though the *National Plan* would issue in a series of 39 action items, its authors and advocates understood that fundamentally 'The Plan had no teeth.'[36] Its effectiveness depended upon what businesses decided to do but, as DEA officials themselves understood, existing arrangements provided no effective link between 'the plan and the firm'.[37] And since Labour attitudes towards business were so ambivalent, the response was bound to be inconsistent, ambivalent and unhelpful. Though convinced that British businessmen were mired in tradition and lacking in enterprise, the government nevertheless bet its future on their improved behaviour. Why, given the fundamentally sceptical view of capitalists in Britain, did Labour allow itself to rely on their goodwill and responsiveness? It would seem that the party was overly impressed with the willingness of industry to talk with government. Organised business had already signed on to tripartite negotiations aimed at growth under the Tories and they signalled a readiness to continue the practice after the election of the Labour government. What Labour missed, or chose to ignore, was that for most businessmen the primary objective was to get government involved in discussions which would lead to a moderation of wages. They were far less interested in changing their own behaviour. For their part, representatives of industry hoped that Labour would be better able to secure the cooperation of the unions in a policy of wage restraint than the Conservatives had been. In fact, the very first solid achievement of the Department of Economic Affairs was the 'The Joint Statement of Intent on Productivity, Prices and Incomes' agreed by the government, the unions and the employers and issued with great fanfare in December 1964.[38]

Business signed on to the subsequent *National Plan* in much the same spirit, but turned a deaf ear to the government's calls for a revitalisation of management and to its ongoing campaign for increased productivity.

And with some reason, for Labour's efforts to court business support came with an attitude of suspicion and were routinely combined with specific policies that business found onerous and inhospitable. These included both the usual policies to which businessmen typically objected, like higher taxes, but also a series of more intrusive policies designed to affect the direction of business activity. Thus Labour's plans to reform corporation tax and to introduce taxation on capital gains provoked predictable criticisms from industry and the City.[39] But businessmen found reason to object as well to a variety of policies that seemed to them to suggest a desire to control business very directly and that appeared also to contradict the rhetorical emphasis on the priority to be accorded to growth. Thus while industry was strongly urged to increase investment and expand its facilities, the Labour government sought simultaneously to implement a very rigorous regional policy that essentially told business where it could and could not invest.[40] Not only did the state seek to control the location of new building by granting or withholding Industrial Development Certificates, it also provided through the Regional Employment Premium (REP) substantial subsidies to firms willing to locate in 'development areas'.[41] These were complemented by positive discrimination against firms wanting to locate in areas like London and, more generally, against businesses engaged in services rather than manufacturing.[42] Wilson was personally quite hostile to efforts to build more office space and regarded such investment as an indulgence by the rich. The main device designed to tilt investment away from services and towards manufacturing, however, was the Selective Employment Tax, the brainchild of the economist Nicholas Kaldor and a pet scheme of the DEA, which was introduced in 1966.[43] The SET imposed a tax on all firms based on the number of workers employed, but firms in the manufacturing sector would have it refunded. The immediate effect was deflationary, but the long-term effect was supposed to be to encourage employment in manufacturing at the expense of services.[44]

The combination of new and restructured taxes and enhanced efforts to discriminate between regions and sectors led business to feel that Labour was less interested in growth than in control. In Labour's strategy for planning, industry leaders were first labelled as key obstacles to growth. They were then to be shamed into adopting a policy of expansion but, in the end, blocked from investing in the most desirable locations and in the service sector, where the opportunities for growth were most attractive. If the *Plan* itself lacked teeth, Labour's detailed policies often did bite, but they bit in ways business found burdensome and may have done as much to inhibit as to inspire growth. And in candid, private moments Labour ministers acknowledged that the government's policies were often contradictory. Thus Richard Crossman confided to his fellow guests at a party in July 1966 that, as Tony Benn recalled, 'almost all our social policies ran counter to the idea of rapid growth. He pointed out that pushing industry into development districts, maintaining the green belt, standard tariffs for electricity and gas, and a whole host of other things which we accept uncritically as being part of a civilised community actually held back growth.' 'It was stimulating . . .', noted Benn, but mainly it was revealing of the fact that for Labour 'growth' was only one objective among many.[45] Even the official definition of the DEA, founded to engineer faster growth, insisted that a 'very important task' was 'to secure balanced regional development and balanced industrial expansion'.[46] However desirable 'balanced' growth might be, the very concept of balance implied a preference for stability and security and a policy of defending against the potentially disruptive impact of economic transformation.

Labour's deep ambivalence about business and its reluctance to allow business to lead the process of growth was matched by an equally strong commitment to protect the prerogatives of the trade unions and, by implication, the interests of the workers they represented. If businessmen sought to use the practice of tripartite bargaining to extract from government a commitment to control wages, unions were determined to use the same structures and practices to veto policies, like wage controls, that might threaten their members' incomes and to block initiatives and policies that might threaten their jobs. The Labour government largely acquiesced, buoyed in their stance by their view that what mainly retarded growth was the backwardness and conservatism of business. They also worked assiduously to keep the focus off trade unions and their restrictive practices as possible obstacles to growth. Thus the DEA persisted in urging employers to agree to 'productivity agreements' with the unions even after George Brown was informed that the nation's largest union, the Transport and General Workers Union (TGWU), never broached the issue in negotiations and typically bargained in a 'non-productivity' manner.[47]

The DEA also discouraged the publication of research comparing productivity in Britain and its economic rivals. The report in question, based on research undertaken not in the DEA but in the Ministry of Aviation, estimated that 'it takes at least three Britons to do the work of two Frenchmen, Germans or Swedes' and concluded that 'widespread overmanning in British industry is the most formidable obstacle which faces the economic Departments . . . in their attempts to increase industrial efficiency'.[48] The department specifically charged with increasing productivity and spurring growth resisted publishing the data and refused to give the argument credence.

Though the Labour government would itself be moved to break with the trade unions over unofficial strikes and ultimately to propose new trade union legislation in its famous paper, *In Place of Strife*, its approach to planning consciously and carefully protected the position of the trade unions. The practice of planning under Labour thus came to consist of an utterly impractical combination of imaginary goals, the exhortation and shaming of business, detailed controls that were bound to provoke resentment and resistance from those same businessmen, and a refusal to contemplate policies that might upset the unions. The package was internally contradictory, lacked mechanisms for successful implementation, and was thus presumably bound to fail in the best of circumstances.

Labour's approach to planning was nevertheless utterly consistent with the party's outlook, structure and past practice. The party's critical stance towards business, for example, was central to the 'socialism' of all factions within the party. There was very little faith, on the Labour left or on the Labour right, in the market per se, in business as it was organised in twentieth-century Britain, or in capitalists as a class. Again, the difference between left and right was a matter of emphasis and temperament: the left wanted to bash business and wage rhetorical class war relentlessly; the right tended to feel that capitalism had already been, or was in process of becoming, transformed out of existence and so did not merit a frontal assault. Crosland, for example, believed that the major economic problems had been solved, but largely due to the fact that businessmen were themselves no longer in charge. He did not take them seriously. When it came to framing economic policy, moreover, Gaitskell as well as his critics on the left and later Harold Wilson had agreed on the inadequacies of the market and of business left to its own devices and firmly believed that the solution to the nation's remaining economic ills lay with government or with enlightened public policy. Businessmen were, at best, an interest that had to be reckoned with, but they were never seen as partners in generating economic growth.

The fact that people beyond the orbit of the Labour Party were now turning to planning was understood, therefore, as vindication of the party's historic antipathy to the market and private capital. But planning for Labour had to proceed on Labourist principles, which in practice meant that the interests so central to the party and its vision of the world had to be put at its centre. The unions had to be consulted, and had to approve, not merely those policies that implied or presaged a direct intervention in industry, but also broader macro-economic policy stances that might stimulate or dampen demand and thus increase or diminish the demand for labour. The unions also, and inevitably, would have to be directly involved in fashioning any policy aimed at controlling wages. They would have to approve it and sell it to their members; and in some variations, they would be expected actually to administer it. Planning as conceived and executed in the Wilson governments of 1964–70 was thus a very direct and accurate projection of the nature of the Labour Party onto its key policy initiative. Its blindnesses were those embedded in Labour's outlook and structure; its preferences grew logically from the party's historic commitments and its institutional legacies; its flaws, then, were not incidental but essential to its origins and purposes.

Given the limitations of Labour plans for planning, failure was likely even in the best of circumstances. Of course, the circumstances were not at all ideal and events conspired to force the abandonment of the *Plan* well before its flaws had time fully to emerge. The outcome was for that reason ambiguous, susceptible as always to varied interpretation. To some, especially those outside the party or without firm ties to its institutions and heritage, the failure of Labour's planning effort was confirmation that planning could not work and that the market was a far more effective mechanism for guiding the economy than the state. To others, especially within the core of the Labour party, the death of the *Plan* proved merely that the forces arrayed against socialism were strong indeed and required even greater efforts to overcome them. To still others, the experience was evidence of a major failure of will on the part of Wilson and the Cabinet over which he presided. And to those seriously invested in planning and eager to preserve hope, but unwilling to engage in a serious critique of planning's flawed underpinnings or of the party's leadership, the failure was to be explained largely in terms of contingent forces, accidents that need not have happened and that could be avoided in future. Since the historical record could be interpreted in such different ways, efforts to understand the legacy of the planning experiment of the 1960s did not necessarily lead to the conclusion that Labour needed a major updating or retooling. Labour as a party was in any event almost inured to failure and rather surprised at its occasional success. The existing stock of arguments used to explain defeat, delay and disaffection could thus be pressed into service yet again, explaining the retreat from the *Plan* and the abandonment of the DEA in the standard tropes of inner-party discourse. The fate of planning would in consequence be made to serve different and even contradictory uses. It could in theory serve as an object lesson in the futility of state inter-vention, though few in the party were inclined to see it that way. It could and would be taken, particularly by the left, as proof of the struc-tural inadequacy of Labourism and the need for a more radical policy of nationalisation and state control. More pragmatically, it could be harnessed to a critique of Wilson's personal leadership and a campaign to replace him and those around him.

Because the experiment was not allowed fully to run its course, it was impossible to decide clearly on its meaning. The record itself offered evid-ence that could be read in many different ways. Because the decision to adopt macro-economic measures that effectively killed the *Plan* were by necessity made at the very top of government, however, Wilson features prominently in any rendition of the story and his role virtually invites criticism. The too-easy critique of Wilson obscures, however, the more fundamental problems with the planning effort and neglects the external constraints confronted by the government as well as the power of those with whom they had to deal. The circumstances were in fact genuinely adverse: the balance of payments problem inherited from the Tories persisted into the period of Labour rule and began to worsen, severely limiting the government's options. At the same time, the political response to financial crisis showed clearly that key interests – the City, the Bank of England and the Treasury especially – did feel threatened by Labour's plans. They therefore responded to the perceived threat by insisting repeatedly that the government adopt measures to deflate and to restore confidence.

The climax would come in July 1966, not long after Labour's decisive electoral victory, and the details starkly reveal the asymmetries of power and influence within British economic and political life. Even before the election in March 1966, there had been talk in financial circles of a looming crisis.[49] Afterwards, it seemed to materialise as the calculations became ever more grim and elicited renewed calls for cutbacks. The key intervention seems to have come from the new Governor of the Bank of England, Leslie O'Brien, who visited Wilson on 8 July and told him of mounting 'exchange losses . . . on a scale endangering the parity'. 'At the same time,' according to Alec Cairncross, 'the Treasury was pressing on the Chancellor [James Callaghan] the need for drastic action.'[50] Though the DEA's top officials resisted strongly, they lost the argument.[51] O'Brien would again weigh in on the side of restraint by writing on 12 July to Callaghan and warning him that without stern measures – measures he conceded would have the effect of 'raising the level of unemployment' – 'a collapse of the sterling parity . . . will be inevitable'. Three days later, the Governor met with Wilson and Callaghan together and claimed that 'a critical situation had been reached . . .'.[52] In response, Wilson forced upon the Cabinet, and upon George Brown in particular, a set of deflationary policies that were widely understood to render the *National Plan* inoperative because its underpinnings in macro-economic policy had been dramatically scaled back.

The 'virtual abandonment of the National Plan' was, of course, profoundly disappointing to the planners.[53] Brown himself offered his resignation and was soon after moved to the Foreign Office. But the precipitous nature of the decision actually allowed the planners to avoid confronting the weaknesses in the project itself and to place the blame for failure on others. Thus Roger Opie, who worked in the DEA, penned the oft-quoted, brief epitaph: 'conceived October, 1964, born September 1965, died (possibly murdered) July 1966'.[54] Who did the deed? The Treasury clearly had a hand in it; so, too, the bankers and the financial community whose views they both shaped and echoed. But they were abetted by Wilson, who was criticised for a failure of will, or imagination, at two critical moments: first, when upon taking office in 1964 he chose to take the orthodox position and chose not to devalue; and second, in July 1966 when he again opted for deflation over devaluation and sacrificed the centrepiece of the party's economic strategy. The arguments for and against devaluation were complex and remain a matter of debate, as does Wilson's broader culpability, but what is obvious is that the ability to blame external circumstances or to fix responsibility upon the Treasury, the bankers or Wilson himself, allowed supporters of planning to avoid a critical examination of the flaws within their own vision and practice.

The effect was that Labour experienced another turning point where it decisively failed to turn, to learn or to reform itself. Instead, the Labour government clung to office and presided over almost four more years of frustrating efforts to stimulate growth through a series of often confused and contradictory state interventions in the economy. In fact, something akin to planning would continue during the last four years of the Labour government, but it would proceed outside the planning department, the DEA, under different names and guises than previously, and without a formal plan. There would be very little discussion of the *National Plan*, no effort to make a new plan nor even an effort to update the old *Plan*, for the planners understood that further talk of this sort would likely 'bring planning into final disrepute', as Michael Stewart – Brown's replacement – would tell his officials.[55] But planning and state intervention in the market continued nonetheless and the belief in it was undiminished within the party at large.

The ability of planning's advocates to locate responsibility for its failure outside the process itself was thus a key factor allowing the Labour government to proceed as if planning might still work. It was also made possible by the fact that under Wilson the effort to plan the economy and to foster growth was not focused entirely on the Department of Economic Affairs or the *National Plan*. On the contrary, a distinguishing feature of Wilson's administration was that economic strategy was to proceed on several fronts simultaneously. Planning itself was to be interdepartmental and involve the DEA, the Treasury, the Board of Trade and Neddy, with lots of work done by the so-called 'little Neddies' working on specific industries. Controls on building remained the prerogative of Housing and the Ministry of Transport would also be involved in decisions about the location of industry, though these departments were not regarded as central to the planning effort. Labour's (and especially

Wilson's) peculiar interpretation of Britain's economic difficulties, and of what was required to overcome them, also dictated a broad and diffuse approach. Since what supposedly held back the economy was institutional and cultural conservatism, then what was needed was prodding here and there to unleash the forces of science and technology. Hence the Labour government's strong desire to open up the bureaucracy and to create a new and more modern civil service – an achievement that would signal an end to the traditional caution and conservatism that infected industry as well as the state. The government was for this reason determined in particular not to allow the Treasury to dominate policy-making and they succeeded in pushing the issue to the point where, in 1968, even the future head of the civil service conceded that it would soon be necessary 'to re-think the functions of the modern Treasury . . .'.[56]

Keeping the Treasury at bay was considered necessary to allow innovative policies to emerge inside and outside government and to afford time and money for them to be pursued effectively. The most important initiatives were, of course, those over which the government would have control. Early on it was expected that these would emanate from the DEA, but over the long term it was the Ministry of Technology to which the planners and modernisers would look for leadership.[57] Thus while the DEA would not be formally wound up until 1969, it was increasingly overshadowed by the Ministry of Technology (Mintech) and the financing institution created to work alongside it: the Industrial Reorganisation Corporation (IRC).[58] Indeed, when George Brown fumed about the need to encourage innovation at industry level, he was told that was not DEA's task but rather the job of Mintech.[59] Along with the DEA, Mintech and the IRC were the major institutional innovations of the Wilson governments and all were aimed at using the power of the state to encourage faster growth. As the former lost its lustre, the latter blossomed. Mintech had been set up in 1964 under the direction of Frank Cousins, the union leader, and was taken over by Tony Benn in 1966. The IRC came later and would be used by the Ministry of Technology to further its aims of restructuring industry, improving (and in some cases actually replacing) management, and encouraging the greater use of science and technology.[60]

Still later, the IRC would be augmented by the additional powers granted the government under the Industrial Expansion Bill of 1968 –

regarded by business as socialism by stealth and by its supporters as 'a formidable beast . . . a "great leap forward" into socialism'.[61] Underlying the work of both these institutions was the assumption that essential to increasing growth rates was the better use of new technology by British firms. In Labour's view, this was being impeded by the traditional conservatism of industry and by the failure properly to incorporate research and development into the work of the firm. Far too much of the nation's R&D effort went towards military purposes, it was argued, and most British firms were too small to undertake serious R&D or to apply technological advances successfully. Mintech and the IRC were thus to seek out and facilitate 'structural changes which will eliminate wasteful duplication and permit economies of scale in production, marketing and research'. Guided by these assumptions, they would proceed to underwrite several major high-technology ventures, including Concorde and a sustained effort to promote a British-based computer industry to rival that of the United States. They also helped to engineer a series of consolidations and mergers designed to create companies that could compete effectively with their European and American rivals. In addition, Mintech and the IRC saw themselves as exercising a broad set of 'industrial sponsorship functions' and they were therefore organised so as to have connections with virtually every major industry.[62] The aim was to ensure that whatever contact government had with private industry was used as leverage to encourage technical innovation, increased productivity and the adoption of modern management techniques.

These sustained but diffuse efforts produced few concrete results and were in any event undermined by other features of government policy. Their significance lies then not in their achievements but in what they reveal about Labour's ongoing commitment to planning and also to public ownership. Public support for nationalised industry may have begun seriously to wane, but Labour still pinned its hopes for revitalising the economy on the state and state-sponsored initiatives. The details had shifted, of course: the earlier faith that public ownership per se would bring greater efficiency, equity and productivity was replaced by more refined notions about the need to reshape industry within key sectors through a more complex mix of policies. The planning process as carried out in the DEA and embodied in the *National Plan* was likewise replaced by policies run out of other departments, mostly Mintech. These would include government-sponsored consolidations, direct and indirect state subsidies to key firms developing innovative technologies, selective state investment in research and development, increased government share ownership in order to move companies in the right direction and, eventually, compulsory planning agreements bargained out between employers, unions and the government.[63] The new policies relied less on public ownership and explicit planning and might, for that reason, be regarded as less rigorously socialist or collectivist. But in other respects the more recent formula was more radically interventionist than the earlier. This new repertoire of policies would be reworked and reimagined, especially after 1970, but its core would persist and come to serve as the inspiration for a new and more left-wing programme for the party and for what came eventually to be called the 'Alternative Economic Strategy'.[64]

Curiously, then, Wilson's fascination with technology and with planning was not merely a programme that could heal the differences between left and right, 'fundamentalists' and 'revisionists'. It was, rather, a particular vision of 'the modern' and of what a party with Labour's basic orientation could contribute to making Britain's economy more open to talent, more dynamic and hence productive. It was a strategy that appeared to respond to the changes Britain was experiencing at least as effectively as any programme that party's revisionist wing might come up with, for it would allow Labour to direct change rather than merely accommodate to it. Yet it was also a confirmation and reaffirmation of Labour's distinctive traditions and political identity and a rejection of the case for a revisionist type of modernisation. At the same time, the planning effort begun under Wilson – with its objective of getting deep within industry in order to engineer growth – was something of a departure that would contribute, indirectly and often unwittingly, to a programmatic and ideological shift to the left. That shift was not, of course, merely a matter of the autonomous drift of policy and ideas but also a product of changes in the structure of the party and in the relative strength of the interests represented within it. Central to the move to the left, in particular, was a transformation in the role of the unions within the party, of the left and the rank and file within the unions, and of ordinary party members' allegiances. These, too, were largely set in motion under Harold Wilson's leadership, but again, often indirectly and unwittingly.

Notes and references

1 The conventional wisdom has viewed Wilson's policies as basically a compromise rather than a genuinely coherent and innovative perspective. For a strong dissent, see Ilaria Favretto, '"Wilsonism" reconsidered: Labour Party revisionism, 1952–64', *Contemporary British History*, XIV, 4 (Winter 2000), 54–80.

2 Douglas Jay, *The Socialist Case* (London: Faber & Faber, 1937), quoted in Lawrence Black, 'The Political Culture of the Left in "Affluent" Britain, 1951–1964', PhD Thesis, London Guildhall University, 1999, 220. See also Black, *The Political Culture of the Left in Britain, 1951–64: Old Labour, New Britain* (New York: Palgrave, 2002).

3 On the classically narrow reference groups of British workers, see W.G. Runciman, *Relative Deprivation and Social Justice: A Study of Attitudes to Social Inequality in Twentieth-Century England* (London: Routledge & Kegan Paul, 1966).

4 Labour Party, *Labour and the New Society* (London, 1950), 3.

5 Letter to the editor in *Labour Woman* (July, 1959), 94, quoted in Black, 'Political Culture', 211.

6 Cited in Black, 'Political Culture', 213.

7 C.A.R. Crosland, *The Future of Socialism* (London: Jonathan Cape, 1956), 521–2.

8 See James E. Cronin, *Labour and Society in Britain, 1918–1979* (London: Batsford, 1984), 139–40.

9 The proportion fell from 39.8 per cent to 38.7 per cent. The percentage for the years before and after 1959 are not strictly comparable because the Standard Industrial Classification system was altered in 1958. The change moved some jobs from mining and manufacturing to various services. This does not mean, however, that the services necessarily grew more rapidly in previous years, since the basis of allocating jobs to industries retrospectively would have the likely effect of moving jobs from manufacturing to services for earlier periods as well. The most reliable method is to stick with the accepted classification systems for the years they were in effect. The data are derived from the *Annual Abstracts of Statistics* (London: Central Statistical Office).

10 *Social Trends 1972* (London: CSO), 74.

11 See John Goldthorpe, David Lockwood, Frank Bechofer and Jennifer Platt, *The Affluent Worker in the Class Structure* (Cambridge: Cambridge University Press, 1969); *The Affluent Worker: Industrial Attitudes and Behaviour* (Cambridge: Cambridge University Press, 1968); and *The Affluent*

Worker: Political Attitudes and Behaviour (Cambridge: Cambridge University Press, 1968).

12 See H. Mercer, N. Rollings and J.D. Tomlinson, eds, *Labour Governments and Private Industry: The Experience of 1945–1951* (Edinburgh: Edinburgh University Press, 1992).

13 Roger Opie, 'Economic Planning and Growth', in Wilfred Beckerman, ed., *The Labour Government's Economic Record: 1964–1970* (London: Duckworth, 1972), 159. Opie was himself on the staff of the Department of Economic Affairs. The term 'purposive planning' was apparently preferred by Sir Robert Shone, director of the National Economic Development Council, but it is hard to see the difference. See PRO: CAB124/1440.

14 Jim Tomlinson, 'Conservative modernisation: Too little, too late?', *Contemporary British History*, XI, 3 (Autumn 1997), 18–38; Astrid Ringe, 'Background to Neddy: Economic planning in the 1960s', *Contemporary British History*, XII, 1 (Spring 1998), 82–98.

15 It has been suggested that the issue of 'controls' was the critical factor underlying the shift of voters, particularly women and the middle classes, away from Labour and toward the Conservatives in the early 1950s. See Ina Zweiniger-Bargielowska, *Austerity in Britain: Rationing, Controls and Consumption, 1939–1955* (Oxford: Oxford University Press, 2000).

16 Ben Pimlott, *Harold Wilson* (London: HarperCollins, 1992), 274ff; Richard Coopey, 'Industrial Policy in the White Heat of the Scientific Revolution', in R. Coopey, S. Fielding and N. Tiratsoo, eds, *The Wilson Governments, 1964–1970* (London: Pinter, 1993), 102–22.

17 Harold Wilson, *Purpose in Politics* (London: Weidenfeld & Nicolson, 1964), 264. On the recurring theme of modernising Britain, see Scott Newton and Dilwyn Porter, *Modernization Frustrated: The Politics of Industrial Decline in Britain* (London: Unwin Hyman, 1988), esp. 147–59.

18 Thomas Balogh, 'The Apotheosis of the Dilettante', in Hugh Thomas, ed., *The Establishment* (London: Anthony Blond, 1959), 83–126.

19 Wilson, *Purpose in Politics*, 265.

20 Though it was never strictly accurate that the Conservatives were hostile to science or lacked interest in improving management. See PRO: CAB124/1433, 'Central Economic Planning' (1961–1963); and the extremely interesting memo on 'The Modernisation of Britain', PRO: CAB129/111, C. (62) 201, 3 December 1962; and the discussion in Rodney Lowe and Neil Rollings, 'Modernising Britain, 1957–64: A Classic Case of Centralisation and Fragmentation?' in R.W.W. Rhodes, ed., *Transforming British Government*, Volume I: *Changing Institutions* (London: Macmillan, 2000), 99–118.

21 Steven Fielding, 'White Heat and White Collars: The Evolution of "Wilsonism"', in Coopey et al., *The Wilson Governments*, 29–47.

22 Favoretto, '"Wilsonism" Reconsidered', refers to Wilson as part of a broader 'centre-left technocratic group' that was neither fundamentalist on issues like public ownership nor truly 'revisionist' in the fashion of Crosland, but something distinct and coherent.

23 The idea for a new department was widely discussed within the Labour Party and the recognition that new policies would require institutional innovation was a mark of the seriousness of the discussion. That this particular innovation should fail does not discredit the understanding behind it. See, for example, the Crosland Papers, File 4/10 on the work of the Fabian Society committee on 'Treasury Reorganisation' chaired by Shirley Williams.

24 *The National Plan*, Cmnd. 2764 (London: HMSO, 1965). See also PRO: EW25/100, 'The National Plan' (1965).

25 See Peter Paterson, *Tired and Emotional: The Life of George Brown* (London: Chatto & Windus, 1993), 165–91; George Brown, *In My Way: The Political Memoirs of Lord George-Brown* (London: Gollancz, 1971), 95–123; Sir Fred Catherwood, *At the Cutting Edge* (London: Hodder & Stoughton, 1995); and Donald MacDougall, *Don and Mandarin: Memoirs of an Economist* (London: John Murray, 1987). Brown's personal difficulties, moreover, were well known. Wilson, for example, was happy to have people give wide currency to his quip that 'If G.B. misses any more meetings through "morning sickness" we will be wondering if he is going to give birth to a "littly Neddy".' See Samuel Brittan's diary, LSE Archive, 22 January 1965.

26 Bill Rodgers, *Fourth among Equals* (London: Politico's, 2000), 77.

27 Christopher Clifford, 'The rise and fall of the Department of Economic Affairs, 1964–69: British government and indicative planning', *Contemporary British History*, XI, 2 (Summer 1997), 94–116.

28 See PRO: PREM13/2126, 'Department of Economic Affairs and the Treasury' (1968) for copies of the original 'Concordat' and subsequent debates and discussions; see also PRO: EW4/50, 'Cooperation between Treasury and Department of Economic Affairs', and PREM13/275, 'Relations between Treasury and the Department of Economic Affairs'. In fact, the papers of the DEA are filled with references to the strained relationship with the Treasury.

29 PRO: EW1/72, D.A.V. Allen to Sir Eric Roll, 28 March 1966.

30 Diary of Samuel Brittain, LSE Archive, entries for 17 December 1964 and 13 January 1965.

31 Lord Croham, speaking in the 'Witness Seminar: The Department of Economic Affairs', edited by Christopher Clifford and Alistair McMillan, *Contemporary British History*, XI, 2 (Summer 1997), 129.

32 PRO: EW24/93, C.A.E. Goodhart to MacDougall, 6 September 1965.

33 See 'The Requirements of Economic Planning: An Outline', prepared by the Labour Party Finance and Economic Policy Sub-Committee, March 1963, in the George Brown Papers, Bodleian Library, C. 5000.

34 MacDougall, *Don and Mandarin*, 158–60.

35 George Brown Papers, C. 5000. Officials and economists often placed very high hopes on the benefits to be gained from the deployment of management consultants. According to one estimate, fully a third of the increase in productivity between 1950 and the early 1960s could be ascribed to the use of consultants. See PRO: FG2/88, 'Future Work of the National Economic Development Council' (1963–64). Just how that figure was arrived at remains a mystery, though a roughly similar estimate was offered by an NEDC official: 'Studies we have made', he said, 'suggest that the use of their [consultants'] services can often increase output per worker by one-third in individual firms.' See PRO: FG2/15, 'NEDC – Preparation of the First Report (1963), "Growth of the UK Economy to 1966" '. Such views were widespread: in 1966, the Minister of Technology, Frank Cousins, was moved to make the 'case for a crash programme to provide the services of management consultants more widely . . .' in order to increase productivity. See PRO: HF12/3, 'National Productivity Conference' (1966).

36 Opie, 'Economic Planning and Growth', 172.

37 PRO: EW24/71, Memo on 'The Plan and the Firm', from J. Grieve Smith to MacDougall, 6 October 1965.

38 PRO: EW8/1.

39 R.W.R. Price, 'Budgetary Policy', in F.T. Blackaby, ed., *British Economic Policy, 1960–1974* (Cambridge: Cambridge University Press, 1978), 144–9; Jonathan Boswell and James Peters, *Capitalism in Contention: Business Leaders and Political Economy in Modern Britain* (Cambridge: Cambridge University Press, 1997), 53.

40 Stuart Holland claims that when the regional planning piece of the *National Plan* was being put together, he was called on to give advice because nobody in the DEA had any expertise. Holland was then working on a thesis on the North-South problem in Italy and seems to have based his advice on his analysis of that experience. It was perhaps better than nothing, but Lancashire and Wales were not the *mezzagiorno*. Interview with Stuart Holland, 7 October 2002. See also Stuart Holland, *Capital Versus the Regions* (New York: St Martin's, 1977).

41 Jeremy Hardie, 'Regional Policy', in Beckerman, ed., *Labour Government's Economic Record*, 229–30.

42 See PRO: EW24/93.

43 PRO: EW24/19, 'Fiscal Incentives, 1964–65', contains files on the extensive discussions within the DEA that led to the adoption of the scheme.

44 SET and REP were also supposed to increase productivity in both services and manufacturing. Productivity would increase in services by forcing firms to shed workers and deploy existing labour more efficiently; it would increase productivity in manufacturing by providing jobs in the newer and more rapidly expanding firms employing the latest technology. It was also argued that because the British economy was faced with a chronic labour shortage, the only way to expand was to direct employment to the less developed districts, where there were underutilised supplies of labour. See the note from Opie to MacDougall, 24 March 1965, in PRO: EW24/19.

45 Tony Benn, *Out of the Wilderness: Diaries, 1963–1967* (London: Hutchinson, 1987), entry for 14 July 1966, 453.

46 PRO: EW1/26, 'The Work of the DEA' (1964).

47 Terry Pitts, Labour Party Research Secretary, to George Brown, 14 July 1966, in George Brown Papers, C. 5010.

48 Sam Hays, Ministry of Aviation, to J. Jukes, DEA, 30 September 1965, in 'Productivity – International Comparisons', PRO: EW24/27. The correspondence sparked by Hays's intervention is fascinating. Jukes responded that overmanning was 'not conclusively demonstrated' and there were other factors, including poor management (21 October 1965); while Hays countered that 'overmanning itself is an aspect of management combined with the national preference for security and immobility rather than for rapid economic advance' (26 October 1965). DEA officials, having just published the *National Plan* using highly questionable numbers at every level, proceeded to find all sorts of problems with Hays's data. The DEA's take on the problem – and neither version seems to have been published – placed the blame on management: 'The quality of industrial management is the most intangible yet probably by far the most important factor in improving industrial efficiency.' A certain amount of 'overmanning' was recognised, but progress in eliminating it, the DEA argued, 'can be made only with the co-operation of the trade-unions . . .' (Draft article on 'Productivity', March 1966). An earlier calculation by NEDC estimated the restriction of output at 30 per cent. See PRO: FG2/80.

49 PRO: PREM13/851.

50 Alec Cairncross, *The Wilson Years: A Treasury Diary, 1964–1966* (London: Historians' Press, 1997), 147 and ff. Cairncross was Director of the Economic Section of the Treasury.

51 See PRO: EW25/128 for MacDougall's resistance.

52 O'Brien to Calaghan, 12 July 1966; and 'Record of a Meeting at 10 Downing Street . . . July 15, 1966', in PRO: PREM13/853. The exchange would seem to be at odds with Wilson's later claim that O'Brien 'was a non-political Governor'. Perhaps in contrast to his predecessor, Lord Cromer, this was true, but his intervention in July 1966 certainly had a decisive political impact. See Harold Wilson, *The Labour Government, 1964–1970. A Personal Record* (London: Weidenfeld & Nicolson, 1971), 251. The crisis of July 1966 also coincided with rumours of a plot to replace Wilson and threats of resignation from Brown. See Pimlott, *Harold Wilson*, 422–31.

53 PRO: EW24/96.

54 Opie, 'Economic Planning', 170.

55 Michael Stewart, 16 November 1966, in PRO: EW24/96. Prior to July 1966, however, officials were optimistic and seriously considered a further planning exercise. See the discussion in PRO: EW24/93.

56 Burke Trend to Wilson, 27 March 1968, in PRO: PREM13/2135. Trend was referring specifically to the implications of the Fulton Report.

57 This is certainly how Tony Benn understood it, even years later. Interview with Tony Benn, 30 September 2003.

58 See P. Mottershead, 'Industrial Policy', in Blackaby, *British Economic Policy*, 418–83 for a thorough and judicious review. For insights of a rather different sort, see Tony Benn, *Out of the Wilderness*, and *Office without Power: Diaries, 1968–1972* (London: Hutchinson, 1988).

59 See PRO: EW24/93.

60 See PRO: EW16/22.

61 Michael Shanks, writing in *The Times*, 29 January 1968, excerpt kept in PRO: FV11/14, 'Establishment of the IRC and Mintech Policy'.

62 See the organisational charts laying out 'the allocation of Mintech's industrial sponsorship functions' and also that of the IRC in PRO: FV11/14. It was assumed that the system would cover virtually all of British industry. The idea of 'sponsoring' departments having a quasi-supervisory role in the development of industry would seem to date from the Second World War and was central to Labour's thinking during the 1940s and, it would appear, long after as well.

63 Planning agreements would come to be associated closely with Tony Benn, but Stuart Holland, the key architect of Labour's emerging new strategy, downplays Benn's contribution. Benn himself stresses the contribution of trade unionists while playing down Holland's role. Whatever their precise roles, it was Benn who became the standard-bearer for planning agreements, for public ownership and for the entire Alternative Economic Strategy.

Interviews with Stuart Holland, 7 October 2002, and with Tony Benn, 30 September 2003.

64 See John Callaghan, 'The rise and fall of the Alternative Economic Strategy: From the internationalisation of capital to "globalisation" ', *Contemporary British History*, XIV, 3 (Autumn 2000), 105–30.

CHAPTER 3

Interests, conflict and the party of progress, 1964–70

Though the link between planning, technology and Labour was largely the invention of Harold Wilson, it was of course not his creation alone. It built both upon Labour's long tradition of support for public ownership and state intervention and upon the fascination with technology and the fixation on the need to 'modernise' Britain that were so ubiquitous in the late 1950s and early 1960s. In forging the connection between these discourses and promising a 'socialist inspired scientific and technological revolution', Wilson accomplished a decisive shift, almost a reversal, in the political identities of Labour and its Tory rivals.[1] He also effected, perhaps without fully intending or realising it, a simultaneous redefinition of right and left within the Labour Party.

Wilson's own position within the spectrum of Labour Party politics was fluid and he was not firmly anchored on either the left or the right. Nor was he trusted by the left or the right or, for that matter, by the centre to which he truly belonged. Wilson had, of course, been elected leader in 1963 as a man of the left, but had largely surrounded himself in Cabinet during 1964–70 with ministers from the right of the party. He was hard to pin down, preferred to deal rather than confront; and he was protected by the redoubtable Marcia Williams, later Lady Falkender. He had been careful not to identify himself too closely with either side during the factional disputes of the early 1960s and was unusually skilled at playing off the left and right to his own advantage. Nevertheless, the policy innovations associated with planning, science and technology, and with the reform of the administrative machinery that Wilson undertook – e.g. the creation of the Department of Economic Affairs and the Ministry of Technology and the broader reform of the civil service – helped to transform the poles of political discourse in a manner that effectively boosted the left, and did so in a more or less lasting way. Whatever his intention, Wilson managed to redefine issues so that the left was no longer backward-looking but rather the standard-bearer for progress.

This was new. In the earlier debates between revisionists and so-called fundamentalists – they would prefer to call themselves simply socialists – the revisionists had little difficulty in portraying themselves as the 'modernisers' interested in updating the party, its programme and structure, and in identifying their rivals as the opponents of change. In the debates of 1959–62, therefore, the revisionist case carried with it the implication of progress, of wanting Labour to confront the changes that had occurred in British society and to bring its appeal and structure into greater conformity with the needs of the modern world and of contemporary electoral politics. Implicit was the identification of those who resisted efforts to revise Labour's outlook as people who were clinging nostalgically to the past and to policies that suited past realities. Equally important was the assumption that during the 1950s it was the Conservatives who had somehow become more modern and had crafted a message more palatable to the concerns of present-day voters and a set of policies that addressed contemporary problems more effectively. These identifications became more pronounced and threatened to become permanent after 1959, as Macmillan, reluctantly and diffidently it seems, adopted the rhetoric of modernisation and as the Tory government itself moved towards a policy of planning the economy while Labour was repudiating the efforts to revise party policy.[2] Wilson's genius, and his central achievement, was to reverse these perceptions of the two parties' competing identities very quickly and very decisively.

What made the reversal possible was Wilson's ability to call upon a Labour tradition of a much more enduring character. That was the belief that business was fundamentally not a force for progress in Britain. Businessmen and the firms over which they presided were widely seen as hidebound and inefficient, resistant to innovation and more interested in preserving the prerogatives of managers and directors, and of shoring up hierarchies within industry, than in creating new products, inventing new processes, applying new technologies or seeking out new markets. The critique of business as an institution and of capitalists as a class – a fundamental presupposition for socialists – had become a staple part of the broader understanding of 'the Establishment' and its place in Britain's class structure during the 1930s and 1940s and it continued to be a part of public discourse into the post-war era, and not only on the left. Even the sustained economic growth of the economy during the 1950s did not translate into increased respect for the ability of capital to generate prosperity; and the focus of the late 1950s and early 1960s on Britain's lagging growth rate merely reinforced old images about the inefficiency and backwardness of business.

So the desire to boost the rate of growth of the economy led quickly to the conclusion that businessmen were not up to the task and that leadership by the state was essential. Hence the enormous popularity of planning and the reworking of the argument for public ownership and for government intervention. The rationale for nationalisation offered by Labour had become tired and unconvincing by the mid-1950s and socialists were consistently forced to defend the nationalised industries from charges of inefficiency and excessive bureaucracy. This stance was a major incentive for revisionists within the party to contemplate the abandonment of Clause IV. With the sudden emergence of growth as the most salient domestic policy issue, however, and with the existing structure, ethos and practice of business increasingly regarded as a major impediment, planning, public ownership and state intervention began to take on a new meaning and a new lustre. These were no longer merely the shibboleths of true believers in the New Jerusalem but rather the essential tools required for economic progress in an age of heroic science and dazzling technological advance. In the rhetoric of Harold Wilson, progress would come through unleashing the powers of science and technology by freeing them from the constraints of capitalist inefficiency; and the state was critical to this process. In the emerging discourse of the early and mid-1960s, then, progress was linked with science, technology, enlightened management, meritocratic recruitment and, most critically, with planning, the state and the Labour Party. Business, by contrast, was associated with restriction, caution, hierarchy, inequality and, equally critically, with political Conservatism. Neither set of connections was entirely fair or accurate, but that was never really the issue. The issue was that the set of associations conjured up by Harold Wilson helped to reposition the Labour Party as the party of progress. Within the party, these new arguments also gave the left a plausible and novel claim to being in the vanguard of efforts to generate economic growth.

The mantle of progress was large and could equally be used to cloak the actions of the centre and the right within the party, of course, for many of the policies dear to the party's revisionist wing could also be construed as essential to the project of modernising Britain. Because planning was not simply nationalisation and because its effective execution presupposed considerable technical expertise, it attracted support from the centre-right of the party as well as the left. Thus it was George Brown who ran the DEA, while Tony Crosland and Bill Rodgers were at his side. Equally important, the push for planning could easily be accompanied by, and reinforce, a broader agenda of liberal and egalitarian social reform. Crosland and Roy Jenkins, for example, could push to reform education and to liberalize legislation on divorce, homosexuality and capital punishment using a similar rhetoric of progress and modernisation. Indeed, it may well be that the most lasting achievements of the Wilson governments of 1964–70 were in these arenas rather than on the altogether more difficult question of managing the economy and engineering growth. But what was most remarkable overall was the way in which political discourse in the 1960s moved in favour of Labour as a party and, more specifically, towards policies both in the economic sphere and on social issues that were more or less appropriately regarded as left-wing and progressive. This shift did not guarantee the success of any particular policy, but it did set the direction of change so that, whether particular policy devices worked or not, the party would continue to move towards the left and its vision. It is unlikely that Harold Wilson had this in mind when he put together his arguments about science, technology, planning and Labour, but it seems to have been the long-term effect.

The ideological reorientation of the Labour Party, and of party politics more generally, did not coincide with any transformation in the interests that made up the party's base, however. Nor did it alter the structure of the party that made it so hard to translate ideas into practical policies. Wilson might well insist, as Richard Crossman reported, that 'If we are modernising the trade unions, modernising Parliament, modernising industry, we mustn't fail to modernise our own Party too.'[3] But the leadership around Wilson did not seriously bestir themselves over the state of the party's organisation, over the tensions between the government and the National Executive or over the peculiar and anomalous role of the party conference and the unions' predominance within it. It should therefore come as no surprise to discover that the attractive modernising gloss laid onto Labour policy commitments did not make the party's policies any more effective. In practice, therefore, the Wilson governments were confronted with stubborn social and economic realities that the party's existing repertoire of policies was not capable of solving. The record of the government was thus highly contradictory: a mix of bold visions and familiar but intractable problems, of fresh starts and repeated setbacks, of innovations that would run into the ground, of promises not delivered, of a regime thinking big and looking to the future but increasingly caught up with the management of short-term crises. The government had many successes. Indeed, when Wilson chose to call an election in the summer of 1970, he did so confident of victory. But the contradictions, limitations, reversals and internal disputes that had marred the record of the Wilson governments ultimately undermined the confidence of the party's supporters and eroded support among the electorate at large. This unhappy pattern might well have owed more than a bit to Harold Wilson's particular style, but it also had much deeper roots that require untangling and explanation.

When Labour left office in 1951 there was a sense that the party and its leaders were tired and in need of a rest; soon it became clear that in fact Labour faced a problem of generational succession. The party of Attlee, Bevin, Cripps and Morrison would become something very different and the battle for the succession between Bevan and Gaitskell was a struggle about how different it would be. Gaitskell's personal triumph did not really settle the issue, as the bitter debates over Clause IV, nuclear weapons, the organisation of the party and the Common Market were to reveal. By the time Wilson was elected, by contrast, the questions that divided revisionists from the left had become less compelling and Wilson's rhetoric linking science and socialism, technology and planning, seemed to transcend prior differences. Under Wilson, then, it became newly possible for leading figures of the left and the right to cooperate and hold office together. The effect was to allow Wilson to create a Cabinet that drew upon an unusual array of talents from all sides of the party. The resulting administration tilted slightly left in outlook, while its composition was weighted slightly towards the right of the party. And the outcome was a collaboration that, while often disturbed by the clash of powerful egos, nevertheless produced a wide range of policy innovations.

Its failures, when they came, would not come because of a lack of talent. Alongside Wilson the top positions in the Cabinet were held by James Callaghan, the Chancellor, and George Brown, the deputy leader who ran the Department of Economic Affairs and then moved over to the Foreign Office. Just beneath these three was an impressive array of ministers who carried major departmental responsibilities and each of whom made considerable, and largely independent, contributions: Michael Stewart, Tony Crosland, Richard Crossman, Roy Jenkins, Barbara Castle and Frank Cousins.[4] Again, left and right were closely balanced, as was Wilson's wont, and ideology had to contend routinely with ego, but the line-up inspired considerable public confidence.

The effect was a long list of reforms that helped to bring Britain into the twentieth century. Education, for example, was utterly transformed by the introduction of comprehensive schooling and by the vast expansion of higher education, most visibly the founding of the Open University. Social services were upgraded as well, with pensions increased enough to make it possible for ordinary men and women to live out their lives without experiencing the impoverishment that typically accompanied old age.[5] The laws affecting marriage and sex were liberalized as well: divorce was made easier, especially for women, and abortion became more readily available; censorship was rolled back, and homosexuality decriminalised. The death penalty was at long last abolished, at first just for a time but then permanently; and despite repeated calls for the reintroduction of hanging it was never brought back.[6] Flogging was ended as well. Reforms were also carried out in local government and in the civil service, even if these proved only the first of many such restructurings. Even on the more difficult questions of racial discrimination and gender equity, the government made at least modest efforts: the Race Relations Act of 1965 outlawed discrimination in public places and established the Race Relations Board; and the Race Relations Act of 1968 extended protection to the areas of housing and employment.

Shortly before leaving office in 1970 the government also secured passage of the Equal Pay Act, pushed so forcefully by Barbara Castle.[7] In 1959, Roy Jenkins had asked rhetorically 'Is Britain Civilized?' and proceeded to elaborate a programme of reforms to make it so.[8] Between 1964 and 1970, the Labour government distanced themselves from common prejudices – and, to some extent, from public opinion – long enough to initiate the process. Overall, the legal and institutional frameworks within which British citizens lived their daily lives were slowly brought up to date; and as these frameworks changed, so did the look and feel of life in Britain. The popular culture of the 1960s was freer and looser and much more demotic and less deferential than before; and working people finally began to be able to enjoy the fruits of the post-war prosperity. Material progress, modernisation and the 'progressive' character of Labour in government seemed for a time to go together naturally.

The Wilson government also adopted what could reasonably be regarded as a more forward-looking and 'modernising' stance on Europe. The Labour Party and the broader 'labour movement' were deeply ambivalent about whether to join the Common Market, but it was never strictly a left–right divide. Gaitskell, after all, had opposed Macmillan's application for membership and carried most of the party with him. Crosland, the intellectual leader of the 'revisionists', was at best lukewarm; Douglas Jay, firmly on the right, was firmly against. The young Tony Benn was mildly in favour; Crossman not a believer but not strongly opposed; Barbara Castle very against. Wilson was himself unsure and shared Gaitskell's worry that closer ties with Europe would damage relations with the Commonwealth. The left was traditionally eager to lessen Britain's dependence on, and closeness to, the United States. This might have led to a more favourable view of the European connection, but the left also feared that, as Wilson put it in the Commons in 1962, 'the whole conception of the Treaty of Rome is anti-planning, at any rate national planning'.[9] The unions were against, but not uniformly so. On balance the right looked upon Europe slightly more favourably than the left, but the balance was close and there were many exceptions and anomalies.

These mixed feelings towards membership in the Common Market were in part a reflection of the fact that reasonable men and women could disagree about the relative merits of the choice confronting Britain.

Membership might open markets and let in the stiff breeze of competition that might well stimulate British industry to improve its performance, but it might also foreclose options elsewhere. In retrospect, the decision has taken on an air of inevitability and sceptics and opponents appear from a distance as myopic, insular and conservative. Although that perception does not do justice to the complexity of the arguments made at the time, it is nevertheless true that a not insignificant element in the resistance to Europe was a rather narrow and backward-looking vision of Britain and its interests. When Gaitskell and, on occasion, Wilson, chose to attack Europe, they found themselves echoing positions that were distinctly unenlightened and garnering support that they would normally be embarrassed to court or even to acknowledge.

Labour's conversion to Europe, temporary and superficial as it turned out, came about in 1966 and was engineered primarily by Wilson and Brown. In January 1966, even before the March election, a secret committee of officials was set up under Eric Roll to review the likely impact of membership.[10] The government began edging towards a new position later that spring and in the Queen's Speech pronounced itself 'ready to enter the European Economic Community provided essential British and Commonwealth interests were safeguarded'.[11] What seems to have decided the issue was a confluence of factors. First, a cadre of supporters had emerged in and around the Foreign Office – Con O'Neill, John Robinson, Michael Palliser, Michael Butler and others – and they worked steadily not only to keep the European option open in the face of French opposition but to treat the choice as almost inevitable.[12] The ongoing argument about Britain's post-imperial role in the wider world also began to tilt towards Europe and seemed to confirm the views of officials. Despite Wilson's admiration for President Kennedy and his subsequent close ties to Lyndon Johnson, Labour even under Wilson had never been entirely comfortable with the 'special relationship' – a Tory invention, after all. The Atlantic Alliance had thus typically been coupled in Labour Party thinking with a continuing commitment to the Commonwealth. Faith in the economic and political future of the Commonwealth may well have been an illusion, but it was a useful vision that allowed the party to support a Britain that remained 'Great' but that was nonetheless on the side of progress and the development of the former colonies. The crisis over Rhodesia's unilateral declaration of independence was a dire threat to this outlook and policy and helped to produce a new sense of realism in which the choice between Europe and the Anglo-American connection would again be seriously posed. To Labour leaders like Brown and Michael Stewart, joining up with Europe was 'the only way to make sure that Britain kept a place at the top table'.[13] Wilson was coming to agree and he was strangely reassured by de Gaulle's moves to obstruct or control the process of integration, most notably the Luxembourg Declaration of January 1966. Worries over diminished sovereignty abated as the French backed away from federalism; and Wilson would take to arguing – perhaps to influence de Gaulle, perhaps to convince himself and his party – that 'a growing parallelism is becoming apparent between British and French interests'.[14]

The economic calculus also shifted. Wilson's lingering fears over the possibility of planning within Europe were eased significantly by the publication in March 1966 of Robert Marjolin's report on 'medium-term economic policy', which Stuart Holland interpreted as an 'attempt to get the French indicative planning model adopted by the Common Market'.[15] The possibility of continuing to plan, and perhaps to plan more effectively, inside the Common Market became more appealing as the prospects of British planning on its own dimmed with the deflationary 'July measures' imposed a few months later. It was while pondering the effects of these austerity measures that George Brown told Castle and Benn, 'We've got to break with America, devalue and go into Europe.'[16] Less than a year after the proclamation of the *National Plan* it was now no longer taken seriously and the government became desperate for some mechanism to generate growth. Europe was in this light an alternative source of dynamism from which the British economy might benefit. Wilson himself held out the prospect of Britain and Europe forming 'a new technological community' that could overcome American technological domination, especially in aircraft and computers.[17] The 'white heat of technology' would thus be created in a common European forge.

It nonetheless took time for Labour to execute the turn to Europe. The decisive Cabinet meeting was held at Chequers in late October 1966 with Brown in the lead and Wilson disingenuously posing as undecided, hard-headed and somewhat above the fray. The outcome was a decision to 'probe' the attitudes in various European capitals through a series of visits by both Brown and Wilson. The decision to launch the tour was itself a major step on the path towards a formal application and as it proceeded in early 1967 Wilson became increasingly committed.[18] Despite a meeting with de Gaulle that gave no easy comfort, Wilson had now staked out a position that led ineluctably to a second effort at entry. Cabinet discussions continued after the 'Probe' but, as Barbara Castle confided to her diary, Wilson and Brown 'have so cleverly set the scene that it will be impossible to come to any decision but to have a try'.[19] The plan to apply for membership was announced on 2 May 1967 and approved overwhelmingly by Parliament on 10 May. De Gaulle was once more dismissive, but a final veto did not come until November.

By then Britain was faced with an altogether more serious financial crisis that compelled Wilson and his Chancellor, Jim Callaghan, finally to devalue the pound. With devaluation accepted and the European option foreclosed, the government would look elsewhere for solutions to the nation's economic difficulties. The conversion to Europe was not forgotten, but the later years of the Wilson government would be dominated by the problem of inflation, which could well have dissipated the economic benefits of devaluation, by battles over incomes policy and by the related, but even more bitter, struggle over trade union reform. These conflicts threatened to tear apart the party or, more precisely, to divide the party's leaders from their trade union allies. Healing the resulting divisions would mean a series of further shifts in party policy that would once again put in doubt Labour's commitment to Europe.

Nevertheless, for a time Europe had been a part of a wide-ranging modernising agenda for Labour and it seemed a fitting accompaniment to the domestic measures adopted by the government in a broader effort to 'modernise' and 'civilise' the nation.[20] To 'modernise' is not, of course, equivalent to building socialism, even if socialism conceives itself as the most progressive or modern of causes. Progress on cultural issues or in matters of social mores, however laudable, was inevitably less important to Labour's core constituencies than the question of the economy. Unfortunately, the Wilson government's achievements in these other spheres could not be translated into success in resolving the economic problems on the handling of which the government and the party would ultimately be judged and found signally to have failed.

It was not from want of trying, however. In fact, the Wilson government remained incredibly activist and persisted in its efforts to encourage growth, even when the external circumstances were least accommodating, through careful efforts to control the macro-economic environment and selective interventions in key parts of the economy. Even if the latter were more interesting and innovative, the government's shifts on macro-economic policy inevitably held centre stage. Absolutely central to either sort of economic management was the question of devaluation. For three years Wilson and Callaghan, backed by officials in the Treasury and representatives of the Bank of England, had resisted devaluation and preferred a mild deflation while others, particularly the planners in the DEA, had come to favour it. The first Wilson government's rather narrow majority and his understandable reluctance to make his first major move an abandonment of the value of the pound led to a decision not to devalue upon taking office in 1964. That choice would plague the government for years after, however, because the decision to protect the pound forced the government to adopt economy measures that undermined all of its efforts to generate growth and its promises to improve benefits and social services. Critics inevitably argued that Wilson was too deferential to the interests of capital, and the City in particular, attacked his timidity and insisted that he, and the government, had missed a unique opportunity to change the framework of economic policy-making. Whether or not the critique of Wilson was justified, the choice not to devalue was enormously consequential. By forcing the government to give priority to the control of inflation, it imposed strict limits on spending. In consequence, promised improvements in pensions, social services and housing were less than hoped for and reforms like the raising of the school-leaving age had to be postponed. Though the government's overall record on the provision of social services was impressive, some of its supporters were nevertheless disappointed that more was not done. Even more damaging to the government, however, was its increasing fixation on the control of wages.

Employers had long contended that the key to the control of inflation, and hence to the growth of exports and the solution of the balance of payments problem, was wage restraint. Conservatives tended to agree, as did many economists and officials at the Treasury and even within the Ministry of Labour. The link between wages and costs was obvious and hard to deny and many within the labour movement were ready to concede that moderating wage claims was essential to a successful economic

policy. Gaitskell had certainly understood this; and the Labour governments of 1945–51 had as well: indeed, they had been able to secure trade
union agreement to voluntary limits on wages in 1948–50 and were
thus positioned to implement a massive rearmament programme with
minimal impact on prices. Success in this case turned on the fact that
the union leaders agreed with the government's broader aims, believed
they received compensatory benefits in the form of social policy, were
consulted from the beginning and could count on the compliance of their
members. Trade union leaders also understood that the policy would
be temporary and that when the crisis passed they would return to the
historic pattern of collective bargaining with minimal state involvement
and no legal enforcement of contracts.[21]

The unions were reluctant to make wage restraint compulsory or
permanent, however, and so throughout the 1950s they strongly resisted
proposals to control wages. Successive Conservative governments vacillated; they feared incurring the wrath of the unions and so shied away
from proposals for mandatory controls, but they were desperate to find
some mechanism through which they could enlist the unions in the
cause of policing wage claims. The machinery ultimately created to
undertake planning – the NEDC and various little 'Neddies' – was one
possibility and it is clear that employers agreed to participate in the
endeavour largely in the hope that it would lead to some form of wage
control. But by the time the Conservatives left office in 1964, little
progress had been made and the unions were increasingly adamant in
resisting efforts to limit their members' freedom to extract what they
could in a buoyant labour market.

The Labour government was no more eager to impose controls over
wages, but was pushed to do so by the persistence of inflationary pressures. The Wilson government, moreover, could rationalise or justify
incomes policies with several more specific arguments. First, the Labour
government's heroic effort to plan and to stimulate growth would mean
that the pay-off from wage restraint would be quick and visible; and in
consequence the unions could be confident that the policy would be
temporary. Both Conservative and Labour governments were aware that
periods of economic expansion had routinely been cut short by balance of
payments difficulties and that this stop-go pattern hindered long-term
investment and innovation. The challenge was to ride out these difficulties

and give growth measures time to work so as to allow capital accumula-
tion to result in productivity increases that would reduce costs and
encourage exports. Because Labour's economic policies were supposedly
more aggressive about growth, a Labour government would be more
capable of getting over this timing problem. Labour also felt that its
unique relationship with the unions would generate the trust essential
to making incomes policies work and, more concretely, that a Labour
government would be simultaneously implementing social policies – on
pensions, housing, social services and education – that would disproportionately benefit working people and convince trade unionists of the
virtue of cooperating on wages. In addition, a Labour government could
presumably be trusted to monitor prices and rents on behalf of the less
well-off. Armed with these views, Labour thus moved to impose a series
of incomes policies: a non-binding 'statement of intent' on wages and
prices agreed in 1964 by the TUC and the Federation of British Industries
was followed by the establishment in 1965 of the National Board for
Prices and Incomes. When it became clear that the Board's norms would
be regularly exceeded and the policy rendered useless, the government
began to add an element of compulsion – insisting on an 'early warning
system' by which the government would be notified of wage claims and
claiming the right to delay their implementation. By July 1966 a reluctant
government had been forced to declare a 'wage freeze' through to
December 1966, to be followed by a policy of 'severe restraint' for another
six months. A brief relaxation was replaced in late 1967 by another
period of restraint from April 1968 until the government lost the general
election in June 1970. To judge by the numbers, the initial 'freeze'
worked reasonably well, while the other efforts very clearly failed. Taken
together, however, this series of successive policies proved that the call
for wage restraint was not temporary but recurring, and almost inevitably
generated opposition from the unions and their members.[22]

This resentment, and the resulting resistance, to incomes policy was
genuinely based on principle and on deeply-held views about Labour's
identity as a party. These principles were backed up by the institutional
clout of unions within the party. There were also thorny practical
questions about whether wage controls could be made to work. Rising
prices, it was argued in Labour circles, were not due solely to excessive
wage demands but were also due to excessive profits, to monopolies or to

inefficiencies endemic to private ownership. In any event, Labour was a workers' party and simply could not in good conscience resist the claims of workers for better wages. And whatever conscience dictated, the unions were willing to remind Labour leaders that they simply would not tolerate restrictions on their historic rights. Privately, moreover, leaders of the unions and of the Labour Party sensed that union members might well refuse to go along with wage controls even if their leaders were fully consulted and involved. In that case, the policy would fail and the leadership would be exposed as impotent; and neither outcome was desirable.

Even more important, by the mid-1960s the economic and social climate had changed drastically since the years of austerity just after the war and the organised working class was deeply affected. If working people had rather modest expectations, focused largely on security, coming out of the Depression and war, by the 1960s they began to want more. Despite the discourse about affluence in the last years of Conservative rule, mass consumption did not really come to Britain until the last years of Tory rule. In terms of the ownership of television sets, refrigerators and cars, for example, the breakthrough came only in the 1960s. And it came first, of course, for the young, who began to emerge as a distinct sector of the market with their own tastes and priorities and with a greater willingness to rely on hire purchase. Shifting family patterns helped as well: as fertility dropped, young couples had more time to accumulate possessions before beginning to have children; and fewer children meant more money for other things. The gradual increase in female employment had a similar effect, again more noticeably among younger workers.

Just as workers were beginning to acquire a taste for more and better consumer goods, however, they faced at least two threats to their well-being. The first was inflation, which threatened to eat away at wage gains even as they were being won. The second was income tax, from which many workers had previously been exempt. As workers' wages rose and tax thresholds were not adjusted upwards, more and more workers were caught in the web of income tax. In 1948 the average adult male worker, married with two children, was not liable to income tax at all and paid but 3.5 per cent in National Insurance contributions; by 1964, a worker in the same relative situation would pay 4.5 per cent of earnings in income tax and another 5.2 per cent in National Insurance.[23] Soon he would pay even more in tax and so would be motivated to push wages still higher. The cumulative effect of all of these changes on industrial relations was to increase wage militancy and to make it much more difficult for union leaders to count on their members' acquiescence to deals struck at higher levels. The problem had begun to emerge as early as the mid-1950s, when a wave of unofficial strikes swept the motor car industry and then spread to other branches of engineering. The strikes tended to be led by shop stewards, who were more responsive to the shop floor than were union leaders at regional or national level. Shop steward organisation expanded massively from the mid-1950s, filling in the interstices of an industrial relations system characterised by fragmented, haphazard and overlapping union structures. The more aggressive and thoughtful trade union leaders, like Jack Jones of the TGWU and Hugh Scanlon of the Engineers, recognised that shop stewards were an integral part of successful union organisation. So although shop stewards were often a source of difficulty and discontent, they had critical support among officials of several major national trade unions and in the Trades Union Congress.[24]

The upsurge in strikes continued into the era of the Wilson governments and led to a search for means by which to control unofficial strike action and to resist the constant upward pressure on wages. An obvious solution was to find mechanisms that would buttress the power of trade union officials and make them responsible for disciplining their members. But union leaders, though eager to be consulted on matters of economic policy and committed to 'corporatist' bargaining with employers and the state on a wide range of issues, were not ready to be drawn into arrangements that might limit their flexibility and credibility. If unions agreed to wage controls, they would be liable to criticism from members and could face the ultimate sanction of losing office; and if they agreed but failed to make it work, they would be faced with criticism from all angles. Union leaders also understood intuitively that it strengthened their own hand in negotiations to be able to say that this or that policy simply would not go down with the members.

Efforts to enlist the unions in the policing of strike action and in setting and administering wage controls were thus on the whole unsuccessful. In response, perhaps even in desperation, the government began to entertain notions of restructuring the unions or imposing legal restrictions on union behaviour. To that end the Wilson government in 1965 appointed Lord Donovan to head a Royal Commission on Trade Unions and Employers' Organisations which conducted elaborate inquiries into the structure of British industrial relations.[25] Its report in June 1968 disappointed, for it largely endorsed the existing system of 'collective laissez-faire' and recommended but minor changes, like the setting up of a standing Commission on Industrial Relations (CIR). The government were determined to do more and proceeded to craft a new policy 'aimed at putting teeth into the Donovan Report'.[26] It was clear to Wilson and to Barbara Castle, the new Secretary of State for Employment and Productivity, that the TUC would dig in its heels, but Castle and her allies came to see that 'we would never get anything positive out of the TUC and that the Government would have to risk giving a lead'.[27] At a weekend meeting held at Sunningdale in mid-November 1968 the outlines of an approach were agreed among key ministers, officials and academic advisers: legislation would be passed giving the government that authority to involve itself in industrial disputes by requiring pre-strike ballots, by declaring a 28-day 'conciliation pause' and by allowing the CIR to impose settlements when the issue involved inter-union rivalry. It also called for 'penal clauses' and fines for disregard of the rules and decisions set down by government or the Commission. These restrictions on union behaviour were to be accompanied, however, by a substantial extension of trade union rights that would strongly encourage membership and by public funding of a 'development scheme' for trade unions.

The aim was clearly a bargain in which the legal rights of the unions would be enhanced in return for procedures that would make unions and their members more accountable to their leaders and that would subject their behaviour to greater control and regulation. If successful, the deal would create a more efficient and centrally organised trade union movement better equipped to make corporatism work. But the arrangement would require that the existing leadership of the unions, and their members, be convinced to acquiesce in this restructuring. Wilson and Castle knew they would encounter opposition from many within the unions but believed, as Castle told Crossman, that the move 'will be popular . . . [and] there will be no real opposition in the Party . . .'.[28] They were mistaken on both counts, for they underestimated the intensity of opposition from the unions and failed to foresee that the party and even the Cabinet would be unwilling to countenance a possible break with the unions. In part, they were listening to the wrong people. Castle, for example, was surrounded by officials who had become disillusioned with the unions' repeated inability, or unwillingness, to rein in local militants. She and Wilson also assumed incorrectly that the top leaders of the TUC could manage opposition from constituent unions. George Woodcock, the General Secretary, was being brought on board with the offer to chair the new Commission on Industrial Relations and he apparently told Castle 'that he didn't think there was anything there [in the White Paper] that need alarm the trade union movement' and that, as she recorded at the time, 'he personally was happy with the package that had been put to the TUC'.[29] Despite appearances and public pronouncements, she concluded, 'he isn't really basically opposed . . .'.[30] Indeed, Woodcock was bargaining over the details of running the CIR while the TUC General Council was seeking to block the entire enterprise.[31] Victor Feather, soon to succeed Woodcock, was equally supportive in private but acted differently in public. He took Wilson's adviser Gerald Kaufman into his confidence in January 1969 and told him that although 25 members of the General Council were opposed to the proposals in the White Paper, with just 16 for, 'there is no belly for a fight except perhaps on the part of Frank Cousins'.[32] Kaufman immediately informed Wilson and Castle, who continued to believe they could prevail. Both should have known better. Feather had an abiding hatred for Castle going back to their shared youth in Bradford.[33] And Wilson should have understood that Feather, new to his position and lacking credibility on the shop floor, could not override more militant leaders like Jack Jones or Hugh Scanlon.

So the government had miscalculated; and over time it became clear that it was the party and the Cabinet, in the end including Wilson, that had 'no belly for a fight'. Within the TUC, Cousins and Jack Jones took the lead in fighting what they regarded as 'repressive legislation' and urged 'total opposition to any legislation restricting the right to strike'.[34] Within the Cabinet support for the White Paper evaporated as ministers figured out that it meant a possible split with the unions. The emerging divisions over strategy did not follow traditional left-right lines. Castle, after all, had long been a standard-bearer for the left; and Wilson was thought to be fundamentally in sympathy with her; and there was a thoroughly respectable line of reasoning on the left of the party about the need to sacrifice sectional interests on behalf of the working class as a whole and the broader project of social reform and economic growth. Crossman, also on the left, was, however, strongly opposed – in part he was miffed at not being consulted before the draft was completed – and sought to modify the White Paper's proposals to demonstrate his influence and importance. Crosland, long the top thinker on the right, claimed to agree with Castle on most of it, but was on the other hand not eager for a fight and so waffled. Benn, who had yet to make the transition from the centre to the left of the party, told Castle reassuringly 'I'm your friend.'[35] Roy Jenkins, who might be assumed to be a firm supporter, was diffident. But the central player in the drama was Jim Callaghan, former Chancellor and now Home Secretary, party treasurer and confidante of key trade union leaders. Long a fixture of the right, he committed himself early on to defend the prerogatives of the trade unions and apparently saw his stance as an opportunity to recoup his position after the debacle of devaluation and thus to advance his claim to leadership of the party. He conspired effectively with Feather and with Douglas Houghton, chair of the Parliamentary Labour Party. Younger ministers also split in somewhat atypical fashion and their words and actions did not always coincide: Peter Shore argued that 'On the left it was absolutely clear to anyone who thought about it that you had to have an incomes policy . . . We had to drive this into the heads of a lot of blockheaded trade unionists.' Structural reform of the trade unions was to him a prerequisite of sensible policy-making. Nevertheless, he went on to oppose *In Place of Strife*. Roy Hattersley, starting from a very different place, would reach the same conclusion: he insisted that although he had 'no philosophical opposition to the imposition of more rigorous laws to control the conduct of trade unions and their members', he believed the effort would fail in practice and 'would unite the whole of the trade union movement against the government'.[36] On balance, support was lacking on all sides, but Wilson and Castle proceeded nevertheless.

When Cabinet met to discuss the proposals in early January 1969 Callaghan admitted to having talked to friends in the trade union movement and argued forcefully against the package in the White Paper: 'Frankly I think it is absolutely wrong and unnecessary to do this', he told his colleagues.[37] Eventually the Cabinet acquiesced to the publication of the White Paper. But with the Cabinet split and senior figures actively flouting collective decisions, the opposition only mounted. The TUC organised a campaign against possible legislation and mobilised a demonstration of 100,000 in Trafalgar Square on May Day. A special TUC conference was set for Croydon in early June. Discontent predictably arose within the parliamentary party as well and on 26 March Callaghan, with TUC cooperation, got the NEC formally to oppose the government's policy. A fresh round of discussions was begun in April and it soon emerged that Wilson would settle for a set of changes in union rules and procedures aimed at preventing unofficial strikes and inter-union disputes in exchange for the government dropping the 'penal clauses' in the proposed legislation. By late May Cousins would tell his fellow General Council members that 'the stage has almost been reached of either the General Council or the Government backing down'.[38]

Even as he prepared to back down, Wilson kept insisting that what was at stake was the very authority of the government. 'His political judgment', he informed the General Council in May, 'was that the real question was whether the Labour Government – or any Labour Government – could continue . . .'[39] At a critical Cabinet meeting a few weeks later he said that to accept the TUC's position would be a major blow: the government 'would lose all credibility at home and abroad; and their authority would crumble'.[40] But the government nevertheless did capitulate. On 17 June the Cabinet refused to back Wilson and Castle and essentially told them to make a deal. For Castle, it was the 'most traumatic day of my political life'.[41] The TUC made a minimal gesture by agreeing to adopt rule changes that would strengthen its ability to intervene in disputes, but ruled out the government's key proposals and forced the abandonment of penal clauses or any other enforcement mechanism. Instead, the unions gave a 'solemn and binding undertaking' to discourage unofficial strikes. Meeting with the TUC the next day, Wilson was reduced to asking them not to claim victory: 'He hoped that the outcome would not be regarded as a victory for either side, but as a victory for good industrial relations.'[42] The government would claim, of course, that its initiative had prompted the TUC to undertake reform on its own and that the result would be more effective than legislation. But nobody believed it.

Wilson's defeat at the hands of the unions was a decisive moment in the party's history and a vivid display of the limits placed by its structure and outlook on what its leaders could do in government. It is certainly appropriate to assess the merits, and the flaws, in Barbara Castle's plan to restructure the unions and to create a framework within which union leaders would be expected to operate – in relation to their members, to employers, to the government and implicitly to the public. But the fact that her proposals barely got a hearing before being banished from the agenda of Labour Party politics illustrates the veto power exercised by the unions over the party's programme and the constraints that union power placed on the government's freedom to manoeuvre. There was an ironic justice to this public demonstration of the party's inability to manage the unions: Labour had come to office pledged to use the levers of the state to improve economic performance, but increasingly found that the tools at its disposal were inadequate for the task. In desperation, Wilson turned to the party's historic allies in the trade unions to impose sacrifices on their members in order to achieve the government's economic objectives. Their refusal to do so was a fitting reminder, therefore, of the broader failure of the government's strategy and of how weak were the instruments through which Labour hoped to steer the economy and stimulate growth. The modernisation project, or this particular variation of it, had been derailed by the very character of the party that sought to pursue it.

The humiliation of the Wilson government would have long-term and very serious consequences. Within the Labour Party the failure encouraged critics of the government to push alternative policies. In the unions, the victory led to a sense of empowerment that encouraged local activism and helped to sustain wage militancy and strike action. During the mid-1960s roughly half a million workers went on strike each year; roughly three times that number engaged in industrial action in the five years beginning in 1968 and union membership expanded by well over a million. The effect, despite tortuous government efforts to hold down wages, was an average increase in real wages of nearly two-thirds between 1968 and 1974. Direct action thus paid off handsomely, and workers were perhaps disloyal, but they were not foolish in resisting government efforts to hold down working-class living standards in an effort to produce growth for the economy as a whole.[43]

The waxing strength of trade unions, demonstrated on the shop floor, the picket line and in membership figures, provided a stark contrast to the apparent paralysis of government. The lesson taken from the comparison was that Labour in government was worth rather less than power in the hands of the labour movement more broadly conceived. The fact that the unions' influence within industry might be at least partly dependent upon the existence of a Labour government or, in a long-term sense, on the recognition of unions' role in society institutionalised by the Labour governments of 1945–51, was of course largely ignored in the heady enthusiasm surrounding direct action in the late 1960s and early 1970s. Conversely, the benefits to be gained by working with rather than against a sympathetic government were dismissed or forgotten. Still, the strike wave of 1968–72 and the huge wage increases it produced underscored the fact that British workers were basically underpaid and that post-war growth and full employment had to a large extent been bought at the price of working-class living standards. It indicated just how low material expectations had been for the generation that came to maturity during depression and war, how restrained workers and their unions had been throughout the first two post-war decades, and how little impact the supposed culture of affluence had had on many workers until very recently. Indeed, given the extremely high density of trade union membership in Britain and the incredibly low rates of unemployment that prevailed through the 1960s, a push for much higher wages was almost inevitable and might well have been expected much earlier.

Rather, it required the prospect of higher growth held out repeatedly by both parties and the excited rhetoric about progress, modernisation and increasing productivity perfected by Wilson for workers finally to decide to use their clout in the labour market to extract an increased share of the national product. The effect of this change in working-class behaviour – predictable, reasonable, but truly novel in Britain – on established ways of conducting politics was enormous. Most obvious was the erosion of authority of the leaders of the Labour Party and the downward shift in power to others within the labour movement broadly conceived: to constituency activists; to union leaders; and to shop stewards and the rank and file. The process was undoubtedly reinforced, indeed partly inspired, by the widespread agitations of students and youth in the 1960s and by the growth of a 'new left' that initially operated on the margins of the party and the unions but whose influence was eventually felt inside those institutions. The generation of 1968 contributed, in particular, a new and increasingly radical language with which to articulate discontent with the party and the unions and imported a spirit of insurgency to accompany it. The effectiveness of the 'New Left' was further increased by the fact that the institutions of British Labour were quite permeable. The leaders of the Labour Party and of the unions had fought bitter battles over the years to exclude communists from their ranks and, unlike their counterparts on the Continent, had even resisted the charms of the 'popular front'.[44] In 1952 the Parliamentary Labour Party adopted standing orders to prohibit factional activity by the Bevanites and these were extended into the 1960s.[45] But by the 1960s the will to enforce such restrictions was lacking and a series of revolts within the PLP signalled a weakening of the disciplinary regime. With the battle over *In Place of Strife*, it collapsed utterly.

Prohibitions and proscriptions were even less effective in the unions and the constituency parties. Despite the efforts to keep communists at bay, party members were locally active and also influential at national level in a number of key unions. So, too, were activists influenced by the New Left but not belonging to the Communist Party but to smaller and often more diffuse organisations or to no organisation at all. Policing the boundaries of the party and the unions against such an amorphous threat was quite impractical even if it had been desirable. The openness of local organisations – both unions and local parties – combined with the alleged sovereignty of the party conference to lure the New Left into Labour's formal organisation. Winning majorities at conference was a formidable task, of course, though it was at least possible to imagine circumstances in which the rank and file could make their presence felt; and even if winning was unlikely, it was nevertheless possible to parti-cipate in debate. The changing social composition of the trade unions further opened the labour movement to a diversity of opinion. Unions in Britain had become remarkably successful at recruiting white-collar and public sector workers and those who entered the labour movement through these institutions were often highly educated and articulate, and frequently more ideological than their working-class comrades. Their presence within the unions and the party helped to blur the distinction between workers and intellectuals that had long existed in the movement and to mute the resulting proletarian suspicion of intellectuals that had often been used to marginalise arguments and proposals unwelcome to the leadership. And finally, the openness of Labour as a party and of the trade unions made it easier for a new generation of enthusiasts to join and to feel that they would be taken seriously. The effect was to create a new cadre of members and potential leaders who would revitalise the party in the period during and after Harold Wilson's period as leader.

The displacement of power within the party and the unions, however, also made more transparent the rather peculiar arrangements by which Labour was held together. Once exposed to the light of outside criticism, moreover, these were hard to explain and even harder to defend. The link between Labour and the unions was extremely intimate and had served not only to sustain the party in good times and bad, but had brought to the unions – and indirectly to those they represented – a quite genuine voice in the way economic and social policy had been made and implemented in the post-war era. But were the resulting 'corporatist' dealings between unions, employers and the state truly compatible with democracy? They could be defended easily enough as a mechanism for securing input and ultimately consent to public policies from those most directly affected, but what of those indirectly affected? What of the public at large? So long as the unions made modest claims on their members' behalf, such awkward questions were seldom asked. But when union members, encouraged by the more militant among the leadership, took to demanding what the market would bear, sympathy ebbed, scrutiny increased and the questions asked became more hostile and pointed. Even harder to defend than corporatist bargaining was the role of the unions in the deliberations of the party: block votes cast by union leaders on behalf of millions of members who were seldom consulted or even informed of how their votes were to be cast were pretty much indefensible. Again, so long as the unions were seen to behave with moderation, the system was accepted. But when the unions chose to resist the Labour government, it was only logical to ask for whom did they speak and on what authority? Labour as a party would not have existed without the unions; and socialists could probably never have been elected to office without a union-backed Labour Party. Over decades, therefore, the relationship had paid off for the party and the unions; but there would be costs as well. The changing balance of advantage can be measured, at least crudely, by the public's attitudes towards the unions. Until the mid-1960s the unions enjoyed considerable public sympathy; from the late 1960s on more and more people began to buy into the notion that the unions had too much power.[46] As that perception grew, the advantages of Labour's connection to the unions dissipated.

Whatever its effects on living standards, the strike wave beginning in the late 1960s therefore began simultaneously to erode support for corporatism, for unions in general and for Labour's apparent dependence on the unions. It also provided the occasion for an influx of potentially troublesome younger activists whose presence would continue to transform Labour Party politics beyond the life of the Wilson governments of 1964–70. Somewhat surprisingly, however, it did not lead to an immediate change of leadership. The reason was that despite all of the government's failed initiatives and embarrassing reversals, the economy eventually began to improve. The combined effects of the austere budgets of 1966 and 1968 and of the decision to devalue in November 1967 finally bore fruit in a record of moderate growth, continued low unemployment and, by 1969, a balance of payments surplus. Devaluation had not come easily: just five days prior to the announcement of 18 November the Treasury's top economist recorded that Wilson was 'still against' the move, but that at long last the 'Chancellor has changed round and now sees the futility of going on'.[47] Callaghan, though accepting the inevitable, conceded that 'This is the most agonising reappraisal I have ever had to do and I will not pretend that it is anything but a failure of our policies.'[48] It was in fact not in itself a failure but rather a belated recognition of past failure, and as such it would be registered most obviously in Callaghan's replacement by Roy Jenkins. Devaluation was also, however, a genuinely new beginning and undoubtedly the right thing to do for the economy, for it allowed a brief relaxation of the balance of payments constraint and thus an opportunity for the economy actually to expand.[49]

The political impact was a recovery in the fortunes of the Labour Party that led Harold Wilson to call an election for June 1970 in the expectation that Labour would prevail over the Tory Party led by the not very popular Edward Heath. Wilson was not foolish in this decision: his optimism was justified in terms of economic data, polling data and by-election results. Although there was reason to fret about likely 'Labour defectors', there was also evidence that new voters, whose numbers had been enlarged by recent changes in electoral law, were strongly predisposed to vote Labour. The party and the government were thus genuinely shocked by the Conservative triumph. In retrospect it is obvious that the recurring difficulties of the Wilson governments had taken their toll on the party's support within the electorate at large and especially among its core constituencies.[50] Harold Wilson had hoped to make Labour into the 'natural party of government', but the successive crises, rebellions and intrigues that plagued his administrations rendered that impossible. Nevertheless, the party had scored impressive successes in a range of policy areas and where they had failed, they could easily pin the blame on their opponents or on circumstance. Ironically, then, the party moved into opposition in a schizophrenic state of mind: Wilson and his fellow Cabinet members felt the worst was over and that they had come through difficult times with their policies and principles more or less intact; their opponents, by contrast, felt aggrieved at what they saw as the repeated sacrifice of principle. Those new recruits to the party or the unions tended to side with the latter, though they were less bitter than hopeful and determined to ensure that the future of Labour would be vastly different than its recent past. From that resolve would come a protracted era of internal debate, wide swings in policy, a revolution in the structure of the party, and repeated electoral disasters.

Notes and references

1 See Ilaria Favretto, ' "Wilsonism" reconsidered: Labour Party revisionism, 1952–64', *Contemporary British History*, XIV, 4 (Winter 2000), 54–80; and Jim Tomlinson, 'Labour and the Economy', in D. Tanner, P. Thane and N. Tiratsoo, eds, *Labour's First Century* (Cambridge: Cambridge University Press, 2000), 61.

2 Tomlinson, 'Conservative modernisation 1960–64: Too little, too late?', *Contemporary British History*, XI (1997), 18–38.

3 Richard Crossman, *The Crossman Diaries: Selections from the Diaries of a Cabinet Minister, 1964–1970*, edited by Anthony Howard (London: Hamish Hamilton and Jonathan Cape, 1979), entry for 2 October 1966, 223.

4 Other Cabinet members included Ray Gunter, Douglas Jay, Arthur Bottomley, Herbert Bowden, Tom Fraser, Fred Peart, James Griffiths, Frank Soskice, Anthony Greenwood, William Ross and Douglas Houghton, along with Lords Gardner and Longford. Tony Benn, as Postmaster-General, was outside the Cabinet but would soon become an insider.

5 Pat Thane, *Old Age in English History: Past Experiences, Present Issues* (Oxford: Oxford University Press, 2000).

6 On several of these issues, the government did not itself propose legislation but rather supported, or allowed its followers to support, private members'

bills. The effect, however, was to put the weight of the government behind these liberal, 'civilising', initiatives. See Peter Thompson, 'Labour's "Gannex Conscience"? Politics and Popular Attitudes in the "Permissive society"', in R. Coopey, S. Fielding and N. Tiratsoo, eds, *The Wilson Governments, 1964–1970* (London: Pinter, 1993), 136–50.

7 Labour's response to immigration, by contrast, was rather less liberal. For a thoughtful account see Kathleen Paul, *Whitewashing Britain: Race and Citizenship in the Postwar Era* (Ithaca: Cornell University Press, 1997).

8 Roy Jenkins, *A Life at the Center: Memoirs of a Radical Reformer* (New York: Random House, 1991), 169.

9 Quoted in Hugo Young, *This Blessed Plot: Britain and Europe from Churchill to Blair* (London: Macmillan, 1998), 183. See also Ben Pimlott, *Harold Wilson* (London: HarperCollins, 1992), 434, citing Uwe Kitzinger, *The Second Try: Labour and the EEC* (Oxford: Pergamon, 1968), 85.

10 Young, *This Blessed Plot*, 186. Wilson would also use Tommy Balogh and his assistant Stuart Holland as personal emissaries to people in Paris thought to have influence with de Gaulle. In fact, Balogh reported to Wilson as far back as 1962 that there were sufficient 'escape clauses' in the Treaty of Rome to allow Britain to do as much planning as it wanted. What the Common Market lacked, he explained, was a 'provision for the enforcement of plans for the whole Community . . .'. That was asking rather a lot, however. Much later, Holland would complain to Wilson via Marcia Williams that Balogh only wanted Holland to 'find arguments against entry, not for it . . .', Holland to Marcia Williams, 27 April 1967. These and other letters are in the file on the Common Market in the Harold Wilson Papers, Bodleian Library, c. 873.

11 Cited in Barbara Castle, *The Castle Diaries, 1964–70* (London: Weidenfeld & Nicolson, 1984), entry for 20 April 1966, 116.

12 Young, *This Blessed Plot*, chapter 6.

13 This is Crossman's summary of their view. See his *Diaries*, 22 October 1966, 233.

14 The wording is from 'Possible approaches to de Gaulle', memo of 26 April 1967 sent by Stuart Holland to Marcia Williams, 27 April 1967, Wilson Papers, c. 873. It was meant to pick up on Wilson's own prior comments on the issue and elaborate their implications.

15 Stuart Holland, 'Britain and Europe since 1945', lecture to the Institute for Contemporary British History, 26 March 1997. Holland began working for Tommy Balogh in January 1966 and apparently brought Marjolin's report – *Premier Project de Programme Economique a Moyen Terme* (1966) – to Balogh's and Wilson's attention. He reasserted the importance of this document in an interview with the author on 7 October 2002. For his part,

however, Marjolin regarded his venture into 'medium-term economic planning', which he dates from 1964, as having 'remained largely a dead letter'. See Robert Marjolin, *Architect of European Unity: Memoirs, 1911–1986* (London: Weidenfeld & Nicolson, 1989), 347.

16 *Castle Diaries*, entry for 18 July 1966, 147.

17 Cited in Young, *This Blessed Plot*, 193.

18 George Brown, *In My Way* (London: Victor Gollancz, 1971), 206.

19 *Castle Diaries*, entry for 20 April 1967, 244.

20 Richard Heffernan, 'Beyond Euro-scepticism? Labour and the European Union since 1945', in Brian Brivati and Richard Heffernan, eds, *The Labour Party: A Centenary History* (London: Macmillan, 2000), 386–8; Pimlott, *Harold Wilson*, 432–42.

21 The presence of Stafford Cripps was critical to this achievement. His successor, Gaitskell, had a much rougher passage, though he was also faced with the grim reality of rearmament. See, among others, Peter Clarke, *The Cripps Version: The Life of Sir Stafford Cripps* (London: Allen Lane, 2002), 509; and Brian Brivati, *Hugh Gaitskell* (London: Richard Cohen, 1996), chapter 5.

22 See Roger Middleton, *Government versus the Market* (Cheltenham: Edward Elgar, 1996), 564–5; and Leo Panitch, *Social Democracy and Industrial Militancy: The Labour Party, the Trade Unions and Incomes Policy* (Cambridge: Cambridge University Press, 1976), 5.

23 Middleton, *Government versus the Market*, 512.

24 On Jones's attitude towards shop stewards, see Robert Taylor, *The TUC: From the General Strike to the New Unionism* (London: Palgrave, 2000), 203–8.

25 *Report of the Royal Commission on Trade Unions and Employers' Organisations, 1965–8*, Cmnd. 3623 (London: HMSO, 1968). The most thorough account of the battles over incomes policies is still Panitch, *Social Democracy and Industrial Militancy*. On the struggle over *In Place of Strife* in particular, see Pimlott, *Harold Wilson*, 510–46.

26 George Woodcock, General Secretary of the TUC, 'Minutes of the TUC General Council Meeting, 23 October 1968', TUC Papers, Modern Records Centre, University of Warwick, GC1.

27 *Castle Diaries*, entry for 16 November 1968, 551.

28 *Crossman Diaries*, entry for 1 January 1969, 495.

29 *Castle Diaries*, entry for 19 December 1968, 574; and 'Note for Record (of phone call from Castle to Wilson)', 3 January 1969, PRO: PREM13/2724.

30 See her remarks as reported in the *Crossman Diaries*, entry for 1 January 1969, 496.

31 *Castle Diaries*, entries for 19 December 1968 and 6 January 1969, 575 and 583.

32 Kaufman to Wilson 14 January 1969, PRO: PREM13/2724.

33 Anne Perkins, *Red Queen: The Authorised Biography of Barbara Castle* (London: Macmillan, 2003), 14–16 *et passim*.

34 Jones, quoted in the Minutes of the TUC General Council meeting, 18 December 1968.

35 *Castle Diaries*, entry for I January 1969, 581.

36 Perkins, *Red Queen*, 279, 282. Hattersley was commenting just after the discussions between Castle and her advisers that had taken at Sunningdale in November 1968. On Shore, see Edward Pearce, *Denis Healey: A Life in Our Times* (London: Little, Brown, 2002), 539.

37 See the *Crossman Diaries*, entry for 3 January 1969, 497; Cabinet Minutes, C1 (69), 3 January 1969. PRO: CAB128 (hereafter Cabinet Minutes).

38 Minutes of the General Council, 21 May 1969. Cousins was commenting on a meeting held that morning with the Prime Minister.

39 Report of the meeting between the Prime Minister and the General Council, 21 May 1969, GC15/1.

40 Minutes of the Cabinet Meeting of 17 June 1969, CC28 (69).

41 *Castle Diaries*, entry for 17 June 1969, 672.

42 Minutes of the Meeting between the General Council and the Prime Minister, 18 June 1969, GC17/3.

43 J. Cronin, *Industrial Conflict in Modern Britain* (London: Croom Helm, 1979), 141–51, 211, 227 and 238.

44 On the importance of the Popular Front to the fortunes of Communism across Europe, see François Furet, *The Passing of an Illusion* (Chicago: University of Chicago Press, 1999) and also Eric Hobsbawm, *The Age of Extremes* (New York: Vintage, 1994), chapter 5.

45 See, in general, Eric Shaw, *Discipline and Discord in the Labour Party: The Politics of Managerial Control in the Labour Party, 1951–87* (Manchester: Manchester University Press, 1988).

46 See David Broughton, *Public Opinion, Polling and Politics in Britain* (Hemel Hempstead: Harvester Wheatsheaf, 1995), 169; and Ivor Crewe, Anthony Fox and Neil Day, *The British Electorate, 1963–1992* (Cambridge: Cambridge University Press, 1995), 251ff.

47 Alec Cairncross, *The Wilson Years: A Treasury Diary, 1964–1969* (London: The Historians' Press, 1997). Entry for 13 November 1967, 244.

48 Callaghan, quoted in the *Castle Diaries*, 16 November 1967, 325.

49 See Kathleen Burk et al., 'The 1967 devaluation', *Contemporary Record*, I, 4 (1988), 44–53.

50 See the Wilson Papers, c. 1086 for the special poll on the attitudes of 'The New Electorate' as well as the subsequent report by Research Services Ltd in its 'March Political Survey' (April 1970) which identifies the 'Labour defectors' as 'older people and those from manual households'.

CHAPTER 4

Wilson, Heath and Benn remake the Labour Party

Labour's defeat in 1970 came as a surprise, a fact surprising enough to require an explanation. The simplest explanation is that the government was misled by data.[1] The numbers were better in the run-up to the election than they had been since 1966. The figures on the state of the economy were much improved, and polls purporting to read the mind of the electorate were also better. Wilson was buoyed in particular by better returns on trade, balance of payments, inflation and economic growth and was convinced, along with his fellow Cabinet members, that the difficult medicine administered in successive tight budgets and the hard but necessary choices – especially the devaluation of 1967 – had finally begun to pay off. The government was also cheered by its recovery in the opinion polls: Wilson was preferred over Heath as prime minister by fully 20 points early in the campaign. The party also took comfort from recent successes in local government elections.

The polls pointing to a Labour victory were nevertheless too recent to be truly convincing, while the good economic news was recent and would prove short-lived. And the memories of division, defeat, disillusion and retreat of the past several years lingered just below the surface. As Roy Jenkins reflected thoughtfully: 'My belief in a Labour victory had been firm, but skin-deep, for I had not believed in it long ... My new belief [in a possible victory] had had no time to settle and harden and was therefore easily broken through.'[2] Still, Cabinet members were genuinely shocked to have quickly become 'Yesterday's Men' and at how quickly they had to vacate their quarters. They realised, too, how painfully dependent they had become on the perquisites of office. Wilson himself was effectively homeless, the Callaghans had to bounce from one lodging to another; Jenkins missed his staff and his car terribly; and Crosland was shocked to find out how difficult it was to complete a telephone call without a secretary. The new reality was quickly registered, of course, but there was a great deal of regret and denial about it all.

The key political question was how Labour would respond to its defeat. There was a widespread and vague sense within the party that Labour's defeat had been largely self-inflicted, that the loss was perhaps a fitting rebuke for failures in government, and that it might require a rethinking of party policy and strategy. But that sort of reflective response was by no means universal or, if it was, it did not persist and would not result in any fundamental reassessment of the party's philosophy, programme or style of governance. Wilson, for example, argued strongly against a 'post-mortem' because, as he put it, there was no dead body to pick over. Inevitably, most former ministers were defensive and reluctant to engage in a bout of self-criticism and so would tend to agree with Wilson's position. The effect on the party overall was in consequence asymmetrical: the centre-right, probably over-represented in the Cabinet and now in the Shadow Cabinet, were relatively complacent in opposition; the left, on the other hand, was more ready to criticise and determined to push its agenda. On balance, therefore, the reaction of the party was to reaffirm its beliefs and historic loyalties but in the process to restate these 'traditional' attitudes in a more aggressive and left-wing direction.

The complacency of the centre-right was abetted by a selective amnesia that allowed them to forget just how badly their recent perform-ance had been. The government had keenly disappointed its supporters in abandoning the *National Plan* in 1966; it looked very much out of its depth during the crises that preceded and accompanied devaluation; and its defeat over *In Place of Strife* was understood at the time to be disastrous. Indeed, Wilson had predicted in June 1969 that if industrial relations reform failed, 'the unions would lose all credibility and so would the government', which would effectively become a 'lame duck government seen at home or abroad to have lost control and to be unable to govern'.[3] When the government pulled back from its confrontation with the unions just a few days later, Wilson and his colleagues chose to claim it a victory, but it was widely understood as the very opposite. Nevertheless, Labour's leaders went on to forget just how badly they had been beaten in the contest. They had taken on the unions and they had lost; once again they failed to carry a policy previously declared to be absolutely critical – like planning, like correcting the balance of payments problem, like maintaining the value of the currency. And, as might well have been predicted, the collapse was followed by an outbreak of industrial militancy. But Labour in power seemed oblivious to the likely cumulative impact of its repeated policy failures or of the inevitably growing perception that the party was unable to get its core constituency, the unions, to go along with what it proclaimed as the national interest.

Why this blindness to the political consequences of failure? The answer surely lies in the fact that the centre-right of the party, no less than the left, were deeply committed to the Labour Party as an institution and as a set of values and to the two central features of the party's identity. The first was the critical link with the trade unions, the connection that made plausible the party's claim to represent the working class while providing it with a natural base of electoral and financial support. The second was the commitment to planning and public ownership, a policy that not only set Labour off from its opponents but which served to move the party beyond the simple defence of working-class interests and institutions towards a vague but genuine aspiration for social and political transformation. The failures of the Wilson governments constituted a direct challenge to both of these pillars of Labour's identity, but the party recoiled from the prospect of giving up on either. Planning may have failed, but to concede so would be to acknowledge that Labour had no policy truly its own. Likewise, the unions' refusal to consider reforms that might allow for a dampening of industrial conflict may have gravely compromised the government's claim to rule and turned a potential asset – the ability successfully to work with unions in a partnership for stability and economic growth – into a liability; but severing or renegotiating the historic ties to the unions was simply not on the agenda.

Faced with undeniable difficulties over its relationship to the unions and over its preference for planning and public ownership, then, the party would choose not to jettison but to reassert these commitments and hence to reaffirm its identity. The continued, and indeed deepened, connection to the unions would be critical to Labour's future. The outcome was, of course, virtually ensured by the party's prior history, for Labour was linked by a sort of umbilical cord to the unions and only through them to the working class. Its leaders knew instinctively that their claim to legitimacy as the defender and promoter of working-class interests was premised on the connection; and they reckoned as well that without union money and logistical support the party's organisation and electoral capabilities would collapse. Within the culture of the labour movement, then, a permanent rift or dissociation with the trade unions was more or less unthinkable. Nor was it desirable, for all sections of the Labour Party truly understood its mission as that of securing for working people, most reliably represented by unions, a more prominent place in the running of the state and of the economy. That goal had been especially compelling when the unions and the people they spoke for were genuinely disenfranchised, as was surely the case prior to 1945. It was a goal, moreover, whose achievement promised not only a better deal for workers but also a better, more just and egalitarian society. Indeed, the great breakthrough of 1945 might be understood as the moment when the particular and sectional interests represented by Labour could be effectively proclaimed as embodying the national interest as well. Socialism was the rhetorical and programmatic route to this broadening, nationalisation and public ownership its means and also its emblem, and the actions and policies of Labour in office its outcome and ultimate justification.

The polity left in place by the post-war Labour governments was more inclusive and open towards the unions, but the implications of its resulting corporatist bias, and its effects on policy-making, were little understood. The practice was considered pragmatically and regarded as a highly useful mechanism for the articulation and representation of interests, a mechanism less authoritative but in crucial respects more informative than mere voting.[4] How else to ascertain the collective interests and considered views of working people than by consulting the groups who claimed to speak on their behalf? No more direct contact was feasible or promised equivalent representation of organised interests, and no politician – no Conservative in particular – had the confidence to boast a more intimate connection or a more accurate reading of popular sentiment. However, the passion and moral power that had sustained the drive to obtain recognition for the interests of labour inevitably ebbed once inclusion became more routine. The argument that successful policy-making required consultation and winning the prior consent of the governed was not unconvincing, but it was certainly uninspiring. And it would prove very difficult in practice to combine corporatist bargaining and consultation with effective policy-making, as Conservative and Labour governments were to learn to their dismay.

The rationale for corporatism was also undermined by full employment, which gave unions and their members unprecedented leverage that could be exercised directly in the industrial sphere. In a very short time, unions went from a position of weakness to a position of real strength and the traditions and practices built up over decades of weakness were ill-suited to the demands and opportunities presented by a vastly altered economic climate and a state recently opened up to union influence. In particular, the voluntarist traditions evolved to defend the unions from employers and the state were hard to reconcile with the unions' insistence on being a partner with the employers and the state in the making of economic policy. The more thoughtful union leaders understood the dilemma. Thus George Woodcock, TUC General Secretary for much of the 1960s, took a moment in 1963 (it seems) to outline both the traditional union stance and the novel complications that arose in the new context of the 1960s: 'There can be no formal limits or restrictions on wage bargaining; on trade unions having the right to get as strong as they can by a system of voluntary association including the closed shop. There can be no justification at all', he continued, 'for any external limitation of a legal or any other kind on a union's right to organise, to formulate their policies and to pursue them as relentlessly as they can.' But, he then conceded, 'today there is a limit to what unions should do – can rightly do – without making it impossible for the government to do the right things too'. At the root of the problem was the fact that it could no longer be assumed that the interests of the unions and their members could automatically be consistent with the universal, or the national, interest. Unfortunately, union leaders themselves did little to bring these distinct interests into line; on the contrary, they were quite willing to assert the separate character of working-class, or at least trade union, interest. Again Woodcock was unusually clear about this: 'we are not going to take our policy from anyone else . . .', he insisted. 'When I say we have to fit in with a conception of national interest, I do not mean a conception of national interest given to us by anyone else, neither by the Labour Party nor the Conservative government.'[5] Len Murray, General Secretary from 1973, would make the same point even more bluntly: 'Trade unions', he lectured in 1970, 'are disposed to question the absolute sovereignty of the state and to regard it at least for some important purposes as a federal society in regulating the affairs of which the government has an important but not necessarily an overriding authority.'[6]

This emerging challenge to the authority of the state or to the privileged position of political parties and government in defining the national interest was a challenge also to accepted notions of parliamentary sovereignty and to conventional understandings of the British constitution. Historically, it was a distinctly novel phenomenon. Back in 1926 the then Conservative government had chosen to define the General Strike in constitutional terms, but it was a partisan and tendentious construction that the unions and the Labour Party vehemently and effectively denied.[7] For unions themselves to assert their doubts about the sovereignty of the state was an altogether different matter that signalled a genuine transformation in their status. The leaders of the Labour Party were slow to grasp the potential danger, however, even if Wilson would occasionally construe union resistance to government policy as a challenge to his, or his government's, authority. Instead, party leaders registered the increase in union strength and in the underlying clout of workers in a tight labour market as a positive development that could be utilised by a Labour government. Labour thus sought to incorporate the unions within their otherwise rather thin repertoire of techniques through which to exercise control over the economy. They were willing, in fact, to delegate extensive responsibilities for managing the system of industrial relations to unions accountable only to themselves, their odd rulebooks and their occasionally vocal but often passive members, and to defer to the unions on a wide variety of issues.

Labour's inherited commitments bedevilled the government's broader economic strategy as well, but again reversing course was out of the question. Wilson's rhetorical joining of technology, planning and growth had served to make the traditional commitment to public ownership compatible with modernisation and economic progress. The subsequent abandonment of the *National Plan* and the formal apparatus of planning, though damaging, could nevertheless be attributed to circumstances, to the power of entrenched interests or to a failure of political will. In consequence, the aspiration to plan and to enlarge the state's role in industry persisted among large sections of the party. Frustrated at the failure of industry to respond to repeated prodding, moreover, the vision of planning held by Labour's experts on industry gradually became less 'indicative' and more compulsory. When challenged, therefore, the commitment was expanded rather than abandoned.

The reinforcement of established identities and commitments on the part of Labour even after the general election defeat was further encouraged by the erratic but provocative behaviour of the Conservatives in power. Indeed, the possibility of Labour moving away from its prior loyalties and commitments and embarking on a programme of 'modernisation' was precluded by the Heath government, which proved no more adept at handling the nation's economic problems and its mounting industrial relations crisis than had Labour. Heath's multiple and cumulative failures led Labour to believe that its own difficulties were but temporary and perhaps less serious. In fact, as early as November 1970 the polls showed 45 per cent dissatisfied with Heath's performance, with only 39 per cent approving; and Labour had a 4 point lead as well. Opinion fluctuated for a short while thereafter, but by June 1971, just a year after the Conservative victory, the judgement on Heath had turned ever more sharply negative – 57 per cent versus 31 per cent – and Labour's lead in the polls was up to 17 per cent. Both Heath and the Conservatives would recover a bit in late 1973, but for most of its time in office the government was on the defensive.[8] Labour's revival, then, was due largely to external events – specifically, the difficulties that beset the Conservative government. The political consequences of its 1970 defeat were thus contradictory: Labour was chastened by its rejection and its leaders were determined to heal the divisions that seem to have caused it. There was a resolve as well to avoid the mistakes of the previous government and for the left that meant fewer compromises and a steadier progress toward socialism. But Heath's failure was interpreted to mean that the path on which Labour had set out was not mistaken; rather, they needed to push ahead more forcefully. Hence the effect of the party's rethinking after 1970 was not to move in a new direction, as had been discussed at least after 1959, but rather to reassert its traditional values and approach – to rally around the trade unions, to insist on the need for corporatist bargaining, to respond to Tory criticisms of state intervention by calling for more of it, and to sharpen up the differences between the parties.

Heath had taken office bearing a distinctive new look – the aggressive posture associated with the image of 'Selsdon man' – and amid talk of a break with Labour's corporatist style of governance and of a decisive turn to the market. The government promised to reverse the interventionism of the previous government, to cut both taxes and spending and to ease the burden of regulations on business initiative. It simultaneously moved forward with its own variant of industrial relations reform, outlined while in opposition in a pamphlet promising a 'Fair Deal at Work'. The Tory plan was considerably more forceful and punitive than what had been proposed in *In Place of Strife*. But Heath's initiatives would almost all come to naught, partly through a lack of will and political acumen, partly because of the unexpected strength of the opposition his plans elicited, and because he had the very bad luck to preside over the beginning of the end of the post-war boom and the oil crisis that followed the Yom Kippur War. In response, the Heath government reversed course on both industrial policy and industrial relations, in the process earning it the enmity of its core base of Conservative supporters and winning no converts from the left or the centre of the political spectrum.

Heath's troubles thus had a curious impact on the politics of Labour in opposition. By initiating a break with the post-war consensus on the role of the state and of the unions, the Conservatives provoked Labour to a vigorous defence. And by failing to follow through on its initiatives, the Tories helped to convince Labour and the unions that they were right to resist, correct in their understanding of how the economy worked and of what needed to be done to move Britain forward. Reappraisals of a more self-critical sort were in this way short-circuited and Labour in Britain continued on the path set by its previous choices and commitments and the political identity that grew from these. The distinctiveness of this pattern is important. Across the advanced societies the all too frequent failures of social-democratic parties and their subsequent defeats by parties of the right have typically led to debates and reassessments that have issued in new appeals and policies meant to attract the centrist voter and thus to nudge the party towards the political centre. Labour, by contrast, responded to failure and defeat by tacking to the left; and it was to some extent the manner of Heath's failing which actually encouraged Labour and the unions to proceed in directions that would end up accentuating the party's long-term difficulties and massively complicate its own efforts to cope with mounting economic problems upon its return to office in 1974. It was not, of course, all Heath's doing. Labour's unique political culture and its peculiar internal structure predisposed the party to respond as it did; and it would have required a leader far more willing to lead than Wilson for it to have done otherwise. But the choices made after 1970 would have real consequences. Labour would learn all the wrong lessons from its period in opposition and so would manage in the late 1970s to repeat all the failures of the late 1960s, but with even more disastrous results.

A closer examination of the effect of the Heath government on Labour's evolution would begin with the Conservatives' willingness to break with the immediate past. The Conservatives entered office in 1970 increasingly uneasy about the prevailing pattern of policy-making and ready at least to contemplate a departure from the consensual style of corporatist bargaining and state intervention in the economy. Heath and his team were especially eager to unleash the spirit of entrepreneurship which they felt was so lacking in the behaviour of British firms. Where Labour saw industry as constrained by narrow, class-based attitudes and the complacency of an elite based not on merit but inheritance, of course, the Conservatives saw business as held back by inadequate profits caused by excessive taxes and intrusive regulations. Heath wanted as keenly as Wilson to modernise the economy and, according to a key Treasury adviser, Brendan Sewill, adopted a strategy that 'was no less than an attempt to change the whole attitude of mind of the British people: to create a more dynamic, thrusting, go-getting economy on the American or German model'.[9] The plan was to inject dynamism into the economy through increased incentives, decreased state involvement and more intense competition; and when competition resulted in bankruptcies or lay-offs, the government must resist the call to subsidise 'lame ducks'. In pursuit of these goals, the government began to dismantle the institutions of control and intervention bequeathed to it by Labour. They got rid of the Industrial Reorganisation Corporation, downgraded the NEDC, repealed the Industrial Expansion Act, abandoned the regional employment premium and the selective employment tax, and at least edged towards the privatisation of the nationalised industries. The Conservative government also reapplied for membership in the European Common Market in the hope that exposing British firms to European competition would encourage innovation and the adoption of more modern and sophisticated management.

The vision of the Heath government was to this extent as grand and expansive as Wilson's had been; and both regimes displayed the same impatience with the inadequacies of the private sector. Heath and Wilson also, it would seem, shared a similar lack of resolve in implementing their visions. Thus when Heath's prescribed remedies – lower taxes, fewer regulations, less state intervention – failed to produce results, or were confronted with short-term problems whose solution could not be left to the workings of the market, they were hastily abandoned. Almost immediately upon taking office, for example, the government had to choose between letting Rolls-Royce, that symbol of British engineering excellence and a source of 80,000 jobs, go bust or undertaking what would prove a prolonged and expensive rescue. They reluctantly opted for a bailout. The following year the government found itself asked to take over Upper Clyde Shipbuilders. In this case, the issue was presented not by management but by an organised and militant workforce who had taken physical control of the yards. The prospect of disorder, violence and, if the enterprise went under, mass unemployment and spreading discontent in the west of Scotland ultimately convinced the government to come up with the £35 million needed to save the shipyards.

Ad hoc reversals called for a rationalisation and ultimately a more formal adjustment and restatement of policy. The result was the Industry Act of 1972. The Industry Act gave back to government much of what it had just recently given away. John Davies, former CBI Director and now head of the Department of Trade and Industry, explained now that 'in a new and changing world industrial and commercial environment, the government cannot stand aside when situations arise which industry and the financial institutions cannot meet alone. We have decided to take powers to help industry to modernise, adapt and rationalise . . .'[10] Davies was silent about equity and social justice, or the self-evident virtues of state intervention, themes Labour would have stressed, and the new line was sold not as an installation of socialism but as the beginnings of a 'new capitalism'. In practice, Conservative policy would involve more businessmen and fewer retired trade unionists than what had transpired under Labour. But the effect was similar: by 1973–74 the Conservative government that had come to office pledged to restore the market was operating a policy of state-led economic modernisation. Tony Benn, increasingly wedded to dirigiste policies himself, could thus ironically welcome the Conservatives' conversion and the new Industry Act and not unreasonably promise in Parliament that 'We shall make use of the powers of the Bill when we come into power again more radically than the right honorable gentlemen will use them' (22 May 1972).

The Heath government's handling of industrial relations and of incomes policy followed similar trajectories to not dissimilar destinations. Again, Heath sought to break out of a pattern of repeated failure. Since the late 1940s policy-makers had understood that growth depended upon exports whose expansion could be easily jeopardised by rising prices or by a shortfall of investment caused by monetary and fiscal policies imposed to right the balance of payments. Devaluation was always an option and Labour achieved positive results when it did so in 1949 and again in 1967. But it was seen as a last resort because it diminished the value of assets held in sterling and that threatened powerful interests both at home and abroad. The Heath government would itself be forced into a de facto devaluation when in 1971 the United States abandoned the Bretton Woods system and Britain was forced to float the pound in response. The preferred solution, however, was not devaluation but rather an effort to find other mechanisms to keep prices low by preventing, or slowing, the increase of wages.

While Labour had operated a successful policy of wage restraint during 1948–50, by 1950 the policy could no longer command support from union members and was allowed to lapse. During the 1950s, Conservatives in government occasionally considered the need for wage controls but feared confrontation with the unions and backed away. By the early 1960s, however, the problem had grown more serious and in response the Tory government first adopted a 'pay pause', then offered up a 'guiding light' norm, and finally turned to a National Incomes Commission. The newly established NEDC, supposedly designed for indicative planning, was also seen by policy-makers as 'a way of involving the unions in an incomes policy'.[11] None of these involved statutory or binding controls. These interventions did, though, betray a new urgency that would be picked up by the incoming Labour government. The issue would consume tremendous time and energy during the 1964–70 governments, but nearly all their efforts failed. Clearly frustrated at the difficulty of operating a successful incomes policy within the existing framework of relations between unions, employers and the state, the Wilson government turned from efforts to control incomes to a plan for altering the structure and working of the trade unions, *In Place of Strife*. That effort also failed and thus left the incoming Conservative government with an enduring problem and, perhaps, a historic opportunity.

The idea of reforming the structure of trade unions had strong support among Conservatives, who had begun pushing Labour on the issue during the mid-1960s, and so it was almost inevitable that the Heath government would try to do what Harold Wilson had failed to do. Its resolve to pursue industrial relations reform rather than wage controls was made more intense by its ideological preference for the market and its aversion to state control. So while insisting that they were opposed to a formal incomes policy, the Conservatives pressed forcefully for the alternative: a new and comprehensive legal framework that would, they hoped, produce more responsible behaviour from the trade unions. Upon taking office the new government was greeted by a wave of strikes, including a crippling dispute on the docks. As early as August 1970 Heath was telling his colleagues in Cabinet that the 'reform of industrial relations . . . was of the first importance'.[12] The Cabinet were willing to consult both sides of industry about the shape of legislation but at a meeting on 1 September the general secretary of the TUC issued a firm no to the government, which went ahead anyway.[13] The Industrial Relations Act, prepared with haste and made public in December 1970, was a complex piece of legislation that would have formally recognised the 'right to strike' and afforded workers protection against unfair dismissal. But these new rights were more than counterbalanced by restrictions on union behaviour and the creation of a large apparatus of state control. The Act would create a registrar of trade unions that would record and supervise union rules; it provided for the elaboration of a model Code of Industrial Relations; it asserted the presumption that collective agreements were binding; and set up a Commission on Industrial Relations that could resolve demarcation disputes and also work out and impose binding settlements of disputes. Most important, the Act established a National Industrial Relations Court and a series of Industrial Tribunals that were to deal with instances of 'unfair industrial relations practices' and that could impose financial penalties on offenders. The Court could also, at the request of the government, impose 'cooling off' periods for as long as 60 days and require compulsory strike ballots. The Act was certainly in the spirit of *In Place of Strife*, but it went much further and granted the government substantially greater power to intervene in the workings of trade unions and the conduct of collective bargaining.

The Industrial Relations Act became law in August 1971; a year later it was put on ice and came to be largely disregarded in the daily practice of industrial relations. Union opposition had begun before the contents of the bill were made public and escalated from there. Close to 150,000 protesters joined a 7-mile march into central London in February 1971 and in March a special TUC meeting urged affiliates not to register under the Act. The question of registration proved to be the Act's fatal flaw: unions would not be compelled to register under the new Act, but were expected to do so. When the TUC recommended against and most unions followed its lead, the entire legitimacy of the Act was thrown into doubt. Its detailed and punitive application to disputes among dockers and railwaymen also undermined confidence in the legislation and confused and contradictory court rulings led Conservatives and many business-men to wonder about the wisdom of criminalizing behaviour that was not typically thought to fall within the criminal law.

The Act had also proved quite useless in dealing with the most significant conflict of the period, the miners' strike of January–February 1972, which forced the government to capitulate to a 21 per cent increase in wages. The strike had been approved by a ballot of members and sanctioned by the NUM leadership. The government chose not to invoke the Industrial Relations Act largely because it was official, but also because of 'the special circumstances of a mining dispute', and because the sections of the Act governing boycotts and secondary picketing had not yet come into effect.[14] It was therefore particularly unable to cope with the mass demonstrations and flying pickets that effectively spread the strike from the coalfields to coke depots and power stations. At the Saltley coke depot in the West Midlands, for example, 'a crowd of some 7000' – including the young militant Arthur Scargill – blocked lorries and shut down the facility in early February.[15] On 17 February the authorities counted no less than 321 sites around the country that were being picketed, mostly mines and collieries but also numerous power stations.[16] Sympathy action by the railway union and by the TGWU added further to the crisis by preventing supplies of coal and oil from getting to power stations. Heath was compelled to back down in the face of this show of force and solidarity. He shared his dilemma with the Cabinet: a tough stance would alienate moderates within the unions and make resistance still fiercer, he explained, and if that happened, 'the Government might find themselves unable to sustain the life of the community unless they surrendered to the miners'. But capitulation, he understood, 'would present the militant leadership of the miners with so clear a victory that no democratically constituted Government could hope to sustain their authority for long without seeking a fresh mandate from a General Election'.[17] They did capitulate, however, and as a result the Conservatives' efforts to discipline the unions through legal regulation lay in a shambles by spring 1972. The final stimulus to the effective abandonment of the strategy and of the Act was the jailing of London dockworkers – the 'Pentonville Five' – in July 1972 and their subsequent release. Putting workers in jail proved very unpopular and convinced the government to back off from enforcement of the Act and to throw its weight behind a joint effort of the CBI and the TUC to work out procedures for a voluntary system of arbitration.[18] As with the voluntary policies adopted after Wilson's failure over *In Place of Strife*, these were not taken seriously by either side or by the public.

Watching its efforts at legal reform of industrial relations unravel, the Heath government edged inevitably towards wage controls, where it would again recapitulate the sorry experience of the Labour government. A voluntary norm of N-1, in which each settlement was to be 1 per cent lower than the last, was proclaimed for the public sector, but the settlement of the miners' strike would make a mockery of its calculations. From March to November 1972 the government engaged in talks first with the TUC and then also with the CBI aimed at a broader but still voluntary policy for all of industry, but failed to secure agreement on a workable plan. In desperation, Heath imposed a statutory incomes policy in three stages: Stage I was a freeze on wages as well as on prices, rents and dividends that lasted from November 1972 into the following spring;

while Stage II involved the setting up in April 1973 of a Pay Board and a Price Commission that would supervise wage and price increases. Stage III began in November 1973 and placed a limit on pay increases of £2.25 a week (roughly 7 per cent), but allowed further increases of 40p for every percentage point by which inflation exceeded the 7 per cent standard. It also provided some room for flexibility when the circumstances involved equal pay or 'unsocial hours'. The introduction of these threshold payments beyond the 7 per cent limit was a reasonable enough decision on its own terms, but in the context proved counter-productive because it established an automatic link between rising prices and rising wages at the worst possible moment, when skyrocketing oil prices were pushing up prices all around. The effect was to ensure that wages and prices would move in lock step at comparable and extremely high rates of increase.[19]

The policy enjoyed modest success for the first year: it was politically popular, most workers acquiesced despite formal union opposition; and the wage and price increases were kept down. But Stage III proved a disaster. Within days of its announcement the miners began an overtime ban for increases that would have broken sharply with the norm applied to other workers. The miners had begun negotiations in the summer, before the new norms were announced, and put in demands that would involve increases of up to 50 per cent for at least some workers. The government had anticipated the need to give the miners more and for that reason built some flexibility into the policy. But the flexibility did not provide enough room to make a deal with the miners. The miners were further encouraged in their firmness by the sharp jump in oil prices, which put them in a more powerful position than ever before because of the increased demand for coal. They insisted on more and the government began looking for a way to meet the miners' demands without jettisoning its entire pay policy. Efforts were made to get the TUC to agree that even if the miners got a settlement out of line with the norm, it would be regarded as exceptional and not used as a lever to get more for other workers. But the TUC had already come out against the policy and, although they professed to understand that the miners were a special case and would not necessarily form the basis for a new standard, they believed a more precise commitment would be a de facto endorsement of the policy. This the unions refused to do.

The government had responded to the miners' action by declaring a State of Emergency almost immediately (13 November 1973) and a month later decided to institute a 3-day week that would commence after the holidays. The aim was to prevent shortages of power and fuel during the winter months. Despite reasonably determined efforts on both sides, negotiations failed to produce a compromise. The miners' leaders held a ballot on 4 February that revealed 80 per cent of the membership to be in favour of a complete stoppage beginning five days later. Two days later Heath called a general election for 28 February in an effort to secure a mandate for a tough stance towards the unions.[20] His pitch to the voters was not entirely negative: over the past 18 months the government had sought to bargain with the TUC on a range of issues and promised to do more in the future. And it had backed off the enforcement of the Industrial Relations Act and held out the prospect of revision. But the basic message was nonetheless clear and contentious: the nation was asked to repudiate 'the danger from within' and 'the abuse of industrial power'. Wilson responded with an unusually deft touch. Since the beginning of the dispute he had been corresponding with Heath in a fashion that was meant to become public about possible compromises and Labour's leader largely succeeded in portraying the government as unyielding, provocative and 'extremist'.[21] Labour did not truly expect or even very much want to win, but hoped at least to blunt Heath's appeal and deny the Conservatives a mandate.[22] Voters reacted by refusing to give either Heath or his Labour opponents a clear victory. The Conservatives polled slightly more votes than Labour, 37.8 per cent versus 37.1 per cent, but Labour won 301 seats to the Conservatives' 297. Neither side secured enough votes or seats to form a majority government. After several days of uncertain manoeuvrings, Wilson just barely managed to form a government on 4 March. Labour would be returned to office, but the election 'was scarcely an endorsement of Labour's programme . . .' and 'could not provide a mandate for decisive action in the battlegrounds of industrial relations and prices'.[23] But these were precisely the issues the new government would be forced to confront. It was not an auspicious beginning.

Labour's difficulties would come soon enough. More interesting in 1974 was what the multiple failures of the Heath government and its apparent tendency to execute U-turns on key policies meant for British politics more broadly. For the Tories it was to be interpreted as a lesson in the futility of compromise and constituted presumptive evidence that the pattern of corporatist policy-making rendered society 'ungovernable' because it just would not work. The defeat would ultimately mean the end of Edward Heath and the rise of Margaret Thatcher, who would lead the party on a long march to the right. Indeed, Thatcher in office was absolutely determined to avoid becoming another Heath; and her aversion to compromise probably owed as much to her considered reflections on Heath's failures as to her unusually combative personality.

The rise and progress of Margaret Thatcher still lay in the future, however, and the more proximate impact of Heath's difficulties was on the Labour Party. The inability of Heath to engineer a move away from state intervention and towards the market was widely noted and understood at the time as a decisive argument for the necessity of an activist state. Tony Benn, for example, gloated in *The Sunday Times* (27 March 1973) that Heath had done the critical 'Spadework for Socialism' and 'has performed a very important historical role in preparing for the fundamental and irreversible transfer in the balance of power and in wealth which has to take place . . .'. The fact that the Conservative government ended its days taking more and more of British industry under its control and spending enormous sums to do so suggested that Labour's collectivist preferences were appropriate and necessary. Heath's repeated defeats at the hands of the unions were likewise interpreted as proof that the balance of forces in industry, and society broadly, gave to the trade unions an enormous influence in the running of the economy and something like a veto power over policies and legislation with which they disagreed. While Conservatives – and others outside the peculiar culture of the Labour Party – might well come to view that influence as a problem, the unions felt it was merely their due. And although some Labour leaders might harbour private doubts, as a group they were committed to the belief that Labour as a party was uniquely able to work with the unions and so uniquely capable of running the country. The Heath government's failures therefore constituted the essential background to the conduct of internal political debate within the Labour Party and they served indirectly to create a climate that would prove unusually favourable to the left.

But the advance of the left within the party during 1970–74 was not merely a reflection of external events. It was also a product of Labour's distinctive history, culture and institutional structure, which predisposed the party under stress or in defeat to fall back upon old loyalties, to revive and update old beliefs, and thus to reinforce what was distinctive about its politics and its strategy of governance. This pattern was especially evident in the early 1970s, when the hard lessons that might have been learned from the experiences of the two previous Wilson governments were overwhelmed by more immediate reactions or absorbed within a framework that minimised their significance. A different political culture, less encompassing and insulating and more open, might well have produced a fuller or different reckoning. The centre-right leadership of the party was, however, not ready to undertake such a reckoning, for it would threaten their positions as well as their beliefs, and so they reacted at only a superficial level, registering surprise and disappointment but no serious determination to rethink or to envision a genuinely alternative course. The party as a whole vacillated between support for the leadership and its moderate, if tarnished, policies and a willingness to line up behind the policies and strategic approach of the left.

Inaction at the top provided a critical opening for those who wanted to reaffirm and extend the party's socialist commitments. The initiatives the party did take during its time in opposition, therefore, were those emanating from the left, which emerged from defeat to argue that the modest shift to the left begun under Wilson – with his vision of planning, state intervention and increased-public spending – needed to be taken further and pursued with much more rigour. The left of the party – Tony Benn, Michael Foot, Ian Mikardo, Judith Hart and many less well-known activists – moved quickly in 1970 to push not only for a more radical set of policies but also for guarantees that they would be carried out. Benn was energised by the defeat and ready to assume a novel role at the head of a movement to reshape the party. When Benn proclaimed just after the defeat that he and his wife had 'never been happier', Tony Crosland explained to his puzzled spouse what it foretold: 'He *is* happier in Opposition. There's no other time he can make his move.' The standard-bearer of revisionism understood that Benn was out to remake the party and to become leader: 'no one doubts his sincerity in seeing himself as a Messiah. The trouble with fanatics – why one should never underestimate them – is they're so assiduous.'[24] The old warhorse Michael Foot was likewise newly energised, though he was perhaps less assiduous than Benn. Most important, the leaders of the left were able to mobilise extremely widespread support. The membership of the party had been falling in the aggregate, but many of those lost had never been active locally and they were more than replaced by new recruits who were active in constituency parties and who were well to the left of Wilson and the parliamentary leadership. The unions were also more open to the left than ever before. Their top leaders were still smarting from the battle over *In Place of Strife* and so on balance unwilling to provide support for the party leaders. Instead, they often backed the critics of the leadership and joined in the push to the left, at least on policy. Perhaps equally important, the party organisation itself put its weight behind the efforts of the left. Wilson had long had a strained relationship with the party and its central staff, and there was palpable disappointment among those charged with the party's day-to-day operations with the government's behaviour and performance. Ron Hayward, Terry Pitt and Geoff Bish – the most prominent of party officials – were to play important roles in setting the agenda for reorienting programme and policy, in recruiting 'experts' – most more or less on the left of the party – to advise on new directions, in preparing background papers, and in putting into a coherent framework the sometimes inchoate sentiments and preferences articulated in policy debates.[25]

Formally, the discussions took place within, and under the auspices of, the National Executive Committee. The NEC had the responsibility for making policy that would be ratified by conference. In practice, the NEC led and largely orchestrated the annual party conference and it had broad discretion in selecting what issues to work on between conferences and what resolutions to send to conference for its action. After the defeat of 1970 the NEC undertook a broad reassessment of policy and organised the inquiry through its Home Policy Committee and, especially, through its sub-committees on Industrial Policy and the Public Sector.[26] These committees were given new prominence after 1970 and unusually broad terms of reference, and they were allowed to co-opt members from outside the party. They enrolled a wide range of experts, many of them academics unaffected by the practical considerations that constrain politicians and civil servants. The list at various times would include names already familiar or soon to be so: Titmuss, Kaldor, Balogh, Wedderburn, H.A. Clegg, Derek Robinson, Bill McCarthy, Michael Barratt Brown,

Richard Pryke, the expert of nationalised industries, and Stuart Holland, who assumed an unusually prominent role in the process of revising Labour's programme.[27] The committees' subsequent deliberations would constitute simultaneously an inquest on 'what went wrong' after 1966 and a forum for working out an ambitious set of policies for the next Labour government.

The effort was complicated and protracted, but by 1973 the party had in place a vision and a plan that differed markedly from the more tepid offerings available in recent decades. Tony Benn, conference chairman in 1972, introduced the first fruits of the party's rethinking by asserting authoritatively that 'the era of so-called "consensus politics" is over. It was never real.'[28] *Labour's Programme 1973* made clear the new, or recently clarified, polarisation of British politics and called for a dramatic shift of power and wealth towards working people and a major expansion of public ownership. It committed an incoming Labour government to extensive controls over prices, to substantial increases in pensions and social services, and to a highly intrusive programme of state intervention in industry. At the heart of the programme for industry were two proposals: for a National Enterprise Board (NEB) whose remit would far exceed that of the Industrial Reorganisation Corporation recently abolished by the Conservatives; and planning agreements. The NEB would buy shares and begin to exert control of key firms in manufacturing. The aim was to use this control to guide investment and somehow to stimulate other companies to match their efforts. The NEB would begin by taking over the management of those enterprises in which the government already had substantial investment – BP, Rolls-Royce and ICL – and add to that controlling interests in another 25 leading companies. Public ownership and control would no longer be confined to lame ducks or declining industries but extended into the growth areas of the economy, thus providing government with leverage to further the process of growth. The effect would be dramatic. As Judith Hart explained:

The National Enterprise Board will take the sector leaders of profitable manufacturing industry into public ownership and control. It will do so in order to exercise direct influence on their strategies for investment, for prices, for exports and for location of new plant in the regions.
To be effective, it must be on a substantial scale and that means that

at the end of a five-year term one-third of the turnover of the top 100 manufacturers, who account for about half of our net manufacturing output and two-fifths of their profits and about half their employment, should be invested with the board.[29]

Planning agreements would further extend the state's role by forcing companies to reach agreements on their investment programmes and pricing policies for the coming five years. Firms would be expected to share with government and the unions information on profits and costs, on products and markets, and to make binding agreements. Government would assist the efforts of firms by offering financing, if necessary, and by approving plans for expansion and prices. Firms that did not cooperate with these 'programme contracts' would see their plans blocked, subsidies cut off, or price increases disallowed, and they could be temporarily taken into state control by the appointment of an Industrial Commissioner (later termed an Official Trustee).

The intent was to provide the government with 'the real tactical instruments' for planning that had been unavailable to the Department of Economic Affairs and to the last Labour effort at planning and thus to revive planning itself. The objective remained what it had long been, that of 'overcoming a defensive investment psychology in management' by supplementing Keynesian macro-economic policy with 'purely micro and purely imperative planning', as Stuart Holland laid it out. In his view the NEB would own outright 'a complement of State firms . . .' that would act 'as pace-setters', and it would also take shares in leading companies thereby 'harnessing' their energies to the cause of growth as well. 'Planning agreements' would be required of all large companies. The effect would be to transform the role of the state in the economy: it would not only be an industrial consultant and banker, but 'also part "plain bully" . . . in indicating to leading private companies that they may be nationalised through the State Holding Company [NEB] if they do not cooperate'.[30]

These dramatically interventionist proposals had a supposedly European provenance – the French were understood to have pioneered the use of programme contracts, while the closest thing to the NEB was the Italian Industrial Reconstruction Institute (IRI) – but they had also been anticipated by the experience of Tony Benn at Mintech. In particular, the element of compulsion grew almost inevitably from the frustration felt by Benn (and others) at their inability to cajole or persuade business into behaving properly. Benn's prior experience and his current sponsorship were in this respect critical, for they lent the proposals an air of legitimacy they might not otherwise have enjoyed. The proposals were also designed to appeal to the party's core constituency, the trade unions, for they were to be given a central role in the tripartite system that would bargain out the details of planning agreements.[31] And it was Benn who argued most forcefully and effectively that the entire package needed to be implemented fully and quickly in order to forestall the resistance of officials, especially at the Treasury, and of the business community. To avoid these diversions and delays, he advocated the rapid passage of an omnibus Industrial Powers Bill that would serve as an 'enabling act' to allow the government to proceed with its economic policy.

Whatever the precise origin and whatever the model, talk of an enabling act, of compulsion, commissioners and detailed government control made Labour's plans for increasing public ownership and state intervention anathema to business; and they were hardly more welcome to the more cautious leadership of the party.[32] Even before the programme was adopted, Wilson felt compelled to promise to veto the pledge to nationalise 25 companies when it came to crafting the next election manifesto, and after Labour's narrow victory in 1974 the government would find tortuous ways of fudging the proposals made in opposition. Nevertheless, *Labour's Programme 1973* was adopted with overwhelming support at conference and with great fanfare. It was a great triumph for the left, 'the finest Socialist Programme I have seen in my lifetime', according to Michael Foot.[33] It remains something of a mystery how and why the left prevailed so easily and so rapidly.

Part of the reason for the left's success, surely, was the weakness of its opponents. The party's leaders were genuinely exhausted by six years in power and at least temporarily retreated from the fray to lick their wounds, recover their confidence and put their personal lives and finances in order. Wilson, for example, took several months to write a self-serving and highly profitable memoir of the previous administration. When Labour's front bench did rouse itself, moreover, it had much to do in Parliament opposing the controversial initiatives of the Heath government and thus paid too little attention to internal party affairs. Wilson was particularly guilty in this respect, for his natural tendency was to fudge and finesse. He had witnessed Gaitskell's bruising battles with the party conference a decade earlier and was convinced that it was better to pander to conference and then to ignore its more troublesome resolutions than to fight head on over matters of principle.[34] Wilson knew well enough what was happening: his old friend Tommy Balogh had written to him in March 1973 warning him about the radical and controversial nature of the proposals coming from the Industrial Policy Sub-committee and soon to become official party policy, but Wilson chose not to respond.[35] He let the process go forward and then, later, relied on private polling of Labour supporters to convince himself, and others if they challenged him, that he must resist committing the party to taking over the nation's top 25 companies.[36] But otherwise he acquiesced in the new direction and therefore failed to give a lead to those discomfited by the party's turn towards the left.

Nor did others from the centre or the right of the party take up the challenge. Tony Crosland did enter the fray late in the day and argued forcefully on the NEC against the left's 'blanket threat' of large-scale nationalisation.[37] Crosland's intervention evoked little response, however, for he lacked serious allies at the critical moment. Denis Healey, for example, came to recognise that the promises being made in opposition would be impossible to fulfil in government, but he spoke up even later than Crosland, whose intervention was already too late. The crucial absence was Roy Jenkins, who was universally recognised as Wilson's main rival and the leading figure on what remained of the Gaitskellite wing of the party. Jenkins's style was, however, distinctly aloof and superior and he was very poorly suited to waging factional battles. Still more important was his increasing isolation from the bulk of the party, particularly outside the parliamentary party. The reason was Europe, and it is fair to say that the problem of Europe utterly crippled the right in the programmatic battle with the left. Jenkins and his closest allies were firmly committed to British membership in the Common Market and came over time to regard the commitment as a sign of their intellectual sophistication, worldliness and modernity and hence a matter of high principle. Jenkins himself professed a 'settled mind because of historical necessity', but conceded that the pose 'was probably infuriating to those with a different view'.[38] The fact that opponents of the Common Market were so frequently prone to play the nationalist card, however, and to indulge in bouts of rhetorical chauvinism, undoubtedly reinforced this self-righteous attitude on the part of the pro-marketeers. Even the less explicitly nationalist stance of Tony Benn, who announced in 1972 that 'the whole Common Market argument is about democracy', was regarded as unseemly populism that could easily drift into demagoguery.[39] Made firmer in their convictions by distaste for their opponents' arguments, Jenkins and his allies led a defection from the ranks in which some 69 MPs defied the whip and voted with the Heath government to join the Common Market in October 1971.[40] Another 20 were convinced to abstain.

'This treachery', as Barbara Castle labelled it, was made inevitable by the increasing hostility of the majority of the party to the government's application for membership in the Common Market.[41] The Labour government had, of course, itself sought to enter Europe in 1967, but the application had been rebuffed by de Gaulle. Even in 1967, however, support for entry had been lukewarm. Many within the unions feared that European competition would force employers to lower wages or to lay off workers. The left within the party continued to fear that the capitalist and free-market character of the Common Market would prevent the government from making greater use of methods of state control over the economy and thus from effective planning. The increasing convergence between the positions of the unions and those of the left in the late 1960s and early 1970s meant that opposition to Europe became more widespread. Equally important, the growing passion of those opposed to entry contrasted sharply with the lack of genuine enthusiasm among many of its advocates. Jenkins and his numerous protégés felt deeply, but others did not: Crosland, for example, agreed with Jenkins on a wide range of issues, but regarded Europe as a minor issue; Wilson, too, was much more pragmatic than principled in his approach; and Denis Healey switched back and forth. Most significant was the posture adopted by Callaghan. Though firmly on the centre-right of the party, Callaghan had never been a strong supporter of Europe and in the early 1970s threw in his lot with the opponents and the defenders of 'the language of Chaucer'.[42] There was clearly a strong element of opportunism and careerism involved in the positions taken by Wilson and Callaghan, but the fact that self-interested calculation led them away from Europe testifies strongly to the drift of opinion in the party and the unions.

Despite what Wilson told a special party conference in July 1971, it seems likely that, had Labour remained in office after 1970, it would have entered Europe on much the same terms agreed by Heath.[43] It is also possible that, had the Heath government been more conciliatory on other matters, Labour's opposition might have been more muted. But Labour was not in power and the proposal to join up was now a Tory initiative; and the very same Tory government was busy rushing towards the free market and towards confrontation with the unions. In the context, support for Europe diminished still further in the ranks of Labour and opposition became more vocal and militant. And it did not dissipate even after the crucial votes were cast on 28 October 1971. Indeed, the party leadership decided in March 1972 not to accept membership as a fait accompli when and if they returned to power, but rather to use the occasion to reopen negotiations and then, critically, to submit the new terms to a referendum for ratification. It was this decision that prompted Jenkins to resign as deputy leader and shadow chancellor and with him a younger cohort of the centre-right exited the front benches. 'From now on,' as Bill Rodgers remembers it, 'Labour Europeans were to be outsiders in the party.' The centre-right would now be deeply split and weakened, and deprived of the status and leverage with which to mount an effective resistance to the sustained leftward movement within the party.[44]

The political battle over Europe not only served to weaken the right; it also demonstrated that while divisions within the party between left and right were bitter, the lines between them were not hard and fast; nor were they marked by intellectual consistency. This tactical fluidity and ideological ambiguity were displayed even more dramatically on the question of how to deal with the unions. Indeed, left and right outdid each other in their efforts to support the unions. Again, the context provided by the Heath government was critical: by taking on the unions directly, the Conservatives allowed Labour and the unions to patch up their differences in a sustained campaign of opposition to the government's attempt to create a new legal framework for industrial relations. Thus, in a move rich with irony, Barbara Castle helped to lead the resistance to Tory legislation that differed only slightly from her own proposals in *In Place of Strife.*

The question of how best to work with the unions was of paramount importance to the entire Labour Party and superseded prior commitments and long-standing predispositions. In the past, the left had often found itself at odds with the leadership of the unions and it was usually the right and the parliamentary leadership who profited directly from the unions' unique institutional role in the party and the use of the block vote. This customary relationship had ceased to hold from the late 1960s, as a generation of more left-wing leaders came to power in the bigger unions and as the rank and file became more militant and engaged. The party leadership needed the unions more than ever, however, for its claim to legitimacy was premised on its ability to bring the unions into the policy-making process and thus to make the system work. Labour could not escape its corporatist inheritance, for it had nothing with which to replace it. On the contrary, when the relationship with the unions became strained and threatened to break after 1966, the prospect threatened the entire Labour project and elicited efforts from all sides to repair the rift.

Callaghan's position was symptomatic. Though firmly on the right of the party and ill-disposed towards industrial militancy, Callaghan's long-standing ties to the unions encouraged him to oppose Castle and Wilson in their efforts to reform industrial relations. He grasped intuitively that a breach with the unions would be disastrous: it would rob the party of its most reliable allies and cut it off from its roots and from the resources needed to run the organisation; it would demonstrate to voters that Labour had little to offer if it could not deliver the trade unions; and it would in any event be counter-productive, because the party could not prevail in a genuine contest with the unions. It lacked the will and capacity. After Labour's loss in 1970, it was widely believed that the priority was to re-establish close working relations with the unions in order to avoid a repeat of the battle over *In Place of Strife*. It was even more essential to have union cooperation if Labour was to make a credible claim to be able to control inflation and engineer growth in increasingly troubled times.

Bringing the unions back into the fold was thus a task from which nobody within the party dissented; and it was an effort that transcended left, right and centre. Tony Benn, for example, made an offer of collaboration very early on; Callaghan was a consistent supporter; and Wilson understood that it had to be done. But the unions were not easily wooed. TUC leaders remained angry over the Wilson government's policies and were resolved to oppose any legislation that threatened to define and, it was presumed, to limit union rights and privileges and to make unions legally liable for industrial action undertaken by their members. They were equally opposed to incomes policies, both because they genuinely believed that controlling wages without equivalent controls on prices and profits was unfair, and because they feared the reactions of the rank and file. Industrial militancy in fact escalated throughout the Heath administration and union leaders were not in a position to halt it. The decisive event was of course the miners' strike of 1972, which not only embarrassed the government and prepared the ground for a U-turn on incomes policy, but also underscored the power of direct action.

The miners' strike also served to illustrate the fact that rank-and-file militancy was not merely economic, but had a political dimension as well. Arthur Scargill, who helped to design the tactic of flying pickets used to shut down coal depots, was no mere industrial militant, but firmly on the political left. Likewise, many of the shop stewards and local activists and officials who pushed for greater insurgency at shop-floor level were sympathetic to the left and not a few were close to the Communist Party. Indeed, in December 1973 the CP's industrial organ-iser Bert Ramelson boasted that the party, largely through its leadership of the Liaison Committee for the Defence of Trade Unions and of the so-called 'broad left' grouping within the unions, 'have more influence now on the Labour movement than at any time in the life of our party'.[45] The influence of the broad left extended beyond the unions and encour-aged those who came within its orbit to direct their energies back towards the trade unions. It thus helped to steer young middle-class radicals – most of whom would hold white-collar jobs and join white-collar unions rooted in the public sector – and also feminists to pursue their goals by first enlisting the support of the unions.[46] Undoubtedly, it was the waxing sense of economic grievance, fuelled by inflation and by widening horizons of comparison, together with workers' growing sense that direct action brought better, quicker and more tangible gains than patient cooperation, that was primarily responsible for both the increase in strike militancy and in support for the left within the unions. But whatever the cause, TUC leaders understood that they did not want to get in the way of such movements and the surge of energy that often lay behind them, and were determined not to be put in that position, either by a hostile regime like Heath's or even by a friendly government like Labour. Again and again, therefore, the TUC emphasized its commitment to the system of 'free' collective bargaining and its opposition to interference by the state.

Nevertheless, the unions also recognised that it was far better to have the ear of ministers than to be ignored, and to maintain their right to be consulted on matters of public policy. The TUC, in short, was as fully committed to corporatism as was the Labour Party. A rapprochement with Labour was to this extent inevitable, but it still required hard bargaining to get there. The first steps were taken in the opposition to the Conservatives' trade union legislation: joint strategy was to be worked out by a Liaison Committee, which would bring together TUC leaders and Labour MPs. Ironically, then, 'the anti-trade union measure that was to provide the instrument for destroying the Labour movement has in fact', in the words of Michael Foot, 'supplied the lever for reforging its unity and its chances of recovery'.[47] A reconstituted Liaison Committee, with five members each from the Shadow Cabinet, the TUC and the National Executive, was set up in January 1972 to coordinate policy more broadly and on a continuing basis. On the union side, the key mover behind the committee was Jack Jones of the TGWU. He brought along reluctant TUC allies and would prove to be the most consistent supporter of the effort to craft an agreement between the party and the unions. On the other side, both the NEC and the parliamentary leadership were eager partners and politicians rushed to take credit for bringing the two sides together: Benn claimed to have made the first overture; Callaghan rightly asserted a longer and closer relation to top union officials, and hence a more decisive role. Wilson was also keen to repair the divisions which were seen to have cost Labour the last election and that were regarded as having the potential, if unresolved, to cost it the next.

But union support did not come cheap and TUC leaders insisted that the first item on their joint agenda be the working out of detailed pledges from the party's representatives on the contents of a new industrial relations bill. When these were secured, the Liaison Committee was allowed to discuss broader issues of social and economic policy, but again very much on the unions' terms. The process adopted was to compare Labour's new and much discussed programme with the TUC's 'Economic Review for 1972' in order to discern where the two plans might differ. Happily, it was decided, 'there are no policies . . .' over which there was 'genuine disagreement' and so an agreed programme was possible.[48] In fact, the unions were committed to a series of quite major initiatives: better pensions, efforts to improve the lot of the low-paid, increased investment in housing and the health services, redistributive tax policies, and the creation of a new arbitration and conciliation service. The unions also insisted that government should control prices by imposing a freeze on rents and by subsidies on food and transport.

By February 1973 Wilson and Victor Feather, TUC General Secretary, had put together a joint statement along these very lines, 'Economic Policy and the Cost of Living'. The document became the centrepiece of the so-called 'social contract' between Labour and the unions. It enumerated all of the policies a Labour government would follow, but said very little about what the unions would do in return. From the beginning, the TUC spokesmen on the Liaison Committee avoided even discussing the possibility of controls on wages. Jones explicitly warned his erstwhile partners that 'It would be disastrous if any word went out from this meeting that we had been discussing prices and incomes policy', and Barbara Castle noted sympathetically that 'So bruised and sensitive were the trade unions that any mention even of a voluntary policy was taboo.'[49] The union position was essentially that if the government managed through price and rent controls, subsidies and successful macro-economic policy to reduce inflation, wage pressure would diminish more or less automatically and that in response individual unions, encouraged by the TUC, would behave responsibly. The objective was to create 'the right climate' for bargaining and for possible talks between the government and the unions. Further than that the unions refused to go.

Even an impending general election, in which trade union behaviour and prerogatives would be central topics of debate, did not move the unions to make further commitments. At a meeting in early January 1974, party representatives on the Liaison Committee virtually begged for more and were utterly abject in accepting union positions across the board. The party's draft 'campaign document', it was explained, 'was built on . . . "Economic Policy and the Cost of Living" and every item has been checked against that statement'. Union leaders, therefore, should be pleased with the result. In return, the party needed and so 'would welcome a statement from the TUC which would go beyond a description of what might happen if the collective bargaining climate were changed; and comprise a statement of intention by the TUC that it would respond in a changed collective bargaining climate'. But the unions would have none of it: 'The TUC was not going to give an absolute firm pledge on wages.'[50] When the Labour election manifesto was agreed for the election of February 1974, Callaghan was thus left on his own to craft the formula for incomes policy: 'as it is proved', he explained, 'that the Government is ready to act – against high prices, rents and other impositions falling most heavily on the low-paid and pensioners – so we believe that the trade unions *voluntarily* (which is the only way it can be done for any period in a free society) will co-operate to make the whole policy successful'.

However asymmetrical and out of balance the duties assumed by the party and the unions, the very fact of the social contract allowed Labour to position itself as uniquely capable of ruling with, rather than in confrontation against, the trade unions. In the elections of February and October 1974, the stance was to prove a distinct asset, not enough to generate mass support for Labour but sufficient to oust the Heath government. Over the long term, the social contract would suffer great strains and, in the end, it would break down with disastrous results. But in the early and mid-1970s it was Labour's lifeline and the basis of its continued claim to office. The process that led to the agreement on the social contract was also important in the development of party policy. The terms demanded by the unions were to a large measure consistent with the thrust of left-wing proposals for extending public ownership, for increasing support for social services, and for effecting a 'fundamental and irreversible shift in the balance of power and wealth'. This compatibility led union representatives on the NEC to work closely with the left of the party on the creation of a more radical programme; and it ensured union support for the programme at conference as well. The effect of the de facto alliance, however, was to ratchet up the promises made by the party by combining commitments to both long-term and structural policies advocated by the left and aimed at economic restructuring and redistribution, and short-term promises on prices, wages and on social expenditures insisted upon by the unions. In the past, the left of the party had been willing to ask unions to postpone immediate gains and accept sacrifices for the ultimate goal of socialist transformation. That tradition was now forgotten. By 1973–74, the party had been forced, largely because of its link to the unions, to offer immediate gains *and* a programme of structural transformation. Whether such a combination was ever economically feasible, it was a very great burden to place upon a government that would come to power at the very end of the long post-war boom. Expecting a government without a clear Parliamentary majority or an electoral mandate actually to implement these policies was utterly fanciful.

Still, the renewed connection to the unions was welcomed by the centre and the right of the party, whose leaders would again be predominant in the Cabinet, just as eagerly as it was embraced by the left. In fact, the new practice of regular consultation between the unions and the party at the very highest levels provided the party leadership with an alternative base of political support that was perhaps more reliable than the party organisation itself and more pliable than the NEC. Indeed, some on the left actually tended to regard the Liaison Committee and the social contract with suspicion. Benn, for example, confided to his diary in September 1973 that 'Jack Jones has completely abandoned his serious left-wing position'; he was now 'against the adoption of the socialist programme because he is sticking to the bread and butter issues . . .'.[51] The judgement was unfair to Jones, for he was committed to much more than that, but it is true that the unions were less interested in the grander visions of the left than in securing the practical agreement of a future Labour government that it would not set itself against the unions. And this is clearly how the party leadership saw the matter. To them the precise terms of the social contract were much less important than the message its existence conveyed about who Labour was and how they would govern. The social contract was in this respect a desperate reassertion of the distinctive identity of the Labour party as the party which had at its core an organic relationship to the working class, nurtured over decades and made real by the allegiance of the trade unions to Labour's cause and, in turn, by the unusual institutional clout that the structure and ethos of the party afforded to the unions. It was a fitting product of Labour under duress, a joint creation of the left, the centre and the right and of both the political and industrial sides of the Labour movement. Labour would rightly be judged on its success, for its effectiveness, or lack of effectiveness, would be a highly appropriate measure on which to base an assessment on what Labour had offered to its supporters and to the nation at large. If the judgement proved harsh, as it would, it was not for that reason unfair.

Notes and references

1 See David Butler and Michael Pinto-Duschinsky, *The British General Election of 1970* (London: Macmillan, 1970).

2 Roy Jenkins, *A Life at the Center* (New York: Random House, 1991), 284.

3 H. Wilson, 'Memorandum', 1 June 1969 in PRO: PREM13/2726, cited in Robert Taylor, *The TUC: From the General Strike to New Unionism* (London: Palgrave, 2000), 174–5.

4 The corporatist character of post-war British politics received its first serious treatment in the writings of the American political scientist, Sam Beer. His most authoritative formulation can be found in Beer, *British Politics in the Collectivist Age* (New York: Knopf, 1965). For an updating, see Keith Middlemas, *Politics in Industrial Society* (London: Andre Deutsch, 1979); and Beer, *Britain against Itself: The Political Contradictions of Collectivism* (New York: Norton, 1982).

5 Taylor, *The TUC*, 146.

6 Murray, 'Trade Unions and the State' (1970), cited in Taylor, *The TUC*, 237.

7 The Labour Party's intense commitment to working within the constraints of the existing system has been often noted and repeatedly criticised, most notably in Ralph Miliband, *Parliamentary Socialism: A Study in the Politics of Labour* (New York: Monthly Review, 1964).

8 Poll data taken from George Gallup, *The Gallup International Public Opinion Polls: Great Britain 1937–1975* (New York: Random House, 1976), Vol. II: *1965–1975*.

9 Sewill, quoted in Robert Taylor, 'The Heath Government, Industrial Policy and the "New Capitalism" ', in Stuart Ball and Anthony Seldon, eds, *The Heath Government, 1970–1974: A Reappraisal* (London: Longman, 1996), 141.

10 Davies, 22 March 1972, quoted in Taylor, 'The Heath Government . . . and the "New Capitalism" ', 152.

11 Leo Panitch, *Social Democracy and Industrial Militancy: The Labour Party, the Trade Unions and Incomes Policy, 1945–1975* (Cambridge: Cambridge University Press, 1976).

12 Minutes of the Cabinet Meeting, August 1970, CM10(70).

13 Minutes of the Cabinet Meeting of 3 September 1970, CM12(70).

14 Cabinet Minutes, 27 January 1972, CM (72).

15 Cabinet Minutes, 10 February 1972.

16 Gen 85 (72), 1st Mtg, 8 March 1972, with 6 March 1972 Memo of the Secretary for Employment on 'The Law on Picketing', in PRO: CAB130/567.

17 Cabinet Minutes, 18 February 1972.

18 See Martin Holmes, *The Failure of the Heath Government*, 2nd edn (London: Macmillan, 1997), 14–36; Michael Moran, *The Politics of Industrial Relations* (London: Macmillan, 1977); Colin Crouch, *Class Conflict and the Industrial Relations Crisis* (London: Heinemann, 1977); Robert Taylor, 'The Heath Government and Industrial Relations: Myth and Reality', in Ball and Seldon, *The Heath Government*, 161–90; and, more generally, Phillip Whitehead, *The Writing on the Wall: Britain in the Seventies* (London: Michael Joseph, 1985).

19 Alec Cairncross, 'The Heath Government and the British Economy', in Ball and Seldon, *The Heath Government*, 133–6.

20 For Heath's account of the decision and its disastrous consequences, see Edward Heath, *The Course of My Life: An Autobiography* (London: Hodder & Stoughton, 1998), 511–16.

21 See Wilson to Heath, 23 November 1973; Heath to Wilson, 27 November 1973; Heath to Wilson, 27 January 1974; Wilson to Heath, 5 February 1974; Statement by James Callaghan and Ron Hayward, 'The Miners, Mr Heath and the Communist Party', Labour Party News Release, 23 January 1974; in the Harold Wilson Papers, c. 955.

22 Bernard Donoughue, *The Heat in the Kitchen* (London: Politico's, 2003), 107–15.

23 David Butler and Dennis Kavanagh, *The British General Election of February 1974* (London: Macmillan, 1974), 266, 268. For the numbers, see 275–6.

24 Susan Crosland, *Tony Crosland* (London: Jonathan Cape, 1982), 210. The judgement is endorsed, with rather more animus, by John Golding in his posthumously published, *Hammer of the Left: Defeating Tony Benn, Eric Heffer and Militant in the Battle for the Labour Party* (London: Politico's, 2003).

25 Though their personal and collective contributions are seldom assessed, the names of key staff members keep recurring in accounts of the party's move to the left. See, for example, Michael Hatfield, *The House the Left Built: Inside Labour Policy-Making, 1970–75* (London: Gollancz, 1978).

26 See, for example, 'The Need for Standing Advisory and Sub-Committees', Home Policy Sub-committee of the National Executive Committee, Labour Party Research Department Memoranda, Memorandum 26 (RD26), November 1970 in *Archives of the British Labour Party* (Harvester Microfiche).

27 Holland's book, *The Socialist Challenge* (London: Quartet, 1975) was to play an important role in laying out the theoretical argument for the left's programme. His influence within the party preceded the book, however, by several years. See Patrick Seyd, *The Rise and Fall of the Labour Left*

(New York: St Martin's, 1987), 25–7. For a fuller, but still not complete, roster, see the 'List of those invited to the Industrial Policy Conference', Industrial Policy Sub-committee, Labour Party Research Department Memorandum, RD265, February 1972 Archives. In an interview with the author on 7 October 2002 Holland claimed largely to have written *Labour's Programme 1973* and the drafts which preceded it.

28 *Report of the Labour Party Annual Conference 1972*, 103.

29 Quoted in Hatfield, *The House the Left Built*, 210. Holland, interview 7 October 2002, argues that this was not the same as nationalisation, though it was difficult at the time to discern the distinction.

30 Stuart Holland, 'Planning Strategy, Tactics and Techniques', Industrial Policy Sub-committee, RD442, October 1972 Archives. The phrase 'plain bully' was attributed to Andrew Schonfield, who used it to describe French practice, but it was an innovation to apply it to British strategy and even more innovative to advocate it so baldly.

31 Interview with Tony Benn, 30 September 2003.

32 On the business response, particularly after Labour returned to power, see Jonathan Boswell and James Peters, *Capitalism in Contention: Business leaders and political economy in modern Britain* (Cambridge: Cambridge University Press, 1997), 127.

33 *Guardian*, 3 October 1973.

34 See Ben Pimlott, *Harold Wilson* (New York: HarperCollins, 1992), 575.

35 Balogh to Harold Wilson, 8 March 1973, Harold Wilson Papers, c. 769.

36 Wilson Papers, c. 1295.

37 Kevin Jefferys, *Anthony Crosland: A New Biography* (London: Politco's, 2000), 168.

38 Jenkins, *A Life at the Center*, 309. For a thoughtful assessment of Jenkins's personal strengths and corresponding liabilities and of his key supporters, see Ivor Crewe and Anthony King, *SDP: The Birth, Life and Death of the Social Democratic Party* (Oxford: Oxford University Press, 1995), 52–60; and, more recently, Giles Radice, *Friends and Rivals: Crosland, Jenkins and Healey* (London: Little, Brown, 2002).

39 Benn, 2 October 1972, *Report . . . 1972*, 104.

40 See Jenkins, *A Life at the Center*, 307–11; and, for the party political context, Eric Shaw, *The Labour Party since 1945* (Oxford: Blackwell, 1996), chapter 5.

41 Barbara Castle, *Fighting All the Way* (London: Macmillan, 1993), 449.

42 Callaghan spoke about 'the language of Chaucer, Shakespeare and Milton' at Southampton on 25 May 1971 in a controversial speech that signalled his

willingness to lead the opposition to Europe. See Kenneth Morgan, *Callaghan: A Life* (Oxford: Oxford University Press, 1997), 392–7.

43 Radice, *Friends and Rivals*, 195–6.

44 Bill Rodgers, *Fourth among Equals* (London: Politico's, 2000), 134–5.

45 Ramelson, quoted in Taylor, *The TUC*, 231.

46 Interview with Anna Coote, 17 July 2003.

47 Foot, foreword to Eric Heffer's, *The Class Struggle in Parliament* (London: Gollancz, 1973), cited in Hatfield, *The House the Left Built*, 48.

48 TUC-Labour Party Liaison Committee, 'Policies Compared', Labour Party Research Department Memorandum, RD438, October 1972 Archives.

49 Jones and Castle quoted in Taylor, *The TUC*, 210.

50 TUC-Labour Party Liaison Committee, Minutes of 4 January 1974, TUC Papers.

51 Tony Benn, *Against the Tide: Diaries, 1973–1976* (London: Hutchinson, 1989), entry for 26 September 1973, 62.

CHAPTER 5

The overwhelming burden of office, 1974–79

Labour returned to power in March 1974 as a minority government that had won slightly fewer votes than the Conservatives. Six months later they would be confirmed in office with just 39 per cent of the popular votes and a bare three-seat majority that would not last.[1] It was not the basis upon which to implement controversial new policies like those embodied in *Labour's Programme 1973*. Nor could it provide the kind of support that would have made it possible for the government to ask for patience with intractable economic problems or for sacrifice in the common interest. But that is what Labour would be forced to do; and that is what they simply could not do effectively.

The weakness of Labour's position was rooted in a perceptible shift in voter allegiance. The elections of 1974 showed that voters had begun to lose confidence in both of the major parties and, by implication, in the way the political system seemed to operate. From 1945 to 1970 Labour and the Conservatives had between them routinely garnered the support of nearly nine in ten voters in successive general elections. In both of the elections of 1974, by contrast, a quarter of voters did not support either Labour or the Tories. And the change was to be more or less permanent: from 1974 to 2001 the combined share of the votes of the two largest parties has not once topped 80 per cent and has averaged less than 75 per cent.[2] In 1974, it was the Conservatives who suffered most directly from the voters' decision to withhold support and Labour thereby profited temporarily. But in the long run Labour would be punished even more severely, for it was Labour that tried one more time to make the post-war pattern of governance work in the teeth of a storm of discontent produced by a worldwide economic crisis that nobody really understood. It was Labour, then, that would become the lasting victim of the process of electoral 'de-alignment'.[3]

What lay behind the weakening ties between the parties and the electorate? Long-term social factors might well have served to loosen the connections between parties and their historic constituents and to have reduced the core of party support and expanded the ranks of voters without secure political attachments. But, as most commentators recognised, the pace of social change tends to be gradual – 'glacial' even – while the drop in party allegiance was precipitous. Logically, then, the haemorrhaging of support for both Labour and the Tories would seem to have been a conscious rejection of what the parties were doing or proposing to do. And the simultaneity of the shift suggests that what turned voters off was in all likelihood not the things that distinguished the parties in the minds of the electorate but what they did that looked and felt similar. The two parties were clearly different: the Tories and Labour spoke for the interests of different clusters of social groups and they proclaimed visions that diverged sharply around questions of public versus private provision, the role of the market, rates of taxation and, to a lesser extent, Britain's foreign policy and defence posture. But what both parties shared was a corporatist style of governance operating within a broad consensus on the need for the state to manage the economy with the aim of securing full employment, relatively modest levels of inflation and, as a means to these ends, higher rates of growth. 'Corporatist bargaining' and a modicum of state intervention constituted the formula that united the parties in this long-term consensus. Of course, neither side was entirely comfortable within this consensus. Conservatives chafed at their responsibility to run the economy at full employment, their business supporters especially unhappy at the leverage a buoyant labour market gave to unions, and so there were periodic outbursts of enthusiasm for the free market from within their ranks. 'Selsdon man' was the classic manifestation. Labour, especially the left, likewise would have preferred to jettison the post-war consensus and pursue strategies designed to move more decisively towards socialism. During the 1960s, moreover, the entire party became suffused with a desire to accelerate growth and break the structural constraints that appeared to hold it back. But neither side defected fundamentally from the broad consensus on the ends of policy and the correspondingly consensual process of choosing and implementing particular policies.

By 1974 unhappiness over the outcomes produced by this corporatist style of government led many voters and even some politicians themselves to question its effectiveness and to doubt as well the objectives for which it was designed. The need for a fundamental rethinking was thus present within both parties, even if practical considerations precluded its success. The earliest aspirations of the Heath government, for example, involved a break with state-centred policies and a turn to the market. Clearly, however, the Conservatives were not sufficiently committed to the market to trust its workings at a time of worldwide economic uncertainty and so pulled back from its implications. A more complete embrace of laissez-faire would have to await the change of leadership provoked by general election losses of February and October 1974. Even then, it would take Margaret Thatcher some time before her ideological stance became as clear and coherent as it appears in retrospect to have been. Labour's sharp move to the left while in opposition was equally a recognition of the diminishing returns produced by the now standard practice of consensual politics and corporatist bargaining. It was surely ironic, however, that Labour's reorientation should be accompanied by the so-called 'social contract', which aimed to overcome the divisions of the late 1960s and break out of the impasse of recent policy-making but which in fact reinforced the corporatist bias that had produced these failures.

Voters questioned the pattern of governance less openly and articulately. Increasingly, though, they found fault with both parties and became gradually less 'identified' with their leaders or policies. Over time the share of voters who labelled themselves as 'strong' or 'very strong' supporters dropped both for the Tories and for Labour. In 1964 39 per cent strongly identified with Labour and in 1966 44 per cent did so; by 1974 support had fallen back to less than 37 per cent. Those strongly identified with the Conservatives likewise fell from over 36 per cent in 1964 to just over 30 per cent in 1974. The social bases of support began to alter as well, though not symmetrically. The Conservatives' traditional edge among women was still visible in 1964, when they led Labour by

40 per cent to 37 per cent; but it had been reversed by 1974, when more women identified with Labour by roughly 35 per cent to 31–32 per cent. This was not to prove a permanent shift, but it did replace what had been a long-term predisposition. Class attachments held up better, at least for Labour, but the trend was disturbingly similar: in 1964 roughly 59 per cent of unskilled workers – class D in the classification system – strongly identified with Labour, in 1974 about 53 per cent did so. Among the so-called C2s, or skilled workers, approximately 53 per cent were firmly in Labour's camp in 1964 and 48–49 per cent remained there in 1974. Those who were disaffected did not, however, switch their support to the Conservatives. Apparently, the Conservatives' confrontational policies towards workers and the unions served to keep most within the Labour camp, but they stayed without real enthusiasm. By contrast, Conservative support among the professional and managerial classes fell dramatically from over 63 per cent (strong and very strong identifiers combined) to under 40 per cent in October 1974, a sign that a substantial section among their core constituency had begun to lose faith.[4]

The polls also indicated a move away from historic preferences, antipathies and polarities. In 1964, for example, 48 per cent of voters perceived 'a great deal' of difference between the parties; by February 1974, just over a third felt that way. If partisan differences were less, presumably parties mattered less than other institutions; but voters' attitudes towards those institutions were not static. In 1964, less than a quarter of those polled felt that the unions, but not business, was too powerful; while a similar proportion, 27 per cent, believed it was business that had too much clout. By 1974, just 12.5 per cent of respondents felt business was too powerful but nearly a third, or 31.9 per cent, believed the unions to be. Of course, at both points over 40 per cent said that both had too much power. On balance, though, it was the alleged excessive power of the unions that was increasingly the focus of attention and worry. As of September 1966, 64 per cent of those polled by Gallup thought that overall the trade unions were 'a good thing' for the country; by September 1974 only 54 per cent thought so.[5]

If Labour's trade union connection was a liability, so was its programme. In early 1974 a MORI poll showed that while substantial majorities favoured Labour's promises to raise pensions and that commitments to limit property speculation and rent increases were also popular, a mere 6 per cent of voters were supportive of the party's key innovation in economic policy-making: the National Enterprise Board. Another, roughly simultaneous, poll, showed that even Labour supporters opposed further nationalisation.[6] But the Conservatives fared no better. Indeed, disapproval of the government's record was a consistent feature of Heath's unfortunate period of office, and by 1974 the Conservatives were seen by a majority of the electorate to 'benefit a single class' within society – 65 per cent, as compared to the 45 per cent who thought of Labour that way. The policies of the Heath government were understood as a form of class warfare and were thus off-putting to voters. As of 1974, then, the programme and stance of Labour was beginning to push voters away, while the practical consequences of Tory rule were simultaneously costing the Conservatives critical electoral support. Indeed, during the election of February 1974 it was revealed that nearly four in ten voters 'thought that neither party was the most competent to handle the two most urgent problems [prices and strikes]'.[7] In short, the established political order was beginning to come undone, even if there was no clear sense of what might be invented to replace it. The Labour governments of 1974–79, led first by Wilson and from 1976 by James Callaghan, would preside over events that would take the process much further and see the post-war political order utterly discredited. The effect would be to give to the Conservatives under Thatcher a unique opportunity to put their stamp upon a new political order.

This historic failure was perhaps not totally predetermined, but the range of choices open to Labour were very few and very restricted. The economic crisis the government faced was deep and structural, poorly understood by economists and no better grasped by policy-makers; and it was not of the government's making. The scope of the possible was in the circumstances very limited. Nor was it possible for Labour to respond fully to the caution signs sent by voters. Party leaders were not fools and could read the disturbing results of the two elections of 1974 as well as the troubling analyses of pollsters and academic commentators; and they understood intuitively that their support was thin and tentative. Wilson, after all, was a seasoned and wily politician, and his successor Callaghan was just as experienced and in certain spheres more skilful. But Labour's leaders had to listen to other voices with more direct access: to the unions with whom they had agreed the social contract, for example, and to the party itself, which had just passed a very radical programme. The government would also have to pay attention to the largely impersonal but still powerful voices of the world economy and, even more, to the very clear messages delivered by the financial community and ultimately the International Monetary Fund. It was not an easy time to be in government.

Labour's first task on assuming office was to prove that it could engineer industrial peace. Achieving that would be essential to getting re-elected with a larger majority. The Industrial Relations Act was repealed and replaced by the Trade Union and Labour Relations Act of 1974. When Stage III of the Tories statutory incomes policy expired in July 1974, the policy lapsed formally and the Pay Board was abolished. Meanwhile, the government had settled with the miners on very favourable terms and soon oversaw, or acquiesced in, generous agreements with the 'railwaymen, engineering workers, Ford manual workers, merchant seamen and local government white-collar staff . . .'.[8] By October 1974 the average annual rate of wage increases was 22 per cent, while the price index was up by 17 per cent.[9]

The government also sought to make good on its specific pre-election pledges stemming from the social contract. Barbara Castle noted approvingly that Wilson 'had changed: as the "custodian of the Manifesto" he just couldn't twist and turn any more' and instead he was 'playing it straight down the line of party policy'. 'That it was a more left-wing policy than we had ever had before . . .' apparently did not deter him, for its honest pursuit was required for party unity.[10] Wilson and Healey thus used the two budgets introduced before the autumn election to raise pensions, unemployment and sickness benefits, to add £550 million to subsidies on food and another £70 million for housing subsidies; and to double the value of the regional employment premium by providing an additional £118 million.[11] Though taxes were increased modestly and made slightly more progressive, the budgets were on balance clearly expansionary and would inevitably fuel inflation. Nevertheless, in the short term the government was visibly seen to have met the most pressing commitments made during the election and to have fulfilled its side of the social contract.[12] These efforts, whatever their long-term consequences, helped the government win a slightly increased majority in the election of October 1974.

While the choices made prior to October 1974 were made primarily to satisfy the terms of the social contract, it is clear that the government also genuinely hoped to prevent or lower unemployment and, if possible, to grow its way out of the economic crisis it faced. These policies were not dictated by the social contract but were certainly consistent with it and with the party's essential political identity and orientation. Thus at a time when other governments were using deflationary policies to combat soaring inflation, Labour stuck to its principles and gave priority to preventing unemployment. It can be argued that the effect was counter-productive, for as UK inflation rates kept rising, unemployment inevitably followed and the government was faced with both higher prices and job losses. But the government's stance was chosen consciously and it fitted within the essential framework of previous economic policy as well with the social preferences and the philosophy of the party and its supporters. In fact, the government would continue to work desperately to maintain jobs throughout its time in office, and to that end undertook costly interventions to keep failing firms afloat. While the effort largely failed, it was neither irrational nor indefensible.

However, the context within which Labour chose to expand social protections and defend jobs was highly inauspicious. The inflationary effects of the jump in oil prices would continue to work their way through the world economy for several years and monetary instability was an inevitable consequence. Expansionary policies that ran counter to the conventional wisdom of the financial community were particularly unwelcome and elicited harsh disapproval. Equally important was the Labour Party's precarious hold on office. After October 1974 the government had a wafer-thin majority that would soon be eroded through by-election losses. From 1977, the party was forced to accept a pact with the Liberals and when that broke down, it ruled as a minority virtually powerless to undertake legislative initiatives. Towards the end, it was kept in office only by the fear that a vote against the government would bring Margaret Thatcher to power. But by then the party was united on nothing more than a common detestation of the Tories, and in consequence it was extremely vulnerable to disaffection within its ranks. The difficult decisions forced upon the government, largely by external circumstances, guaranteed that its fragile unity would be repeatedly tested and found wanting. Three crises merit particular attention: the first was over the

Common Market; the second arose when Tony Benn was demoted and the party's radical industrial policy effectively abandoned; and the third came when the government was forced to apply for a loan from the IMF which would be granted only on very severe terms. As these crises unfolded and as political expediency enforced successive departures from Labour's cherished beliefs and aspirations, the government and the party suffered enormously. The effect was a progressive weakening of the party as an institution, a sapping of its sense of confidence and claim to rule, a fatalism about its future and a growing belief that it might not matter so much if it failed. When the party experienced a fourth and final major test in the 'winter of discontent', it failed utterly.

The debate over British membership in the Common Market was to prove critical in setting the direction of the 1974–79 government. Labour had moved back and forth over Europe in a somewhat knee-jerk partisan fashion. When the Tories first broached the idea of membership in the early 1960s, Labour's leader Gaitskell had baulked at accepting terms negotiated by his adversaries and so led Labour against. Wilson, who on principle was neither strongly pro- nor anti-Europe, nevertheless was moved by the arguments for membership to initiate a second application in 1967, although it was again blocked by the French. When the Heath government carried through a successful application, the party reverted to opposition in large part because they were loath to support Heath on anything. The defection of a significant number of pro-European Labour MPs, led by Roy Jenkins, produced great bitterness on the left, not because of the clash of principle so much as because Labour support had saved the Heath government and its cherished project. Labour in opposition therefore ratcheted up its criticism of Europe and promised if returned to office to renegotiate and submit the results to a vote of the British people.

The idea of a referendum – or a general election fought on that issue alone – had been proposed by Tony Benn and at first infuriated supporters of the Common Market. The left, by contrast, was complacent in its assumption that a vote would produce an anti-European verdict and it was misled by opinion polls to that effect. It seems that the general unpopularity of the Heath government carried over into a temporary but superficial popular opposition to Europe. In February 1974 fully 58 per cent believed that it was a mistake to join the Common Market, and only

28 per cent thought it the right thing to have done. Opposition continued through 1974 and into 1975: a year on, in February 1975 50 per cent still thought membership 'wrong' and only 31 per cent were in favour.[13] But popular opposition was neither deep nor well reasoned and it was largely dissipated by the process of negotiation skilfully carried out by Wilson and Callaghan. As Foreign Minister Callaghan argued forcefully for British interests and his conduct of the negotiations convinced sceptics in his own party and in the country at large that he had won important concessions. British objections to the Common Agricultural Policy of course got nowhere, but deals were struck over dairy products from New Zealand, over steel quotas, over West Indian sugar imports and the entry of other products from Commonwealth countries. Agreement over the British budgetary contribution was more difficult to achieve, but at the Dublin summit of March 1975 a deal was struck giving Britain a substantial rebate of its excess payment. The British team also won support for a regional development fund, which could henceforth be used to further regional policy in Britain. It was an important victory, for a central plank in the left-wing critique of the Common Market was that, as a quintessentially capitalist institution, it would put a stop to Labour's efforts to interfere with the market and direct investment and employment to the regions.

Wilson and Callaghan combined to sell the deal first to Cabinet, then to Parliament and finally to the voters. The job was easier than expected, for the prolonged engagement with Britain's European negotiating partners led to a growing sense that continued membership was a given and withdrawal unlikely. Ongoing discussion implied that adjustments were possible and likely, both then and in the future, and led to a recognition that Europe was less a hostile force committed to the free market than a collection of diverse nations some of which were actually run by socialists or social democrats. Callaghan's initially aggressive negotiating posture, followed up by detailed discussions that were more amicable, further smoothed the path towards success. Particularly helpful was the relationship Callaghan struck up with Helmut Schmidt, the German Chancellor, who addressed the Labour Party conference in late November 1974 to urge socialist solidarity across Europe.[14] The erosion of the anti-European position was recognised by anti-marketeers like Michael Foot, who proposed to Wilson that Cabinet members and MPs be free to speak their minds on either side without restriction or fear of recrimination. On 23 January Wilson announced his support for an 'agreement to differ' on the question of the Common Market.[15] The move was tactically very wise, because it removed at least some of the sting from the ensuing debate and promised to make reconciliation afterwards more likely. After a thorough debate Cabinet voted on 18 March by 16–7 to support the new terms and recommend them to Parliament, which also agreed in April by a vote of 396–170 – overall a very solid endorsement, but with significant defections on both sides. In fact, more Labour MPs voted against (145) than for (137) and the government had been forced to rely upon the votes of the opposition, but the majority was nonetheless commanding.

The referendum was set for 5 June 1975 and the result – a 2–1 margin in favour – was surprisingly unambiguous. The campaign was a novel phenomenon, with leaders from both parties split both ways.[16] Left-wing opponents like Benn found themselves in de facto alliance with Enoch Powell and, on occasion, sharing a platform. On the centre-right, the effect was not so much the pairing of opposites as an experience in finding genuine common ground. Roy Jenkins, for example, became head of an all-party organisation, Britain in Europe, and worked happily alongside Tories like Heath, Maudling, Whitelaw and Douglas Hurd and also Liberals such as Jo Grimond, Jeremy Thorpe and the up-and-coming David Steel, as well as like-minded members of the Labour Party, e.g. William Rodgers and Shirley Williams. Victor Feather, who had recently retired as head of the TUC, was also a member and his presence served to counteract the strong opposition in certain sections of the trade union movement. For his part, Jenkins revelled in the centrism of it all and in retrospect regarded the referendum as 'the event I most enjoyed during 1974–76'.[17] Wilson and Callaghan played modest parts in the campaign, and so did the new leader of the Conservatives, Margaret Thatcher, who delegated the task of mustering support to others. The effect, however, was momentarily to loosen up party loyalties, to generate a genuine and substantive debate, and to produce a decisive result. To people of centrist leaning like Jenkins, the referendum campaign was a lesson in the futility of partisanship and the virtues of consensus and it would serve as a precedent for the launching of the Social Democrats some years later. For Wilson it was another successful fudge that kept the party together under his leadership and got him past yet another troublesome hurdle.[18]

The campaign also again exposed sharp splits within the parties, however, and especially the growing division within Labour. Wilson had hoped that the agreement to differ would smooth over intra-party differences, but the energy with which both left and right fought for their positions precluded that happy outcome. The very day after the Cabinet took its decision, over 80 MPs opposed to membership met and proclaimed their intention to work for a 'No' vote; and a memo signed by Ian Mikardo – but drafted by Barbara Castle working closely with Michael Foot, Tony Benn, Judith Hart and Joan Lestor – urged the NEC to utilise its weight and the party machinery to the same end. It was proposed as well to call a special party conference that was expected to provide a forum for opposition. Ron Wayward, Labour Party General Secretary, indicated his willingness to put the machinery of the party behind the 'No' campaign if the NEC voted that way. Wilson was outraged and regarded the prospect of the party campaigning explicitly against the government as 'intolerable'. A deal was struck at the NEC meeting of 26 March 1975 and the party organisation stayed neutral, but the campaign itself was intense and bitter.[19] Over the course of the debate, Tony Benn would emerge as the clear leader of the opposition and his stature would rise accordingly; as the argument proceeded, moreover, it was cast in increasingly broad terms. Jenkins boasted that the pro-Europeans chose not 'to play down the importance of the issues or to suggest that all that was at stake was a narrow trade policy decision. It was political Europe in which we were interested.'[20] The left saw the issue in equally grand terms. As Benn explained to his constituents:

> The powers of the electors of Britain, through their direct representatives in Parliament, to make laws, levy taxes, change laws which the courts must uphold, and control the conduct of public affairs, has been substantially ceded to the European Community whose Council of Ministers and Commission are neither collectively elected, nor collectively dismissed by the British people, nor even by the people of all the Community countries put together.[21]

The fight against membership in the Common Market was in this formulation nothing less than an all-out struggle to preserve democracy in Britain and the nation's independence.

But by fighting so hard, casting the argument so grandly, and then losing so decisively, the left, Benn in particular, suffered serious damage when the result went the other way. Defeated over Europe, the left was hard-pressed to make the case within the party that their other policies would, if pursued rigorously and effectively, win voters. They had had their chance to speak directly to the electorate and it appeared that they had lost the debate.[22] The effect was to reinforce the view, on the centre and right of the party, that however much support the left might have in the constituencies, on the NEC and at conference, the appeal of their policies was distinctly limited. They must be appeased, but they need not be listened to. The left, of course, drew a rather different conclusion. They regarded the behaviour of Wilson and Callaghan to be another instance of dishonesty and betrayal – and it certainly did contradict the expressed will of more than one party conference – and became even more resolved to develop mechanisms to keep the leaders honest and to ensure that their stance in office was consistent with the position of the party.

The referendum thus served to widen the rift between the left and centre-right of the party. It also served as a critical moment in the defeat of the industrial policy of the left, at least for the life of the Labour government of 1974–79. When Labour took office in March 1974, Tony Benn was made responsible for Industry, where he was assisted by Eric Heffer and Michael Meacher. The appointment seemed a guarantee that the government would move forward decisively on the radical industrial policy worked out in opposition. That policy centred on increased government intervention in industry and, to make that happen, a large extension of public ownership. As a practical matter, the policy required the creation of a powerful and well-financed National Enterprise Board and the implementation of a process for concluding 'planning agreements' with private corporations. The likelihood of a short Parliament and a quick election and the pressing need to address issues like the repeal of the Conservatives' Industrial Relations Act meant that legislation on industry was put off through the spring and summer of 1974. Nevertheless, the government felt compelled in July 1974 to issue a White Paper, *The Regeneration of British Industry*, outlining its future plans for industrial policy.[23] The paper itself was a compromise, largely because it was intended to serve two divergent purposes: it was meant in part to reassure the party that the government took its commitments seriously; and partly it was drafted with an eye to the coming election in the autumn of 1974 and, as Wilson explained, to 'limiting the possibility of election scares on this issue'. The draft which had been written within the department was undoubtedly crafted with more concern for the policy itself than for its presentation and it was rejected by Wilson as 'sloppy and half-baked, polemic, indeed menacing, in tone'. The Prime Minister proceeded to put himself in charge of a committee to rewrite it. The result was a document that announced the government's faith in the 'mixed economy' while proposing a National Enterprise Board that would be indeed powerful but not 'marauding' and a planning agreements system that would be fundamentally voluntary rather than compulsory. The White Paper was clearly intended to downplay some of the more fearsome aspects of the new industrial policy and to reassure business, even if it retained the core of the left's proposals. These would in turn be incorporated again in the manifesto on which Labour fought the October 1974 election.[24]

After the election there seemed no excuse for further delay and legislation went forward in the new year. The Industry Bill introduced in February 1975 was at least as radical as the White Paper, giving the government the authority to force businesses to share information with trade unions and providing massive funds for the state to use in its efforts at industrial reorganisation: specifically, the department would have £1,000 million to provide aid and support for industry. The NEB would initially be given wide latitude and, crucially, £700 million, with the possibility of calling on an additional £300 million, to facilitate its interventions. A mechanism for working out planning agreements was also created. Before any of this could become effective, however, Wilson took two decisions about who would run the government's industrial policy that would put severe constraints on its implementation. The first was the choice of Donald Ryder as chairman of the NEB. A highly successful businessman, Ryder was no ideologue and shared little of the left's enthusiasm for bringing about a decisive shift of 'wealth and power' via the government's policy for industry.

Rather more significant was Benn's removal as Secretary of State for Industry. Benn was a charismatic figure whose presence on the left added a lustre to its cause. He was charming and articulate and had accumulated useful experience in office. The press was unusually fascinated by his persona and his actions, and he garnered attention that was often resented by his fellow Cabinet members and rivals within the party, even on the left. Wilson had long regarded him as a protégé, but was no longer charmed by 1974–75; he was convinced that Benn was out for his job and massively irritated at what he saw as Benn's disregard for the principle of 'collective responsibility'. Reprimanded in late 1974 for having publicly opposed government policy on South Africa, Benn was for his part convinced that Wilson 'hates my guts'. Whatever Wilson's personal view, he waited until after the referendum of June 1975 to act on it. Benn had played a very prominent role in the battle over Europe and it was widely accepted that Wilson's victory in that poll gave him the authority to reshuffle his Cabinet and shape it more to his liking. Anticipating Wilson's action, Benn had apparently begun to encourage his supporters to organise a campaign on his behalf even before the outcome of the referendum – held on 5 June – was known. Letters poured in from union branches, trades councils and constituency parties claiming in nearly identical language that Benn's only crime was loyalty to the manifesto and a willingness to stand up to 'big business'.[25]

Wilson cleverly took aim not only at Benn but at two representatives of the left – Benn and Judith Hart, Secretary for Overseas Development – and he offered Benn another Cabinet post. The plan was for Benn to swap offices with Eric Varley, who ran the Department of Energy, while Hart was offered Transport, but without a seat in the Cabinet. The response was interesting and of real consequence. Benn tried to put off responding to Wilson while rallying his friends and colleagues on the left, like Michael Foot, Barbara Castle and Peter Shore, who were duly enraged. But when Foot, Castle and Benn visited Wilson, they fixed upon the fate of Hart. Benn, for his part, eventually accepted his fate on the grounds that it was better to stay in government and fight for the left's programme than to resign. Hart, for her own reasons, actually did resign. The result was a coup for Wilson, a 'brilliantly cunning' move Barbara Castle told him admiringly, but a serious defeat for Benn, for the left and for the industrial policy they supported.[26] Benn confided to his diary that it was not unlike being 'assassinated'.[27] It would seem that Benn suffered considerably, both for his brilliance and for his popularity outside the Cabinet, and that he had no really good option available. The job he got was important enough that he would look bad in refusing it, though in taking it he comfirmed the view voiced by Bernard Donoughue 'that there was no humiliation which Benn would not swallow in order to stay in the Cabinet'.[28] His friends were angry on his behalf, but at least some were sufficiently resentful of his prior success and good fortune that they could not quite bring themselves to come resolutely to his defence. Castle's own musings on why she and others failed to rally to Benn's cause is revealing: 'I suspect we were more than prepared for Wedgie's move. We have all suffered from his habit of writing Labour policy by ministerial edict. The Department of Industry enabled him to be all things to the Labour movement with none of the restraints the rest of us face. "The prima donnas can look after themselves . . ." '[29] The characterisation of Benn's behaviour may have been unfair and ungenerous, but the attitude she betrayed was undoubtedly not hers alone. Benn himself concluded from the affair that he could no longer trust Michael Foot and henceforth, as he put it, 'must not rely on Michael for anything more than cover'.[30]

With Benn gone from Industry, the government's industrial strategy was deprived of its driving force and largely recast.[31] (Heffer and Meacher left the department as well.) In the context, the enormous pressure to use the powers and the cash available to the ministry and the NEB to conduct rescue missions and prop up lame ducks became irresistible, since every intervention of this defensive sort could be justified on the grounds of saving jobs. In consequence, the record of industrial intervention under the Labour government would be noted not for its aggressive moves to regenerate industry and to invest in new technologies but for its defensive struggle to keep failing firms alive and to prevent job losses. Despite all the rhetoric, only one planning agreement would be signed, and that with Chrysler, one of the companies bailed out by the state. Otherwise, the planning agreements strategy was whittled down into more protracted and ultimately ineffective discussions within 'sector working parties'. These relatively 'innocuous' interventions would pale into insignificance alongside the 'expensive bail-outs, of sometimes questionable permanent value' of larger firms.[32] Indeed, the need for the government to get involved in the motor industry arose even before the Industry Bill had been introduced. In December 1974, it emerged that British Leyland faced imminent bankruptcy. While a committee was established to investigate the pros and cons, the government committed itself with a financial guarantee of £50 million on 18 December 1974. The government chose in effect to take the company into public ownership at an ultimate cost of hundreds of millions of pounds. Even as the funds started flowing towards Leyland, Chrysler informed the government of its decision to cut production and jobs. Again, the response was a rescue plan worth £162 million in return for a promise from Chrysler not to leave Britain and to sign a planning agreement. Despite the agreement, the firm would later be sold to Peugeot-Citroën without the government being informed. Further monies would be spent on Rolls-Royce, on shipbuilding and aerospace, but few of the ventures were profitable and they were all costly. They did little to generate economic growth, and nothing at all to shift the balance of wealth and power.

Treated in isolation each of these decisions might have been justifiable, if not on grounds of profitability, then on the basis of protecting jobs. With the worldwide economic crisis ongoing and unemployment increasing, intervention aimed at growth and transformation was inevitably overwhelmed by the more pressing need for state subsidies designed to prevent the worst from happening.[33] The effect, however, was to reinforce the defensive cast of Labour policy, to underscore the fact that Labour's entire orientation was to defend what was rather than to move towards something new. The party recoiled from policies that might jeopardise the living standards and the social rights won through earlier trade union efforts and Labour policies; and it sought to avoid or mitigate changes in the economy that might cost the jobs of existing workers even if they might create investment in new industries producing for new markets and providing jobs for a new generation. Likewise, it was central to Labour's thinking that union membership and the institutional perquisites of the unions must be protected, whatever the cost and consequence. This was what Labour was all about; it was the *raison d'être* of the social contract and it inspired party policy across the spectrum. That the defensive should prevail over the transformative was thus merely to confirm the party's political identity, its rootedness and pragmatism. Both the origins of the left's radical industrial policy, therefore, and its rejection or abandonment were equally products of the nature of the Labour Party as an institution.

What was most difficult to reconcile with the party's identity, and what did most to reveal and to further its fragmentation, were the Labour government's repeated decisions to curtail social expenditure in 1975–76. These formed the background to the third critical moment in the government's tenure. Labour's pitch to the electorate in February 1974 was premised on the social contract with the unions. It was a deal in which the party agreed to refrain from statutory incomes policy while in office, to restore and augment union rights and, most important, to use the powers of the state to increase the social wage in the hope that the unions would respond by moderating wage claims and, where possible, discouraging the resort to strikes. The government was thus pledged to increase public spending as the price for industrial peace. Healey's budgets of March and July 1974 began to fulfil the pledge and, as one insider confessed, 'the first months of the new government were characterised by our spending money which in the event we did not have'.[34] Healey's third budget, in November 1974, though no longer aimed at winning an imminent election, was nevertheless still quite generous. He was distraught at the mounting evidence of unemployment and argued passionately that 'deliberately to adopt a strategy which requires mass unemployment would be no less an economic than a moral crime'.[35] The budget was thus focused on combating spreading unemployment and so sought to pump additional funds into industry. The stimulus was further increased in January 1975 when the government brought out a Public Expenditure White Paper promising greater expenditure and increased subsidies theoretically aimed at job creation.[36]

These decisions to increase spending came at a highly inopportune moment: the oil crisis was working its effects across the economy and driving up prices; and the desire to avert industrial conflict combined with the phasing out of incomes policy to produce generous wage settlements. The effect was rapidly rising prices: inflation was running at 9 per cent in 1973; in 1974 it rose to 16 per cent and in 1975 to just above 24 per cent. By March 1975 the prospect of an inflation rate of 25 per cent shocked the Cabinet into a rethink and Healey, prompted by his Treasury advisers, came up with a plan for £1 billion in expenditure cuts. The ensuing battle in Cabinet was ferocious. Barbara Castle complained that it 'was 1966 all over again. The moral appeared to be: "A Labour Government can never increase the social wage".' Roy Jenkins, by contrast, not only favoured the cuts but also was eager to confront the unions with the need for wage controls. 'This was not 1966', he argued, but worse: 'the situation is incomparably more serious'. And Benn was enraged: 'These cuts mean we are abandoning the Social Contract.' The Chief Whip, Bob Mellish, predicted a serious rebellion: 'How will the Commons take it?' he asked. 'This means the virtual destruction of the Manifesto and the impossibility of continuing the Social Contract. You are going to see the most major revolt in your history', he told his colleagues.[37]

In the event, Healey got his cuts and the reaction among MPs and even within the unions was more muted than anticipated. The party was pre-occupied with the referendum campaign and, perhaps more important, there was a feeling that the cuts were probably inevitable. The unions, as Barbara Castle noted at the time, 'were not looking for a showdown with us . . .' and so acquiesced.[38] Over the long term, however, the party would be split deeply over the turn to expenditure cuts and, even more, by what the turn entailed. In recognising the need to rein in public spending, the party leadership were tacitly accepting a diagnosis of the nature of the economic crisis that entailed giving up their most cherished beliefs in Keynesian policies and accepting the logic of their long-time foes and rivals in the Treasury. Indeed, the Treasury was itself in the process of a conversion that would take it away from a lukewarm attachment to Keynesian demand management to a fixation on the size of the public debt – symbolised by the Public Sector Borrowing Requirement (PSBR) – and, finally, to monetarism. That the Treasury's trajectory traced a path similar to that of the financial community was proof enough to some that the entire concern with expenditure was a capitalist conspiracy. But the origins and motivations behind the concern did not matter in the end. What mattered was the course of the economy, which seemed truly out of control and in need of correction. The Labour government signalled its willingness to begin the retreat from public spending in April 1975 and at that moment set a course that guaranteed internal division and, ultimately, ineffectiveness. As Edmund Dell, a former Labour minister has argued, 'Healey's budget had, for the first time since the war, given the battle against inflation priority over full employment. It was a turning point in Britain's post-war economic history.'[39] Its political significance was signalled by the Chancellor's warning that the TUC's guidelines, laid out in *Collective Bargaining and the Social Contract*, were ineffective, with the clear implication that the government would also now have to back off its promise not to resort to incomes policy. If Labour now chose to put the defeat of inflation at the top of the agenda, it would have to secure agreement from the unions to hold down wages. The vague hints from the TUC that lower prices would create a more favourable climate for the moderation of wage claims would no longer suffice and the government and unions were forced in the direction of a new and less voluntary wages policy.

Initially, the revival of incomes policy could be understood, and would be sold, as a continuation of the social contract rather than its repudiation. And it was not unreasonable to argue that the Labour Party had delivered on its promises in 1974 and early 1975 – e.g. replacement of the Conservatives' Industrial Relations Act, the increase in food and housing subsidies, efforts to hold prices and rents in check, reflationary budgets and the favourable disposition of wage claims – and that the unions should respond with more rigorous efforts to refrain from inflationary wage settlements. The government had also begun to deliver on a range of other policies dear to at least some sections of the party, especially issues affecting women. During 1975–76, for example, legislation would be passed dealing with sex discrimination, violence against women, women's right to sit on juries and equal treatment over pensions.[40] Even more important than what the government had done, or was in process of doing, on social issues was the fear of the alternative. The prospect of a Thatcher government was anathema to the unions and the labour movement and again and again over the next several years union leaders would be convinced to accept hitherto unacceptable policies on the grounds that it was necessary to keep the Labour Party in office. This was certainly what inspired Jack Jones, the leader of the TGWU and the person most responsible for making and maintaining the social contract. He was impressed that upon taking office the Labour government had moved steadily to implement its campaign promises and told his colleagues on the TUC General Council in June 1974 that Labour had by then 'already gone a long way in carrying out their obligations . . .'. For that reason 'The aim [of the TUC] must be to keep the Labour government in office . . .' Joe Gormley, the miners' leader, was even more forceful, insisting that 'The relationship between the TUC and the Labour Party was so important that members [of the TUC] should do nothing to jeopardise the return of a Labour Government.'[41]

Aware of the party's precarious hold on power and of the country's dire economic circumstances, Jones and his allies on the TUC gradually moved towards acceptance of the idea that wages had to be kept down. Thus, although dismayed at the budget cuts of April 1975, he nevertheless argued that 'if the TUC wrote off the social contract on account of the budget they would in effect be writing off the Labour government', and that would be a serious mistake. Jones feared not only the prospect of a Conservative government led by Thatcher but also the possibility of a split within the party and a resulting coalition government. Such an outcome would do 'very severe damage to the Labour party and lead to the possibility that Labour would not be in power for generations'. Len Murray, TUC General Secretary, agreed: he referred to the TUC's 'very intimate relationship with the Government' and argued that in their deliberations the unions should be 'proceeding on the assumption that the General Council wanted to keep the Labour Government in office . . .'. David Basnett of the GMWU was equally committed to preserving existing arrangements between the government, the party and the unions: 'The social contract', he explained, 'meant the TUC having a voice in the management of the economy and in decisions about social priorities, and to abandon it would be to lose something very valuable to the movement.'[42] The memory of 1931, with its overtones of loyalty and betrayal and conspiracy, made it imperative to preserve unity within the party and between the party and the trade unions. So rather than let the recent budget become the pretext for abandoning the social contract, Jones and Murray and their allies used their considerable influence to work with the government on developing a new and acceptable incomes policy. The government was pushed in the same direction by the economy and by explicit warnings from the Treasury and the financial community. When Wilson turned his attention back from the referendum and the subsequent reshuffle he found an economy deteriorating rapidly, with inflation hitting 25 per cent in May 1975. Denis Healey, the Chancellor, told the Cabinet on 20 June that the economy was 'heading for the precipice' and that a massive crisis bringing high unemployment loomed just over the horizon. Treasury officials came forward with a statutory incomes policy that would have clearly broken with the social contract, while the Number 10 Policy Unit, headed by Bernard Donoughue, elaborated 'a voluntary policy backed by sanctions' – not much of a difference really.

On 30 June the Governor of the Bank of England, Gordon Richardson, intervened. He went first to see Healey and then the two of them visited Wilson, who was told that the pound was collapsing and that this proved the need for a statutory policy.[43] Richardson reportedly told Donoughue that it was time 'to end the nonsense of getting the consent and coopera- tion of others, the trade unions and the Labour Party. We must act now.'[44] Wilson came close to acquiescing, but his advisers – Donoughue and Joe Haines, it seems – held out and in the end the Prime Minister opted for the voluntary policy. The government began actively consulting with Jones and Murray, who drove a hard bargain, and Jones and Healey then worked to bring along Hugh Scanlon of the Engineers. The TUC finally agreed on a flat rate wage increase of £6 that would in theory be 'voluntary' but that would in fact to be backed up by sanctions held in reserve. The plan was supposed to run for only a year, followed by a return to 'free collective bargaining', though it would be renegotiated and extended into 1978.

The £6 limit, though often breached in practice, did have a slight moderating effect on wages and inflation, which declined to 16.5 per cent in 1976. The improvement was not enough, however, and the financial crisis continued to worsen. The government had difficulty grappling with the critical state of the British economy because there was very little agreement, or in some cases understanding, of the nature and extent of the problem. The hostility and suspicion towards business within the Labour Party meant that, even on the right of the party, there was little sympathy for the plight of corporations facing declining profits. Indeed, the programme of the left had been premised on the argument, advanced most forcefully by Stuart Holland, that capitalism had entered a new, multinational stage in which governments needed additional powers to confront and counteract the overweening dominance of the corporations that had outgrown national controls.[45] It was difficult to reconcile that diagnosis with the complaints of the Confederation of British Industry about high taxes, price controls, burdensome regulations and unreason- ably high wages. Labour thus continued to believe contradictorily that business was inefficient, undercapitalised and lacking in managerial drive for markets and profits and, at the same time, overly big and power- ful and prosperous. Holders of financial wealth were regarded with even greater antipathy, especially foreign bankers and investors. Most important, the Labour government and most of its supporters were highly suspicious of the two institutions that regularly served as the spokesmen for financial interests and fiscal orthodoxy: the Bank of England and the Treasury. When the Bank and the Treasury brought warnings about the value of the pound and the confidence of foreign investors, the first reaction was to dismiss them as coming from the camp of the enemy.

Divergent interests and views not only precluded agreement on what was wrong with the British economy but, inevitably, also hindered the creation of a consensus about how to fix it. And as usual, there was evidence to support a variety of views. British business was, as the left insisted, inefficient, amateurish and resistant to innovation; and investment was too low to generate the growth required to sustain full employment. On the other hand, taxes and spending were high by international standards and they were increasing, and the government had inherited a tradition that predisposed it to tell business what to do, where to invest and how to behave. Unions, as employers complained and trade union leaders boasted, were very deeply entrenched and they did use their influence to block moves that might lead to job losses. Wages, moreover, were not high by international standards but they had risen; and extensive overmanning meant that the wage bill overall was quite high. Finally, bankers and foreign investors were indeed unsympathetic to the objectives of the Labour government, but they were also responding to clear signals from the real economy. The Treasury instinctively responded to the same stimuli, but out of conviction and bureaucratic habit rather than self-interest. Actors saw what they wanted, and acted in response to what they selectively saw. Even the great big, new fact of the moment – the historic increase in the rate of inflation – was interpreted and assessed according to prior visions, predispositions and interests. The financial community, overwhelmingly focused on the value of their monetary assets, was appalled; industry was concerned about the costs, both of labour and of raw materials, but only so far as they could not be recovered in prices. Workers were even more ambivalent: as consumers they worried about inflation, but as employees they could be mollified with appropriate increases in wages; while the organised labour movement tended to privilege full employment over price stability.

However inflation was perceived, it worked its effects nonetheless. As prices rose and wages rose in response, ratcheting prices up still further, exports became more expensive and so less competitive. The bill for imports, on the other hand, had risen massively with the price of oil and so the balance of payments worsened drastically. The net effect was to cause a depreciation of the currency, which was both a reflection of international competitiveness and a means to recovering it. The weakening of the pound was at first disguised by the willingness of oil producers to leave a large share of their assets in sterling, but soon they began to move their money around and into more stable currencies experiencing lower rates of inflation. Apparently the Treasury and the Bank of England agreed that the pound needed to be devalued and adopted a stance that ensured its drop.[46] But the government still needed to cover the balance of payments and hence to borrow. It was now forced to defend its creditworthiness and to make policy in the knowledge that its every move would be scrutinised by the international financial community and that wrong moves would be quickly and painfully punished. Labour faced a classic crisis, for it found that it was no easy matter to maintain, and even harder to restore, confidence and that in the end they would be forced to take stronger measures than might have been required of a government of different hue.

In the meantime, however, the Labour government had to endure the effect of several obviously wrong moves. In November 1975 the Cabinet had agreed on a further £3 billion in expenditure cuts and elaborated its plans in a February 1976 White Paper on Public Expenditure. Much to its embarrassment, however, the White Paper was rejected in Parliament when a number of Labour MPs rebelled. The government then proceeded to bring its supporters back into line by calling for a vote of confidence, but the message had already been sent that Labour was deeply divided and could not be relied upon to take the measures necessary to bring inflation under control. Days later, on 16 May 1976, Harold Wilson resigned as prime minister.

Wilson's abrupt departure provided at least a fleeting opportunity for Labour to reassess and perhaps alter its course or, at a minimum, retrace and correct recent missteps. But in what direction might it have moved? The contest over the leadership revealed indirectly the party political constraints that limited Labour's room for manoeuvre. It drew in the four major figures of the centre-right – Callaghan, Jenkins, Healey and Crosland – and two from the left – Michael Foot and Tony Benn. The outcome was never much in doubt; nor even the likely finalists. Healey was only recently feuding with the left and saddled as well with the immediate responsibility for the government's increasingly stringent budgets; resentment against Jenkins's stand for Europe was still raw and his moment had clearly passed. Crosland's had perhaps not yet come, for he still had not held one of the top positions in government, and he was in any event unsuited by temperament to the task of 'gathering troops' and often left people thinking that he 'didn't care whether he got to No. 10 or not'.[47] On the left, it was conceded that Benn's time had also not yet come and he had only a short while back been on the losing side of the referendum over Europe. In the third ballot, held on 6 April, Foot won 137 votes from his fellow Labour MPs, but Callaghan polled 176 and was elected leader.[48] Callaghan was the least controversial choice, the candidate least likely to break with Labour's past or, most importantly, with its traditional approach to governing. He had shown his commitment to the role of the unions within the Labour Party in the battle over *In Place of Strife* and was demonstrating the same loyalty in carrying out the terms of the social contract. Callaghan prevailed as 'the least challenging candidate of the centre-right' and the one least likely to deviate from the path followed since 1974.[49]

Callaghan's accession as prime minister was thus a clear victory for continuity in personnel and in policy. He made a few Cabinet changes – unceremoniously getting rid of Barbara Castle, appointing Crosland Foreign Sercretary, a bit later nominating Jenkins to the presidency of the European Commission and, critically for the future of the party, making Michael Foot Leader of the House of Commons. It had long been Callaghan's dream to become prime minister, but in realising it he also inherited the mounting crisis. Even before he had the opportunity to put his stamp on policy, the government was forced to produce yet another budget that, whatever the reasoning behind it, would be widely interpreted as yet another wrong move. Despite Healey's efforts to get his colleagues to accept expenditure cuts, the April 1976 budget was on balance mildly reflationary. Expenditure was increased on employment schemes and social security benefits, while the standard rate of income tax was to be reduced from 35 per cent to 33 per cent. The inspiration was in theory Keynesian but also transparently partisan; and the effects counterproductive. What attracted greatest attention in the budget was a minor feature that came to symbolise the government's predicament. Part of the tax cut was made contingent on the government reaching a satisfactory agreement with the TUC on an extension of incomes policy. Critics on the right noted the troubling constitutional implication: that the government's most cherished prerogative, the determination of the nation's finances, was to be shared with union leaders who might or might not be responsive to their members but who had definitely not been elected by the voters. Even the left, who regarded it as their job to defend the rights and secure the input of the unions, recognised that such explicit linkages exposed the unions to potential criticism. As Brian Sedgemore argued in the Commons, making concessions to other taxpayers conditional upon union decisions 'is likely to bring odium on the trade union movement'.[50]

The budget thus accentuated the perception that the government was beholden to the unions and unable to function independently. The perception was not without foundation. From the beginning, the government had been determined to work cooperatively with the trade unions and the unions, for their part, were determined to have their views taken seriously. To that end Foot had been made Employment Secretary with the understanding that he would serve as the unions' eyes, ears and voice in Cabinet. As Edmund Dell later recalled, 'Through him the trade unions were directly represented around the Cabinet table.'[51] The unions already had an institutional link with the government via the National Economic Development Council (NEDC), but in that venue their representations were matched by, and had to compete with, those of the employers. From 1974 the union connection was further strengthened by the fact that the TUC/Labour Party Liaison Committee, founded while the party was in opposition, continued to meet regularly during the lifetime of the government and provided the TUC with more direct input. Senior ministers would thus regularly report to, and be called to defend themselves before, top TUC officials.[52] The arrangement reinforced the perception that the government was not really in control of its own policies and underscored the 'constitutional' issue raised by the April 1976 budget. Labour's connection to the unions was, of course, nothing new; but it was now more nakedly visible. And the effect was harmful to both sides: 'By placing the unions so centrally in the political stage,' a noted expert in industrial relations argued in retrospect, 'it prepared the way for the devastating political reaction.'[53]

Negotiations over Stage II of incomes policy took place in May 1976 and went reasonably smoothly. The inflexibility of the £6 limit was modified and a more flexible system adopted. Weekly wage increases would range from £2.50 for the lowest paid to £4 for the better paid. The effect would be that those earning £60 or under would get 5 per cent or better and workers on average would receive about a 4.5 per cent rise. TUC leaders were not happy with the arrangement. Jones was 'terribly dissatisfied', both 'because I knew the figures were inadequate' and because he had all along preferred a flat rate on grounds of fairness.[54] Len Murray echoed his concern and warned that 'there could be a price too high for the trade union movement to pay for a Labour Government . . .'. But this was not it, and he concluded instead that 'this was an honourable agreement, and one they [the TUC] must ensure was honoured'. There would be no further agreement to hold down wages after this, however, and the TUC would insist on holding the government to its pledge to facilitate 'an orderly return to free collective bargaining'.[55]

Unfortunately, the Stage II agreement was insufficient to restore investor confidence and the pound continued to fall in value and to do so further and faster than even the advocates of a lower exchange rate wanted. In June the government was forced to obtain a de facto loan from the central banks, a $5.3 billion standby credit which, if taken up, would have to be repaid in December. That deadline more or less guaranteed that Britain would next have to seek assistance from the IMF, from whom the government had already secured a loan of $1.8 billion the previous January. It is clear in retrospect that the implications were pretty well understood at the time, at least by Healey and Callaghan and by the financial community in Britain and abroad, even if it took months for the logic to be fully revealed. Since $2 billion of the June credit had come from the United States and since the United States played a critical role in the IMF, the negotiation of the loan had of necessity involved representatives of the US Treasury. They were keen to see 'that Britain put its house in order and that if it did not do so it should be forced to go to the IMF and accept IMF conditions'.[56] To avoid this, or perhaps to prepare for it, Healey orchestrated yet a further round of cuts totalling £1 billion in late July. In order to increase the impact of the 'July package' the government also chose to impose a 2 per cent surcharge on employers' National Insurance contributions. While the measure did add muscle to the package, it also brought bitter controversy. Cabinet members had not been fully consulted and were very angry; and businessmen were upset both at the lack of consultation and at the sudden increase in the cost of employing workers. Both business and the unions would come to regard the surcharge as a tax on employment and so much resent it. The effect was less useful than hoped for and the bankers in particular remained unimpressed. Indeed, as Edmund Dell has argued, the shape of the package 'convinced the market that there really was no way of persuading this government to come to its senses'.[57]

Decisions taken in the spring and summer of 1976 not only ensured that the government would need recourse ultimately to the IMF but also that the process would be extremely painful both politically and economically. By that autumn the government had largely exhausted its reserves of support within the ranks of the unions and it had conjured up a powerful resentment from the left of the party who saw the leadership as having sold out on the industrial policy, having outmanoeuvred them on Europe, and having turned against the welfare state. The disenchantment of the left was registered most dramatically on the NEC and at party conference. Relations with the NEC were particularly difficult, in part because Barbara Castle, no longer bound by collective responsibility and embittered after being sacked by Callaghan in April, was now willing openly to attack the government. Repeatedly, the NEC came close to outright rebellion and it used its control of conference to ensure that criticism in that venue would be intense. The party conference at Blackpool was unusually nasty and gave short shrift to the explanations and exhortations of ministers. Healey was booed and ridiculed; and the chair of the parliamentary party, Cledwyn Hughes, regarded the event as 'an almost unmitigated disaster'.[58]

The display of dissent within the party, though understandable enough, nevertheless itself probably worsened the economic situation. The government was now caught between the need to satisfy its supporters and preserve unity within the party and the Cabinet and with the unions, and the equally pressing need to satisfy its creditors. The two goals were just not compatible. Even as the government was negotiating a distinctly non-inflationary agreement on wages with the TUC in the spring, for example, it was moving in Parliament to pass legislation nationalising the aerospace and shipbuilding industries. The debate in

July about cuts in expenditure revealed a deeply divided Cabinet that was resolved not to cut again. In September, despite efforts by the TUC to keep wage settlements within the agreed limits, strikes broke out at British Leyland, among seamen and then at Ford. So Labour failed to reap the credit it deserved for what were in fact serious efforts to trim expenditures and reduce borrowing. Its failure was no doubt partly a reflection of the hostility of the press and of a financial community profoundly unsympathetic to a putatively socialist regime; and partly it was due to tactical mistakes. But Labour's commitments to public ownership and state intervention, to the defence of trade union prerogatives and behaviour and its determination to fulfil the terms of the social contract, were not inadvertent errors but entirely appropriate manifestations of the party's basic identity. Nor was the tendency to faction unique to the 1970s. Its problems, then, were not incidental but fundamental; and its fate probably beyond the capacity of any individual or group within the party to influence.

It was nevertheless Callaghan's unhappy personal fate to preside over Labour's increasing difficulties and embarrassments. He might well have been a better leader than Wilson, but he was destined to lead at a moment when better was simply not good enough.[59] The nation's financial position continued to deteriorate from the time he took office through the autumn of 1976. By September the Minimal Lending Rate (MLR) was put up to 13 per cent and Callaghan and Healey had decided it would be necessary to approach the IMF for a further loan of £3.9 billion.[60] The ensuing negotiations and the parallel debate within the government exacerbated Labour's divisions, pushed the Cabinet to adopt unwelcome policies that seemed to violate the party's first principles, forced a reluctant recognition of the limits of Keynesian policies and policy-making, and left voters with the distinct impression that the government was not really in charge of the nation's affairs. The impression might well have been unfair, but politics is seldom fair.

Callaghan inaugurated the debate with a famous intervention at the party conference in Blackpool in late September.[61] He told the assembled activists things that they were not at all happy to hear, particularly from a Labour Prime Minister. 'Britain has for too long lived on borrowed time, borrowed money, borrowed ideas', he proclaimed. 'For too long, perhaps ever since the war, we postponed facing up to fundamental choices and fundamental changes in our society and in our economy.' More specifically, 'the cosy world we were told would go on forever, where full employment would be guaranteed by a stroke of the Chancellor's pen, cutting taxes, deficit spending, that cosy world is gone'. Even more boldly Callaghan proceeded to argue that unemployment was actually 'caused by paying ourselves more than the value of what we produce'. If employment was to recover and industry to revive, moreover, business would have to make a profit. He concluded that it was therefore wrong of his comrades 'to think that you could just spend your way out of a recession and increase unemployment by cutting taxes and boosting Government spending. I tell you in all candour that that option no longer exists and insofar as it ever did exist, it worked by injecting inflation into the economy.'[62]

The speech, labelled courageous by a few, was widely interpreted and routinely denounced as a repudiation of the Keynesian views within which Labour had operated its economic policy since the 1940s. Whether it was intended so grandly, the effect was to announce publicly that the government now intended to follow a different path and that the historic association between Labour, full employment and increasing social expenditure no longer held or at least that the party's commitment to full employment would in future have to be balanced by a resolve to combat inflation. The immediate political consequence was to isolate Callaghan and Healey even further, dividing them not only from the left but also from their erstwhile allies on the Croslandite right of the party. But Callaghan's speech also signalled a willingness to speak openly and a desire to produce something of a consensus from among his Cabinet colleagues. He would not fudge as Wilson surely would have. Instead, he would conduct a debate over economic policy and public expenditure in which his opponents would have their say and, as Healey put it, 'talk themselves to a standstill'.[63] Callaghan would prevail in that effort, but it would take until Christmas; and it would do him little good in the long term.

After a further interest rate increase to 15 per cent in October and continued deterioration in the position of the pound, the final debate over the government's response to the financial crisis began in earnest with the arrival of a team of negotiators from the IMF on 1 November 1976. The IMF representatives met repeatedly with their counterparts from the Treasury and demanded a reduction in public borrowing (measured by the PSBR) of £3 billion in 1977–78 and £4 billion in 1978–79. Meeting those goals would mean eliminating roughly 6–8 per cent of public spending and hence deep cuts in social expenditure. The government responded by offering £2 billion in cuts for 1977–78. Both sides dug in and bargained forcefully while the Cabinet agonised over what to do. Callaghan, for his part, was a tough negotiator and he was buoyed in his resistance by his belief that the problem was not the level of expenditure and borrowing but rather the use of sterling as a reserve currency, and by his naive hope that his good relations with Helmut Schmidt, the German Chancellor, and with President Ford and his Secretary of State, Kissinger, would allow the government to resist and in the end to outmanoeuvre the IMF.

On the surface the debate seemed to pit the Treasury team, headed by Healey, against the left on the one hand, and the Keynesian right on the other, with Healey emerging as the ultimate victor with Callaghan's support. At a deeper level, the key struggle was between the left and the rest. Benn, Foot, Peter Shore and their supporters responded to the IMF crisis with a thoroughgoing assault on the policies of the government and the elaboration of what they called the Alternative Economic Strategy (AES). The AES grew logically from the left's understanding that British capitalism had failed the nation and that the moment was ripe to push forward government control and public investment.[64] The instruments were already at hand in the form of the National Enterprise Board and the planning agreements system. What was needed was a willingness to utilise these devices and a massive infusion of funds obtained through taxes and borrowing sufficient to allow a doubling of investment. To give the policy time and market space within which to work, however, would in turn require quite strict import controls. The left's proposals were internally consistent, they had the backing of an influential group of Cambridge economists, and they were in keeping with the broad thrust of the party's industrial strategy. But were they feasible?

As the AES was never tried, there is no way definitively to answer that rhetorical question, but the government would be forced to arrive at a tentative assessment in order to decide on the IMF loan.[65] Central to the outcome were the arguments put forward by Callaghan's Policy Unit, run by Bernard Donoughue.[66] The Prime Minister used the group to develop what proved to be extremely effective counter-arguments against Benn and the AES. The attack on the alternative strategy focused less on details than on broad assumptions about the nature of Britain's economy and its role in the world. Fairly or not, Benn's proposals were portrayed as implying the declaration of a state of emergency and the creation of a 'siege economy'. By cutting itself off from its trading partners, it was argued, Britain would invite retaliation that could only be devastating for an open economy critically dependent on exports and imports. It would damage the country's political standing as well and provoke a rift with its allies, ultimately depriving Britain of what remained of its influence on the course of world events. Most pointedly, it was argued that the voters had just opted to stay in Europe and that to institute import controls would effectively ignore and reverse that decision and, in the process, violate the terms of membership in the Common Market. The left was vulnerable on both of the central points in the argument and its failure to offer an effective response was an indication of 'serious deficiencies' in its 'analysis and alternative programme'.[67] Increasing public spending by either borrowing or taxing would be hugely controversial and probably inflationary; and autarchy was simply not workable for a trading nation that had, only recently, confirmed its commitment to the international economy.[68] And by showing itself so willing to reverse by fiat the verdict of the recent referendum, the left allowed itself to appear undemocratic. The result was a decisive rejection of the Alternative Economic Strategy. Even before the IMF discussions, Denis Healey had ridiculed the approach and supposedly 'just fell about laughing' when Brian Sedgemore proposed it. When the debate commenced in earnest, the full weight of the Treasury and the Policy Unit proved too much for Benn who, though articulate, 'was pulverised' in the Cabinet discussion of 1 December.[69]

With the effective defeat of the left, the range of dissent within the Cabinet was much narrowed. Crosland, in the last great struggle of his life, fought hard against the acceptance of cuts on the scale demanded by the IMF. He argued that the extent of the crisis was much exaggerated and that it was not a question about the real state of the economy but about the confidence of the bankers. Indeed, he claimed that the 'only serious argument for the cuts was one in terms of international confidence', but confidence would not be restored for long if the social contract failed to hold. Refusing to be cowed by the Treasury, he maintained that their calculations were unreliable and that Britain could face down the IMF. He reasoned that 'Politically the IMF could not refuse the loan . . .', for 'it was even more passionately opposed to protectionism than it was attached to monetarism'.[70] In Cabinet he even insisted that 'Our weakness is our strength, it is a test of nerve, and the IMF must give us the loan.'[71] Tony Benn backed a different set of policies, but agreed on calling the IMF's bluff.[72] There was further convergence among long-time opponents in that Crosland coupled his defence of public expenditure, and of Keynesian strategy generally, with a willingness to consider a modest form of import controls. The plan did not win broad acceptance, however, for in the end the left would not compromise on their more extensive proposals for restructuring and because Crosland's supporters on the right backed away, unwilling to go even a short way towards protection. Crosland himself climbed down, though not graciously. Callaghan informed him he was going to support Healey in the end and Crosland in turn told the Cabinet that he remained unconvinced and that the decision 'was wrong economically and socially'. But he would back the Prime Minister because he should not be seen to fail: 'The unity of the Party depends on sustaining the Prime Minister and the effect on sterling of rejecting the Prime Minister would be to destroy our capacity.'[73]

The political argument, however grudging, proved effective with others as well. Foot announced his support for Callaghan and his acquiescence effectively communicated to his colleagues that the TUC were willing to go along as well.[74] For the TUC, for Foot, for Crosland and for many more, the spectre of 1931 and the possibility of a disastrous split within the government loomed large and proved decisive. When pushed, therefore, the majority of the Cabinet felt they had no choice but to rally behind the Prime Minister. In doing so, however, they were not abjectly caving in to the IMF. In fact, Callaghan himself met with Johannes Witteveen, head of the IMF, on the morning of 1 December and made it clear that the Fund was asking too much. After a sharp exchange, a compromise began to emerge. The next day Healey proposed a package of cuts amounting to £1 billion for 1977–78 and £1.5 billion for the year following. In addition, the government would sell £500 million worth of shares in BP and use the proceeds further to reduce borrowing. The final agreement was marginally less favourable and came to roughly £3 billion in cuts over the two years. After further debates on just where the cuts would fall, a Letter of Intent was signed and submitted in late December.

The terms of the loan were nevertheless in the end much less harsh than first demanded and, in fact, the cuts fell largely on defence and so spared most social programmes. The deal thus came closer to what critics like Crosland had proposed than to the IMF's original numbers. It seems clear that this was roughly where Callaghan wanted to end up as well. His Policy Unit had come up with figures close to Crosland's, for example, and it had also briefly expressed some support for limited import controls. Though this particular proposal came to nothing, it was part of a broader strategy that was designed to steer a course between what were seen as two unacceptable extremes: 'the suicidal extremism of the Treasury and the protectionist extremism of Mr Benn', according to Donoughue, who was presumably putting on paper what was in Callaghan's mind.[75] Moreover, Callaghan would persist in his efforts to free sterling from the burden of serving as a reserve currency so as to prevent a recurrence of the crisis and he secured agreement on that the following February.[76] The final outcome of the resort to the IMF was thus less dire than critics feared, and the economic effect was probably salutary. The process was painful politically, however, and is likely to have weakened the overall legitimacy of Labour's claim to govern. But for those familiar with the details and the process it seemed not such a bad deal.

The problem was that although there had been a thorough thrashing out of alternatives within the Cabinet, no comparable understanding was available to the public or even to the broad ranks of the government's supporters. The stark fact, driven home by the Opposition and by the press, was that a Labour government had been forced to plead with foreign bankers to bail it out. It appeared an ignominious defeat even if the government had in the end secured reasonable terms. The dramatic nature of the event ensured that dramatic conclusions would be drawn as to its meaning. Callaghan's conference speech had appeared to argue the end of Keynesian policy-making; the IMF loan then confirmed its passing. The repeated cuts that climaxed in the IMF agreement and the imposition of 'cash limits' on spending were even more potent symbols that Labour had been forced to change and that the era of expanding social provision was over. The precise details of Labour's policies and their distributional consequences were less important than the image of a

Labour Chancellor cutting spending again and again, and apparently in response to outside pressure. What, then, remained of Labour's appeal and its claims to govern after the IMF loan?

Two different answers were on offer: one from the government and a second from the left of the party. The left could claim that its prescriptions had yet to be tried and so could not be said to have failed. The failure, rather, was the refusal of the government to follow agreed party policy and instead to back away from the industrial strategy and from the party's historic commitments to expanding public expenditure paid for largely through progressive taxation. The need, then, was to use the crisis produced by inflation to move forward, not to retreat. The left was undeterred by the awkward fact that its alternative strategy had been thoroughly debated in Cabinet and then rejected; nor was it moved by the expressed preference of voters to remain in Europe and the implied rejection of their autarchic approach. Defeat, and voter rejection, were easily explained as the inevitable result of the treachery of the party leaders, who chose not to argue the case for the party's socialist policies but to capitulate to conventional opinion. So the left 'added two names to the list of guilty men, betrayers of socialism, Callaghan and Healey', and continued to push for the programme agreed while in opposition.[77]

Even after the industrial strategy was shelved and the IMF loan agreed, the left persisted in arguing for greater state involvement in industry, increased spending to that end, and more generous social provision. In July 1977, for example, the Liaison Committee called again for a variation of the alternative economic strategy, with more public investment, state control of banking and insurance, a wealth tax and a weakening of ties to Europe. Demands for faster and more extensive reflation came repeatedly from the left – sometimes from the NEC, at other moments from *Tribune*, the Liaison Committee, or from Tony Benn. In November 1977, for example, Benn insisted that the Energy Department he headed should have first claim on the proceeds from North Sea Oil and that it be allowed to use them to increase public investment. The Treasury, eager to use the same money to reduce taxes and borrowing, saw the matter differently and ultimately prevailed, but Benn's resilience and tenacity were remarkable.[78] He was clearly sustained by the support he received from the party outside Westminster. Not surprisingly, then, he lent his name and support to a major effort to empower those forces.

He contributed mightily to the campaign to make MPs and the leadership of the party more directly responsible to the party, as embodied in its activists and represented formally by its National Executive and by the annual Labour Party conference. That movement would take time to mature, but in the long run it would prevail and its success would immensely complicate relationships between the party, its representatives in Parliament and its leadership and, more importantly, the connection between the party and the broader voting public.

The government's case was more practical, if rather less inspirational. Callaghan and his colleagues could plausibly claim to have averted a much more extreme outcome and to have survived a very difficult set of circumstances. In fact, the IMF package did restore confidence; within a very short time the nation's finances were in much better shape, the balance of payments was in surplus by the second half of 1977, and the pound had recovered much of its value. Inflation abated significantly, declining from 24.2 per cent in 1975 to just 8.3 per cent in 1978. In October 1977 Healey was able to offer a mildly expansionary budget and to announce that the last tranche of IMF funds would not be needed. By January 1978, the government's White Paper on Expenditure was to propose 'resumed and continued expansion'. On balance, Callaghan and Healey could plausibly claim that they had successfully brought the economy through the crisis induced by the oil shock of 1973−74 and managed the transition from an era of steady expansion to a period of slower growth for the world economy as a whole and for Britain.

They could argue as well that they had done so fairly and in a manner that spread the pain equitably. The government's policies did force a decline in the share of public expenditure in overall GDP, from 46.4 per cent in 1975 to 42.9 per cent in 1979.[79] Social expenditure thus inevitably declined as a share of the national product as well, from 24.7 per cent in 1974 to 23.9 per cent in 1979. But social spending had increased as a share of total public expenditure and, despite the straitened circumstances, had grown by almost 2 per cent in real terms. The burdens of the late 1970s were real, but reasonably shared. In seeking to distribute burdens equitably and to protect what it regarded as the core social programmes, the government saw itself as continuing to operate in the social-democratic tradition. It is likely, in fact, that rather too much was made of Callaghan's famous speech to the party conference in 1976 purportedly announcing the end of the Keynesian era: though he breached party orthodoxy momentarily, neither he nor his colleagues fully abandoned their faith in Keynes or their commitment to the welfare state. Keynesian wisdom might need to be tempered and adjusted, but it did not need to be abandoned. On the contrary, when the effects of inflation had been contained and the nation's finances restored, Callaghan and Healey were eager to undertake a modest expansion and resume the effort to improve social provision.[80]

The government also sought credit for its success in bargaining with the unions. The social contract was undoubtedly battered by successive expenditure cuts and the IMF loan, but it had strong and sustained support from key union leaders. These leaders, Jack Jones most prominently, had been able to deliver union support for the two elections of 1974 and for two instalments of incomes policy, and they had engineered the reluctant acceptance of expenditure cuts by the trade unions. To them the prospect of a Tory, or even a coalition, government was anathema and the need to keep Labour in power imperative. The TUC also clearly enjoyed its influence with the government and desperately feared losing it. As a result, its leadership chose to keep working closely with the government even after the IMF loan. The Liaison Committee continued to meet regularly, and the union leaders enjoyed continued access to ministers at the very top of the government. TUC pressure would prove important, moreover, in encouraging the government to reflate sooner rather than later, and its influence was clearly noticeable in budgetary priorities pursued during 1977–78.

What the union leadership could not do was to deliver pay restraint beyond Stage II, which ended in the summer of 1977. Instead, the TUC formally refused to endorse a policy for 1977–78 but nevertheless allowed the government to proclaim a 10 per cent norm which, according to Jones, was 'not agreed but tacitly accepted by the unions', and the unions then worked to calm or contain disputes that arose from its implementation.[81] They would have much more difficulty accepting the 5 per cent norm imposed the following year, and the unions would in fact make little effort to enforce it. Still, at least through the summer of 1978 it was not unreasonable for the government and the TUC to insist that the social contract had delivered in terms of lower inflation rates and relative industrial peace; and that regular consultation with government had ensured the effective representation of working-class interests in the formulation of key public policies.

The choices that had been forced upon the Labour government nonetheless did real damage to party unity and to the party's relationship with the unions and their members. Ultimately, the damage would issue in divisions and conflicts that would undermine whatever the government had achieved and, more significantly, the entire rationale for a Labour government. Difficulties arose almost immediately after the IMF agreement was concluded. As of early 1977 Labour held but the merest majority over the Conservatives and no majority overall in Parliament. They got through by constructing ad hoc majorities and that meant depending upon minor parties and rogue MPs who were by definition unreliable allies. The government had to govern, however, and it proceeded to outline the terms of the IMF deal in a White Paper on Public Expenditure presented to Parliament in March 1977. The left within the party, mainly the Tribune Group, used the occasion to demonstrate its discontent and to embarrass the government, which lost a vote on the White Paper on 17 March. With a vote of no confidence looming a week hence, Labour made a pact with the Liberals that kept it in office, but with very little room for manoeuvre. Its policies, which until now it had to work out with one eye upon the party's supporters and another on the financial community and in constant dialogue with the unions, had also now to please the Liberals as well. The pact would continue in force until August 1978. The deal with the Liberals provoked yet another row within the party, as the left – apparently encouraged by the staff at party head-quarters – mobilised against it and Tony Benn once again considered resigning in protest. The pact proved in the end quite useful tactically, allowing the government to carry on for more than a year with rather more security of tenure than before. Still, Callaghan's command of Parliament was tenuous and over the course of his premiership the government lost more than 30 votes in the Commons and his command over his own party was equally shaky.[82]

The Callaghan government was on even less secure grounds in its dealing with the unions and the rank and file workers whom they represented. Throughout the late 1960s and 1970s the dominant figures in the trade unions were Jack Jones of the Transport and General Workers and Hugh Scanlon of the Engineers. Both were traditionally men of the left and their rise to prominence was critical to the party's dramatic shift to the left in the early 1970s. But after 1974 both were determined to keep the Tories out and Labour in. Jones had been largely responsible for putting together the social contract; together Jones and Scanlon had made it work and kept the unions in line behind the government's policies. By 1978 both Jones and Scanlon were preparing to retire and their replacements, Moss Evans and Terry Duffy respectively, were to play very different roles. Neither had a background on the left and so neither could command automatic support from that quarter; and both still needed to prove themselves to their own members. Thus, although their politics were on the whole more centrist, they were far less willing or able to deliver the support of their unions or of the TUC overall for the policies of the government.

By mid-1978, therefore, support for continued pay restraint was waning. The annual Trades Union Congress formally rejected incomes policy and so, too, did the Labour Party conference. The government nevertheless went ahead with the imposition of a quite unrealistic 5 per cent norm. As Len Murray, head of the TUC, explained subsequently, 'We warned Callaghan that he would have industrial trouble if he tried to impose a 5 per cent wages policy . . .' but he 'was over-impressed by the quality of the Treasury printout and started thinking with his head rather than his stomach.'[83] Murray's recollection was perhaps clearer than the messages conveyed at the time. Roy Hattersley, for example, has reported a dinner meeting with TUC leaders – among them Moss Evans, Alf Allen and Murray – at which Healey was told, in effect, 'Look, none of us can carry this in our unions. But if you blind it through, you'll get away with this.'[84] It was nevertheless a mistake to put much faith in such advice, for if no union leader would publicly defend the new norm, it would not be obeyed. In fact, probably the best argument for the 5 per cent norm was that it was really a fake: Callaghan was expected to call an election in the autumn of 1978 and the norm would send a message of toughness and fiscal responsibility to voters but it would never have to be implemented.

Callaghan would confound expectations, however, by deciding not to call an election until the next year. His reasoning was in part very sensible, in part utterly delusional. Labour was within striking distance of the Tories in the polls and Callaghan himself was consistently preferred to Thatcher, but a detailed review of the situation in marginal constituencies was much less favourable. There was reason as well to hope that the economy would continue to improve and no reason to think that Mrs Thatcher would suddenly become cuddly and popular. On the other hand, it was foolish to ignore the warning signs from the unions or to expect that, at a time of rising prices, workers would abide by a norm of 5 per cent wage increases. Callaghan was certainly aware that the balance of opinion and influence within the unions had moved against him, and he knew how much the success of previous policies had been due to the diligent efforts of supporters who were no longer there. It was a major misjudgement by a politician whose judgement was usually very acute. And the mistake was truly his own, for a majority of the Cabinet and most of the key union leaders had advised him differently. His error would prove costly, both for him and for the entire Labour Party. Even so, an NOP poll still had Labour ahead by a slim 1 per cent as late as December 1978. It was only in January, when the government's pay policy was in ruins amid a wave of strikes by public sector workers, that the Conservatives jumped ahead and took an 18 per cent lead.[85]

What followed the decision to carry on through early 1979 was not only predictable, but perhaps inevitable. The 'winter of discontent' was a popular repudiation of the very premisses of Labour's historic link with the trade unions, of the social contract, and of the government's incomes policy. Labour had long claimed that in representing the collective interests of working people, as filtered through the unions, it was better able to serve the entire nation. This identity of interests was partly mythic, always tendentious and recently uncertain, but over the years it had been reassuring as rhetoric and acceptable in practice, particularly when it produced reasonable compromises on potentially divisive social and economic disputes. It remained viable so long as the sectional interests it privileged were constrained in their demands and had needs that could be satisfied without jeopardising broader interests. But it ceased to command assent when the sectional interests of particular groups took precedence over what was understood as the national, or the people's, interest. This was increasingly likely as the centre of trade unionism shifted from manufacturing to services funded by the taxpayer and as the site and strategy of industrial conflicts was relocated in response.[86] It was now less often a contest between capitalists and workers than a struggle that pitted public sector workers against the state and the public it was supposed to serve. At that point Labour's corporatist formula and its link with the trade unions lost support and, in the absence of acquiescence from a willing public, the inherent flaws in the arrangement – e.g. the questionable right of organised interests to special treatment, the effective loss of authority and even sovereignty that beset a government which gave the unions (or anyone else) effective veto power – became issues in themselves and made the strategy even more unworkable. The cumulative effect was to prove disastrous for Labour and for the unions; and it would be the making of Margaret Thatcher.

The manner of the Labour government's demise was entirely consistent with its history, structure and identity. It had been guided from the outset by the corporatist pursuit of 'the social contract' and it would end in a desperate attempt to continue that policy when it no longer worked. The effort began to fall apart when workers at Ford went on strike on 25 September in support of a claim that vastly exceeded the 5 per cent norm. Ford was willing to settle, but the government threatened sanctions against the firm if, and when, it finally did, for a bit over 17 per cent. The absurdity of penalising the company for an agreement forced upon it by unions, who were supposedly allied with the government, was evident. When the government pressed the case for sanctions in Parliament on 13 December, defections from the left of the party ensured that its position was rejected. The defeat demonstrated that the government's policy had little behind it but fond wishes and rhetoric; and the lesson was not lost on other workers. Even before that, oil tanker drivers had begun action on behalf of a claim for a 40 per cent increase. In short order lorry drivers, workers at British Leyland and manual workers for local authorities had joined in with similarly large claims.

The government's growing impotence was reflected in its inability to get the union leadership to serve as a moderating influence. Healey, Foot, the Employment Secretary Albert Booth, the Transport Minister William Rodgers and Callaghan himself were deeply involved in intense negotiations, but to little effect. A document of 14 November 1978 containing *TUC Guidance to Negotiators*, which would have at least urged moderation upon unions, split the TUC General Council down the middle and so was not approved and not issued.[87] Still worse from the government's perspective, the strikes that broke out in December and January were routinely made official by union leaders eager not to be seen as out of sympathy with their members. Repeated attempts to get the TUC to urge restraint produced only frustration.[88] At a formal meeting at the Chancellor's on 19 December Callaghan and Healey alternately pleaded and threatened, and hinted at compromise. Healey, for example, desperately explained that the government's policies had kept unemployment lower in Britain than in other countries and had brought down prices; and tax cuts and improved benefits meant that living standards had risen 7.5 per cent over the previous year. Healey also hinted that any combination of policies that kept wage increases under 10 per cent might be acceptable. The TUC was unmoved.[89] Callaghan for his part stressed pointedly that a government of a different hue would be tempted to respond to industrial unrest with less sympathetic understanding and that continuing it 'could lead to an attempt at legislation which could set back the trade union movement for a decade'. Ministers continued to make the case for restraint over the next two months, as disputes dragged on with little or no help from the union leaders. The TUC refused to help and instead began to insist upon direct input into the preparation of the next budget.[90] The government's position was increasingly desperate, but its stance elicited only the most modest concessions from the unions. As the crisis was winding down in mid-February, Murray would explain why the TUC had offered so little support: 'the government should understand', he said, 'that the TUC would not and should not promise more than it could deliver'.[91]

And that was clearly not much. Throughout January and February 1979 strikes had mounted, settlements escalated and what little public sympathy there was evaporated. The lorry drivers and water and sewer workers were joined by railwaymen and train drivers, and mass picketing at ports and depots blocked the transportation of essential supplies. A coalition of unions representing public sector workers – the National Union of Pubic Employees (NUPE), GMWU, COHSE and TGWU – brought out 1.5 million workers on 22 January in a 'day of action' and began selective stoppages throughout the public services. Schools and hospitals were soon affected and the disputes began to impede other essential services: dustmen did not remove the rubbish; ambulance drivers ceased to respond to (at least some) emergency calls; and grave-diggers in Liverpool refused to bury the dead – an action even the Labour Prime Minister thought betrayed 'heartlessness and cold-blooded indifference'.[92] The press turned violently hostile to the unions: 'They Won't Even Let Us Bury Our Dead', screamed the *Daily Mail* on 1 February 1979; a day later the same paper announced the 'Target for Today: Sick Children'.[93] The press was, of course, largely Conservative in orientation and undoubtedly exaggerated the extent of inconvenience to the public, but the bare facts were nevertheless hard to defend or to reconcile with a favourable image of trade unions acting in the broader national interest.

The government response was abject. A secret committee at the heart of the government supervised a Civil Contingencies Unit aimed at maintaining administration and minimising the effects of the industrial stoppages upon the public. Its regional committees kept in touch with local (and national) union leaders to ensure that food and medical supplies got through. Its success helped to convince the government not to impose a state of emergency, but this sensible decision made the government's response appear more 'supine', as Callaghan himself later described it, than it actually was. Callaghan's personal behaviour also contributed to the sense that the government was responding inadequately: he visited Guadeloupe and then Barbados in early January, came back looking tanned and rested, and upon his return responded to press queries in a manner that seemed to make light of the crisis. In fact, the government took the matter very seriously, but were at a loss over what to do. They had used up the existing repertoire of policy devices, narrow as this was, and were left without viable options. Bernard Donoughue has recalled how, amid the crisis, activity at the centre of the government machine came to a virtual halt: 'the flow of official papers ceased', and 'Number 10 was silent, the atmosphere one of quiet despair, like a ship holed and sinking. Neither the civil service nor ministers had any ideas on how the Government should go forward.'[94] Whether or not Britain was literally 'ungovernable', the Government acted as though it was, and there was undoubtedly a widespread sense of what Ralph Miliband had called 'desubordination'.[95] All the Labour government could do, it seemed, was to seek help from the unions. Their requests were for a long time unrequited, however. On 16 January Callaghan issued a statement that in effect abandoned the 5 per cent norm, at least for underpaid workers in the public sector, and hinted at some effort to ensure 'comparability' between the public and private sectors. The initiative ushered in a further series of inconclusive meetings, but meanwhile industrial unrest worsened.

Eventually a deal was cobbled together that meant very little in practice but that was politically quite significant. The government met with the TUC at the end of January and Callaghan, agreeing that the 5 per cent norm had been unrealistic, proposed an agreement over a broader policy against inflation and over a code of conduct for trade unions. Shortly after, on 3 February, he went further in his commitment to the establishment of a Comparability and Relativities Board. Two days later he met with the General Council and reiterated his suggestions. After another week of hard bargaining, on St Valentine's Day the government and the TUC issued a joint statement, a new 'concordat' on 'The Government, the Economy and Trade Union Responsibility'. The agreement, to which the TUC signed up only reluctantly, called for a union code of conduct, for an annual assessment of the state of the economy and its implications for wages and prices, and for a sustained effort to reduce inflation to 5 per cent by 1982. The concordat had little immediate effect and strikes continued to run their course until they were settled, typically on very generous terms. As if to underline the state's incapacity, civil servants chose to strike at the end of February on behalf of a demand for roughly 25 per cent and the government inevitably conceded.[96] In late March the government set up its comparability commission, which would be chaired by Professor Hugh Clegg and which would proceed to announce a series of generous awards in September, months after the Labour government had been replaced. The 'winter of discontent' had merely petered out; it was never met and dealt with either by government or by the TUC.

The concordat mattered politically, however, for two rather contradictory reasons.[97] First, it constituted a recognition, even by the TUC, that the behaviour of the unions had become a legitimate cause for public concern. The proposed guidelines on union conduct were to encompass the issues of strike ballots, picketing and the need to maintain essential services. Just talking about these had previously been unacceptable to the unions and the government had shied away in response; putting them on the table gave credence to the charges that union behaviour was becoming irresponsible. It was a point that the press and the Conservatives had made repeatedly. For Labour and the unions to concede its validity was devastating to the case for Labour's approach to managing the relationship with the unions, which had been the basis of its claim to govern since at least 1974. At the same time, the government's inability to come up with anything other than an updating of the social contract was a further confession that it had reached the limits of its effectiveness. Its corporatist policy-making offered no real alternative, despite the fact that this alternative had proved so ineffective so very recently. In a classic understatement Callaghan told the TUC that 'Current events had . . . cast doubt on the partnership between the two sides of the Labour movement which had been so successful in previous years.'[98] The idea that a repackaged social contract would nonetheless provide the basis for another appeal to the voters was quite fantastic, but it was the logic of Labour's thinking and its practice and a highly apposite expression of its structure and identity as a party.

Ironically, the end would not come over Labour's ineffective handling of strikes but over Welsh and Scottish devolution. The government position was rejected in referenda held in both countries on 1 March and from that moment the government could no longer count on sufficient support from MPs representing the Celtic nations for it to stay in office. A vote of confidence was scheduled for 28 March and, despite frantic manoeuvring, it was lost by a margin of one. A rather lengthy election campaign ensued. Labour, typically, fought with itself over the manifesto and put up a dispirited and lackadaisical effort. The party's only hope, after so much difficulty in governing and so many internal splits and disagreements, was that the harsh image of Mrs Thatcher would turn away voters. It probably did, but not enough to counteract all those turned away by Labour's record. The Conservatives won a solid if unspectacular victory: they took the popular vote by roughly 44–37 per cent and won 339 seats to Labour's total of 268.

The election of May 1979 must be understood as a genuine and ultimately quite reliable referendum on Labour's fundamental outlook, its strategies and its detailed policies. No doubt Callaghan and his colleagues had made tactical mistakes over the previous year – on the timing of the election, on whether to seek a vote of confidence on this or that particular issue, on what Callaghan should say after his trip to the Caribbean, on whether to declare a state of emergency, and so on – but the mistakes were minor and in most cases quite in keeping with Labour's basic approach to governance. To the extent that the election had turned on personality, moreover, the popularity contest between Thatcher and Callaghan was very much to Labour's advantage. Labour's defeat, then, was considered, reasonable and deeply meaningful. Regrettably, it was well earned.

Notes and references

1 On the two elections, see David Butler and Dennis Kavanagh, *The British General Election of February 1974* (London: Macmillan, 1974), and *The British General Election of October 1974* (London: Macmillan, 1975). In February Labour won 37.1 per cent of the popular vote, the Tories 37.8 per cent; in October Labour got 39.2 per cent to the Conservatives' 35.8 per cent.

2 See Vernon Bogdanor, 'The Fall of Heath and the End of the Postwar Settlement', in Stuart Ball and Anthony Seldon, eds, *The Heath Government, 1970–1974: A Reappraisal* (London: Longman, 1996), 382, and Anthony King, ed., *Britain at the Polls, 2001* (New York: Chatham House, 2002), 233. The combined share of the vote garnered by the two major parties has continued to fall even with the much altered fortunes of the parties – from just under 74 per cent in 1997 to 72.4 per cent in 2001.

3 The classic study of 'de-alignment' was Ivor Crewe, Bo Sarlvick and James Alt, 'Partisan de-alignment in Britain, 1964–74', *British Journal of Political Science*, VII (1977), 129–90. Subsequent studies placed less emphasis on 'de-alignment' in general and more on the long-term atrophy of Labour support. See, for example, Crewe, 'The Labour Party and the Electorate', in Dennis Kavanagh, ed., *The Politics of the Labour Party* (London: Allen & Unwin, 1982), 9–49. A still more long-term view is on offer in Anthony Heath, Roger M. Jowell and John K. Curtice, *The Rise of New Labour: Party Policies and Voter Choices* (Oxford: Oxford University Press, 2001).

4 These data come from the compilation of results from successive British Election Studies in Ivor Crewe, Anthony Fox and Neil Day, *The British Electorate, 1963–1992* (Cambridge: Cambridge University Press, 1995). The British Election Studies represent the most comprehensive set of opinion polls available and have the great virtue of having asked roughly the same questions to comparable samples of voters over an extensive period of time. The studies have asked voters whether they identify with various parties and whether they do so a little, strongly or very strongly. I have tended to merge the latter two responses and called them simply 'strong' and focused on changes in the overall size of this group. Other measures, of course, produce slightly different results and impressions.

5 George Gallup, *The Gallup International Opinion Polls: Great Britain, 1937–1975* (New York: Random House, 1976), Volume II: 1965–1975, 887–8, 1353.

6 Michael Hatfield, *The House the Left Built: Inside Labour Policy-Making, 1970–75* (London: Gollancz, 1978), 228–9.

7 Butler and Cavanagh, *The General Election of February 1974*, 139–40.

8 David Coates, *Labour in Power? A Study of the Labour Government, 1974–1979* (London: Longman, 1980), 59–60.

9 Martin Holmes, *The Labour Government, 1974–79* (New York: St Martin's, 1985), 13.

10 Barbara Castle, *The Castle Diaries, 1974–6* (London: Weidenfeld & Nicolson, 1980), 61.

11 Homes, *The Labour Government*, 8–10.

12 See Samuel H. Beer, *Britain against Itself: The Political Contradictions of Collectivism* (New York: Norton, 1982), 93.

13 *Gallup Polls*, 1296, 1386.

14 Kenneth Morgan, *Callaghan: A Life* (Oxford: Oxford University Press, 1994), 421.

15 Harold Wilson, *Final Term: The Labour Government, 1974–1976* (London: Weidenfeld & Nicolson, 1979), 98–9.

16 David Butler and Uwe Kitzinger, *The 1975 Referendum* (London: Macmillan, 1976).

17 Roy Jenkins, *A Life at the Center* (New York: Random House, 1991), 377 and ff.

18 Ben Pimlott, *Harold Wilson* (London: HarperCollins, 1992), 652–60.

19 Anne Perkins, *Red Queen: The Authorised Biography of Barbara Castle* (London: Macmillan, 2003), 384–8; *Castle Diaries*, 19, 20, 24 and 26 March 1975, 345–57. Mikardo came close to implicating Castle and other dissenting ministers when he told that NEC meeting that the motion they were debating was not really his: 'I didn't even draft it. I was just the postman.'

20 Jenkins, *Life at the Center*, 392.

21 Quoted in Coates, *Labour in Power?*, 231.

22 As Coates, *Labour in Power?*, 230–2, has forcefully argued.

23 *The Regeneration of British Industry*, Cmnd. 5710 (July 1974), *British Parliamentary Papers*.

24 Wilson, *Final Term*, 33–6; Coates, *Labour in Power?*, 89–94; Holmes, *The Labour Government*. 38–9.

25 Harold Wilson Papers, c. 533.

26 *Castle Diaries*, 10 June 1975, 413.

27 Benn, *Against the Tide: Diaries, 1973–76* (London: Hutchinson, 1989), entry for 9 June 1975, 390.

28 Donoughue, cited in Pimlott, *Harold Wilson*, 668.

29 *Castle Diaries*, 416.

30 Benn, *Against the Tide*, entry for 11 June 1975, 399.

31 See David Coates, *Labour in Power?*, 110–13.

32 M. Artis, D. Cobham and M. Wickham-Jones, 'Social Democracy in hard times: The economic record of the Labour government, 1974–1979', *Twentieth Century British History*, III, 1 (1992), 55. For more detail, see Artis and Cobham, eds, *Labour's Economic Policies, 1974–1979* (Manchester: Manchester University Press, 1991), especially M. Sawyer's chapter on 'Industrial Policy'.

33 Holmes, *The Labour Government*, chapter 3.

34 Joel Barnett, *Inside the Treasury* (London: Andre Deutsch, 1982), 23, cited in Holmes, *The Labour Government*, 8.

35 *House of Commons Debates*, 12 November 1974.

36 Holmes, *The Labour Government*, 21.

37 Castle's, Jenkins's, Benn's and Mellish's remarks are all recorded in *Castle Diaries*, entry for 25 March 1975, 353.

38 *Castle Diaries*, entry for 21 April 1975, 371.

39 Edmund Dell, *A Strange, Eventful History: Democratic Socialism in Britain* (London: HarperCollins, 2000), 462.

40 Interview with Anna Coote, 17 July 2003.

41 TUC General Council Minutes of 26 June 1974, TUC Papers, Modern Records Centre, University of Warwick.

42 TUC General Council Minutes of 25 June 1975.

43 Edward Pearce, *Denis Healey: A Life in Our Time* (London: Little, Brown, 2002), 435.

44 Bernard Donoughue, *The Heat of the Kitchen* (London: Politico's, 2003), 164.

45 Stuart Holland, *The Socialist Challenge* (London: Quartet, 1975).

46 Holmes, *The Labour Government*, 81–4.

47 The judgements are reported in Susan Crosland, *Tony Crosland* (London: Jonathan Cape, 1982), 311. See also Kevin Jefferys, *Anthony Crosland: A New Biography* (London: Politico's, 2000), 187–99.

48 On Foot's surprisingly good showing, see Mervyn Jones, *Michael Foot* (London: Victor Gollancz, 1994), 393–5.

49 Giles Radice, *Friends and Rivals: Crosland, Jenkins and Healey* (London: Little, Brown, 2002), 240.

50 Sedgemore quoted in Richard Whiting, *The Labour Party and Taxation: Party Identity and Political Purpose in Twentieth-Century Britain* (Cambridge: Cambridge University Press, 2000), 254.

51 Dell, *A Strange, Eventful History*, 435.

52 The format of the minutes of the TUC-Labour Party Liaison Committee indirectly makes the political point. The minutes regularly attribute remarks to particular ministers and NEC representatives, thus exposing and recording their differences and presumably diminishing their collective impact. The TUC, by contrast, speaks with one, highly authoritative, voice. See, for example, the minutes of 6 December 1976, when the committee discussed the impact of the IMF loan: 'The TUC emphasised the importance of maintaining the social contract and the industrial strategy and of avoiding any division in the movement which could prejudice the Labour Party in Government.' Truly a curious example of dialogue. The Liaison Committee's minutes are reproduced and included in the minutes of the NEC Archives.

53 William Brown, 'Industrial Relations', in Artis and Cobham, *Labour's Economic Policies*, 226.

54 Jack Jones, *Union Man* (London: Collins, 1986), 307.

55 TUC General Council Minutes, 5 May 1976.

56 Samuel Brittan, cited in Holmes, *The Labour Government*, 87.

57 Edmund Dell, *A Hard Pounding: Politics and Economic Crisis, 1974–1976* (Oxford: Oxford University Press, 1991), 229–30.

58 Quoted in Morgan, *Callaghan*, 535.

59 See Morgan, *Callaghan*, chapter 22, for a convincing discussion of Callaghan's considerable strengths as prime minister, and also Bernard Donoughue, *Prime Minister: The Conduct of Policy under Harold Wilson and James Callaghan* (London: Jonathan Cape, 1987).

60 Though the official documents remain closed, the story of the IMF loan has been examined thoroughly and thoughtfully in a range of works making extensive use of interviews and/or personal reminiscences. See, among others, Morgan, *Callaghan*, chapter 23; James Callaghan, *Time and Chance* (London: Collins, 1987), esp. 434–44; Denis Healey, *The Time of My Life* (London: Michael Joseph, 1989); Pearce, *Denis Healey*; Benn, *Against the Tide*; Dell, *A Hard Pounding*; Barnett, *Inside the Treasury*; Kathleen Burk and Alec Cairncross, *'Goodbye, Great Britain': The 1976 IMF Crisis* (New Haven: Yale University Press, 1992); Stephen Fay and Hugo Young, *The Day the £*

Nearly Died (London: Sunday Times Publications, 1978); Holmes, *The Labour Government*; Coates, *Labour in Power?*; Artis and Cobham, *Labour's Economic Policies*; Mark Harmon, *The British Labour Government and the IMF Crisis* (London: Macmillan, 1997), and, most recently, Donoughue, *The Heat in the Kitchen*. Morgan's biography is especially useful for he has had unique access to the Callaghan papers as well as extensive opportunity to interview key participants.

61 See Morgan, *Callaghan*, 535, on the provenance of the speech. Peter Jay, Callaghan's son-in-law, apparently came up with the key themes and phrases while the Prime Minister's Policy Unit, headed by Bernard Donoughue, apparently took the lead in framing it.

62 *Report of the Labour Party Annual Conference 1976*, 185–94.

63 Healey, *Time of My Life*, 431.

64 See, *inter alia*, Home Policy Committee (NEC), 'Alternative Economic Strategies', Labour Party Research Department Memorandum 900, December 1976 Archives.

65 See John Callaghan, 'The rise and fall of the Alternative Economic Strategy: From the internationalisation of capital to "globalisation"', *Contemporary British History*, XIV, 3 (Autumn 2000), 105–30.

66 See 'The I.M.F. Negotiations' (PU/229) 5 November 1976; 'The I.M.F. Negotiations' (PU/230) 16 November 1976; and 'The I.M.F. Negotiations: A Compromise Package' (PU/235) 26 November 1976; cited in Morgan, *Callaghan*, 536, notes 59–61.

67 Coates, *Labour in Power?*, 242.

68 To be fair, Benn and Peter Shore argued plausibly that import controls were compatible with both European commitments and with GATT. See Benn, *Against the Tide*, entry for 1 December 1976, 663; and also Burk and Cairncross, '*Goodbye, Great Britain*', 89.

69 See Holmes, *The Labour Government*, 96, citing Neil Kinnock on Healey's response and a summary judgement by Fay and Young, *The Day the £ Nearly Died*, 38; and also Benn, *Against the Tide*, 661–9.

70 The words are actually Susan Crosland's paraphrase of arguments he presented in Cabinet. See Crosland, *Tony Crosland*, 377–8.

71 Benn, *Against the Tide*, entry for 23 November 1976, 654.

72 Interview with Tony Benn, 30 September 2003.

73 Benn, *Against the Tide*, entry for 2 December 1976, 674.

74 Murray was clearly a major ally of Callaghan at this time. See Callaghan, *Time and Chance*, 437; and also the Minutes of the Liaison Committee for

6 December 1976, at which Healey declared himself 'grateful for the tone of the Liaison Committee's discussion'.

75 'The I.M.F. Negotiations' (PU/230), loc. cit.

76 Morgan argues that there were not three key factions in the debate – Callaghan/Healey; the left around Benn and Foot, and the Croslandite Keynesians – but four, with Callaghan developing his own 'alternative strategy' based on escaping the burden of the sterling balances. Perhaps, but since the outcome Callaghan engineered was so very close to the position advocated by Crosland and ultimately bargained out by Healey, it is not obvious that Callaghan, Healey, Crosland and their various supporters were truly stable factions in any meaningful sense. Nevertheless, the arguments and differences felt real enough at the time. Though Crosland articulated a position that quite closely approximated the outcome, his role remains interesting and controversial. For the left, his opposition was token and 'he collapsed like a house of cards. It was a pathetic thing, quite frankly.' Others were impressed with the opposite: 'That was the day Croslandism died . . . It was a tormenting time for him. I watched him, torturing himself.' [The judgements are reported in Holmes, *The Labour Government*, 98.] On the right, on the other hand, his lack of realism was itself cause for denunciation: to Edmund Dell his 'arguments were a forlorn defence' of a philosophy that no longer worked and 'to those who heard them they appeared desperate and unconvincing'. [See Dell, *A Strange, Eventful History*, 459.] More generally, see Radice, *Friends and Rivals*, 243–69.

77 Dell, *A Strange, Eventful History*, 462.

78 Morgan, *Callaghan*, 577.

79 Roger Middleton, *Government versus the Market* (Cheltenham: Edward Elgar, 1996), 506.

80 As Burk and Cairncross, '*Goodbye, Great Britain*', 228, conclude: 'There was little change of heart in the Labour Party.' This was perhaps less true of Callaghan than of Healey. See, for instance, Healey, *The Time of My Life*, 432–3.

81 Jones, quoted in Holmes, *The Labour Government*, 110.

82 Morgan, *Callaghan*, 564.

83 Len Murray, *The Observer*, 2 September 1984, cited in Robert Taylor, *The TUC: From the General Strike to New Unionism* (London: Palgrave, 2000), 238–9.

84 Pearce, *Denis Healey*, 515–16.

85 See Colin Hay, 'Narrating crisis: The discursive construction of the "Winter of Discontent" ', *Sociology*, XXX, 2 (May 1996), 254.

86 See Steve Ludlum, 'The Impact of Sectoral Cleavage and Public Spending Cuts on Labour Party/Trade Union Relations: The Social Contract Experience', in David Broughton et al., eds, *British Elections and Parties Yearbook 1994* (London: Frank Cass, 1995), 15–28.

87 Minutes of the TUC General Council Meeting of 14 November 1978.

88 These contentious and unproductive meetings are discussed in detail in Taylor, *TUC*, 238–46.

89 Reported in the Minutes of the TUC General Council Meeting of 20 December 1978.

90 Minutes of the TUC General Council Meeting with Ministers – including Healey and Foot – of 24 January 1979. This was part of a series of meetings that were to 'culminate in a measure of agreement on the Government's Budget proposals . . .'.

91 Minutes of the TUC General Council Meeting of 14 February 1979.

92 Callaghan, *Time and Chance*, 537.

93 Cited in Hay, 'Narrating Crisis', 262–3.

94 Donoughue, *Heat in the Kitchen*, 267.

95 Ralph Miliband, 'A state of desubordination', *British Journal of Sociology*, XXIX, 4 (December 1978). The idea that democratic states had become 'ungovernable' was much debated and regularly assumed in the mid- to late 1970s and the British government's inability to deal with industrial unrest, under both Conservative and Labour administrations, was typically cited as evidence. See, for example, Michel Crozier, Samuel Huntington and Joji Watanuki, *The Crisis of Democracy: report on the governability of democracies to the Trilateral Commission* (New York: NYU Press, 1975); and also the remarkably hysterical interviews gathered together in 'Is democracy dying?' *US News and World Report*, 8 March 1976. For a more balanced but not dissimilar account, see Samuel Beer, *Britain against Itself* (New York: Norton, 1982). Clearly, one man's 'desubordination' is another's 'ungovernability'.

96 Donoughue, *Heat of the Kitchen*, 269–70.

97 See Pearce, *Denis Healey*, 521–2, for a slightly more favourable assessment of the concordat. He notes correctly that the unions' agreement that there should be limits on picketing and boycotts and other restrictions on union behaviour was an achievement. But it was, of course, without practical effect and doubts can surely be raised about whether action would ever have resulted from the new stance.

98 Minutes of the TUC General Council Meeting, 14 February 1979.

CHAPTER 6

Defeat, divisions and defections, 1979–83

Margaret Thatcher's victory in May 1979 was less than it might have been. The failures of the Labour government of 1974–79 had been cumulative and massive and its image had suffered repeated defacing at the hands of its erstwhile backers among the unions and its own dissidents. The combined effects were more than enough to guarantee repudiation by the voters. Despite these advantages, Thatcher won a solid victory, but no 'landslide'. The Conservatives won just under 44 per cent of the vote while Labour polled 37 per cent, the same share it received in February 1974; in Parliament the Tories had 60 more seats than Labour and an overall majority of 43. The biggest losers were actually the Liberals and the Welsh and Scottish Nationalists, whose combined share of the vote declined from just under 22 per cent in October 1974 to less than 16 per cent in 1979 and whose representation in Parliament dropped from 27 to 15 seats. The Conservative performance was strong, but there was no reason to assume that Thatcher's triumph would usher in nearly two decades of Tory rule. Thatcher herself was regarded as an electoral liability by her campaign managers and her free market preferences did not commend themselves to most voters or even to a majority of her own party. That she would win three successive victories and that her effort to recast the relationship between state, society and economy would prove enduringly successful was almost unthinkable in 1979. What ultimately made Thatcher so dominant were her considerable political talents, the coherence of her vision and the consistency with which she sought to advance it, some very good luck, and – probably most important – the prolonged crisis into which Labour descended.

None of this was certain and nothing was predetermined in 1979. What had become fairly clear by that date, however, was that Labour's vision and style of governing were seriously flawed. The disasters of the last Labour government were impossible to deny or to explain away and cried out for explanation. Unfortunately, the debate about the party's recent failures and, implicitly, about what to do next, led at first not to clarification and renewal, but to doubt, recrimination and further bloodletting in full view of an increasingly impatient and sceptical public opinion. Traditionally, Labour's leaders had come from the centre-right of the party, while its most passionate supporters and activists espoused grander and more radical views. In the aftermath of 1979, that centrist leadership – especially Callaghan – was demoralized and discredited; those more solidly on the right were angry at the unions and understood that they were isolated within the ranks of the party as well. The left was resurgent in the party and, to a somewhat lesser extent, in the unions, and faced little or no effective resistance in either arena. The effect was a further shift to the left in programme, vision and party practice; a de facto withdrawal on the part of the centre-right faction represented by Callaghan; and the literal departure of the revisionist right to form the new Social Democratic Party. The outcome illustrated with particular clarity the character of the Labour Party and its distinctive outlook, and its resulting corporatist commitments – all of which militated against a move towards the political centre and instead facilitated a move to the left. In so doing Labour effectively narrowed its appeal still further, cut its ties to the political centre and drove out leaders who were out of sympathy with the party's present direction. The result was the horrendous election of 1983, Labour's worst defeat since 1931, and the emergence of full-blown Thatcherism, ready after 1983 to implement its programme with a vengeful determination and to do whatever it could to weaken permanently Labour's institutional bases of support within the unions and in local government and, even more, to banish socialism from the British political agenda. Those who controlled the Labour Party during the first Thatcher government, and presided over its growing isolation, would leave a legacy not easily reversed.

Not all of the debates about what went wrong were especially rancorous and in fact there were informed and sustained discussions among academics who took the long view of Labour's history and the evolution of the working class. These could have provided a useful guide to the social changes confronting Labour as it confronted Margaret Thatcher but, significantly, they did not have much impact on arguments and decisions within the party itself, at least in the short term. A particularly important intervention came from Eric Hobsbawm, who used the occasion of his Marx Memorial Lecture in 1978 to ask, 'Is the Forward March of Labour Halted?' Hobsbawm's rather simple title masked a quite complex argument that was premised on the importance of economic and social change, but that also paid due regard to culture and politics. To Hobsbawm there was no denying that at the core of Labour's steady growth throughout the twentieth century was a large and, for a time, expanding manual working class upon which was grafted a distinctive way of life, characteristic and widely shared patterns of sociability, and collective organisation. All of this had come together politically in a solid allegiance to Labour as a party. Class sentiments and support for Labour had begun to come apart, however, as its social base began to contract. The number of workers stopped increasing, then began a slow decline; and gradually white-collar work became more and more prevalent. The industries – manufacturing, mining, the railways and the docks – where the trade unions were best organised and where loyalty to Labour was strongest declined even more precipitously. Workers remaining in these trades, moreover, were able to extract decent wages even as their numbers shrank and so gradually were able to raise their living standards. Those who laboured in the newer and more prosperous industries did still better. Overall, the organised workers became better off and their struggles and claims less compelling to outsiders. Increasingly, too, the unions confronted not private management, but government and, at least implicitly, the public they represented. The spread of public ownership and the involvement of the state in industrial relations, especially when it adopted incomes policies, also meant that few industrial disputes featured the stereotypical foes in the class struggle – the bosses and the workers – and more and more brought unions into conflict with representatives of the public. Incomes policies had a further fragmenting effect, for they resulted in the narrowing of the wage differentials that workers had constructed so painfully and defended so vigorously. Industrial disputes became in consequence more sectional and less broadly based.[1] Because 'the strength of a group [now] lies not in the amount of loss they can cause to the employer', Hobsbawm argued, 'but in the inconvenience they can cause to the public, i.e. to other workers', their cause was less likely to engage popular sympathies.[2]

Hobsbawm's article pre-dated by a few weeks the onset of the 'winter of discontent', which ensured that the forfeit of public opinion by the unions and the Labour Party would be more than temporary. But the loss of support for Labour was in his view a secular process rooted in the irreversible transformation of the economy: the decline of old industries, the rise of the service sector and of white-collar jobs, upward social mobility and the dissolution of working-class communities. The formulation thus resembled the earlier argument about the impact of 'affluence' on industrial behaviour and on voting. But while affluence was largely a prospect when it was first discussed in the late 1950s and early 1960s, by the late 1970s it was increasingly real. So, too, the structural changes that were gradually turning the 'workshop of the world' into a post-industrial society. When the 'affluent worker' studies began to appear in the mid-1960s the British economy was still recognisably what it had been in the 1940s and 1950s. The huge industrial concentrations in mining, shipbuilding and other branches of heavy industry remained; and hundreds of thousands continued to labour in industries like textiles that were fated to diminish in importance. There had been a steady, but again not spectacular, increase in the numbers of women working and a shift from manual to white-collar work as well. Nevertheless, the big industries that made up the bulk of British industry were still largely intact into the mid-1960s, and structural change had only gradually begun to shrink them. Nor had the slow growth of earnings made possible a distinctly new and higher level of mass consumption. Ironically, however, the moment when the collection of data for the affluent worker studies was completed was precisely when Britain began seriously to change. Throughout the 1960s and 1970s, the pace of transformation would accelerate. By 1978–79, the social structures underpinning long-term political alignments had been substantially reconfigured.

Central to the transformation was the sustained, if slightly uneven, increase in living standards. The successive bouts of inflation and the varying impact of incomes policies meant that periods of advance would be mixed with occasional setbacks, but over the long run real wages increased considerably: from the mid-1950s through the mid-1960s real wages grew by less than 1 per cent annually; from 1966 to 1973, by contrast, they leapt fully 28 per cent. During 1974–79, and despite the incomes policies and austerity measures that brought a brief reversal after 1976, real wages grew another 10 per cent.[3] The social wage also increased, and with more equitable distributional effects. Into the 1950s, even after the heroic creation of the welfare state in the immediate post-war era, social expenditures were but a mere 14 per cent of GDP; and as late as 1959 they were just 15.2 per cent of national income. By 1970, however, they had grown to 20 per cent and by 1974 to nearly a quarter of GDP. The constraints on government spending imposed during 1974–79 brought that figure down slightly, but Labour's political preferences ensured that defence and administration fared worse than social services.[4]

Rising incomes translated directly in expanded opportunities for consumption and working people proved as susceptible to the lure of the capitalist marketplace as anybody. By the mid-1960s many workers had cars and almost all had televisions, but a majority lacked refrigerators and only a few had telephones; by 1979 all of these items were ubiquitous. Home ownership, long the preserve of the middle classes, had also been brought within the reach of at least the better off among the working class. The possibility of landing a substantially better job also improved. A massive study of social mobility based on data from 1972 demonstrated that nearly half of British men ended up in social classes different from where they started. After allocating occupations to one of three broad categories – the service class (professionals, managers, high-level administrators, owners), the intermediate class, or classes (supervisors, small businessmen and most white-collar workers), and the working class – researchers found that 27 per cent of working-class children had moved into the intermediate ranks and 16 per cent all the way into the professional class; while more than a quarter of the children of the privileged service class had fallen in social standing. A follow-up study a decade on showed even greater social fluidity, despite the hard times that had intervened.[5] The gains in income and social mobility had been made, moreover, against a background of industrial decline. Employment in industries like coal mining and textile production, for example, had remained quite high into the mid-1960s, but eventually had to shrink. Between 1966 and 1979 the labour force in textiles dropped from 757,000 to 479,000; those working in mining and quarrying declined from 569,000 to a mere 337,000. The expansion of jobs elsewhere, and on the whole better jobs, was thus very dramatic. The new jobs offered rather more openings for women than for men: between 1965 and 1979 approximately half a million men left employment while nearly 1.75 million women joined.[6] Even so, there were new jobs and an expansion of opportunity for both men and women, if not in the industries and occupations from which Labour and the unions had traditionally drawn their support.

By the time Labour fought the 1979 election, therefore, its appeal had to contend with social trends that were in the main adverse to its message. The rhetoric of class solidarity was hard to reconcile with what appeared to be the highly sectional practice of trade unionists; and the apparent need for collective advance through the efforts of unions and a sympathetic government had diminished as individual prospects improved. Labour retained, however, two critical resources that still worked in its favour, though not as unequivocally so as in the past: union membership and public housing. Remarkably in Britain, union membership had continued to increase in the face of a persistent decline in the number of workers employed in the traditional bastions of trade union strength. As the ranks of the miners and textile workers thinned, their places within the ranks of the unions were taken by employees in new industries, by white-collar workers, by women and, in particular, by those working in the public sector. These categories overlapped, of course. Between 1966 and 1979 the labour force grew very slightly overall, but the membership of unions increased by roughly 3.2 million to 13,447,000, which represented better than 55 per cent of the entire labour force. Since union membership was the best predictor of Labour voting, and since the leaders of the unions were desperate to keep Thatcher out and Labour in, the waxing strength of trade unionism gave Labour a distinct electoral advantage.

A second, at times reinforcing, source of Labour support came from the fact that so many working people were also council house tenants. Throughout the post-war era private home ownership continued to increase, but so, too, had the building and letting of council houses, if at a slower pace. Both owner-occupancy and rental from public authorities had expanded at the expense of private rental accommodation. As of 1979, over 54 per cent of housing was privately owned, while roughly a third of the housing stock was rented from local authorities.[7] Since the majority of private homes were presumably owned and occupied by the middle class and the bulk of council house tenants were undoubtedly working class, it would appear that Britain was divided into two distinct housing classes, both to some extent beholden to the state for their housing.[8] Private owners benefited substantially from mortgage tax relief, while council housing was built with public money and then heavily subsidised. The link between government and council tenants was, however, far more visible and of more direct political significance; and the effect was to predispose tenants to vote Labour, the most consistent advocates for public spending on housing. Still, home ownership was beginning to be a possibility for a growing section of the working class. Thus, while council tenants remained a constituency linked by self-interest and, often, also by political loyalty to Labour, other workers were now detached, or semi-detached, from that allegiance. More important, as the possibility of owning one's home became more widespread, the aspiration to home ownership became ever more widely diffused and significant numbers of council house tenants looked to buy the houses they occupied. There were initiatives from within the Callaghan government to consider the sale of council houses, but for most of the party the prospect was anathema and as a result it got nowhere.[9]

On balance, then, social trends during the 1960s and 1970s seemed to have worked against Labour as it had traditionally defined its interests and identity, though perhaps not uniformly and not always with great force. Certainly, Labour just could not by the late 1970s take for granted the routine support of as large a section of the electorate, or even of the working class, as had regularly supported the party in the past. As Hobsbawm would note in response to his critics, the size of the Labour vote had by 1979 dropped from its historic high of close to 14 million in the early 1950s to just 11.5 million in 1979.[10] The figure would in fact dip further during the 1980s as the party quarrelled in opposition, splintered and further isolated itself. But the loss of support to 1979 was itself sufficient to ensure a Tory victory. The terms on which that victory had been achieved were yet a further indictment of Labour's approach to government. In that election the Conservatives won by distancing themselves from the style of government that had marked both Labour and Conservative administrations since the 1950s but that by 1979 had become unambiguously the property of the Labour Party. In 1974, the two closely fought elections showed that the electorate was sceptical about the nostrums and the recent practice of both parties. By 1979 voter antipathy was refocused and now directed overwhelmingly at Labour; and even if Thatcher's monetarist prescriptions failed to win universal assent, it was widely understood that a vote for Thatcher was a repudiation of Labour, its policies and its particular approach to governance.

If the recognition of Labour's failure was widespread both outside and inside the party, the internal debate was nonetheless on balance neither sociologically insightful nor politically helpful. The left was unusually bitter, but became fixed on what it regarded as the betrayals by the party leadership and thus focused on so-called 'constitutional' issues that were a code, and a recipe, for fratricidal war. As people like Tony Benn saw it, the social analysis of the party's weakness – 'wet sociological pessimism', he once labelled it – failed to get at the main problem.[11] Labour, the left insisted, had in place a fundamentally correct programme that could meet the mounting economic crisis and begin the transition to socialism, but its leaders lacked the will to fight for it and to make it happen. The Wilson and Callaghan governments had been essentially duplicitous, appearing to agree with party policy but repeatedly avoiding implementing the programme while in office. Instead, they listened to the constraining voices of Treasury officials, paid too much heed to the whims of the financial markets, and let themselves be deflected from their purpose in a futile pursuit of investor confidence. The lesson was obvious: Labour's representatives in Parliament, and the leadership especially, must be made accountable to 'the movement', however defined. For more than two years after the historic defeat of 1979, the left would preoccupy itself with internal party reforms designed to ensure compliance with the party's programme. It was an odd, if understandable, fixation that failed to engage with the deeper roots of the previous Labour government's failures and with the need to redefine not only Labour's message and policies but also its historic attachments and outlook.

The left's stance was also somewhat disingenuous in that it assumed that it was feasible to carry out the party's radical programme while lacking any serious mandate from the electorate and, for a long period, even a parliamentary majority, and in the teeth of an international economic slowdown brought on by the massive increase in the price of oil. Years later, Benn might concede this and claim that what he really wanted back then was for Wilson and Callaghan to lead and to 'educate' the public, and in this way to begin winning support for radical policies.[12] But in the aftermath of the 1979 defeat the talk was not about education but about betrayal. The position of Callaghan's critics also ignored the extent to which they themselves participated in all the government's decisions and had had their say in critical debates – e.g. on the IMF loan and the alternative economic strategy – and how involved they had been in drafting the 1979 manifesto, even if they were forced to give way to Callaghan on key issues.[13]

Most important, they ignored the fact that their own policies committed them to just the sort of corporatist pattern of governance that had failed Wilson, Callaghan and the Cabinets they led. The preference for corporatism was widely shared by left and right and it was the entire Labour Party that had decided that the defeat in 1970 had stemmed from the feud with the trade unions and that the relationship needed to be repaired. The response was the social contact, proposed and fully supported by Benn, Foot and other spokesmen of the left but actually bargained out by Wilson and Callaghan, and implemented faithfully by a not very left-wing Cabinet. The social contract was the apotheosis of corporatism, of Labour's stance as the party of the trade unions whose first duty was the defence of working-class interests as defined and represented by the unions. By a similar logic, the one genuinely new item on Labour's agenda in the 1970s – industrial democracy – drew support from the left and the right and it, too, was envisioned as working only in and through the trade unions.[14] Not just the Labour right, then, but the left as well put the unions at the centre of their vision of a just society; and virtually everyone in the Labour Party regarded it as right and proper that the unions should have a special role to play in setting the goals of the Labour Party and the priorities of Labour in power. It was corporatism ennobled and raised to the level of a political philosophy *and* a historic necessity. The left was certainly more committed to socialist advance beyond, but also through, corporatism than were their comrades and rivals on the centre-right. But for both the left and the right, advance would come only after the defence of what already existed on the ground in the factories, mines and offices where unions functioned in the everyday.

The implication of the entire Labour Party in the corporatist approach to governance meant that effective critique had to come largely from outside. It is true that Tony Benn spoke passionately in favour of democracy and against the creeping authoritarianism of British government and claimed explicitly that he was against 'corporatism' and the 'corporate state', by which he meant the practice of enlisting the unions to deliver the compliance of their members to incomes policies worked out from on high. But he never seems to have questioned the right of the unions to veto government policy on incomes or on matters quite unrelated to wages, prices and jobs.[15] On the right, Roy Jenkins came a bit closer to a fundamental criticism, arguing in his famous Dimbleby Lecture of November 1979 that 'the idea that the British people want a trade-union-dominated and -nominated government on top of the power the unions today exercise at the work place is far from the truth'.[16] Still, Jenkins had long been associated with governments that behaved quite in the fashion he now opposed and the social-democratic alternative to which he soon attached himself represented a continuation, rather than a reversal, of the approach that had distinguished recent Labour governments. Equally important, voices like his were increasingly marginal to the debate within the Labour Party.

Almost by default, then, a more basic criticism of Labour's corporatist style of rule was left to the Conservatives. Thatcher, and her mentor Keith Joseph, had effectively used their time in opposition to hammer out and articulate a thoroughgoing criticism of the statist and corporatist biases of past Labour and Conservative regimes alike.[17] Their aim was partly to consolidate their position among fellow Tories and partly a partisan attack. It was also part of an effort to provide an intellectual underpinning to a policy of disengagement, in which government would retreat from its responsibility for economic management geared towards maintaining full employment and would sharply limit its commitments to spending on social protections. The 'winter of discontent' seemed a fitting confirmation of their arguments, and they could cite the self-evident failures of the effort to coordinate social and economic policy with the unions in the more narrowly partisan game of attacking the Labour government and its trade union allies.

In January 1979, for example, Thatcher would give an interview to *The Observer* in which she combined a demagogic antipathy to the trade unions with a genuine understanding of the debilitating effects of corporatist practices.[18] She sharply contrasted her overall objective with that of Labour: 'My goal was, and is, not the extension but the limitation of government; the goal of the Labour party is all-pervasive government.' But, she proceeded,

> Limitation of government doesn't make for a weak government – don't make that mistake. If you've got the role of government clearly set out, then it means a very strong government *in that role*. Very strong indeed. You weaken government if you try to spread it over so wide a range that you're not powerful where you *should* be because you've got into areas where you *shouldn't* be.

The corporatist bargaining that brought government involvement into the very details of wage negotiation in this view weakened the authority of government and put it in thrall to forces that were fundamentally irresponsible: the unions. 'We said the unions must be responsible and realistic because they have such great power. They must use their power responsibly, otherwise it will be taken away.' In a clear reference to the strikes then gripping the nation, she went on to say that 'I don't know of any idea or ideal in trade unionism in a free society which implies that one group is entitled to hold the rest of the nation to ransom by threats, so that the country degenerates into a running tribal warfare between competing trade union groups.' Even before taking office, Thatcher met with trade unionists and made clear that her views were different. As Len Murray of the TUC would later recall, 'We were horrified . . . Conservative leaders have always been able to recognise a vested interest when they saw one. But she did not seem keen on institutions, whether it be the TUC, the CBI, Whitehall or even the City of London.'[19] Thatcher's arguments allowed the Conservatives to begin preparing for a break with the policy of consultation and consensus-building that had characterised all post-war governments. In place of consensus would come conviction, and the central convictions were that the role of government had to be rethought and redefined and that 'trade union power' would have to be dealt with.

It was unfortunate for Labour that the critique of corporatism came from outside, for it meant that it had to be wrong and so could be safely ignored. Still worse, Thatcher's critique was accompanied by policies transparently aimed at curbing the power of the unions. In the context, the only appropriate response was defence, and resolute defence precluded reform. Thatcher in this sense pushed Labour into defending what was to many indefensible and helped to freeze Labour into a posture of almost blind resistance and an adamant refusal to engage in reflection and reorientation. It is always hard to turn around an institution with such a long history and rich tradition as the Labour Party. The context of opposition and factional strife that defined the first years of the Thatcher government compounded the difficulty and rendered the project nearly impossible.

What Labour could and did do, however, was to pursue the arguments dividing it to a logical, if tragically counter-productive, conclusion. If the disagreements within the party had been merely over policy, the outcome might have been less dramatic, but policy differences had become inextricably linked to the question of the institutional arrangements that had long given Labour its unique definition. And since authority and office were won or lost within the party's institutions, it was also a struggle for power. Labour's defining character trait and often its greatest strength had been that it was more than a party, that it was the embodiment of a set of interests that existed prior to, and outside of, politics and whose key manifestation was the trade union movement. The party itself was a uniquely appropriate institution that allowed the trade union interest to predominate, but also to coexist with interests that were more ideological and hence less socially rooted. Party activists were thus often middle class, and an ability to wield the rhetoric of socialism was essential to party leadership. But the unions had a special and unrivalled place in the party – a position recognised by their role in constituency organisations, on the National Executive and especially at conference, where union block votes constituted fully 90 per cent of the total. Secure in their representation throughout the party, the unions had nevertheless long deferred to the parliamentary party on matters of high politics and had not interfered with the choice of leader, the appointment of ministers and shadow ministers, or the perquisites of MPs. There was in fact a major constitutional fudge involved in the arrangement, for in theory the party in Parliament was committed to the policies agreed at conference and to the detailed supervision of the executive (NEC). In practice, the Parliamentary Labour Party had been left largely to its own devices.

The relatively comfortable relationship that had long prevailed between the party leadership and the 'labour movement' had not proved capable of surviving the challenge of governing in the 1960s and 1970s, however, and it showed itself vulnerable as well to the changing character of local party membership and union activism. To engineer growth in the seemingly stagnant 1960s, both Conservatives and Labour were compelled to enlist the aid of unions and employers in agreeing to innovations that might boost productivity and to that end had established institutions like the National Economic Development Council (Neddy), which accorded unions direct access to top leaders of business and government. Labour's planning efforts of 1964–66 had made these contacts even more important and thus conferred upon the unions a right to consultation greater than ever before. When planning failed and was replaced by a more traditional policy of controlling wages so as to stimulate exports, the union connection had become still more important. The unions' collective failure to deliver shop-floor compliance, reflected in their inability to control the shop stewards and unofficial strikes, prompted Labour's leaders to seek a reform of the structure of the unions which provoked, as they might have anticipated, a huge and crippling rift. To heal that wound the party agreed to the social contract, which had further enhanced the influence of the unions in the counsels of government. The role of the unions in making and breaking policies and even governments therefore grew steadily until peaking in the era of the social contract. The enhanced leverage of the trade union movement, however, inevitably rendered its disagreements with the policies of the Wilson and Callaghan governments more visible and damaging; and the multiplication of points of contact and influence served to multiply as well the points of potential antagonism. The gradual shift of unions to the left magnified the danger, and more or less assured that the relationship between the unions, the party and its leaders would become more and more difficult to manage.

The compromise that had long allowed Labour to think of itself and to act as both a social movement and as a party of government was also threatened by the intensified efforts of local party activists to make their voices heard on policy and to enforce compliance from MPs and the party's leaders. Labour activists had always differed from ordinary Labour voters: they were often, though not always, more middle class and literate and interested in politics; they were more committed and tended on the whole to be somewhat more left-wing.[20] They were also relatively impotent, because they were routinely overwhelmed at conference by the block votes of the unions and ignored by MPs in the long stretches between elections. Three factors changed this. First, there was the leftward movement of opinion within the unions. This was a reflection of the growth of local, shop-steward influence *and* of the election of more left-wing trade unionists to national leadership positions. Hugh Scanlon had been chosen to lead the engineering union in 1967, Jack Jones as head of the TGWU in 1969, by which time the miners and post office workers were also led by the left. A new generation of leaders meant that the union block vote was up for grabs and occasionally could be brought behind the more left-wing proposals emanating from the constituencies. Second, the local parties themselves were transformed, unevenly but noticeably, by a stream of new recruits: some were well-educated professionals, often employed in the public sector; at least some were working-class militants who had become active as shop stewards or local union organisers or officials; others were feminists who after some initial hesitations realised that Labour was an appropriate place in which to invest their political energies; and quite a few were part of the new political generation of 1968, veterans of student radicalism and partisans of a 'new left'.[21] A small number of these new members were allied to various Trotskyist sects, like Militant; rather more were in the orbit of the Communist Party; most had no such affiliation. But in general they were not averse to cohabiting with the far left in local parties. Entry by organised factions was facilitated by the decision of the Labour Party annual conference in 1973 to eliminate the list of proscribed organisations and, in effect if not intent, to open the party to new influences.[22] Finally, the left in the constituency parties found extremely effective allies on the National Executive Committee, which ceased to be a mere echo of the leadership and became in the mid-1970s an alternative and a source of criticism. The key figure was, of course, Tony Benn, who rather tendentiously claimed that under the leadership of the left the NEC had become 'a serious centre of socialist thought and criticism, loyal to the government but critical of some of its policies'.[23]

The apparent betrayal of Labour Party policy by the 1974–79 government raised the issue of the leaders' relationship to the 'movement' in a very dramatic fashion and further fuelled efforts to restructure the party. The party's General Secretary, Ron Hayward, was moved to remind the leadership to 'take serious note of what the other parliament says, the parliament of the party outside the House of Commons'.[24] If the labour movement was in this construction sovereign, then it was critical and appropriate to ensure the party's control over its representatives in government. What made this effort to redefine the relationship between leaders and led so successful was the fact that by the late 1970s it was being pushed effectively by organisations dedicated explicitly to the task of 'democratising' the Labour Party. By 1979–80 there were nearly a dozen groups loosely linked in the Rank and File Mobilising Committee, but the two most important were the Campaign for Labour Party Democracy and the Labour Co-ordinating Committee. The Campaign for Labour Party Democracy (CLPD) had been founded in 1973 as a more or less direct response to Harold Wilson's explicit refusal to accept the party programme and was focused rather narrowly on constitutional issues. The Labour Co-ordinating Committee (LCC) was launched in 1978 by close allies of Tony Benn – Michael Meacher and Frances Morrell in particular – and focused its attention on policy.[25] As questions of policy and party organisation inevitably merged in practice, so, too, the groups came together in the aftermath of Labour's 1979 defeat to ensure that the party was restructured in a manner that could guarantee the implementation of the policies of the left.[26]

The CLPD was a unique political phenomenon, an organisation that was run by leaders apparently uninterested in personal advance and willing to devote their energies to decidedly unglamorous efforts – drafting model resolutions, circulating petitions, boning up on arcane procedural rules, attending innumerable meetings to work out tactics, and instructing followers in how to respond to opponents and how to make the arguments needed to win votes. At the core of the CLPD were its founder Vladimir Derer, a Czech immigrant long active in the Labour Party, Vera Derer, Victor Schonfield and Francis Prideaux, who together undertook the task of establishing links with the trade unions, Jon Lansman – a Cambridge graduate soon to be made famous by Denis Healey's charge that he was responsible for disrupting speeches in the 1981 campaign for the deputy leadership, Peter Willsman of NUPE and Andy Harris, GLC representative for Putney and 'meetings organiser' for the organisation. Another key member was Chris Mullin, who would become editor of *Tribune* in 1982. The Campaign was urged on by, and in turn secured substantial support from, the left in Parliament and on the NEC – Benn, Joan Maynard, Jo Richardson, Ernie Roberts, Dennis Skinner, Audrey Wise – and they also secured a modest base among trade unionists. By 1980 over 160 trade unions or union branches had affiliated, along with 17 trades councils. The CLPD also received public support from highly placed union officials like Bernard Dix of NUPE, Bob Wright of the AUEW, Eric Clarke of the Miners, and Jack Dromey and Ron Todd of the TGWU. Financial backing came mostly from these organisations but also from a broad mix of other public and private sector unions.[27] Many of these unions had moderate or right-wing leaders at national level, but lower-level officials who were willing to push hard for a left-wing agenda. Support for constitutional reform grew in particular as trade unionists reacted with anger to the Callaghan government's incomes policies and what they regarded as the apparent failure of the social contract.[28]

The Campaign doggedly pursued three reforms in the structure of the party: mandatory reselection of MPs, election of the party leadership, and control by the party itself – i.e. the NEC – rather than the parliamentary leaders over the manifesto presented to voters at general elections. A proposal to subject all MPs and candidates for Parliament to a regular process of selection or reselection first came to the floor of conference in 1974 and received a surprising 2 million votes; thereafter it was reintroduced repeatedly until it passed by a large margin in 1979. The demand for the election of leader emerged first as an insistence that the leadership be elected by the party conference. Seeing that as unwinnable, the CLPD switched to various proposals for an electoral college. After complex manoeuvring and bargaining, that proposal was accepted in principle at the 1980 conference. A plan to set up an electoral college in which the unions would cast 40 per cent of the votes, the constituency parties 30 per cent and the parliamentary party 30 per cent was approved at a special conference at Wembley in January 1981 where, as one commentator wryly observed, 'the trade union block voted for the predominance of the trade union block vote'.[29] The effort to wrest control of the manifesto from the exclusive control of the leaders failed by a narrow margin, but the principle that conference decisions be incorporated in the appeal to electors was registered strongly, and it was fully and dutifully implemented in the run-up to the 1983 election.

Success was bought at a steep price, however, and the political costs would burden the party for at least the next three elections. There was first and foremost the split within the party that led to the founding of the Social Democratic Party. In addition, the triumph of the left on matters of organisation, which was celebrated as a victory for party democracy, was widely perceived outside the ranks of Labour as a violation of democracy. A plausible case could be made that Labour's constitutional fudge had long deprived the party as a whole of its proper influence and that deference to the parliamentary leadership by the party organisation rendered MPs and Labour governments unaccountable and irresponsible. Certainly, the idea that the party's electoral platform would be approved by the party itself was hardly revolutionary. Nor was the principle of re-selection or the demand that the leader be elected by the party rather than simply its representatives in Parliament. Socialist and social-democratic parties in other democratic nations followed such practices as a matter of routine. However, the context within which constitutional change was achieved within the Labour Party could be, and often was, construed as something other than an advance for democracy. Two factors were critical: first, the exceptional role played in the party by trade unions; and second, the unrepresentative character of local party organisation. Labour looked bad and undemocratic whenever public attention was focused upon the role of the block vote and the men who wielded it; and despite some misgivings, by the 1970s and 1980s the left was largely content to leave that in place. Having begun to win conference votes based on union support, the left chose to ignore the fact that the unions' role was arbitrary and fundamentally indefensible and to forget the principled objections of the Labour left before 1960. On the contrary, it developed a rhetoric in which the decisions of conference, where the block vote was utterly dominant, were treated as nearly sacred. And when it came to specifying who would cast votes in the electoral college set up to choose party leaders, the left was happy to grant the unions 40 per cent, or even 50 per cent, of the total.

So the most basic flaw in the informal constitution of the party was glossed over and instead the left concentrated on enhancing the power of constituency parties, both in the electoral college and in the process of parliamentary selection. Members of constituency parties represented but a small fraction of Labour supporters, however, and their views were not necessarily typical. To accord them a greater role, the left had argued, would lead to increased membership, and to greater input into policy and the recruitment and selection of candidates for office. It thus should not have offended democratic sensibilities. But to accord local activists the dominant role, and to privilege their opinions over ordinary Labour voters, who were ultimately responsible for electing MPs, was presumptuous and provocative. Again, what was most significant was what was not done. Just as the left conveniently ignored the question of rethinking the role of the unions, so it ignored the possibility of some sort of primary system through which the ordinary Labour voters would be given a say in candidate selection. More pointedly, it rejected the principle of 'one man, one vote'. In the context of what was possible and indeed necessary, therefore, the left's proposals for democratising the party could easily be portrayed as another cynical attempt to entrench a particular point of view and to impose it on those who disagreed.

The constitutional victory of the left thus served in critical respects to undermine the party's historic claim to be the party of the people, the party of democracy. Indeed, Labour would in practice cede the issue to Mrs Thatcher, who practised an unaccustomed populism – an 'authoritarian populism', as Stuart Hall would argue persuasively – but an effective populism nonetheless.[30] The conduct and outcome of Labour's internal battles over party structure were increasingly seen as evidence of intolerance, conformity and a narrowing of the range of permissible opinion in a party that had long been characterised by a vigorous tradition of dissent, a tradition that historically had sustained the left when it could muster very few actual votes. Now it seemed that the left was unwilling to give the same rights to its opponents. Proof of this undoubtedly one-sided picture seemed to be provided by the spectacle of the secession by the so-called 'gang of four' and the founding of the Social Democratic Party. The presence of the Social Democrats as a supposedly 'sensible' and centrist alternative to Labour and to the Conservatives was to prove essential to Margaret Thatcher's ability to win three successive victories and hence to the consolidation of the Thatcherite project. The birth of the Social Democratic Party was a decisive setback for Labour. But the exit of the right produced few tears and few regrets from the left when it happened in early 1981. Indeed, when what was then merely the 'gang of three' published their Open Letter on 1 August 1980 denouncing the left and adumbrating the possibility of a third party, Stuart Holland responded that 'If they think they will have a damaging effect by leaving, they are wrong.'[31]

The 'gang of three' – David Owen, Shirley Williams and William Rodgers – would become four when joined by Roy Jenkins upon his return from Brussels. The 'gang of four' were stalwarts of the Labour right and all had served in Cabinet. Had Labour somehow won the election of 1979, they would probably have been in government yet again. But since the early 1970s, they and other MPs on the right of the party had become increasingly isolated and they found themselves regularly at odds with the party programme. As Shirley Williams candidly admitted in her letter of resignation, she had fought within the party for years, but 'We have almost always been defeated and we have been defeated by larger and larger majorities as the years have gone by. I see no prospect that that will change.'[32] Williams, Owen and Rodgers were at odds with the majority on virtually all key issues: they had no sympathy for the 'alternative economic strategy' or the policies of widespread state intervention it pre-supposed; they were committed to protecting the welfare state but also alert to the need for, or at least to demands for, fiscal responsibility and lower taxes; they were committed to Europe and frustrated at Labour's turn against it; and they would soon find themselves in especially strong disagreement with the left's defence policies as well. What really drove them to exit the party, however, was the series of constitutional reforms that threatened to make them irrelevant. They grasped intuitively that if MPs could be sacked by their constituency parties, they would in all likelihood lose their seats in Parliament. Moreover, if the voice of MPs in the selection of party leader was reduced to a mere 30 per cent of the total, the chance of choosing someone from the centre-right of the party would be virtually nil and their minority status would become perman-ent. The restructuring of the party meant that the 'gang' and their allies could no longer envision a future within a party that was being forced to become more uniformly left-wing. Careerism and principle converged, a powerful mix that produced a decisive break.

The occasion for the defection was well chosen, even if the decision had been taken some time before. The 1980 conference had approved mandatory reselection of MPs and parliamentary candidates and accepted a proposal to establish an electoral college to choose the leadership. A decision on its precise composition, however, had been put off until a special conference to be held at Wembley on 24 January 1981. Callaghan, who was already without real authority since the 'winter of discontent' and his defeat at the hands of Mrs Thatcher, had failed to forestall these changes. Instead, he had reluctantly accepted the idea of an electoral college at a fateful meeting of the Commission of Enquiry on Party Organisation at Bishop's Stortford in June 1980 and in the process signalled his inability to fight on. His last and rather defiant act was to resign as leader in November 1980 and so provide the parliamentary party with a brief window in which it could select a new leader without the intrusion of the electoral college. Denis Healey was the logical successor and probably commanded more genuine political support among MPs, but victory went instead to Michael Foot. Foot was the more popular personally and he was seen as far more likely to unify the party than the combative and at times bullying Healey.[33] But it was precisely Foot's role as a mediator within the party that incapacitated him as a possible leader for the nation. Simon Hoggart, the sketch-writer, noted right away that Foot, so persuasive in Parliament, was a surprisingly 'rotten performer on television': 'His anxiety to address himself to all sections of the Labour Party prevents him from addressing himself to the electorate, which must occasionally feel like an onlooker in some obscure family quarrel.'[34] If only it had been so obscure.

The election of Foot, whose tenure was to usher in a further period of electoral decline, represented yet another victory for the left and made the founding of a third party almost inevitable.[35] The final break came in January, when the 'gang of four' responded to the Wembley decision with the so-called Limehouse Declaration of 25 January 1981, announcing the formation of a new Council for Social Democracy. A full-page advertisement in *The Guardian*, published on 5 February, was signed by a hundred supporters and drew an enthusiastic response. Buoyed by utterly fantastic opinion polls, the Council became the Social Democratic Party on 26 March 1981; before the end of the year 26 Labour MPs and one Conservative had signed on. For the next several years the spectre of the SDP, soon in alliance with the Liberals, would hang over the electoral system and threaten to transform it. Its poll numbers would soar, slump and soar again and at two successive general elections it would siphon often a quarter or more of the vote from the two major parties, adding an element of instability that made outcomes unpredictable. The main practical impact of the new party would be to detach Labour from centrist voters and to reduce the share of the total vote needed to ensure the Tories successive victories, but that was not yet known in the spring of 1981. The SDP, and later the Alliance, would ultimately fail to break the mould in which British politics was set, but the venture would have important long-term effects nonetheless. It would create more space for ideas and constituencies that lacked sufficient voice in the two main parties. The centrist parties were more open to women, for example, and to women's issues; they were more willing to feature environmental concerns; and they effectively placed a range of constitutional issues permanently on the political agenda.[36] The Tories could perhaps afford to ignore these issues and the groups backing them; Labour could not and so would be forced to respond. Most important, the centrist alternative would eventually force Labour back in that direction. The effect then was to begin to recast the mould of centre-left politics, though the process was to be protracted.

In the meantime, the intense bitterness of the constitutional struggle would continue to divide left from right, to begin also to pull apart relationships within both left and right and to produce what many experienced as a truly poisonous atmosphere throughout the Labour Party. On the right, the growing recognition by the 'gang of three' that it would be necessary to fight or to leave divided them from potential allies who could not contemplate a break. Even before the decision to leave had been made, the future leaders of the SPD fell out with people like Callaghan, Healey and Hattersley, who were charged with having failed to give effective leadership in the internal battles over policy and party structure. After initial puzzlement and hesitation, for example, the right had settled upon the principle of one man, one vote (OMOV, as it was labelled) as the only viable counter to the demands of the left for mandatory reselection and an electoral college, and the only alternative that might rally support. But Callaghan had already conceded the argument by agreeing to a compromise in June 1980 and Healey and Hattersley had done little to protest. The subsequent contest for party leader was similarly an occasion for dissension. Healey waged a dispirited campaign, but then responded to his loss to Foot by agreeing immediately to become deputy leader and pledging his loyalty to the team. The right thus splintered first over whether and how to resist the left; later, they turned against one another over whether to join the SDP. To those who left Labour and joined the Social Democrats, every like-minded person who chose to stay was an embarrassment; for those who stayed, their prior associations with people who were now traitors and wreckers undermined their position within the ranks of the party.

But the left fared no better. The 'outside left' centred on the CLPD was suspicious not only of MPs and the parliamentary leadership, but also of an older Labour left who had remained content to play the role of loyal opposition. The newer left played to win and proof of that was their determination to follow up victories over policy with structural and procedural reforms designed to guarantee compliance. More established figures like Barbara Castle, Ian Mikardo and, especially, Michael Foot, thus had a rough time with the rank-and-file militants; and they were in turn suspicious and resentful of Tony Benn, the 'outside left's' insider. Hence Castle's lack of sympathy when Benn was moved from Industry to Energy by Wilson in 1975 and the increasingly bitter estrangement of Foot and Benn. For his part, Mikardo worked closely with the left on matters of policy and he would support Benn's campaign for the deputy leadership in 1981, but he was less adamant on issues of structural reform. In 1978, for example, he fashioned a compromise that called for a two-stage reselection process in which a vote of no confidence in the sitting MP would be required before a local party could go on to select a new candidate. His allies on the left regarded the effort with distrust and antipathy. Efforts to engineer compromise solutions to disagreements within the party were regularly denounced and in the process antipathies were aroused even among allies. A classic example was the experience of the Commission of Enquiry pushed so assiduously by David Basnett of the GMWU and appointed by the NEC. Though the commission would decide that, 'in the absence of consensus', it would 'make no recommendation' on constitutional issues, it nevertheless furthered the cause of the left by demonstrating the wide support their proposed changes commanded.[37] The committee was in fact dominated by the left – at least by Benn's informed and careful count – and its proposals, argumentation and evidence largely ratified the left's achievements. Indeed, Callaghan had got himself in considerable trouble by seeming to acquiesce to the compromises that began to emerge from the committee's deliberations. Nevertheless, the activists of the Campaign for Labour Party Democracy were sharply critical and fearful of the outcome of the exercise, and in response they joined with other left and 'far left' groups to set up yet another organisation, the Rank and File Mobilising Committee. Its goal was to oppose compromise and to press for the full complement of reforms: mandatory reselection, NEC control of the manifesto, and an electoral college with a much-diminished role for the parliamentary party.[38] Politics conducted in this spirit further polarised and embittered the debate over the fate of the Labour Party.

As new leader Foot would therefore inherit a party more fractured and factionalised than ever before in its history. It was the problem that would define his leadership and he never came close to solving it. Foot had long been the most articulate voice of the left in Parliament and he was extremely popular outside as well. Foot was also very close to union leaders like Jack Jones and in practice served as their watchdog and representative within the government of 1974–79. Nevertheless he had served *in* that government and, unlike Benn, chose not to dissociate himself from either its successes, more visible before 1979 than after, or its failures. He was above all committed to maintaining party unity and to that end would work with both left and right. For this stance he inevitably incurred the enmity of the left, who demanded far greater consistency. His willingness to have Denis Healey as his deputy was met with suspicion by the left and they took the appointment of a Shadow Cabinet drawn largely from the right of the parliamentary party as a further portent of the ultimate failure of Foot's efforts to preserve party unity: 'The illusion of reconciliation is over. Michael Foot cannot bridge the gap between this Shadow Cabinet and the rank and file of the party', declared the chair of the CLPD.[39] Foot's compromise plan for an electoral college system, according to which the PLP would get half the votes, also got nowhere. Most important, his recurring pleas for party unity went unheeded. When, for example, in March 1981 he desperately begged Tony Benn not to challenge Healey for the deputy leadership, Benn found the argument not 'very credible' and proceeded to run.[40]

The contest in 1981 between Benn and Healey aptly summarised the state of division within the party and, of course, further exacerbated it.

To Benn and his supporters, the election of Foot and then Healey was a deliberate effort to pre-empt the electoral college and to reverse the 1980 conference decision on the election of leader. Benn understood that Foot's popularity precluded a direct challenge, but he could argue plausibly that it made no sense to have a leader more or less committed to party policy and a deputy leader utterly opposed to it. As Mikardo pointed out in supporting Benn, 'Denis Healey's policies are anathema to much of the party and have been rejected by conference.' Benn's adviser Valerie Wise put the issue more forcefully when she admitted that the aim was a thoroughgoing purge of the previous leadership: speaking of Healey and Hattersley, she said that 'the sooner they go the better because the trouble with those people is that they are very much identified with the last Labour government and with previous Labour governments who betrayed the working people of this country . . . I have a gut feeling that we're not going to get rid of all the people who should leave.'[41] Clearly, Foot's exhortations about the need for unity were not being heard. Throughout the summer and early autumn of 1981 Labour was consumed with the deputy leader election. At the outset, Benn doubted his chances but as the struggle wore on, he gained increasing support, and by the eve of the actual vote, he detected around him and began to share in 'a sense of confidence . . . which I have never had before'.[42] In the final count, Healey won by a fraction of a percentage point.

Benn's impressive result was probably the high point of the left's influence in the party, but he had also succeeded in alienating many potential allies. Just weeks before announcing his intention to run, for example, Benn had joined the Tribune Group of MPs, but immediately managed to anger his new comrades by refusing to listen to their advice not to run. Robin Cook, a young and promising man of the left, helped to draw up a letter to Mikardo urging a collective discussion about the possibility of a challenge to Healey, but Benn issued a pre-emptive press release early the next morning, before the proposal could be aired. The effect was to head off a discussion in which Benn would surely have been told by colleagues on the left to desist from the challenge to Healey. Appropriately, it was the 'soft left' in Parliament whose refusal to support Benn cost him the election. A key figure was Neil Kinnock. Kinnock was a rising star on the left who had already aroused suspicion by casting a deciding vote on the NEC to defer a decision on control of the manifesto

– a move characterised as 'a significant crime' by Jon Lansman of the CLPD – and who now led a group of MPs to abstain on the second and critical ballot and, in the event, throw the election to Healey. Kinnock's betrayal made him the target of an effort to deny him a place on the Executive in 1982, an effort that nearly succeeded.[43] Eventually, the disenchantment and alienation of people like Foot, Cook and Kinnock would come back to haunt the left; as of the 1981 conference, the effect was merely to highlight Labour's divisions for the viewing public.

Debates over policy and constitutional arrangements within Labour abated somewhat after the contest over the deputy leadership. Top party and trade union leaders met – again at the ASTMS retreat at Bishop's Stortford – in January 1982 and David Basnett announced afterwards that 'Peace has broken out in the Labour Party.'[44] But the peace was an uneasy compromise on terms that were largely unworkable and it gave way inevitably to periodic outbursts of anger and resentment. The left had conquered a great deal of territory, and even if its advance had slowed, it remained powerfully entrenched. Its opponents, both centre-right and so-called 'soft left', might have begun to regroup, but progress was slow and halting and had to take into account the new institutional power of the left. The result was a series of inconclusive skirmishes, several false starts, many close votes, repeated posturing, but no fundamental alteration of course until well after the next general election defeat.

At the 1981 party conference, for example, an important shift had been registered in the trade union stance and on the NEC. A new though still secret alliance of centre-right union leaders organised to secure the election of a new NEC on which the left would no longer command an automatic majority. The effort was led by the St Ermin's Group, named for the hotel in which they met, and included Terry Duffy, Scanlon's successor in the AUEW (engineers), Sid Weighell of the railwaymen (NUR), Bill Sirs of the steelworkers (ISTC), Bryan Stanley of the Post Office Engineering Union (POEU) and his deputy, John Golding, also an MP, and Frank Chapple of the electricians.[45] Golding was the main organiser, working closely with Roger Godsiff and John Spellar. Despite this realignment, however, NEC committees would continue to be dominated by the left – a concession by Foot aimed at securing party unity. But the left would lose two more seats in 1982 and the right-wing, or self-styled 'moderate', members of the NEC proceeded systematically to remove Benn and Eric Heffer from the chairmanships of the Home Policy and the Organisation Sub-committees respectively. Even before that, the party leadership and the NEC had begun to mount a counter-attack on what it regarded as the undemocratic and extra-parliamentary, if not anti-parliamentary, left. In the House of Commons Michael Foot was provoked in December 1981 into denouncing Peter Tatchell, the recently selected Labour candidate for Bermondsey. Tatchell was gay, more or less openly so; he had spoken forcefully of the need for 'extra-parliamentary struggles to carry out a left-wing programme' and had written a piece in *London Labour Briefing* arguing that

> Debates and parliamentary divisions are fruitless cosmetic exercises
> given the Tories' present Commons majority. And if we recognise this,
> we are either forced to accept Tory edicts as a *fait accompli* or we must
> look to new more militant forms of extra-parliamentary opposition
> which involve mass participation and challenge the Government's right
> to rule.[46]

Foot repudiated Tatchell's views, but made the mistake of saying that he was not and would never be 'an endorsed member' of the party. In fact, he had been a member for some time and was already selected as a candidate. Foot was forced to amend his statement but, having made his position clear, he felt compelled to stick to it and in December 1981 convinced the NEC not to endorse Tatchell's candidacy.

At the same meeting the Executive also voted to begin an inquiry on the Trotskyist Militant Tendency. Tatchell was not a member of Militant, neither were most of the activists in the Campaign for Labour Party Democracy or other groups causing trouble for the leadership. But just as a relatively small number of activists were often able to play a role in constituency parties out of proportion to their numbers, so Militant could, with modest numbers but discipline and coordination, play a disproportionately large role in local parties across the country. So while its significance was often exaggerated, it was not entirely without impact; more important, it came to symbolise the efforts and the politics of the 'hard' or 'outside left' more generally. And while that identification was partly unfair, it is also the case that by the early 1980s Militant and similar sects were participating fully in coalitions – e.g. the Rank and

File Mobilising Committee – that had the effect of blurring the distinctions between various 'lefts', hard versus soft, inside versus outside, those who accepted the parliamentary road to socialism and those who did not.

There had been an earlier inquiry into Militant undertaken by Reg Underhill, Labour's national agent, in 1975 and he had concluded then that Militant was indeed a party within a party. The NEC, however, voted not to publish the report and not to act on it, prompting Underhill to leak it to the press after his retirement in 1979. Foot was himself directly involved in the decision to bury Underhill's report, but by late 1981 he too had come around to the position that Militant was indeed a threat. Its local power bases, especially in Liverpool, were too important for the leadership not to intervene and the issue of Militant's presence in the party had become closely intertwined with the question of extra-parliamentary resistance. The resulting inquiry concluded that Militant was indeed more than a newspaper and, in fact, was a 'well-organised caucus centrally controlled' with 'its own programme and policy' and hence 'in conflict with . . . the Party constitution'. Its report called for groups wishing 'to be recognised and to operate within the party' to register. The clear intention was to use the registration process to deny access to revolutionary groups like Militant on the grounds that their aims were incompatible with the party constitution. In July letters were sent to unaffiliated organisations asking them to register, a policy approved subsequently by the 1982 conference. Unfortunately for the party leadership, Militant responded in a very clever fashion. In a letter sent to the party's national organiser on 16 October 1982, the group refused to apply for registration because the request, when sent out, had yet to be approved by conference. It further claimed it was not an organisation with members and discipline but merely a newspaper; and it claimed, in addition, that the NEC's attempt to expel it was unconstitutional.[47] The party's lawyers and the courts agreed and effectively abandoned the effort to use the proposed register to get rid of Militant. Instead, the NEC was forced to adopt the far less attractive expedient of declaring Militant a proscribed organisation – an action they could take legally – and then, after further disputation and uncertainty over determining its membership, proceeded in February 1982 to expel the five people listed as editors of the newspaper, none of whom happened to be from Liverpool.[48]

It was a very modest gain for so much effort and demonstrated the difficulties that even a determined leader – and Foot was not one – would face in any effort to reorient the party. The question of registration nonetheless did serve to sow divisions within the left: the Campaign for Labour Party Democracy, for example, split bitterly over whether to register and decided by a narrow margin to do so. The majority reasoned that conference had, after all, approved the new rule and conference decisions were in their view supreme. The Tribune Group chose to register as well, although the decision prompted key resignations. A dispute over the editorial policies of the group's newspaper produced a further row and yet more dissension within the left. Chris Mullin, a long-time member of CLPD and close ally of Tony Benn's, had been appointed editor of *Tribune* in May 1982, but his attacks on the caucus's ineffectual policies angered long-time members and provoked an effort by the paper's shareholders to remove the staff-appointed directors and replace them with directors willing to control Mullin's alleged excesses. Foot was called upon to mediate and a compromise was worked out, but again the differences within the party, and in this case within the left, had been fought out in full public view.[49]

If the left were on the defensive over Militant and gradually losing their domination over the National Executive after 1981, their influence remained undiminished in the local parties, at conference and at party headquarters. Ron Hayward, Geoff Bish and other staff members were largely in sympathy with the left, even if they did not agree on the full programme and were willing to countenance the proscription of Militant.[50] These party officials had been deeply alienated from the Callaghan government for supposedly ignoring party policy in making decisions and, even more, for the leadership's reluctance even to put forward party policy in the manifesto. Bish complained in 1979, for example, that the NEC and the party apparatus had been treated by the government as 'a mere pressure group, just one among many. The outcome of our numerous delegations, representations, statements and resolutions was thus little different from those of many other pressure groups: a few minor successes, perhaps, but little of real substance in the way of changing the *direction* of Government policy.'[51] The creation and adoption of the 1979 manifesto was seen as the ultimate rebuke. Staff at party headquarters had worked for years on a prospective document, but at the last minute Callaghan's Downing Street advisers produced their own version without any consultation. Bish regarded the new version as 'appalling. Not only did it ignore entire chapters of Party policy: it overturned and ignored many of the agreements . . . laboriously hammered out within the NEC-Cabinet Research Group.' Callaghan's draft prevailed nevertheless, with only minor amendment, and confirmed the fundamental 'unwillingness of the Labour Government to concede to the Party any real measure of . . . joint control in terms of policy or strategy'.[52]

Hayward was likewise moved by the conduct of the Callaghan government into abandoning the traditionally neutral stance of a party official and joining instead in the recriminations that so marked the 1979 conference. His public criticism followed closely the arguments made by the left: 'we did not . . . select, raise the money, work to send an M.P. to the House of Commons to forget whence he came and whom he represents . . .'. Hayward then turned ominously on those threatening to leave the party to tell them that they could easily be replaced: 'I have got a queue a mile long that wants to go to the House of Commons.' Still more pointedly, at least from the point of view of the leadership, he argued that 'if it is going to be said . . . that we lost the election because of the winter of discontent . . . you have got to ask the first question: why was there a winter of discontent? Because the Cabinet, supported by M.P.s, ignored Congress and Conference decisions . . .'[53]

Even as the left's majority on the NEC slipped away, therefore, the staff at headquarters remained committed to the policies argued out and adopted over the previous decade. And it was they who would be primarily responsible for putting together *Labour's Programme 1982*, which contained the numerous pledges later incorporated in the 1983 election manifesto. The lingering resentment over the drafting of the 1979 manifesto encouraged the party leadership to acquiesce, though more cynical calculations were at work as well. Golding, leader of the right on the NEC, thus claimed later that he knew already that the election was lost. If so, he and his allies reasoned, the contest should be fought on the programme of the left so that it would be clear where the responsibility for defeat should be placed. But in fact the right had no real option, for the left's policies still enjoyed strong support and Foot, in particular, was committed to them.

The parliamentary party more broadly, and many in the Shadow Cabinet in particular, were less enthusiastic and Geoff Bish was right to assert that they had been 'bounced into accepting a document they did not want. They did not like the policies and it showed.'[54] The 1983 manifesto was big – 'the longest suicide note in history' according to Gerald Kaufman – and gave more hostages to fortune than any previous manifesto. It largely reiterated the left's commitments to extensive state intervention in the economy, to a revitalised planning effort based on the unabashedly corporatist National Economic Assessment exercise – yet another tripartite process to be agreed between the government, the employers, and the unions – to industrial democracy, to reflation, to devaluation, selective import controls and withdrawal from the Common Market, and to a defence policy based on unilateral disarmament.[55] Foot agreed with most of these commitments, Healey with far fewer. Outside the shadow cabinet Jim Callaghan, the former prime minister, was particularly opposed to the party's unilateralism and publicly denounced the new policy on the eve of the election at a meeting in Cardiff on 25 May. His speech was actively disloyal, but his sentiments were undoubtedly shared by many Labour MPs – and even Foot expressed reservations over details of the party's programme. The leadership would therefore have to fight the election of 1983 on the platform of the left despite the fact that the organisational advance of the left within the party had by that time been checked. That they did so ineffectively was hardly surprising and it was not a betrayal, but an accurate reflection of who they were and what they believed.

The influence of the left within the party had thus been checked and its progress temporarily halted by 1983, but had not been reversed. On the contrary, Labour's shift to the left seemed by 1983 to have become a more or less permanent feature of the political landscape. The repeated efforts of the left had given Labour a set of programmatic commitments that were not easily shed; the party's recent dismal record in government, moreover, produced a widespread belief that any future Labour government would have to govern from the left rather than the centre. The party's new institutional structure, with new procedures for reselection and election of party leader in place, seemed a further guarantee that Labour MPs would in future be of more uniformly left-wing disposition. Labour's position on the political spectrum of British politics was also defined, as always, in large measure by the policies and positions taken up by its opponents. The radicalisation of both Labour and the Tories under Thatcher had left the political centre vacant, but the SDP rushed in and, together with the Liberals, occupied the space where Labour might have made electoral gains. In the near term, the continuing presence of the Alliance made the option of a move towards the centre much less attractive than electoral logic might otherwise have indicated. That would change after 1987, but only then and only slowly.

Even more important was Mrs Thatcher, whose aggressively right-wing policies began to redefine the boundaries and assumptions of politics. The initial impact of Thatcher was paradoxically to force the Labour Party and the trade unions into an oppositional stance from which they could not easily extract themselves – a position that made it extremely difficult for them to adapt and respond to new circumstances. Thatcher had boasted to *The Observer* that 'I'm not a *consensus* politician or a *pragmatic* politician. I'm a *conviction* politician.'[56] Her convictions would bring her government into sharp conflict with the entire tradition of post-war economic and social policy and with the Labour Party: the Tories under Thatcher sought to lower taxes and restrict expenditure to an extent that threatened the institutions of the welfare state – education, social security and even the health service; they renounced the government's commitment to, and responsibility for, full employment, and seemed willing to watch unemployment rise to levels unknown since the 1930s; the government began to privatise the industrial assets which the state had acquired over several generations and in which Labour invested so much hope, and money, and also to sell off the public housing that Labour (and some Tories) had seen as the best means of providing decent housing for the working class; and Thatcher chose not to bargain with, but to attack, the unions whose role in the nation's economic and social life and in the polity Labour had endeavoured to defend and extend.

Thatcher appeared to threaten everything Labour stood for and her broad-based attack necessitated an equally broad and militant defence. Again and again Labour would be moved to call for open and mass opposition. The resulting mobilisations would fall far short of the goal of stopping Tory policy, but the rhetoric of resistance to Thatcher would come to permeate the discourse of the entire Labour movement – left, right and centre. As early as the spring of 1980 the National Executive had produced a fighting document, *Peace, Jobs, Freedom*, and called a conference on 30 May to publicise it and to encourage the fight against Thatcher. As the conference chair, Lena (Baroness) Jeger, explained, 'we called this meeting today because of the deepening crisis in our country – a crisis of worsening unemployment, of soaring inflation, of increasing deprivation for the poorest people and a loss of confidence and hope which threatens the very fabric of our society . . .'. She urged endorsement of the NEC's document and campaign as 'the measure of common ground that unites us in our total condemnation of the worst Government this country has endured since the Thirties'.[57] It was imperative, given the nature, extent and cause of the crisis, to resist and to refuse to accept the policies of the Thatcher government. Ron Todd of the TGWU asked rhetorically, 'Do you really think – and does Maggie Thatcher think – that we are going to acquiesce in the destruction of a trades unions organisation in Britain?'[58] The answer was obviously a resounding no. The TUC had already given much the same answer in 1979, when it called for a massive effort to turn public opinion against Thatcher. It would deliver the same message again at Wembley in early 1982 when it urged unionists not to cooperate with the Tories' new Employment Act.[59]

These clarion calls for resistance to Thatcher were meant to inspire, to rally the troops, but they utilised a language that in effect precluded careful analysis and any effort to re-evaluate past policy. Eventually, Thatcher's demonstrable successes would force Labour and the unions to come to terms with the changes her governments had wrought, but the task in her first term was to stand firm, to fight back and not to accept her victories as inevitable. The logic of resistance was almost irresistible, for Thatcher was still far from achieving victory prior to 1983. Inflation continued to rise after the Conservatives took office, at least for a time, and unemployment also rose steadily. In the midst of the economic crisis of the early 1980s, opinion polls showed massive dissatisfaction with the Thatcher government. To concede prior to the 1983 election would have been premature; in fact, despite the defection of the SDP and the massive bad publicity generated by Labour's internal squabbles, it was still possible to believe that Thatcher's rule would be short-lived. And then, in April 1982, came war in the Falklands, which utterly reversed party fortunes. The Labour Party in Parliament – Michael Foot most prominently, Healey more worriedly, the future leader Neil Kinnock at excessive

length – strongly condemned the Argentinians and supported the sending of troops, but also expressed the hope that the mere threat of military
action would produce a diplomatic solution. On the left of the party, the
newly Bennite *Tribune* explicitly opposed the invasion.[60] When it went
ahead, successfully if controversially, Thatcher began to pull ahead in
the polls. Over the first three quarters of 1981 – the period of most intense
factional strife within Labour – Labour continued to have a slight edge
over the Tories; and the lead actually increased in size from roughly 4.5
per cent to 8 per cent during that time. It then shifted; by early 1982 the
new SPD-Liberal Alliance had pulled slightly ahead of both Labour and
the Tories, with opinion almost evenly balanced between the three. After
that everything changed and the Tories jumped out to a lead of roughly
10 points over Labour and 20 points over the Alliance. Soon the economic numbers began to improve as well. By 1983, Thatcher was ready
to win another term with a handsome parliamentary majority.

Nevertheless, Thatcher's apparent vulnerability prior to the Falklands
was an invitation to maintain, or even step up, resistance to government
policies. Resistance was made still more urgent and compelling by a
growing sense that the government's international policies were
reactionary, immoral and positively dangerous. During the late 1970s
relations between the United States and the Soviet Union had begun to
deteriorate and détente was replaced by what was not unreasonably
termed 'the second cold war'.[61] The Soviet invasion of Afghanistan in
1979 worsened relations still further, and prompted in response a US-led
boycott of the 1980 Olympics. Rather more significant was the NATO
decision to counter the Soviets' new SS-20 missiles by installing a new
generation of nuclear weapons, Pershing and Cruise missiles, across
Europe. The re-escalation of the arms race coincided with increased concern over nuclear power, brought home graphically by the near disaster
at Three Mile Island just outside Harrisburg, Pennsylvania in March
1979. The Campaign for Nuclear Disarmament, largely inactive during
the 1960s and 1970s, quickly revived and led a series of mass marches
that attracted broad support within the Labour Party. Michael Foot was a
regular marcher and speaker; so were Neil Kinnock and Tony Benn. All
three participated in a demonstration in London in June 1980 that drew
80,000. Protest against the new missiles continued to build, culminating
in the famous women's occupation of Greenham Common begun in

September 1981, and in ever bigger mass rallies.[62] Soon after, the Labour Party conference adopted a strongly unilateralist position. The mobilisation against war would continue until the missiles were deployed in 1983 and it would add immeasurably to the feeling within the labour movement that the resistance to Thatcher was a noble and pressing cause. The effect was to reinforce a rhetoric of struggle and polarisation that worked to the advantage of the left and kept at bay efforts to reconcile Labour with the newly-emerging social and electoral realities.

Labour was, it would seem, structurally and ideologically unable to undertake such efforts. It was paralysed by its identity and its institutions. Instead, the party pursued a strategy that gave Margaret Thatcher a victory of historic proportions in June 1983. The Thatcher government was returned with 397 seats to Labour's 209 seats. The Tories had won 42.4 per cent of the vote, while Labour's share was down to a mere 27.6 per cent, just two points ahead of the Alliance of Liberals and Social Democrats. Foot fought valiantly in the campaign, but he was sadly ineffective. He had come under repeated attack from his enemies and his erstwhile friends in Parliament and in the press; at one point the party's General Secretary, Jim Mortimer, had even felt it necessary to announce that 'At the campaign meeting this morning we were all insistent that Michael Foot is the leader of the Labour Party and speaks for the party . . . The unanimous view of the campaign committee is that Michael Foot is the leader.'[63] The leadership had been saddled with a manifesto in which it had little or no faith, and it reaped the fruits of four years of bitter and crippling internal strife that had gripped the party following the disastrous ending of the Labour government of 1974–79. The only good news in 1983 was that it would be difficult for things to get much worse.

The news that truly mattered in 1983, however, was that voters had rendered yet another negative verdict on what Labour had to offer. The effect would be to close off another option, another pathway, for the beleaguered party of the people. In 1970 the electorate – taking its cue from the party itself – repudiated the Wilson government and its strategy of growth through planning, state intervention, technical modernisation and incomes policy. In 1979 the voters, and again much of the party and many union members, had decisively rejected the Callaghan government, with its more defensive corporatism symbolised by the social contract with the unions and, later, with voluntary pay restraint. The policies simply had not worked. In 1983 the party offered something different – a more definitively left-wing programme promising a more interventionist alternative economic strategy, a massive redistribution of wealth, withdrawal from Europe, and a unilateralist, non-nuclear defence strategy. This would involve a fundamental break with NATO and the United States. It produced the worst result since 1931. The varieties of 'Labourism' seemed by 1983 to have been exhaustively explored, debated and dismissed by voters.

Advocates of each of these articulations of Labour Party policy could argue plausibly that their strategy had not been given a fair test and that it should not therefore be abandoned. The 1964–70 governments, it was easily argued, had been blown off course by the balance of payments, by bad advice from the Treasury and the bankers on how to deal with it, by a lack of cooperation from business and finance, and by tactical miscalculation; but all these problems could be rectified next time around. Supporters of Callaghan could argue with equal force that the government had done its best to fulfil the terms of the social contract and done much good as a result. They could say, too, that for a time the government had succeeded in controlling inflation without recourse to mass unemployment, but that ultimately the oil crises and resulting world slump had imposed burdens too great for any regime to bear. The left could and did insist that the defeat of 1983 was not a sign that voters could not be won to a more radical vision but rather a judgement on the divisions in the party and its perceived competence. They could also point to the fact that the Shadow Cabinet transparently did not support the party programme wholeheartedly and so failed to defend it adequately; and they could justifiably complain of Callaghan's disloyalty on defence, expressed in the middle of the campaign. All of these objections and qualifications are reasonable, but they suffer fatally from the counterargument that history is always messy; there are no properly controlled social experiments and no rigorously scientific tests in the real world of politics; and people have to draw conclusions and make choices based on what was, not on what might have been under ideal circumstances.

That is certainly what would happen in the Labour Party, as a new generation willing to challenge both the left and the right began to emerge from the defeats of 1979 and 1983. It was from this cohort of young politicians, who were just beginning to define their futures in terms of the

Labour Party, that the core of what became New Labour began to take shape. Blair's Australian lecture in 1982 was an apt illustration of the response that would inspire the effort to 'modernise' the party and inform the development of New Labour. The lecture was delivered shortly after Blair's by-election defeat at Beaconsfield in May 1982, which had been fought in the middle of the Falklands crisis. As preparation for that contest Blair had visited party headquarters and been thoroughly briefed on policy. He was apparently very unhappy about what he was told and became more unhappy when he sought to defend the party's policies, on defence especially, on the doorstep.[64] The arguments he laid out in Australia were in part a reflection on that experience and revealed a future party leader who was clearly not comfortable signing up with any of the dominant factions and traditions of the party.

Blair was not alone in his experience or his reaction to it; and between 1979 and 1983 those who would inevitably constitute the future of the party were shocked into an understanding that things had to change radically and that neither the old right, nor the established and sensible centre, nor the old or new left had the answer. Thus on the night when the young Gordon Brown was first elected to Parliament, he would be found sitting in his flat 'in front of the telly, utterly dejected. He had just achieved something he'd worked on for a decade, but victory had turned to ashes . . . "It is a bloody disaster"', he commented.[65] This was no moment for rejoicing, or for complacency about the leadership and direction of the party with which he had cast his lot. Another new left veteran, Mo Mowlam, happened to be interviewed in a Channel Four documentary on the 1983 election and confessed to finding herself in 'an untenable position'. Though she approved the manifesto, she agreed that 'We haven't got the electorate to the point of supporting that manifesto. We are in a ridiculous position.' Unlike Benn and others who put the blame elsewhere, she was extremely self-critical and recognised that the party had stopped listening to the voters and needed desperately 'to get back to listening'. She went on: 'It's not a very popular thing to say: on the left, we've pushed a number of things through, we've partly split the party and we haven't taken the electorate with us.'[66] The implication was clear enough.

The experience of defeat, discord and defeat again would have an equally dramatic effect on an extensive roster of young and aspiring politicians and activists. Alastair Campbell, the journalist who later emerged as Blair's key spokesman and the man held mainly responsible for New Labour's excessive 'spinning' of the news, learned the import-ance of effective presentation while chronicling Labour's failures during 1979–83. 'What people don't understand about Alastair', a friend later noted, was 'that he was blooded at a time when Labour was an electoral liability'.[67] The choice to join and work for Labour at such a moment had to be a disenchanted one, and had to be accompanied by a plan to remake it. Peter Mandelson – though, unlike people like Brown or Jack Straw or Mowlam, never really part of the new left – had come to a similar point of despair by 1981, when he told a friend that the likes of them would never get to sit on the Labour benches in the House of Commons. In response, he temporarily gave up politics for the media – a turn that would have ramifications for a long time to come. Straw was first known as a student radical, then went on to work for Barbara Castle and eventually inherited her seat in Parliament. He traced a trajectory very much like Gordon Brown's, from the student left to the 'soft left' to the camp of the mod-ernisers. In 1980 he was heard demanding that the UK immediately leave the Common Market and in 1981 he prominently supported the left's position on the selection of leader. But after Benn's unsuccessful chal-lenge to Healey later that year, Straw came to believe that the left was largely responsible for the party's lack of support from voters. By 1983 he had moved a long way and a perceptive journalist noted that he had already 'become less radical, less impressed by the shrivelled kingdom of a truly Socialist Party, which he and the rest of the left, after having long sought it, are now entering'.[68] The young, 'workaholic' Australian, Patricia Hewitt, moved along the same path at about the same pace. A student radical, then active on behalf of the elderly and women and then a leader of the National Council of Civil Liberties, she attended party conferences in the early 1980s as a highly visible supporter of the left on matters of policy and on issues like mandatory reselection and control of the manifesto. But then she was selected as the party's candidate for Lei-cester East, saw the 1983 election up close, lost, and was appalled and transformed. Her response was to craft a blueprint for restructuring the party and its approach to campaigning and organisation and to send it to the two leading candidates for the leadership – Neil Kinnock and Roy Hattersley.[69] Kinnock and Hattersley might have vastly differing views on policy and programme and on the party's 'aims and values', but it did not matter.[70] They might be the next generation of leaders, but it would be people like Hewitt and her disillusioned but determined cohort who would actually do the work of defining the Labour Party of the future. Hewitt's generation had been decisively shaped by the experiences of 1979–83 and they would in turn reshape the party.

Notes and references

1 On the increasingly sectional character of industrial disputes, see Samuel Beer, *Britain against Itself* (New York: Norton, 1982).

2 Eric Hobsbawm, 'The forward march of Labour halted?', *Marxism Today* (September 1978), reprinted with critiques and responses in Martin Jacques and Francis Mulhern, *The Forward March of Labour Halted?* (London: Verso, 1981), 1–19.

3 See J. Cronin, *Labour and Society, 1918–1979* (London: Batsford, 1984), 199. For a summary of the history of wage controls and their effects on earnings, see Roger Middleton, *Government versus the Market* (Cheltenham: Edward Elgar, 1996), 564–5.

4 Thus the share of social expenditures in public expenditure overall increased slightly during 1974–79. The data come from Middleton, *Government versus the Market*, 506.

5 See John Goldthorpe, *Social Mobility and Class Structure in Modern Britain* (Oxford: Oxford University Press, 1980), which analyses the results from 1972, and *Social Mobility and Class Structure in Modern Britain*, 2nd edn (Oxford: Oxford University Press, 1987), which is based on 1983 data. The interpretation of these results remains controversial. Goldthorpe took pains to argue that despite the high absolute rates of mobility, there were still substantial barriers to equal opportunity in Britain. Peter Saunders, on the other hand, has argued that it is unrealistic to expect much higher rates than those revealed in the study. See Saunders, *Unequal but Fair? A Study of Class Barriers in Britain* (London: IEA, 1996). The arguments are not so contradictory that both cannot be in part correct. Yet another cause of interpretive conflict, of course, is the fact that most social mobility studies are based on data about men and their fathers and do not focus on women. It seems likely that a proper inclusion of women's experience would alter the picture, though it would probably muddy the outcome, for women typically move into intermediate occupations, whatever their parents' backgrounds.

6 OECD, *Labour Force Statistics 1965–1985* (Paris: OECD, 1987), 448–9.

7 *Annual Abstract of Statistics 1981* (London: CSO, 1981).

8 See Patrick Dunleavy, 'The urban basis of political alignment: Social class, domestic property ownership, and state intervention in consumption processes', *British Journal of Political Science*, IX (1979).

9 Kenneth Morgan, *Callaghan: A Life* (Oxford: Oxford University Press, 1997), 502.

10 Hobsbawm, 'Observations on the Debate', in *The Forward March of Labour Halted?*, 169.

11 Benn was referring to the work of Jeremy Seabrook and Trevor Blackwell, of whom he wrote: 'They have been writing a lot of stuff, in effect saying that the Labour Party is finished, the old working-class alliance has gone and working-class consciousness has declined. It is a sort of wet sociological pessimism coming allegedly from the right. They are mesmerised by Thatcher with her messianic message . . .' Benn was rather more impressed with Eric Hobsbawm. See Tony Benn, *The End of an Era: Diaries, 1980–90*, Ruth Winstone, ed. (London: Hutchinson, 1982), entry for 11 November 1982, 251, and, on Hobsbawm, entry for 15 July 1980, 19.

12 Interview with Tony Benn, 30 September 2003.

13 See John Golding, *Hammer of the Left: Defeating Tony Benn, Eric Heffer, and Militant in the Battle for the Labour Party* (London: Politico's, 2003), 82–8; Morgan, *Callaghan*, 686–90.

14 Though left and right agreed on the importance of extending democracy into the workplace, unions were often ambivalent because of the fear that worker directors elected outside the unions, and with non-unionists voting, would undermine trade union claims to speak authoritatively on behalf of the workforce. This rather ultra-left, workerist stance that viewed industrial democracy as class collaboration would be met by agreeing that unions should control and select worker representatives on boards of directors. See the Bullock Report of January 1977 – *Report of the Committee of Inquiry on Industrial Democracy*, Cmnd. 6706 (London: HMSO, 1977) – and the highly critical account in Edmund Dell, *A Strange, Eventful History: Democratic Socialism in Britain* (London: HarperCollins, 1999), 463–6. The widespread support for industrial democracy can be seen in the highly sympathetic analyses offered by Giles Radice, *The Industrial Democrats: Trade Unions in an Uncertain World* (London: Allen & Unwin, 1978), and *Community Socialism* (London: Fabian Society, 1979), Fabian Tract 464.

15 Tony Benn, *Arguments for Socialism* (Harmondsworth: Penguin, 1980), 145–6; 'Tony Benn: An Interview with Eric Hobsbawm', in *The Forward March of Labour Halted?*, esp. 88.

16 See Roy Jenkins, 'Home Thoughts from Abroad', Dimbleby Lecture, 22 November 1979, in Wayland Kennet, ed., *Rebirth of Britain* (London:

Weidenfeld & Nicolson, 1982), 2–29; and Jenkins, *A Life at the Center* (New York: Random House, 1991), 476.

17 Gillian Peele, 'Contemporary Conservatism and the Borders of the State', in Dieter Helm, ed., *The Economic Borders of the State* (Oxford: Oxford University Press, 1989), 153–79.

18 Interview for *The Observer*, 12 January 1979, in Christopher Collins, ed., *Margaret Thatcher: Complete Public Statements on CD-ROM* (Oxford: Oxford University Press, 1999).

19 Len Murray in *The Observer*, 2 September 1984.

20 See Patrick Seyd and Paul Whiteley, *Labour's Grass Roots: The Politics of Party Membership* (Oxford: Clarendon, 1992), esp. 23–4, on studies of the politics of constituency parties. Seyd and Whiteley themselves did a much more extensive survey, but for a later period (1989–90), and demonstrated that although activists were more left-wing than Labour voters, the differences were modest on most issues. Issues on which major differences existed were private education, public spending and (possibly, but not definitively), defence. (211–18)

21 Seyd, *The Rise and Fall of the Labour Left* (New York: St Martin's, 1987), 40–50.

22 *Report of the Labour Party Annual Conference 1973*, 11. See also Eric Shaw, *Discipline and Discord in the Labour Party* (Manchester: Manchester University Press, 1988), 172–7.

23 Benn Interview with Hobsbawm, 84.

24 *Report of the Labour Party Annual Conference 1979*, 191.

25 The two organisations would subsequently take very different paths, with the LCC becoming a base for the 'modernising' wing of the party and moving decisively away from the left. See Paul Thompson and Ben Lucas, *The Forward March of Modernisation: A History of the LCC, 1978–1998* (London: LCC, 1998).

26 See Seyd, *Rise and Fall of the Labour Left*, and David Kogan and Maurice Kogan, *The Battle for the Labour Party* (London: Kogan Page, 1982), on these organisations and their activities.

27 These included the television technicians (ACTT), the white-collar union ASTMS, the Fire Brigades Union (FBU), the printers' union (NATSOPA) and selected branches of the boilermakers and railway engineers (ASLEF), as well as the foundrymen, the major clerical union (APEX), the Post Office Engineering Union (POEW), the National Graphic Association (NGA), the electricians, furniture workers, the construction workers (UCATT), the communication workers (UCW) and the shopworkers (USDAW).

28 Kogan and Kogan, *Battle for the Labour Party*, 41–4.

29 Simon Hoggart, *On the House* (London: Robson, 1981), 128.

30 See Stuart Hall, 'Popular Democratic versus Authoritarian Populism: Two Ways of "Taking Democracy Seriously"' (1980), 123–49, and 'Authoritarian Populism: A Reply to Jessop, et al.' (1980), 150–9, in Hall, ed., *The Hard Road to Renewal* (London: Verso, 1988); and Bob Jessop, Kevin Bonnett, Simon Bromley and Tom Ling, 'Authoritarian populism: Two nations and Thatcherism', *New Left Review*, 147 (September–October, 1984), 32–60.

31 The letter appeared simultaneously in *The Guardian* and the *Daily Mirror*. Holland's remark is quoted in Ivor Crewe and Anthony King, *SDP: The Birth, Life and Death of the Social Democratic Party* (Oxford: Oxford University Press, 1995), 47.

32 Shirley Williams to Ron Hayward, cited in Crewe and King, *SDP*, 98.

33 The contrast in personalities, which worked consistently to Healey's disadvantage, is widely conceded. See, for example, the discussion of the contest by his biographer: Edward Pearce, *Denis Healey: A Life in Our Times* (London: Little, Brown, 2002), 539–42.

34 Hoggart, *On the House*, 148.

35 It has been suggested that Foot's narrow margin was provided by right-wing Labour MPs who might in normal circumstances have voted for Healey but who were actually seeking an excuse to bolt the party. See Crewe and King, *SDP*, 74–5.

36 On the SPD and women, see Anna Coote and Beatrix Campbell, *Sweet Freedom* (Oxford: Basil Blackwell, 1987), 149–50. The Alliance fielded slightly more women candidates than the other parties and received slightly more votes from women as well, according to the data in Crewe and King, *SPD*.

37 See the *Report of the Labour Party Commission of Enquiry 1980* (London: Labour Party, 1980); and, for its impact, Seyd, *Rise and Fall of the Labour Left*, 124–6.

38 Kogan and Kogan, *Battle for the Labour Party*, 71–3.

39 Quoted in Mervyn Jones, *Michael Foot* (London: Gollancz, 1994), 457.

40 Benn, *End of an Era*, entry for 24 March 1981, 112.

41 Wise, quoted in Jones, *Michael Foot*, 468.

42 Benn, *End of an Era*, entry for 26 September 1981, 153.

43 Robert Harris, *The Making of Neil Kinnock* (London: Faber & Faber, 1984), 133, 182–8.

44 The meeting was held at the ASTMS conference centre at Bishop's Stortford. See Jones, *Michael Foot*, 482; and, for a more detailed account, Benn, *End of an Era*, entries for 13, 14 and 15 June 1980, 5–10.

45 Additional support came from Roy Grantham (APEX), Hector Smith (NUBF), Bill Whatley (USDAW), Tom Jackson (UPW), Joe Gormley and Sid Vincent of the NUM and at critical moments Sam McCluskie of the seamen's union. See Golding, *Hammer of the Left*, 178–9.

46 Harris, *Making of Neil Kinnock*, 170.

47 Peter Taaffe to J.E. Mortimer, 16 October 1982, cited in Shaw, *Discipline and Discord*, 237–8.

48 For the complicated details, see Shaw, *Discipline and Discord*, 235–44; and also Peter Shipley, *The Militant Tendency: Trotskyism in the Labour Party* (Richmond: Foreign Affairs, 1983), a slanted account that nevertheless reproduces key documents; and the *Report of the Labour Party Annual Conference 1982*.

49 Seyd, *The Rise and Fall of the Labour Left*, 165–6; Jones, *Michael Foot*, 502–3. Mullin had made himself unpopular by publishing articles with titles like, 'The death of the Tribune Group' and 'The Tribune Group: Is there life after death?'.

50 Hayward was described as 'a man of infinite vanity' by Bernard Donoughue, who obviously did not share his politics. Barbara Castle did, however, and worked closely with him in the 1970s. She recorded his tendency to 'make Delphic, and hardly deferential, utterances' to Wilson and regarded his 'manner' as 'at moments almost impertinent'. His public criticism of Callaghan at the 1979 party conference was certainly not deferential. See Bernard Donoughue, *The Heat of the Kitchen* (London: Politico's, 2003), 102; and Barbara Castle, *The Castle Diaries, 1974–1976* (London: Weidenfeld & Nicolson, 1980), 19 March 1975, 346.

51 Geoff Bish, 'Working Relations between Government and Party', in Ken Coates, ed., *What Went Wrong?* (Nottingham: Spokesman, 1979), 164.

52 Bish, 'Drafting the Manifesto', in Coates, *What Went Wrong?*, 197, 201.

53 *Report . . . 1979*, 189.

54 Bish was quoted in *The Guardian*, 25 July 1983. See Eric Shaw, *The Labour Party since 1945* (Oxford: Blackwell, 1996), 167.

55 Eric Shaw, *The Labour Party since 1979: Crisis and Transformation* (London: Routledge, 1994), 12–13, suggests that the 1983 manifesto said less about public ownership and was in general less left-wing than it might have been. It was nevertheless widely judged an electoral liability.

56 12 January 1979, interview for *The Observer*, in *Margaret Thatcher: Complete Public Statements*.

57 *Report of the Annual Conference and Special Conference of the Labour Party 1980*, 231.

58 *Report . . . 1980*, 273.

59 Robert Taylor, *The TUC: From the General Strike to New Unionism* (London: Palgrave, 2000), 246–7.

60 Martin Westlake, *Neil Kinnock: The Biography* (London: Little, Brown, 2001), 192–4; Pearce, *Denis Healey*, 567–70.

61 For a lucid account, see Fred Halliday, *The Making of the Second Cold War* (London: Verso, 1983); and *From Kabul to Managua: Soviet-American Relations in the 1980s* (New York: Pantheon, 1989).

62 See Jill Liddington, *The Road to Greenham Common: Feminism and Anti-Militarism in Britain since 1820* (Syracuse: Syracuse University Press, 1989).

63 Jim Mortimer, 27 May 1983, quoted in Jones, *Michael Foot*, 510.

64 John Rentoul, *Tony Blair: Prime Minister* (London: Little, Brown, 2001), 83–4; John Kampfner, *Blair's Wars* (London: Free Press, 2003), 5–6.

65 Paul Routledge, *Gordon Brown: The Biography* (London: Simon & Schuster, 1998), 111.

66 Julia Langdon, *Mo Mowlam: The Biography* (London: Little, Brown, 2000), 134–5.

67 Kamal Ahmed, 'The executioner', *The Observer*, 31 August 2003.

68 Edward Pearce, *Hummingbirds and Hyenas* (London: Faber & Faber, 1985), 92.

69 Westlake, *Kinnock*, 247–9. Hewitt described herself as a workaholic who left Australia because there were so few like her. See Andy Beckett, 'My generation', *The Guardian*, 17 April 2003.

70 As part of the Policy Review launched by Kinnock after the defeat of 1987, Hattersley would be explicitly charged with drafting a summary of 'socialist aims and values'.

CHAPTER 7

Labour in the shadow of Thatcher, 1983–87

The tragedy of Neil Kinnock was that he was forced again and again to confront the wrong foe. The battles he fought were not of his choosing, but he fought them nonetheless. And in fighting them he began the long process through which Labour would eventually get itself back into power. But he would be deeply scarred by the experience and would in the end forfeit the opportunity to lead a new Labour government. His enemies were two: Mrs Thatcher and the left within the party. Thatcher was more than enough, but the fact that he was compelled to struggle with his erstwhile allies within the Labour Party made the effort to oppose Thatcher all the more difficult. The internal battles Labour engaged in were, in addition, a distraction and a source of division that would be ruthlessly exploited by the party's opponents. They made the Labour Party 'a profoundly unhappy place' and poisoned the legacy with which Kinnock had to work: as one commentator wrote at the time, 'Neil Kinnock had a dreadful inheritance, but if it had been less dreadful Neil Kinnock wouldn't have got it.'[1] Kinnock was faced with the need to lead, or be seen to lead, the political crusade against Thatcher. But this was an imperative that served as well to sustain Kinnock's rivals within the labour movement even while her victories progressively undermined the core of Labour's support, its institutional base, its rhetoric and its programme. Kinnock was constrained as perhaps no previous or subsequent leader of the party. The measure of his achievement was that, despite the impossible tasks and the narrow limits imposed on him, he did what was required to allow the survival of Labour through its most difficult decade and to prepare it for a proper resurrection after his resignation in April 1992.

That Michael Foot would be replaced as leader was understood even before the catastrophe of 9 June 1983. In the run-up to the election there was talk of his removal, and the scale of the defeat guaranteed it. Kinnock was the first leader to be selected by the electoral college and his triumph must have been galling to those on the left who had campaigned so hard for the reform. Though Kinnock had historic ties to the left of the party and in 1983 still largely agreed with its programme, his NEC vote against the left's proposal for control of the manifesto, his refusal to support Benn's challenge to Healey, and his stance on the Militant Tendency made it obvious to all sides that he was not truly one of them. He was too willing to compromise, reluctant to discount the impact of electoral defeat, and ultimately wedded to a thoroughly parliamentary path to power. He still managed to receive support from the left, although not the so-called 'hard left', in the leadership election, but with Benn temporarily out of Parliament there would be no serious challenge from that quarter.[2] Because he was not Benn, moreover, Kinnock also attracted votes and support from the centre-right of the party. He benefited even more from the massed weight of the unions. His victory in the leadership was assured at virtually the beginning of the contest: the union leaders Clive Jenkins and Moss Evans arranged to nominate Foot for re-election on the understanding that he would stand down and they would then throw their support to Kinnock. With the votes of major unions already largely decided and with Kinnock's broad appeal in the constituencies, the outcome was never in doubt.[3] When the votes were counted up, Kinnock had won over 70 per cent; his nearest rival, Roy Hattersley, came in at just under 20 per cent. Hattersley was duly elected deputy and the 'dream ticket', delicately balancing left and right, was in place in time for the party conference. Foot was happy enough with the succession and relieved to be leader no longer. The party conference registered its approval forcefully: Kinnock's first speech as leader, Benn recorded in his diary, 'was pretty vacuous . . . but he got a huge ovation'.[4] For a brief moment, the battle within the party was adjourned.

The Thatcher government ensured that the battle would revive soon enough, however, for victory in the election of 1983 made an already bold regime even more aggressive. The result was a series of confrontations that vastly complicated Kinnock's efforts to nudge the party back towards the centre and towards the votes it had lost to the Conservatives, the Liberals and especially the Social Democrats. The contests took place in contexts carefully chosen by the Thatcher government and on issues where Labour's stance, or that of its allies in the unions or its representatives in local government, were hard to defend. To this extent the second Thatcher government had advantages not available to it during the first term. The first Thatcher government had been forced to focus its attention on the economy and made the defeat of inflation its overriding goal. For a time this objective seemed unreachable, for Thatcher took office at the beginning of the second oil crisis. Prices were out of control across the advanced economies. The Tories also inherited the responsibility for paying for the awards of the Clegg Commission on comparative pay levels in the public service. The commission had been Labour's way out of the 'winter of discontent' and it had involved the promise of comparing work and rewards in the public and private sectors and compensatory settlements for underpaid public sector employees. The awards were frequently in excess of 20 per cent and added enormously to inflation. Yet a third, if temporary and deliberate, boost to inflation came from the Conservative government's decision to cut income tax and to make up the difference with a near doubling of VAT, which translated directly into the price index. The single-minded pursuit of lower inflation nevertheless succeeded after a time, aided by a rapid retreat of oil prices and a worldwide slowdown in economic growth. By 1981, inflation had begun to ebb and the most pressing problem appeared to be steadily rising unemployment. Calls for reflation or a relaxation became widespread. The Thatcher government chose to do the opposite, however, and the budget of March 1981 was uncharacteristically harsh and, by most reckonings, pro-cyclical – i.e. it deepened the recession at a moment when other governments, committed to more conventional economic policy objectives, might have tried to fight it. The decision produced a public rebuke from 364 university-based economists. The effect on the economy was to make unemployment worse, while continuing to drive down the rate of inflation.

Increasing unemployment had its uses, however, for it fell most harshly on the traditional industries where unions were strongest and where Labour voters were heavily congregated. Unions were as a result drastically weakened: they lost members and they lost bargaining power on the shop floor. The ability of unions to resist what was happening to them, and to their members, was further constrained by the impact of Conservative trade union legislation. For TUC leaders, the overriding reason to accept the social contract and to sustain the Labour government in office after 1975 had been the fear that the Tories would impose legislation regulating the activities of the trade unions. These fears were quickly confirmed: the Thatcher governments would pass four separate acts designed to reform trade union practice. Thatcher was extremely careful, however, not to provoke a confrontation of the sort that had brought down the Heath government. Instead, the Tories under Thatcher proceeded incrementally: the 1980 legislation restricted picketing and made secondary action unlawful; it granted compensation to workers who ran foul of the closed shop and made it harder to establish closed shop arrangements; and it allocated government money to carry out votes within unions. The 1982 act went a bit further: it imposed further restrictions on the closed shop; made unions liable for damages resulting from illegal strikes and industrial action; and it narrowed the range of acceptable industrial disputes to disagreements with employers on pay and conditions and thus ruled out strike action designed to affect third parties – e.g. government or other employers.

The Tories' legislation predictably brought cries of outrage and repeated calls for 'days of action', but it was implemented nonetheless. The unions were hampered by the fact that, after the 'winter of discontent', they enjoyed diminished public support. They were crippled as well by the way in which rising unemployment undermined their industrial strength; and they were further thwarted by the care with which the government waged its campaign to curb union power. Despite her reputation as a combative foe, Thatcher avoided confrontation and proceeded one step at a time, all the while allowing unemployment to do indirectly what Edward Heath had been unable to accomplish directly. With a solid electoral victory in 1983, it became possible for the Thatcher government to move more decisively against its opponents. Thatcher had already rid herself of troublesome colleagues when she purged the Cabinet 'wets' in September 1981. In her second term, secure within the party and newly secure with voters, the broader objectives of Thatcherism could be pursued more vigorously and transparently.

Labour had for so long been dependent on the unions that any weakening of the unions would immediately disadvantage the party. The Thatcher government's successive efforts at trade union 'reform' were carefully calculated to do just that. The legislation passed in 1984, for example, was overtly political in intent: it went beyond issues like the closed shop and imposed much clearer rules on how unions were to be run and, most important, required that the membership approve by ballot the use of union funds for political purposes. The hope was that the members would not agree to having their money funnelled to the Labour Party. The Tories would be disappointed when, after a notably effective counter-mobilisation, the trade unionists en masse chose instead to continue their affiliation with the Labour Party, but by that time the unions were themselves a weakened and much chastened force.[5]

The critical event in the process of weakening the unions was the defeat of the miners' strike in 1984−85.[6] It was the miners who had pioneered a new level and style of industrial militancy in 1972 − with flying pickets and secondary boycotts − and it was they who had effectively brought down the Heath government in 1974. The Thatcher government were determined to exact revenge, but careful not to move prematurely. During her first term, Thatcher faced down strikes by steelworkers in 1980, by civil servants in 1981, by health workers in 1982 and by water workers the next year; and in January, 1984 the staff at GCHQ Cheltenham were denied the right to unionise, due to alleged national security considerations. Public sector unions, so central to the 'winter of discontent', no longer had privileged access to, or sympathy from, the state. But the Tories backed away from a confrontation over pit closures in 1981 and avoided taking on the miners until Thatcher's second term. They did so only after key pieces of legislation were in place, when coal supplies were abundant and contingency plans had been made to protect the movement of coal throughout the country.

The thoroughness with which the government prepared for battle was not matched by a comparable tactical intelligence on the part of the miners. Arthur Scargill, who succeeded to the NUM presidency in 1982, had first become known as a militant local leader during the conflicts of the 1970s, and he was very much on the left of the labour movement. Immersed in the insular world of the miners, he failed to grasp that the conditions which had facilitated the union's earlier victories had altered

fundamentally, and that in Margaret Thatcher he faced a far more determined enemy than Edward Heath. Upon taking office in 1982 as NUM
president, Scargill moved its headquarters from London to Sheffield – a
suitably democratic gesture that nonetheless signalled what would
become a pattern of ignoring unpleasant political realities at the national
level and focusing instead on the local, the familiar and the reassuring.
This was reinforced by the fact that the national context was far less
hospitable: the government were proceeding with plans to build up coal
stocks for a future dispute; closures were continuing; and in September
1983 Ian MacGregor, the scourge of the steel industry's workers, was
appointed to head the National Coal Board. Discontent in the coalfields
simmered, but in ballots held in October 1982 and again in March 1983
over 60 per cent of miners voted not to strike. The government presumably took note of the pessimism among the miners; Scargill did not.

The strike broke out in March 1984 when pickets were called out in
Yorkshire in response to a move to close a local pit and a plan for more
extensive closures. The stoppage soon spread to Scotland, South Wales
and Kent and quickly became a de facto national strike. The NUM argued
correctly that the government planned to close a large number of pits and
so felt justified in utilising pickets to spread the dispute into a national
confrontation. But Scargill never chanced a vote, and his refusal to
ballot the members gave the government a terribly effective propaganda
weapon. Kinnock was appalled at the tactics of the miners' leaders and
their determination to press ahead with a prolonged stoppage in the face
of the sure knowledge that the Coal Board could hold out indefinitely. He
also grasped immediately that Scargill was making an enormous tactical
mistake by not holding a ballot and told him explicitly that what the
Tories wanted most was 'no ballot . . .', for they foresaw 'enormous political profit for them if they can use the taunt of no ballot'. Indeed, not just
the Tories but the 'people in the street' felt that the consultations undertaken by the miners' executive did not have 'the validity of the national
ballot that was being called for'. Scargill nevertheless resisted and
confided to the party leader that he might only get the support of 54–57
per cent of the members, and possibly less, and fretted over the impact
of such a narrow margin.[7] Even after Kinnock went public with his support for a ballot, the NUM refused. It was a fatal mistake that undermined
the legitimacy of the miners' case and raised profound doubts about

Scargill's leadership. The sense that he, and the strikers, might not be speaking for the entire workforce was further reinforced by the fact that coal continued to be mined and transported from the more profitable pits in Nottinghamshire.

The dispute dragged on for a year and the consequences lingered long after. Its conduct was marked by violence on the picket line, partly provoked by the police but made almost inevitable by the miners' tactics. The Labour Party was pressured by the Conservatives, and by a hostile press, to condemn the violence and Kinnock did so, but even-handedly – noting police provocations as well as aggressive picketing – and thus to little effect. The government were not convinced of his sincerity, nor were the public and the press, while the miners and their more ardent supporters regarded Kinnock as disloyal for uttering at least an implicit criticism of the strikers. The party conference, moreover, rallied enthusiastically behind the miners and seemed by dint of that to endorse not only their demands but also their strategy and tactics, with Kinnock reluctantly acquiescing. In Parliament Labour consistently argued for compromise and lobbied assiduously for a settlement with both sides. But compromise proved impossible and the strike began seriously to weaken as winter approached and coal stocks remained high. In December 1984 Scargill and the left urged a general strike, but received little response. By January the drift back to work was increasing; and the strike formally ended on 5 March.

Scargill never admitted defeat, but the outcome was nevertheless a rout for the government. The miners had fought valiantly, but against superior forces. The police were especially well organised and they had been deployed in vast numbers. The state knew what to expect of the miners and prevented them from carrying out their plans. Coal remained plentiful and, where necessary, it was supplemented by oil. Scenes of miners clashing with police were broadcast nightly and generated massive sympathy for the strikers from within the labour movement but less sympathy outside it. Thatcher's uncompromising rhetoric about 'enemies within' had a similar polarising effect.[8] But truly effective support for the miners was lacking, largely because the unions were already weakened by years of recession, and what assistance was forthcoming was further hemmed in by the constraints of the new trade union legislation. Volunteers brought food and tea to strikers and their families and collected large sums of money; there were frequent rallies and mass mobilisations, but the impact on a resolute government was minimal. After a year, the bulk of the miners had chosen to return to work, though some found no jobs to go back to. The union was defeated; the industry itself was now ready for a dramatic and terminal decline. Still, the issue did not go away within the Labour Party, for Scargill and his supporters launched a campaign towards the strike's end for the party to promise that if elected it would reinstate all miners who lost their jobs and reimburse the unions for fines incurred during the strike. Kinnock resisted mightily, arguing that binding a future Labour government to such a course made no sense; and that it was in effect an 'incitement' to breaking the law. The proposal was deferred when first raised in December 1984, but reiterated by Scargill in the summer and then endorsed by the TUC in September 1985. By then, however, the tide of opinion even within the party had begun to swing around and it became possible for Kinnock to launch a more sustained and effective critique of the NUM's conduct of the strike. At the 1985 party conference he delivered a forceful speech insisting that the dispute had been poorly planned, ill-timed and not 'really thought out'. Though Kinnock lost the vote, the margin was closer than expected and the result widely regarded as a victory for Kinnock and a defeat for Scargill. It was nonetheless only a modest victory and it was gained over the wrong enemy; and it was barely noticed in the context of the broader defeat both for the miners and their leadership and, more generally, for trade unions.

The intensified campaign to weaken trade union influence within industry and as a source of support for Labour provided a clear and apt illustration of how the Thatcher government's objectives evolved and grew as the possibilities for success expanded. The elaboration of full-blown Thatcherism was, of course, facilitated by the fact that Margaret Thatcher was not an ordinary politician: she declared herself a 'conviction politician' and her convictions were broader and more ideological than those of most other politicians, for whom conviction typically means a determination to win and little more. Thatcher was not immune to the lure of office, nor was she unwilling to compromise and retreat when necessary. But she was also unusually ready to move forward when the opportunity appeared; and her ideological orientation told her what to do. Between 1979 and 1983 the Thatcher government was clear enough in its intentions, but it had to be cautious in its proposals. After 1983, an electoral mandate, a recovering economy, a cowed Conservative Party and a split opposition opened up the possibility of a genuinely transforming government. In consequence, projects only dreamed about in opposition became practical proposals, and over time Thatcher would have an impact that changed permanently the framework within which politics were fought and policies worked out.

Perhaps the classic example of the expansion of the Thatcherite project was the issue of privatisation. The preference for the market over the state was central to Thatcher's view of the world; and antipathy towards the nationalised industries was a staple in the belief system of post-war Conservatism. But Conservatives, including Thatcher, had shied away from a direct attack on the public sector and focused instead on questioning its efficiency, limiting its growth and crippling its ability to compete with the private sector. Once in power, however, Thatcher and her supporters began to hatch schemes for dismantling the nationalised industries, and when their plans met with little resistance, they moved towards a wholesale stripping of state assets. They discovered a formula for rewarding their supporters with heavily discounted shares in what used to be public enterprises and in effect removing from the state, and from any future Labour government, the leverage over the economy which the control of major industries might have offered. The programme expanded until very little was left of what had taken years to put together, and it increasingly became a campaign to create a new 'enterprise culture'. Tories had long talked of creating a 'property-owning democracy', but had done rather little to achieve it. Under Thatcher, however, the rhetoric began to correspond a bit more to reality: in the decade after 1979, the number of individual shareholders tripled, from 3 million to 9 million. Norman Lamont, the future Chancellor, boasted that 'The number of people owning shares in British industry is not much less now than the number of people who belong to trade unions.'[9] Share ownership remained rare among workers, of course, but it was not unknown, and the impression created by the government was that capitalism was now increasingly democratic.

Even more successful was the effort to privatise formerly public housing. Again, the desire to increase private home ownership was not new and previous Conservative governments had sought to ease restrictions on private building and to provide financial incentives to allow individuals to own their own houses. Nevertheless, the aspiration to home ownership continued to be beyond the means of most working-class families throughout the 1960s, while the sustained pressure to provide accommodation meant that both Conservative and Labour governments kept building council housing. Under Labour governments the balance of public policy was tilted towards public housing; under the Conservatives private ownership received greater support. Through 1979, however, the net effect was to increase both private home ownership and its opposite – council housing built with public funds and let out at subsidised rents – and to shrink the private rental market. After Thatcher came to power, this balance was altered and the preference for private housing was accentuated. The big innovation was the decision to allow council tenants to buy their homes at substantial discounts. Labour councils, which had largely built and long run the council estates and who were often the beneficiaries of the votes of grateful tenants, resisted at first, but the programme was popular and proved hugely successful. Over a million units were sold up to 1988 and more after that; by the late 1980s roughly 65 per cent of the population lived in owner-occupied housing.

The selling off of previously nationalised industries and of council housing generated revenue, created great wealth for a few and modest gains for many, dispersed the ownership of property more broadly, and brought considerable short-term benefits to the party in power. But privatisation was more than that. Thatcher had infamously said that there was no such thing as society, but in fact her policies aimed to change society. Thatcherism sought not only tactical political advantage and temporary relief for the Exchequer and the taxpayer, but aimed much further: she sought to remake the social and institutional foundations of politics. Labour policy-makers had long regarded the public sector as a key resource in economic management, even if they did not often use it effectively. But shrinking it back Thatcher would deprive them of its potential use in the future. Likewise, as late as 1979, roughly a third of the population still lived in publicly-subsidised housing and these millions of working-class council tenants were the core of Labour's electoral support. Conservatives hoped that by transforming tenants into homeowners they would deprive Labour of an enduring material link to a large block of voters, who would henceforth be, if not floating voters, at least open to different appeals and to the possibility of voting Conservative.

A defining feature, then, of the expansive version of the 'Thatcherite project' as it emerged after the election of 1983 was its focus upon reshaping the political landscape by eroding the institutional and social-structural underpinnings of Labour support. Thatcher once defined her goal as being 'to get rid of socialism as a second force in British politics' – a far grander objective than winning the next election – and she came close to achieving it.[10] Neil Kinnock's daunting task was to preserve Labour's position as a viable party of opposition. He seems quickly to have realised that the more ambitious goal of displacing Thatcher in the next election was unattainable, and he would focus instead on protecting Labour's sources of electoral strength. But that was especially hard, for Labour's strengths were also, ironically, its greatest points of vulnerability. The unions, for example, provided the bulk of the party's funds, much of its membership and support 'on the ground', and huge numbers of votes. But the union link implicated Labour in whatever the unions chose to do; and the 'block vote' wielded by trade union leaders at Labour Party conferences was an embarrassment. The party's involvement in local government was similarly ambiguous. The party received lots of votes from council tenants and municipal employees; and experience running local government was a critical training ground for future Labour leaders. But the party's connection to local governments in the large urban centres allowed the Tories to hold Labour responsible for whatever ill-chosen actions local councils might decide upon. The party leadership was therefore not merely forced onto the defensive by Thatcher, but they were often forced to defend the seemingly indefensible. This was obvious with the miners' strike, in which Kinnock was beside himself with anger over Scargill's tactics but forced to back the union in public in order to appease sentiment within the party. It would be equally the case in the battle over local government, where Kinnock was compelled to fight alongside allies whose behaviour was often hard to defend and for policies that were not viable.

Upon taking office in 1979 the Tories had begun systematically to decrease financial support for local authorities, forcing them to cut spending or increase local rates. The more left-wing councils imposed substantial rate increases, to which the government responded with the Rates Act 1984, which capped local taxes on property. Officially, 16 councils were 'rate-capped' by central government; in addition, councillors in Liverpool chose to act in solidarity. The resulting confrontation pitted Labour's local strength against the prerogatives of the state controlled by the Tories. The triumph of the centre was inevitable, for it was based upon the most basic fact of British politics: the supremacy of Parliament and the derivative character of local government within a unitary state. But the constitutional argument, however clear, was not convincing to activists who regarded the directives of central government as dictation rather than democracy and who hoped to capture 'the local state' and turn it against the policies emanating from Westminster.

That construction was particularly appealing to those in control of local authorities. The most spectacular and visible victories of Labour's left may have been at national level – over the Labour Party's programme and over its institutions – but the left had also achieved a series of more prosaic victories in local elections across the country. Long the object of disdain from previous generations of left-wing activists and regarded as corrupt or at least complacent by voters and activists, local government took on increased importance during the 1970s, as local spending increased and the government sought to rein it in.[11] The creation of a second tier of larger metropolitan authorities in the 1970s, moreover, and the steady turnover in the leadership of local government at all levels, provided unprecedented opportunities for the new generation who joined the party in the aftermath of 1968 and emerged as a 'new urban left'.[12] The most popular model was London, where the left had been voted in on a radical programme in 1981. The most prominent insurgent there was Ken Livingstone, who worked closely with the radical journal, *London Labour Briefing*, and was chosen to lead the Greater London Council. Another emerging figure destined for high office was David Blunkett, who became leader of the Council in Sheffield. Rather more infamous was Derek Hatton, the de facto leader of the left in Liverpool.

The differences between London, Sheffield and Liverpool meant that the move to the left took distinctive forms in the divergent localities. London was massive enough to be home to a large number of organised workers and unions, but it was also the centre of finance, publishing, services and government. Its style was never 'proletarian', and its feel was diverse and cosmopolitan. Left-wing politics in London for that reason took on a less traditionally socialist aspect and instead focused upon issues that appealed to a wide range of Londoners, like the fares charged by London Transport, or on providing voice and access for the different ethnic communities that made the metropolis their home. The GLC had in fact little responsibility for providing services but considerable capacity to levy taxes; and it used its funds to give grants to organisations representing minority groups, gays and lesbians. Livingstone himself broke with the national consensus on ostracising the supporters of Sinn Fein and the IRA. The tabloids were endlessly fascinated with 'Red Ken' and his off-hand comments and the council was denounced as the plaything of the 'loony left'. On a more serious note, the GLC began to busy itself with questions of local economic development, setting up a London Enterprise Board and publishing in 1985 a detailed blueprint for economic revitalisation, *The London Industrial Strategy*. Sheffield, by contrast, was a bastion of the traditional working class and had a strong local socialist tradition on which to draw for inspiration. The left on the council, led by Blunkett, turned its focus to local economic development and job creation; it also encouraged the growth of cooperatives, the improvement of social services – though benefit increases were targeted rather than universal – and a greater involvement of local residents in their provision and administration. For a time, it seemed that Sheffield 'had found an effective alternative to Thatcherism: a decentralised municipal socialism which would provide a catalyst, drawing together business, commerce, trade unions, community groups and workers to save the declining steel and engineering industries'.[13]

The Liverpool example lacked the attractions of what was happening in London, which was broad and multicultural and at least fun even if not very effective in regenerating the local economy, or in Sheffield, where local government policies modestly improved the lot of ordinary people. The left in Liverpool was dominated by representatives of the Militant Tendency which, as a Trotskyist organisation, was less interested in delivering on reform than in exposing the inadequacies of capitalism and the futility of efforts to reform it.[14] It was intrinsically more confrontational because it believed confrontation would 'heighten contradictions' and further the struggle for socialism. The Liverpool Council chose therefore to confront the Thatcher government directly over expenditure and rates. Liverpool was a seriously depressed city suffering from long-term industrial decline, and its citizens were often desperately needy. The council persisted in spending more than it raised and in June 1985 passed a budget it could not pay for while refusing to set rates. Despite advice from party headquarters that even the council's own accountants were not legally free to go along with such an improvident decision, it refused to back down.[15] By August Liverpool's impending bankruptcy led the council to send provisional redundancy notices to its more than 30,000 workers. The tactic was counter-productive; it caused alarm and anger among trade unionists and led ultimately to its repudiation by the Labour Party at national level.[16]

The defeat of Militant in Liverpool was indicative of the broader failure of the left-wing challenge in local politics. Local Labour politicians across the country had at first responded to the Conservative legislation on rate-capping with a decision not to comply. At a special conference in Sheffield in July 1984 local parties were urged to 'resist, using all the options available, the imposition of rate-capping . . .'. Party officials understood that in refusing to cooperate 'local authorities will be moving very much into uncharted territory as far as the law is concerned', but they ventured forth the nonetheless.[17] By the summer of 1985, however, the campaign had collapsed and the local authorities gradually came into line with government policy. That was not enough for Thatcher, however, who proceeded with the outright abolition of the Greater London Council and other metropolitan governments in 1986. The GLC celebrated its demise with a giant festival and in defeat Livingstone became enormously popular, but the net result of the left's tireless work and broad-based gains in local politics was the elimination of the venues in which they had succeeded so well. Thatcher had once again gone after the institutional bases of Labour's power and in this case decisively took them away.

Not before causing the new Labour leadership great discomfiture and political embarrassment, however. The campaign over local government expenditure exposed the deep fissures within the Labour Party, brought into sharp relief the widespread influence of the left within the party and illustrated in painful detail Kinnock's inability to deal with it. The key symbol was the Militant Tendency, and the battleground would be in its stronghold in Liverpool. Under Michael Foot's leadership the NEC had reluctantly moved to curb Militant's activity prior to the 1983 election, but that effort proved ineffective. Legal challenges delayed action and the will to carry out a full-blown purge was absent. When Kinnock assumed leadership in 1983 he was determined to direct his attention towards Thatcher and loath to dissipate whatever goodwill he enjoyed in internal party battles. Unfortunately for Kinnock and his new team, the battle over local government had afforded Militant a new cause, new visibility and an issue over which they, or rather the position they took, enjoyed wide support. Liverpool had long been a stronghold for the Trotskyist faction and they were a predominant influence within the Liverpool District Labour Council, which in turn gave direction to the Labour Group on the council. Labour had first won control in Liverpool in 1983, then consolidated its hold in 1984. In response to government demands for cuts, the council had adopted an 'Urban Regeneration Strategy' involving no reductions in services and instead proposing to provide 5,000 new council houses, which would also create jobs for those who would build them. Kinnock urged restraint and told the representatives from Liverpool to work within the law. They responded that resistance to cuts would open up a 'second front of popular protest' alongside the miners' strike and ultimately bring down the government. When the government came through with an additional £30 million in subsidies, the Liverpool councillors seemed to have prevailed and Kinnock was forced back on the defensive.

Emboldened by their success and fêted at the Labour Party annual conference in October 1984, the left in Liverpool set out to defy the government again the following year. In the interval much had changed, however, and their continued resistance backfired. In local authorities across the country – including London – local councillors had abandoned their campaign of non-compliance when faced with financial penalties and disqualification from office; and they had reluctantly chosen to set legal rates. Liverpool was defiant, however, and missed the legal deadline for setting rates and then did so at a level that left a deficit of £100 million. In July 1985 Kinnock warned representatives from Liverpool and Lambeth, the one London borough still holding out, against the politics of 'gestures', for 'gestures don't bring housing repairs or meals on wheels'.[18] The financial crisis built over the summer and by the autumn it was clear that Liverpool would run out of money and be forced to lay off local authority workers. With jobs at stake, the unions began to turn on the council and its policies and when the council decided in late September to send out redundancy notices, renting a fleet of taxis to do so, they were outraged. At the party conference a few days later, Kinnock effectively used the incident to turn on Liverpool and on Militant. In his speech, delivered with much fanfare at Bournemouth on 1 October, Kinnock described the events in Liverpool as the inevitable result of factions committed to making 'impossible promises'.

> I'll tell you what happens with impossible promises. You start with far-fetched resolutions. They are then pickled into a rigid dogma, a code, and you go through years sticking to that, outdated, misplaced, irrelevant to real needs, and you end up in the grotesque chaos of a Labour council – a *Labour* council – hiring taxis to scuttle round a city handing out redundancy notices to its own workers.

Amid howls of outrage from the left, Kinnock pressed his advantage: 'you can't play politics with people's jobs and with people's services or with people's homes . . . The people will not, cannot, abide posturing. They cannot respect the gesture-generals or the tendency-tacticians.'[19] The speech was a decisive moment in Kinnock's tenure. It was widely praised by the press and sympathisers within the Labour Party and denounced by his intended victims. Eric Heffer walked out; Benn left right after it ended, noting that 'It was all part of his strategy, going back to 1983, to kill off any left-wing challenge' to his leadership.[20] Unlike much of what he had done since 1983, however, this effort would prove effective.

Just after the conclusion of the party conference, the NEC launched an inquiry into Liverpool's finances and a compromise was proposed. But again it was rejected by the Liverpool council, which proceeded to draw up yet another budget that differed only modestly from the proposed deal. The effect was merely to rebuke the party leadership and it was understood as such. Kinnock's response was not subtle: people who act this way, he explained, 'can be excluded from membership' in the Labour Party; rather more bluntly, he explained, 'It is generally recognised that Militant Tendency is a maggot in the body of the Labour Party . . . I want them out . . .'[21] The outcome was the suspension of the Liverpool District Labour Party and the appointment of a committee to inquire into its conduct. The committee was split, but a clear majority found 'serious and deep-seated problems in the functioning and practices' of the party in Liverpool; it was decided in February 1986 to restructure the local party and to seek the expulsion of 16 members of Militant.[22] Questions over the nature of Militant as an organisation – the group formally denied that it was more than a newspaper and membership was secret – which had hampered previous purges were this time swept aside. Eventually nine of its supporters were expelled. The process was nevertheless bloody and protracted.[23] Left-wing members of the NEC chose at one point to withdraw and deprive the proceedings of a quorum at a hearing scheduled in March; later in April, the rules were changed and a new hearing set for May. It would drag on for two days and net only three expulsions. Still, the pattern was established and over time the leadership managed to settle scores with dozens on the left. At the annual conference of 1986 a new National Constitutional Appeal Committee was created to review complaints against party members and a new offence added to the rulebook – that of engaging 'in a sustained course of action prejudicial to the party'. On that standard and with a more efficient structure of control, the purge of the left went forward more smoothly.

Even so, it dragged on for years; and when it involved the selection, reselection or deselection of candidates for Parliament it became public, nasty, politically embarrassing and at times counter-productive. However undemocratic and unrepresentative the beliefs of Militant and its supporters, Kinnock's campaign against the group was often heavy-handed and marked by a rather cavalier disregard of normal procedure.[24] There was arguably no alternative. The structures of the Labour Party allowed rather small and unrepresentative groupings to carve out local niches of influence within constituency parties. The leadership, if it wanted to win, had to craft an appeal to voters with very different views who had, in effect, no proper voice within the party's structure. Appealing to these putative supporters meant, in effect, overriding the views of those who were most active in the party. It was not a pretty thing, but it was the precondition of the party's ability to continue as the main opposition to Thatcher. And it came at a price. The tragedy for Labour was that its leader was forced to demonstrate his authority and prove himself by standing up to his own supporters in struggles designed deliberately to weaken the party. The attack on the miners, after all, was not merely a battle over the economics of the coal industry; and the effort to control the spending of local authorities was no mere exercise in fiscal responsibility. Ironically, in both cases the government also sought consciously to weaken institutions from which Labour drew its strength. In opposing the resistance of the miners and local councillors, Kinnock was conceding that these institutional underpinnings would in the end have to be abandoned and that Labour, if it were to win again, would not only have to be rebuilt, but that it would have to be recreated on a new basis. How thoroughly Kinnock, his allies or opponents grasped this stark reality remains unclear, for they inevitably fought the battles of the moment with the slogans of the moment. But they would grasp their significance over time; and over time it would become obvious that Kinnock's agenda for reshaping the party was informed by an understanding that the basis of the Labour Party had been thoroughly transformed by Thatcher, by the economic restructuring she oversaw and encouraged, and by the changing contours of the political landscape that she did so much to overhaul.

Kinnock, the new and untested leader of the Labour Party, would therefore be repeatedly forced by Thatcher to fight on terrain she had chosen, with unreliable and often openly disloyal allies, and for policies not of his design. An effective response to Thatcher required that Labour under Kinnock refashion its appeal and its policies and redefine its relationship to its core supporters, its key constituencies and the unions with which it had been so long identified. It had, in short, to remake itself. Complicating the task enormously and delaying its implementation were two critical facts: the continued threat from the Social Democrats and the enduring strength of the left within the party. These two realities prevented Kinnock from moving Labour towards the centre until after 1987, both because that political space was already occupied and because so many in the party refused to move in that direction. Eventually, the threat from the Social Democrats and the Alliance would recede. They had polled extremely well in the election of 1983 and almost forced Labour into third place in the popular vote, but they suffered ups and downs over the next several years. They exerted a consistent appeal as the party that eschewed extremism of either the left or the right, but internal squabbling and a fundamentally incoherent programme would ultimately put a brake to their rise in 1987. Still, in Kinnock's early years as Labour leader he had to struggle mightily to prevent the Alliance from replacing Labour as the main opposition party.

The influence of the left within the party was likewise not easily or quickly diminished. It was rooted in the demographic changes in party membership during the 1970s and its strength was entrenched by the institutional reforms that followed. By 1979–81 the left was therefore deeply embedded in the party's multi-level political structure and it had strong support on the National Executive Committee. Though the left's control of the NEC had been broken in 1981, it continued to be strongly represented and as of 1983, when Kinnock became leader, it still controlled the party's programme, it still had strong support in the constituencies and it continued to have influence within a number of trade unions, especially the public sector unions. The left was also very strongly represented in local government across the big cities and profited as well from the slow but steady growth of 'new social movements' and of identity politics – i.e. from feminism, environmentalism, anti-racism and opposition to nuclear weapons. The intense hatred of Thatcher and the accompanying belief that her assault upon the left, the unions and the welfare state merited full-scale resistance and no compromise further buttressed and sustained the standing of the left within the party, for calls for moderating the party's image and appeal were easily criticised as caving in to Thatcherism. However ill-advised Kinnock might have thought the miners' strike, therefore, he was forced to give lip-service to the cause because it was viewed, not unreasonably, as the front line in the battle with Thatcher. Similarly, however much he loathed and feared the implicit challenge to the sovereignty of Parliament inherent in the campaign of non-compliance on the part of the rate-capped local authorities, the spirit of resistance to Thatcher elicited wide support, and a special Labour Party conference had explicitly endorsed the defiant stance of the local councillors. Only when the passions aroused by these issues were spent, only after the strategies adopted by the left proved counter-productive, and only after Kinnock felt strong enough to challenge both the miners and Militant – as he so forcefully did at the annual conference in 1985 – could the argument truly begin about how to move the party in a new direction. Even then, Kinnock and his allies were obliged to move slowly and carefully.

The reorientation of Labour's policy, programme and organisation would therefore take time and would require sustained debate, patient efforts to reshape the party's organisation and a thorough purge and restaffing of the party at the highest levels. It presupposed as well that Kinnock put together a coalition in support of his quest to remake the party. Kinnock's problem was that in his campaign to change the party he would need a different set of allies, a different coalition, from the one whose support had brought him initially into the leadership. He had triumphed in 1983 with firm union backing, with large-scale support from the left within the constituencies and with solid, but not over-whelming support from within the parliamentary party. That combina-tion would not and could not last: the backing of the union leaders was only as strong as their hold over a potentially restless membership; the constituency parties were strongholds of Bennite sentiment and on most issues far to the left of Kinnock. And the battle over local government inevitably pitted the new urban left and many local parties against the leadership in London. Over the long run, moreover, Kinnock would require more support from his fellow MPs: they were the professional politicians who needed to align their career prospects with Kinnock's fortunes if either were to advance. They were the ones who would have to serve under Kinnock in the Shadow Cabinet and, if Labour attained office, in government.

Kinnock's second coalition would nevertheless remain anchored by the unions. Indeed, TUC leaders were ahead of Kinnock in their appreci-ation of Thatcher's impact and of what it meant for the future of the trade union interest. Union leaders might have been extremely disappointed with the Wilson and Callaghan governments, but they knew well enough the difference between a Labour government with whom they could deal and a Tory government out to reduce their power and influence. More important, the unions were being decimated by massive job losses in manufacturing during the early 1980s and their leaders knew instinct-ively that they now lacked industrial muscle. Even as they waged their campaign of resistance to Tory policies in early 1980, they sensed that the views of union leaders were, as they euphemistically put it, far 'in advance of the wider membership'. TUC leaders recognised that it was therefore important 'to insure against too wide a gap' opening up between leaders and led.[25] This profound sense of weakness meant that the trade unions could neither sustain opposition to the government nor exert real leverage with employers. Indeed, the very survival of the unions and of collective bargaining seemed at stake in the early 1980s and made it essential that the unions help Labour to do whatever was necessary to return to power. As early as September 1983, TUC leader Len Murray began advocating a 'New Realism' that took into account Thatcher's recent victory at the polls and the wide support the Tories enjoyed in their efforts to curb the power of trade unions. He argued that unions needed to get back to basics and back in touch with their members in order to begin again to rebuild union strength. It was a concession that many did not want to hear and in the subsequent din raised by the miners' strike the argument would make little headway. But it was a counsel that could not forever be ignored.[26] It ensured that, whatever the public stance of the unions during the miner's strike, the leaders of the major unions would be solidly behind Kinnock's efforts to bring unity to the party, to pull it back from the controversial policy stances of the early 1980s and to refurbish its image and recast its appeal. Despite a slight shift from the centre-right to the centre-left during 1983–84, therefore, the unions would remain at the core of Kinnock's base. As the battles over direct action played themselves out during Kinnock's first two years of leadership, union backing for Kinnock would become still more reliable.

That backing would be essential for Kinnock's management of the NEC. The left had won considerable support on the NEC in the late 1970s and used its leverage to secure passage of constitutional reforms by the annual conference and also to maintain pressure on the leadership faithfully to implement the party's left-wing programme. The left's control had been broken in 1981 by the concerted efforts of more moderate union representatives, John Golding in particular, and Benn was subsequently removed as chairman of the all-important Home Policy Committee. Still, the NEC remained precariously balanced and the left on the Executive could count on regular affirmations of its policy stances by majorities at conference. Kinnock's election in 1983 did little to change that balance and the NEC remained torn between an instinct to support the new leader and, as Kinnock himself understood, 'a slight majority against the Leadership on most issues which involved a significant alteration in the policy and constitutional position of the Party'.[27] Thus although there was a strong desire, on the left and the right of the party, not to embarrass the new leader and to maintain the appearance of unity, the price of unity at least through 1985 was continued adherence to the programme and rhetoric put in place by the left over the previous decade.

Between 1983 and 1985, therefore, the Kinnock leadership was embattled and unable to impose its will upon a recalcitrant party. Over the long term the generation whose first taste of politics was the bitter taste of defeat during 1979–83, and who would emerge from the experience ready to back Kinnock's reforms and create a new Labour Party, would ensure victory for Kinnock's policies. But that cohort was still in formation and not yet ready for a major role. In the short term Kinnock needed a coalition among those already in positions of influence. He succeeded by recruiting new allies from what was referred to as the 'soft left' of the party. The 'soft left' was in fact largely Kinnock's creation, for it was made up of people who in the early 1980s were often indistinguishable from the 'hard left' or, as Blunkett preferred, the 'firm left'.[28] If there was a core, it probably consisted of those Tribunite MPs who, led by Kinnock, had refused to support Benn's bid for the deputy leadership in 1981. The Tribune Group had for decades been the major embodiment of the left, but it refrained from the kind of factional activity that would have made it liable to the charge of being a party within the party and so remained basically a parliamentary caucus. The organisation became more prominent as the ranks of the left swelled inside and outside Parliament and in 1981 Tony Benn had signed on as a new member. Almost immediately, however, he angered his colleagues by standing against Healey for the deputy leadership and provoking a contest that was not unreasonably regarded as a challenge to Michael Foot. In response, Tribune split and Kinnock emerged as a leading member of those who refused to support Benn. In the ensuing battle Kinnock showed genuine pluck and argued forcefully that Benn's decision was a distraction that would damage the 'Party electorally' and 'prolong the conflict within' it.[29] The contest evolved into a major campaign during the summer and autumn of 1981 and the left put enormous pressure on erstwhile allies, like Kinnock, to rally around Benn. Kinnock had sharp exchanges with Arthur Scargill, for example, and he was repudiated by a majority in his own constituency party in Bedwellty. He was not moved, however, and in the end led a group of 16 MPs from the Tribune Group who, having voted for John Silkin on the first ballot, abstained on the second and effectively threw the election to Healey.

Kinnock's position was extremely delicate and he was in consequence relatively isolated during 1981–82. He was also compelled to work extremely hard to justify his opposition to Benn. Indeed, the immediate effect was a period of nasty recrimination, as Benn's supporters accused Kinnock and his fellow abstainers of betrayal. The split over the deputy leadership election was the moment at which the soft left, until now largely sympathetic to Benn and in awe of the left's recent successes, began to detach itself from what was increasingly regarded as the hard left. Even within Benn's camp there were second thoughts. Vladimir Derer, for example, the driving force behind the Campaign for Labour Party Democracy (CLPD), argued after the deputy leadership contest for unity and for a moratorium on inner-party struggle. It was now 'important', he explained, 'that those who fought for constitutional reform should be the ones to initiate moves that would make unity possible' and that it was necessary to keep a 'low profile in all elections for Party offices'.[30] An uneasy truce settled over the party, though it masked a continued domination of policy-making by the left and a growing but still often unspoken understanding on the soft left of the electoral liabilities that these left-wing commitments incurred. Kinnock's elevation as leader obviously advanced the cause of those who, like him, were sympathetic to the policies of the left but unwilling to reconcile themselves to repeated electoral disasters. His first moves as leader were appropriately designed to put Labour on a permanent campaign footing and to begin building an effective electoral machine. But his efforts were resented by the left and not much appreciated by others. More important, they were soon overshadowed by the heroic struggles that characterised the second Thatcher government – the miners' strike and the battle over rate-capping – and that delayed Labour's reckoning with the disastrous results of the election of 1983.

Those conflicts had nonetheless demonstrated vividly the inherent limitations of the strategy of the left and they played a decisive role in helping to define the central issues facing Labour as a party and in encouraging the further emergence of the soft left. If voters had failed to rally to a left-wing programme in 1983, the public response to the extra-parliamentary agitations of the next two years was even less favourable and was registered in continuing adverse polling numbers showing that, while the policies of the Thatcher government were unpopular, Labour was even less popular. The effect was to stimulate a reconsideration of strategy among at least some adherents of the left and to drive them toward Kinnock or the soft left.

Three key converts, whose trajectories were emblematic, were David Blunkett, Tom Sawyer and Michael Meacher. Blunkett's leadership of the Sheffield Council brought him a seat on the NEC in 1983, where he routinely sided with the left. Though he, along with Meacher and Sawyer, was reported to have begun a slow drift towards the leadership in late 1984, well into 1985 Blunkett still sought to play the role of mediator.[31] He took a position designed to bridge the gap between Kinnock and the miners' more aggressive supporters and he likewise worked with Derek Hatton and the Liverpool councillors to find a compromise that would fudge the differences between them and the national leadership. Blunkett was in fact largely responsible for the appointment of the Stonehouse Commission, which in 1985 visited Liverpool, reviewed its finances and recommended cutbacks and a rate increase to save jobs and avoid bankruptcy. But when Blunkett went up to Liverpool that November and sought to sell the deal, he was roughly treated by Militant supporters who rejected the Commission's report. The effect, as he later put it, 'was seminal. It was when the left outside Militant decided that it was prepared to take them on.'[32] By March 1986, Blunkett was willing to support the formal expulsion of Militant supporters from the party. His shift was symbolically very important: as a leader of the new urban left he had enormous credibility among constituency activists, which was where Militant and the Bennite left had long drawn critical support.

Sawyer and Meacher also served to bring key groups behind the leadership. Sawyer, for example, was deputy secretary of the National Union of Public Employees (NUPE) and a well-known representative of the trade union left on the NEC. He had played a key role in Benn's campaign for deputy leadership in 1981 among trade unionists and also in Benn's return to Parliament as MP for Chesterfield in 1983.[33] Again, he regularly voted with the left on the NEC but, like Blunkett, he was turned off and turned around by the behaviour of Militant in Liverpool. Many members of his own union worked for the local authority in Liverpool and not a few were appalled by the threat that the council's policies posed to their jobs.[34] It was Sawyer who, in response, in late 1985 proposed an investigation into the activities of Militant in Liverpool and he himself volunteered to take part. The result was a compromise of sorts, but very much on Kinnock's terms: with Sawyer as a critical swing vote the committee agreed that the conduct of Labour Party affairs in Liverpool was indeed irregular and that at least a modest purge was in order. Sawyer would later recall the 'atmosphere of intimidation fuelled by parading Council security guards and hundreds of non-delegates' who packed the meetings. 'Some of the things I saw', he concluded, 'have more in common with the extreme right in European politics than the left.'[35] Kinnock was delighted at Sawyer's turn and declared that, 'From now on, majority is spelled S.a.w.y.e.r.' Sawyer's loyalty would be proved repeatedly in subsequent debates and he was eventually to become general secretary of the party under Tony Blair.[36]

Meacher's conversion was equally significant, not only because of his long and close association with Benn and the left but also because of his ties to the left within the parliamentary party, where Kinnock was relatively weak. Together with Frances Morrell, Benn's political assistant, Meacher had helped to set up the Labour Co-ordinating Committee in 1978, an organisation committed to maintaining, explaining and elaborating Labour's increasingly left-wing programme. The LCC worked effectively to close the gap between activists and thinkers, between parliamentarians and the party outside Parliament, and between the trade unions and the Labour left.[37] Meacher went on to run as the Bennite candidate for deputy leader in 1983 and thus threatened to disrupt the smooth accession of the dream ticket of Kinnock and Hattersley. He was badly beaten, however, and came out of the fray deeply wounded – he had in fact been ridiculed by Kinnock as 'kind, scholarly, innocuous – and as weak as hell'. He was also subjected to a campaign of damning leaks clearly inspired by Kinnock and his allies. Nevertheless, Meacher had genuine roots on the left and considerable support in the PLP; and he had even served in the 1974–79 government. He was thus not simply a creature of the Bennite insurgency or the constituency left and he almost inevitably developed a working relationship with Kinnock as a member of the Shadow Cabinet. Meacher, like Sawyer and Blunkett, had been shifting his allegiance away from the left as its fortunes in the party and in the country began to ebb. For him, however, the decisive break came not over rate-capping and Militant but over the miners' strike. The controversial proposal to reinstate laid-off miners and to compensate the union for its losses was to be debated at conference in September 1985 and when the NEC met to consider its position, Kinnock publicly called on Meacher to oppose it for fear that it would put an end to 'any prospect of a Labour government'.[38] Meacher acquiesced and effectively signed on to the Kinnock team for the duration. His role was essential in reconciling MPs committed to left-wing policies, especially on social provision, to the Kinnock leadership.

The split between the soft left who chose to support the party leadership and others on the 'firm left' was not merely a matter of individual decisions to change their stance but also involved institutions. The editorship of *Tribune*, for example, was also transferred from the left to the soft left with the replacement of Chris Mullin by Nigel Williamson in November 1984. Mullin had been a supporter of Benn and had broken with the Tribune Group of MPs when he took over the newspaper in 1982. Williamson re-established the link with this quintessentially 'soft left' faction and effectively announced the group's switch in an essay on 'Working to Win' published in *Tribune* in January 1985. Of probably greater significance was the movement towards Kinnock of the Labour Co-ordinating Committee, which had been set up to advance the formulation of the party's left-wing programme and to apply pressure to see that it was implemented. Its organising secretary, Nigel Stanley, explained that its province was the battle of ideas: 'It is actually winning support for socialist ideas.'[39] Because the LCC spanned the key constituencies whose allegiance had been essential to the advance of the left and because it consistently nurtured its relations to the left in Parliament, its political reorientation behind Kinnock's leadership brought him critical allies. The LCC formally decided in 1982 that the party's programme was appropriately 'left' and that the task ahead was to win voters. By 1983, it was writing to Kinnock arguing for the 'Modernisation of the Labour Party'.[40]

As individual defections added up and as the stance of groups like the LCC altered, it became obvious that the balance of advantage within the Labour Party had begun to change. In May 1985 Patrick Seyd, an academic and party activist in Sheffield, wrote about the emergence of a new 'Bennism without Benn'. The argument was that Labour had in place a set of left-wing policies and the priority was now to win support for it. Benn was a lightning rod and a distraction, and so, too, were the activities of the hard left. A 'realignment of the left' behind Kinnock would allow the leadership to focus on winning the next election while ensuring continued access and influence for the left. Providing Kinnock with a bloc of soft left supporters on the NEC and in the parliamentary party would have the added benefit of serving 'to detach him from the embrace of the parliamentary right'.[41] For his part Kinnock was happy for the extra backing but keen to maintain his independence: 'I am not a prisoner of the right. I lead the party in the way I want to lead it and I am under obligation to no faction, grouping or wedge in the Party.'[42] What Kinnock did not say, but might well have said, was that with his position within the party more secure, he could now lead it much more effectively away from the policies dear to the hard and the soft left alike, and towards the political centre.

The sense that the tide had turned against the left was thus palpable by late 1985 and no one felt it more acutely than Tony Benn. As early as March 1983, Benn had met with Meacher and Frances Morrell and they informed him that 'we were defeated; we had no troops'. Soon defeat became personal, as Benn lost his own seat in the June election, and he was then forced to watch Kinnock win an easy victory in the leadership context and to see his surrogate, Meacher, soundly defeated for deputy leader. By September he confessed to his diary that he was 'feeling a bit depressed at the moment. I think the real effect of losing my seat is apparent, and no doubt being out of the leadership election has caught up with me. It is a fact that I have lost a platform and an income, and have no absolute certainty that I will get back.'[43] By 1985 he understood that the contest had turned even more decisively against his position. He met in May of that year with Ralph Miliband, the most senior and respected academic critic of the Labour Party, and a group of '*New Left Review* people', including Perry Anderson, Tariq Ali, Hilary Wainwright, John Palmer and Robin Blackburn. Miliband regarded the Bennites as 'the independent socialist left' that 'wanted socialism without rocking the boat'. It needed to be 'strengthened' in its resolve and supported in its struggles against both the 'ultra-left' and the moderates, stretching from 'Hattersley to Hobsbawm', who were ready to support Kinnock. But whatever the others at the meeting thought about the Bennites' prospects, Benn himself was clear: 'There has been a major political shift and we have to accept it without bitterness.'[44]

It was impossible to contemplate the recent turn dispassionately, however, as Benn revealed a month later. At a lunch with his long-time aide, Frances Morrell, with the new editor of *Tribune*, Nigel Williamson, and with Tom Sawyer, Benn was put very much on the defensive on the question of whether he and his allies were genuinely committed to winning elections and defeating Thatcher. Williamson attacked Ted Knight and Chris Mullin in particular for arguing that the next Labour government would be no better than the last and hence, by implication, not worth electing. He also told Benn that in 'putting forward maximalist demands', he was using a classic 'Trotskyite trick to "expose" other people . . .' rather than actually seeking to influence policy. Morrell concluded the debate about what policies Labour should fight on with a taunt to her old mentor: 'Why should you set the agenda?' she asked. Benn would later record the meeting in his diary, admitting that 'It was awful and I regret having gone.'[45]

For the best part of two years, then, Kinnock had been forced onto the defensive – by Thatcher, by his unease over how to respond to the miners' strike and the resistance to rate-capping, and by the continued, if diminishing, influence of the left within the party. But eventually he had put together a coalition behind the central theme of his leadership, which was to make Labour electable once more, and he was ready to move the party towards that end. It is not clear that in late 1985 or early 1986 either Kinnock or his closest allies truly understood what that task would require, however. They seemed to feel at first that it was a matter of presentation and that the policies themselves were perfectly defensible. They learned quickly that it was crucial as well to give the impression that the party as an organisation was prepared to lead, its leaders prepared to govern, and that meant creating party unity and purging those who most threatened it. Only later did it become clear that policy itself needed revision and that the image of the party could not be restored until its programme – and, in order to achieve this, its culture and institutional structure – had been changed as well. Neither Kinnock nor his closest allies 'had a crystal clear and detailed view of all of the changes . . .' that would be required. And only very late in the day would it become painfully clear that Kinnock himself would not lead Labour to 'the promised land' and that he, too, would have to go. All this still had to be learned, and if the scope of change had been properly understood in 1985, it is not at all obvious how many – particularly on the soft left – would have signed on for the project. But politics involves choices, learning and occasional leaps of faith. Supporting Kinnock in his effort to revive the party's electoral fortunes was for many a genuine leap, and in the context of 1983–86 a rather courageous one, onto a path whose destination remained largely unknown. It was facilitated by the simple and very honourable desire not to keep losing and not to allow Thatcher and the Tories to keep winning. But even that was not simple. The desire to win was in fact not at all universal within the party and Kinnock was right to acknowledge 'an element which has treated realism as treachery, regarded appeals to unity as an excuse for suppression of liberties and scorned any emphasis on the importance of winning elections as a con- taminating bacillus called "electoralism" '.[46] Kinnock's first achievement, in retrospect, was to make it respectable to aspire to victory.

Wanting to win was, of course, not the same as actually being in a position to do so and Kinnock grasped early on that the effort to make Labour electable again would require 'profound changes in the policies and in the organisation of the Labour Party'. The task would not be quick or easy, however, for 'in the Labour Party, the leadership had no instrument for inaugurating and pursuing change on the scale and in the direction that was needed'.[47] The creation of a coalition loyal to the new leadership was the first prerequisite for Kinnock's sustained effort to reshape the party and while his election as leader seemed to mark the emergence of such an alliance, it was but a first step. The alliance backing Kinnock's election was far too broad and too fragile to become the basis of an effort to reshape the party and so had to be reconstituted during 1984–85. Prior to that the pressing need to deal not only with Margaret Thatcher, but with the furious opposition to Thatcher, further delayed the process of renovation and, indeed, almost derailed it entirely. Thatcher's aggressiveness seemed to confirm the left in its diagnosis of the ills of British capitalism and in its repudiation of the moderate policies characteristic of previous Labour governments. Thatcher also provoked a period of intense confrontation that further discredited counsels of moderation and reinforced the appeal of the left, which by now was deeply rooted in the institutions of the party. Only repeated failure in the confrontation with the Thatcher government had weaned the party from the left and its more radical strategic vision and elicited a break between a soft left willing to back Kinnock and a more hard left committed to continuing the struggle for socialism. Only after the accession of the soft left to the coalition arrayed behind Kinnock was it possible for the new leadership, which by this time was not quite so new, to begin to move the party to the political centre by recasting its image and remaking its programme.

This time lag would mean that very little progress had been made by the general election of 1987, which Labour again lost by a wide margin. Kinnock himself expressed regret at the delay but argued that forcing the pace of change would have been counter-productive: as he explained to an interviewer in 1994, 'if you make the change at a speed that is not agreed or acceptable to the Labour movement, then you smash into the wall of the block vote or uproar in the constituencies'.[48] It was clear in retrospect that whatever direction reform and restructure would take, it would face serious obstacles. What was not so clear at the time, however, was in just what direction Kinnock, or those around him, wanted to take the party and, whatever the chosen path, how far they would want to go on it. Hindsight makes the eventual outcome too obvious and obscures the fact that those who chose to stick with Labour in the early 1980s, its lowest point in decades, and to seek to rebuild it, had but the vaguest notion of what rebuilding would entail and how much would have to be changed. What Kinnock was clear about, from the very beginning, was the need to improve the party's organisation and campaigning ability so as to enhance its capacity to present its ideas and programme. Presentation was essential to making the party electable once again, and Kinnock broke decisively and immediately with those on the left who appeared willing to contemplate successive defeats secure in the knowledge that their programme was correct and that eventually history, if not the voters, would judge them right.

The very first fruits of the choice to become electable were the appointments Kinnock made to his own staff and to the staff and structure of the party's headquarters. Dick Clements, former editor of *Tribune*, became head of the leader's personal office; and Charles Clarke, son of the distinguished civil servant 'Otto' Clarke and a former leader of the National Union of Students – where he first did battle with the hard left or, in this case, the 'broad left' organised by the Communist Party – and long-time member of the Labour Co-ordinating Committee (LCC), was appointed Kinnock's personal assistant and in short order took over Clements's job. Henry Neuberger was inherited from Foot's staff and took responsibility for economic policy; and the formidably talented John Reid was hired to do political research. Another important appointment was Patricia Hewitt, who became press secretary *extraordinaire*. Though still quite young, Hewitt had extensive experience working for what are now called 'non-governmental organisations' – first, when still fresh out of university, for Age Concern and then, from the age of 24, serving as the head of the National Council for Civil Liberties for nine years. She, too, had been active in the LCC and as an unsuccessful Labour candidate in 1983 had suffered the consequences of the party's disastrous campaign. Reflecting on the experience, she had concluded that 'The Labour Party lacks virtually all the requirements of a successful national political party.'[49]

Very quickly both Clarke and Hewitt produced blueprints for party reorganisation and began to put their imprint on at least the style, if not the policy substance, of the new leadership. Understanding the need to impose some discipline upon the garrulous Kinnock and to provide a measure of protection from a potentially hostile press, Hewitt famously told a reporter from the BBC that 'We're out to control people like you' and proceeded to veto a plan for the leader to appear on the popular *Weekend World* programme on 9 October 1983. To the extent possible, Hewitt imposed a monopoly on communications between the leader and the media while Clarke asserted control over Kinnock's schedule, insisting to his boss 'that you never make a commitment to anybody for your diary . . .'.[50] At the same time the Kinnock team sought to ratchet up the party's focus on winning over potential voters by establishing the Campaign Strategy Committee, which had the additional advantage of bypassing the potentially troublesome NEC and allowing the leadership a relatively free hand in how it chose to present issues to the public. The left might still determine Labour Party policy, but Kinnock and his allies increasingly managed to exert greater control over which policies were talked about, which policies were conveniently forgotten, and how policy would be explained to potential voters.

The leadership's efforts to control the flow of information and hence to influence the image of the party were distinctly limited, however, by three factors: first, they could not easily impose their reading of events on a press whose job it was to be critical; second, they had absolutely no ability to prevent the Conservatives from focusing attention on those aspects of the Labour Party that were deemed least attractive; and third, Labour still spoke with many voices. The party could in fact do little to influence the press, although it could and did begin a more concerted effort to use television rather than the print media to get is message across. Nor was it possible to deter the Tories from attacking the party.

Where Kinnock and his allies could in theory make change was within the party they led. This proved to be a difficult and protracted task and progress would come very slowly. An essential prerequisite to exerting tighter control over message was tightening and rationalising the party organisation. When Kinnock took over, party headquarters at Walworth Road was split into ten separate departments, each with its own head, and the general secretary, Jim Mortimer, lacked the strength or the will to coordinate their work effectively or to impose a strategic goal upon their often overlapping agendas. Mortimer's plan for redundancies, a move dictated by the party's dire financial difficulties in the aftermath of the 1983 election defeat, had been rebuffed by the NEC. A subsequent 'Review of Reviews', submitted in June 1984, summarised and restated previous advice on how to streamline the party's organisation, but it, too, met an indifferent fate. Part of Kinnock's problem was his tenuous hold on the NEC and the unions, both of which had tilted back slightly to the left during 1983–84. The unions went so far as to inflict a stinging defeat on Kinnock at the 1994 conference over a proposal to introduce the principle of one member, one vote (OMOV) into the reselection process in constituency parties. Kinnock reacted by moving more deliberately on issues of constitutional reform which, if pressed too fast, might produce tactical alliances between the unions seeking to preserve their collective influence and the hard left committed to restricting the freedom of manoeuvre of the leadership and the parliamentary party. Kinnock also began systematically to bypass the NEC on policy-making by the device of 'joint policy committees'. Throughout the 1970s and early 1980s the major source of policy innovation was the NEC and its sub-committees, most especially the Home Policy Committee. In December 1983, however, Kinnock managed to secure agreement on the setting up of several joint policy committees, each of which would have a more limited remit and would be composed of representatives of the NEC, the TUC and the Shadow Cabinet. The ostensible objective was to provide a more integrated policy-making process; the unspoken aim was to reduce the influence of the NEC and the left – something he could still do only indirectly, and by stealth.

Not until Mortimer's retirement in 1985 was it possible to restructure the party's central organisation in a more thoroughgoing fashion. By then Kinnock's support on the NEC was more secure and he had little difficulty getting his way over Mortimer's replacement. The job went to Larry Whitty, a former civil servant with extensive background in the trade unions. He had been for several years responsible for running Trade Unions for a Labour Victory, the group that kept Labour afloat financially, and he thus knew well who mattered and who did not within the unions and how to get things done through them. Whitty belonged to a cohort of young union officials – Tom Sawyer was another – who had worked to modernise the structure and finances of the trade unions in a turbulent era of growth, consolidation and then precipitous decline, and who had come to believe that a similar process was required for the Labour Party machine.[51] To them, modernisation was not an especially political issue, but an organisational necessity. Working closely with Hewitt and Clarke, Whitty moved rapidly to reshape the party's organisation: its diffuse department structure was jettisoned and three new 'directorates' – for research, organisation and communication – were established. Geoff Bish stayed on as director of research and policy; and Joyce Gould was put in charge of organisation; but the key appointment was Peter Mandelson as director of communications. Mandelson would join with Hewitt and Clarke as together they became the three central players in the drive to 'modernise' the Labour Party from within. Mandelson had a background in television that was more than symbolic, for Kinnock had begun to write off the newspapers and placed his hopes increasingly on television. While Clarke had first informed Mandelson of the opening at party head-quarters, he was initially regarded as Roy Hattersley's candidate. The NEC was sharply divided – there were two other strong candidates, Dennis McShane and Nita Clarke – and the vote was close in the end, but Mandelson performed exceptionally well in his interview and Kinnock had by then come round as a supporter. His appointment was a clear signal of Kinnock's determination to make Labour an effective campaign organisation.[52]

Mandelson, Hewitt and Clarke would jointly oversee a revolution in how Labour functioned as a party and, equally important, in how it was seen to function by the press, who saw these matters up close, and by the public.[53] Labour under their influence sought to alter its image and the image of its leader; the party began an effort to communicate its message more simply and effectively to voters by making better use of television and by paying attention to what was seen as well as to what was said; and they redefined the audience to whom they were appealing. In all of this they were self-consciously 'modern' in a manner that distinguished them sharply from early generations of party leaders and officials and in no sphere were they so modern and so professional as in that of measuring and reacting to public opinion. Traditionally, Labour had been suspicious of polling for it seemed to imply a readiness to abandon principle and to pander to voters by telling them only what they wanted to hear. Labour politics should be a crusade, a movement, a matter of commitment, not a preference to be marketed or a product to be sold. The practice of polling elicited special animus from the left of the party, for opinion polls so often revealed the wide chasm that separated voters and the party faithful, particularly on issues like nationalisation and disarmament, and provided a rationale for overriding questions of ideology and of principle in the interest of winning elections. The critics were to some extent correct, as the progress of the 'modernisers' would demonstrate. Kinnock's new team began in 1985–86 exploring how to make the case for Labour's existing repertoire of policies. When that failed decisively in the 1987 election, they would be forced to move on to reconsidering those policies themselves. Still, the move was not automatic; nor did its gradual unfolding prove that the modernisers began with the aim of revising the party's programme and abandoning its historic commitments. At the beginning was merely the desire to win again – the full agenda of revising what the Labour Party stood for followed from that.

In fact, the energy with which Clarke, Hewitt and especially Mandelson pursued the task of equipping Labour with a 'modern' apparatus for fighting and winning election campaigns suggests that they truly believed, or at least allowed themselves to believe, that this might well suffice to defeat Thatcher. The first step was to go outside the party for professional advice. As early as 1984 Hewitt had urged the hiring of an advertising agency to run the party's 'Jobs and Industry' campaign and she was already looking ahead to the next election.[54] It was Mandelson, however, who in the autumn of 1985 began to put together a new organisation and to implement an entirely new approach to political communication within the party. He had been contacted by Philip Gould, a young advertising and political consultant, and the two had agreed the main outlines of a plan that Gould summarised in a report later commissioned by the party. The aim of this so-called 'Communications Review' was to propose how Labour should organise itself for future campaigns.[55] Even before it was presented, however, a meeting was arranged for 23 November 1985 in which key officials reviewed polling and other data on the task confronting the party. The problem, as Gould recounted, was

> the fault-line between Labour and its potential supporters, the apparently unbridgeable gap between what Labour had become and what the British electorate now wanted. While Labour was still talking the language of nationalisation, unilateralism and high taxes, the British public was buying council houses and shares in the newly privatised British Telecom and British Petroleum, and revelling in the success of Britain's born-again military might.[56]

From there the discussion proceeded to the question of target voters, particularly people aged 25–44 whose historic ties to Labour were weak or non-existent, who believed that society was increasingly scary and hostile and whose response was to focus upon 'me and my family'. In the main these people were simply indifferent to Labour's traditional appeal; but they were actively hostile to Labour's positions on defence, trade unions and taxes. Younger people were even more antipathetic to Labour: 'The only time the Labour Party was good was in history, what they've read at school . . . But that's not the case any more.'[57] The implications were dire and demanded a dramatic response.

Gould's follow-up report, similar in tone, was ready by December and built upon this analysis of Labour's massive liabilities. He then made two quite significant arguments. The first and most obvious was that the party's existing campaigning organisation was a shambles and needed major restructuring along professional lines; the second, and potentially the more controversial, was that the way forward was to create a new group that would, in effect, be outside the existing party apparatus. The message was not only that reform and repackaging were critical but that the party as constituted just could not do it. Instead, Gould proposed the creation of what became in March 1986 the Shadow Communications Agency (SCA), which he would run using volunteers (and space) from BMP (Boase, Massimi, Pollitt), the advertising agency that had designed the campaign in defence of the Greater London Council. This informal group would formally advise the larger, official Campaign Management Team, chaired by Robin Cook, but day to day it would interact with Mandelson and the leadership around Kinnock. The SCA would help to develop slogans and symbols, test out concepts and proposals and provide guidance to the party on presentation. That guidance would be based on opinion polling of a familiar quantitative sort supplemented by qualitative research, i.e. the use of focus groups to discern more precisely what voters thought, feared and hoped for and how different messages would be received and interpreted. The SCA also undertook to educate the party on social trends and to identify target constituencies, their interests and aspirations. They would become the party's sociologists in residence who sought to analyse the social structure of both the electorate and of the Labour Party and who would serve as the vehicle by which Labour policy, programme and rhetoric were aligned with perceived or projected changes in society.

The team assembled by Kinnock was distinctive and it proved highly effective. His personal office, dominated by Clarke and Hewitt and aided by the economist John Eatwell, gave the leader resources that had been unavailable to his predecessors. The appointments of Whitty and Mandelson at Walworth Road did not solve all the problems of the party's formal organisation but at least put in place a set of people who understood them and who could begin addressing them. The creation of the SCA, moreover, provided a level of professional expertise that had long been missing within the party and its location outside the party's formal structure gave it a flexibility essential to waging a fast-moving, media-driven, modern election campaign. Most important, the moves enabled Kinnock to get on with the election campaign without having to do battle over every line of the manifesto and every slogan with the NEC which, even when it was loyal, was cumbersome and inefficient and by custom and belief unwilling to play the role that the new team took upon itself. Mandelson and his allies at the SCA were thus able to move rapidly to remake the image of the party. At the group's very first official meeting in March 1986, for example, there was a candid discussion of the baggage attached to Labour: 'There is more imagery attached to the Labour Party than to other parties . . .' and its 'imagery owes more to history, ideology and an apparent multiplicity of "spokespersons"' than was desirable. The Tories, by contrast, were linked in people's imagination 'more to individual aspirations' and, ironically, they were seen as having no 'ideology'.[58] Since, according to the results of the focus groups, 'Self-interest is the prevalent ethos among the target audience', Labour had a huge problem. As a very first step, the modernisers – as they defined themselves – set out to find a new symbol for the party and unveiled the red rose at the next party conference. The aim was to be 'inspirational' and to avoid frightening voters. The new team also began to recruit media celebrities – writers, artists, rock stars – as part of an effort to recast its image: it would be in future the party of the thoughtful, tasteful and creative and not merely the poor and the aggrieved.[59] Ken Follett was asked to chair the 'Writers' Group'. His wife Barbara Follett would take it upon herself to make-over Labour candidates for Parliament, advising on dress, grooming and presentation. Over time quite a number of future MPs, men and women alike, would be 'Folletted'.[60] A parallel effort was also begun to see to it that 'the competing "noise"' of the angry, of the left, of 'Scargill/Grant/Hatton' was 'turned off', although that proved quite difficult to achieve in practice.[61]

Perhaps most impressive was the extent to which the campaign's organisers were sensitive to the party's liabilities and to the ways in which it was open to Tory attack. Early on it was conceded that neither Kinnock nor Hattersley were 'seen yet as the statesmen the British public likes to see in their prime ministerial candidates'.[62] Kinnock could be a highly effective speaker when addressing audiences of the party faithful, but he was too long-winded to do well in parliamentary debate and comparable venues. He had famously failed, for example, to land a serious blow on Thatcher at a highly vulnerable moment in the row over Westland in January 1986 and it was obvious that he was best when controlled. Deciding how to market Kinnock and make him appear more authoritative was thus a top priority. It was equally important, however, to anticipate attacks and devise appropriate responses. Again, focus groups led Mandelson and the SCA to worry over defence, 'the Party's links with the trade unions', the so-called 'loony left' and the broader sense that Labour was 'a party in disarray'.[63] Balancing these liabilities were several historic strengths – the party's identification with the National Health Service and the welfare state, for example – and the fact that Margaret Thatcher was herself extremely unpopular: people simply

disliked her 'personality, which is cold verging on the positively vindict-
ive'.[64] Labour had hoped that it would be possible to attack the Conservatives on the issue of unemployment, which remained high, but by
1986–87 economic recovery had set in and party researchers learned that
the public, or large sections of it, had become inured to the plight of
those unable to find work and were more concerned with their own circumstances. The conclusion drawn from these findings was that Labour
should run a campaign that was fundamentally negative: 'Overall theme.
Mrs Thatcher is extreme . . . is hectoring, out of touch and out of the
consensus mould of decent Toryism.' 'Neil Kinnock', on the other hand,
'is the mainstream.' The campaign was at the same time defensive, as officials sought to parry the blows of the Tories by obscuring their position
on defence and by trying to distance themselves from, and to discredit,
the left within the party. A characteristic example was the response of
Patricia Hewitt to the by-election defeat at Greenwich in early March 1987.
She wrote in a leaked and widely-quoted letter:

> It is obvious from our own polling, as well as from the doorstep, that the
> 'London effect' is now very noticeable. The 'Loony Labour Left' is now
> taking its toll; the gays and lesbians issue is costing us dear amongst the
> pensioners and fear of extremism and higher taxes/rates is particularly
> prominent in the GLC [Greater London Council] area.[65]

It was a curious strategy in that it lacked a centre – a positive vision
of what Labour offered that could command the support of the party and
its leaders. Labour had numerous policies, some of which Kinnock and
his allies supported and some of which they shunned, but the election
of June 1987 would be fought on other grounds: as a referendum
on Thatcher. It was also fought with great flair: Kinnock was energetic,
eloquent and impassioned, and the party's media effort was regarded as
extremely successful. The first major campaign event was his speech at
Llandudno, which was much praised and quoted. The party's initial
broadcast, directed by Hugh Hudson, made extensive use of the footage
from that event and featured Kinnock and his personal qualities rather
than the party. It was regarded as a great success and so rebroadcast
towards the end of the campaign. Kinnock's handlers also did their best
to rebut criticisms of party policy, though they were repeatedly thrown
onto the defensive. The issue of the 'loony left', however unfairly framed

and reported, had been aired fully and to damaging effect during and after the Greenwich by-election in early March and so continued to hang over the campaign for the general election of June 1987. The two other issues about which party strategists had worried – defence and taxes – also arose in due course. Kinnock made a key blunder on 24 May in response to a question from David Frost about Labour's non-nuclear defence policy. He explained plausibly enough that in the event of a Soviet invasion or occupation the choice would be between 'exterminating everything that you stand for' or 'using the resources that you've got to make any occupation totally untenable'. He was confident that 'any effort . . . to occupy the United Kingdom . . . would be utterly untenable'. His candour was not appreciated, however, for it was simply impolitic for the leader of the Labour Party to appear capable of contemplating the possibility of a Soviet occupation with such equanimity. However sanguine he might personally be about the outcome of popular resistance, it was hardly reassuring about the party's defence policy. A few days later campaign officials arranged a press conference designed to defuse the issue, but considerable damage had been done. The party also suffered grievous harm from Kinnock's discussion of taxes during the campaign's last week: he admitted that if elected the party would reverse the government's recent reduction of 2p in the basic rate and also increase National Insurance contributions. Though tax had long been identified as a potential liability for the party, the campaign had not succeeded in preparing a proper response.[66]

Without a more positive message and beset by the difficulties of defending policies that were deeply unpopular, even the most effective campaign strategists – and Labour's might not have been quite as effective as they were reputed to be – could not prevail. In fact, the election was a disaster. Thatcher won a third successive victory with 42.3 per cent of the votes; Labour came a distant second with 30.8 per cent; and the Alliance won 22.6 per cent. Labour picked up 20 seats, but the Conservatives retained a majority of over 100 seats. The Labour share of the vote had increased just 3.2 per cent over the low point of 1983 and the Tory vote remained at almost the same level. What Labour had effectively done was to see off the threat from the SDP, or rather the SDP-Liberal Alliance. When the campaign began, the Alliance were between two and four points behind Labour in the polls, not far off from their final tally in the 1983 election. But the Alliance was hampered by the problem of the 'two Davids', in theory co-equal leaders but in truth not, by the fact that the two parties did in fact differ substantially in outlook, and by indecision over whether to focus their attacks on Labour or on the Conservatives. Most important in determining the Alliance's fate, however, was the fact that the Labour campaign was much better than in 1983; and its mistakes, though harmful, were not devastating. The effect was 'a sudden surge of belief that Labour was doing much better than expected' and a return of voters temporarily lured away by the prospects of the Alliance.[67] As the election approached, the gap between Labour and the Alliance widened and at the end Labour was more than eight points ahead in the popular vote. Labour emerged with 229 seats; the Alliance with a mere 22.[68] This was no small achievement, for it would mean that Labour would continue to provide the only real alternative to the Tories both inside and outside Parliament and it would guarantee that, if and when the Conservatives began to lose support, it was Labour that would be in position to pick it up. But that prospect seemed as far off as ever. As Larry Whitty noted just after the election, 'Throughout the campaign . . . the Tory vote remained stubbornly steady.'[69] Labour had failed to make inroads in the Conservative vote despite a clear and often convincing focus on the unattractive character of the party's leader. The conclusion was clear enough: however abrasive Thatcher's personality, her policies and her government's handling of the economy and their conduct of the nation's affairs commanded wide support and Labour's alternative did not.

In the post-mortems on the 1987 election all sides agreed that the campaign itself was a great success. Whitty, as the voice of the party organisation, congratulated Mandelson and said that his 'efforts, political judgement and imagination have made this the most effective campaign the party has ever waged'. Kinnock concurred and asserted that it had been 'the most successful campaign in the history of the party'. Roy Hattersley, a bit more caustically, argued that 'The 1987 election was, in terms of policy and personalities, a total failure. But it was a public relations triumph.'[70] The fact that a supposedly brilliant campaign produced such dismal results, however, convinced the leadership that the transformation of the party had to be pushed ahead still further. Patricia Hewitt admitted after the election that there had been an 'over-emphasis on anti-Thatcher', implying that it was necessary to offer the voters something more. It would be necessary as well to deal with the fact that, as Nick Raynsford put it, there were '. . . too many worrying skeletons in the Labour Party cupboard deterring voters . . .' from opting for Kinnock.[71] Defence, taxes, the role of the 'loony left' and the perception that Labour was still a divided and fissiparous party were the main 'skeletons', and getting rid of them would require more than deft handling by the party's press officers. It would also require the development of a new set of policies that would assure the electorate that Labour had truly and permanently changed under Kinnock. It was to that task that the Kinnock leadership turned in the aftermath of defeat.

Notes and references

1 Edward Pearce, *Hummingbirds and Hyenas* (London: Faber & Faber, 1985), 80–1.

2 Kinnock supposedly regretted that Benn was unable to challenge him for the leadership in 1983, for if he had, 'the result of the leadership election would quickly have defined the character of the party'. Kinnock, cited in Martin Westlake, with Ian St John, *Kinnock: The Biography* (London: Little, Brown, 2001), 210.

3 Robert Harris, *The Making of Neil Kinnock* (London: Faber & Faber, 1984), 212–18.

4 Tony Benn, *The End of an Era: Diaries, 1980–1990*, edited by Ruth Winstone (London: Hutchinson, 1992), 320.

5 See Patricia Hewitt, 'Political Fund Ballot Campaign', 31 July 1984, in the Kinnock Papers, Churchill College, Cambridge, Box 90 KNNK/90.

6 The most authoritative account is probably M. Adeney and John Lloyd, *The Miners' Strike, 1984–85: Loss Without Limit* (London: Routledge, 1986).

7 The quotes are directly from Kinnock; the estimate of 57 per cent is inferred from Kinnock's statements in response to Scargill as recorded in the transcript of a 'Telephone Conversation between Neil Kinnock and Arthur Scargill', 9 April 1994, Kinnock Papers, Papers on the Miners Strike, KNNK 3/23. On 19 April 1984 the NUM formally altered the rule that 55 per cent of workers vote yes in order for a strike to be called and substituted 50 per cent, but the executive still did not hold a ballot. See Westlake, *Kinnock*, 288, 298.

8 *The Times*, 20 June 1984.

9 Cited in Peter Riddell, *The Thatcher Decade* (Oxford: Blackwell, 1989), 118.

10 *Financial Times*, November 1986.

11 See, in general, Barry Jones and Michael Keating, *Labour and the British State* (Oxford: Clarendon, 1985).

12 John Gyford, 'The new urban left: A local road to socialism', *New Society*, No. 64 (1983), 1066; M. Boddy and C. Fudge, 'Labour Councils and New Left Alternatives', in Boddy and Fudge, eds, *Local Socialism* (London: Macmillan, 1984); and Patrick Seyd, *The Rise and Fall of the Labour Left* (New York: St Martin's, 1987), chapter 6.

13 David Blunkett, with Alex MacCormick, *On A Clear Day* (London: Michael O'Mara Books, 1995), 130.

14 See Peter Jenkins, *Mrs Thatcher's Revolution: The Ending of the Socialist Era* (Cambridge, MA: Harvard University Press, 1988), 246–50.

15 Kinnock Papers, Box 193 KNNK/193.

16 For a detailed account, see Peter Kilfoyle, *Left Behind: Lessons from Labour's Heartlands* (London: Politico's, 2000), especially 141–66.

17 See the note, 'Rate-Capping. A Note on Political Strategy', NEC Local Government Committee (Geoff Bish, secretary), Labour Party Research Department Memorandum 3094, August, 1984, in Labour Party Papers, Labour History Archives and Study Centre (LHASC), University of Manchester.

18 *The Times*, 27 June 1985, cited in Westlake, *Kinnock*, 322.

19 *Report of the Labour Party Annual Conference 1984*.

20 Benn, *End of an Era*, entry for 1 October 1985, 424.

21 Kinnock, speaking in late November 1985, quoted in Westlake, *Kinnock*, 329.

22 See the 'Report of the Investigation into Liverpool District Labour Party', February 1986, in KNNK/90; NEC Minutes, 26 February 1986.

23 Eileen Jones, *Neil Kinnock* (London: Robert Hale, 1994), 74.

24 See Richard Heffernan and Mike Marqusee, *Defeat from the Jaws of Victory: Inside Kinnock's Labour Party* (London: Verso, 1992), chapter 10 for a detailed and engaged account; and Eric Shaw, *Discipline and Discord in the Labour Party* (Manchester: Manchester University Press, 1988), chapters 11–12, for a less engaged view.

25 Minutes of the Meeting of the TUC General Council, 21 May 1980, TUC Papers.

26 Robert Taylor, *The TUC: From the General Strike to New Unionism* (London: Palgrave, 2000), 246–53.

27 Neil Kinnock, 'Reforming the Labour Party', *Contemporary Record*, VIII, 3 (Winter 1994), 536.

28 Blunkett, *On A Clear Day*, 128.

29 Kinnock to Ian Mikardo, 13 April 1981, KNNK/418.

30 CLPD Annual Report for 1981, KNNK/418.

31 See Heffernan and Marqusee, *Defeat from the Jaws of Victory*, on the earliest reports of 'the realignment of the left', 64.

32 Quoted in Andy McSmith, *Faces of Labour: The Inside Story* (London: Verso, 1996), 172–3.

33 Benn, *End of an Era*, entry for 19 November 1983, 326.

34 McSmith, *Faces of Labour*, 173–6; Shaw, *Discipline and Discord*, 269–70.

35 *The Guardian*, 20 May 1986.

36 Interview with Lord Sawyer, 10 October 2002.

37 The LCC was launched by a committee of 17, including Meacher, Bob Cryer, Bryan Gould, Stuart Holland, the intellectual architect of Labour's Programme 1973, Jeff Rooker, Brian Sedgemore and Audrey Wise. Together with Benn's two key aides, Morrell and Francis Cripps, this collection ensured a close relationship with the left in the parliamentary party.

38 Westlake, *Kinnock*, 309.

39 Quoted in David Kogan and Maurice Kogan, *The Battle for the Labour Party* (London: Kogan Page, 1982), 51.

40 Paul Tompson and Ben Lucas, *The Forward March of Modernisation: A History of the LCC, 1978–1998* (London: LCC, 1998), 3.

41 Patrick Seyd, 'Bennism without Benn', *New Socialist* (May, 1985).

42 *Tribune*, 20 Setember 1985. The most extensive and critical discussion of this issue of 'realignment' is Heffernan and Marqusee, *Defeat from the Jaws of Victory*, 64–70.

43 Benn, *End of an Era*, diary entries for 27 March 1983, 279; and 25 September 1983, 318.

44 Benn, *End of an Era*, entry for 5 May 1985, 407.

45 Benn, *End of an Era*, entry for 25 September 1985, 318.

46 Kinnock, 'Reforming the Labour Party', 540.

47 Kinnock, 'Reforming the Labour Party', 536.

48 Kinnock, 28 February 1994, interview with Tudor Jones, cited in Jones, *Remaking the Labour Party: From Gaitskell to Blair* (London: Routledge, 1996), 114.

49 Cited in Westlake, *Kinnock*, 248.

50 She spoke to the BBC reporter on 7 October 1983. See Westlake, *Kinnock*, 251–3.

51 Interviews with Lord Whitty, 14 November 2002, and Lord Sawyer, 10 October 2002.

52 Donald Macintyre, *Mandelson and the Making of New Labour* (London: HarperCollins, 1999), 90–5.

53 The three worked closely together, but the relationship was occasionally strained and would disintegrate in the end. Mandelson and Clarke fell out when Mandelson sought his own seat in Parliament in 1989 and Clarke had already eased Hewitt out of her job in late 1988 and into a new position in charge of policy, from which she quickly departed to join the Institute for Public Policy Research. They all kept reappearing, however, and were never far from the centre of the New Labour project for long. On the falling out in 1989–90, see especially Philip Gould, *The Unfinished Revolution: How the Modernisers Saved the Labour Party* (London: Little, Brown, 1998), 99–102; also Macintyre, *Mandelson*, 185–6, 238–40; and Westlake, *Kinnock*, 472–3.

54 Hewitt, memo of 23 July 1984, KNNK/304.

55 Philip Gould to Robin Cook, 4 October 1985, KNNK/304.

56 Gould, *Unfinished Revolution*, 49–50.

57 The data and analysis were furnished by Leslie Butterfield and Paul Southgate from Abbott Mead Vickers, Roddy Glen of Strategic Research Group, and by representatives of the firm BBDO. See Gould, *Unfinished Revolution*, 49–54.

58 Report of meeting of Campaign Management Team, 25 March 1986, KNNK/304. The Conservatives' ability to portray themselves as above ideology was not new, but rather their characteristic ideological stance. For a thoughtful analysis, see E.H.H. Green, *Ideologies of Conservatism: Conservative Political Ideas in the Twentieth Century* (Oxford: Oxford University Press, 2002).

59 The strategy is laid out in various letters contained in KNNK/304.

60 Interview with Anna Coote, 17 July 2003. Barbara Follett helped to found the Labour Women's Network in 1987 and became director of Emily's List UK in 1993.

61 'Communications Strategy: Next Steps', nd (but presumably December 1985), KNNK/304.

62 Robert Worcester, of MORI, to Chris Powell, 9 January 1986, KNNK/304.

63 See Worcester to Powell, 9 January 1986 and the SCA presentation, 'Communicating the Party's Strategy', February 1987, KNNK/307.

64 See 'Communicating the Party's Strategy', February 1987, and 'Labour Party – Policy and Advertising Research. Summary Report', 31 March 1987, KNNK/307.

65 The leak occurred on 4 March 1987. The excerpt is quoted in Heffernan and Marqusee, *Defeat from the Jaws of Victory*, 74.

66 Westlake, *Kinnock*, 411–2, 415, recounts both episodes.

67 Bill Rodgers, *Fourth among Equals* (London: Poltico's, 2000), 256.

68 Ivor Crewe and Anthony King, *SDP: The Birth, Life and Death of the Social Democratic Party* (Oxford: Oxford University Press, 1995), 366–82.

69 See Whitty's report to the NEC, 'General Election 1987', GS56/6/6/87, NEC, 24 June 1987 LHASC.

70 Quotes from Macintyre, *Mandelson*, 167–8. As Macintyre makes clear, however, there were some, like Charles Clarke, who did not share this enthusiasm for what Mandelson and the SCA advisers had done.

71 See Hewitt to Bryan Gould and the Campaign Management Team, 16 July 1987; Nick Raynsford, 'Lessons from the Defeat', June 1987, in KNNK/585.

CHAPTER 8

• • • • • • • • • • • • • • • • •

'Modernise' and lose, 1987–92

Labour's 1987 election campaign had demonstrated in painful detail the limits of what could be achieved simply by improving presentation. The experience argued strongly for the need to move further and to reshape more thoroughly the party's programme, its detailed policies and its image. This would require nothing less than a new identity. From this radical understanding would emerge the Policy Review, a process that would serve to reverse the recent domination of policy-making by the left and proceed to equip Labour with a conceptual framework, a rhetoric and a programme on which to base a renewed claim to the right to govern the nation. Almost as soon as the devastating general election results were in, therefore, voices were raised about the importance of revising policy. Kinnock had suggested the need to 'pull some teeth' and the recurring problem of having to defend policies that were widely recognised as inapplicable and unpopular had deepened the resolve among those most involved in the campaign to rid the party of commitments that seemed to bring only trouble. Mandelson retired for a period of reflection after the campaign and emerged convinced that the party's weakness lay in the product, not the presentation: 'Labour cannot offer more of the same even better packaged . . .', he argued. It was the programme itself that had to go; and what the party needed was 'an intellectually driven process of change' that would do for Labour what Bad Godesberg had done for the German Social Democrats.[1] Philip Gould chimed in soon after in a report to the NEC on the campaign and what should follow. He proposed that 'working groups be established to prepare reports in all areas' of policy and that the SCA carry out simultaneous research into the broader processes of social change in order to determine 'what are the real motivations influencing voting behaviour'.[2] The debate about policy would thus be conducted much like the campaign, with focus groups trying to discern where voters were at. It was taken for granted, implicitly at least, that the party would go to where the voters were rather than expect voters to be moved towards the party by the strength of its arguments. The idea was quickly translated into a plan of action by Tom Sawyer of NUPE – also chair of the NEC's Home Policy Committee – who put forward a proposal for a sustained effort to reassess policy that would combine the work of so-called Policy Review Groups with a consultative exercise designed to elicit the views of party members and the public.[3] The plan was proposed in July, approved by the NEC in mid-September, and adopted by conference later in the month, though without great enthusiasm.[4] Sawyer went on to head the exercise, which would consume the efforts of most of the party's top leaders for the next two years. Kinnock largely set the process in motion and would preside over it, though he kept himself above the details and would occasionally betray a lack of engagement with the task. He was convinced that Labour needed new policies and equally determined to see them in place, but Kinnock was a politician first and foremost and so more comfortable selling policy than making it up.

It was widely understood that the aim of the Policy Review was to shed past commitments and to dissociate the leadership from positions that it was assumed were costing the party votes. The actual content of the new policies was to this extent rather less important than the symbolic effect their adoption would have, or was supposed to have, in proclaiming that the party had been transformed and that it was no longer in the grip of the left or in thrall to the unions. The elaborate staging of the review was intended therefore to underline for the public that Labour was different and no longer to be feared. Staging was also critical in creating a show of unity that would demonstrate that Labour was not still in the throes of an internal war and that it could display the self-discipline voters demanded in a possible government. Agreeing on a new set of policies was therefore only the first and the more formal objective of the exercise and the process was designed to do much more.

Taken together, these were far-reaching aims and the Policy Review went a long way towards achieving them. That it did not succeed completely merely underscores the scope of the task it was invented to correct.

The Policy Review was effectively carried out by seven study groups that were also chosen largely with an eye to presentation: there were groups on 'A Productive and Competitive Economy', 'People at Work', 'Economic Equality', 'Consumers and the Community', 'Democracy for the Individual and Community', 'Britain in the World' and the 'Physical and Social Environment'. Membership included representatives of the Shadow Cabinet, the NEC and the trade unions as well as co-opted out-side experts. The structure had been carefully designed to produce con-sensus among the key actors in the party. If the NEC and the unions were built into the process, it was felt, they would have less cause to complain about its outcome; and if the unions and the NEC were in support, then the party conference would approve as well. Getting the leaders of the parliamentary party involved was equally essential, for it would guaran-tee that considerations of practicality and the electoral impact of policy were not neglected. And guaranteeing that the question of presentation, and of getting elected, would remain central was the fact that the daily management of the review – the provision of logistical support and the organisation and presentation of research – was in the hands of the same party officials who had largely run the 1987 campaign. Mandelson, for example, would play a major role and he would again enlist the aid of the Shadow Communications Agency. Hewitt and Clarke remained active as well and served as surrogates for the leader; and the staff at party head-quarters would be commandeered and reshaped for the effort.[5]

Since the aim was to have a new set of policies adopted, approved, put into slogans and then talked about in time for the next general election, it moved fast and was kept rigidly on schedule. In consequence, the time and the space allowed for genuine consultation was minimal. The effort was formally designated as 'Labour Listens' and it involved meetings around the country at which members of the review groups would hear the opinions of ordinary citizens and constituency activists. Inevitably, the inputs were inconsistent and uneven, with correspond-ingly little impact, and the staged events served mainly as public relations. Colin Byrne, Mandelson's assistant who was often delegated to carry out the process, remembers it as this 'odd thing, which was basically about taking shadow ministers to town halls the length and breadth of the country to be shouted at by complete lunatics . . .'. The campaign nevertheless had a further, if unacknowledged purpose. As Byrne explained, 'At the time we thought, "Why are we doing this?" But it was quite clear afterwards that it was a strategy so he [Mandelson, but also his allies] could report back to the NEC: "People hate our policies: we've listened. People hate our policies".'[6] In short, Labour Listens was organised and carried out so as to reinforce the message that Labour desperately needed to change and to make that change seem both legitimate and inevitable. It was never meant seriously to solicit opinion from party activists and constituency parties, for they were the last people from whom the leadership wanted to hear.[7] Even after the review was completed and approved, local party members remained further to the left than the leadership and they were thus highly sceptical about the aims and the outcome of the review itself. They did ultimately come to accept the need to win elections, but were still reluctant to remake the party's programme in order to do so.[8]

In the end, the transformation of Labour's policies would be substantial, if not exactly revolutionary. On economic policy, for example, the effect of the review process was to moderate, to soften and to remove specific promises that could be seized on by opponents to frighten away voters.[9] The Policy Review therefore downplayed the party's plans for state intervention, spoke of 'social ownership' rather than nationalisation and regulation rather than planning or control; and in particular the party hedged on the commitment to take recently privatised industries back into public ownership. Labour as a party was nevertheless not ready as yet formally to abandon its support for state ownership and intervention. Indeed, while an early draft of the statement of 'philosophical' principles underlying party policy, *Democratic Socialist Aims and Values*, had expressed support for a mixed economy, even this rather uncontroversial statement of the obvious met with objections at the NEC and so was watered down in a subsequent revision.[10] The final report of the Policy Review, *Meet the Challenge, Make the Change*, approved overwhelmingly at the annual conference of 1989, likewise echoed the party's long-standing critique of finance and the City and the narrow, short-term mentality of business. The argument and the enemy were familiar: 'if short-termism is the disease, then it is the City which is the source of the infection'.[11] What was different was the determination not to do anything very dramatic about it.

Despite a reluctance to move too far or too fast, the deliberations undertaken by the review eventually issued in positions that pushed the party's programme towards the centre, struck a note of moderation and fiscal responsibility and stressed, perhaps tendentiously, the identification of socialism with 'social justice' and 'freedom'.[12] Thus the review proposed a fairer tax system that would provide relief to both the middle and working classes and promised, predictably, to close loopholes. It carefully avoided more aggressive policies aimed at redistribution and implicitly accepted the large changes in the structure of taxation – from direct to indirect taxes like VAT and the massive reduction in top rates – brought about by Thatcher.[13] Kinnock himself insisted that the party 'will not spend, nor will we promise to spend, more than the country can afford'.[14] There was also a clear shift of emphasis when discussing just what the state would do to revitalise the economy. The Labour Party, a top official proclaimed, now 'recognises the market's role in spurring innovation and consumer choice' and so it had come to accept that government's role was to create a framework for growth that would ensure adequate investment, proper training and infrastructure. This would entail the adoption of a genuine programme for growth, if not exactly a plan – the so-called Medium Term Industrial Strategy – and an enhanced Department of Trade and Industry to direct it. It would require the implementation of several new policy initiatives: more incentives for research and development; loans at below-market rates for small business; a national training fund financed by a 0.5 per cent payroll tax; and a national minimum wage. There would be new entities to oversee these innovations as well: British Technology Enterprise, a British Investment Bank, Skills UK, and a Fair Wages Commission. But for all the grand talk about new policies and agencies, and despite the continued identification of Labour as the party of production and of industry, the practical focus was increasingly shifted to supply-side interventions in the labour market – primarily education and training programmes, which would allow Britain to develop as a 'talent-based economy'. The state under a future Labour government would be, as Kinnock had termed it, an 'enabling state' that would create the conditions for growth and, in particular, give workers the skills they needed to get the jobs they lacked; it would not be a state that directly employed large numbers of workers or that decided where to invest and what to produce.[15]

The Policy Review also moved delicately towards redefining the relationship between Labour and the unions. There was, of course, a widespread desire within the labour movement to repeal the restrictive trade union legislation passed by the Thatcher governments. But even the union leaders recognised that most of the Thatcher reforms had won wide public acceptance and that a return to the pre-1979 pattern, in which unions enjoyed tremendous influence at the workplace and in politics and were protected by a wide range of immunities, would send the wrong signal to voters. A compromise solution was not easily reached, however. TUC representatives agreed to a modest restoration of trade union rights and a broader commitment to a 'charter for employment rights' for individual workers largely modelled on the European Social Charter.[16] The convenor of the review group in charge of issue, Michael Meacher, was nevertheless committed to something closer to the old approach and eager to demonstrate the party's loyalty to its trade union supporters and its continuing resistance to Thatcher. The draft of the *People at Work* document produced under Meacher's auspices would thus be rejected by the NEC in May 1989 for not going far enough in revising existing party policy. A further compromise was worked out after consultations with Derry Irvine, the Labour lawyer, who proposed the establishment of separate industrial courts to deal with the conduct of disputes. A suitably amended version of the report was approved at conference. It was not the most successful or popular piece of the review, but it began the process of shifting Labour's identity away from its historic connection with the trade unions.

Perhaps the most difficult shift to orchestrate was over defence policy; and the result was indirect and indecisive. The people who had run the 1987 election campaign were in no doubt that the party's defence policy not only lost votes directly but contributed to a more diffuse, but ultimately very damaging, sense that Kinnock and the Labour Party could not be entrusted with the nation's welfare. Campaign organisers had sought to finesse the issue by suggesting that the Tories' reliance on nuclear weapons weakened Britain's conventional forces, but the line simply did not take. A revision of party policy after the election was thus inevitable. Gerald Kaufman chaired the Britain in the World group and superintended the transformation. The basic strategy was to argue, sensibly enough, that the world was changing and Labour's policy should evolve with it. The emergence of Mikhail Gorbachev as the new Soviet leader led very rapidly to a de-escalation in the rhetoric of the 'Second Cold War' and to serious talks about arms control. The famous meeting between Gorbachev and Reagan at Reykjavik seemed to offer Labour an opportunity to argue for a new approach. The party's existing unilateralist policy was premised on the notion that the UK should renounce nuclear weapons in order to signal its aversion to nuclear war and to push the United States and the USSR to do likewise. However unlikely the prospect of that happening, it was the rationale for giving up 'something for nothing'. If the United States and the USSR were giving up weapons on their own, however the British stance was largely irrelevant.

Labour was nevertheless reluctant to alter its position, however, and the review of defence policy dragged on longer than other aspects of the review. Of course, if profound changes in the international climate were in the making, it made sense to study and evaluate them before proposing a new policy. In addition, waiting and remaining silent had at least the virtue of avoiding the sorts of gaffes and waffling to which Kinnock had been prone on the issue. His personal difficulty in articulating a new policy undoubtedly sprang in part from his past and passionate commitment to disarmament, which made it difficult for him to switch without inviting charges of opportunism. Unfortunately, delay also allowed time for confusion to deepen and for the opponents of change to resist. Indeed, in a series of interviews and meetings in the summer of 1988 Kinnock seemed to take both sides, first advocating a shift towards a multilateralist position and then seeming to back away, and in the process he conjured up opposition to the party's emerging policy from both the hard and the soft left, from Tony Benn and his allies as well as from Ken Livingstone and David Blunkett. A predictable side-effect was the embarrassing reaffirmation of the party's unilateralist position at the 1988 conference.

In the end it was the Soviets who facilitated the turn on defence policy. Kaufman and his study group continued to discuss the issues and arranged a trip to Moscow for February 1989. In a carefully staged event in Red Square, Soviet spokesmen affirmed their support for multilateral negotiations leading to multilateral reductions in nuclear weapons. Kinnock could now claim with greater credibility that he, and the party, retained 'the aim of renouncing nuclear weapons'. The debate had been 'about the best way of doing that' and the Soviets had now said it was through negotiations involving the United States and NATO. A Labour prime minister would not 'ever again' have to 'make the tactical argument for the unilateral abandonment of nuclear weapons without getting anything in return . . .'.[17] The review document put together by Kaufman elaborated the new policy in some detail and it was endorsed by the NEC and then by conference in 1989.

In fact, the entire package of changes – assembled in *Meet the Challenge, Make the Change: A New Agenda for Britain* – was overwhelmingly approved at the party conference in 1989. The exercise had produced at least a grudging consensus, if not enthusiasm, and even at the NEC the debate was muted. Tony Benn noted that at the NEC meeting of 8–9 May he 'was as cheerful as I could be; and there was no hostility because the majority against was so enormous'. A bit more strife and drama might actually have served the leadership well, for it would have underscored more forcefully the extent of the shift in party policy. Benn himself was in no doubt about the significance of the choices that had been made: 'It was a remarkable two days. The NEC has abandoned socialist aspirations and any idea of transforming society; it has accepted the main principles not only of capitalism but of Thatcherism; and it thinks that now the Party has a chance of winning office.'[18] Kinnock himself came to believe that the 'modernisers' had been in the end too timid and should perhaps have gone further; and over the next two years policy statements would move still further away from the commitments of the past. Still, the conclusion of the Policy Review was a major act of 'revision' and an enormous step in fashioning a new Labour Party. It might not yet be 'New Labour', but it was not the same party that Kinnock had inherited in 1983.

The major reason for thinking the Policy Review could perhaps have gone further was that by 1989 the left within the party had been very much weakened. Benn, provoked by the transparent revisionism of the Policy Review, had decided to mount a challenge for the leadership in 1988. Aided by Kinnock's lacklustre performance in the early stages of the Policy Review and his missteps over defence during that summer, the prospect of a divisive contest produced considerable anxiety among Kinnock's supporters. Still more worrying for Kinnock was John

Prescott's decision to contest the deputy leadership at the same time. But support for Benn melted away; the move to Prescott was contained; and Kinnock and Hattersley emerged with a solid victory.[19] Even the revival of local – and often extra-parliamentary – resistance over the poll tax failed to revive the left's fortunes within the party and, possibly most important, the declining salience of defence issues deprived the left of the sense that the fate of the earth was in the balance. Over time the effort to mobilise against Thatcher ebbed as well; by 1985 she had triumphed over the unions and in 1987 she had prevailed in a third general election. Thatcher might not have converted the nation to her world-view, but she had beaten her opponents handily; and her economic policies seemed finally to be working.[20] All this served to deprive the left of the will and the issues with which to fight the internal battle within the party.

The weakening of the left within the Labour Party was also accompanied by, and perhaps furthered by, a gradual change in the climate of opinion among the intellectual left. If the reorientation of the Labour Party under Kinnock was premised upon his ability to put together a coalition in support of his reforms in party management, it would require more than that if it were to succeed. It would mean also that the party would have to find and elaborate a new outlook and a new political rhetoric. These were no more easily achieved than the realignment of party factions, for discourse can be as powerful as any more formal institution. Nevertheless, the ongoing debate about Labour, its place in society and in the effort to reform or transform capitalism, would ultimately issue in a new intellectual consensus that would allow Kinnock and his allies to relocate the party within the political spectrum. The evolution of the debate can be seen clearly in the trajectory of discussion among the intellectual left, where Kinnock's revisionism would find surprising but critical support. Elaborating a left-wing rationale for moving to the political centre would prove a distinct advantage in a political organisation like the Labour Party, with its particular history, identity and inherited predispositions.

The intellectual left – a shorthand for what was undoubtedly a socially complex and evolving cultural force – had a long, complicated and ambivalent relationship with the Labour party.[21] As David Marquand has argued, 'the relationship between the Labour Party and the progressive intelligentsia, on which it depended for ideas and which alone could validate its claim to be a potential party of government rather than the vehicle of a social interest, had always been tense, uneasy and ambiguous'.[22] In particular, the party's working-class leaders had frequently displayed resentment at the role of intellectuals within the movement and the feelings were often reciprocated. Left-wing, or socialist, intellectuals had in fact solid reasons for regarding the party as a poor vehicle through which to realise their aspirations for socialist transformation. More often than not, therefore, intellectuals – academics, journalists and artists alike – stood to the left of the party leadership on issues and routinely criticised Labour for its willingness to compromise, and for its lack of daring and imagination. Even intellectuals on the right of the party, like Tony Crosland, were moved to criticise the party's stodginess and cultural conservatism, its lumbering organisation, and its apparent lack of intellectual rigour and political principle.

This traditional suspicion of the party and its leaders on the intellectual left, especially the Marxist left, had been much intensified during the 1960s. Despite a brief flirtation with Harold Wilson, who was subsequently attacked all the more intensely for having verbally seduced at least some left-wing intellectuals, Labour's record in office offered major grounds for criticism.[23] The party's planning efforts failed dismally, for example, and it seemed that the government was too willing to acquiesce to the views and wishes of finance and to the dictates of the Treasury. Wilson's support for the United States in Vietnam was another cause for disillusionment, especially to the 'new left' emerging in and around the universities, even though the war in Indo-China never became a truly mass issue in Britain. The government's growing rift with the unions over unofficial strikes and over the union leadership's inability to rein in shop stewards was a further spur to discontent and it served briefly to align the intellectual left with the trade unions – a novel alliance in the history of the party. The dramatic confrontation over *In Place of Strife* in turn drove the unions into the unaccustomed stance of directly resisting a Labour government in power and served to endear them, or at least some of them, to an intellectual left that had previously been unimpressed by their typically moderate behaviour.

Specific complaints about Labour's failings were often harnessed to, and incorporated within, broader assessments that implied that the entire party and its strategic vision were flawed. To Ralph Miliband, for example, the party's repeated failures stemmed from the choice, made early in its history, to privilege the parliamentary road to socialism.[24] From that flowed a deference to existing institutions, an unwillingness to contemplate radical constitutional change and a fetishising of elections over 'direct action'. The effect was to discourage large-scale popular mobilisations, industrial conflict and protests that did not contribute directly to electoral success and that might, in the extreme, scare away voters.[25] For Perry Anderson, Tom Nairn and the *New Left Review*, Labour's failing was more ideological than strategic.[26] The Labour Party, in their view, lacked the sort of coherent world-view that Marxism provided for socialist parties on the Continent. Instead, Labour in Britain made do with a vaguer, less sophisticated outlook that stressed a shared proletarian sense of resentment and distrust of the establishment, a simplified 'us/them' political sociology, and a willingness to place loyalty to the class or the 'labour movement' above ideological rigour. 'Labourism', in this account, was not a proper, guiding ideology but a sign of its absence; and socialism remained in Britain an aspiration and an ethos rather than a programme and a plan of action.[27]

These influential critiques, when taken at face value, led to a profound pessimism about the Labour Party that was often confirmed by the party's behaviour in office. Such arguments offered little hope that the party could be turned around and implied that joining the Labour Party was a largely futile exercise.[28] Despite the pessimism of the leading lights of the intellectual left, however, hundreds of new leftists – including feminists, peace activists and environmentalists – took the more prosaic, but ultimately more hopeful, decision to join the Labour Party in the 1970s and early 1980s. Though they might remain strongly influenced by the critique of Labour and labourism, they would nevertheless become the troops with which Benn and the left within the party fought their battles against the leadership.

The advance of the left within the party might have been gratifying to the intellectual left outside the party, but it did not fundamentally dispel or refute their belief that it was a futile effort; and the even more spectacular and simultaneous advance of Thatcherism seemed actually to reinforce their view. Labour's inability to stem the tide of popular opinion as it moved right seemed all of a piece with its previous failure to move politics and policy to the left when, it was assumed, it had the opportunity to do so. Ironically, though, this highly critical stance would ultimately assist Labour in coming to terms with Thatcher's success and the party's failure and aid the protracted and often painful process by which Labour eventually began to rethink and regroup. Tony Benn and his activist supporters would continue to insist, despite the evidence of defeat, that a more forthright and resolute defence of the party's programme would win elections and they would persist in believing that the pursuit of a radical programme while in office would be possible and effective. The academic left did not, and instead they reverted to a more sceptical view that led to very much the opposite political conclusion.

The intellectuals' critique of Labour was rooted in the belief that bringing about socialism was no easy thing and that powerful structures in state and society and deeply embedded cultural assumptions made the task close to impossible in a country like Britain. Success, were it ever to come at all, would come only after the sustained pursuit of what, following Gramsci, was termed a 'hegemonic project'.[29] The labour movement, for all its strength and durability, had never evolved into such a movement. While the labour movement as a whole, and party and union activists in particular, were outraged by the emerging Thatcherite project and deeply engaged in resisting it, the intellectual left was fascinated and began seriously to analyse it. Stuart Hall was a central figure in the effort, as he put it, 'to define the character and significance of the political project of "Thatcherism" and the crisis of the left which it has precipitated'. Note the phrasing: the very term 'Thatcherism' denotes an ideology, not a mere policy; hers is a 'political project' whose vision and coherence Labour could only envy; and it was intimately linked to a 'crisis of the left'. Hall's essays date from the late 1970s and early 1980s, the very moment when Benn's supporters within the party were winning one victory after another.[30] Interestingly, Hall's formulations privileged ideology, indirect testimony to what was genuinely new and important about Thatcher, and he recognised the effectiveness of Thatcherite ideology not only in providing an apparent answer to the frustrations of economic policy but in tapping into popular resentments of the sort that Labour was reluctant even to acknowledge. Hall was one of the first to deploy the term 'Thatcherism' and he also invented the notion of 'authoritarian populism' as a means of describing her appeal to ordinary citizens who might in normal times be expected to resent and resist Tory appeals.

Hall's arguments resonated widely and soon became conventional wisdom among left-wing intellectuals and academics. The intellectual left's take on Thatcher was thus a kind of mirror image of its critique of Labour. Where Labour was tasked for its deference and defensiveness, Thatcher represented the unabashed reassertion of class interests. While the political outlook of the Labour Party was crippled by it empiricism and pragmatism and lacked what Perry Anderson had called 'hegemonic thrust', Thatcher was not unreasonably credited with seeking to institutionalise the dominance of Conservatism and to render socialism permanently impotent. The strategy of the Labour Party, Miliband would have argued, was fatally constrained by the party's acquiescing to the routine practices and constitutional niceties of the political system. Thatcher, despite her rhetoric about tradition and Victorian values, sought wherever possible to change the rules of the game and to alter the institutional setting within which politics was conducted.

The debate over Thatcherism on the intellectual left in this sense gave a lead to those in and around the Labour Party who sought to move the party in a new direction. The same writers also provided a framework within which to determine what direction that should be. The stress upon the ideological distinctiveness of Thatcherism also led to efforts to get beneath the surface of politics and political discourse and to probe the material basis of the phenomenon. The effect was salutary, for the discussion of the social and economic underpinnings of Thatcherism meant by definition a re-examination of the social basis of Labour and an effort to think yet again about what social change might mean for the party's future. It meant also a reassessment of the entire 'postwar settlement' and the Keynesian assumptions upon which it was built, and of the particular role assigned to the Labour Party and the trade unions within that political order. From there it was possible to see how the 'trade-unionist and corporatist *offensive* by the labour movement' – e.g. the upsurge of strikes in the late 1960s culminating in the miners' victories in 1972 and in 1974 and the expansion of rights and benefits brought about by the Labour governments of 1964–70 and 1974–79 – had helped to push the 'Keynesian welfare state' into crisis.[31] The rise of Thatcher was from this perspective an almost inevitable response to an emerging economic and political crisis which Labour had 'presided over', perhaps even precipitated, but which in the end had undermined its claim to rule.

Thatcher's appeal was proof that her policies provided at least the promise of addressing the crisis. Her ability ultimately to dominate the political landscape seemed to provide subsequent confirmation of the fit between Thatcherite policies, the political and economic requirements of the moment, and the society in which those needs had become so pressing.

Confronting Thatcherism thus offered an opportunity and an incentive to think more broadly about the sociological sources of Labour weakness and Tory strength. The discussion underscored once more the need to look at the party's relationship to the working class and to query both the connection and the social reality it presumed. The arguments about the transformation of the economy and social structure, first raised in the debate about affluence in the early 1960s and then updated by Hobsbawm in the late 1970s, were revisited yet again, but with a new urgency and an unaccustomed willingness to acknowledge that society really had changed substantially over the post-war era. The discussion was widespread within the intellectual left, but a particularly prominent role was played by *Marxism Today*. *Marxism Today* originated as, and officially remained, the theoretical journal of the British Communist Party, and to the very end it would be subsidised by the party. But under the inspired editorship of Martin Jacques, it became increasingly the venue through which to express unorthodox and truly independent views.[32] Contributors to *Marxism Today* regularly addressed the painful fact that Thatcherism had wide appeal and that Labour's appeal had correspondingly narrowed. Increasingly, this was seen as a reflection of social trends that steadily reduced the size and clout of Labour's core constituencies – manual workers in general, trade unionists and council house tenants especially – and the appeal of its message. Eventually, the journal put forward in October 1988 an analysis which announced an entirely new social and economic reality that *Marxism Today* labelled 'New Times'.[33] The concept 'New Times' betokened a post-industrial, postmodern world that bore scant resemblance to the familiar and traditional world of the labour movement and the Labour Party and that required a new politics.

Central to the New Times analysis was the claim that capitalism had begun to take on a distinctly new character: 'At the heart of New Times is the shift from the old mass-production Fordist economy to a new, more flexible, post-Fordist order based on computers, information technology and robotics' (p. 3). Post-war economic growth had been based, it was argued, on the expansion of mass production which in turn had generated a plethora of reasonably cheap, standardised products that could be consumed by the very same workers who laboured in mass-production industries. Mass-produced goods were also attractive in foreign markets and so led, assuming exchange rates and trade regimes were favourable, to increased exports. The system constituted a virtuous circle of the type identified with Henry Ford – hence 'Fordism', a notion that linked mass production and mass consumption. The labour movement, with its bastions of support in heavy industry, was itself very much implicated in Fordism, and displayed the characteristic features of the Fordist model: a large, mostly male and largely unskilled or semi-skilled working class set to work in factories outfitted not with the latest, but with the next to latest, generation of machinery and earning wages modest enough to sustain a sense of grievance but high enough to consume what was produced.

Unfortunately for British workers, and for the industries in which they worked, the Fordist model had ceased to function effectively in the 1970s and was gradually eroded and replaced by 'post-Fordism'. Industry was increasingly organised so as to make use of more highly skilled workers using computers and other advanced technologies to perform more varied tasks – 'flexible specialisation' – in order to produce more differentiated, high-quality and costly products for more specialised markets. Mass production and mass markets were no longer especially profitable and so investment moved to newer industries employing more advanced technologies and organising production differently. Inevitably, shifts in production entailed changes in employment and so worked a restructuring of the working class. The newer and expanding sections of the working class lived and worked in different places; they were more skilled and prosperous; and they owed little allegiance to the institutions of the labour movement and showed little concern for its traditions and cultures. This transformation within the manufacturing core of the economy, and of the working class, was paralleled by continued changes in the sectoral distribution of employment and in the demography of the labour force. There was a steady expansion of the service sector, where employment patterns differed substantially from those in industry and where large numbers of women worked. At the same time, those sections of manufacturing that still derived their competitive advantage through the use of cheap labour became dependent on immigrants, minorities and women, whose outlook and interests often diverged from the inherited traditions of the labour movement. Overall, therefore, the post-Fordist era saw the emergence of a new and different economy with a workforce that looked, and in fact was, different.

The political implications of this transition to post-Fordism would inevitably be dramatic, although their precise character would be much debated.[34] To some, the understanding that the economy had changed out of all recognition, and with it the working class, was an argument for Labour to become less closely allied with the unions and the old, industrial working class. It should instead move towards the political centre in order to attract votes from the expanding ranks of white-collar workers and professionals, particularly those living in the suburbs and the more prosperous southern part of the country. Labour should therefore distance itself from the rhetoric and policies of the past and abandon nostrums like nationalisation in which few people believed but which scared away potential voters. This new revisionism would remodel Labour by making it less socialist, less collectivist and less hostile to property-ownership and private enterprise.[35] This was basically the Kinnock agenda.

To others, however, the eclipse of 'old Labour' was a signal to move left, but with a reconfigured and reimagined social base. The reasoning was equally straightforward: the Labour party had been in the past the de facto projection into politics of the interests and preferences of the organised, mostly male, industrial working class, and that social base gave the party its distinctive ethos, outlook and programme. The changing nature of the working class – the fact that it was increasingly female and less overwhelmingly 'white' – should logically dictate the adoption of a new and radical programme designed to appeal to women, ethnic and racial minorities and recent immigrants. Labour should become a sort of 'rainbow coalition' of the excluded and marginalised who, together with what remained of the traditional working class, could be mobilised around a fundamentally left-wing programme. The hope was that this 'new socialism' would become 'more than the sum of these movements' and attract a majority of voters.[36] The model for this vision was, of course, the Greater London Council, which had attempted to provide access and assistance to women, people of colour, and gays and lesbians while crafting a programme of local economic revitalisation that might also appeal to what remained of the industrial working class. The policies of the GLC were to become a major source of contention both inside and outside the Labour Party. The GLC's openness and flair made its radicalism attractive and endeared it to many ordinary London voters who would much lament its abolition in 1986. The very same characteristics had allowed Thatcher and the Conservatives to attack London as a stronghold of the 'loony left' and to smear the Labour Party more broadly in the 1987 general election. Ken Livingstone's penchant for controversy – his willingness, for example, to offer legitimacy to the IRA – added a personal element as well and made Livingstone for a time as demonised or, to his supporters, as heroic a figure as Tony Benn had been just a short time before.

The debate to some extent pitted the head against the heart, even if both sides aspired to hard-headed analysis. The 'left' interpretation of New Times was extremely attractive to writers like Stuart Hall, whose academic work in 'cultural studies' led directly to a sympathy with the emerging 'politics of identity' and whose New Left background predisposed him, and them, to view the Labour Party of Wilson and Callaghan with disdain and contempt. But Hall and other contributors to *Marxism Today* could also count and so they understood intuitively that even adding up all of the relatively small groups of people moved by ethnic or sexual identities or involved in new social movements over peace and the environment would never in fact create a majority. And the need quickly to create a new anti-Thatcher majority was stressed repeatedly by others in the debate. Indeed, the need to cobble together a majority seemed imperative in the aftermath of her third successive victory in 1987 and was undoubtedly a factor in making schemes for proportional representation increasingly attractive. A similar counsel of despair at the seeming permanence of Thatcherism presumably lay behind the growing fascination with constitutional reform and the wide support generated by Charter 88, a statement calling for a written constitution and a bill of rights, freedom of information and proportional representation.

There was much talk as well of various alliances and united fronts. Eric Hobsbawm, for example, argued in March 1988 that the left had been 'right from the start to see Thatcherism as something quite different from, and immensely more dangerous than, just another Tory government. It is an experimental model for post-democratic bourgeois society in the 1980s, as fascism (which was a very different species of political animal) was the model for bourgeois regimes in the 1930s which felt that they could no longer afford democracy.'[37] Though Hobsbawm knew well enough to distinguish Thatcher from Hitler, the logic was nevertheless similar: the threat from the extreme right should be met with the creation of a new 'popular front' against Thatcherism. This would necessitate a movement that would encompass many more than the numerous minorities seen as the core of a new Labour Party by supporters of the GLC model of oppositional politics and it would have to be built around a programme that was more centrist than what Labour had so recently offered to voters.

What was most interesting about the debate about New Times, however, and about similar discussions proceeding in venues other than *Marxism Today*, was that they made evident, and reinforced, the loss of faith in both the old, corporatist policies of Wilson and Callaghan and in the more left-wing policies associated with Benn and the so-called hard left. The New Times analysis provided a rationale for a Labour politics that was not merely a projection of trade union interests and that instead took a critical look at what Labour had long stood for.[38] Despite its Marxist provenance and rhetorical style, moreover, it did not give aid or comfort to those on the left who wanted to rekindle the class struggle and reassert the virtues of planning and nationalisation. If the political implications of New Times were often ambiguous, they were clearly not an endorsement of either the inherited wisdom of the centre-right of the party – and its failed corporatist practice – or the rediscovered faith and enthusiasm of the left. These debates and interventions were instead a call for innovation, even if their authors knew not quite where it would lead; and the widespread agreement they elicited within the labour movement was decisive evidence that many within the party, and even the unions, realised the need for a decisive break.

Politicians fearful of their political futures did not, of course, need left-wing intellectuals to tell them that the Labour Party needed retooling, rethinking and repositioning. Labour's leaders were nevertheless desperately in need of a framework within which to accomplish the reorientation of the party, as were the unions and the rank and file of the party, and the arguments of the intellectual left helped to provide guidance and also lent legitimacy to the project. 'Public intellectuals' of the left moved the political discourse surrounding Labour's future away from the foci of the late 1970s and early 1980s – on alternative economic strategies, on the failures of the party's leadership, on the bitter feuding between left and right – and towards a perhaps grudging recognition that the battles of the past should not determine the politics of the future. The claims about New Times might well have been overstated, but they had the great virtue of shifting the terms of the discussion.

It was precisely the same shift that party officials sought to achieve within the party and within the context of the Policy Review. In December 1988, for example, Kinnock explained to review group 'convenors' that their job was to enable the party to 'confront the realities of a post-Thatcher Britain'.[39] A month later Geoff Bish, the Policy Director, insisted that everything in the review should be linked to a vision of the emerging 'world of the 1990s'.[40] The assumption was that Labour might well not defeat Thatcher in the short term but that the party would eventually inherit the world she had created. Resistance had given way to acceptance, even if in coming to terms with Thatcherism Labour would find much in need of repair and reconstruction in her wake. Equally important, the admonition to confront the realities of post-Thatcher Britain was not merely a matter of being practical and anticipating likely scenarios. It was much more: it was a licence to think about social change, to measure the distance Britain had travelled in recent decades, and to acknowledge that by the time Labour came to power again, the society envisioned in earlier Labour plans and programmes would no longer be. 'Manufacturing industry will have declined even more . . . – and the financial and service sectors will have greatly expanded. We will have been in the European Community for almost twenty years . . . We will have to face the challenge of growing competition – with *new markets, new technologies*, and the growing *completion of the European internal market*. We must also adopt to the decline of Britain's oil revenue.'[41] Gone from this formulation were the vain hopes of using North Sea oil revenues to finance a wave of industrial expansion; missing, too, was even the prospect of withdrawing from Europe; and at its very centre was the question of competition within a fundamentally capitalist world market. The starting point of the review, in short, was that everything had changed and that it was possible, as Patricia Hewitt would put it, to 'pretend that the Labour Party was only now being created'.[42] The phrase 'new Labour' had yet to gain currency, but it was surely very much in prospect.

The completion of the Policy Review and the approval of *Meet the Challenge, Make the Change* brought a dramatic reversal in Labour's, and in Kinnock's, standings. Opinion polls started to improve and so did the mood of the party and its leader; and the European elections the following June produced the first large-scale electoral victory in well over a decade – Labour won just over 40 per cent of the vote to the Tories' 34 per cent. The path ahead seemed clear and promising. Thatcher continued to alienate voters and her own supporters; the economic indicators had begun to turn negative and undermined the earlier and triumphalist claims of the Conservatives; and Labour could plausibly claim to have turned decisively away from the unpopular positions it had espoused during the 1980s. Doubts about Labour as a party and about Kinnock as a leader also began, it seemed, to dissipate.

The growing prospect of victory in turn reinforced the determination to achieve it. In practice, that would mean a further push to the political centre in matters of programme and policy; a reshuffling of the Shadow Cabinet to give more prominence to a younger generation of more centrist MPs; and a sustained effort to win the confidence of business. The party's stance on Europe was a particular focus of attention. Even before the party conference in 1989 Kinnock and John Smith, the party's major economic spokesman, were preparing to endorse British membership in the Exchange Rate Mechanism of the European Monetary System. Party policy remained officially sceptical on the grounds that the 'European Monetary System, as presently constituted, suffers from too great an emphasis on deflationary measures . . .' in order to maintain price stability.[43] That position had largely been worked out by the Policy Review group chaired by Bryan Gould, who continued to be lukewarm towards Europe and soft on interventionist economic policies. The party leader and its economics spokesmen – John Smith and his shadow Treasury team – were beginning to think otherwise and believed both that Britain could join the ERM and maintain growth and that joining was useful tactically, for it would send a strong signal to the markets and the financial community that Labour would not tolerate inflation. On 24 October 1989 Smith signalled the shift by referring in a Commons debate to 'the important and prudent conditions that the Labour Party had outlined' for joining – conditions that he only got around to defining almost two weeks later.[44] The detailed conditions mattered far less than the commitment ultimately to join up. They would allow Labour to argue that the Tories had done it wrong while reassuring doubters that Labour would not break fundamentally with Tory policy.

By late 1989 Labour had thus managed to execute a major shift of position on Europe. It had moved a long way from its outright opposition to continued membership in the European Economic Community proclaimed during the 1983 election. The process had been less direct and open, but no less thorough, than other policy shifts undertaken under Kinnock. Almost immediately upon assuming the party leadership Kinnock had begun to soft-pedal the party's controversial position and he assigned Robin Cook, his former campaign manager, to help reorient party opinion.[45] In the June 1984 European elections, for example, the emphasis was put on reforming the European Community rather than withdrawing from it. Kinnock, it seems, had by then come to be influenced by Stuart Holland and other pro-Europeans on the left of the party who claimed that the path to economic recovery actually ran through Europe.[46] There was certainly not much hope for an expansionist and interventionist policy being successfully implemented by a British government acting on its own, so Labour was encouraged to think in terms of a European recovery programme.[47] The accession of Jacques Delors as president of the European Commission made the European option still more attractive, especially with the elaboration of the European Social Charter. The European Social Charter offered a vision of a distinctively 'European model of society' that was not Thatcherite, and not based on the primacy of markets. It also provided Labour with a workable legal framework for industrial relations that might guarantee workers a new and more extensive set of rights than they enjoyed under Thatcher while avoiding a return to the privileges, practices and failed corporatist policies of the 1960s and 1970s. The ERM served a similar political function, for in it the party discovered a device that effectively committed a future Labour government in the battle against inflation while allowing it to maintain a formal, or at least a rhetorical, commitment to economic growth.

The shift on monetary policy was critical in itself and indicated a very different orientation towards Europe and towards the market. It simultaneously made it clear that the programme that emerged from the Policy Review was not fixed and would continue to evolve still further towards the political centre. It was not a fixed position around which the party would now unite and which would form the settled basis of the party's public appeal. It was more of a way station, a temporary compromise on the road to what was still a vaguely understood new political identity.

Commentators at the time, and since, have focused on the precise terms of that compromise and tried to assess its workability and coherence and to decide whether it was an abandonment of the party's socialist heritage or a refinement of that tradition along the lines of European social democracy. It was actually both – it was undoubtedly closer in spirit to Bad Godesberg than to Clause IV or the *National Plan* and to this extent it was an adjustment that brought Labour in line with the policies of other European social democratic parties. But it was also an unmistakable step towards abandoning the party's historic commitments; and as such it could and would lead on to further moves in the same direction. Linking Britain to the ERM was one such step; successively more sanitised reiterations of party policy would come later and represented yet further moves away from Labour's peculiar brand of socialism. *Looking to the Future*, the updated programme unveiled in May 1990, omitted reference to the Medium Term Industrial Strategy altogether – perhaps an aesthetic judgement on the inelegance of the phrase, but in effect backing away from any serious macro-economic goals or explicitly Keynesian strategies. Spending commitments were also made conditional: benefits would be increased 'as rapidly as resources allow', while the commitments to the ERM and to battling inflation were made more absolute. Support for 'charters' spelling out the rights of consumers and of employees was made more formal and, in the process, the language of rights (and implicitly responsibilities) was reinforced. *Opportunity Britain*, the 1991 update, pushed this rhetorical shift still further while the programme itself merely restated earlier commitments in a more popular idiom. Electoral considerations were even more evident in the 1992 manifesto, *It's Time to Get Britain Working Again*, which narrowed and qualified previous commitments on spending, taxation and economic policy-making.[48]

The Policy Review was thus but a first, albeit critical, chapter in the progressive whittling down of what the party promised to do in office.

The process was driven largely by the logic of electoral competition, though the emphasis altered slightly over time. Up to 1989 the goal was to scrap the programme that Kinnock had inherited and to rid the party of what were seen as pure liabilities. The apparent popular success of the review, accentuated by the growing unpopularity of Thatcher, turned the attention of Labour's leader to the prospect of victory and to the need, prior to an election, to reassure business and the middle classes of the party's new moderation on economic and fiscal questions. To do that, however, required a new team who were not in any way tainted with the radicalism of the early 1980s. Internal battles over the shape of the Policy Review proved the testing ground for this next generation. Bryan Gould, the hero – along with Mandelson – of the 1987 election campaign, had been put in charge of the Productive and Competitive Economy review group and he had done much to smooth the way for the substitution of various supply-side interventions for the more aggressive and ambitious set of economic policies previously espoused by Labour. But he remained suspicious of Europe and he also betrayed a lingering attachment to nationalised industries. That led him to maintain the commitment to renationalise the utility industries privatised under Thatcher. Kinnock at a critical moment dispatched John Eatwell, his new economic adviser, together with the young Gordon Brown and the younger Tony Blair, to talk Gould out of his stance. Gould was quite put out, not only because he disagreed and not only because the compromise he had worked out had the support of the unions, but also because the intervention was a signal of Kinnock's preference for a younger generation of more committed modernisers and his growing independence from the soft left whose support had been so critical at an earlier moment. Gould was undoubtedly correct in this, and his own personal fortunes soon began to fade. After the Shadow Cabinet elections in 1989 he was replaced as Industry spokesman by Gordon Brown and moved to Environment, where he was given the unrewarding job of coming up with an alternative to the poll tax.[49]

The elevation of Brown paralleled the rise of Blair, whose star rose at the expense of another member of the soft left, Michael Meacher. Meacher and Blair had served on the Policy Review committee on People at Work. That group had also sought to orchestrate a consensus with the unions, but over the even more delicate issue of trade union rights. Kinnock had been dissatisfied with the report presented near the end of the process and a compromise was only just cobbled together in the summer before conference. Immediately after the 1989 party conference, however, Kinnock appointed Tony Blair as Shadow Employment Secretary and thus as the person responsible for party policy in the area previously controlled by Meacher. Blair moved aggressively to distance the party from its past close association with the unions and did so by forcing the unions to accept the fact that the closed shop was no longer viable. The European Social Chapter, on which important aspects of the Policy Review had been modelled, was very forceful about giving workers the right to join unions, but it also stipulated that they had a right not to join. In return for a firm policy on the right to union membership and recognition the unions had to accept that individuals might well opt out. The outcome was a sign of Blair's determination to break with the traditions of his party and of the labour movement, and of his ability to carry it off. Kinnock was apparently very impressed; not long after he noted Blair's arrival at a meeting and remarked to Harriet Harman, another 'moderniser', 'Here comes the next leader of the Labour Party.'[50]

Brown and Blair were together to play especially important roles in executing Labour's shift in economic and industrial policy and the two were capable of waxing eloquent about the new focus on supply-side interventions. Thus Brown confidently announced to the party conference in 1990 a 'new role' for government – 'not government doing everything, not government doing nothing, not the government of the invisible hand of unrestrained market forces, not the government of the dead hand of centralised power; but the government of the helping hand . . .'. A future Labour government would institute a 'training revolution', Blair told the same gathering; and training would be at the very centre of the party's economic strategy.[51] A year later, Brown invoked and adapted the soaring rhetoric of Harold Wilson when he spoke of the party's proposals on education and training: 'it is not a reheat of the technological revolution that will transform British industry in the 1990s', he explained. Rather, 'it is the liberating potential of the training revolution'.[52] Blair was bolder still: 'This is the mission of socialism for the twenty-first century, planting the seeds of learning in individual men and women to yield a harvest of talent for the nation. This is our vision for Britain.'[53] The replacement of the ambitious and interventionist strategies of economic growth through modernisation of the 1960s and after with the modest, incremental and

very long-term promise of reaping the benefits of better training and education was an appropriate measure of the distance that at least the self-
consciously 'modernising' section of the Labour Party had travelled in
the 1980s. It was a sign, too, of where the modernisers would take the rest
of the party if given the opportunity.

Yet another new face to emerge under Kinnock was that of Margaret
Beckett, who also boasted a background on the soft left but who now
proved herself a key loyalist. When Gordon Brown moved to Industry,
Beckett took his job as Shadow Chief Secretary and became John Smith's
loyal assistant. Despite Smith's background on the right and Beckett's
roots on the left, the two worked closely and together the new Treasury
team imposed a tight discipline on Labour's promises. The leadership's
refusal to endorse new spending commitments became known as
'Beckett's Law' and she was credited with adding the caveat 'as resources
allow' to any and all suggestions for increased expenditures, innovative
programmes and policy initiatives.

For what must have seemed to him the longest time, Kinnock had
laboured largely on his own in his fight to reshape the Labour Party,
aided in his quest by the acquiescence of the NEC and the TUC and the
active support of his personal entourage. He had courted fellow MPs and
won their support, but he found few genuine allies among them. By
1989–90, however, he could begin to count on a new cohort of politicians
who shared more fully his vision of the future of the party. Increasingly,
the party's publicity machinery would therefore focus on the 'favoured
four' now visibly in the leader's camp and now also in charge of
economic policy – Smith, Brown, Blair and Beckett. The four were also
sent out on a campaign to woo, or at least to reassure, business in
anticipation of the forthcoming general election. The so-called 'prawn
cocktail offensive' began shortly after the 1989 conference and filled
Smith's calendar for much of the next year. It was followed by the formal
launch of 'Industry 2000', through which Brown and Blair organised a
series of meetings with industrialists. Meanwhile, Mo Mowlam, the
party's new City spokesperson – the job that had first brought Blair to
public attention – is said to have logged no fewer than 150 lunches with
bankers and businessmen over an 18-month period.[54] Labour leaders
were keen on being viewed by industry and the City as newly solid on the
key economic issues; and they certainly added a few pounds. Whether

the effort succeeded in allaying fears of a Labour victory would become clear only at the next election.[55]

But the general election had to wait until 1992 and in the intervening time one small thing and one very big thing happened. The small thing, although to some it was not small at all, was that the highly-effective group of personal advisers clustered around Kinnock began to break apart. Patricia Hewitt, for example, was first moved around and then chose to leave and work for the Institute for Public Policy Research. Still more dramatic was the departure of Mandelson, whose decision to secure a seat in Parliament broke apart his relationship with Charles Clarke, Kinnock's personal assistant. Mandelson secured the nomination of the Labour Party in Hartlepool in December 1989. Even before that result was known, Clarke told him that if he was selected, he would 'have to decide immediately when to leave . . .' his job at party headquarters. After Kinnock was drawn into the dispute, Mandelson was prevailed upon to stay through the European elections and the 1990 conference. But then he was gone.[56]

Mandelson's replacement as communications director, John Underwood, actually took up his duties even before his predecessor had left. It was an example of the confusion and unhappiness that attended Mandelson's leaving and an augur of things to come. Kinnock had opposed the appointment of Underwood, a former TV producer, and apparently preferred Colin Byrne, Mandelson's assistant and protégé. The association with Mandelson doomed Byrne's chances with the NEC and party staff members, however, and it was they who made the choice for an outsider. But Kinnock was unwilling to do without the talents of either Hewitt or Mandelson and he remained in touch with both. Hewitt, though working for the IPPR, would in fact be co-opted to help coordinate the 1992 election campaign. Mandelson had his own local campaign to run, but nevertheless stayed in London sharing a flat with Byrne and Julie Hall, Kinnock's press secretary. Underwood not unreasonably felt undermined by the trio's presence and their continued ability to speak authoritatively to the press about the party's actions and policies, and in response he developed closer relations with NEC members and Walworth Road staff. He in effect distanced himself from Kinnock, further undermining his own ability to speak with the authority long enjoyed by Mandelson. Confusion and lack of coordination were rampant and after a difficult year Underwood resigned. He was replaced by David Hill, long-time assistant to Roy Hattersley, and Clarke banned further contact with Mandelson who was by now more absorbed in Hartlepool. Byrne resigned a few months later and a degree of stability finally settled over the party apparatus by the end of 1991.

It was by now very late to be beginning to chart an effective election campaign, however, and the bitterness created by two years of nasty personnel issues lingered. Philip Gould of the Shadow Communications Agency continued his attempts to put a shape to Labour's efforts, but in very unpropitious circumstances. He pulled together a coordinating group that met secretly on Thursdays and then passed on directions to party officials who had to carry them out wondering whence they came. Of course they knew and were unhappy about it. Efforts to involve larger numbers in more meetings failed to correct the problem, however, and throughout the campaign there would be a de facto split between the SCA types who had Kinnock's ear and the people hired to do the hard work of the campaign. As Gould would later argue, 'The campaign team was riven with suspicion bordering on paranoia; lines of command were confused; and the leader of the party was isolated from his own campaign team.'[57] The key loss was Mandelson: his great strength residing in the fact that while he had a very close relationship with Kinnock he had also remained a fixture located physically at the very heart of the party machine. Coordination happened through his person; with him gone, it could have been achieved through a properly functioning organisation, but it was not. By all accounts Labour would proceed to wage a competent, but flawed and overly-defensive, campaign in 1992. It would be good enough, but not good enough to win.

The other, and truly big, event that occurred before Labour could put its new image and programme before the voters was the resignation of Margaret Thatcher on 22 November 1990. Thatcher had been Kinnock's nemesis for most of the 1980s; it was surely ironic that her final triumph over the Labour leader was won by her leaving. By 1990 Thatcher had clearly become a liability for her own party. Her governments and their policies had forever altered the political landscape and even the social underpinnings of politics and most voters were content with her accomplishments. Very few desired to return to the economic disarray of the late 1970s and early 1980s, which was routinely blamed on Labour;

the weakening of the trade unions enjoyed broad support; and nearly everyone who bought a house from the local authority or who purchased shares in a privatised firm was intent on holding fast to their new property. But as numerous surveys showed, Thatcher signally failed to change people's values: they continued to opt for preserving social services rather than lowering taxes, even if they often voted otherwise; and they refused to endorse her individualist and competitive vision of society. Most important, they did not like her. Arrogance and intolerance were written all over her face and the resolve she displayed against Argentina over the Falklands did not play well when turned on her political opponents at home, some of them former allies and fellow Conservatives. Antipathy to Thatcher, and her regime, intensified considerably after 1987. Emboldened by its third victory over what seemed an impotent opposition, Thatcher became seriously overcommitted to the highly unpopular poll tax. Thatcher also grew increasingly critical of Europe, particularly the new Europe emerging under Jacques Delors's tenure as president of the European Commission. Delors's vision of a 'European model of society', in which social protections were privileged over competition and which enshrined a substantial package of rights in its 'Social Charter' was anathema to Thatcher. She feared that socialism, now effectively banished from Britain, would sneak back in through Europe: as she put it in her famous Bruges speech in September 1988, 'We have not successfully rolled back the frontiers of the state in Britain only to see them reimposed at a European level . . .'[58] Thatcher's obstinacy over the poll tax and increasingly shrill and even xenophobic stance towards Europe transformed lingering popular resentment into outright hostility so palpable that even her Tory colleagues deserted her. When they did, her fall was rapid.

Thatcher was replaced by John Major, whose ascendency she had sponsored. Regarded as thoroughly loyal to his patron prior to assuming office, Major's defining feature as Prime Minister was that he was very much the antithesis of Thatcher. Where she was brash and fearsome, he was 'a disarmingly ordinary bloke'; where she was stubborn, he compromised; and very quickly Major distanced himself from the more controversial initiatives of the third term.[59] The effect on Labour was devastating. Philip Gould heard of Thatcher's demise and immediately 'felt numb. I knew it was all over.'[60] Labour's entire strategy of rebuilding, reshaping and moderating itself was premised upon Thatcher and the need to fashion itself as the alternative. Kinnock's personal image, for example, had been reconstructed deliberately to contrast him as 'caring' and Thatcher as obviously not, to paint her as fanatical and him as not. Even in 1987, party strategists regarded Thatcher's strident personality as the Tories' biggest liability and her behaviour since had underlined how right that view was. Suddenly that liability was removed and the Conservatives could present to voters a likeable face with a reassuring message: he would preserve the gains of the Thatcher revolution but moderate its impact and remove its hard edges. Within days of Major's accession the polls turned around and put the Conservatives ahead of Labour. Labour would regain ground in the spring of 1991 and actually force Major to delay by a year the calling of the election. But Labour would proceed to lose its lead in the polls yet again, and when the leadership began preparing for the general election in earnest in December 1991, they would confront a formidable task.

The campaign did not go well, though while it was in progress it appeared that Labour might well win.[61] For most of the campaign the opinion polls gave Labour a narrow lead and the economic news was not good, rendering largely ineffective the Tories' charge that Labour was not competent to manage the economy. But the Conservatives were still able to frighten voters just enough to convince just enough of them not to take a risk with Labour, not to jeopardise whatever personal gains they had made over the previous decade, and not to trust their fate to Kinnock and the party he led. Just how and why they succeeded would be much debated inside and outside the Labour Party after the election, but there would be no arguing with the claim by Larry Whitty, Party Secretary, that the party's fourth successive defeat was 'one of the most disappointing in the history of the party . . .'.[62] It was not merely a loss, but it seemed an unnecessary and undeserved loss, because Labour had done so much to win. And it was routinely asked, if Labour could not win in 1992 against a lacklustre opponent with a lagging economy, when could they win? To some pundits and to many disconsolate supporters, 'Never, was the simple answer. Never, ever, ever.'[63]

Labour lost the election of April 1992 partly because Kinnock had never quite attained the stature of a possible prime minister. That failure, however, was itself largely based on a fear of who or what lurked behind

Kinnock and a sense that he lacked the authority to prevail within the party. Indeed, the fear of Labour had such deep roots that the Tories needed only to remind voters for it to become a deciding factor. And the campaign itself, though by many measures highly effective and professional, served to reinforce the message on which the Conservative victory would be built. The most basic fear about Labour was that it remained committed to high taxes and uncontrolled spending and would revert to both if elected. Party leaders had worked hard to display their fiscal rectitude and to minimise spending commitments in the run-up to the election. However, the party unity that Kinnock so desperately craved had been purchased at the price of including in Labour's programme plans to increase pensions and child benefits and these would have to be paid for with increased taxes: a new top rate of 50p and a rise in the ceiling for National Insurance contributions. These commitments had preceded the Policy Review, survived it and were reaffirmed in subsequent documents. John Smith, the Shadow Chancellor, was unwilling to abandon these quite modest promises and was prepared to defend them. It was agreed that the best approach was to be forthright and patient, explaining the reasoning behind the pledges and pointing out the many who would benefit and the relatively smaller numbers who would pay more.

But that tactic was to prove to be a source of disagreement, difficulty and even embarrassment. The Conservatives had long understood that to attack Labour as the party of 'tax and spend' was their best strategy and during the summer of 1991 put out a claim – based upon totalling up all sorts of random statements made over several years – that Labour's promises would cost £35 billion more than was available. In January, as the campaign neared, the Chancellor, Norman Lamont, reiterated the charge while inflating it by another £2 billion. In a poster labelled 'Labour's tax bombshell' the Tories proceeded to divide the dubious total into an extra £1,000 for every taxpayer. The Tory claims were demonstrably and maliciously wrong. They nevertheless struck a chord with voters and prompted the press to take a closer look at Labour's actual plans. Closer and more dispassionate examination showed that the Tories calculations were inaccurate, but they also made it clear that Labour did plan to raise taxes significantly in order to pay for additional spending. They key questions were by how much and on whom the increases would fall. One reliable estimate had it that a person making £100,000 a year would pay more than £1,000 per month in additional taxes. Since few taxpayers had incomes that high, what was to prove more important was the determination of how many would pay more and how many would not. That was specifically a question of the threshold at which National Insurance contributions, which were set at 9 per cent, stopped being deducted. The cut-off point had been £20,280, which meant that Labour would effectively raise taxes on anyone earning more than that while those earning less would escape unless and until their incomes rose to that level.

Kinnock understood intuitively that raising taxes on anyone making roughly £21,000 was dangerous, for it affected many 'aspiring', middle-class voters whose support Labour had to have. He began inching away and at a famous dinner held on 15 January 1992 at Luigi's Restaurant in Covent Garden he suggested that the increase in National Insurance contributions might be phased in. This was a major slip, largely because Smith had not agreed but also because the resulting numbers did not add up, and so Kinnock was forced to disown his own proposal. The ensuing confusion served to fix in voters' minds several damaging notions: that Labour would indeed raise taxes; that Labour was not being fully candid about the matter; and that the party was not united on this and perhaps on other issues.

Officially the campaign had not yet begun, but already the terms of debate had begun to shift against Labour. Long before the election Labour strategists understood that their strength lay in the party's historic com-mitment to the public services, the NHS in particular, and that the Tories were extremely vulnerable to charges that they would destroy or weaken the health service. It was equally clearly understood that Labour's weakness was tax and that the Tories would attack. The Conservatives themselves realised that, as Maurice Saatchi put it later, 'If they'd [the Labour party] dealt with it [tax], we had nothing else.'[64] The plan was to defuse the tax issue by confronting it head on. The party decided to present a Shadow Budget early in the campaign, to showcase the event as proof that the party was fit to govern and to get the issue out of the way so that the campaign could focus on other issues. The tactic was not univer-sally agreed – Philip Gould, head of the Shadow Communications Agency, had long argued for a more aggressive approach; and Gordon Brown, Smith's closest colleague, thought the Shadow Budget notion very risky as well – but Smith was determined and Kinnock was determined to support Smith. The reasoning behind the tactic was not implausible: being direct and honest with the public had its merits and there was evidence that voters were willing to pay for better services; putting the matter to rest early in the contest was surely desirable. But such reckoning underestimated the intensity of the likely Tory counter-attack and its potential resonance with voters; and it rather naively assumed that the press, in most cases Conservative in sympathy, would allow the question of tax to die down.

Labour was also caught off guard by the details of the pre-election budget presented by Norman Lamont on 9 March 1992, just two days before the general election was called. A tax cut was widely anticipated and Labour's strategists assumed it would be a straightforward 1p or 2p off the basic rate. An across the board cut could be sold as being of benefit to rich and poor alike, but in fact the major benefits would flow to the Conservatives' core, middle-class supporters. Labour had prepared to attack this as crude electioneering and to promise to reverse it in the Shadow Budget. In its stead Labour would propose a cut in the rate of National Insurance contributions from 9 per cent to 8 per cent, a move that would reward those on lower incomes while softening the blow on middle-class incomes that would otherwise result from raising the ceiling on those very contributions. In the event the Chancellor surprised and confounded Labour by choosing to leave the basic rate unchanged at 25p and to introduce a new, lower rate of 20p for the first £2,000 in income – a tax break for all taxpayers that disproportionately benefited the lower-paid. Labour now had to decide whether to acquiesce in an obviously popular and even progressive tax policy or to promise to reverse it in order to make its sums come out right. The problem was the need to finance the party's pledges on pensions and child benefits; and the Tories had cleverly put Labour in the position of having to raise taxes either on the poor or the middle classes in order to keep those promises.

When the Shadow Budget was presented on 16 March the choice had been made to spare the poorest and put the burden more squarely on middle-class taxpayer. The 1p reduction in National Insurance charges was thus abandoned and with it the effort to soften the impact of Labour's tax plans on those who made over £21,000. It was a principled choice and the entire presentation earned plaudits from the press and brought at least a sense of relief to the Labour campaign team. And the polls remained upbeat, at least for a time: four polls conducted shortly after the Shadow Budget gave Labour an average lead of just over 2 per cent.[65] The Tories, however, began to make headway after an effective counter-attack, unleashed on 22 March, in which they claimed that the average taxpayer would now face an increase of £1,250 per year. The figure was inflated, but it stuck, and seems to have had a corrosive effect on the minds of voters who would be repeatedly reminded of the tax issue by the largely Tory press.

Labour strategists were not fools, of course, and proceeded quickly to move attention away from taxes and towards other issues – health in particular. Unfortunately, the last three weeks of the campaign were marked by flaws in execution that might not have mattered if the underlying trends were clear and positive but that, in a close and shifting contest, hurt. The focus on health, for example, was based upon an election broadcast featuring a young girl who had apparently been forced to wait for an ear operation due to NHS underfunding. The story was about a real child, Jennifer Bennett, whose father had written to Robin Cook about it. But Labour's publicity machine mishandled the story about 'Jennifer's ear' and found itself contradicted by her doctor and criticised by her mother and grandfather, both of whom were Conservatives. Though the effectiveness of the broadcast was its claim to authenticity, there was confusion and hesitation about whether to release or confirm the details of the actual case. Press commentary was biting, Cook and Kinnock were placed on the defensive and what should have been Labour's most devastating blow was turned against the party. Philip Gould, architect of the move, would later claim that the public's reaction was on balance favourable, but it was undoubtedly less positive than it could and should have been.

What kept Labour's mood up throughout most of the campaign was that the Conservative campaign was also considered ineffective. Norman Lamont performed poorly when responding to Smith's Shadow Budget and William Waldegrave stumbled over 'Jennifer's ear', in both cases allowing Labour to escape the full consequences of its own errors. Major was unable to get any traction in his efforts until well into the contest, when he mounted a soapbox and assumed the role of underdog. It was to prove an unusually effective pose, for it served to keep the attention on Kinnock and on what would happen if Labour were elected. By all accounts Kinnock was himself a liability to his party. He seemed in and through his person to carry tremendous baggage: even though he had devoted much of his career to exorcising Labour's past he appeared to embody it. His garrulous personality and long-winded style undermined his steady efforts to appear statesmanlike, and however controlled the performance, every once in a while the real Kinnock broke through unrestrained. The classic example during the election was the infamous Sheffield rally on 1 April 1992, where Kinnock bounded onto the stage in a burst of triumphalist enthusiasm. At a stroke, it seemed, 'The vision of a Labour Camelot gave way to the atmosphere of a Welsh rugby club . . .', and Kinnock's carefully constructed public personality was revealed as very much a construction.[66] The entire point of the rally, of course, was to create the sense of an impending victory; and indeed the last stages of the campaign were dominated by a resolve to remain cautious, not to make any mistakes and to further the image of Labour as responsible and ready to form a government.[67] The indirect effect was to deter Labour from responding in kind to the sharp attacks the Tories and their supporters in the press were making. Nor did they grasp that the contest had evolved and that, by the end, the vote would not be a judgement on the Tories' record but an assessment of what a Labour victory might mean. That, in turn, led to increased scrutiny of Labour's plans and proposals and to renewed fears about Labour's competence to govern.

And as the election drew to an end and the polls narrowed, worries over the outcome were further magnified by the prospect of a hung Parliament. The possibility that no party would have a majority and uncertainty about what sort of government that would produce seem to have frightened voters and led quite a few to turn at the last minute away from Labour and back towards the Conservatives. Labour's stance probably compounded the problem. Dismayed at the possibility that Conservatives might prevail indefinitely over a divided opposition, an array of left and liberal writers and politicians had begun in the late 1980s to take seriously arguments in favour of coalitions and of proportional representation, an electoral system that would make coalitions more likely. Most Labour politicians were wary, if not opposed outright, but a few – Kinnock, for one – were intrigued, and a few more – Robin Cook and Patricia Hewitt among others – believed on principle. The issue had not been a major concern of the Policy Review, but in 1991 the NEC had appointed the Plant Commission to investigate the case for and against electoral reform. When the issue arose during the 1992 campaign, Kinnock was seen to waffle. On 'Democracy Day' (2 April 1992), sponsored by Charter 88, the Labour leader invited the Liberal Democrats to participate in the deliberations of the Plant Commission; a few days later he backed off. Prior to the campaign the questions of electoral reform and coalition government were not high on Labour's agenda. As the election progressed, however, and as an uncertain outcome began to loom, they took on genuine importance. While Labour gave a mixed and varying message on the prospects of a 'hung Parliament' and a possible coalition, moreover, the Conservatives were very clear and forceful. The Tories went on to accuse Labour of trying to sneak into office by encouraging anti-Tory tactical voting for the Liberal Democrats and insisted that they would not join any coalition. Major, who had had difficulty finding an effective message and a distinctive voice, became eloquent on the supposed constitutional issue: 'If I could summon up all the authority of this office,' he intoned gravely, almost hysterically, 'I would put it into this simple warning – the United Kingdom is in danger. Wake up, my fellow countrymen! Wake up before it is too late.'[68]

Major's call for voters to 'wake up' resonated with the fundamental thrust of the Tory campaign, which was designed to instil or revive fears of the possible consequences of a Labour victory. It was in fact Major himself who on 30 March had conjured up the spectre of a 'Nightmare on Kinnock Street' and thus provided the inspiration for the *Sun*'s notorious special the day before the election. And it worked.[69] On 9 April 1992 Labour experienced its fourth consecutive general election defeat. The Conservatives polled 41.9 per cent and won 336 seats; Labour got just 34.4 per cent and won 271 seats; while the Liberal Democrats received 17.8 per cent of voters and won only 20 seats in Parliament. The Tory margin over Labour was 7.5 per cent. The result was a real improvement over the 11.5 per cent gap of 1987, but it was still very far short of victory. Under Kinnock's leadership and with his constant prodding Labour had worked for nearly a decade to remake itself, to shed its most controversial policies, to banish its troublemakers, and to re-establish its connections to ordinary voters. The party had desperately courted public opinion, its leader had become a new person; and it had denied itself the evident pleasures of faction and of internal squabbling in the interests of presenting itself as unified and fit to govern. But it proved unable to reassure voters and so failed to gain their trust. What would this dire outcome mean for the future of the party? Kinnock, at least, would have to go, but what of his policies, his reforms and his protégés? Would the party press on with 'modernisation' or revert to another vision, another moment in its past? Would the Tories continue their domination of British politics? Those were the questions Labour would ask itself while it mourned the results of the 1992 election and poured over their meaning. They would continue to loom large in the party's assessment of its most recent failure and the choice of a new leader to succeed Kinnock.

Notes and references

1 Mandelson speaking to the XYZ Club, 15 June 1987, quoted in Donald Macintyre, *Mandelson and the Making of New Labour* (London: HarperCollins, 1999), 174. On Bad Godesberg and its significance in the evolution of European social democracy, see Donald Sassoon, *A Hundred Years of Socialism* (New York: The New Press, 1996); and Gerassimos Moschonas, *In the Name of Social Democracy*, translated by Gregory Elliott (London: Verso, 2002). Even after the programmatic change of 1959, however, the SPD would be compelled to steadily reshape its organisation as well. For a useful comparison between Germany and Britain on these issues, see Susan Scarrow, *Parties and their Members: Organizing for Victory in Britain and Germany* (Oxford: Oxford University Press, 1996).

2 Philip Gould, 'SCA Campaign Appraisal and Next Action', 12 July 1987, KNNK/585.

3 Sawyer's plan was actually drawn up by Adam Sharples, who was on the NUPE staff and who, in an earlier life, had played in a rock band with Tony Blair at Oxford.

4 Martin Westlake, *Kinnock: The Biography* (London: Little, Brown, 2001), 424–5.

5 Gerald Taylor, *Labour's Renewal? The Policy Review and Beyond* (London: Macmillan, 1997), 42–67. See also Colin Hughes and Patrick Wintour, *Labour Rebuilt: The New Model Party* (London: Fourth Estate, 1990); and also Martin J. Smith and Joanna Spear, eds, *The Changing Labour Party* (London: Routledge, 1992).

6 Byrne, quoted in Macyntire, *Mandelson*, 204–5.

7 Sawyer in effect conceded that the review proceeded without regard to what local activists felt and defended it by claiming that 'political discussion [within local parties] is either non-existent or more of a political virility test'. See Tom Sawyer, 'Dear member', *New Socialist* (June–July, 1989), 11.

8 See Patrick Seyd and Paul Whiteley, *Labour's Grass Roots: The Politics of Party Membership* (Oxford: Clarendon, 1992), 40–55, on party members' political beliefs as revealed in an extensive survey conducted in late 1989 and early 1990.

9 For extremely useful assessments of the politics and economics of the Policy Review and subsequent revisions of party programme, see Mark Wickham-Jones, 'Anticipating social democracy, pre-empting anticipations: Economic policy-making in the British Labour Party, 1987–1992', *Politics and Society*, XXIII, 4 (December 1995), 465–94; Patrick Seyd, 'Labour: The Great Transformation', in Anthony King, ed., *Britain at the Polls* (London: Chatham House, 1992), 70–100; M. Smith, 'A Return to Revisionism? The Labour Party's Policy Review', in Smith and Spear, *The Changing Labour Party*; Smith, 'Understanding the "politics of catch-up": The modernization of the Labour Party', *Political Studies*, XLII, 4 (1994); and Colin Hay, 'Anticipating accommodations, accommodating anticipations: The appeasement of capital in the "modernization" of the British Labour Party, 1987–1992', *Politics and Society*, XXV, 2 (1997), 234–56.

10 The statement was drafted by Roy Hattersley. On the objection and later revision, see Westlake, *Kinnock*, 433. For the final version, see Labour Party, *Democratic Socialist Aims and Values* (London: Labour Party, 1988). The statement was largely a formality and had little impact on the more detailed work of the Policy Review groups.

11 Labour Party, *Meet the Challenge, Make the Change* (London: Labour Party, 1989), 12.

12 See, for example, *Social Justice and Economic Efficiency* (London: Labour Party, 1988), the theme of which was the dependence of the latter on the achievement of the former.

13 Taylor, *Labour's Renewal?*, 86–7.

14 Kinnock, in *Meet the Challenge, Make the Change*, 8.

15 Labour Party Policy Directorate, *Campaign Briefing*, 75 (Special Issue), June 1988, KNNK/46.

16 *Campaign Briefing*, June 1988, KNNK/46.

17 Kinnock, writing in February 1989; and speaking at the NEC in May 1989, quoted in Westlake, *Kinnock*, 438, 444.

18 Tony Benn, *The End of an Era: Diaries, 1980–90* (London: Hutchinson, 1992), 563–4, 567–8.

19 Macintyre, *Mandelson*, 190–5; Westlake, *Kinnock*, 451–70.

20 In 'Has the Electorate Become Thatcherite', in Robert Skidelsky, ed., *Thatcherism* (London: Chatto & Windus, 1988), 25–49, Ivor Crewe makes a strong case that voters had not been converted. See also Dennis Kavanagh, *Thatcherism and British Politics: The End of Consensus?* (Oxford: Oxford University Press, 1987). For more recent and somewhat different asessments, see Richard Heffernan, *New Labour and Thatcherism: Political Change in Britain* (London: Macmilan, 2000), and Peter Kerr, *Postwar British Politics: From Conflict to Consensus* (London: Routledge, 2001).

21 See Richard English and Michael Kenny, 'Public intellectuals and the question of British decline', *British Journal of Politics and International Relations*, III, 3 (October 2001), 259–83, and Kenny, *The First New Left: British Intellectuals after Stalin* (London: Lawrence & Wishart, 1995), who treat the intellectual left as part of the broader category, public intellectuals; and also Radhika Desai, *Intellectuals and Socialism* (London: Lawrence & Wishart, 1994). A more inside view is provided in *Out of Apathy: Voices from the New Left Thirty Years On* (London: Verso, 1989), edited by the Oxford Union Socialist Discussion Group. On the left's long-term ambivalence about whether to join or challenge the Labour Party, see Eric Hobsbawm, *Politics for a Rational Left: Political Writing, 1977–1988* (London: Verso, 1989), 77–8.

22 David Marquand, *The Progressive Dilemma: From Lloyd George to Blair*, 2nd edn (London: Phoenix Giant, 1999), ix.

23 In an otherwise highly critical account of Labour up to and including 1964, for example, Tom Nairn ended on a note of cautious optimism about the recently elected Wilson government. 'It is very unlikely', he argued, 'that revolutionary changes will occur with dramatic rapidity under the Labour regime. Nevertheless, change is underway, and it could eventually have a revolutionary meaning . . . Because the Labour government may play a positive part in this process – whatever its limits, however contradictory its role – socialists everywhere should see its advent with a certain hope, a certain critical confidence, and not merely as the futile repetition of an old illusion.' See Tom Nairn, 'The Nature of the Labour Party', in Perry Anderson and Robin Blackburn, eds, *Towards Socialism* (London: Fontana, 1965), 216–17.

24 Ralph Miliband, *Parliamentary Socialism* (London: Allen & Unwin, 1961).

25 A broader and more social-scientific variation of the argument, applied to socialist and social-democratic parties more generally, can be found in Adam

Przeworski and John Sprague, *Paper Stones: A History of Electoral Socialism* (Chicago: University of Chicago Press, 1988).

26 See Perry Anderson, 'Origins of the Present Crisis', 11–52, and Tom Nairn, 'The Nature of the Labour Party', 159–217, in Anderson and Blackburn, *Towards Socialism*. For a brilliant riposte, see Edward Thompson, 'The peculiarities of the English', *Socialist Register 1965* (London: Merlin, 1965), 311–62. For a recent restatement, see Gregory Elliott, *Labourism and the English Genius: The Strange Death of Labour England* (London: Verso, 1993).

27 A very useful formulation is found in H.W. Drucker, *Doctrine and Ethos in the Labour Party* (London: Allen & Unwin, 1979).

28 'Entryism', as practised by groups like Militant, presupposed a rather different theoretical orientation.

29 Michael Kenny and Martin J. Smith, 'Interpreting New Labour: Constraints, Dilemmas and Political Agency', in Steve Ludlam and M.J. Smith, eds, *New Labour in Government* (London: Macmillan, 2001), 237.

30 Stuart Hall, *The Hard Road to Renewal: Thatcherism and the Crisis of the Left* (London: Verso, 1988).

31 Bob Jessop, Kevin Bonnett, Simon Bromley and Tom Ling, 'Authoritarian populism, two nations, and Thatcherism', *New Left Review*, 147 (September–October 1984), 41.

32 Jacques estimates that the journal needed financial support of roughly £35,000–40,000 per year even at the height of its popularity in the late 1980s. The relationship to the party was complex, however, and in 1982 there was an effort to shut the magazine down. Still, as late as 1989 the journal's editors would repackage the 'New Times' argument into a *Manifesto for New Times: A Communist Party Strategy for the 1990s* (1989). The document was to be discussed at the Party's 41st Congress, which was scheduled for November 1989 but did not convene. Interview with Martin Jacques, 13 November 2002. The journal was wound up in 1991 when the CPGB ceased to exist. For a brief but enlightening retrospective, see Jacques, 'The last word', *Marxism Today* (December 1991).

33 'New Times: A Marxism Today special on Britain in the nineties', *Marxism Today* (October 1988).

34 See, for example, Stuart Hall, 'Brave new world', *Marxism Today* (October 1988), 24–9.

35 Giles Radice, *Labour's Path to Power: The New Revisionism* (London: Macmillan, 1989); and *Southern Discomfort*, Fabian Pamphlet 555 (London: Fabian Society, 1992).

36 Hilary Wainwright, *Tale of Two Labour Parties* (London: Hogarth Press, 1987), 254–5. See also Anthony Heath, Roger Jowell and John Curtice, *The Rise of New Labour: Party Policies and Voter Choices* (Oxford: Oxford University Press, 2001), who refer to the strategy as a 'coalition of the two lefts', 83–4.

37 Eric Hobsbawm, 'Rethinking Labour: No sense of mission', *Marxism Today* (April 1988), 14–17. More generally, see Hobsbawm, *Politics for a Rational Left*, in which he defends a strategic orientation based upon the need to create a broad 'popular front' against Thatcher.

38 This was actually the theme of a piece by Tony Blair in *Marxism Today* in 1991 in which he called for an agenda 'without the old failings of collectivism'. See Blair, 'Forging a new agenda', *Marxism Today* (October 1991), 32–4.

39 Kinnock to Convenors, 7 December 1988, KNNK/46, File 3.

40 Bish to Convenors, January 1989, PD:1910, KNNK/46, File 2.

41 *Campaign Briefing* (June 1988), KNNK/46.

42 Hewitt, 'The Strategy for Phase 2' (1988), KNNK/591, cited in Westlake, *Kinnock*, 426.

43 *Meet the Challenge, Make the Change*, 14.

44 Smith in the *Sunday Correspondent*, 5 November 1989; and in *Hansard*, 24 October 1989, cited in Andy McSmith, *John Smith: A Life* (London: Mandarin, 1994), 199–200.

45 Jon Kampfner, *Robin Cook* (London: Victor Gollancz, 1998), 58–9.

46 Stuart Holland, 'Britain and Europe since 1945', presentation to the Institute for Contemporary British History, 26 March 1997; interview with Stuart Holland, 7 October 2002. The discussions between Kinnock and Holland led to Kinnock's piece, 'Why Europe?' *New Socialist* (February 1984). The pro-European left inevitably fell out with Tony Benn and other anti-Europeans.

47 See Stuart Holland, ed., *Out of Crisis: A Project for European Recovery* (Nottingham: Spokesman, 1983).

48 On these refinements, see Taylor, *Labour's Renewal?*, 102–33.

49 Bryan Gould, *Goodbye to All That* (London: Macmillan, 1995), 208–9 and *passim*.

50 John Rentoul, *Tony Blair: Prime Minister* (London: Little, Brown, 2001), 153–8.

51 *Report of the Labour Party Annual Conference 1990*, 75.

52 *Report of the Labour Party Annual Conference 1991*, 40.

53 *Report . . . 1991*, 70.

54 See Julia Langdon, *Mo Mowlam: The Biography* (London: Little, Brown, 2000), 180–2, on Mowlam's considerable success in the effort.

55 Wickham-Jones, 'Anticipating social democracy, pre-empting anticipations', 476.

56 Macintyre, *Mandelson*, 238–40.

57 Philip Gould, *The Unfinished Revolution: How the Modernisers Saved the Labour Party* (London: Little, Brown, 1998), 114.

58 Quoted in Hugo Young, *This Blessed Plot: Britain and Europe from Churchill to Blair* (London: Macmillan, 1998), 347.

59 The phrase is from John O'Farrell, *Things Can Only Get Better: Eighteen Miserable Years in the Life of a Labour Supporter* (London: Doubleday, 1998), 222.

60 Gould, *Unfinished Revolution*, 106.

61 Eric Shaw provides a comprehensive and very thoughtful analysis of the campaign. See Shaw, *The Labour Party since 1979: Crisis and Transformation* (London: Routledge, 1994), 129–51. The role of the press has been much debated. See, for example, James Thomas, 'Labour, the tabloids and the 1992 general election', *Contemporary British History*, XII, 2 (Summer 1998), 80–104.

62 Whitty, 'The General Election 1992', 12 June 1992, KNNK/180. The report was discussed at the NEC meetings of 18 and 24 June 1992, NEC Minutes, LHASC.

63 O'Farrell, *Things Can Only Get Better*, 230.

64 Quoted in Gould, *Unfinished Revolution*, 117.

65 These include the ICM/Guardian poll conducted on 17 March and published on 18 March, giving Labour a 43–38 advantage; the Gallup/Telegraph poll conducted on 17–18 March and published on 19 March, which had the Conservatives up 40.5–38.5; the NOP/Independent poll conducted 17–18 March, published 19 March and showing Labour up by 42–38; and the MORI/Sunday Times poll conducted 18–20 March, published on 22 March and giving Labour a 41–38 lead. See Table 7.1 in David Butler and Dennis Kavanagh, *The British General Election of 1992* (London: Macmillan, 1992), 136.

66 Quoted in Butler and Kavanagh, *General Election*, 125.

67 Gould, *Unfinished Revolution*, 152; Westlake, *Kinnock*, 560.

68 On the strange impact of the 'constitutional issue', see Gould, *Unfinished Revolution*, 151; Butler and Kavanagh, *General Election*, 130; and Westlake, *Kinnock*, 564–9.

69 Just what worked has been much debated. Was it the steady Tory attack, the strong anti-Labour bias of the media – as Kinnock claimed in his resignation speech – or the underlying weaknesses in Labour's programme upon which Tory tactics had played so effectively? See Westlake, *Kinnock*, 588–90; Martin Linton, 'It Was The *Sun* Wot Won It', *New Statesman* (22 March 1996); John Curtice and Holli Semetko, 'Does it Matter What the Papers Say?', in Anthony Heath, Roger Jowell and John Curtice, eds, *Labour's Last Chance? The 1992 General Election and Beyond* (Aldershot: Dartmouth 1994), 43–64; and David McKie, 'Fact is Free and Comment is Sacred, or Was It The Sun Wot Won It?', in Ivor Crewe and Brian Gosschalk, eds, *Political Communications: The General Election Campaign of 1992* (Cambridge: Cambridge University Press, 1995), 124–30.

CHAPTER 9

· · · · · · · · · · · · · · ·

The fitful progress of 'New Labour'

The defeat of 1992 was cruel, for it seemed so undeserved. Labour had fought a solid, if not flawless, campaign; its leader acquitted himself well overall, though with exceptions; and the programme the party offered voters was, if not inspiring, at least unobjectionable. Most important, Labour's opponent was distinctly unimpressive. And yet Labour still lost, and for the fourth successive time. The loss was hard to accept and still harder to explain, and the effort to make sense of it would provide yet another occasion for rethinking the party's past, its image and its philosophy, and for the recriminations that accompany such clarifying and polarising moments. The moment was truly ambiguous and did little to clarify what should be done, however, for the party's most recent failure not only confirmed that Labour's old image and programme were not viable but also raised doubts about the party's new identity that had been crafted so carefully and fought for so bitterly.

Much to his credit Neil Kinnock did not hesitate to offer his resignation as party leader and to accept a full share of the responsibility for the defeat. As a result, the debate about why Labour lost proceeded apace with the selection of a new leader. The effect was perhaps to blunt slightly the encounter between the partisans of continued 'modernisation' and those who felt the party had already made sufficient accommodation with a hostile reality, a suspicious electorate and a nasty press. The disagreements were nonetheless intense. Kinnock's clear preference was to continue the transformation of the party. To that end he announced during his resignation speech on 13 April a determination to stand for election to the NEC in the autumn so as to continue the campaign to reshape the party. In May he went on to propose the adoption of 'one member-one vote' for the selection of MPs and the election of party leaders, the one reform that would in a stroke recast the relationship between the party and its historic base of support in the unions.

By coupling his resignation with an insistence on altering the institutional structure of the party, Kinnock gave his continued blessing to the 'modernising' project. By pushing forward the selection of a new leader he also seemed to foreclose, at least for the moment, the possibility of a campaign in which fundamental policy questions would be reopened. That meant that Kinnock acquiesced in John Smith's accession to the leadership, for no other candidate would have time to organise an effective campaign. Over the years Kinnock had been personally closer to Bryan Gould, who would unsuccessfully challenge Smith, but it was not unreasonably assumed that Smith was more committed to the reorientation of the party initiated by Kinnock. Smith was not a committed 'moderniser' at heart, but a fairly traditional centre-right moderate. He had nevertheless loyally supported Kinnock and presumably his instinctive caution and his political outlook would prevent a reversion to the more left-wing politics of the 1980s. Gould, by contrast, was more likely to reconsider the party's new direction and possibly reverse recent policy decisions on the economy and on Europe. That might well have provided an opening for the left to regain the initiative. The 'modenisers' could not countenance that prospect and threw their support behind Smith's candidacy. The Gould campaign failed decisively, unable to garner even 10 per cent of the vote.[1]

The formal post-mortem on the election would thus be held in the midst of the transition from Kinnock to Smith. The NEC held a special meeting to discuss the election on 18 June 1992 and continued its deliberations the following week. The meeting became the occasion for the expression of considerable resentment at the modernisers and their campaign techniques. An early article in *Tribune* had claimed that the campaign had been taken away from politicians and run by a 'tight clique of [Kinnock] supporters', Philip Gould and Patricia Hewitt most prominently, whose 'glitz and gloss approach, far from enabling Labour to compete on equal terms with the Tories, positively obscured our message'.

The lesson was obvious: 'Labour can dispense, lock, stock and barrel, with the well-meaning, metropolitan, ministrations of the Shadow Communications Agency and go back to real politics.'[2] John Prescott, apparently resentful at the modest role he had been assigned in the campaign, joined the attack as well; and his critique was repeated and endorsed widely by the left, who resented not only the campaign but the entire drift of recent policy-making. The discussion within the NEC was equally contentious and Philip Gould's presentation was, he wrote later, 'the worst' experience in his long association with the Labour Party.[3]

Party officials nevertheless stood by the campaign team and argued, as had been widely admitted during the contest, that the campaign was well run but the task simply too great. The reason was Labour's inherited image. Larry Whitty, the General Secretary, conceded that among many 'Labour weaknesses', the central problem was that the party continued to be 'judged by its history'.[4] It was regarded by voters as 'the party of the past' that would, if given the opportunity, 'turn the clock back'.[5] David Hill, Roy Hattersley's trusted aide who had been put formally in charge of the campaign, agreed that Labour carried 'too much baggage from the late 70s and early 80s to persuade people that they could fully trust us'. As the SCA's subsequent research would confirm, 'Labour lost because it was still the party of the winter of discontent; union influence; strikes and inflation; disarmament; Benn and Scargill'.[6]

The argument that what caused Labour's defeat was its past, and that the key lesson of the campaign was the need for further change, was put especially forcefully and publicly by Tony Blair, who after the election defeat began to emerge as the most forceful advocate of the case for further 'modernisation'. Blair's intervention went beyond a defence of the modernisers' campaign tactics and of the 'modernised' programme presented by Kinnock and insisted on the need for a more profound shift in the Labour's Party's identity. Just after the defeat he proclaimed that 'The lesson, in my view, is clear: neither to stand still and simply change leaders; nor, certainly, to go lurching back to the early 1980s; but to continue and intensify the process of change.'[7] On 30 June he elaborated further: 'The true reason for our defeat is not complex. It is simple. It has been the same since 1979: Labour has not been trusted to fill the aspirations of the majority . . .' In this Blair echoed his friend Mandelson, who claimed that 'It was a credibility gap, not a policy chasm, that Labour had to bridge in

1992.'[8] The gap in trust was based on the fact that the interests, and presumably the perceptions, of this elusive majority had evolved over the post-war years and Labour's policies had not. As Blair reasoned,

> When the majority were have-nots, and the vested interests that held
> them back were those of wealth and capital, the idea of people acting
> together, through the state, to reform social conditions and redistribute
> power became a strong political force . . . But the state, as it grew, itself
> became a potential vested interest . . . [and] the majority of people, as
> they prospered, earned more and began to pay the tax to fund the state,
> became more sceptical of its benefits . . .[9]

The modernising agenda was premised on a particular assessment of social and economic change. The British people were in the modernisers' view becoming more middle-class and Labour needed to align itself, and its programme, with what were assumed to be their aspirations. As Mo Mowlam would put it a few months later, 'we exist as a party to make people as affluent and as free as possible . . . Until the Labour Party can mentally make the leap that says aspiring to be middle class is positive, the public will always have trouble believing that we want to represent them or want to help anyone less fortunate . . . People want more money, a decent house, a good car – and so do all of us in the Labour Party.'[10] John Smith, not given to temporary and unconsidered enthusiasms, made much the same point in February 1993, asserting that the party's object-ive was 'the advancement of the individual, their [sic] freedom, auto-nomy, ability to participate, and capacity to prosper'.[11] Gordon Brown had already pointed out the electoral implications of this perspective in a speech to the Tribune Group in the summer of 1992: Labour might have been by tradition a class party, but now 'we must create a modern party with membership roots in every community . . .'. 'The truth is', he went on, 'that our natural constituency is far broader than what our comment-ators call our traditional constituency, and there is no contradiction between them. Our natural constituency is the majority who benefit from a just society.'[12] Brown's argument avoided the sociological reductionism common in other formulations in which being middle-class translated automatically into individualism, a reluctance to pay taxes and resent-ment at public provision. The middle classes, Brown suggested, were not merely self-interested but had reasons of their own to support the quest for social justice. Still, he and his fellow modernisers clearly envisioned an electoral majority that would include large numbers of those who had done well out of the Thatcher revolution and the social and economic changes of the 1980s and 1990s; and that is what they urged their comrades to imagine as well.

The modernisers had yet to capture the imagination, let alone the hearts, of the rest of the party, however, and found themselves often rather isolated. It was a curious situation: Blair and Brown were clearly the rising stars of the Labour Party and easily secured prominent positions within the Shadow Cabinet. Brown became Shadow Chancellor and was therefore the party's key spokesman on economics and Blair shadowed the Home Secretary and would use the position to great advantage. But Blair and Brown and their close friend Mandelson, now MP for Hartlepool, were unable to dominate the party so long as Smith remained in charge. They had allies: Jack Straw was drawing closer and was very forceful about it, Harriet Harman had long been, Mo Mowlam threw in her lot with the modernisers, and many of the class of 1992 were attracted as well. Blair and Brown also had many admirers in the mainstream press and their arguments were increasingly well presented in sections of the left-wing press – e.g. in the steady flow of publications from the rejuvenated Fabian Society and in new ventures like *Renewal*, sponsored by the Labour Co-ordinating Committee.[13] *Marxism Today* had, however, gone silent. Gradually, these new assets would have a decisive effect. But with the departure of Kinnock the modernisers had lost their grip on the party machine. The key figures in turning the party around from the mid-1980s had been Charles Clarke, Patricia Hewitt, Mandelson and, at one remove, Philip Gould. All owed their positions ultimately to Kinnock and served on his personal staff, on the staff at party headquarters or, in the case of Gould, as a paid adviser reporting to these insiders. But they were an unstable combination and by 1989 Hewitt had left and Mandelson was on his way out. Hewitt would come back to play a major role in the 1992 campaign but was out again when that ended; Mandelson was by then in Parliament but out of favour with the new leadership; Clarke was just out; and Gould was beaten up, depressed and soon seeking solace and inspiration in the Clinton campaign headquartered in Arkansas. So the informal access and influence that Brown and Blair had previously enjoyed was no longer available.

The case for modernisation was at least temporarily short of spokes-people. It would thus fall to Giles Radice, for example – a fixture of the old Labour right rather than a proper moderniser – to make the argument at the time of the 1992 party conference. His Fabian pamphlet, *Southern Discomfort* (September 1992) quickly sold out at the annual gathering and served for a brief period as the most coherent and current exposition of the argument for a further reform of the party's programme and a fur-ther effort to reach new voters.[14] Equally important, the reforming faction also had formidable rivals and opponents within the party and often found themselves in a minority within the Shadow Cabinet, where the remnants of the soft left – Blunkett, Meacher, Bryan Gould (for a short time), and especially Robin Cook – would mount a determined resistance to further steps to 'modernise' the party's programme. Prescott, though from a very different background, was equally resistant and openly so. Margaret Beckett, despite her decision to contest the deputy leadership with Prescott on the basis of a 'Modernisation Manifesto', was an unreliable ally.[15] She would even wobble in her support for Smith, who had effectively given her the job as deputy leader, during the highly charged campaign for OMOV, or one-member, one-vote. Given the pre-carious balance, it would be Smith's wishes that would regularly prevail and effectively determine how far, how fast, and indeed in precisely what direction the party would proceed.

Doubt would persist on these matters even after the post-mortem on the recent defeat. To some it was a sign that the debate had been too brief and too superficial. But it went on long enough to demonstrate that the main rival visions of what the party was and should become each still retained considerable appeal and so remained potentially viable. Inevitably, the debate about the failures of the 1992 campaign also provided yet another opportunity to try out the arguments behind the alternatives and another occasion for politicians to seek to reposition themselves vis-à-vis the leadership, the party programme, ordinary party members, and potential voters. David Blunkett, for example, gave the argument about why Labour lost a populist twist and suggested that the party needed a tougher image to appeal to the 'traditional' working class. The lingering doubts about Labour, he implied, and the reasons 'people do not trust us' were not just about the party's economic competence but also about 'whether it tolerates the intolerable – anti-social behaviour, freeloaders, and the like . . .'. Better to be 'denouncing the thugs . . .', he believed, than putting out images of 'soft music, green vistas' and reassuring words.[16] Blunkett, his credentials on the left secure from his years in Sheffield, could thus make a move towards 'the people' on the basis of an appeal to their supposed traditional values. Tony Benn's analysis differed markedly, of course, and he gestured towards his dwindling band of allies: the increasingly isolated fragments of the left and groups organised around racial, ethnic or sexual identity. He thus called for greater unity of the left on the assumption that a rainbow coalition would be the foundation of an electoral majority.[17] Clare Short made a rather more predictable pitch to the party faithful, claiming that because of its shift to the political centre under Kinnock, 'Labour was seen as having lost its soul, its identity, its integrity'.[18] It therefore had failed to connect with voters in 1992 but could somehow, she reasoned, reconnect if it were outfitted with a firmer set of principles and commitments.

The argument had no clear resolution and no declared winner, but the fact that it occurred was an unambiguous sign that there would be strong resistance to any immediate further steps towards 'modernising' the party. Indeed, the Shadow Communications Agency would be wound up in the autumn of 1992 and a new advertising firm hired. Far more important was the fate of Kinnock's effort to push the party into altering its procedures by adopting OMOV as its preferred method for making decisions. He wanted to force a vote at the 1992 conference, having calculated that the unions would be hard-pressed to mobilise so quickly and that the party would be unwilling to rebuke its new leader at his first conference. But Smith chose not to back Kinnock and put the matter off until the 1993 conference. In preparation, a study group – the Union Links Review Group – would assess the proposal in the broader context of relations between the party and the unions. As a matter of course, the trade union interest would be well represented, though Mo Mowlam and an often frustrated Blair also served on the committee; and together they pushed steadily for the reform of the union connection.

The delegation to committee would come to typify the Smith era.[19] Under Kinnock the old system of policy-making by the National Executive and its sub-committees had been replaced by a system of joint committees with representatives from the NEC, the Shadow Cabinet and the unions. Over and above these was the TUC/Labour Party Liaison

Committee that had been set up to manage relations between the party and the unions under the social contract. The Policy Review followed this pattern, which was set out early in Kinnock's tenure. Whatever its actual flaws, the review process was declared a success and led to the decision to institutionalise the style of consultation and deliberation that the Policy Review had embodied and, it was implied, vindicated. To this end a National Policy Forum would be established to undertake a 'rolling' review of policies and programmes. The result was to reduce massively the independent role of the annual conference and the initiative of constituency activists in setting party policy and to put controversial issues into the hands of experts and professional politicians. They would thus be taken out of the reach of partisans, activists and party staff. Kinnock developed the tactic a step further with the appointment in 1990 of the Plant Commission on Electoral Reform. The Commission was formally charged with reviewing different systems of voting for Parliament and for the proposed new assemblies for Scotland and Wales; its unstated purpose was to signal to supporters of proportional representation, including the Liberal Democrats and quite a few Labour Party members, the party's open-mindedness on issues of constitutional reform while deferring any specific commitment.[20]

Smith continued the shift away from policy-making by the party and by the politically engaged with the creation of special committees or working parties on the party/union connection, on party finance and on Europe. His most significant initiative, however, was the wholesale delegation of the review of social and economic policy to the Commission on Social Justice.[21] The Commission, chaired by Sir Gordon Borrie, was asked to 'identify a fairer tax and benefits system that will stand the test of time'.[22] It was run on a practical and daily basis by the moderate left-wing think tank, the Institute for Public Policy Research (IPPR), which had been set up in 1988–89 with Patricia Hewitt, Kinnock's former press officer, serving as a deputy director. She and David Miliband, who served as the secretary of the Commission, did much of its actual work – soliciting its submissions, organising its consultations, commissioning research and drafting working papers, and writing its reports. The commission reflected the ongoing transformation of the party both in its procedures and its conclusions. It drew upon the expertise of social policy academics and input from the anti-poverty lobby but also welcomed advice from the unions. Its interim reports were widely circulated and so there was at least a modicum of debate and consensus-building.

But because the effort occurred outside the party, full-time officials inevitably played a diminished role. There was both a political and a financial imperative behind the move. Both Larry Whitty and Geoff Bish resisted the approach represented by the institution of the National Policy Forum and the regular setting up of ad hoc committees and would have preferred a different strategy.[23] But Smith inherited a party with declining membership, uncertain income, substantial debt and a large staff that could not be sustained. Whitty announced in May 1992 that the party was nearly out of money and needed to cut staff and programmes.[24] Almost immediately Smith commissioned a study of the party's internal organisation and undertook moves to streamline its machinery.[25] Geoff Bish, the director of research, and Joyce Gould, director of organisation, would be retired in the spring of 1993.[26] A shrunken party machine had of necessity to rely on others for ideas and policy initiatives. That would mean in practice that when proposals appeared on the agenda of the party's leaders, they were not there because of internal pressure or support and so could be accepted or rejected all the more easily.

Policies crafted outside the party were also more likely to break with party traditions and taboos and so, more often than not, lent support to those who advocated changing party policy. The Social Justice Commission's final report was a very revealing example of this tendency and of the growing ascendancy of the arguments and intellectual approach favoured by modernisers. The report sought to escape from past commitments to the welfare state by reframing the debate about social provision and its impact on society and the economy. This it did by inventing three distinct approaches from which flowed three different visions of the nation's future: that of the deregulators, the levellers and the investors. The deregulators – most obviously identified with the Tories – were deeply implicated in society's inherited inequalities and saw 'no limit to how high earnings at the top will rise – and no limit to how low wages at the bottom will fall . . .'. Growth would come through the efforts of 'dynamic entrepreneurs, unshackled by employment laws or social responsibilities' and so the main task for government was to open markets and create the space within which individual capitalists would compete and succeed. It was also easy enough to identify or, as some might argue, to caricature, the levellers, many of whom had long found their political home on the left of the Labour Party. These were people who were 'concerned with the distribution of wealth to the neglect of its production; they develop policies for social justice independent of the economy'. The investors, by contrast, 'believe we can combine the ethics of community with the dynamics of a market economy'. The critical need was for investment, not so much in industry as in education and in 'strong social institutions, strong families and strong communities, which enable people to grow, adapt and succeed'.[27] The invocation of community, the priority given to production over redistribution, the centrality of education – these were the themes increasingly struck by the party's modernising faction, especially by its most articulate spokesmen – Brown and Blair. Equally telling was the framing device deployed in the report, which set up the Tories as one extreme, the doctrines of socialism or 'old Labour' as another, and then laid out a new and better approach, in effect a third and more rational option that could be portrayed not merely as a middle way but as a different and better way. The answer was not yet called the 'third way', but the style of thinking and argumentation would lead almost inevitably to some such formulation.

The actual proposals of the Social Justice Commission did in fact define more a middle position than something especially original. It repeated plans for improving education at all levels – from pre-school children to adults needing training and wanting 'lifetime learning'. Of the two specific promises Labour had made in 1992, on child benefit and pensions, it supported the first and backed off the second with a proposal for a 'pension guarantee'. The Report also proclaimed Labour's support for 'a modern form of full employment' – though neglecting to define what was meant by 'modern' – and proposed various supply-side meas-ures to achieve it. And on tax the Report favoured 'fairness', conceded 'that no one should pay more than 50 per cent of their income in tax', and argued for a closer integration of tax and benefit systems to eliminate the 'poverty trap' and to facilitate the movement into paid employment.[28] None of these proposals was new or surprising and they did typically split the difference between pre-established positions. Still, simply rais-ing alternatives to existing Labour policies served to expand the party's agenda and the repertoire of possibilities for a future Labour government.

The Report also proposed one quite new and specific policy initiative – new at least in Britain and in the ranks of Labour – and launched a key concept into circulation within British political discourse. The policy was 'welfare to work', which the Report's authors were at pains to distinguish from right-wing proposals for 'workfare' inspired by the American example; and the broader concept was 'social exclusion', a genuinely novel way of talking about poverty that put the emphasis on work and community rather than on the distribution of income and wealth. Both would have a future in the emerging politics of 'New Labour'. More important, the Commission and its Report marked a very real advance in the efforts of the modernisers to begin to shake up the thinking of the party, particularly on questions like universalism. To this extent it was an accurate measure of the slowly shifting balance between the party's contending factions during John Smith's brief period of leadership.

The close balance within the party revealed itself in how the party operated, in policy, and in personnel. Smith's cautious style contrasted sharply with the intensity of Kinnock, whose initiatives became crusades if only because he was so embattled. Even Smith's supporters worried a bit over his relaxed management of the party: Nick Raynsford, for example, complained just after the 1992 conference of 'an atmosphere of calm bordering on the complacent . . .'. 'The party', he suggested, 'appears to be substituting a state of anaesthetised torpor for the previous mood of hyperactive aggression'.[29] Others simply thought Smith was a bit 'lazy'.[30] But there was no real reason for Smith to hurry and to create excitement and potential opposition. The Conservative government, though weak, had a sufficient majority to ensure that it would not fall to a series of clever parliamentary manoeuvres. Smith, moreover, had the luxury of coming to the leadership after the battles of the 1980s had been resolved: the issue of Militant, the difficulty of responding effectively to the miners' strike, and the reorientation of the party's programme through the Policy Review. The memories and scars left by those struggles meant that he inherited a party desperate for unity. A particular irony in the situation was that Smith, though from the right of the party, was surprisingly popular on the left.[31] This was perhaps in part due to the fact that, unlike Kinnock, he was never one of them and hence was immune to the familiar charge of betrayal. Smith had also made his career in Parliament rather than in the party and so he had fewer opportunities to alienate those with whom he disagreed. Smith's tenure, then, was widely perceived as a moment of consolidation and reconciliation.

Where Smith did press forward with the reforming agenda of Kinnock and his allies was in the battle for OMOV. The path he followed to that end was nevertheless deeply worrying to those most committed to it. To begin, he chose to put the matter off from 1992 to 1993, thereby guaranteeing that the union leaders who opposed the move would have an opportunity to mobilise opposition. He then oversaw the appointment of a committee to work out the details of the new electoral system, the Union Links Review Group, on which the trade unions were relatively over-represented. Third, Smith himself played little role in the committee's deliberations and left his allies on the issue, like Blair, to fend for themselves until virtually the last minute. Smith did hold discussions with top union leaders, but was apparently quite taken aback by their steadfast opposition, which began early and continued to mount as the decision approached. Bill Morris of the TGWU provided a glimpse of what was to come in his speech to the 1992 conference: 'Colleagues,' he warned, 'a Labour Party without its trade union links would be a party without its roots, a party without a cause and indeed a party without a soul.'[32] Smith was apparently surprised to find that the union leaders listened politely to the position of the party leader and then proceeded first to negotiate, then to mobilise in opposition. During the summer before the 1993 conference the influential Manufacturing, Science and Finance Union (MSF) came out against the measure. So, too, did the GMB, NUPE and the TGWU; and it appeared for a time quite likely that Smith would lose the vote. He even talked with his closest staff members about the possibility of resigning as leader. Even at this late date the one reform absolutely essential to the modernisers' agenda looked to be very remote.

Smith would prevail in the end, but in a manner that illustrated graphically the close balance 'between the modernisers and those who favour the status quo'.[33] The proposal that passed at conference was a compromise brokered at the last minute and sold to the unions at a considerable cost. During 1992−93 various plans were debated and discarded because they preserved too little or too much influence for the unions. The system in place, adopted in 1981, had established an electoral college for the selection of party leaders in which the unions cast 40 per cent of the votes, MPs 30 per cent and constituency parties another 30 per cent. A similar, and more cumbersome, process had been put in place for the adoption of candidates for Parliament. Smith initially wanted a new system in which the party's leader and deputy leader would be chosen by an electoral college in which half the votes were accorded to MPs and Members of the European Parliament (MEPs) and the other half to local party members voting on OMOV principles, effectively eliminating both the block vote and the unions' special influence altogether. Predictably, the plan got nowhere.

The compromise that eventually emerged grew from a proposal backed by John Prescott which would give union members who paid the political levy to their union the right to join the Labour Party at a reduced rate and thus participate in the process of selecting candidates. Smith indicated his initial support for the principle and reworked it into a plan for the election of leader instead: the new system would have an electoral college in which MPs and MEPs, constituency parties and unions would each have a third of the votes, with the union votes based on those signing up for the party on the so-called 'levy plus' basis and voting as individuals. The plan would also mean that the selection of candidates for Parliament would be conducted on the OMOV principle, applied to local members and to members affiliated through the unions on the levy plus basis. The casting of union votes at conference, already reduced from 90 per cent to 70 per cent of the total, would also be determined by a variation on OMOV in which the allocation of conference delegates would be apportioned according to prior votes by union members.[34] The Review Group backed the complicated plan at its meeting of 14 July and Smith then undertook to win passage at conference.[35]

The great irony, of course, was that the proposal to reduce the unions' influence within the Labour Party had to be passed by a party conference still dominated by those very same unions. Their leaders were being asked to acquiesce in what could well be seen as their own weakening. In earlier moments in the party's history the very thought would have been heretical. What rendered it at least conceivable in the early 1990s was the much diminished role of the unions within the economy and of union votes within the electorate, and the fact that trade union leaders were willing to do almost anything to get rid of the Tories. The debate over OMOV in the aftermath of the 1992 defeat was thus more open and more unfettered by adherence to tradition than a similar debate would have been a decade, or even a year or two, before that. It was possible, in fact, to contemplate a real break between the unions and the party, a 'friendly divorce' that would allow the unions and the party to remain allies but sever the constitutional connection.[36] The problem, of course, was that genuine separation would deprive Labour of the financial support on which its very existence depended and would require, in its stead, either a massive increase in paid membership or the public funding of political parties. Neither was imminent, if even desirable, and so some sort of compromise was the only possible outcome. The question was on what terms, and it was on this issue that the modernisers had cause to worry.

To Blair and Brown and like-minded reformers, the package Smith proposed yielded too much to the unions and left the trade unions with a more privileged position than was appropriate to a remodelled party. The 70 per cent of conference votes that they retained – it would subsequently be reduced to 50 per cent – was the most egregious example, but there were fears as well that the unions' continued formal role in the election of party leaders was also a mistake. Blair, who played a prominent role in the Review Group and in the public debate over the issue, was especially disappointed. He had been very forceful in January 1993, saying that 'We have block votes for everything. That's all got to go . . .' and that what was needed was 'not a process of adjustment' but a more fundamental 'project of renewal'.[37] He believed that the bargain Smith and Prescott brokered was not a good one and that a firmer lead could have produced a more thoroughgoing transformation. In fact, there was evidence that ordinary party members were convinced as early as 1989–90 of much of the case for reforming the trade union connection: Seyd and Whiteley's well-known survey showed that over 80 per cent thought that 'the Labour Party leader should be elected by a system of one party member, one vote' and 72 per cent felt that 'The trade union block vote at conference brings the party into disrepute.'[38] Even more telling was the one proper sampling of trade union opinion. The engineering union (AEEU) polled 2,000 of its members in 1993 and found that only 21 per cent supported a union role in the selection of MPs.[39]

As the party's primary economic spokesman Brown had still greater cause for upset because, in convincing the unions to back him at conference, Smith had appeared to make unnecessary and potentially damaging concessions on economic policy. Thus at the TUC meeting on 7 September Smith delivered a speech that undercut the sustained effort to strike a pose of fiscal moderation by reiterating Labour's commitment to full employment and by promising an extension, or restoration, of trade union rights curtailed under Thatcher. Smith proclaimed that 'The goal of full employment remains at the heart of Labour's vision for Britain. Labour's economic strategy will ensure that all instruments of macro-economic management . . . will be geared to sustained growth and rising employment.' In failing to couple this goal with a pledge to combat inflation, Brown felt, Smith was reverting to the Keynesian policies that had failed so decisively in the past. In addition, Smith offered his support for a minimum wage and for the right to union membership for all workers, including those working part-time, and from 'the first day of employment'. In his effort to win reluctant trade union support for his modest reform of the union link, Smith had apparently set aside the caution that Brown was determined to maintain over macro-economic policy and that Blair, in his tenure as Employment spokesman, had displayed over trade union rights. Smith's policies were not quite a reversion to the past. What he proposed on the issue of union membership was in line with European standards and the Social Chapter, which Labour publicly supported, and he would later qualify his support for full employment. But there is no doubt that he had been forced to bend to the lingering power of the trade unions in his quest for party reform. As one ardent moderniser later put it, 'the price of victory was a large nod in the direction of old-fashioned Labourism . . .'.[40] Since it was precisely that culture that the modernisers believed had to be eliminated from the party, the price was judged to have been far too high.

As it was, Smith barely won the vote at conference and the device that guaranteed victory very much tainted its achievement. The leadership went into the conference just shy of a majority and Smith, desperate to win, let it be known that he would resign if he lost the vote. Even that ploy did not immediately prevail, but at the last moment the MSF was convinced to abstain. The grounds were contrived and not entirely credible: the union was opposed to OMOV but since the proposal put to conference also contained a provision requiring that women be nominated for half of the open seats judged to be winnable, the executive chose not to cast its 4.5 per cent of the total vote. With that abstention, the measure would pass narrowly, but the process had demonstrated Smith's dependence on the very forces he sought to escape.

So, too, did the conference debate preceding the vote. As Smith and his aides prepared for the crucial test, they decided that it made more sense to have John Prescott make the case for the leadership than to have it put either by a moderniser, like Brown or Blair, or by the deputy leader, Margaret Beckett, who proved to be not at all solid on the issue. Prescott's intervention became a famous occasion in which he simultaneously demonstrated his curious but effective grasp of the language, his passion for the cause of the day, and his loyalty to the leadership. In his bravura performance, the ex-seaman proved he could play to the crowd and its moods by beginning with a nod to women. On the question of increasing women's representation among MPs, he declared that 'I will be a moderniser for the sake of that argument'. On the union link, he reiterated Tom Sawyer's complaint about how some party members, presumably the 'modernisers', had forced the issue onto the agenda when in reality there was no problem.[41] He got in a further jibe by claiming that the very same people had been largely responsible for the 1992 defeat: 'They lost. . . ,' he said, 'and a little more humility from them would and should have been expected.' But, he proceeded, since the issue had been raised and since the Tory enemy and a hostile press were watching, the party now had to vote for OMOV and against the block vote. It was not the principle that mattered, therefore, but the need to thwart the press and the Tories. He declared,

> Last night, the Tories reminded us of the connection between the trade unions and the Labour Party. There is no doubt that this man, our leader, put his head on the block by saying, basically: 'I fervently believe' – because that is what he believes – 'in the relationship, and a strong one, between the trade unions and the Labour Party.' He has put his head on the block. Now is our time to vote. Give us a bit of trust and let us vote to support him.[42]

Conference delegates reluctantly gave Smith his triumph and his head, and they willingly gave Prescott their hearts. The impact of the debate was to some extent contradictory. To have the replacement of the block vote by the principle of one member, one vote endorsed by a quintessentially 'old Labour' figure like Prescott undoubtedly gave the result an added legitimacy and made it easier for many to accept. Nevertheless, the close result, the dubious manouevres that produced the majority in support, and the rhetoric used to sell it gave the modernisers a genuine cause to worry over the party and its future and, of course, over what role they themselves would play in a party that seemed increasingly likely to win the next election but reluctant to continue the process of internal reform.

The battle over OMOV was therefore important in itself, but even more important for the lesson it taught about the party's inherited political culture and its institutional structure. The modernisers had learned, or were learning, that Labour's policies and programme, over which they had fought repeatedly and successfully during Kinnock's tenure as leader, were firmly rooted in its organisation and in its pervasive culture. The resistance elicited by the proposal to abandon the block vote revealed the resilience and enduring potency of the unions within the party and of the ethos that justified the unions' unusual status. As Will Hutton had pointed out even before the 1993 conference, 'the grip of "labourism" on the old guard in the party remains tight'.[43] In fact, 'Labourism' was not just an old prejudice, but deeply embedded in the party's identity and preferred policy options. The obvious lesson was the need to make a more thorough break, to remake the 'underlying culture of the party', and to remove its organisational peculiarities in order to prevent a resurgence of support for the policies that were held to be responsible for the crises of the 1970s and the disasters of the 1980s.[44]

Already the modernisers were being forced to retreat, or at least to adopt a slightly different rhetorical pose, on economic policy. Repositioning the Labour Party on economic policy was a top priority for those who believed, as Kinnock and his allies surely did, that it was the party's economic record and strategy that had disqualified it in the minds of voters. Labour was widely seen in the 1980s as the party of high taxes and high spending, and it was perceived as dependent on the unions and so unable to resist their demands for inflationary wage increases or to curb the propensity to strike. The party was regarded as unsympathetic to the aspirations of those who wanted to improve themselves, hostile to home ownership and to private consumption, and addicted to state regulation. Whatever the truth or fairness of these characterisations, they had to be addressed and the Policy Review was meant to do that. Party policy on privatisation was subtly adjusted; its commitment to reversing the

Tories' trade union legislation deflected; spending promises were pared down; and Labour policy on tax became less radical and redistributive. The few commitments to 'tax and spend' that managed to survive the Policy Review and that found their way into the 1992 manifesto and the Shadow Budget would come back to haunt the party during the campaign. The effect was a determination to purge even these residual commitments to redistribution. Most important, the party's strategy for generating growth was redesigned fundamentally: the old focus was on macro-economic policy and Keynesian in inspiration; the new approach was post-Keynesian in theory and its emphasis was on supply-side socialism and measures to improve skills, training and education.[45] Gordon Brown actually went so far as to criticise the Tories for engineering a demand-led boom that had not been prepared for by investment in skills and training, arguing that 'a consumer boom without prior, adequate and sustained investment effort was bound to be untenable'.[46] Labour also began gradually lowering expectations about its own ability to reduce unemployment.

The reorientation of economic policy had inevitably led to a parallel shift on Europe. The alternative economy strategy of the late 1970s and early 1980s had been premised on the imposition of selected import controls – a semi-autarchic vision fundamentally incompatible with continued membership in the Common Market. Soon after becoming leader Kinnock therefore began a steady, if also stealthy, retreat from that exposed stance. The move had been greatly aided by the evolution of the European Community itself. With Jacques Delors's accession to the presidency of the European Commission and the articulation of the concept of a 'European model of society', the European connection became more attractive even to the left within the party. Delors had been welcomed as a hero at the 1988 TUC meeting and encouraged the unions to think of their future in European terms. The Social Charter, proclaimed in 1989 and incorporated as the Social Chapter in the Maastricht Treaty in 1991, was an especially appealing commitment to a set of social rights. Thatcher's antipathy virtually ensured its embrace by the rank and file of the trade unions and the Labour Party. The promise that a Labour government would sign up to the package of rights accorded to employees in the charter was particularly helpful in reconciling the unions to the framework of industrial relations put in place by the Conservatives' trade union legislation. During his brief stint as Employment spokesman, for example, Tony Blair had pushed through a new policy on the closed shop by holding out the prospect of enhanced protections of employees and their right to organise and join unions contained in the Social Charter. As Alan Tuffin of the Communication Workers Union explained, the unions were opting for 'individual workers' rights, rather than trade union rights as such'.[47]

Labour's rethinking on Europe went still further in the early 1990s, as Smith and his advisers edged towards support for the European Monetary System and the Exchange Rate Mechanism that was intended to make it a reality. The appeal was first, that it was likely to happen anyway and would probably be in place if and when Labour ever returned to power and thus hard to reverse. Second, a prior commitment to maintaining ERM would have the effect of reassuring business and the investing public that a Labour government would be fiscally responsible and could be trusted rigorously to combat inflation.[48] When Smith became leader and Brown took over as Shadow Chancellor, support for ERM quietly continued. At the same time the pursuit of fiscal orthodoxy intensified and prior commitments were dropped. 'I scrapped the Shadow Budget', Brown later recalled, and he had 'told John Smith we were not going back to it. . .'. He would go public with a new plan in early November 1992. By then, however, he was able to claim that it was the deterioration in the economy – rather than any abandonment of principle or tactical consideration – that produced the shift recently.[49] In truth, the entire basis of economic policy, both for Labour and for the government, had been undermined.

What had changed was 'Black Wednesday', 16 September 1992, when Britain was forced to withdraw from the ERM. The Major government had cast its lot with the effort to link the major European currencies, but it became increasingly clear over the summer and autumn of 1992 that the pound was overvalued. After pouring £1.8 billion into a futile effort to hold the rate and after interest rate hikes to 15 per cent, the Chancellor Norman Lamont was compelled to announce that Britain was leaving the system. The decision was to become a turning point in British politics, the moment when the Conservatives lost their reputation for being the party that could successfully manage the economy and when it became possible for the public to think that Labour might actually do better.

Smith and Brown were devastating in their criticism. On 24 September Brown pointedly reminded the House of Commons that 'The Conservative Party ran a general election campaign on the slogan "You can't trust Labour" and has shown itself completely unworthy of trust.' He went on to claim that 'Ministers who continue to hold responsibilities now cannot command respect. They may hold office for five years, but even after five months they have lost all authority to govern. They have failed the country and they will never be trusted again.'[50] Public opinion rapidly turned and by January 1993 Labour was ahead of the Tories by an average of eight points in three key polls. Labour's lead would widen to roughly 20 points by the following December and the gap would remain in that range until the election of May 1997.[51]

But the collapse of Tory policy simultaneously deprived the Labour leadership of the most compelling reason for moderating the party's own economic policy and for its parallel move towards Europe. The evolution of Labour's economic policy during the late 1980s and early 1990s was not simply a response to the success of the Conservatives', for it retained distinctive emphases, but it was undoubtedly based on the sense that the Tories had got something right and that Labour in the past had got things very wrong. The result was a convergence on critical issues like the ERM and on the inapplicability of Keynesian remedies for slow growth and continuing unemployment. Thus the National Institute of Economic and Social Research could plausibly report in 1990 that 'the economic policy differences between the two major parties are narrower now than they have been for about twenty years'.[52] The decision to leave the ERM changed all this; and now that Tory policies were suddenly seen to be failing, the logic behind convergence disappeared. The economy was languishing in the early 1990s and inflation had begun to rise again. The economic gains registered under Thatcher were quickly forgotten and replaced with a growing popular resentment. Fears that Labour might do no better apparently prevented this discontent from revealing itself in the 1992 general election, but when the centrepiece of Conservative strategy collapsed shortly after, public support for the government rapidly dissipated.

The Tory discomfort, following and confirming the earlier discard of monetarism, led within the Labour Party to at least a minor revival of Keynesian thinking, while the persistence of high unemployment led to a renewed attention to the goal of full employment. During 1993–94 remnants of both the hard and the soft left combined with the leadership of several major unions to push the party into support for a more expansionist set of economic policy commitments. Bryan Gould, though no longer in the Shadow Cabinet and soon to leave British politics altogether, helped to put together a Full Employment Forum, which was launched on 12 March 1993 and became 'an immediate success, in terms of both the support it attracted and the impact it had on policy statements from the Labour leadership'.[53] Important backing for a more aggressive policy also came from the Labour Members of the European Parliament. Stuart Holland, the architect of the original Alternative Economic Strategy, had gone to work for Delors and the European Commission in 1991 and soon produced a report on 'economic and social cohesion' that seems to have become the inspiration for a plan to use EU funds to stimulate a coordinated European Recovery Programme.[54] The assumption behind the proposal was that recovery was impossible if the different national economies and governments went their separate ways, but that acting together the European nations could coordinate fiscal and monetary policy with a programme of infrastructural investment to promote growth and jobs. Specifically, the EU would issue federal bonds for a series of 'trans-European transport and communications networks (TENs), research and development projects, regional development schemes for the environment and for urban renewal and support for small and medium-sized enterprises (SMEs)'.[55] These ideas found partial expression in the Commission's 1993 White Paper on *Growth, Competitiveness and Employment*.[56] The central point of the White Paper was the need to enhance competitiveness through improving skills and education and thus preparing Europe for the transition to a high-tech, information-based economy. The report even gestured towards the need to make labour markets more flexible. However, it also contained modest proposals for coordinated expansion and public investment and it was these measures that appealed to the majority of Labour's representatives at Strasbourg, who were beginning to emerge as the best organised and most effective opponents of the modernisers. The proposals also found echoes within Britain on the left of the party and won support among the trade unions.[57]

This 'Euro-Keynesian' challenge arose at precisely the moment when Smith and Brown were least able to fend it off. The increasing disarray of the Tories and the deepening of the nation's economic woes led to a relaxation of the discipline that had recently constrained Labour policy and that had largely forced it to abandon its Keynesian preferences. In response, Brown was forced to adopt at least some of the fashionable Euro-Keynesian rhetoric. In November 1992, for example, he called for a 'jobs and growth recovery programme for Europe'; in February 1993 he spoke of 'our commitment as a Labour movement to full and fulfilling employment for all'; and later that year he was largely responsible for a Labour Party proposal to the EU calling for the establishment of a 'counter-cyclical European Recovery Fund to generate jobs by improving communications, the environment and training'.[58] Smith went even further to conciliate the supporters of reflation when he famously reasserted the party's commitment to full employment at the 1993 TUC meeting.

The momentum behind this reversion to an older approach to economic policy was quickly halted, however. Having won his conference victory on OMOV, Smith began to back off from his unequivocal endorsement of full employment. Brown, despite a dip in his popularity within the party, remained determined to resist demands for increased spending and for a return to Keynesian policies. And for both Smith and Brown the continuing difficulties of the Tories made the prospect of a Labour victory and a Labour government increasingly real and this realisation stiffened their resolve not to give hostages to fortune. At the European level, the recovery plan was never likely to get past the watchful eye of the Bundesbank and the Council of Ministers duly put it to rest. The proposal had arisen in the aftermath of the Maastricht Treaty and was seen at the time as a necessary counter to the deflationary impact of the criteria for convergence leading to monetary union. When the prospects of ratification looked bleak, the plan was widely trumpeted. As voters fell into line and prospects for the treaty improved, it became unnecessary and the normal EU preference for fiscal prudence was restored.[59]

The battles over the party's link with the unions and its economic strategy were nevertheless unambiguous signs that the party's conversion to its new image and programme was largely superficial and merely tactical in inspiration, a product of electoral calculations that could and did change. Most important, the experience of 1992–93 revealed the extent to which the reorientation undertaken during the Kinnock leadership was in crucial respects incompatible with the party's institutional structure and its ethos and culture. Many within the Labour Party still thought of it as the party of the workers and of the 'labour movement' and operated within a mental framework that was 'Labourist' and putatively 'socialist', however vaguely those terms were now defined. Equally significant was the fact that the unions still clearly regarded the party as their creation and property. When as staunch an ally of the Kinnock leadership as Tom Sawyer, the NUPE offical, warned the party of breaking with the unions – 'No say, no pay' he argued – and when John Prescott felt compelled to wrap his support for OMOV in a rhetoric of continued party/union collaboration, it was obvious that the effort to create distance between the party and the unions had met with only partial success.[60]

The party was so resistant to the efforts of the modernisers because its identity was built into its structure and reinforced by its myths and beliefs. The union connection, in particular, was not a choice or a policy but the very foundation of the party. Its Labourist ethos, which meant at its core the defence of the interests of Labour as embodied in institutions like the trade unions, flowed naturally from this foundation. And holding this very unique institution together was the organisational glue provided by a shared commitment to Clause IV, to nationalisation, to what passed as socialism.[61] The practical conclusion to which the modernisers were increasingly driven was that a genuinely new model Labour Party had to be created on a new institutional basis and within a new ideological framework. Reform had to be more thorough and had to involve a visible and conscious break with the party's past and with its inherited structures and procedures. Despite the heroic exertions of Kinnock and the rather more plodding efforts of Smith, the party had yet to learn thoroughly the lessons of its previous failures and defeats. Or so it appeared to those who would soon emerge as 'New Labour'.

The struggle to modernise the party was thus far from won: rather, it was proceeding on several fronts and meeting with differing and uneven results. On the critical issue of leadership, however, it was moving inexorably forward. It was increasingly obvious, for example, that the two most likely successors to John Smith were Brown and Blair. Brown had already outshone the party leader when forced to substitute for the Shadow Chancellor after his first heart attack in late 1988. Upon Smith's return in January 1989, the *Sunday Express* noted mischievously 'How quickly the spotlight moves on.' 'Almost every day of his absence, he

[Smith] has heard glowing reports of the brilliant way in which his deputy, Dr Gordon Brown, has stood in for him.'[62] There was even speculation in 1992 that Brown would challenge for the leadership. He chose not to, presumably out of a mix of loyalty and strategic calculation, but Blair claimed afterwards that he should have fought and believed, according to a confidante, 'that Brown would have won'. 'Tony's view', it was later reported, 'was that the party wanted to be led ... and if you sold it an out-and-out modernising message it would take it.'[63] Blair's position was perhaps slightly too optimistic and it was transparently self-interested, for it would serve to rationalise his own subsequent determination to stand for the leadership when it might otherwise have been thought to be Brown's turn. But it was also a plausible reading of the prospects of a leading contender for the future leadership of the party.

Brown's only serious competition could and would come from his friend and close ally, Blair, and it was during Smith's tenure as leader that Blair began to edge out Brown in the contest over the eventual succession. It was partly based on matters of presentation and partly a reflection of Blair's maturation as a politician and his waxing ambition. But the choice was also influenced by more serious, if contingent, matters. It was Brown's fortune and fate to have the most important job in the Shadow Cabinet behind that of leader of the opposition, but serving as Shadow Chancellor was a potential liability as well. Brown was rightly held responsible for the party's increasingly niggardly stance on taxing and spending and, in particular, for seeming to renege on promises to increase pensions and child benefits. He was forced to act as watchdog over the proposals that issued from other members of the Shadow Cabinet and earned only resentment for these efforts. In addition, Brown was especially vulnerable over the party's position on the ERM and the related question of devaluation. Kinnock, Smith and Brown were in agreement that Labour needed to reassure the markets prior to the general election and that it should not be seen as the party of devaluation. But because the pound was objectively overvalued in 1992, it was also understood that some adjustment was probably inevitable. Kinnock's advisers, John Eatwell and Meghnad Desai, had in fact been planning to raise interest rates as soon as a Labour victory was declared and to begin discussions of devaluation. Kinnock, just having lost the election and so no longer having to guard against possible indiscretions, had himself written in July to the *Financial Times* arguing for just such a realignment.[64] But Brown had held firm to the party's prior public commitment on the issue and so was in a very weak position to attack the Tories after Black Wednesday. He spoke forcefully against the government, but his colleagues knew it was largely an effort to cover his previous attachment to the very same, but now discredited, policy.

Brown's time as Shadow Chancellor was for all these reasons a period in which his stature visibly rose with the public and the press while his stock within the party fell. By contrast, Blair had a very good run in opposition, particularly in his role as Shadow Home Secretary, and the experience benefited him both within and outside the Labour Party. To begin with, Blair had been very aggressive in arguing that the meaning of the defeat in 1992 was that the party should change more, modernise more, and not regress. He was outspoken as well on the question of the block vote. Brown, holding a slightly more elevated post and so more exposed, seemed just a bit less forceful and in effect ceded to Blair the leadership of the modernising camp. Brown, Blair and Mandelson continued to work closely, but the attention began to fall more upon Blair. A telling moment occurred the day after Smith's election as leader when a profile of Blair, *en famille*, appeared in *The Sunday Times* and posed the question of whether Labour had chosen the wrong man: 'Yesterday Labour elected a new leader. Some feel the Party should have skipped a generation and gone for Tony Blair.'[65] Blair had in fact thought seriously about standing for the deputy leadership in 1992, but chose not to, heeding the advice of Kinnock and Hattersley that he would be better placed eventually to become leader by not becoming deputy to Smith. Instead, Blair pressed for the post of Shadow Home Secretary, not ordinarily a stepping stone to greatness, but in his case a very effective platform. It was a position that allowed him to speak regularly on domestic affairs and to become far better known. Even more important was the opportunity it afforded for recasting the image of the party on social issues.

Labour was not always and invariably the party of social liberalism. Neither the traditional working class whom the party sought to represent, nor the trade unions through whom these workers often spoke, were immune to 'traditional' values, to the claims of 'king and country', to occasional displays of intolerance or even to the authoritarian populism of Mrs Thatcher. Labour's most recent prime minister, James Callaghan, gave voice to that aspect of Labour's political culture in a famous speech at Ruskin College in October 1976 in which he criticised progressive trends in education and argued for a return to standards.[66] Nevertheless, ever since the reforms undertaken by the Labour government of 1964–70 and associated most clearly with Roy Jenkins, the party had been by and large committed to a liberal agenda on issues of crime, education, divorce and homosexuality as well as on matters of social policy. The impact of the generation of 1968, who entered the party in the early 1970s and became the core of the left-wing challenge to the leadership, was to confirm this stance. The policy reorientation initiated by Kinnock had begun to shift party policy in each of these areas, but only gradually and indirectly. The move away from Keynesian demand-management and its replacement with supply-side socialism emphasising skills, training and education meant that Labour's education policy was given a new theoretical and rhetorical underpinning. The party remained committed to increased opportunities and to at least some modest increases in spending to make that happen, but the objective was now more practical and hard-headed. On social policy Labour was also forced by the exigencies of electoral competition and by the prospect of tight budgets to temper its commitment to spend more money. The National Health Service, it was obvious, would require an infusion of cash, but if so, other areas of social provision would have to make do with less, or at least lesser increases. The logic was an end to the principle of universal provision, the introduction of more carefully targeted benefits, and a drive for more efficient delivery. The Commission on Social Justice represented the first steps in an effort to justify this less generous programme by emphasising personal responsibility and the importance of community and family. Policies and arguments of this sort could not, however, be expected to inspire the party faithful or even to distinguish Labour from the Tories. They were expedient, perhaps necessary or even inevitable, but the rhetoric did not soar and the analysis failed to bite. The exercise was largely a matter of defence, not yet a matter of conviction.

Labour's stance on crime was similar, and probably even less inspiring. The party's philosophy was to emphasise quite reasonably the social causes of crime and to point out ways of relieving them. Labour also favoured rehabilitation and opposed the death penalty, and in recent years had become more likely to identify with ethnic minorities and their complaints about racial bias among the police. The Tories rightly judged that these positions, however worthy and defensible, left Labour slightly out of touch with a rather illiberal electorate who worried about crime, sympathised with the police and wanted to see criminals punished, and that Labour was on this account vulnerable to the charge of being 'soft on crime'. Tony Blair was to change all this and to alter the political discourse so as to make crime an issue that worked for Labour and against the Tories; and he did it with feeling and a touch of political genius.

Under the Tories both the crime rate and the size of the prison population had steadily risen. Labour's existing approach to the issue rendered the party's criticism ineffective, however, and encouraged the Conservatives to press ahead with proposals designed to mark them out as the party of law and order. John Major's 'back to basics' theme was part of this strategy, so were the increasingly illiberal and punitive legislative initiatives of Kenneth Clarke and Michael Howard, successive Home Secretaries. Nevertheless, the bare facts could be mobilised against the government if the case were made properly and by the right person. Despite his experience as a long-haired rock musician, Blair was largely immune to the spirit of the 1960s; his private life was a model of respectability; and he was a convinced Christian. Moreover, for a Labour politician he was unusually sympathetic when faced with constituency complaints about hooligans and muggings. He spoke with conviction about 'Friday nights made absolutely impossible for people; old people afraid to live within their own home, never mind go out on the streets, young people often intimidated by other young people . . .'. '[T]hese things', Blair insisted, 'are wholly unacceptable . . .'.[67] In late 1992 he set about reworking Labour's approach to crime with these complaints and sentiments in mind. By early 1993 he had decided to adopt a new, harsher, but more populist line: Labour, he argued, needed to be both 'tough on crime and tough on the causes of crime'. The phrase was originally Brown's, but Blair made it his own. He gave it a decidedly Christian inflection, adding along the way that 'Christianity is a very tough religion', and made a convincing connection between crime and the broader question of community.

The public breakthrough came in February 1993, when the news was filled with the tragic story of Jamie Bulger, the two-year old led away to his death by two 10-year-olds. The horror was caught on tape with a surveillance camera and shown repeatedly on television. Blair gave a speech on 19 February that was presumably heartfelt but that also captured the public reaction and put Labour, for once, on the same side. As Blair put it,

> The news bulletins of the last week have been like hammer blows struck against the sleeping conscience of this country, urging us to wake up and look unflinchingly at what we see . . . These are the ugly manifestations of a society that is becoming unworthy of that name. A solution to this disintegration doesn't simply lie in legislation. It must come from the rediscovery of a sense of direction as a country and most of all from being unafraid to start talking once again about the values and principles we believe in and what they mean for us, not just as individuals but as a community . . . The importance of the notion of community is that it defines the relationship not only between us as individuals but between people and the society in which they live, one that is based on responsibilities as well as rights, on obligations as well as entitlements.[68]

The stress upon community was not itself an innovation. Blair and Brown and many others within the Labour Party had been using the term with increasing frequency. It was a concept that served well to distinguish Labour from Thatcherite conservatism, with its disdain for 'society' and its fetishising of the market. Faced with the 'market fundamentalism' of the Tories a number of centre-left thinkers had begun arguing in the 1980s that markets themselves were social constructs and that they required institutions and non-market values to work. To exalt the market over society actually threatened to destroy the very framework that made markets and capitalism possible. Notions about the limits of markets and the importance of revitalising civil society and, in the process, redefining the meaning of citizenship and with it the role of the state, began to inform Labour Party discourse from the early 1980s and were particularly prominent in the rhetorical framing of the Policy Review.[69]

The approach was also of considerable practical use in explaining new policies on employment, social security, education and crime. It would provide a theoretical grounding for the supply-side interventions in the market proposed by Labour as part of the Policy Review; and it furthered the impression that social provision under Labour would be based on 'reciprocity' rather than hand-outs. Gordon Brown was eloquent on the issue in his Sovereignty Lecture of 1992:

> I want to argue that we require an entirely new settlement between individual, community and government; that a modern version of socialism must retrieve the broad idea of community from the narrow notion of the state; and that we must ensure that the community becomes a means by which individuals can realise their potential . . . Indeed, democratic socialism was founded on the belief in the value of community; its main inspiration is the ethos of community, not a theory of economy.[70]

Blair's decisive contribution was to make the idea of community unusually concrete and to draw from it a powerful, even a harsh, message. Earlier usages betrayed a defensive cast of mind that Blair discarded. Community in Blair's hands became a demand for decent behaviour, a 'bargain' in which 'opportunity' would be paired with 'responsibility' and would produce a set of social relations within which, as he explained to readers of *The Sun*, 'There is no excuse for crime.'[71] Within a very short time, Blair's repositioning of Labour policy was reflected in polls showing that voters thought Labour would be more effective in handling crime than the Conservatives. The reversal became more or less permanent as Blair repeated his message at the 1993 party conference and argued that 'for millions of our citizens the democratic freedom they value most is freedom from crime and the fear of crime'. It was for that reason that 'Labour is now the party of law and order in Britain . . .'.[72] Blair also worked hard to steer the party in Parliament away from direct attacks on Tory legislation on crime and into a strategy of picking away at details. Blair did not become a social conservative: his positions on the death penalty, divorce, women's rights, gay rights and race relations were consistent with the party's liberal and libertarian views. But at a time when voters' were becoming increasingly concerned about crime and told to regard it as an indicator of the quality of life, they became convinced that Labour would do something about it.[73]

Blair's achievement on crime was a further indicator of the shifting balance within the party between the modernisers and their opponents. The battle between the two visions was complex and at times revealed, or even created, alliances that cut across established political or ideological differences. Overall, the era of John Smith did not see the emergence of debate on fundamental questions, but rather produced skirmishes and subtle manoeuvring over a range of issues that vaguely traced the fault line between the modernisers and the so-called 'long gamers', but which seemed often to be based largely on temperament and style. It was in truth a more significant split.[74] The decreased pace of change under Smith and the tenacious resistance that the modernisers confronted on major issues led Alastair Campbell, political editor of the *Daily Mirror* and soon to be Blair's press secretary, to characterise the modernisers as 'frantics'. What made them frantic was their not unreasonable belief that the momentum for reform and for what Blair would later call 'permanent revisionism' was slowing all around them. In this apparently calm moment, they increasingly felt that 'the party does not know what it is for, other than to oppose the Government in Parliament'.[75] A steady and competent opposition, the modernisers intuitively understood, might well win the next election, but the resulting government would be a short-lived and unhappy affair. As Tony Wright argued, if the party remained unreformed, a newly-elected Labour government 'will be blown out of the water in record time, its precarious majority threatened by those who will lose no time in raising the familiar cry of betrayal, its core base of electoral support revealed as dangerously eroded, and a Conservative Party . . . having rediscovered that its . . . mission is to be in power'. Labour required 'a project', a 'larger framework of ideas' if it were to become capable of articulating a set of goals that could last beyond the next general election and so become politically dominant in the way the Conservatives had been in the 1980s.[76] This desire not simply to win, but to win repeatedly and to dominate the political arena was a uniquely grand aspiration for a party – or a faction within a party – that had lost four successive general elections and that was almost more comfortable in opposition than in government. It was nevertheless how the modernisers had come to envision their 'project', and these aspirations not only made them impatient at the pace and pattern of advance, it also made them uniquely alert to what stood in the way of achieving them. In particular, they became aware during 1992–93 of the strength of their opponents within the party and they were reminded more than once of the myriad ways in which the party's institutions and its political culture provided a series of veto points over proposals for change and enshrined in its formulations a rhetoric with which to cloak that resistance.

It was thus at precisely the moment when the victory of the modernisers was becoming ever more likely that they were becoming more and more determined of the need to wage a bitter battle to remake and take control of the party that they seemed destined to lead. Brown and Blair were by far the two most dominant figures in the Shadow Cabinet and were likely to lead the party sooner or later; they were more and more the public face of Labour and its future; and they and their supporters were making policy in the key areas. Smith had delegated the revamping of social policy to a committee and a think tank run by modernisers; economic policy was in the hands of Brown and even when he was pressed from the left Smith backed him; and Blair had not only redefined the party's image on crime but had begun to position Labour as the genuine voice of the nation, speaking the values of community, and instinctively taking the side of ordinary people. Smith's own manifesto for the leadership had been largely drafted by Brown and Blair and it was obvious that although there were alternatives to modernisation, none offered a coherent vision that could mount a challenge to what the modernisers were saying.

And yet the modernisers were in fact often frantic about their prospects, worried over complacency and the party's evident tendency to backslide. Blair, according to the TUC leader John Monks, was in this period visibly irritated and 'impatient . . . It was as if he wanted to pick the Party up and shake it by the scruff of the neck. He was angry. Angry with the small c conservatism of the Labour Party. Angry at its resistance to change.'[77] Blair and Brown both frequently confided their frustrations to their ally on the NEC, Tom Sawyer: they were 'really desperate under John's leadership', Sawyer has recalled, 'because there was nothing happening . . .'.[78] Time might well have been the modernisers' friend, and so it turned out, but the passage of time might just as easily have become their enemy, for rising stars cannot continue to rise and will not rise when part of a weak and ineffective government or within a party with whose basic instincts they are at odds. Blair, Brown and their fellow reformers reasonably feared that the opportunity to transform Labour and to make it into the kind of party that could govern long enough and forcefully enough to put its stamp upon the nation's life might be squandered through Smith's 'masterly inactivity' and, more ominously, that the chance might not come again.

That possibility was underscored by the obvious fact that the party was largely at peace with itself while Smith was leader. The struggle over OMOV was intense and closely fought, but for most it was not a crusade. Smith's threat to resign if he lost it was thus largely regarded as a bluff on which he was quite unlikely to follow through. Intense factional strife was clearly not a good in itself, but to the modernisers complacency was equally an enemy. Especially worrying, however, was the resentment recently manifest against the modernisers themselves – and against the very concept of modernisation – and the accompanying sense that it was they who were disturbing the party's new inner peace and self-confidence. The recriminations that followed the 1992 defeat had offered numerous outlets for this resentment and put those most closely implicated in the campaign, Gould and Hewitt, very much on the defensive, but it persisted long after Smith's election, Black Wednesday and the reversal of party fortunes.

A nasty but characteristic outburst had accompanied Brown and Blair's trip to the United States in January 1993, for example. They were accused by John Prescott of wanting to 'Clintonise' the party and Smith was so irritated that he called for Peter Mandelson in order to deliver an indirect, if blunt, message to the two pilgrims. In Mandelson's account, Smith complained that 'All this Clintonisation business, it's just up-setting everyone. Stop boat-rocking with all this talk of change and modernisation. It will just divide the party. If we remain united we'll win. Do just shut up.'[79] Clare Short joined in with talk of a clique of 'secret, infiltrating so-called modernisers' seeking to use the Clinton victory to push Labour into adopting policies and strategies alien to its traditions.[80]

The charges had a basis in fact, for the links and contacts between Labour and the Democrats were legion and the most recent electoral results in the United States suggested that Labour had much to learn from the encounter. As Philip Gould has conceded, 'the Clinton experience was seminal for the Labour Party' and made a particularly deep impression on the modernisers. Gould had himself slipped off to Arkansas just after the 1992 defeat; several other Labour staff members – Margaret McDonagh, John Braggins, Alan Barnard – worked for the Clinton campaign and reported on its success. Gould and Patricia Hewitt wrote approvingly of the strategy of the 'New Democrats'; Clive Hollick studied the Clinton effort and on his return proposed a 'new Labour Party, new policies on tax and trade union links'. The Labour Co-ordinating Committee compiled a report that contrasted the Democrats' success with Labour's recent failure; Geoff Mulgan, who had written frequently for *Marxism Today* and later headed up the think tank, Demos, and Yvette Cooper, a former aide to Smith, authored a study comparing the British and American elections and found the Labour effort wanting; and even Margaret Beckett visited Washington and returned impressed. Mandelson, of course, was a still bigger fan and found the Clinton approach to running an election campaign a model that Labour would do well to emulate.[81]

The Clinton influence was no secret, however, and it took only when it reinforced what was happening, or needed to happen, in Britain. Mandelson, for example, did not require the example provided by James Carville in 1992 in order to decide how to manage Kinnock's campaign in 1987; and he and Gould, Hewitt and others had been doing since the mid-1980s what the Democrats only discovered later. What the election of Bill Clinton did was to demonstrate that these tactics could be made to work. This was critically important in 1992, for the advocates of modern campaigning had just lost the election in Britain and were desperately in need of proof that their attention to mass media, their efforts to present a clear and coherent message, and their willingness to tailor the message to the audience of prospective voters could produce victory.

Perhaps even more important was the influence of Clinton and the 'New Democrats' in ratifying recent shifts in Labour policy and encouraging further moves in the same direction. During his trip to the United States in January 1993 Brown made contact with some of the 'policy-wonks' around Clinton, like Robert Reich, and would later spend summer holidays on Martha's Vineyard discussing the virtues and possibilities of supply-side socialism.[82] The effect was to reinforce Labour's emphasis on education and training as the central feature of its new economic policy. The willingness of Clinton's advisers to consider alternatives to welfare 'as we know it' and to offer a more liberal version of workfare also served to alert Labour's modernisers to the potential of a new bargain over work and welfare and a new policy of 'welfare-to-work'.[83]

Even more important, however, were the lessons of the Clinton strategy on issues like crime and on the broader question of traditional values. Clinton famously took time from his campaign to fly back to Little Rock and approve an execution. Tony Blair would not be forced to go to such lengths, but it seems quite clear that his stance on crime and his muscular vision of community and the need for responsibility and reciprocity owed much to his understanding of Clinton's electoral strategy.[84] The essence of the Clinton strategy was to reconnect with the broad middle class by escaping the Democrats' prior identification with the poor and with policies that were portrayed as benefiting mainly the poor or racial minorities, and by embracing a new populism. For the modernisers in the Labour Party, this translated into an effort to create 'a populism of the centre rather than the left'.[85] The lessons from America were the very same lessons the modernisers had been trying to sell to their comrades since the mid-1980s. Labour had to move beyond its shrinking base in the industrial working class by reaching towards and capturing the centre, which was middle-class in reality and in how it thought of itself. Blair articulated the view very clearly when he argued that 'We play the Tory game when we say we've got to speak up for the underclass rather than the broad majority of people in this country.'[86] He put the insight into effect with his initiative on crime, which he launched a mere three days after returning from the United States. The new stance allowed Labour to claim to be on the side of ordinary people on an issue of great saliency. The manoeuvre also provided the party with a unique opportunity to speak on behalf of society, to lament the 'shredding of the social fabric', and to proclaim that only Labour was capable of 'repairing this break in civil society' because to do so required 'a Party which believes in it'.[87]

It was of course Margaret Thatcher, with her bold assertion that 'There is no such thing as society', who made it possible for Labour effectively to put in a claim as the defender of society. But it had taken Labour a very long time to evolve an effective answer to the Conservatives and to counter their neo-liberal faith in free markets and a diminished state. Its Labourist ethos, its socialist aspirations and its collectivist predisposition all stood in the way of a new formulation that would reconnect Labour and society. Labour had first to free itself of the taint of extremism in the aftermath of the Bennite insurgency, the miners' strike and the sectarian antics of Militant; it had then to jettison the policies and programme which separated it from all but its most loyal supporters; it required as well the creation of a new and more moderate programme that would appeal to the centre ground and to at least some of those who had done well out of Thatcherism. After all that, it still needed to win voters' trust and confidence and allow voters to identify with the party instinctively. The general election of 1992 demonstrated that Kinnock was unable to do that.

Over the next two years, however, the party finally succeeded in its efforts to forge a new connection with the majority of the British people. How? To some extent, John Smith's reassuring competence removed the lingering fear that Labour would ruin everything if it were elected. He was massively aided in this achievement by the Conservatives' cumulative failures in government, beginning with Black Wednesday, and their increasing disarray as a party. It seems not unreasonable to suggest, however, that while Smith was building confidence in the party's leadership, the arguments of the modernisers about community and responsibility were beginning to resonate, to provide the intellectual framework within which to situate Labour's reshaped programme and a language that could convince a sceptical electorate that the party's remaking was sincere and lasting. The modernisers, in short, were winning the argument inside and outside the party and they were about to prevail. That they should worry over the inevitable resistance was further proof that they were serious, determined and very likely to win the battle for control of the Labour Party and, after that, much more. They fretted because they knew, as all serious politicians know, that timing is critical. In the event, the long game was foreshortened and time was about to run out on John Smith and to give the modernisers their chance.

Notes and references

1 The speed with which Kinnock moved to resign led some to argue that the fix was in and to regret the lost opportunity for debate. The fact that it was once more the leaders of the big trade unions who pronounced for the eventual winner, even before Kinnock had resigned, seemed to confirm that there was a conspiracy afoot and to this extent harmed Smith early in his campaign. See Andy McSmith, *John Smith: Playing the Long Game* (London: Verso, 1993), 203–5. On the challenge by Gould, see Bryan Gould, *Goodbye to All That* (London: Macmillan, 1995), 253–62.

2 Phil Kelly in *Tribune*, 17 April 1992. See also Anthony Bevins in *The Independent*, 25 April 1992. These are cited in Philip Gould, *The Unfinished Revolution: How the Modernisers Saved the Labour Party* (London: Little, Brown, 1998), 155–60.

3 Gould, *Unfinished Revolution*, 158.

4 Minutes of the NEC Meeting of 18 June 1992 HASC.

5 Report of the General Secretary (Whitty), 'The General Election 1992', 21 June 1992, Kinnock Papers, KNNK/180.

6 Gould, *Unfinished Revolution*, 158, citing his own report to the Labour Party, '1992 General Election: Evaluation and Implications', September 1992.

7 Tony Blair, 'Pride without prejudice', *Fabian Review*, CIV, 3 (May 1992), 3.

8 Peter Mandelson, 'Why Labour Lost', *Fabian Review*, CIV, 3 (May 1992), 6.

9 *The Guardian*, 30 June 1992.

10 Mo Mowlam, 'What's wrong with being middle class?', *Fabian Review*, CV, 2 (January–February 1993), 4–6.

11 *The Independent*, 7 February 1993.

12 Brown, speech in Central Hall, Westminster, 9 July 1992, cited in Paul Routledge, *Gordon Brown: The Biography* (London: Simon & Schuster, 1998), 166.

13 The Fabians were aboard the modernising project from the beginning and played an important role in the Policy Review. The LCC would emerge as an especially strong advocate as well and in 1993 actually published a *Manifesto for Modernisation*.

14 Giles Radice, *Southern Discomfort* (London: Fabian Society), Fabian Pamphlet 555 (September 1992).

15 Colin Brown, *Fighting Talk: The Biography of John Prescott* (London: Simon & Schuster, 1997), 238, 249–60.

16 David Blunkett, 'Review of the General Election 1992', 16 June 1992, KNNK/180.

17 Tony Benn, 'Labour: Why We Lost and How to Win', June 1992, KNNK/180.

18 *Tribune*, 3 July 1992.

19 Andy McSmith, *John Smith. A Life, 1938–1994* (London: Mandarin, 1994), 329–31. (This is the second edition of McSmith's biography, revised and republished after Smith's untimely death in May 1994.)

20 Martin Westlake, *Kinnock: The Biography* (London: Little, Brown, 2001), 522–3; John Kampfner, *Robin Cook* (London: Gollancz, 1998), 71–2. Kinnock himself was undecided on electoral reform but was forced by the prospect

of dealing with the Liberal Democrats to keep the option open. Some of his closest allies, like Patricia Hewitt, were in favour and had been involved with Charter 88. Other modernisers, like Brown and Blair, were determinedly opposed. On the support within the Kinnock camp, see Richard Heffernan and Mike Marqusee, *Defeat from the Jaws of Victory: Inside Kinnock's Labour Party* (London: Verso, 1992), 319–20.

21 Commission on Social Justice, *Social Justice: Strategies for National Renewal* (London: Vintage, 1994). See also Gerald Taylor, *Labour's Renewal? The Policy Review and Beyond* (London: Macmillan, 1997), 137–68; Paul Anderson and Nyta Mann, *Safety First: The Making of New Labour* (London: Granta, 1997), 213ff; and S. White, 'Rethinking the strategy of equality: An assessment of the Report of the Commission on Social Justice', *Political Quarterly*, LVI, 3 (July–September 1995), 205–10.

22 John Smith, speech of 30 April 1992, quoted in Anderson and Mann, *Safety First*, 213.

23 Interview with Lord Sawyer, 10 October 2002.

24 *The Times*, 23 May 1992.

25 For a summary, see David Pitt-Watson and Arthur Hay, 'There is more to winning than politics: A management report on Labour', *Renewal*, I, 4 (October 1993), 12–24.

26 *The Independent*, 7 February 1993.

27 Excerpted in Taylor, *Labour's Renewal?*, 151–2.

28 Anderson and Mann, *Safety First*, 215–6.

29 Nick Raynsford, 'Sleepwalking into oblivion', *Fabian Review*, CIV, 6 (November 1992).

30 Interview with Lord Radice, 9 October 2002, who suggested that this view was fairly widespread among Smith's colleagues in Parliament.

31 McSmith, *Smith: A Life*, 313.

32 Morris, speaking on 30 September 1992, in the *Report of the Labour Party Annual Conference 1992*, 189.

33 Letter of local Labour leader to *The Times*, 6 January 1993, cited in McSmith, *Smith: A Life*, 303.

34 For details, see Steve Ludlam, 'Norms and Blocks: Trade Unions and the Labour Party since 1964', in Brian Brivati and Richard Heffernan, eds, *The Labour Party: A Centenary History* (London: Macmillan, 2000), 230–4; and Paul Webb, 'Reforming the Labour Party-Trade Union Link', in David Broughton et al., eds, *British Elections and Parties Yearbook 1994* (London: Frank Cass, 1995), 1–14. For background, see Lewis Minkin, *The Contentious*

Alliance: Trade Unions and the Labour Party (Edinburgh: Edinburgh University Press, 1991). For a broader, comparative perspective, see Ludlam, Matthew Bodah and David Coates, 'Trajectories of Solidarity: changing union-party linkages in the UK and the USA', *British Journal of Politics and International Relations*, IV, 2 (June 2002), 222–44.

35 *Labour Party, Trade Unions and the Labour Party: Final Report of the Review Group on Party-Union Links* (London: Labour Party, 1993).

36 Donald Sassoon, 'The union link: The case for friendly divorce', *Renewal*, I, 1 (January 1993), 28–35.

37 Blair on BBC1, 17 January 1993, quoted in John Rentoul, *Tony Blair: Prime Minister* (London: Little, Brown, 2001), 207.

38 Patrick Seyd and Paul Whiteley, *Labour's Grass Roots: The Politics of Party Membership* (Oxford: Clarendon, 1992), 50–1.

39 Routledge, *Brown*, 179.

40 Paul Thompson, 'Labour's year of not living dangerously', *Renewal*, II, 1 (January 1994), 1–8.

41 See Tom Sawyer, 'Roots and resources', *Fabian Review*, CIV, 4 (July 1992), 3–4.

42 Prescott, 29 September 1993, in *Report of the Labour Party Annual Conference 1993*, 161–4. A slightly different version – neither more nor less grammatical but not quite the same – was reported in the press and quoted, for example, in Rentoul, *Tony Blair*, 214. Presumably reporters faced the same difficulty as those who transcribed the text for the conference report. The effect is nevertheless clear enough, whichever wording is recalled and preferred.

43 Will Hutton, 'Constitutional change and the modernising of Labour', *Renewal*, I, 3 (July 1993), 51–2.

44 See Geoff Mulgan, 'Creating an enabling party', *Renewal*, I, 1 (January 1993), 66, on the need to change the party's culture.

45 On the theoretical underpinning, see N. Crafts, 'Post-neoclassical endogenous growth theory: what are its policy implications?', *Oxford Review of Economic Policy*, XII, 2 (1996), 30–47.

46 Gordon Brown, *Where There is Greed: Margaret Thatcher and the Betrayal of Britain's Future* (Edinburgh: Mainstream, 1989), 23.

47 Tuffin, speaking to a Fabian Society conference in November 1990, quoted in Stephen Tindale, 'Learning to love the Market: Labour and the European Community', *Political Quarterly*, LIII, 3 (July–September 1992), 291–2.

48 On the logic of the move, see Peter Burnham, 'New Labour and the politics of depoliticisation', *British Journal of Politics and International Relations*, III, 2 (June 2001), 127–49.

49 Brown made the statement in an interview with his biographer on 28 July 1997. See Routledge, *Brown*, 168, and, for the announcement of 9 November 1992, 173–4.

50 Routledge, *Brown*, 171.

51 Broughton, *British Elections*, 243–4. The polls whose results are summarised here were done by ICM, MORI and Gallup.

52 Cited in Eric Shaw, 'The Wilderness Years, 1979–1994', in Brivati and Heffernan, *The Labour Party*, 131.

53 Gould, *Goodbye to All That*, 276.

54 See Stuart Holland, *The European Imperative: Economic and Social Cohesion in the 1990s* (A Report to the Commission of the European Communities) (Nottingham: Spokesman, 1993); Holland, *Beyond Maastricht: A New Strategy for Jobs and Recovery for Europe* (London: MSF, 1993); and also Ken Coates, 'A European recovery programme', paper to the European Parliamentary Labour Party, 25 September 1992, cited in Anderson and Mann, *Safety First*, 402.

55 Michael Barratt Brown and Ken Coates, *The Blair Revelation: Deliverance for Whom?* (Nottinghan: Spokesman, 1996), 166–9.

56 The White Paper was Delors's last major initiative. For the context and impact, see George Ross, *Jacques Delors and European Integration* (New York: Oxford University Press, 1995), 221–6.

57 See Anderson and Mann, *Safety First*, 88–97; and also Gerard Strange, 'British trade unions and European Union integration in the 1990s: Politics versus political economy', *Political Studies*, L, 2 (June 2002), 347–9.

58 Gordon Brown, 'First principles', *Tribune*, 26 February 1993; Labour Party, *Economic Renewal in the European Community* (London: Labour Party, November 1993).

59 See Ed Balls, *Euro-monetarism: Why Britain Was Ensnared and How It Should Escape* (London: Fabian Society, December 1992); and 'Where next after euro-monetarism?', *Fabian Review*, CV, 1 (January–February 1993), 7–8.

60 Sawyer made the remark at a NUPE conference. See McSmith, *Smith: A Life*, 278. For a fuller discussion, see Tom Sawyer, 'Roots and Resources'.

61 H.M. Drucker, *Doctrine and Ethos in the Labour Party* (London: Allen & Unwin, 1979), 30–1.

62 *Sunday Express*, 26 January 1989, cited in Routledge, *Brown*, 151.

63 Cited in Rentoul, *Tony Blair*, 180.

64 Anderson and Mann, *Safety First*, 86–7.

65 Barbara Amiel, 'Labour's Leader in Waiting', *The Sunday Times*, 19 July 1992. For context and reaction, see Rentoul, *Tony Blair*, 186–7; Jon Sopel, *Tony Blair: The Moderniser* (London: Michael Joseph, 1995), 136–7.

66 Kenneth Morgan, *Callaghan: A Life* (Oxford: Oxford University Press, 1997), 502–3.

67 Blair, interviewed on *The World This Weekend*, 10 January 1993, cited in Rentoul, *Tony Blair*, 192.

68 Blair, speech to the Wellingborough Labour Party, 19 February 1993.

69 See Raymond Plant, *Equality, Markets and the State*, Fabian Tract 494 (London: Fabian Society, 1984); Bernard Crick, *Socialist Values and Time*, Fabian Tract 495 (London: Fabian Society, 1984); Crick and David Blunkett, *The Labour Party's Aims and Values: An Unofficial Statement* (Nottingham: Spokesman, 1988). For a useful discussion, see Geoffrey Foote, *The Labour Party's Political Thought: A History* (New York: St Martin's, 1997), 329–35.

70 Gordon Brown, 'The servant state: Towards a new constitutional settlement', *Political Quarterly*, LXIII, 4 (October–December, 1992), 394, 399.

71 *The Sun*, 3 March 1993.

72 Tony Blair, 27 September 1993, *Report . . . 1993*, 183.

73 Anthony King, 'Why Labour Won – At Last', in King, et al., *New Labour Triumphs: Britain at the Polls* (Chatham, NJ: Chatham House, 1997), 193–5.

74 It was occasionally argued that the distinction between modernisers and traditionalists was a false one, but that very claim was typically the first move in an effort to criticise one's opponents. See, for example, Peter Hain, 'Neither mod nor trad', *Fabian Review*, CV, 4 (July–August, 1993), 6–7. More plausible arguments for the relevance of the distinction were made by Blair, 'Why modernisation matters', *Renewal*, I, 4 (October 1993), 4–11; and Paul Thompson, 'Modernising Labour', *Renewal*, I, 3 (July 1993), 2.

75 *The Sunday Telegraph*, 7 February 1993.

76 Tony Wright, 'What new politics?', *Renewal*, II, 1 (January 1994), 75–81.

77 Monks, quoted in Sopel, *Tony Blair: The Moderniser*, 129.

78 Interview with Lord Sawyer, 10 Ocobter 2002.

79 Donald Macintyre, *Mandelson and the Making of New Labour* (London: HarperCollins, 1999), 274.

80 Short, 9 January 1993, quoted in Rentoul, *Tony Blair*, 196.

81 See Sopel, *Tony Blair: The Moderniser*, chapter 6; Rentoul, *Tony Blair*, 194–8; Macintyre, *Mandelson*, 367–8; and Philip Gould, *Unfinished Revolution*, 176–7; Routledge, *Gordon Brown*, 175–7.

82 James Naughtie, *The Rivals: The Intimate Story of a Political Marriage* (London: Fourth Estate, 2001), 220–1.

83 Desmond King and Mark Wickham-Jones, 'From Clinton to Blair: The Democratic (Party) origins of welfare to work', *Political Quarterly*, LXX, 1 (January–March 1999), 62–74.

84 As Philip Gould and Patricia Hewitt wrote about the New Democrats' model, 'Their fusion of economic interventionism . . . and social conservatism may or may not be appropriate here. Even if it were, acceptance of capital punishment will not be.' See Philip Gould and Patricia Hewitt, 'Lessons from America – learning from success: Labour and Clinton's New Democrats', *Renewal*, I, 1 (January 1993) 45–51.

85 Gould and Hewitt, 'Lessons from America'; and *Tribune*, 8 January 1993.

86 Blair, 26 May 1993, quoted in Rentoul, *Tony Blair*, 197.

87 Tony Blair, 'Crime and Society', in *What Price a Safe Society?* (London: Fabian Society, 1994), Fabian Pamphlet 562: Proceedings of the 1994 Fabian New Year School, 2–4.

CHAPTER 10

'New Labour's' moment

The architects of what would come to be called New Labour – basically the most committed of the party's 'modernisers' – may have chafed during John Smith's tenure as leader, but it was very hard to argue with his success. Under John Smith's leadership the Labour Party went from puzzled agony over the loss of 1992 to a confident expectation of victory whenever John Major might choose to call the next election. The pivot was Black Wednesday in September 1992: after that date Labour never lost its lead in the opinion polls. Even during the controversy surrounding the block vote popular support remained firm, and in January 1994 five separate polls gave Labour an average lead of 20 points over the Conservatives. Over the next six months Labour's lead would be translated into massive victories in local elections that typically saw the Tories pushed into third place behind the Liberal Democrats, and it was dramatically confirmed in the elections to the European Parliament on 9 June 1994, when Labour won more than three times as many seats as the Tories and Liberal Democrats combined.[1] By then, of course, John Smith had died and Blair's leadership campaign was well under way, but the polls remained undisturbed.

Nor was the surface of Labour Party politics much disturbed once the 1993 conference battle over one member, one vote (OMOV) had been concluded. Smith was presiding over a large and growing lead and the party had the unaccustomed pleasure of watching the Tories self-destruct as they sought in vain to define a post-Thatcher identity. Issues that might well have caused dissension within the party – like the Maastricht Treaty – were smoothed over by Smith's deft management and the

Tories' ineptitude, especially over the economy and taxation. The decision to abandon the ERM continued to have serious repercussions and to force the government into a series of difficult measures. Labour's Shadow Chancellor, Gordon Brown, responded with great effectiveness and in January 1994 produced a long list of Tory tax pledges that had been broken. Later that month Harriet Harman, a member of Brown's team, elicited a formal response from the Treasury admitting that recent rises would mean that people would be paying more of their income in tax under the Conservatives than they had under Labour in 1979 – 35 per cent versus 32.3 per cent. Shortly after, the Treasury also conceded that ordinary families would be paying yet another £1,160 in tax as of April 1995.[2] The public debate undermined the Tories' credibility, for they had based their 1992 election campaign on a relentless attack on whether Labour could be trusted on the economy and, specifically, on issues of taxing and spending. The effect was to reinforce the shift towards Labour.

When Smith died unexpectedly on 12 May 1994 he thus bequeathed a party largely at peace and savouring the prospect of regaining national office for the first time since Thatcher's victory 15 years before. The contest between modernisers and their opponents was put on hold for the moment and the unfeigned grief elicited by Smith's death would prolong that moment for a while longer. It also soon created a new agenda in which the battle over the party's programme, outlook and constitutions was at least temporarily replaced by a struggle for the leadership. Very quickly, it became clear that 'It's got to be Tony . . .', as Smith himself had put it as recently as 9 May, but there were details to be worked out, rivals to be beaten or brought on board, and a campaign to be waged.[3] The manoeuvring of the next few weeks would reveal much about the party's future leader; it would also rearrange the party's hierarchy and establish the terrain on which the next stages of the struggle to control the party would be fought out. The question of who would lead Labour would have inevitable consequences for the debate about whether efforts to modernise the party should be continued, intensified or allowed to dissipate. But the contest was first and foremost about who could best lead the Labour Party back into office; and it would for that reason constitute only an indirect referendum on the issues that had been at the heart of internal party politics for the past decade.

Blair's victory would mean the de facto triumph of the modernisers, but the terms of the victory would mean that their dominance would still have to be consolidated after the selection of leader. Blair clearly understood this and for that reason mounted a campaign that was powerfully effective but also quite cautious. The first task, dictated by caution but perhaps also by loyalty, was to deal with Gordon Brown. Brown and Blair had for several years been regarded as the two most obvious choices for the Labour leadership after Smith, but it was equally clear that standing against each other would be dangerous. It would split the modernisers, embitter them against each other and in the process weaken the cause; and it would provide an opening for a candidate who did not share their agenda. Such possibilities existed in the persons of Robin Cook and John Prescott, and maybe even Margaret Beckett.[4] Resolving the potential conflict between Blair and Brown was therefore critical in ensuring a commanding victory for the modernisers. It fell to Brown to stand aside, but Blair and Mandelson worked hard to make it happen and to make it relatively painless. Although the outcome left Brown feeling seduced and abandoned by his closest allies, it also secured his place as Blair's nearly equal partner in the emerging New Labour project and in any future government. The arrangement was imperfect, for it produced continued tensions and prolonged the rivalry between the two into government. But it also kept the two stars on the same team and brought enormous strength and talent to the top of the party.[5]

A seemingly decisive role was played by the press, which began speculating on the party's next leader well before Smith was buried, and Blair was more successful in this arena than his rival. Blair and Brown were both effective on television and Brown was very successful in managing his relations with the press and with broadcast media, but Blair was even better and his performances evoked a more positive reaction. The experience of propagating Labour's new policy on crime was indicative: Brown invented the soundbite – 'tough on crime, tough on the causes of crime' – but it was Blair who delivered it so well and got the credit. Blair struck a chord with voters that Brown, though articulate and presentable, simply did not. It was thus not surprising that a few days after Smith's death three different polls gave Blair a decisive edge in the race to succeed the fallen leader, for the public response to Blair had been that much more favourable. Blair also knew enough to play to his strength, telling supporters that 'the only thing that matters in this campaign is the media' and admitting to Brown that while he might well be the party's preferred candidate, it was he, Blair, who would do better with the electorate at large.[6] Blair and Brown both had friends in the media and surrogates adept at their handling, but Blair was again better placed. Alastair Campbell, who became his press spokesman and close adviser, was extremely well connected and effective and Mandelson, though torn between his friends, would work assiduously for Blair's candidacy.

Mandelson would also play a critical, if controversial, role in resolving the question of Brown's stance. He had undoubtedly decided immediately that it would be Blair and he and Blair talked often during the contest. But his long prior attachment to Brown pulled in another direction and so he maintained at least the appearance of neutrality while seeking to broker a deal between the two. Brown and his allies believed that as the senior moderniser his claim to leadership was prior and more solid, and it was claimed as well that there had been a 'secret pact' dating from 1992 in which it was agreed that neither would oppose the other and at least implying that Brown was to have the first crack at winning the top prize. The Brown camp believed that Mandelson was conniving with Blair simultaneously to break the agreement and to deploy it as an argument against Brown himself running. It would seem that whatever agreement existed was vague and ambiguous and that Mandelson was merely recognising the changed political reality in shifting his support to Blair. But Mandelson also worked to engineer the manner of Brown's retreat. With the press moving decisively to Blair, Mandelson briefed reporters and dissembled to colleagues to the effect that Brown still could win. To Brown he spoke with two voices: with one voice he noted discouragingly how far ahead Blair was and laid out the obstacles to overtaking him: it would require a 'media onslaught' aimed at 'explicitly weakening Tony's position'. With another voice he offered his services for just such an effort. In the end, though, the real point was to work with Brown to craft a 'strategy to exit with enhanced position, strength and respect'.[7] Central to the plan was the need to build Brown up so as to make his subsequent withdrawal look like an act of statesmanship rather than abject surrender in the face of inevitable defeat.

That meant giving contradictory signals to the press and to Labour Party colleagues and confidantes; and playing this tricky game did not endear Mandelson to Brown. It also furthered his reputation for devious-ness. It did in some sense work, however, for after a brief period of hesitation and agonising Brown decided to take himself out of the contest. He and Blair had a famous, if anticlimactic, dinner at Granita in Islington on 31 May and the next day Brown formally announced his decision.[8] The two sides actually put in writing their understanding that Brown's decision to withdraw would be met by a commitment on Blair's part to make Brown's 'fairness agenda . . . the centrepiece of Labour's programme'.[9] With the deal consummated, Blair's leadership campaign could begin in earnest or, to be more precise, it could go public, for those closest to Blair were aware of his intentions from the very beginning and had been lining up support and refining their arguments. But with Brown officially on board the effort could become more open and aggressive and Blair immediately drafted a memo outlining just what a Blair candidacy and a Blair leadership would look like. He reiterated, for his own benefit and those privileged few with whom he shared his thoughts, what made him different: his 'strong convictions around Christian socialism'; his commitment to 'family . . .' and to a view that there was 'more to life than politics'. He would bring these differences with him into the party leadership; he would press on with the process of 'change and renewal' aimed at centring the party on 'traditional values but modern application; honouring the past but not living in it' and '[b]reaking through old left/right barriers'. His socialism was thus 'not a set of rigid economic prescriptions but a set of values based on a belief in society and commun-ity'; and this unique focus dictated a need 'to re-create [the] terms of community and social cohesion . . .'.[10]

These themes – vague, lofty, but apparently sincere – would dominate the Blair leadership campaign and the package, appropriately marketed, was more than sufficient to ensure victory. His opponents in the end were John Prescott and Margaret Beckett, both of whom also sought the deputy leadership should they fail to win the top slot. The campaign was managed formally by Jack Straw, who was emerging as a leading figure among the modernisers, and Mo Mowlam, who brought a bit more char-isma and quirkiness to the venture. Peter Kilfoyle, who had done battle over many years with Militant in Liverpool, also played a prominent role; as did Harriet Harman. Blair's personal retinue – people like Anji Hunter, Alastair Campbell, Philip Gould, David Miliband, Tim Allan and Peter

Hyman – were active but not as visible as the politicians. Perhaps the least visible, but probably also the most important, was Mandelson. It was Mandelson who decided that Blair should announce his candidacy from his constituency in Sedgefield; it was Mandelson who spoke daily with Blair; and it was Mandelson who advised Blair on when and where and how much to speak. His role was kept semi-secret, however, both because of his reputation for media manipulation and because key supporters, like Mowlam, threatened to quit if he were involved, or known to be involved. There was a bit of winking and nodding at work here, for surely people knew of his importance, but it was nevertheless thought best to keep his role hidden.[11] At his victory celebration on 21 July Blair would go out of his way publicly to thank 'Bobby', a code name for Mandelson, and by the next day the press made the identification for those who still did not know. But until then the pretence was maintained.

Even before Brown withdrew, the polls revealed that Blair was far ahead among those who had a vote – Labour MPs and MEPs, members of constituency parties, trade unionists – and even further ahead with Labour voters and the electorate. The contest soon revolved around two issues only. The first was the matter of how strong Blair would emerge from the campaign: would he stumble to victory or win going away, what compromises and what promises would he make along the way, and what mistakes might he make en route to victory? The second was the question of deputy leader – an issue Blair could perhaps influence but which he could not at this point actually control.

On the first question the campaign was a considerable success. Though criticised as insubstantial, the Blair camp conducted the contest very effectively. An extremely supportive press helped, but Blair's performances were good, if not spectacular. And he gave no hostages to fortune. He was not forced to make concessions or promises that could be turned against a future Labour government that he would lead. In particular, Blair handled the issue of whether to further the transformation of the party with great caution. When, early on, Gordon Brown seemed to invoke the spirit of old Labour, Blair balanced this by carefully restating his commitment to the new. Blair's manifesto, *Change and National Renewal*, was built around the themes laid out in his June memo and did not provide the level of specific detail that might have given offence and provoked controversy. While Prescott appealed rhetorically to the traditional forces in the party and Beckett came close to promising the unions that she would seek to overturn the Tories' trade union legislation, Blair did neither. He made clear his commitment to modernisation but did not clutter up his appeal with specifics and possible diversions. In consequence, Blair came through the campaign relatively unscathed and so more or less unencumbered.

The votes for leader prefigured the choice of deputy. Blair won 57 per cent of the vote overall and he prevailed in all three sections of the party: among MPs and MEPs he got over 60 per cent; among party members just under that (58 per cent); and better than 52 per cent of trade union votes. Prescott got just under a quarter overall (24.1 per cent), Beckett a bit less than 19 per cent. Prescott would get the deputy leader's job by a solid, though not overwhelming, margin. The outcome was what Blair preferred, largely because Prescott had proved his loyalty to the leadership over the block vote back in 1993 and Beckett, quite conspicuously, had not. Prescott was also a more effective bridge to the trade unions. He had a working-class background and had risen through the trade unions and with their sponsorship; and he spoke their language with great forcefulness. But he had also come to recognise that if it were ever to win, Labour needed to change. His status as deputy leader would certainly cause awkwardness in the future, partly because his style differed so totally from Blair's, partly because it was hard to design a proper job for him in government and, even more, because Brown was the effective deputy leader – and to some almost co-leader – of the party rather than Prescott.[12] But the arrangement also brought great benefits, particularly within the party, where Prescott's style often played much better than the leader's.

Blair therefore emerged from the leadership contest with his reputation enhanced, with a solid mandate, with his most powerful rival firmly a member of the team, with a loyal deputy who brought with him a following of his own, and without having compromised on the key issues on the modernisers' agenda. He would proceed to surrounded himself with a Shadow Cabinet with impressive credentials: Prescott was a popular deputy; Brown had the top economic job; Cook was tapped for foreign affairs; George Robertson for defence; Straw got the newly important position as Shadow Home Secretary; Blunkett got education, which was to be central to Labour's plans and its rhetoric; and Harriet Harman health and social services. Mowlam was unhappy with the Northern Ireland portfolio, but the appointment worked well, at least for a time. It was a strong team that could perform effectively in the Commons and on the hustings and at party conferences. Blair's allies were dominant, but not to the extent that powerful rivals were left outside. Robin Cook, Michael Meacher and Clare Short – each further to the left than New Labour – had been brought inside and so not were tempted towards disloyalty until well into the second term. This coexistence was facilitated by the fact that Blair and Brown also got to appoint their closest collaborators to staff positions in which they owed loyalty only to them. Both Blair and Brown had powerful personal offices, with highly skilled researchers, policy advisers and officials responsible for dealing with the press. Blair would also assert control over party headquarters, where he replaced Larry Whitty with Tom Sawyer in the post of general secretary.[13]

Crucially, Blair had not been forced, as Smith had been in his quest for support over OMOV, to make any serious gestures or concessions on economic policy; he got union votes without agreeing to restore their privileged status on the shop floor, within the party, or in the counsels of a future Labour government; and he was able to pose as more sympathetic to the need for social provision without abandoning the implicitly contrary rhetoric about fiscal prudence, responsibility and community. The strategy was to become characteristic of Blair's leadership both in opposition and in government. He not only sought to win, but made sure that the terms of successive victories did not jeopardise the next battle. His rhetoric might be grand but his promises were pared down so as to give no ammunition to those likely in future to charge betrayal. Blair would in fact go further and seek to alter fundamentally the political culture of the Labour Party and the recurring tendency to be on the look-out for betrayal on the part of its leaders. He was determined as well to reduce the role of the institutions in which that culture was embedded and as far as possible to eliminate the customs, procedures and platforms that might be used to launch or sustain such criticism.

Secure in his position as leader and relatively unscathed from the effort to get there Blair moved decisively to put his stamp on the party and, in the process, to reassure voters that this was not the old Labour Party. In his manifesto Blair made clear his belief that the party still needed to win the voters' trust and that 'We need to change the tide of ideas.' The politics of reassurance would thus be more than a matter of being cautious while in opposition and seeking to avoid arousing the fears on which the Conservatives were sure to pounce. Rather, it would entail an unusually aggressive effort to win the public argument about who should govern and why, a sustained effort to elaborate a new philosophy of government that could underpin and reinforce Labour's new policy orientation, and a further effort to restructure the party. It was fundamentally the opposite of the approach adopted by John Smith who had believed, with Roy Hattersley, 'that the party does best when it is at peace with itself'.[14] Blair chose instead to administer what he referred to as 'electric shock treatment' designed to carry the process of reshaping Labour to a point where it could not be reversed.[15]

The effort began shortly after Blair's election when he proclaimed that Labour would no longer be tied, as in the past, to the trade unions which would in future 'have the same access as the other side of industry . . . We are not running the next Labour government for anyone other than the people of this country', he told the BBC.[16] A few days later he made clear his preference for traditional, two-parent families and soon after he took a hard line on questions of education. The effect was a wave of favourable publicity from a normally hostile and pro-Tory press. He also in effect unleashed those like Gould and Mandelson who had been eager for a symbolic break with Labour's past and allowed them to unveil and popularise the phrase, 'New Labour'. The October 1994 party conference would be surrounded by signs and images announcing the birth of 'New Labour, New Britain' and clearly marking the distance between New Labour and the old Labour Party of Wilson and Callaghan, of nationalisation, planning and In Place of Strife, of the social contract and the 'winter of discontent', and of Tony Benn, Arthur Scargill and Militant. The decision to shake up the party had clearly been taken.

The choice carried risks for, as the modernisers had seen during John Smith's tenure, the resistance to further restructuring and to more thoroughgoing shifts in policy, programme and outlook was deeply embedded and remained tenacious. The reform of the block vote had just barely been carried at conference and as the price of victory the unions had extracted from Smith at least a rhetorical reassertion of the commitment to full employment. Even after the adoption of OMOV the unions retained a huge vote that could still be turned against the leadership. Party officials and MPs were also not exactly clamouring for reform and they could cite in their favour the fact that Labour's poll numbers were staggeringly good and had got still better with Blair's election. Why upset all this? The logic of waiting to inherit office was powerful and it reinforced an aversion to a battle that might jeopardise party unity and put its lingering disagreements and uncertainties on display.

But the counter-argument was compelling in a different way. Allowing the forces of resistance to persist while in opposition would more or less ensure their persistence and ultimately their disloyalty when Labour was in power; and the fear of disloyalty would constrain even a government dominated by modernisers. Leaving intact the political culture that suffused the Labour Party and defined its traditions would also limit what the new leadership could do because it would allow opponents to portray innovation as deviation and its advocates as ignorant of the party's history, dismissive of its heritage and willing to threaten 'this great movement of ours'. The historian and long-time Labour party member Royden Harrison provided a typical illustration when he proclaimed that Labour under Blair is no longer 'in this great tradition'. Rather, 'It threatens a regression so pronounced as to amount to an unravelling of the entire history of the Labour Party.'[17] The choice, then, was to confront that very tradition so as not to be tied to it, so as to avoid being held up to it and found wanting, and so as to break decisively with it.

The critical moment in the confrontation with Labour's past, and with the party's understanding of it, was the battle to rewrite Clause IV of the party's constitution.[18] The need to abandon the party's commitment to nationalisation was widely accepted in private, and not only among the modernisers, but very few were willing to say so in public. Detailed memories of Gaitskell's failed attempt may have faded, but the mythology surrounding that historic battle suggested that it was a mistake to challenge this cherished symbol. A few voices nevertheless began to break through the silence. In a clear reference to Clause IV, for example, Gordon Brown promised back in 1992 that, in the ongoing 'battle of ideas', 'some traditional no-go areas will lose their exemption from discussion'.[19] As if on cue, Simon Crine of the Fabian Society soon called on Labour to 'rewrite Clause IV' in 1993 and the Society's study group on the party constitution, the so-called Archer Committee, recommended its replacement in June 1993.[20]

A still more urgent call had been issued in February 1993 in a pamphlet written by Jack Straw and published by his constituency party in Blackburn.[21] The piece was first drafted as a reflection on the 1992 defeat and the question of how to win elections was Straw's essential starting point. He argued strongly that 'The future is the central issue at every election. The argument', he explained, 'may revolve around the past . . . but it is the party that offers what the electorate regards as the best future which wins.' The next election would turn even more decisively on visions of the future, for it would be held in the shadow of the millennium and the Tories would mount attacks on Labour as 'the party of the past, trapped in its past, its task over and done'. Proof of that charge would be the persistence of Clause IV, a potent symbol of beliefs that 'we lack the courage to change'. To dispel the impression of a party wedded to an unusable past required a 'recasting of all the party's objects . . .' and the articulation of a new set of beliefs. It was not a matter of rejecting ideology, Straw claimed, but of updating it. In particular, it was necessary to reconcile the party's moral outlook, which was basically Christian, with its economic ideas, which were at least implicitly Marxist. Straw argued pointedly that 'The clear organisational separation of the Labour Party . . . from the Communist Party was never reflected by a similar ideological distinction.' Even though Labour had long been critical of the authoritarian character of the Soviet and east European regimes, many within the party had in fact long retained a sympathy for the Soviet 'experiment' and harboured the hope that it could be reformed into something more humane and democratic but still 'socialist'. They also continued to think about economic policy in largely Marxist terms.[22] The collapse of the Soviet Union was thus extremely important, for it 'undermined the ideological base of the democratic left to a far more significant extent than had previously been perceived'. Events in Britain and across Europe all told in the same direction: the kind of socialism identified with state ownership and planning was no longer a viable option; and Labour needed to move on and to develop objectives and a programme built upon 'positive freedoms' – with commitments to 'fairness', 'equality', 'free will, choice and responsibility'.

Straw's intervention served to open up the debate on the constitution and elicited considerable support.[23] Will Hutton of *The Guardian*, for example, made a powerful case to the effect that Labour needed a new constitution to become truly credible. Labour's attachment to Clause IV, he argued, was proof to voters that the party was still trapped within the intellectual confines of 'Labourism', 'a view of politics', he explained, that had been 'shaped by Labour's history, an extant neo-marxist ideology and the shape of the British state'. It had to be got rid of: 'The establishment of a congruence between the Party's constitution and its political aims is the essential precondition for the political integrity that the electorate demands.'[24] The case for revising Clause IV in order to establish integrity and consistency and to win voter trust resonated strongly with the views of people like Philip Gould, who had been harping on the issue of trust for a very long time but with particular intensity since the voters had once again manifest their distrust of Labour under Kinnock in the general election of 1992. Blair was clearly listening to the argument and to the polling data on which it was based; and he would echo precisely these sentiments a year later when he insisted that 'a modern party . . . requires a modern constitution that says what we are in terms the public can understand and the Tories cannot misrepresent'.[25]

Blair also agreed with the intellectual case against Clause IV and had argued as early as 1982 that the left needed a 'political philosophy . . . more sensitive, more visionary, in a word more modern, than Marxism . . .', that both left and right within the party had a tendency to avoid the realities of the present and the prospects for the future and instead 'chain themselves to the past'.[26] He would continue to press his comrades to adopt a 'new framework of the public interest' centred on the notion of community as the 'governing philosophy of today's Labour Party'.[27] Blair had been careful not to campaign for the leadership on the issue of Clause IV, but very soon after he began canvassing support. Brown and Blair had long been in agreement that Clause IV should be abandoned and that it should be done quickly in order, as Brown felt, 'to deter large numbers of people from hoisting the flag for Clause IV'.[28] Mandelson claimed that he too 'strongly supported' the move, but he took a moment before agreeing it was the right time.[29] Blair secretly told his future press secretary, Alastair Campbell, of his plan while recruiting him for the job in August 1994 and the very boldness of the gesture won his approval and helped to convince him to take the position. In early September John Prescott was informed and, though initially sceptical, became part of the effort. As

Campbell later recalled, 'There was no way we could have done it without John Prescott – not John reluctantly agreeing, but John actually giving his blessing to it.'[30]

Blair's initiative was made public in his carefully prepared speech at conference on 4 October when he announced that 'it is time we had an up-to-date statement of the objects and objectives of our party . . .' and that 'John Prescott and I, as Leader and Deputy Leader of our party, will propose such a statement to the NEC'.[31] In the next breath Blair also signalled his intention to conduct party affairs in an altogether new way: 'Let it [the new statement] then be open to debate . . . I want the whole party involved and I know this party will welcome the debate . . .'[32] Blair was speaking to conference, the party's policy-making body, but he was telling them that he would consult the party directly, over their heads and over the heads of the trade union leaders who still wielded enormous influence in the party.

The reality of the campaign would be slightly more prosaic, but still dramatic in its effects. Blair and Prescott would work with their advisers – Mandelson, David Miliband, Derry Irvine in particular – to draft new language to substitute for the old Clause IV. The wording would be accepted by the NEC, though not until March, and then approved at a special conference in late April. The conference would necessarily operate by the normal rules and procedures that still privileged the input of the unions and approval would thus depend on those who had traditionally wielded power within the party. The vote would nonetheless be preceded by an exercise aimed at soliciting the views of party members more broadly and designed to pre-empt opponents who presumed to speak in their name without actually determining their opinions. The process got off to a slow start and those resistant to the change made gains at first. In fact, the 1994 conference narrowly passed a resolution to keep Clause IV within days of Blair having announced his plan to revise it. Little progress was made by either side until the new year, but in January the majority of Euro-MPs came out in favour of keeping Clause IV and opposition to the leaders' position began to crystallise in the unions as well.[33] But Blair and his allies responded vigorously and set up a tour of local parties at which the new leader very publicly and effectively rebutted critics and argued for the new constitution. In March the Scottish Labour Party voted in favour of the change and when the special conference met at Westminster on 29 April 1995 the new language was approved by nearly 2–1. The margin was much higher among constituency party members, 85 per cent of whom voted for the replacement of the old Clause IV. The union vote was less decisive, but still in favour, and at least some of the opposition discredited because, as in the case of Unison, the executive did not bother to consult its membership before casting its vote. The outcome was a major victory for Blair and the modernisers and a portent of what was to come.[34]

What was to come along with the rewriting of Clause IV had in fact already begun to appear by spring 1995: it was a broader New Labour offensive designed to shift the political culture in and around Labour and to further remodel its institutions so as to embed a new culture more firmly within the party. The restructuring of Labour Party institutions was inevitably a less exciting, and for the most part, less visible affair, but it was not for that reason unimportant. It was perhaps inevitable that the election of a new leader and the prospect of victory and government would concentrate attention and authority in the hands of the leadership, but New Labour's leaders had a grander ambition. They sought a permanent shift in the party's centre of gravity that would prevent the party as an organisation from giving sustained aid and comfort to critics of the leadership either while in opposition or when it was in power. Blair was obsessed with the party's historic tendency to charge its leaders with betrayal and with the accompanying view that 'every compromise is a sell-out'.[35] He and Brown and other modernisers felt that the established pattern was not only disruptive in the short term but deadly in the long term, for it would make it almost impossible to win re-election. If the pattern were to be broken, it would require a structure of policy-making in which the roles of the National Executive Committee and the party conference were much diminished and taken over by bodies more firmly in the control of the leadership.

The Policy Review had begun the shift away from the NEC and its sub-committees, and its attempt to solicit opinion from ordinary party members and voters through the 'Labour Listens' campaign was a first assault on the power of local, mostly left-wing, activists to dominate the expression of opinion in the constituencies. Conference remained the supreme policy-making body, however, and only gradually was its role chipped away. The adoption of 'one member, one vote' was a second major step in curbing the role of activists within local parties and leaders within the unions. It enshrined the principle of consulting with the membership both in the party and in the unions before the casting of votes; and it applied the principle to the selection of candidates as well as to conference deliberations. Still, the modernisers had seen under Smith that the party conference remained a tough sell and that the unions would demand a steep price for their support. Further restructuring was apparently necessary and it would take two forms. The first was the direct appeal from the leadership to the membership of the party and, in effect, of the unions as well. It was at the heart of the strategy successfully deployed in the campaign over Clause IV, and New Labour's leaders quickly grasped the implications for the routine conduct of party business. The 1994 conference had given the NEC the authority to ballot the membership on specific issues, and although the rewriting of Clause IV required the subsequent approval of a special conference organised along traditional lines, the campaign preceding it had been conducted as a referendum on the leadership's proposal. It was thus a partial step towards turning the Labour Party into a sort of plebiscitary democracy, with the normal and predictable effect of concentrating power at the top, whose proposals and performance would be periodically ratified by the members but not supervised by the membership or their representatives in detail and day to day.[36] As such, it became the model for the process of soliciting input and winning approval for the manifesto.

Gaining control of the party's election manifesto had been a centrepiece of the left-wing effort to restructure the party in the late 1970s and early 1980s. They had failed to achieve it, but the question of who wrote the manifesto and of what was in it continued to excite interest on the left and defensiveness on the part of the leadership. It was the manifesto that took Labour's often elaborate programme and reduced it to a small number of electoral promises; and it was the inevitable and often glaring contrast between the commitments of the manifesto and the policies of government that had been the foundation of recurring charges of betrayal. In retrospect, Harold Wilson's third biggest mistake – the most important was presumably the decision not to devalue in 1964 and the second biggest mistake was his hasty decision to push forward with *In Place of Strife* – was to lose control over the party's programme and manifesto during Labour's period of opposition during 1970–74. The adoption of

Labour's Programme 1973 was the precondition for subsequent charges that he, and later Callaghan, had betrayed the party's programme and manifesto and hence a major stimulus to the Bennite effort to reshape the party constitution. What the Campaign for Labour Party Democracy would call 'the long march backwards' after the Bennite triumphs of 1979–80 was at its most basic an effort on the part of Labour's leaders to take back control of the party – over its programme, over the selection of candidates, and over the manifesto. New Labour's leaders witnessed the progress of that 'march' and did their part to make it successful, but the continued resistance to modernisation repeatedly revealed its limits. The direct appeal to members and the call for a referendum on proposals from the leadership was seen as a way decisively to bypass and get beyond those limits.

Hence the decision in 1996 to submit the draft manifesto to a plebiscite of party members. The idea seems to have come from Philip Gould, who argued in December 1995 that Labour needed to use the next year to 'break through electoral scepticism and resistance' and to recapture 'the sense of crusade and mission we had with Clause IV'.[37] It became policy when Alastair Campbell worked up a plan for 'The Road to the Manifesto', which would start with a series of policy statements and end with ratification by the membership. The result was 'New Life for Britain', issued on 4 July 1996, initiating another round of campaigning. In November the leadership could claim a near universal approval (95 per cent) on a strong turnout (60 per cent of members). Neither the membership, the NEC, nor the party conference were given the option of amending the draft manifesto: they could accept or reject, but not influence, create or even revise.

Who, then, would make policy? As the Policy Review of 1987–89 was drawing to a close, a proposal emerged for a permanent policy-making body – a National Policy Forum – that would bring together key players outside the framework of the NEC, its sub-committees and conference. Smith proceeded to set it up and it did begin to meet, but the essence of Smith's approach had been to delegate and under his leadership critical rethinking was effectively contracted out of the party itself. So little came of the initiative. When the modernisers got control of the party organisation, however, they began to formulate new proposals for the responsibility for policy-making and for the relationship between the leadership and the party as a whole. The exercise was dubbed 'Party into Power' when it began; by the time of its formal adoption in 1997 it was relabelled 'Partnership in Power'. At its core was a reinvigorated National Policy Forum that would conduct ongoing reviews of policy. The Forum would give representation to the NEC – itself reshaped to give more voice to office-holders so as to become 'a new stakeholder body'[38] – to the unions, and to the leaders of the parliamentary party; it would be organised into eight sub-committees; and its results would be presented to conference in the first year, then debated and revised and resubmitted for final approval in the second year of the 'rolling' process. While there would be time for debate and structures would be put in place to elicit rank-and-file opinion, the real work would be done by experts working with the leadership and the initiative would come from the top.

Originally, the intention had been to put this new structure in place in 1996, before the general election, but internal opposition and the pressing need to focus on the impending campaign caused a delay until 1997. Even then, with New Labour in office and conference reluctant to embarrass the government, the plan was accepted only grudgingly. Tom Sawyer, the Party Secretary, argued that the reform was necessary because 'without the ability to reconcile the requirements of democracy of the party with the requirements of running the country, we cannot be a united party'. He confessed, however, his fear that 'the mountain of motions stacked up against *Party into Power*' at the beginning of conference put its adoption in doubt. The proposal in fact prompted intense debate and provoked real bitterness and resentment. Ken Livingstone understood its significance and said so; Mo Mowlam fought back hard on behalf of the leadership; but in the end it was the unions who reluctantly came around and assured passage.[39] Still, they were not happy. John Edmonds, for example, insisted that the debate was not about 'policy-making, it is about trust'; and to him the proceedings demonstrated how little the leadership trusted its members. He acquiesced, but uttered a not very subtle warning: 'So the GMB's message to the NEC', he concluded, 'is that we will be voting for you but, to coin a phrase, we will be watching you as well . . .'[40] The arrangements agreed in 1997 were clearly much more efficient than the old approach to policy-making which rested upon the authority of the party conference and privileged the role of the unions and party activists. But whether the outcome should be more appropriately regarded as an advance in democracy, as Sawyer claimed, or as an exercise in 'Bonapartism', as critics on the left charged, or even 'Leninism', as Philip Gould once let slip, can surely be debated.[41] What was obvious, however, was that the changes were meant to alter fundamentally the behaviour of the party and to make life easier for Labour in government. As Mandelson (and Liddle) wrote hopefully of the party's reforms, 'All this is here to stay, there will be no changing back. With its new instincts and new culture, improving all the time, this new party will not, as in the past, be a source of trouble for the Labour government but will be Prime Minister Blair's strongest ally.'[42] That at least was the objective.

Mandelson's assertion makes it clear that the rationale behind the continuing restructuring of Labour's institutions was to implant 'new instincts and [a] new culture' in an established party with a great respect for its own traditions. Parallel to New Labour's efforts at institutional change was thus a protracted effort to remake the culture of the party, to move the party's system of beliefs further towards the political centre and more closely in line with what were thought to be the views of the voting public. The struggle was complicated by the fact that Blair, Brown and their New Labour allies were now the leaders of the party and so they were always speaking to the public as well as to the party. They were required to work simultaneously to reassure voters, to bring along the party and to achieve a dominant position in the intellectual debates of the centre-left. It was a battle to make the ideas of New Labour hegemonic and to convince a new generation to attach itself to what was increasingly referred to as the New Labour 'project'.[43]

New Labour had several advantages in the competition for allegiance among floating voters and, more importantly, floating intellectuals and journalists. Most important, they spoke to a nation desperate for a new vision of politics. Despite all the talk on the left about Thatcherism as a 'hegemonic project', by the time she was forced out of office she had signally failed to create an 'entrepreneurial culture' or to engineer a return to 'Victorian values'. Thatcher's message had never been inspirational, however much conviction lay behind it, and it was typically accepted with resignation and a sense that, as she herself put it, 'There is no alternative.' Thatcherism was in any event more a rejection of the corporatist philosophy of the past than a vision of the future; and whatever purchase its critique of the state, of socialism, of the unions and of failed incomes policies had had in the 1980s, it no longer worked so well by the mid-1990s. Mrs Thatcher's successor, John Major, undoubtedly put a more acceptable face onto Thatcherism, but the appeal of the basic product had atrophied.

Meanwhile, Labour had seen off the threat from the Social Democrats and had purged its programme of promises that had previously aroused the fears of voters. What remained was to fashion a more positive appeal to voters and to the public. New Labour set out to do that and had at its disposal an impressive array of supporters and resources that were pressed into service on behalf of its new project. Its greatest assets were the talents of the modernisers and their savvy way with the media. New Labour also had in its camp several think tanks and journals that were making the case for a rethinking of politics in terms that closely echoed those deployed by the party's modernising leaders. The Institute of Public Policy Research was a prime example. It had close ties to Labour and to New Labour more specifically; and it had run the Commission on Social Justice at John Smith's request. Its director in the early 1990s was Patricia Hewitt, who had worked as Kinnock's press secretary and retained strong ties to the modernising faction within the party. The Institute's research and publications revealed an ongoing interest in questions of new technology, social change, the expansion of women's employment and its impact on family life, questions of work and leisure and, of course, politics.[44] Another extremely useful organisation was the Fabian Society, which regarded itself as the original think tank and which had been active in the reform of the Labour Party at least since the beginnings of the Policy Review. In 1991 the Fabians turned their staid newsletter, *Fabian News*, into a much more accessible journal, the *Fabian Review*, and gave the modernisers a more polished and seemingly independent voice. *Renewal*, an equally articulate advocate of the modernising cause, was founded by the Labour Co-ordinating Committee in 1993 and later gave itself a subtitle that formally proclaimed its allegiance: as of October 1995 it became known officially as *Renewal: A Journal of New Labour Politics*.[45] In 1996 it set up Nexus, a network designed to give institutional form to the link between academics and policy experts and New Labour.

A roughly parallel, if distinctive, effort had been undertaken by veterans of *Marxism Today*, two of whom – Martin Jacques and Geoff Mulgan

– founded the think tank Demos in 1993. Demos aimed to think big thoughts unfettered by old boundaries and undeterred by old taboos; they were to be the radical innovators who would craft a vision of the future for a new and reimagined party of the left. Under Mulgan's leadership, Demos would bring the thoughts of American communitarian thinkers, like Amitai Etzioni, to a more sceptical British intellectual class, and it would seek to bring Labour and its allies into the post-modern world with its insistence talk of ' "the end of politics", "the end of unemployment", "the end of social democracy", . . . of "traditional definitions of what it means to be a man or woman", and the end of "class-based left-right politics" '.[46] Its remit knew no formal boundaries, and its writers and thinkers were happy to go beyond giving advice on politics and economics and to speculate on *Life after Politics*.[47] Demos's iconoclasm was extremely useful in giving a sense of flair to what was in fact a very workmanlike New Labour programme, and its proclaimed intention of transcending the old boundaries, particularly the categories of left and right, helped to prepare the ground for the later discussion of 'the Third Way'.

None of these ventures attained a wide circulation or a great popular following, but they were read and listened to where it mattered. And because they were not directly controlled by the Labour Party, even if they were closely linked and strongly allied with it, they were more effective for being at least nominally independent. Their easy mix of soft economics, common-sense sociology, and a readiness to engage in policy-making played very well among the academics and journalists, mostly based in London, Oxford and Cambridge, who tend to dominate intellectual life in Britain. The effect was to create in those circles the sense that New Labour was serious, that it was willing to rethink estab-lished orthodoxies and to try new solutions, that it would consult with academic experts like them and that it was therefore the vehicle through which to address issues of political importance in the coming era. The claims of New Labour did not convince everyone, but its arguments and assumptions soon began to dominate political discourse and the language in which politics was conducted. Its distinctive rhetorical style, its manner of posing the choices confronting government and voters, its sense of public morality and the public good, and its caricatures of its opponents and the alternatives they offered have been, of course, regularly contested.

But even critics were forced to concede that 'New Labour has built a new political discourse that has . . . transformed the field . . .'.[48]

But to what end? That is the issue on which New Labour's critics have focused most intently, though the precise complaint had been typically muddled. For some New Labour has simply lost sight of its roots, abandoned socialism, reconciled itself to the domination of capital and become virtually identical with Thatcherism. The implication is that New Labour represents merely capitulation. In fact, New Labour's rapprochement with capital was based on a clear belief that markets might be flawed, but worked; and the rejection of socialism, however defined, was a choice made in the face of a long record of socialist failure. The decision to accept the broad outlines of what Thatcher had wrought was likewise not just a reluctant concession to what was politically feasible but a recognition that much of what the Conservatives had said and done in the 1980s was effective and in some sense appropriate. So New Labour had not forgotten its traditions: rather, it had consciously and explicitly rejected those traditions and the policies to which they were attached.

A more serious criticism was that New Labour, having effectively freed itself from the past and the old objectives of the Labour Party, had not put in place a big idea that could unite the party, inspire voters and guide policy-making into the future. As David Marquand argued, 'In place of an ideology New Labour has a rhetoric – an ahistorical (not to say anti-historical) rhetoric of youth, novelty and a curiously abstract Future.'[49] To Marquand and many others that was not enough. But it was not for lacking of trying. On the contrary, New Labour's leaders and intellectual allies repeatedly lamented the absence of a positive vision of the future and demanded a sustained effort to create 'a hegemonic project' around a dominating theme. As Tony Wright argued in early 1994, 'Labour needs a project . . . a larger framework of ideas'.[50]

For a time the concept that aroused most interest and seemed to offer the greatest promise was 'community'. Brown and Blair had stressed the importance of community and solidarity in order to distinguish Labour's rather modest proposals for a supply-side socialism from Thatcher's transparent disregard for community and society.[51] Brown argued forcefully for the grounding of political morality in a sense of community; and he would assert that 'the most distinctive feature of British socialism historically has been its insistence on the moral basis of politics'.[52] That rather strong claim was put forward in the introduction to an anthology of texts on socialism that he helped to put together and published in 1995. The book was quite long and it contained selections from Robert Burns, Shelley, Thomas More, Matthew Arnold, Keynes, Crosland, Kinnock and many more. But it included no Marxists: there was no Marx, despite those long hours in the British Museum; no Engels, despite *The Condition of the Working Class in England*; not even writers like the part Marxist, part Romantic Edward Thompson. Advocates of class struggle had been erased and replaced in the lore of British socialism by those yearning for a lost sense of community.

The notion of community also fitted well with the emerging rhetoric of responsibility and reciprocity and so helped to justify Labour's new departures on crime and social policy. It would also prove useful in the future in framing arguments about social exclusion and in support of policies to move people from welfare to work as a remedy.[53] It seemed to open up towards a grander vision of a one-nation Britain in which social inequalities would be much reduced and old divisions replaced by a renewed sense of solidarity. 'The idea of community', according to Wright, was a 'concept of unmatched potency and, handled correctly, it is our concept and our territory.'[54] It was thus widely touted, its meaning widely debated, in the early days of New Labour, though the notion also began to encounter opposition from people who felt it cloaked a new social conservatism with potentially authoritarian overtones.[55] But over time interest waned primarily because the concept was so very vague, its very versatility reducing its purchase and its capacity to inspire.[56]

At the beginning of 1996 Blair made a speech in Singapore that introduced yet another new concept into New Labour thinking: the stake-holder society.[57] The idea was less vague than community and promised more. Blair was strongly influenced by Will Hutton's *The State We're In*, a book that had emerged from debates in which New Labour thinkers were already deeply involved.[58] Hutton believed that the source of Britain's economic weakness was its financial system, with its bias towards short-term profits and its neglect of the long-term needs of industry. He built upon two existing bodies of work to produce a compelling diagnosis and a plan to remedy Britain's chronically weak economic performance. The first was a long tradition of research on the uniquely powerful role of the City of London in the economy and the unusual predominance with government of the Treasury. The resulting City/Bank/Treasury axis was responsible, it was claimed, for favouring finance over industry in economic policy-making, raising the cost of capital and limiting the flow of funds into industry.[59] Hutton also drew upon a series of studies of different and apparently more successful varieties of capitalism on the Continent and in Asia.[60] The implication was that the different institutional structures within which these economies were embedded – with typically closer links between business and the state and between finance and industry, and with more cooperative patterns of industrial relations – enhanced economic performance. The solution was to reshape the institutions of British capitalism: specifically to remake the financial system, patterns of corporate governance and employment by empowering all of the 'stakeholders' in the economy – workers, consumers and communities as well as managers, owners, investors, bankers and the public.

Hutton had made a case for structural reform of a potentially radical sort. In Blair's hands, by contrast, the stakeholder society took on a less structural and more individualist character, and it was merged with earlier notions of community and rhetoric about the so-called 'training revolution'. 'The stakeholder economy', he explained, '. . . is not about giving power to corporations or unions or interest groups. It is about giving power to *you*, the individual. It is about giving you the chances that help you to get on and so help Britain to get on too: a job, a skill, a home, an opportunity – a stake in the success we all want for Britain.'[61] Economic growth was at the centre of Blair's argument for stakeholding, for giving people a stake would presumably create a framework of 'trust' that would encourage innovation and investment. Blair's version of the argument made changes in attitude more important than changes in the structure of power. 'We need to build a relationship of trust,' he explained, 'not just within a firm but within a society. By trust, I mean the recognition of a mutual purpose for which we work together . . . We need a country in which we acknowledge an obligation collectively to ensure that each citizen gets a stake in it.'[62] Blair's reworking of the case for stakeholding was a highly effective move, for it took a critique of the economy as it was and harnessed it to Labour's emerging vision and pro- gramme. In the process, it also domesticated the critique and reattached it to themes more comfortable for New Labour.

But a potentially radical message of structural change still lurked behind even Blair's more anodyne formula and would ultimately be its undoing. In New Labour's perspective progress would come not through structural reform of the sort that a thorough commitment to stakeholding would entail but rather from the effect of supply-side measures like training and education that, pursued rigorously, would redraw the contours of British society more or less automatically and, it was hoped, move the balance of employment and economic activity in the direction of higher wages, higher quality and high-tech. Hutton's version of structural transformation and new configurations of economic power was much more controversial and contained echoes of earlier, and by now largely discredited, corporatist schemes. These associations led Gordon Brown, ever sensitive to arguments that could be turned against Labour, to back off the idea almost as soon as it was proposed. The consequence was that despite Blair's deft reworking, stakeholding failed to catch on as Labour's big idea; and by the time of the election of May 1997 it had ceased to feature at all prominently in New Labour's rhetoric.[63]

So New Labour would end up fighting the 1997 election without having settled upon its 'big idea'. Its first two iterations had not quite worked and a third – the so-called 'Third Way' – would not be unveiled until after Labour had regained office. Inevitably, the absence of a bold unifying theme evoked criticism and fuelled the impression that New Labour was more interested in using opinion polls and focus groups to figure out what voters wanted to hear than in deciding what it believed. Particularly resistant to New Labour's charms and rhetoric, and biting in their criticism, were left-wing intellectuals of an earlier generation.[64] Stuart Hall, for example, would look back in 1998 and write scathingly of New Labour's style and substance:

> The attempt to govern by spin (through the management of appearances alone), where you 'gloss' because you cannot make your meaning clear, New Labour's systematic preference for media reality over sterner political realities, indeed, the constant hype about 'hard choices' coupled with the consistent refusal to make them, are all part of the same phenomenon. This is not a superficial 'style' we don't much like, but something that goes to the heart of the Blair project.[65]

The antipathy ran deep; and it was obvious that the very claim to novelty so central to the modernisers' appeal was grating to those who were once themselves a new left and who continued to regard themselves as something of an intellectual vanguard. They were transparently resentful of 'twenty-something Young Turks beaming out ill-will' towards their mostly older opponents and critics on the intellectual left.[66] The irritation was reciprocated by New Labour – by Blair himself, who claimed he was 'never a partaker of the chattering classes' and was overtly hostile to the 'sneer squad'; by younger recruits to the New Labour cause who seemed to cherish the opportunity to strike back and assert that the '68ers no longer hold the monopoly of wisdom and virtue on all things radical'; and by New Left and *Marxism Today* veterans like Geoff Mulgan who, having opted for Blair and New Labour, now deplored the inability of 'parts of the leftwing intelligentsia . . . to acknowledge that history has moved on'.[67]

The critique of New Labour as all spin and no substance was thus quite fully in place even before the party took office, but it would be articulated still more forcefully when, in Mandelson's words, 'New Labour's "spin machine" went into action . . .' after the election victory of 1997.[68] The characterisation was no doubt partially accurate, but New Labour had long been convinced that what others called 'spin' was simply smart politics. The modernisers' repeated efforts to float and debate big ideas was also evidence of an intellectual engagement that indicated a willingness to go beyond mere spin. The case for paying careful attention to media presentation and seeking, where possible, to influence how the media portrayed the party, its politics and policies, was in fact based largely on the experience of not having done so. Labour had traditionally ignored the press and regarded it as instinctively Tory and so largely hostile; and the party had been even more reluctant to acknowledge the growing power of television and the role of advertising. But in doing so they courted and perhaps even ensured failure. Indeed, in the 1980s the public perception of the party was disastrously negative and this image had been reflected in repeated electoral disasters. 'This is the pattern of history that', in Philip Gould's view, 'New Labour is determined to break.'[69] But the break had to come in a political context defined by 'a new media environment and a ferocious press' and so would necessarily involve what detractors would call spin. Blair was, if possible, even clearer on the issue than his fellow modernisers, for to him it was axiomatic that a serious politician had either to spin or to fail. In arguing the case for modernisation back in 1993, for example, he had written presciently that 'To criticise politicians for being able to give a good "soundbite" – when, for most of the news media, a bite is all you get – is like criticising a politician for turning up to a press conference in a suit rather than a pair of pyjamas. Getting the image right is just part of the job; no more, no less.'[70] It is therefore unlikely that Blair was much moved by those who thought New Labour paid too much attention to matters of presentation and communication. To New Labour spin was an inevitable and appropriate response to the evolving technology of modern mass communications and its impact on campaigns, elections and government.

The attack on spin was not, of course, primarily an argument against an obsession with the media and its short attention span. It also made the more telling point that a focus on presentation precluded a serious consideration of larger issues. The question was whether New Labour in fact ignored substance and fixed instead upon the trivial and the superficial. It is certainly true that the party leadership remained acutely aware of public opinion in the roughly three years between Blair's selection as leader and the next general election. A sense of what voters wanted to hear and what messages might scare them away undoubtedly guided Labour's behaviour in Parliament and informed its message. What is not clear is whether the effect was to constrain and limit the range of ideas and arguments or to inspire a creative rethinking disciplined by a more sophisticated sense of the possible.

New Labour was certainly not silenced by the need to reassure voters. On the contrary, the party's new leaders were ubiquitous and eager to talk to whomever would listen. Still more impressive was New Labour's willingness to confront very directly and forcefully Labour's past, to 'challenge the ethos and traditions of the party' and to transform 'the underlying culture of the party'.[71] The rebranding of Labour as New Labour and the debate over Clause IV were the most visible steps in this reckoning and reformulation, but the effort was broader and deeper than these more symbolic moves. It was a bold and ambitious strategy that has typically not been appreciated, either by New Labour's critics or its supporters. In fact, neither electoral calculation nor the requirements of internal party management would have led to the conclusion that New

Labour should make a frontal assault on the party's traditions. On the contrary, attacking the party's inherited beliefs would entail considerable risk and might well provide ammunition to New Labour's internal opponents.[72] By 'conceding the terrain of the past' to defenders of tradition, the modernisers would make it possible for their critics to argue plausibly that the party's new leaders had abandoned that past in the vain pursuit of short-term electoral advantage. Clare Short, for example, would claim predictably that the new leaders had 'very little understanding of Labour's traditions . . .'.[73] The modernisers were keen 'to rip lots of things up . . .', but did so 'without realising they'd have nothing left'.

The modernisers clearly decided, however, that they had more to gain than to lose in criticising, modifying and redefining the party's legacy. The calculation seems to have been that a break with the culture and traditions of the party would allow it to cast a wider net among voters and make a much broader appeal. The break with the past would mean more specifically breaking with Labourism – that amalgam of loyalties and sensibilities occasionally spilling over into a vague socialism that suffused the party and its institutions, sustained it in opposition and, in New Labour's view, prevented it from recognising the imperatives of the present and the promise of the future and from attracting voters who did not share those sentiments and loyalties. The rupture would require that the party's past be reinterpreted so as to query and qualify its identity as 'Labourist' and to legitimise traditions normally regarded as alien to, or at least outside, 'Labourism' and the labour movement. A parallel effort would be required to rediscover forgotten elements within the party's tradition that might become the basis for a new political philosophy and to tease out, from the complicated mix that constituted the party's inherited political culture, those parts that still remained useful. The recovery of neglected components and moments in Labour's past was to some extent the easy part and New Labour was very effective in insisting that the essence of socialism and of Labourism was a set of values and objectives – like equality, fairness, community – and that it was a mistake to confuse these enduring values with the means chosen to achieve them in the past. The association between Christianity and socialism was yet another useful rediscovery, if only because it cost so little and provided an alternative grounding that was moral rather than material and thus inherently worthier than self-interest.

Reassessing the Labourist identity of the party was more difficult, for it put in question the party as a social phenomenon and as a distinctive culture and organisation. The challenge was to be able at one and the same time to praise this 'great movement of ours' and also to transcend it. This would mean a redefinition of Labour's past achievements as triumphs of the people over the narrow interests of their enemies, rather than as victories for one class over another. Recalling the historic connection to Liberalism helped in this shift; remembering 1945 as the culmination of a 'people's war' and a broad reforming consensus was a further step. Opening up space between Labour and the trade unions was still more important; and adopting a style that was less distinctly proletarian mattered as well. These new formulations and postures were meant to signal that Labour was now the people's party, not the embodiment of a narrowly working-class interest. The argument worked, and presumably was intended to work, on three levels. First, it was an invitation to those outside the fold to regard Labour as theirs, not the property of a particular interest. Second, the emphasis on the importance of the progressive coalition of the past was a direct overture to the Liberals, who were being asked to vote for Labour as a 'cousin' who shared their essential values and who might also, depending upon the results of the coming election, be offered a place within a new progressive coalition and a new government. And third, construing Labour as a people's party redefined its social base at a moment when the party's historic base in the industrial working class had massively shrunk and when the contest for political advantage hinged, if not on the political centre, then on the 'broad mass in the middle' of society.[74]

The modernisers had always based their case for recasting the Labour Party as much on sociological as on political grounds. They believed and repeatedly argued that Labour as a party had abandoned the centre and must recapture it, and asserting that society had itself changed and Labour needed to adapt was more appealing, less confrontational and not so easily attacked as opportunistic. By the mid-1990s, moreover, the argument about whether and how Britain's social structure had evolved was largely settled in favour of those who, like New Labour, believed that Britain had changed irrevocably and beyond recognition. Britain was a new society and there was simply no way to deny or even minimise the extent of the transformations its people, or peoples, had experienced over the previous half-century. Thus by one measure, the working class had declined from over 58 per cent of the labour force in 1964, when Labour won, to 49 per cent in 1979, when the party lost decisively, to just over 34 per cent in 1997. At the same time the non-working class sections of the population had grown steadily: between 1979 and 1997 the 'petit bourgeoisie', the 'salariat' and other 'non-manual' occupations grew from 47 per cent of the labour force to over 60 per cent. Thinking and feeling a part of the working class was of course not the sole basis or predictor of political affiliation, but it was a critical foundation. In addition, factors like union membership and home ownership predisposed voters to be more or less sympathetic to Labour. Labour's 'core supporters' were not only typically working class; they also tended to belong to unions and to rent their homes from local authorities. These determinants of voting had shifted even more decisively by the mid-1990s: between 1979 and 1997 union membership dropped precipitously from almost 53 per cent of the labour force to 27.3 per cent; home ownership over the same period rose from 55.3 per cent to 67.2 per cent and the proportion of dwellings rented from local authorities fell from 31.5 per cent to 17 per cent. Logically and inevitably, then, 'the proportion of the working class who were both council tenants and union members had almost reached vanishing point – down from 18 to 3 per cent'.[75] The core of support upon which a Labour victory could be built was thus much diminished by the time New Labour was born and a successful electoral coalition would have to be recreated anew. It would still have to encompass the industrial working class, but it would also have to include far more professionals and many more service-sector employees. It would have to appeal to the mythical 'man polishing his Ford Sierra' whom Blair claimed to have met 'on an ordinary, suburban estate in the Midlands' and who had stopped voting Labour because he had bought 'his own house' and 'set up his own business'.[76] Labour would have to reach beyond its ghettos in the older industrial centres, especially in the north, in Scotland and in Wales, and become more suburban, more southern and more English.[77]

New Labour's leaders and strategists were keenly aware of the shifting social geography of Britain and undoubtedly understood its political implications. That knowledge made the effort to build a new electoral coalition not only plausible but essential. It also meant that while jettisoning Labourism might cause momentary discomfort within the Labour

Party, where its narrow social base was grossly over-represented and the voices of its advocates magnified disproportionately, it would also open up the possibility of attracting a broader range of support. To this extent electoral strategy meshed with principle and both considerations dictated a break from Labour's inherited culture and the policy commitments and preferences that flowed from it. Whether New Labour's effort to distinguish itself from old Labour and its associations would succeed would not be known with any assurance until it had faced the voters in a general election. Even that would render only a tentative verdict on the New Labour project, for the project was defined from the very beginning as protracted and so assessing it would have to be long term as well. What can be said with some assurance, however, was that by 1997 New Labour succeeded in its ideological offensive in attracting attention to its claims, in shifting the debate onto its terrain, in keeping its opponents, within the party and in opposing parties, on the defensive, and in convincing a sceptical electorate to take it seriously. This is not exactly the achievement of ideological or political hegemony, if that is ever possible in a liberal democracy, but it is presumably what a hegemonic project ought to look like early on.[78]

The election took place almost three years after Tony Blair had secured the leadership of the party. The interval was perhaps inadequate to allow for a wholesale conversion to New Labour's ideas – or for the full elaboration of its outlook – but it was sufficient to allow a testing of the party's new resolve to win. It also provided an extended look at how it would operate if and when it took office. From the outset the key figures within New Labour sought to reassure voters that the old Labour Party was not still hiding beneath the façade of the new.[79] That determination had been behind New Labour's ideological offensive and its imposition of a new system of policy-making within the party. It was also reflected in Labour's conduct in Parliament and in its election strategy. The Conservatives made repeated attempts to provoke Labour into taking a stance on taxes or spending or crime that might be played back against them at election time. Blair, Brown and other Shadow Cabinet members refused to be drawn: they avoided voting no on a proposed tax decrease in 1995 and they reversed the party's long-standing opposition to the periodic renewal of the Prevention of Terrorism Act.[80] Where possible, New Labour's leaders tried to limit commitments to even less than what was already promised in the party programme. The result was a curious spectacle: Labour's front bench spoke all the time, at considerable length and, in general, effectively, but they offered less and less detail about alternative policies. Attack was thus not accompanied by counter-proposals. The tactic succeeded, however, largely because of the government's ineffectiveness and the growing rift within the Tory ranks. After Black Wednesday the Conservatives lost their reputation for economic competence; over the next five years they even lost their claim to be the party that lowered taxes. And in 1995 they showed that they had lost their famous will to win: John Major, who lacked the confidence of the party, resigned in June and challenged his critics to stand against him. No challenger emerged, and Major was re-elected, but Labour's pollsters discovered that voters 'felt used, and . . . manipulated' and had seen that the Tories not only had no faith in their leader but that they had no altern-ative either.[81] Over the next two years Major's predicament worsened, as bitterness over Europe split the party and revelations of sex and sleaze made the Tories vulnerable to charges of hypocrisy and, even more devastating, to ridicule.

The Tories's difficulties made it possible for Labour to make inroads among groups it had never before been able to reach. New Labour made a special effort to court business, with Blair and Brown talking endlessly to groups of business people and delivering the message that Labour was now fiscally responsible and business-friendly. Business people and their lobbyists were made to feel especially welcome at the party's annual conference, where they in turn sponsored events, discussions and convivial settings for party luminaries. During the election campaign Blair visited the City of London and professed his belief that 'economic activity is best left to the private sector' and that the 'postwar Keynesian dream is well and truly buried'. Within the week, on 11 April 1997, Labour published its business manifesto, *Equipping Britain for the Future*, and recruited over 80 businessmen to support it.[82] Blair even worked his charm on Mrs Thatcher, seeking her counsel, listening respectfully and earning something like her blessing when she spoke to a private gathering at the Reform Club on 23 January 1997 and said that 'Tony Blair is a man who won't let Britain down'.[83]

An even more sustained effort was made to establish a new and more positive relationship with the media, even with those normally sympathetic to the Conservatives. Alastair Campbell fashioned a strategy to win at least a hearing from sections of the press long antipathetic to the Labour cause. He managed to get Blair invited to address the executives of Rupert Murdoch's media empire in July 1995 and there he argued that 'If . . . the left can liberate itself from outdated preconceptions, strip its essential values out from the means of their application relevant to another part of history, then the modern centre-left is best able to provide security and change.'[84] Two of Murdoch's papers, *The Sun* and the *News of the World*, would in fact endorse Blair in 1997; and during the campaign Blair would be afforded the opportunity to be interviewed twice and to write seven separate articles for *The Sun*.[85] In all six of the ten major national newspapers backed Blair; and their combined readership was twice that of the papers backing the Tories.[86] Even those newspapers that stayed loyal to the Conservatives gave Blair far better and more even-handed treatment than was accorded his much-maligned predecessor, Neil Kinnock.[87]

New Labour never allowed itself to forget the actual voters upon whom its fate would ultimately depend, however. On the contrary, Blair, Mandelson and Campbell were superstitious about even whispering the word 'landslide' for fear that it would breed complacency and lead to mistakes or to abstentions. The polls put Labour solidly and steadily ahead from 1994 on, but careful analysis of large-scale polls, more targeted polls and focus group results all tended to show that support was often soft and that there was still suspicion and scepticism. Philip Gould was nearly obsessed with 'volatile segments of the electorate' that he regarded as essential to victory. In May 1996, for example, he wrote in near panic to Mandelson that 'We are now in the most serious situation that we have faced since Tony became leader. If we continue to implode and disintegrate we can still lose.' As the economy picked up that summer, he worried that 'people are frightened of losing the small gains they have made. In effect they are saying: "Now that we are off the floor and things are a little better, we have something to lose, and Labour may put that at risk".'[88] New Labour remained susceptible to these fears because they knew from the bitter experience of 1992 how easily an election could slip away.

Their response was to reassure voters by simplifying the message and making sure that any new commitments were carefully 'costed' and could be paid for without increases in tax. When party strategists Gould, Peter Hyman, Matthew Taylor and David Miliband debated the 'five pledges' that would become Labour's 'offer' to voters – vote for us and we will deliver these specific results; and if not, throw us out – they were repeatedly test-marketed and the costs carefully toted up. Labour ended up pledging to reduce class sizes, to provide jobs for the young, to introduce 'fast-track punishment' and to 'cut waiting times' in the NHS; the fifth pledge was broader and vaguer but equally important: 'Labour will set tough rules for government spending and borrowing; ensure low inflation; strengthen the economy so that interest rates are as low as possible.'[89] The pledges would in fact evolve: later on Labour would promise to hold a referendum on joining the euro; and there would be more specific promises on taxes and spending. In his speech to the 1996 conference, moreover, Blair would rearrange the pledges into ten vows that would be his 'covenant with the British people'.[90] The specifics thus varied some, but the fundamental message was the same: Labour would make only modest, affordable commitments but could be trusted to carry them out. The modest character of the goals was a precondition for winning the trust of voters; it was also a protection against future disappointment and the likely charges of betrayal that could be expected to follow.

But above all else the aim was to reassure voters and to that end Labour went a step further in early 1997. Memories of the 1997 defeat focused ovewhelmingly on tax and on the apparent success of the Tories' 'tax bombshell' in which they purported to uncover the enormous cost of Labour's proposals and the equally enormous sums needed to pay for them. Anticipating a similar charge Blair and Brown sought to pre-empt it. Since becoming Shadow Chancellor in 1992 Brown had exercised tight control over the plans and promises of his colleagues and of policymakers within the party, and his vigilance meant that by 1997 Labour's promises were few and the means of paying for them clearly specified. He had not ruled out all possible sources of additional revenue, however, and had in fact proposed a windfall tax on privatised utilities that could be used to fund Labour's welfare-to-work programme. But Blair and Brown were eager to provide voters, and financial markets, with even more convincing evidence that Labour was no longer the party of high taxation. That proof, or at least a firm promise, came on 20 January 1997 when Brown announced not only that a Labour government would live within the spending plans of the previous government but that there would be 'No rises in income tax rates'. This was the final plank in the programme Labour would present to voters in 1997. It would be featured prominently in the manifesto and repeated endlessly as the election drew near.[91]

The formal presentation of Labour's case began on 17 March when John Major called for an election six weeks away. It was a long campaign, long enough for New Labour to worry about something going wrong. Blair, Brown, Mandelson and Campbell were at the centre of the campaign and none of them was complacent. Mandelson, for example, never 'totally lost the fear of losing', and Blair was determined not to let anyone in the party forget the disappointment of 1992.[92] Elaborate plans were made to meet any contingency and a sophisticated campaign apparatus, modelled on Clinton's, was put in place at the party's new headquarters at Millbank. Mandelson had followed Blair and Brown to the United States in search of lessons and was overwhelmed with admiration for the Clinton operation. Two of Clinton's key advisers, Stanley Greenberg and Paul Begala, worked closely with the Blair team and reinforced the message that Mandelson and the modernisers had been pushing since 1985. New Labour set up its own 'war room', much like the command centre created by James Carville in Little Rock. Labour, too, had its 'war book', which Begala had helped draft and which Gould inconveniently left at Euston Station. (It was later leaked to the press by the Conservatives, but to little effect.) Labour also learned from the Clinton campaign the need for rapid response and so set up a computer system and a massive databank designed to allow instant refutation of Tory claims or unflattering press reports. There were a few awkward moments, like Blair's *Panorama* interview on 7 April, but overall the campaign was so successful that it was soon regarded as boring. The boredom factor in turn produced an uneasy feeling that the lack of real drama might lead the press to focus on trivial or personal issues for which the campaign was unprepared. More specifically, it was feared that the bitter feuding that characterised the relationship between Brown, who was officially in charge of the campaign, and Mandelson, who also had major responsibilities, would flare up again and become the big news of the campaign. There were worries, too, that Labour might look overconfident and that dissent within the party might resurface and remind voters of the past. Labour also had to negotiate the question of Europe, which could have played either way, and in the process found themselves sounding more nationalist and patriotic than pro-European Tories. Most important, there were recurring moments of doubt about whether voters would accept New Labour's claim not to be the old Labour Party. Blair ended an *Observer* interview by promising 'to be a lot more radical in government than people think', and provoked a flurry of concern, but in the end it, too, did not seem to matter.

On 1 May 1997 Labour, now New Labour, won a resounding victory. The unforeseen did not happen; Labour's internal rivalries were submerged in a common desire to win; and whatever uncertainty might have lurked in the minds of voters was counterbalanced by a sense that the Tories had to go and Labour deserved a chance. Critical to that perception and to that choice was the Tories' complete inability to mount an effective campaign. Major was unable to orchestrate even a temporary unity within the party and came increasingly to be seen as incapable of governing.[93] The contrast with Blair, Brown and the rest of New Labour was striking and voters responded by inflicting a devastating defeat upon the Conservatives. Finally, New Labour could speak of a 'landslide', even if its meaning and significance could and would be debated.[94] Labour won 43.2 per cent of the vote and 418 seats; the Conservatives' share dropped to 30.7 per cent and brought them only 165 seats. The Liberal poll fell slightly to 16.8 per cent, but the geography of the Tory collapse gave them 46 seats, up from 20 in 1992; while the smaller nationalist parties garnered less than 10 per cent of the vote and won a total of 30 seats. Labour's majority was the largest in its history; the Tories' defeat the worst since 1832. Labour had climbed all the way back from its historic defeats in the 1980s. The process of rebuilding had been protracted, painful and transforming, but the outcome was a near total vindication of those who made it happen. Just what this New Labour Party would be, what it would do, and how it would fare, remained to be demonstrated in government. But there would be 'no turning back'.[95]

Notes and references

1 Colin Rallings et al., eds, *British Elections and Parties Yearbook 1995* (London: Frank Cass, 1996), 182, 196. In the European elections Labour won 62 seats, the Tories 18, the Liberal Democrats 2, and three other seats went to even smaller parties.

2 See Paul Routledge, *Gordon Brown: The Biography* (London: Simon & Schuster, 1998), 184–6.

3 The quote is from a conversation between Smith and his adviser, David Ward, reported in John Rentoul, *Tony Blair: Prime Minister* (London: Little, Brown, 2001), 218.

4 For background see John Kampfner, *Robin Cook* (London: Victor Gollancz, 1998); and Colin Brown, *Fighting Talk: The Biography of John Prescott* (London: Simon & Schuster, 1997). Beckett had been Smith's deputy and so entered the race as a quasi-incumbent, but her candidacy was always a very long shot. Beckett's pre-election interview with Nyta Mann in the *New Statesman and Society* (8 July 1994), for example, appeared under the heading, 'Time for no change?' and captured effectively the typical response to her bid for leadership.

5 The saga of Brown's withdrawal and the resentments it bred has been frequently retold. The publication of Routledge's semi-authorised biography of Brown in 1998 gave new life to the story even after the election and it remains controversial. See, among others, Rentoul, *Tony Blair*, 221–48; Donald Macintyre, *Mandelson and the Making of New Labour* (London: HarperCollins, 1999), 286–310; and, most recently, James Naughtie, *The Rivals* (London: Fourth Estate, 2001), 54–75.

6 See Rentoul, *Tony Blair*, 230, for Blair's statement about the media and his discussion with Brown.

7 Mandelson to Brown, 16 May 1994, reprinted in Macintyre, *Mandelson*, 294–5.

8 The dinner was already legendary before the Stephen Frears' dramatisation of the episode in *The Deal*, which was broadcast on Channel 4 on 28 September 2003, the first night of the party conference. The television version adhered closely to the pro-Brown interpretation of events.

9 The text, apparently drafted by Mandelson, was published in *The Guardian*, 6 June 2003.

10 Blair, early June 1994, cited in Philip Gould, *The Unfinished Revolution: How the Modernisers Saved the Labour Party* (London: Little, Brown, 1998), 202–4.

11 Julia Langdon, *Mo Mowlam: The Biography* (London: Little, Brown, 2000), 251–2.

12 Blair's supporters were thus split about the merits of Prescott as deputy. See Rentoul, *Tony Blair*, 243.

13 Mowlam claims to have facilitated Sawyer's appointment, though it was a logical choice in view of his trade union background and his stalwart service to Neil Kinnock while on the NEC. See Langdon, *Mo Mowlam*, 256. Sawyer was eager to join up with the Blair team and even under John Smith had been discussing reform of the party machinery with Blair. Interview with Lord Sawyer, 10 October 2002.

14 *The Observer*, 15 January 1995.

15 Blair apparently told Philip Gould that 'It is time we gave the party some electric shock treatment' over lunch at a ' "brainstorming" session' at Chewton Glen on 9 September 1994. See Gould, *Unfinished Revolution*, 216–18.

16 22 July 1994, quoted in Rentoul, *Tony Blair*, 248.

17 Royden Harrison, *New Labour as Past History* (Nottingham: Spokesman, 1996), 3.

18 The effort has been well-documented. See Tim Bale, ' "The Death of the Past": Symbolic Politics and the Changing of Clause IV', in David M. Farrell et al., eds, *British Elections and Parties Yearbook 1996* (London: Frank Cass, 1996), 158–77; 'Labour's Constitution and Public Ownership: From "Old" Clause Four to "New" Clause Four', in B. Brivati and R. Heffernan, eds, *The Labour Party: A Centenary History* (London: Macmillan, 2000), 292–321, and *Sacred cows and common sense: the symbolic statecraft and political culture of the British Labour Party* (Aldershot: Ashgate, 1999); Michael Kenny and Martin Smith, 'Discourses of Modernisation: Gaitskell, Blair and the Reform of Clause IV', in C. Pattie et al., eds, *British Parties and Elections Review*, Vol. 7 (London: Frank Cass, 1997), 110–26; and P. Riddell, 'The end of Clause IV, 1994–5', *Contemporary British History*, II, 2 (Summer 1997), 24–49.

19 Gordon Brown, 'The battle of ideas', *Fabian Review*, CIV, 5 (September 1992), 1, 3.

20 Simon Crine, 'Unsteady progress', *Fabian Review*, CV, 3 (May–June 1993); *Report of the Archer Committee: A New Constitution for the Labour Party* (London: Fabian Society, Fabian Special, June, 1993); and Ben Pimlott, 'A fitter, leaner Labour', *The Guardian* (22 February 1993).

21 Jack Straw, *Policy and Ideology* (Blackburn: Blackburn Constituency Labour Party, 1993).

22 Tony Wright made a similar argument retrospectively when he suggested that Labour only became a social democratic party in the 1990s. Prior to that it had been a strange hybrid, and 'At the beginning of the 1980s it seemed closer to the communist parties of Europe, and experienced a similar political fate.' See Wright, *Socialisms: Old and New* (London: Routledge, 1996), 136.

23 See Paul Thompson, 'Modernising Labour', *Renewal*, I, 3 (July 1993).

24 Will Hutton, 'Seizing the moment: Constitutional change and the modernising of Labour', *Renewal*, I, 3 (July 1993), 50–4.

25 *Report of the Labour Party Annual Conference 1994*, 106.

26 Tony Blair, 'Australian Lecture' at Murdoch University, Perth, 1982.

27 Tony Blair, 'Forging a new agenda', *Marxism Today* (October 1991), 32–4.

28 Brown, paraphrased in Jon Sopel, *Tony Blair: The Moderniser* (London: Michael Joseph, 1995), 272.

29 Routledge, *Gordon Brown*, 215–6; Gould, *Unfinished Revolution*, 215. Mowlam was also enthusiastic. See Langdon, *Mo Mowlam*, 256.

30 Campbell, quoted in Gould, *Unfinished Revolution*, 221.

31 *Report . . . 1994*, 106.

32 *Report . . . 1994*, 106.

33 See their advertisement in *The Guardian*, 10 January 1995.

34 Rentoul, *Tony Blair*, 259–62.

35 These views came through even in Blair's 'Australian Lecture'.

36 On the benefits and hazards of this model of party organisation, see Patrick Seyd and Paul Whiteley, *New Labour's Grass Roots: The Transformation of the Labour Party Membership* (New York: Palgrave, 2002), 170–7.

37 Gould, *Unfinished Revolution*, 263.

38 Tom Sawyer, speaking to the party conference on 29 September 1997, and quoted in the *Report of the Labour Party Annual Conference 1997*, 11. On the restructured NEC the unions had 12 of 32 seats; within the National Policy Forum 30 of 175 seats were reserved for the unions, though they might end up with more. See Steve Ludlam, 'Trade Unions and the Labour Party since 1964', in Brivati and Heffernan, *The Labour Party*, 232.

39 Mowlam spoke forcefully at conference and had also devoted considerable time to developing the proposals being debated. See Langdon, *Mo Mowlam*, 257.

40 *Report . . . 1997*, 11–28, 192–3.

41 Vladimir Derer, 'New Labour's Bonapartist coup de farce', *Labour Left Briefing* (May 1996); Philip Gould interview in *Tribune*, 6 November 1998.

42 Peter Mandelson, *The Blair Revolution Revisited* (London: Politico's, 2002), 231. (Originally published as Mandelson and Roger Liddle, *The Blair Revolution* (London: Faber & Faber, 1996)).

43 See, for example, Anne Showstack Sassoon, 'Some day my prince will come: Gramsci, Blair and modernising projects', *Renewal*, VI, 2 (Spring 1998), 31–9.

44 On the emerging need for Labour to address women and issues surrounding women's work and the family, see Joel Krieger, *British Politics in the Global Age: Can Social Democracy Survive?* (New York: Oxford University Press, 1999). For a provisional assessment, see Angel McRobbie, 'Feminism and the Third Way', *Feminist Review*, 64 (Spring 2000), 97–112.

45 *Renewal*, III, 4 (October 1995). Appropriately, it carried a long piece by Tony Blair, 'Power for a purpose', 11–16.

46 Nick Cohen, 'Profile: Totally wonkers: Demos, Tony Blair's favourite thinktank', *The Observer*, 9 March 1997. See also Maureen Freely, 'Scrambled eggheads', *The Guardian*, 30 June 1998.

47 Geoff Mulgan, ed., *Life after Politics: New Thinking for the Twenty-First Century* (London: Fontana, 1997). Many of the pieces had first appeared in the *Demos Quarterly*.

48 Norman Fairclough, *New Labour, New Language* (London: Routledge, 2000), 21. See also Alan Finlayson, *Making Sense of New Labour* (London: Lawrence & Wishart, 2003).

49 David Marquand, *Must Labour Win?*, London: Fabian Society, Fabian Pamphlet 589, December 1998).

50 Tony Wright, 'What new politics?', *Renewal*, II, 1 (January 1994), 76–8.

51 Noel Thompson, 'Supply side socialism: The political economy of New Labour', *New Left Review*, 216 (1996). More generally, see Colin Hay, *The Political Economy of New Labour* (Manchester: Manchester University Press, 1999).

52 Gordon Brown and Tony Wright, *Values, Visions and Voices: An Anthology of Socialism* (Edinburgh: Mainstream, 1995).

53 R. Levitas, *The Inclusive Society? Social Exclusion and New Labour* (London: Macmillan, 1998).

54 Tony Wright, 'Now or never', *Fabian Review*, CV, 3 (May–June 1993), 1, 3.

55 See, for example, Phil Shiner and Brendan Nevin, 'Communitarians: New left or moralising right?', *Fabian Review*, CVII, 1 (February 1995), 9–11.

56 It has also been suggested that the stress upon community was undermined by the controversies over the Blairs' decision in 1994 to send their son Euan to the London Oratory and Harriet Harman's 1995 choice of St Olave's in Kent for her son. These exercises of parental choice meant by definition an opting out of the local community; and they also contradicted Labour's long-standing policy in favour of comprehensive schools. See Rentoul, *Tony Blair*, 257–8, 282–4. Blair might well insist that 'The notion of community for me is less a geographical concept than a belief in the social nature of human beings', as he told the *New Statesman* (28 April 1995). But the response

demonstrated vividly both the vagueness of the concept and the potential problems that would arise when one tried to give it a more specific meaning.

57 See Tony Blair's Speech to the Singapore Business Community, 8 January 1996, reported Andrew Marr, *The Independent*, 9 January 1996; his Speech in the Assembly Rooms, Derby, 18 January 1996, reported by Patrick Wintour, *The Guardian*, 19 January 1996; and 'A stakeholder society', *Fabian Review*, CVIII, 1 (February 1996), 1, 3–4.

58 Will Hutton, *The State We're In*, rev. edn (London: Vintage, 1996). The first edition was published in early 1995.

59 The clearest exposition of the argument is Geoff Ingam, *Capitalism Divided? The City and Industry in British Social Development* (New York: Schocken, 1984). The impact on policy is pretty well demonstrated, but the effect on investment and economic growth more controversial. On the former, see James E. Cronin, *The Politics of State Expansion: War, State and society in Twentieth-Century Britain* (London: Routledge, 1991). Also well established is the argument that Britain evolved a peculiar type of 'gentlemanly capitalism' with a predisposition to empire and overseas investment. See P.J. Cain and A.G. Hopkins, *British Imperialism, 1688–2000*, 2nd edn (London: Longman, 2002).

60 The key early text here was Michel Albert, *Capitalism against Capitalism* (London: Whurr, 1993), but there have been numerous additions to the literature in recent years. See, among others, Suzanne Berger and Ronald Dore, eds, *National Diversity and Global Capitalism* (Ithaca, NY: Cornell University Press, 1996); Colin Crouch and Wolfgang Streek, eds, *The Political Economy of Modern Capitalism* (London: Sage, 1997); David Coates, *Models of Capitalism: Growth and Stagnation in the Modern Era* (Cambridge: Polity, 2000); and Peter Hall and David Soskice, eds, *Varieties of capitalism* (Oxford: Oxford University Press, 2001).

61 Blair, Derby speech, 18 January 1996.

62 Blair, Singapore speech, 8 January 1996.

63 Gould, *Unfinished Revolution*, 253–6.

64 The resistance was visible very early on and became more intense the clearer it became that New Labour was intent on winning. See, for example, Martin Jacques, *The Guardian*, 26 September 1996, complaining about Blair's success: 'His project for the party is a triumph, but what about the project for the country?' For useful analyses of the phenomenon, see Michael Kenny and Martin J. Smith, '(Mis)understanding Blair', *Political Quarterly*, LVIII (1997), 220–30; and 'Interpreting New Labour: Constraints, Dilemmas and Political Agency', in Steve Ludlam and Martin J. Smith, eds, *New Labour in Government* (London: Macmillan, 2001), 234–55.

65 Stuart Hall, 'The great moving nowhere show', *Marxism Today*, (November–December 1998), 11. *Marxism Today* ceased regular publication in December 1991, but came out with this special edition to assess Blair and New Labour in 1998.

66 Hall, 'Great moving nowhere show', 13.

67 Blair, quoted in Hall, loc. cit., 14; Geoff Andrews, 'Breaking free: Tomorrow's intellectuals and New Labour', *Renewal*, V, 1 (February 1997), 22–3; and Geoff Mulgan, 'Whinge and a prayer', *Marxism Today* (November–December 1998), 15.

68 Mandelson, 'Introduction', in *The Blair Revolution Revisited*, xiv–xv.

69 Gould, *Unfinished Revolution*, xviii.

70 Tony Blair, 'Why modernisation matters', *Renewal*, I, 4 (October 1993), 4–11.

71 Kenny and Smith, 'Discourses of Modernisation', 125; Geoff Mulgan, 'Creating an enabling party', *Renewal*, I, 1 (January 1993), 66.

72 See Jon Lawrence, 'Labour – The Myths It Has Lived By', 340–66, and Steven Fielding, 'New Labour and the Past', 367–92, in Duncan Tanner, Pat Thane and Nick Tiratsoo, eds, *Labour's First Century* (Cambridge: Cambridge University Press, 2000).

73 Lawrence, 'Labour – The Myths', 361; Short, cited in Fielding, 'New Labour and the Past', 371.

74 David Lipsey, *The Name of the Rose*, Fabian Pamphlet 554 (London: Fabian Society, 1992), 7–8.

75 Anthony Heath, Roger M. Jowell and John Curtice, *The Rise of New Labour: Party Policies and Voter Choices* (Oxford: Oxford University Press, 2001), 15. The data cited above come from the British Election Studies and are reported by Heath, Jowell and Curtice, *The Rise of New Labour*, chapter 2. They also included a useful discussion of the methods used to determine class membership and the distinctions between different systems of classification. Other systems, including the census, would give slightly different sums, but the direction and magnitude of change would be the same.

76 Blair, *Report of the Labour Party Annual Conference 1996*.

77 See Giles Radice, *Southern Discomfort*, Fabian Pamphlet 555 (London: Fabian Society, 1992).

78 See David Halpern and Stewart Wood, 'Comparable revolutions', *Renewal*, IV, 4 (October 1996).

79 The task was made more difficult because at least some within the party shared the Tories' view. Clare Short, for example, told the *New Statesman* (9 August 1996) that because the modernisers 'think that Labour is unelectable' they chose to dissemble with voters: 'They are saying: "Vote for Tony Blair's New Labour. We all agree the old one was absolutely appalling and you all know that most of the people in Labour are really the old one, but we've got some who are nothing to do with that – vote for us." One, it's a lie. And two, it's dangerous. I think they're profoundly wrong.'

80 See Rentoul, *Tony Blair*, 271.

81 Gould, *Unfinished Revolution*, 245–6.

82 Blair's speech was delivered on 7 April 1997. See David Butler and Dennis Kavanagh, *The British General Election of 1997* (London: Macmillan, 1997), 109.

83 Rentoul, *Tony Blair*, 276–7.

84 Blair, 17 July 1995, cited in Rentoul, *Tony Blair*, 280.

85 Macintyre, *Mandelson*, 372–6.

86 Margaret Scammel and Martin Harrop, 'The Press', in Butler and Kavanagh, *General Election of 1997*, 156.

87 See Colin Seymour-Ure, 'Leaders and Leading Articles: Characterisations of John Major and Tony Blair in the National Daily Press', in Ivor Crewe, Brian Gosschalk and John Bartle, eds, *Political Communications: Why Labour Won the General Election of 1997* (London: Frank Cass, 1998), 131–45.

88 Gould, *Unfinished Revolution*, 275–6.

89 Gould, *Unfinished Revolution*, 267–72.

90 Blair, 1 October 1996, in *Report . . . 1996*, 80–7.

91 See Ross McKibbin, 'Very old Labour', *London Review of Books* (3 April 1997), on the resulting minimalist character of Labour's programme.

92 Macintyre, *Mandelson*, 372.

93 David Denver, 'The Government That Could Do No Right', in Anthony King et al., eds, *New Labour Triumphs: Britain at the Polls* (Chatham, NJ: Chatham House, 1997), 15–48.

94 The basic question was whether the seismic shift in electoral behaviour would last and become the basis for a long-term realignment. For a thoughtful review, see Geoffrey Evans and Pippa Norris, eds, *Critical Elections: British Parties and Voters in Long-term Perspective* (London: Sage, 1999). See also Robert Worcester and Roger Mortimore, *Explaining Labour's Landslide* (London: Politico's, 1999).

95 Ben Pimlott, 'New Labour, new era?', *Political Quarterly*, LXVIII, 4 (October–December 1997), 327.

CHAPTER 11

The New Labour project in practice

There is no doubt as to who lost the election of 1997: John Major and the Tories did; and they had clearly worked at it for nearly five years. But who or what had won? Was it Labour, or 'New Labour'? How much did voters care about the distinction between 'old' and New Labour, so long as they were not the Tories? Tony Blair and his closest allies had no doubt that the party's earlier transformation was critical to its electoral success, but the ease of victory and the utter collapse of the Conservatives could be taken as evidence either way. The argument about 'modernising' the party would therefore continue even as New Labour assumed office. But now, of course, it was the modernisers who were in charge and they would have the authority of the government behind them in the ongoing effort to make the Labour Party into something new and different.

But New Labour also had to rule – to preside over the nation's interests and well-being, to manage its relations with the world, to run the economy, to calculate and decide budgets, to deliver services, and to take responsibility when any of these tasks went wrong. It would therefore be necessary to govern in a manner that would make possible the further modernisation of the party and at the same time prove that it was worth doing. Changing the party would be but a piece of a much broader agenda over which the government would never have complete control. But it was not for that reason unimportant, for New Labour's leaders believed that a reformed party would make it easier to govern, and to govern successfully; and that a redesigned party and a successful administration would in turn make possible the re-election upon which their achievements would ultimately depend. Actual governance and policy-making would thus be combined with continuing efforts to reform the party and with a unique and unprecedented campaign of explaining, justifying and theorising about what was being done in the name of the Labour Party. This characteristically New Labour project would render the experience of governing exciting, consequential and often extremely controversial. Success could of course only be measured definitively over the long term, but a provisional assessment should provide hints as to the likely outcome and ought at the very least to demonstrate that, as the former Cabinet Secretary Sir Richard Wilson has argued, 'it is not possible to understand the workings of the Blair government without understanding what happened before they came to power'.[1] New Labour's past was not merely a prelude, but a living presence and a guiding force in New Labour's practice as a government.

The 'new' in New Labour had been intended to distance the party publicly from past associations and past failures, but it also served to shape strategy and policy. As the party's new leaders understood their history, a major reason for failure was that the party's rhetoric and programme produced hopes that could not be met when it took office. From this perception had flowed a rigid determination to minimise campaign promises so as to reduce the pressure of expectations on performance. The election of 1997 was to be a model of an election effort that gave few such hostages to fortune. But Blair and Brown went still further upon taking office and less than a week into their tenure announced their decision to give the Bank of England the freedom to set interest rates.[2] The move was significant for what it did, but it was even more important as a symbol of how the government would handle the responsibility for managing the economy. Setting the Bank free signalled New Labour's recognition of the limits that the workings of the world economy placed upon the government's ability to steer the economy.[3] It sent a message to investors that New Labour could be trusted to work within such constraints and not to seek to impose its will upon forces largely beyond its control; more tellingly, it told Labour supporters and voters at large that the government could not be expected to intervene where intervention would not work.

The question of what in fact governments can and cannot do in an era of global capitalism is not easy to answer with confidence or precision, nor is it clear whether Labour's abstention from the setting of interest rates enhanced or restricted its capacity for macro-economic policy-making.[4] The political message was nonetheless clear enough: Labour had abandoned its '"heroic" approach to the economy' – an approach embodied in a strategies of nationalisation in the 1940s, of planning and industrial sponsorship in the 1960s, and later in the party's embrace of the highly interventionist Alternative Economic Strategy – and replaced it with a plan to create a stable framework within which more modest measures taken on the supply side of the economy would bring about technological change and economic growth.[5] The real objective of the decision on interest rates and monetary policy was thus not to free the Bank, but to allow the government to avoid making promises it could not keep and accepting responsibilities it could not effectively discharge.

The grant of independence to the Bank of England – and the Monetary Policy Committee that advised it – seems also to have expanded the government's options on Europe. A central motivation behind Labour's earlier interest in joining the EMS, an interest quickly disavowed and even forgotten after Black Wednesday, was to win the confidence of business and finance. By agreeing to subject themselves in government to a monetary discipline of the sort exercised by the Bundesbank over the German economy, Labour's leaders hoped to ease fears over spending, borrowing, taxation and inflation. The decision over the Bank achieved the same ends much more painlessly and perhaps more effectively: the markets were reassured and the government did not have to commit itself to the decisions of the new European Central Bank or to the more rigorous terms of the Growth and Stability Pact agreed as part of the preparation for the introduction and maintenance of the single currency. The new government could also put off into the future what would surely be a difficult debate over whether to adopt the euro. That debate would have elicited emotional appeals to national sovereignty, invocations of Britain's unique history, irrational fears of a European superstate as well as reasonable arguments about the direction of economic policy. These would be inextricably mixed up and confused and might easily provide the feuding Tory opposition with an opportunity to regroup. Once delayed, of course, the choice to adopt the euro would become ever harder; and inertia would threaten to become policy. In 1997, however, the move to devolve power to the Bank was a brilliant stroke that won New Labour the time and space to pursue its more immediate objectives.

The continuing reform of the institutional structure of the party had a similar effect in enhancing the new government's autonomy. The 1997 party conference was inevitably a celebratory affair, with delegates giddy at the thought of a Labour government finally in power again. But the conference was not so delirious as to miss the fact that the terms of 'Partnership in Power' – the plan to reorganise the National Executive and in effect to replace conference as the locus of policy-making power in the party with a rolling series of consultations directed from the top – would make the party as an organisation utterly subordinate to its leaders. It had no choice but to approve, however, for it was unthinkable that a leadership so recently and so overwhelmingly approved by the voters should be rejected by its followers. The outcome, of course, was a further freeing up of the leadership, who would in future have much less to fear from the rank and file of the party or from the unions that still formally wielded real clout within the party and whose role in funding the party remained central and even indispensable.

Making few promises, shedding responsibilities, and taming the party were all part of a design to allow New Labour to escape from its past, its ideological legacy, and its institutional moorings. The effect, it was hoped, would be to allow the party in power greater flexibility in deter-mining, defending and executing policy. The same goal underpinned the new government's efforts to manage the machinery of the state and, especially, its relations with the mass media. Blair created around him a team of advisers who were not reared in the civil service and steeped in its ethos and whose loyalties were to him and to New Labour. His personal staff was at least double the size of John Major's. The Cabinet Office was also expanded. Gordon Brown operated in a similar fashion at the Treasury. The teams assembled at Number 10 and Number 11 were often at odds and famously so, as were at times their bosses, but most of the time they managed to cooperate on the big issues; and it is likely that their combined presence added essential depth to the making of policy and to efforts to sell the government's actions to the press and the public.

The selling of government policy in fact went hand in hand with its formulation. As early as July 1997 a new 'Ministerial Code' was issued insisting that 'all major interviews and media appearances . . . should be agreed with the Number 10 Press Office before any commitments are entered into'.[6] Alastair Campbell, Blair's press secretary, in October 1997 further elaborated in an infamous warning that the Government Information Service had to 'raise its game': 'We should always know', he explained, 'how big stories will be playing in the next day's newspapers' and when 'a story is going wrong,' he added, 'we must respond quickly, confidently and robustly'.[7] A subsequent official report on communications – the Mountfield Report (November 1997) – more or less endorsed the new regime when it argued that 'effective communication and explanation of policy and decisions should not be an after-thought, but an integral part of a democratic government's duty to govern with consent'.[8] This did not mean that Campbell and Blair in fact monopolised communication with the media, for the effort to control was copied by Brown's advisers at the Treasury. Thus Campbell would find himself regularly competing with Charlie Whelan, Brown's spokesman, until Whelan resigned in January 1999. Still, the combined effect of Blair's new team led by Campbell and Brown's parallel efforts – and with Mandelson regularly briefing as well – was a remarkable ability to dominate the news and squeeze out alternative views, whether expressed by the Conservative opposition or by others in the Labour Party or even in the government. According to one estimate, during Labour's first full year in office Campbell and Mandelson got more press coverage than the Foreign Secretary, the Home Secretary and the Deputy Prime Minister combined.[9] Their efforts led almost inevitably to charges that the government was obsessed with 'spin' over substance, and over time would produce a press poised to be sceptical towards whatever news emerged from the government's press machinery. But presumably those who did the 'spinning' were not unhappy at such grudging compliments, at least as the beginning, and took them as a strong if indirect indicator of their effectiveness.

The enhanced capacity of the centre to formulate policy and to communicate its rationale was reinforced by shifts in the formal organisation of government. After 18 years of Tory rule the higher reaches of the civil service were presumed to have been cast in a thoroughly Thatcherite mould. Whether or not that was true – and the new ministers' relationships with civil servants were inevitably mixed – Labour was eager to reshape the machinery of government in order more effectively to carry out its policies.[10] There was a widespread belief within New Labour's inner circles that 'The centre has far less power than is typically ascribed to it.' In particular, the office of the Prime Minister, though formally at the apex of powerful government apparatus, was thought to lack 'the resources necessary to be a commanding and dominating nerve centre'.[11] Hence the need for a further concentration of power at the top. Under New Labour the effort to augment the power of the government would be built around two focal points – one centred on Blair and another on Brown. The policy flowed from the terms of 'the deal at the heart . . .' of New Labour.[12] Those terms were straightforward and easily summarised: 'a command premier would operate alongside a command Chancellor licensed to operate across a wide range of economic and domestic policy' and in pursuit of what Brown regarded as his 'fairness agenda'.[13] And the process of reshaping government in an increasingly centralising direction would be ongoing. Midway through the government's second term, for example, it would be evident to outside observers that 'Blair's centralisation of government in Downing Street has . . . fed Brown's parallel centralisation of government at the Treasury. The one locus of power has enhanced the other . . . in a dialectic of competing centralisms.'[14] The effect, openly admitted even at the beginning, would be 'a change from a feudal system of barons to a more Napoleonic system'.[15]

Creating a more effective centre would mean elaborating mechanisms through which to monitor and control the performance of departments. Two particular strategies were adopted by the new centre(s): direct and detailed control by the Treasury; and efforts to overcome departmental autonomy and inertia by creating interdepartmental task forces and committees. As part of the Blair/Brown compact, the Chancellor would get the right to insist that ministers and departments meet performance and efficiency targets as the precondition for receiving additional funding. The goals and objectives of every department would be spelled out in a series of Comprehensive Spending Reviews that gave the Treasury the ability to dictate the agenda in virtually all areas of domestic policy. Ministers were in turn forced to defend their progress towards these objectives and their budgets against the scrutiny of the Treasury's Public Expenditure (PX) Committee. Alistair Darling, Chief Secretary to the

Treasury, presided at over 100 such meetings with departmental representatives in preparing the first spending review, released in July 1998. Brown and Blair themselves had another 25 meetings as well before agreeing to what Darling boasted was a 'tough settlement' with the departments.[16] That settlement tied budget increases to measures aimed at 'reform and modernisation' and embodied in over 500 targets specified in December 1998.[17] Treasury control was hardly a new phenomenon or practice in British government; but the manner and the extent were intensified under New Labour.

The other approach to penetrating the defences of departments was to identify problems 'which have no single, departmental home' and whose resolution would require coordinated action by several departments.[18] The most notable moves on these lines were the creation of the Social Exclusion Unit and the Performance and Innovation Unit, both located within the Cabinet Office, and the setting up of numerous task forces and reviews. The rationale behind the Social Exclusion Unit was typical: since social exclusion resulted from 'being detached from the organisations and communities of which society is composed and from the rights and obligations that they embody . . .', its reversal required action to reconnect the excluded to the workplace, the educational system, networks for the provision of housing, social services and transport, the National Health Service and government itself. The tasks by definition transcended the responsibilities of any single department and so required that all policies be reviewed for their likely impact on social exclusion. The Performance and Innovation Unit had a similarly broad remit to review policies across established boundaries. These initiatives were explained and defended in a series of reports on *Modernising Government* (March 1999), on *Civil Service Reform* (December 1999) and on the use of new technology, *Wiring it Up* (January 2000), all making extensive use of the new mantra of 'joined-up' government.[19] Previous policies had failed, it was implied, for lack of coordination; New Labour would succeed because its policies would be formulated and implemented in a coordinated and coherent manner. Whether these efforts would succeed would of course not be known for some time, but in the short run they allowed the new government to put a distinctive stamp on policies across the entire spectrum of government activity.

The fundamental thrust of Labour's new style of governing would thus be to centralise and to concentrate power. However, this process was accompanied by highly visible moves in the opposite direction and supposedly designed to limit and disperse power.[20] Immediately upon taking office, for example, the government announced it would accept the European Social Chapter and bring UK legislation and policy into compliance. The European Convention on Human Rights was likewise incorporated into British law. While in opposition New Labour had also committed itself to a set of constitutional changes that it felt compelled to honour, at least formally, when in office. These included devolution in Scotland and Wales and the establishment of regional authorities in England upon which power might be further devolved; a new authority for London and an elected mayor; abolition or at least reform of the House of Lords; and a freedom of information act. New Labour also worked hard, and with success, at engineering a lasting settlement in Northern Ireland. Blair had also promised a commission that would give serious consideration to systems of proportional representation. Taken together, these reforms looked to some like a genuine revolution in Britain's constitutional arrangements. In practice, the changes have not been as great as the list might suggest. Scottish and Welsh devolution have been implemented, but without fundamental upset in relations with the centre; and the power of the new local government in London has been tightly circumscribed. Lords reform has also proceeded, but controversy had persisted over the form a second chamber would ultimately take. Over the long run it is likely that the key changes will prove to be those made to the administration of justice. Moves to unlock information, by contrast, have been and will probably continue to be modest in scope and grudging in implementation; and proportional representation has lost its appeal to a party profiting disproportionately from the existing electoral system. It seems obvious that a government with an overwhelming parliamentary majority has little genuine interest in reforming the constitution so as to give away power it now wields. Long years in opposition had produced a sense of desperation about the prospect of Labour ever ruling on its own again and a willingness to contemplate drastic changes in how Britain was governed. Victory quickly removed the temptation actually to do so, however. What Jack Straw said about one particular item of constitutional reform – 'Freedom of information is for oppositions, not for governments' – could be said of a broad range of proposals that appealed to Labour before 1997 but had little purchase after that year's landslide election.[21] The same fate overwhelmed and silenced rash and desperate thoughts of electoral reform and governing coalitions that would by definition place limits on a Labour government ruling in its own right.

On balance, then, the practice of government under New Labour has been to continue, and even to accelerate, the process of augmenting the institutions and decision-making power of the central state. The changes instituted by New Labour have added a not unreasonable further capacity to communicate its choices, to argue its case and to boast of its achievements. Enhanced authority at the centre, more effective control of news and political imagery and fewer constraints from the party should have, indeed must have, bolstered New Labour's ability to pursue its agenda. But what was the agenda? What has New Labour done, or sought to do, with its huge Commons majorities and its unprecedented predominance over its opponents? What have been its signature policies, and how do they fit together? Here is the fundamental problem for New Labour in office. New Labour came into existence largely as a repudiation of what Labour had long stood for, as a negation of its past, and with a determination not to repeat that past by promising more than it could deliver or by claiming that a Labour government could do more than was in fact possible. That would translate in practice into a very modest set of commitments in the run-up to the election of 1997 and a resolve to keep expectations within reach after that. But this modest stance was undercut by two huge facts: the unexpected scale of the electoral landslide; and the soaring and relentless rhetoric about change emanating from the new government itself. As Peter Mandelson explained in 2002, 'having promised less than we thought we could do, we started hyping more than we were actually achieving' and so the government's genuine achievements 'were lost in a fog of charge and countercharge'.[22]

New Labour was thus caught in the dilemma of having got hold of extraordinary power but still seeming to lack a vision of what it might be used for. This lack was perceived early on, but attempts to remedy it met with indifferent results. The best example, both of the effort and the problems it would encounter, was the discussion of the 'Third Way'. The

Third Way was Labour's most sustained, and in some respects its most effective, effort to spell out its philosophy, its perception of how the world worked and of what role government could play in improving it. Earlier attempts to provide New Labour with a broader theoretical framework had centred on such concepts as community and stakeholding. But the idea of community was terribly vague – 'one of the most indefinite social and political concepts', in Raymond Plant's view[23] – and it carried connotations of social conservatism and self-righteousness. The argument for stakeholding, by contrast, was likely to lead to more specific commitments than the party leadership was willing to make.[24] The most consistent refrain in New Labour discourse was, of course, modernisation, but however clear and inspiring its meaning might be to the hard core of New Labour activists, ordinary people were never likely to be moved by the notion. The Third Way was probably no more exciting as a slogan or a soundbite, but it had rather more to commend it intrinsically than earlier 'big ideas'. For a short time it was to become extremely fashionable in British politics, journalism and academia; and it even exercised a brief attraction outside Britain as well.

The Third Way had clearly been anticipated in prior Labour Party debate: Kinnock had actually used the phrase back in 1985, though in a context that made the meaning different. More importantly, Labour's modernising faction had adopted as their chosen rhetorical device a formulation in which they proposed neither this nor that, but something in between and not extreme and therefore better – a way of thinking and talking that lacked only the label of the Third Way. Blair would use the term with more precision when speaking to European social democrats shortly after his election, but it was Bill Clinton who in his State of the Union address in January 1998 gave the phrase a wider currency by using it to describe a putatively new and distinctive philosophy of centre-left government.[25] The usage would spread across Europe as social democrats scored a series of unexpected electoral victories – Jospin in France in June 1997; Schröder in Germany in October 1998; and d'Alema in Italy in November 1998 – and searched for a means of defining their shared goals.[26] Gerhard Schröder actually literally signed on to the Third Way, or *Der Neue Mitte*, on behalf of the German Social Democrats.[27] Still, the concept was most fully and forcefully deployed by New Labour. As articulated by Blair and his allies – and given more formal academic shape by the sociologist Anthony Giddens – the Third Way was distinguished by four features: its global orientation; its linking of social, economic and political analysis; its consistent modernity; and its rhetorically effective method of structuring the choices facing progressive governments.[28] Its strengths also signalled what critics would deem its weaknesses: its reach seemed too grand, its social and political analyses too vague, its modernity too unquestioning of the value and direction of change, and its alternatives progressive only because of the rhetorical trick of contrasting them with the more extreme positions adopted by neo-liberals.[29]

Precise iterations of the Third Way argument differed in minor, but significant, ways. In Blair's version, the starting point was a set of values: equal worth; opportunity for all; responsibility and community.[30] These were said to be the enduring values at the heart of social democracy and democratic socialism. But, crucially, the means by which to attain these values had of necessity to change as society and economy evolved. Social democrats in the past, Blair argued, had become fixated on specific means of realising their values – state intervention, public ownership and public spending in particular – that by the 1960s and 1970s had become outdated. The Third Way would pursue similar goals but with more modern means: its practitioners would make greater use of the market where it functioned effectively, use the state more sparingly and strategically, and rely more on communities and civil society. The stress placed upon values was not unreasonable, especially for a leadership seeking to articulate a new vision for a party desperately in need of inspiration. It served to impart a moral purpose to what might otherwise have appeared mere expediency. The focus upon values also seemed genuinely to fit well with both Blair's and Brown's styles and beliefs.

In other versions of the argument the emphasis differed. Thus for Giddens the case for the Third Way was premised less on values than on the compelling logic of social, economic and technological change.[31] The world economy was becoming more globalised, with labour, capital, goods and information flowing with ever more speed and freedom across international borders; and it was simultaneously becoming more competitive. More important, competition increasingly centred on the manipulation of knowledge not things, and hence turned on skills, education and technology. It made no sense in this context to oppose this process of globalisation, for it was a source of economic growth and greater opportunity and it was in any case unstoppable. Blair, from a different starting point, had reached much the same conclusion and insisted that 'in a world of rapid change . . . [t]he challenge is to turn change into progress'.[32] The Third Way was a strategy based on the assumption that effective government had to work with rather than against the world economy, with the trends of capitalist development rather than in opposition to them. It would lead, as Blair explained, to an 'active government working with the grain of the market . . .' rather than against it.[33] It would thus not resist the turn towards individualism in contemporary capitalism, but seek to empower individuals to participate effectively within it. This became both possible and progressive because of the convergence between the dictates of the international economy and the demands of social justice. What Giddens called the 'social investment state', by directing public investment into human capital, in people, would simultaneously equip Britain to compete in a global, knowledge-based economy while 'equipping individuals to prosper' within it and to profit from its steady expansion.[34]

At the core of the Third Way, then, was a claim about the pace and path of recent history and the insistence that the new economic and technological environment required a new understanding and a refashioned practice governing the relationship between the state, society and the market. If old-style social democracy, or more full-blooded socialism, believed it could manage or even transform the economy in the interests of the workers and the disenfranchised, the Third Way would involve 'rediscovering an activist role for government . . .' within a framework that left the market centrally responsible for economic well-being.[35] Its aims would therefore be far more modest: advocates of the Third Way would use the state to better educate its citizens, to train them to take the jobs on offer in the information economy; and government would simultaneously prod people into the labour market and provide the social services that made risk-taking and work feasible and attractive. It would also encourage entrepreneurship, police the market in order to facilitate wider participation, and create a stable macro-economic framework for large and small business.[36] This kind of 'supply-side socialism' – or 'active welfare state', aimed at increasing levels of labour market 'activation' – had long been advocated by Blair and Brown and they understood it as the contemporary alternative to Keynesian macro-economic management.[37] Giving people the means to participate in the labour market would also permit a shift of focus from equality measured by outcomes, adult incomes in particular, towards what would come to be called an 'asset-based egalitarianism'. Attention and policy would be redirected towards starting points and initial endowments; the aims of policy would be made explicit and formal by commitments to early childhood education, daycare and the promise to eliminate child poverty, and they would be embodied in practice in programmes like Surestart and the payment of a 'baby bond'.[38]

The Third Way therefore provided a more elaborate rationale for a set of policies that New Labour had been working towards and advocating for some time. It also offered a theoretical underpinning for various initiatives aimed at social cohesion. If social change were so ubiquitous, so unstoppable and so wrenching, then if unchecked it would surely tear society apart – its disruptive consequences leaving large numbers excluded, marginalised and alienated. Government had a clear role in countering these trends by combating social exclusion, using some of the same mechanisms aimed at encouraging work rather than welfare, and by reinforcing a sense of civic responsibility, strengthening the link between 'rights and responsibilities', and working to reduce crime and combat 'anti-social' behaviour. Again, both the rhetoric and the policies had been anticipated in Brown's almost daily commentary on the economy in the late 1980s and early 1990s and by Blair, first as employment spokesman and then as Shadow Home Secretary. The same themes had informed the reasoning of the Social Justice Commission that weighed in at roughly the same moment. But the Third Way would provide a more coherent defence and explanation than had previously been on offer.

An obvious corollary to the Third Way's proposal for a new role for government was the insistence on a new kind of politics. Here, too, the emphasis was typically upon technological change and its possibilities – for connecting and communicating through coordination, for 'linked-up' initiatives and for a 'wired-up' state in constant dialogue with an active citizenry that would be plugged in to the government. The increased, and supposedly freer, flow of information would provide greater transparency and accountability; and decentralising the delivery of services wherever possible would put the state and its bureaucracy into a closer relation to those it was designed to serve. The Third Way was thus meant to combat the erosion of faith in government and the growing disconnection between government and citizens. The guiding premise was the recognition, or the contention, that the era of big government had past, that simply enlarging the state would be counter-productive and that the burden of proof was now on advocates of government intervention to demonstrate its superiority over the market. As Stephen Byers, then at the Treasury, insisted in late 1998, 'The old days of throwing money at a problem and hoping that it goes away are gone.'[39]

The argument about the Third Way was not just a more thoughtful articulation of the assumptions uniting New Labour and hence a better way to present views already worked out. It also helped to shape those views and make them more widely understood. The discourse had, then, a more broadly educative and creative effect, especially within the party and the government. As late as 1994, the modernisers within the Labour Party were a rather small band isolated within the party and largely out of sympathy with its culture. The 'progenitors' of New Labour, it has rightly been noted, 'were tiny in number. Less a mass movement, more a junta who had executed a coup . . .', their fortunes had been transformed only with Blair's election as leader.[40] It was then, but not before, that a substantial cohort of younger MPs and activists signed on to the project. Even then it was not obvious what it was all about besides getting elected once again. Brown and Blair and their allies would work assiduously over the next three years to reshape the party's outlook in a deeper and more basic fashion and to win genuine converts among the public and the pundits. They aimed at hegemony, though it continued to elude them, in part no doubt because of the caution and compromises forced on them by the approach of the general election. The debate about the Third Way offered a further opportunity for New Labour, now in government, to hone its ideas, to practise favoured formulas and to expand their application to the entire range of policy choices that a ruling government had to make. The most important audience in attendance at the debate about the Third Way was thus the government itself and the party it led and represented. Party and government learned in the process what they were about and how policies in diverse fields were meant to cohere into a plan for remaking the nation and restructuring the relationship between the state and the people.

While the Third Way represented a more robust and convincing argument for the broad range of New Labour policies, it was not necessarily convincing to critics and sceptics within and outside the party. The reasons it so often failed to convince were to some extent intrinsic to the argument. The Third Way was intended as a step beyond the rhetorical 'triangulation' that had long been used to explain Labour's turn away from older and more left-wing policies and it was meant to offer a more positive vision. As Blair put it, 'The Third Way is not an attempt to split the difference between Right and Left.' Nevertheless, the structure of the argument continued to work in much the same way, with the same dialectical oppositions and resolutions, as in the past. To Giddens, therefore, the Third Way was a position arrived at in opposition to both the statist 'economic management and planning' of the left and the 'neoliberalism, or market fundamentalism' of the right.[41] Situating the Third Way between such stark alternatives might be tactically useful, but since the space that lay between these oppositions was so vast, it said far too little about what the Third Way actually was; and it virtually invited cynical commentary about its vagueness and vacuity. Occasionally, the Third Way was located with rather more precision using a different set of alternatives. In his brief pamphlet on the topic, for example, Tony Blair conjured up a peculiarly British split – between the new liberalism of the early twentieth century and the democratic socialism that came to replace it – and asserted that the Third Way would reunite these 'two great streams of left-of-centre thought'. But Blair still defined these movements and outlooks in terms of overly-simplified oppositions: 'Liberals asserted the primacy of individual liberty in the market economy; social democrats promoted social justice with the state as its main agent', he explained. Again, the space thus opened was large enough to accommodate almost any particular position; and so, again, it failed to satisfy those who wanted greater intellectual rigour and more specificity in their political philosophy.

This more or less structural weakness within the argument presumably accounts for the quick passing of the fashion for the Third Way and for the decreasing frequency with which New Labour leaders actually used the phrase. By the middle of Labour's second term it was virtually absent. The shift in rhetorical fashion did not mean that the idea ceased to inform policy-making, however. On the contrary, the most obviously New Labour policy interventions – e.g. in welfare policy, on crime, on social inclusion, on public-sector 'reform' – can most reasonably be understood in the terms of the Third Way discussion. Welfare reform, specifically the effort to move people from welfare to work, was undoubtedly the most distinctive policy initiative undertaken by New Labour and it was to some extent the very embodiment of the Third Way. The premiss of the effort was an explicit repudiation of older traditions of the left and the right and the embrace of the quintessentially Third Way principle of labour market 'activation'. The central notion was that work was better than welfare not only because it was more cost-effective but also because people at work were empowered, self-reliant and better able to participate in society and political life. Work was the antidote to 'social exclusion', absence of work its key cause and most visible consequence. Most important, the jobs required to make work widely available would not be generated by government implementing policies of demand management, but by the private sector making use of a growing supply of well-educated, technically sophisticated and trained workers.

The new government sought to demonstrate its commitment to a new model of work and welfare by appointing the iconoclastic Frank Field as 'Minister for Welfare Reform' charged with 'thinking the unthinkable'. (The appointment was not a great success, but was nonetheless a signal of the government's intent.) The new windfall tax on privatised utilities – the only new tax the party dared to propose before the election of 1997 – was also earmarked for the purpose of replacing welfare with work. The emerging programme was labelled the New Deal – a combination of benefits, counselling, training and education, and employment incentives designed to move first the young unemployed, then older unemployed workers, then even lone parents and the partially disabled, into the labour market. The younger unemployed would be given counselling and advice and then several options for entering the world of work: a job in the private sector made possible by a six-month state subsidy to employers with guarantees of training on or off the job; work of similar duration with either a voluntary organisation or an environmental task force that would bring a modest wage or benefit plus £15 a week extra and provision for training; or a full year of technical or vocational education. Participation was mandatory in that refusing these options would eventually lead to cessation of benefits, but the sanction was expected to be rarely used. As the policy was implemented, it was extended with minor modifications to the older unemployed and, without the element of compulsion, to single parents and the disabled.[42]

The New Deal for the unemployed was accompanied and reinforced by shifts and additions within the tax and benefit system designed to achieve the same end. Work was made more attractive by the establishment of a new, national minimum wage and, more significantly, by the introduction of the Working Families Tax Credit and the Childcare Tax Credit. These tax credits more than replaced previous credits and allowances, for they were both considerably more generous and more clearly tied to work. These were also very widely available, and so highly effective at redistributing income to needy families and their children. Lower-paid workers also benefited from a new 10p tax rate for the first £1,500 in income. At roughly the same time the government announced a 'National Childcare Strategy'. The connection to the labour market was critical in the workings of all these policies. By most accounts the programmes were successful in lowering rates of unemployment, in improving living standards and in making childcare more available, and hence in facilitating women's employment in particular. Whether success was due to the policies themselves, or a reflection of structural trends aided by a favourable business cycle, was of course impossible to determine over the short term. What was not in doubt was that these New Labour policies were very different from the sorts of employment policies pursued by previous Labour governments and that they genuinely reflected a new outlook as expressed most clearly in the debate on the Third Way.

At least as important as these specifically Third Way innovations, however, was the broader if indirect impact of the Third Way debate on the framing of government policy, especially its spending decisions. The Third Way was launched more or less simultaneously with the announcement in mid-July 1998 of the first Comprehensive Spending Review, which substantially modified the government's stance on public expenditure. New Labour had committed itself to operating within the budget limits set by the Tory Chancellor for its first two years in office and the government did as promised. After two years of restraint, however, they were ready, able and eager to increase spending. But on what, to what end, and with what guarantees that new expenditure would be effective? The Third Way formally eschewed the 'tax and spend' policies of the past, real or imagined, and insisted that government needed to be made more flexible, efficient and responsive if it were to be trusted with more of the public's money. So increased spending would be very measured and would not be allocated across the board; it would be carefully targeted; and departments would be held responsible for meeting specific performance criteria. Higher spending would also not be used up in higher pay for public sector workers. On the contrary, the spending increases announced in the review were coupled with a formal directive to pay review bodies to take into account the government's inflation target as well as departmental spending limits and output and efficiency targets in setting wages.[43] The TUC was appropriately outraged and demanded an urgent meeting with the Chancellor. The government believed, however, that it would miss a rare opportunity to improve the quality of services if funds were used largely for improved wages for existing workers, and so held firm.[44] It seems likely that New Labour's leaders were steeled in their resolve by their memories of the 'winter of discontent' in 1979, which had grown primarily out of disputes among public-sector workers and which was regarded as in no small degree responsible for bringing Mrs Thatcher into power. These memories might well have been exaggerated and loomed larger in the lore of New Labour than in the memories of voters, though only slightly. In any event, the Third Way provided a rationale for moving in a very different direction and for matching increases in spending with improvements in performance. It thus helped to make the case for raising spending by over 5 per cent per year (after inflation) on education, by nearly that on health and by better than 8 per cent on transport for the three years after 1998.[45]

Ironically, then, the Third Way gave cover to a shift from a policy of restraint in public spending to a far more expansionist programme. Equally important, of course, was the material fact that the economy grew steadily and generated enough additional revenue to allow spending increases without borrowing or major increases in income tax. In addition, the Chancellor made effective use of what were not unreasonably attacked as 'stealth taxes' – increased duties on tobacco and fuel; the phasing out of the married couple's tax allowance, mortgage deductions, various tax credits, and Advance Corporation Tax; the imposition of higher stamp duties and a climate change levy – as well as asset sales that together raised considerable money without recourse to higher income tax rates. The government also imposed the promised windfall tax worth £5.2 billion on the profits of privatised utilities in order specifically to fund the 'New Deal at Work'. But basic rates of income tax remained unchanged, and the entire programme was wrapped up in the rhetoric of the Third Way with its careful attention to achieving a balance between more expenditure and efforts to get more value for money. The result was a genuine effort to rebuild and reinvest in public services after an era of profound neglect and even antipathy. New Labour's effective 'steward-ship of the economy' in this way 'allowed it . . . to make the case for active as opposed to big government and for decent provision of public services', but the public rationale for doing so was framed in thoroughly Third Way reasoning.[46] The actual policy was of course as much 'old Labour' as 'New', but the new discourse made it possible for the policy to be portrayed, defended and perhaps even understood in a new and different way.

In fact, the use of Third Way rhetoric – even if the term itself was not always deployed – was so persistent and pervasive that it might possibly have deprived the government of proper credit for its efforts to invest in, and improve, public services. Thus the recurring talk within the party and the unions about New Labour having lost its way and abandoned its role as advocate of the disadvantaged – itself in part a response less to actual policy and more to the government's novel rhetoric – served to obscure the fact that the government had moved decisively from restraint to expansion as early as 1998 and that its investment in public services continued to grow since that turn. The second Comprehensive Spending Review (2000), for example, proposed still further increases in the fund-ing of public services, with large sums again devoted to health, education and transport. These commitments served as the starting point for the election of 2001 and established the terrain on which it was fought. Although the Labour manifesto and campaign in that contest were less than forthcoming about the issue, the result guaranteed that greater attention would be given to the state of public services and constituted a mandate for further investment. As a direct consequence, the first post-election budget, in April 2002, contained the first clear and unambiguous rise in taxes on income. National Insurance contributions were increased by 1 p and the upper limit upon which they were levied was removed entirely. The extra funds were to be used specifically for investment in the health service. The spending review of 2002 proposed still more increases that would continue to raise public expenditure from 39 per cent of GDP in 2001–02 to nearly 42 per cent by 2005–06. In 2002 the

Chancellor promised £61 billion in new public services investment over three years, plus a further £32 billion in higher pensions and benefits. Education would get 6 per cent more per year; health 7.3 per cent more for each of the next three years. The trend in public expenditure was massive and unmistakable.[47]

These boosts in spending, both before and after the 2001 election, were nevertheless accompanied at each stage by the reinvocation of the rhetoric of the Third Way. 'New resources must be matched with reform', the 2002 CSR document proclaimed, and 'Effective service delivery requires the devolution of power to service providers.' And again, the Chancellor insisted on keeping public sector pay settlements within bounds so as not to use additional funds merely to reward existing workers. On both counts the government's plans ran counter to the wishes of the leaders of the public-sector unions (and presumably their members as well), who welcomed the overall increases in funds but resisted reform. They readily accepted the modest pay increases bargained by the government, but resented the call for further pay restraint. The disagreement posed two huge questions about the fate of the government's plans for improving public services: would the effort become bogged down in endless struggles with public sector unions over pay; and were improved services even possible without reform in the structure of the public sector?

These questions went to the heart of the New Labour project and the debate over the Third Way. If New Labour meant anything, it meant a renegotiation of the Thatcherite settlement of the relationship between state and society. The Tories' excessive reliance on the market would be replaced by a commitment to redesigned public services that would repair the social fabric and restore social cohesion. If it were to succeed in this venture, however, New Labour believed firmly that it needed to prove to a sceptical public that the state was neither parasitic nor harmful to the economy, but that it could enable individuals and assist the workings of the market. The hand of the state would have to rest more lightly on society and especially on business; its exactions had to be more limited; and its demands less intrusive. Most important, it had to provide services efficiently and with new flexibility. New Labour argued powerfully that the old pattern of universal social provision and one-size-fits-all services might have worked for the Britain of the 1940s and 1950s, when the welfare state took on its characteristic modern shape and meshed reasonably well with social structures and social needs, but that it would not work in the post-Fordist, post-industrial world of the new millennium.[48] Needs and risks were more varied and precise; constituencies more fragmented and distinct; and citizens, the consumers of services, had become more diverse and discriminating and they demanded higher standards. If the public sector were to grow in this new world, it had to be reformed. The challenge, then, was for New Labour to develop a strategy for improving public services while transforming them. It was an inherently difficult task, for restructuring causes disruption and imposes transition costs and the process can actually impede the delivery of services. So, more specifically, can disgruntled public employees. In promising better public services, the government was putting its fate in the hands of those who provided them; in pledging the government to reform and restructuring, New Labour alienated precisely those same people and the organisations that spoke for them.

The government would have recourse to several strategies to overcome this dilemma, though each brought its own difficulties. The simplest thing was to issue orders. Under New Labour, and the Chancellor in particular, these took the form of targets, reviews, audits and reports that were designed to apply pressure for results on those receiving increased budgets and that probably did provide a certain 'backbone to policy-making'.[49] But the targets were almost inevitably arbitrary and it might well be that their imposition distorted efforts at reform towards meeting these criteria rather than meeting actual need. The use of targets also contradicted the goal of giving greater autonomy and flexibility to local managers, whether in the schools or the health service, to respond to local conditions. Over time, the government therefore tended to back away from the extensive use of such top-down tactics, but effective substitutes were hard to find.

The alternative to detailed control was, of course, the market and private provision, but this was to prove highly controversial for a Labour government whose leaders had campaigned against the Tories' ideological preference for privatisation and, in particular, its use of the so-called 'internal market' in the NHS. The government did formally abolish the internal market for health services, but it was unwilling to abandon the use of devolved, market-style mechanisms more generally. New Labour attempted to shift the terms of discussion, however, and began speaking not about markets but about 'public-private partnerships', cooperation and decentralisation. The objective was still somehow to make more use of the market and competition in the effort to improve public services. This at times involved subcontracting out services in health and in local government; at times the further development of the autonomy of local providers – local health authorities, newly-established Primary Care Groups, NHS trusts and, later, 'foundation hospitals', within the field of health care, and in education it took the form of local management of school funding. It has also meant recourse to private investment for public projects via Private Finance Initiatives (PFI), particularly in health, local government and transport, as well as the attempt to enlist private funds in improving failing schools through the creation of Education Action Zones (EAZs). These moves were occasionally merely cosmetic; more often, they bespoke a desire to invest money more quickly and to get results faster than would be possible if government acted alone and in the traditional manner. But they were also a reflection of New Labour's attitude towards the state and public provision. New Labour's leaders were convinced that the Labour Party's previous approach to government was too uncritical, too ready to spend without demanding performance, and too deferential to public-sector unions. They were determined not to repeat those mistakes and not to fall into the patterns of behaviour that seemed to follow from these mistaken views.

New Labour was especially keen to avoid the impression of being dominated by the wishes and interests of public-sector workers and their unions. The unions, for their part, were extremely suspicious of efforts to reform the public sector. Subcontracting and privatisation, they feared, would mean at a minimum a loss of influence, perhaps also the sacrifice of cherished benefits and the acceptance of lower wages, and in extreme cases lost jobs. Flexibility to them meant the freedom of managers to hire and fire or, at least, to redesign jobs and to impose new rules and working conditions. The unions wanted none of this. And just as government saw the increased funding made available by New Labour as a unique opportunity to rebuild the public services, so public-sector workers and unions saw the moment as a unique opportunity to restore wages that had been eroded over nearly 20 years of Conservative rule. These differences were difficult to reconcile; and it was not clear that either side had a short-term interest in reconciling. The government had staked its future on improved and reformed public services; the unions understood their future to depend on getting the best deal and the most secure working environment for their members within a well-funded public sector. Added to this genuine conflict of interest was a mutual antipathy that was also unlikely to go away: unions felt mistreated and taken for granted by a government they had helped to elect and continued to fund. During Labour's second term the antipathy between the unions and the government grew steadily. A series of retirements opened up the top jobs in several of the largest unions and these were regularly filled by trade unionists critical of New Labour.[50] The generation of union leaders beaten and tamed by Thatcher was passing from the scene and their replacements were eager to test the government's resolve with their industrial strength. The 'big four' unions – the TGWU, the GMB, Unison and Amicus – had all seen their leadership move to the left by mid-2003 and the new leaders emerged as an 'awkward squad', seriously threatening the government's strategy on the reform and restructuring of the public services. The critics were not all of one mind, of course, and few were willing to endorse the more radical proposals of left-wing leaders like Bob Crow of the railway union (RMT) to cut union funding for the party and direct it elsewhere. Nevertheless, the unions were increasingly prepared to resist New Labour's plans. New Labour's leaders in turn regarded the obstinacy of the unions as the main impediment to their goal of reconfiguring the boundaries between the state and the market and elaborating a new framework and approach to progressive government. The tension was deeply rooted in New Labour's history and it was unlikely to disappear so long as the level and quality of public provision was at the top of the government's domestic agenda; and that would presumably be the case so long as New Labour remained in power.

The difficulty of expanding while reforming public services had been less urgent prior to the election of 2001. From that moment the issue would dominate the government's domestic statecraft – its deliberations, its policy-making, and the response it received from critics and voters. During its first term of office, by contrast, the government's energy and enthusiasm for innovation, its successful spinning and its surprising economic competence combined to divert attention from the extent of additional funding and structural reform that would be required to rebuild and update public services. So, too, did the media's complementary focus on matters other than policy – on the new government's management of the press, for example, or on personalities, personal rivalries and gossip, or on scandal or at least the appearance of impropriety, or on those unforeseen events that inevitably intrude on the routine work of governing. On many occasions, this concentration on the superficial undoubtedly worked to New Labour's temporary advantage. The government's sensitivity to what was news and to what people cared about was also of considerable, short-term political benefit. This ability was demonstrated with dramatic effect, for example, in the government's typically deft response to the death of Princess Diana. Blair had received word of Diana's death at about 2.00 am on 1 September 1997. Over breakfast that morning he had learned that the royal family would say nothing. By 10.00 am he and Campbell had not only decided to fill the void but had already crafted Blair's statement to the nation. The Prime Minister was, he said, 'utterly devastated. Our prayers and thoughts are with Princess Diana's family . . . our hearts go out to them. We are a nation in a state of shock.' 'She was', he ended, 'the People's Princess and that is how she will stay, how she will remain in our hearts and in our memories for ever.' The 'People's Princess' was apparently Campbell's phrase, but the delivery and the instinct about just how to pitch it were Blair's, and it worked spectacularly well.[51]

New Labour's preferred communications style nevertheless also led to a rather perverse attention directed to the very practice of spinning and to New Labour's apparent obsession with managing the news. Thus when the inevitable scandals and embarrassments did occur – Bernie Ecclestone's convenient donation to the party coffers, for example, or Robin Cook's affair with his secretary and the break-up of his marriage, or repeated rumours of antagonism and broken deals between Blair and Brown, or the embarrassments over the Millennium Dome, or Mandelson's unsecured loans from Geoffrey Robinson and, later, his possible interference with Srichand Hinduja's passport application, or any of several lesser but still awkward moments – New Labour's reputation for effective news management had the oddly ironic effect of seeming to make the problems worse and harder to get past.[52] It appeared that the press could not resist taking revenge on its supposed master. Whether these mini-crises ever mattered much to the broader public, they took their toll among those with a more active interest in politics and served to erode at least some of the goodwill with which the government first took office. Most important, these episodes reinforced a perception that the government lacked a serious purpose other than to win and undermined the sense of mission it sought to convey through its policy proposals and through the debate on the Third Way.

The government was indeed gripped by a resolve to win a second and then a third term, and virtually its every effort was undertaken with that goal in mind. The focus stemmed not merely from the desire to hold office but also from the deeply-held conviction that it was impossible to make a real impact on government within a single term. The 2001 election would therefore be regarded as a turning point that would usher in a second term with a markedly different tone. The year preceding the general election offered pointed reminders of just how vulnerable even a media-savvy regime could be to unexpected events. The government was caught off guard, for example, by the intensity of the fuel protests that nearly paralysed the country in the autumn of 2000. In retrospect, the prospect of popular resentment over higher fuel prices becoming fixed on increased petrol taxes and leading to angry demands for their lowering seemed obvious enough, but it was not evident beforehand and required serious attention when it happened. The outbreak of foot-and-mouth disease was less easily foreseen but equally troublesome, for the government would be held responsible for stopping it and compensating farmers who lost animals and for the tourist industry's lost customers. The crisis, which was in no way comparable to the threat previously posed by 'mad cow disease' (BSE), nevertheless caused the postponement of the election and was gravely worrying to ministers and politicians as they prepared to put their case to voters. The difficulties experienced by the government in dealing with these two unforeseen and, on the scale of things, relatively insignificant problems served as reminders of their political mortality and made the leaders of the party and the government alert to shifting voter concerns as registered in opinion polls as the campaign progressed.

What was universally regarded as a dull campaign and an election lacking genuine issues and drama nevertheless conveyed definite messages.[53] The messages were delivered in code, however, by the response of voters to the contrasting themes offered by the major parties. The initial thrust of the Conservative effort, for example, had been on tax: the

Tory manifesto promised £8 billion in tax cuts, including a sharp decrease in petrol duties. The tactic failed to move voters, however, and that failure signalled a de facto willingness to pay more for public services. The apparent attraction of the Liberal Democratic message, which promised increased investment in public services and conceded that higher taxes were needed, reinforced that signal and allowed Labour to absorb the message without having to quite say it out loud. Labour had in fact begun to move in the same direction and made it clear that it was predisposed to increase spending on public services. After the election the government would act on this new perception of what public opinion had made possible.

As the election campaign unfolded, the Tories shifted their strategy to focus on Europe and the supposed threat to British sovereignty implicit in the government's attitude towards the EU and the euro. Again, Labour had not said much and, as it would turn out, was not prepared to do much when re-elected with a large majority. But the Conservatives' failed attempt to conjure up Euro-sceptic fears suggested that popular ambivalence towards Europe was relatively superficial and not critical to voters' choices. The effect, again, was to license Labour efforts to move in whatever direction it later chose. Labour's second landslide, then, was not unreasonably interpreted by party and media as a reason to press forward both on the campaign to invest in the public sector and, if the government so chose, perhaps even to move ahead on Europe.

But the vote also contained a warning, or so it was regularly and not unreasonably argued, in its unusually low turnout. Participation fell by 12 percentage points, to just above 59 per cent, the lowest recorded since 1918. The margin of victory, especially in parliamentary seats, demonstrated the absence of a genuine alternative to Labour, but the lack of enthusiasm generated by the contest suggested that support was wide but not deep and that the potential for disillusionment was very high. It was in fact hard to discern precisely what message voters were sending by staying away from the polls. The race was never expected to be close and so a major motivation for voting was simply not there. In addition, opinion polls done after the election made it clear that abstainers were not any more critical of the government than those who cast votes and that their votes would actually have increased slightly the scale of Labour's victory. More important, Labour did well in getting out the vote in the seats it first won only in 1997 and where the conventional wisdom predicted a close contest in the next election. It also largely kept the gains it had made in 1997 among middle-class and women voters whose attachment to Labour thus seemed to be firming up. The meaning of low turnout was in this sense unclear and its significance possibly exaggerated, though it probably did indicate that the newest and youngest cohort of voters was not especially enthusiastic about New Labour's message, or not enthusiastic enough actually to vote.[54] But the choice also indicated that they were no more interested in the messages on offer from the opposition parties.

The 2001 election thus did not produce a new government, let alone a new set of electoral realities; nor even a fundamentally new set of issues. It did confirm the political landscape displayed so starkly in 1997 and it produced a heightened sense of urgency within the government about the need actually to deliver on its promises to improve public services if it hoped to make the realignment of recent years into a more lasting phenomenon. That meant above all the decision openly to increase taxation, which would come in the next budget. Beyond that, of course, it raised even more forcefully the question of how much reform, or restructuring, would be required in order to secure better performance from the public sector. The debate over reform ran right through the government and the party; while there was virtually no debate among the unions, who regarded reform with fear and disdain. It seems possible that at least some of New Labour's leaders were themselves not fully convinced of the virtues of reform. There was, after all, no disagreeing with the proposition that more money was essential, and a plausible case could be made that sufficient spending over a sustained period was the ultimate key to success. There was by contrast much less consensus on the virtues of reforming the public sector. Restructuring, increased flexibility and local variation were seen – and not only by the unions – to threaten not just workers' rights and wages, but also and more importantly the collectivist ethos that was held to inspire Labour's commitment to public provision and equality. This ambivalence, this unresolved argument, has continued to surround and complicate the government's ongoing efforts to deliver better public services. It seems unlikely to diminish, moreover, for it is truly fundamental: it once more pits New Labour's determination, by now instinctive, to break free of its past, and to be seen to be doing so, against not only its traditions but also against what core supporters have come to define as their vital interests. Just how successfully these contradictory imperatives are reconciled in practice will go far towards determining New Labour's legacy. It is unlikely that it will be resolved and go away, however, for it is endemic to the New Labour project and will become irrelevant only if and when the project is eclipsed, abandoned or overtaken by events.

The most obvious example of the sort of unforeseen event that might push these debates to the side and come to dominate the political agenda was, of course, the attack on the World Trade Center of 11 September 2001. New Labour's response was never in doubt and not long in coming. The government chose to side quickly and openly with the United States, even if it meant teaming up with an administration with whom New Labour shared very little. While the choice was close to inevitable, it would nevertheless prove extremely controversial. Would it also be consequential and affect New Labour in the long term? More specifically, would the foreign policy dilemmas forced upon New Labour by the aftermath of 9/11 distract or divert from the government's domestic statecraft? Or would the new focus on matters of defence and security complement and reinforce New Labour's political philosophy and identity?

At the very least the new importance of foreign policy would add a new dimension to what it meant to be New Labour. Until the attack on the World Trade Center the New Labour story had been largely, though not solely, a matter of domestic policy. In this respect New Labour had been unusually at one with its heritage, for the Labour Party that the 'modernisers' had sought to lead and transform was a party whose unique contribution to British politics had been its attention to society and economy, its role in giving voice and representation to ordinary men and women of the working class, and its attempt to write their needs into the definition of national interest. Labour was the party of domestic reform and New Labour's chosen task was to redefine the limits and techniques involved in that effort. Of course, Labour had always, and of necessity, had a foreign policy and a stance on defence and international relations, but these were not the issues that normally attracted voters to the Labour Party and they had not been a central preoccupation of New Labour. After 11 September, the world and Britain's role in it would for a time figure far more prominently in British politics and in New Labour's imagination. The international crisis would mean that whatever stance New Labour took would henceforth matter a great deal. It would be visible and meaningful; and it would invite intense scrutiny and debate. The fact that its choices after 9/11 were prefigured well before that moment does not mean that the act of carrying them out, and the parallel work of articulating the premisses behind them, were any less significant in defining New Labour as a political phenomenon – to itself, its supporters and its critics.[55]

Although the decision of the Blair government to ally itself with the United States and to adopt an aggressive policy towards terror was long in the making, it still provoked a drastic reordering of the political agenda. The crisis produced by 11 September and its aftermath constituted a major suspension of the assumptions governing the everyday conduct of political business and it imposed on New Labour the need to forge a distinctively New Labour position on foreign and defence policy. The identity that emerged from these choices was of course only partially new, only partly New Labour. The alliance with the United States had been, after all, the centrepiece of foreign and defence policy for the entire era since the Second World War. The special relationship between the two nations might or might not have conferred special status and benefits on the UK, but successive British governments, Conservative and Labour, had stuck to it nevertheless. Alongside this commitment and in opposition to it, however, there had also existed within Labour a lengthy and respected tradition of pacifist and internationalist thinking and a certain animus towards the United States as the embodiment of brash and untempered capitalism and relentless anti-socialism. From the very beginning of the Cold War, therefore, many within the Labour Party had advocated that Britain form, and lead, a 'third force' to mediate between America and the Soviet Union, between the unbridled capitalism of the one and the harsh and dictatorial rule of the other.[56] It was this hope that later inspired the Campaign for Nuclear Disarmament in the late 1950s, and the outlook was shared widely enough to prevail at the party conference in 1960. The critique of US foreign policy and of nuclear weapons was further deepened during the Vietnam War, though Wilson's deft handling of the issue meant that it lacked a clear target and hence a proper outlet. The rekindling of fears of nuclear war in the late 1970s and early 1980s provided the needed focus and led to a revival of unilateralist organisation and sentiment that again captured the party's imagination and came to be reflected in its programmes and manifestos. The elections of 1983 and 1987 put Labour's new unilateralist and non-nuclear defence policy on public display and it became the object of ruthlessly effective attacks by the Tories. As a result, it came to be regarded even by its supporters as an electoral liability, though the position continued to command the moral high ground and to enjoy wide support among party activists.

The party's defence policy had nevertheless proved difficult to defend and so would become a casualty of the Policy Review launched by Kinnock in 1987. By 1989 Labour had moved back, in effect, to its traditional policy of seeking disarmament through multilateral negotiations and, until that succeeded, continuing as a loyal member of NATO to rely on nuclear weapons and on American, and British, readiness to use them. There was a lingering ambiguity in Labour's stance, however, largely because the Cold War ended so precipitously and took the passion out of the debate over defence and foreign policy. The arguments within the Labour Party over social and economic policy had been hard fought and were seen through to the end. Indeed, there was eventually a formal referendum on the replacement of Clause IV. On foreign and defence policy, on the other hand, the arguments gradually ran out of steam. The reliable Gerald Kaufman, former Wilson confidante and fixer, had chaired this critical portion of the Policy Review. Though his efforts were not helped by Kinnock's erratic interventions, he produced a report that backed off Labour's exposed position and essentially defused the issue. What made the retreat possible was the fact that the argument lost salience with the end of the Cold War and the rapid disappearance of the Soviet threat. During the 1990s Labour was in consequence able to combine without serious dissension its continued support for the Atlantic Alliance, its increasing interest and involvement in Europe, and its aspiration for a global order based on peace and international cooperation. The party did persist in its support for a strengthening of conventional forces, the preferred alternative to nuclear weapons, though the leadership also left in place the by then uncontroversial assumption that military spending would decrease overall.[57] The Shadow Defence spokesman, David Clark, supposedly had as his brief the advice 'to keep defence as low a profile issue as possible' and his style was apparently well-suited to the task. He and his Tory opponent, Malcolm Rifkind, were not unfairly caricatured for proposing endless reviews but no new strategy and few weapons. As Matthew Parris noted in July 1993, 'Labour plans to approach future world conflicts armed with a comprehensive range of reviews. Yesterday,' Parris went on, '. . . Clark . . . described just a few of the sophisticated and deadly reviews his party hopes to deploy.'[58]

When New Labour came to power in 1997 this ambiguity was to be glossed over by the vaguely internationalist rhetoric of the Third Way, with its commitments to 'remain outward looking not isolationist' and to pursue 'openness, trade and diplomacy' through 'strong partnerships with the EU, the US and in Asia . . .'. Blair would propose closer international cooperation on 'security and environmental protection' and boast that New Labour's predecessors on the centre-left had been the 'architects of an international order, underpinning security and prosperity for decades'.[59] That these aims might be incompatible or hard to realise was largely overlooked, for they struck an appropriately balanced, judicious and progressive note. The balance was reflected more concretely in the allocation of Cabinet responsibilities: Robin Cook was appointed Foreign Secretary, George Robertson and John Reid became respectively ministers for Defence and for the Armed Forces, while Clare Short was named head of the Department for International Development (DfID). Though Cook had an established record as a unilateralist – he had joined CND as a teenager – by the 1980s his politics had become more flexible and pragmatic: a sceptical commentator noted in 1985 that while he was 'left-wing enough' to have credibility in those circles, 'he is the first realist of that very young generation' beginning to make its mark after the debacles of 1979 and 1983.[60] He seems, moreover, to have been much more interested in social and economic policy than in foreign affairs. His position as Foreign Secretary conferred an appropriately elevated status, but he would probably have preferred to be elsewhere. Cook nevertheless sought to give a distinctive direction to the Labour government's foreign policy with a new emphasis on ethics and human rights. His presence at the Foreign Office was nevertheless counterbalanced by Robertson at Defence. When CND was winning converts everywhere during the late 1970s and early 1980s – including Michael Foot, Neil Kinnock and the young Tony Blair – Robertson had been willing 'flatly to oppose it'. He remained instead 'a believer in the continuation of nuclear defence . . . and . . . a supporter of the Atlantic Alliance – an extremist in fact'.[61] John Reid, for a time a key Kinnock operative and by his own account a 'moderniser' well before Blair, had in the 1990s grown close to the defence establishment and became Minister of State for Armed Forces. The presence of Clare Short might seem to have tipped the balance towards the left in view of her anti-war and anti-nuclear credentials, her resignation from the Shadow Cabinet over the Gulf War, and her assumed role as New Labour's socialist and internationalist conscience. In fact it did not, and in practice this collection of diverse ministers worked together to pursue policies that effectively combined internationalist aspirations with a pragmatic recognition of the realities of global power. The delicate ministerial balance that New Labour struck also ensured that Blair would assume a personal role at key moments and that it would be largely his vision that would impart whatever distinct or innovative cast there would be to New Labour's foreign policy.

Blair's position was strengthened by the fact that Cook got into trouble early on in seeking to import ethical concerns into an arena where the hard-headed calculation of national interest typically prevailed. Cook was embarrassed, for example, over arms sales to Indonesia, where the government might well use them against internal opponents, and by the formal announcement of a new policy on arms sales that did not go down well.[62] He was also put very much on the defensive over the handling of events in Sierra Leone. The British position had been to restore to power the elected head of government, who had been ousted in a particularly nasty coup. But in doing so the government found itself violating an arms embargo largely of its own creation and dealing with possibly unsavoury characters. Blair would insist in response that the good guys had won and that was what mattered, but the effect was to make Cook's ethical foreign policy look tarnished and inconsistent and to reduce his influence within the Cabinet. Cook had also been compromised over personal matters and from that moment dependent for his effectiveness, and even his job, on the support of Number 10.

The Defence ministers had fared better than the Foreign Office team and in July 1998 they managed to produce a Strategic Defence Review that won broad approval. It proposed no major new expansion of weapons or of troop strength, but their upgrading and more careful deployment.[63]

More important and prescient, the Review asserted that Britain must continue to play a role on the world stage. The threat now was not from any single power, as had been the case as long as the Soviet Union existed, but just as real though more diffuse. It came from failed states and rogue powers and from recurring violations of human rights. The theme was roughly in keeping with Britain's continued yearning for great power status, with Cook's and Short's privileging of the ethical dimension in foreign policy, and with Blair's personal sense of mission and morality. It was, though, a more aggressive stance than a Labour government made up of so many former CND supporters might have been expected to adopt.

Whatever the role of the Foreign Office and Defence ministries, it was the Prime Minister who was inevitably called on to represent Britain in the highest counsels of world leaders and Blair clearly found in that role a venue for articulating much the same Third Way message as he delivered at home. The man who would be 'tough on crime and tough on the causes of crime' in Britain would find it an easy transition to recast the message into foreign policy guidance: he would be tough on terror and tough on the causes of terror and would use force to bring peace and justice. Since it was Blair who routinely met with presidents and prime ministers, he had repeated opportunities to frame the government's overall foreign policy stance and to shape its responses to the inevitable crises that make up the reality of international affairs. It was Blair whom Bill Clinton visited just after the election of May 1997, it was Blair who led the delegation to the EU meeting in Amsterdam a few weeks later and it was he who chaired EU sessions during the UK Presidency. It was thus Blair who set the tone and took the big decisions, and it was his interventions that mattered most. A fitting example was the issue of Northern Ireland. It was his personal involvement, endorsed and helped by Clinton, that was largely responsible for the breakthrough that led to the Good Friday Agreement of 10 April 1998.

Blair's most significant interventions were over Yugoslavia and Iraq. Here were two instances of states fairly labelled 'rogue' if not as yet 'failed' and which had clearly violated the standards of the international community and international law. But both were nations that posed little or no direct threat to British, or US, interests in the traditional military sense. On the contrary, no great power seemed to have a real stake in confronting these states. In such a context New Labour's activist and global vision provided a rationale for intervention by the international community – by the United Nations, if possible, and if not, then by whatever 'coalition of the willing' could be assembled for the occasion. The proximate background to this novel and potentially revolutionary conception of the workings of the international order was a transparent frustration with the failures of the early 1990s. Despite the outcome of the Gulf War and the hardships of the sanctions regime that followed it, for example, Saddam Hussein stayed in power and sought repeatedly to escape the consequences of sanctions and to frustrate the work of UN inspectors. In Bosnia, the failure of foreign powers to act in a timely and effective fashion had allowed Serbian 'ethnic cleansing' to proceed unopposed for what seemed a very long time. In opposition, the Labour Party had sharply criticised the Conservatives for their inactivity in the Balkans, with Robin Cook especially vocal. The bombing that brought about the Dayton Accord in 1995 seemed to offer convincing proof that the use of force could succeed and served to confirm New Labour in its predisposition to adopt in the future what it regarded as a policy of humanitarian intervention.

The opportunity to do so came quickly to the new government eager to prove itself on the world stage and to shed previous images of the Labour Party as being soft on matters of defence. In November 1997 the French and the Russians sought a compromise over Iraq, but Saddam Hussein was adamant and actually expelled UN weapons inspectors. Blair was insistent that the Iraqis must back down. Iraq did back down at first, but then reneged, and the crisis festered without resolution. By February 1998 the government had secured a Commons resolution authorising force in response to Iraq's recent declaration that 'presidential sites' were off-limits to inspectors. Robin Cook prominently argued the need for a tough line with the bold claim that 'Saddam is the clearest example of a leader who is also a terrorist.'[64] Kofi Annan stepped in at the last moment and helped to broker a deal, effectively pushing back the date at which there would be recourse to force. But after further manoeuvres over inspections, posturing, threats and demands, Britain and the United States carried out a brief but intense bombing in December 1998.

Over roughly the same period the situation steadily deteriorated in Yugoslavia, as the Serbs sent troops into Kosovo and began what was obviously another campaign aimed at ethnic cleansing. Again, threats, denunciations and ultimata followed one another in predictable succession and came near to producing a resolution in early 1999. In the event the Serb leader Milošević would not agree and ordered his troops to press ahead rapidly, with tens of thousands of Albanians forced to flee their homes. The response was a bombing campaign officially conducted by NATO but urged on, and carried out, largely by the UK and the United States. When that seemed not to be working, it was British leaders who would argue most consistently and forcefully for a ground invasion. The Germans, for example, were strongly opposed and other NATO leaders tended to agree with them. Gerhard Schröder regarded the prospect of a ground war as 'unthinkable', while the Italian premier labelled it 'a totally useless exercise'. But Britain continued to press the case that bombing alone would be insufficient. At Easter Clare Short visited British troops and came away convinced that an invasion was the only solution. In early May Blair and his wife, Cherie, followed up with a dramatic visit to the Kosovo border, where he declared that 'This is not a battle for NATO. This is not a battle for territory. It is a battle for humanity. It is a just cause.'[65] The British position was in fact much more aggressive than the American stance and even caused resentment within the Clinton camp, which thought Blair's behaviour made the President look weak. As the debate over intervention proceeded and troops gradually were put in place, the bombing began to do its work and on 9 June Milošević acquiesced in NATO's demands and gave the order for Serbian forces to withdraw from Kosovo. A ground campaign was just barely averted and the logic of humanitarian intervention, backed by force and the threat of more to come, seemed again to have prevailed.[66]

The argument for intervening in Iraq, Kosovo and perhaps elsewhere had been put with some force and surprising clarity in Blair's famous speech in Chicago on 22 April 1999, delivered in the midst of the apparently ineffective NATO bombing campaign and against the background of a deep split over what to do next.[67] Blair used the occasion to make explicit what was previously merely implicit in New Labour foreign policy. According to Blair, 'unspeakable things are happening in Europe . . . – ethnic cleansing, systematic rape, mass murder'. The war in Kosovo was thus a 'just war' aimed at stopping 'evil' and 'we must not rest until it is reversed'. The problem, of course, was that this kind of war was new and, as Blair conceded, it could scarcely have been contemplated 20 years earlier, when Cold War alliances and preoccupations remained intact. The end of the Cold War and the spread of globalisation had utterly transformed the context, however, and now 'We live in a world where isolationism has ceased to have a reason to exist.' It was now necessary to develop a 'new doctrine of international community'. The doctrine would have wide application: it would provide a guide to economic policy, for example, and so would inspire efforts to better manage international finance by improving the structure and workings of the IMF and the World Bank and, more specifically, by relieving the burden of Third World debt. It would lead in addition to initiatives designed to open up trade and to manage the global environment. The new doctrine would also lead to plans to reshape international institutions like the United Nations and NATO. Most important, it would inform decisions about security, where future actions should be determined not by narrow national interest conceived in traditional fashion but instead 'by a more subtle blend of mutual self-interest and moral purpose in defending the values we cherish . . . – liberty, the rule of law, human rights and an open society . . .'. In defending these values there was obviously a 'pressing' need 'to identify the circumstances in which we should get actively involved in other people's conflicts'. Not interfering in the affairs of others, Blair acknowledged, 'has long been considered an important principle of international order'. But now this 'principle of non-interference must be qualified . . .'. Blair proceeded to list a series of largely subjective conditions for outside intervention: 'are we sure?', 'have we exhausted all diplomatic options?', is it practical and are 'we prepared for the long term?' and are our 'national interests involved?' These were transparently not 'absolute tests' of an objective sort but rather, in Blair's words, 'the kind of issues we need to think about in deciding when and whether we will intervene'. It was also important, Blair suggested, to 'support the UN' as a 'central pillar' of a 'world ruled by law and by international cooperation', but for that to happen the UN itself had to be reformed so as to avoid the 'deadlock' characteristic of the Cold War.

The Chicago speech hardly qualifies as a fully worked out doctrine, at least in any formal and coherent sense. It nevertheless captured well the thrust of New Labour's more activist foreign policy and offered an early view of what would emerge so distinctively and so controversially after 11 September 2001. New Labour had by 1999 already chosen to adopt a more muscular stance towards the world that differed markedly from the party's recent unilateralist past and from the policies typically followed by its European allies. In New Labour's vision British policy would no longer be animated by a traditional imperial or post-imperial mission, anchored in the alliance system of the Cold War, but by a humanitarian vision that would nonetheless be rooted in the very same alliance. Britain would remain close to the United States as a first principle, but seek to serve as a bridge to, and erstwhile leader of, Europe as a second but important objective. It would pursue these alliances less to protect itself than to promote its liberal values. This humanitarian motivation would be premised, however, not on mere goodwill but on a realist and disenchanted view of the world. There were evil regimes that would not be deterred except through force; and the existing framework of international laws and institutions required restructuring and a new set of operating principles if they were to be truly useful in this new era of global interdependence and security threats that spilled over traditional borders and that confounded established definitions.

This 'doctrine of international community' was inherently controversial and elicited a modest debate in 1999, but the success of the intervention in Kosovo and its subsequent ratification by the United Nations meant that the new doctrine was not regarded as quite the departure it in fact was. Nor was its import clear in the immediate aftermath of 9/11, when just about everybody rallied to the side of the United Sates. Thus the French declared themselves honorary Americans; the Germans proclaimed their sympathy; the Russians agreed to help – especially if it meant that Europe and the United States would soften their criticisms of Russian policy in Chechnya; and both NATO and the United Nations fully agreed that the United States had the right to defend itself against al-Queda and the terrorist *jihad* it had proclaimed. The response of the British government went further and included not only solidarity but the promise of practical cooperation in taking action against 'terror'. When it became clear what sorts of action the United States had in mind, however, international support began quickly to dissipate. It took some time for the dimensions and direction of US foreign policy to become clear, but as they did, opposition mounted.

What made American foreign policy after 11 September so controversial – and Blair's support so provocative to opinion in his own party

– were three, related issues. There was first the US insistence not only on bringing terrorists to justice and destroying their ability to launch attacks but also the announced intention to hold states supportive of terrorists responsible for their actions. The principle was logical enough, but its application beyond a relatively clear-cut case like Afghanistan would be extremely difficult. Afghanistan was no problem, for the Taliban regime was intrinsically loathsome and also, it emerged, deeply indebted to and intertwined with al-Queda. And al-Queda had no qualms about declaring itself a terrorist organisation. But what about other organisations that might deploy terror but whose cause enjoyed wider support. And in terms of complicity, what was to be done about the Taliban's sponsors in Pakistan and about al-Queda's supporters and sympathisers in Saudi Arabia, some of them members of the extended royal family and presumably in positions of authority? What of various regimes in the Middle East, like Iraq, Iran and Syrian, that were hostile to Israel and often complicit in the Palestinian use of suicide bombers, but also distinct from, and hostile towards, al-Queda? The decision to label three states – Iraq, Iran and North Korea – that had little to do with one another an 'axis of evil' and, by implication, of terror, further complicated the question of who would have the right to decide just who was a terrorist and which states were complicit in terror.

The second issue was the use of force. Again, Afghanistan was the easy case, although it was not entirely uncontroversial. There was little doubt that the Taliban had harboured bin Laden but there was also little formal proof of it. This asymmetry undoubtedly predisposed the United States to bypass international law, which seemed in any case not equipped or designed for such a task, and instead to attack and destroy the regime. Even so, there was criticism that the US bombing campaign was inherently cowardly, and there were widespread fears that the strategy would cause massive civilian casualties and create a huge humanitarian crisis. The quick collapse of resistance and the visible enthusiasm of the local population led to a muting of these worries and criticisms, but the war had briefly brought into view the divergence between the emerging position of the Bush administration and its allies in Britain and the views of potential critics.

The third and related issue was the role of international institutions and the apparent willingness of the United States to act unilaterally, or with only nominal support from other nations. On this issue also the attack on Afghanistan was exceptional, for the rogue character of the regime led to support for its replacement from the international community even if the deed were done more or less unilaterally by the United States. The success of the operation, however, seemed to reinforce American tendencies towards a unilateral approach to security and foreign affairs. The United States had been clearly unwilling to wait upon a diplomatic settlement with Afghanistan, if only because the prospect seemed so remote. But it was also relatively uninterested in gaining allies for its bombing and subsequent invasion of Afghanistan. The apparent reason for this attitude was that the gap between US military power and the armed might of other powers was now so wide that joint operations would add little and would merely complicate the prosecution of the war. The exception was of course the UK, whose military was no match for that of the United States but which was funded, trained and equipped at levels that made cooperation meaningful. Success in Afghanistan offered an apparent vindication of this strategic choice and encouraged its application elsewhere.

Extending the 'war on terror' beyond Afghanistan made each of these criticisms more urgent and led to growing disaffection with US policy and with the British government's close collaboration with the Bush administration. When the United States turned its attention to regime change in Iraq, it therefore found itself isolated from possible allies, with the prime exception of the UK. Britain, and Blair especially, would for this reason play a critical role in the events leading to war in March 2003. Britain was responsible in large part for pushing the United States into an engagement with the United Nations and securing UN support for renewed weapons inspections, with the implicit threat of force if Saddam failed to cooperate. It was also the British government that, faced with a sceptical public and with a major rebellion on the backbenches, insisted that the United Sates go back to the UN to try to obtain a more explicit endorsement of military action. When that failed and war came and the Iraqi regime was defeated, it was again Blair who talked Bush into a renewed bid to involve the UN in the post-war reconstruction of Iraq. Throughout the crisis it appeared that Blair was the only world leader capable of putting the American case clearly and convincingly and the only one willing to do so.

The choice to ally with the United States and with the Bush administration in the war in Iraq proved the most contentious decision made by New Labour in power. Blair risked his job on the outcome and hence put at risk the future of the government and the entire New Labour project. It was a choice that surprised, puzzled and dismayed both supporters and critics and that provoked enormous debate about Blair, his commitments, even his sanity, and about whether he should continue to lead the party or be replaced, presumably by Gordon Brown.[68] The fateful decision produced a huge and unprecedented wave of popular protest and a large backbench rebellion. Robin Cook, already replaced as Foreign Secretary by Jack Straw in 2001, resigned from the Cabinet and from his position as Leader of the House of Commons just before the war. Clare Short went just after it ended. Both claimed to have been misled by Blair and their criticisms helped to stimulate and sustain the bitter post-war controversy over whether the government's claims about 'weapons of mass destruction' were yet another example of spin shading into dishonesty. Relations with the press, the BBC in particular, turned confrontational and almost violent, and the suicide of weapons scientist David Kelly was an appropriately grim symbol of the toll taken on public discourse. The Prime Minister, fêted in the United States, was subjected to fierce criticism at home and he appeared increasingly isolated.

Dismay over the government's decision might well have been called for. The invasion and subsequent occupation of Iraq were bold and potentially dangerous moves that merited all the debate they in fact elicited. There was, however, far less reason to be surprised or puzzled. Cook and Short, for example, could not have been as naive or shocked or outraged as they later portrayed themselves, for they had been together at the centre of foreign policy-making as it had evolved first in opposition and then during Labour's first term. It was surely obvious to them and to all concerned that the unilateralism of the 1980s had been long discarded by New Labour. New Labour's conduct of foreign policy before the attack on the World Trade Center told fundamentally the same story. The posture adopted towards Iraq in 1998 and towards Kosovo in 1999 hardly indicated a pacifist bent; nor did these policies imply a deference towards the prerogatives of international institutions. Blair and Cook, for example, had been in accord in claiming that no further UN resolution was required to justify bombing Iraq in 1998; and the entire operation in Kosovo had been conducted outside the UN for fear of a Russian veto. Instead, the intervention had been organised through NATO. In consequence, as a ground invasion became more likely and as European leaders voiced doubts and hesitations, the talk turned to assembling a 'coalition of the willing' – precisely the phrase used to describe the forces arrayed against Iraq in 2003.[69] The implication in each of these cases was that neither the United Nations nor NATO nor any other existing international organisation could or would undertake what was regarded by the Labour government as a necessary and justified task. Without the means for their achievement, internationalist aspirations and multilateral efforts had thus been forced to give way even before 11 September; it was unlikely they would prove more robust or practical after that.

The case for intervention in Iraq in 2003 was thus well and thoroughly rehearsed several years prior to that crisis. It was nevertheless a decisive moment in New Labour's history, an occasion when the implications of previous choices were manifest and when, confronted with the full logic of its position, the party was forced to choose once again and to define itself once more. It became clear as the prospect of war loomed ever closer that many in the party would prefer not to make the choice at all and not to be required to define their political identity in terms of the war in Iraq. The outcome was in this sense both highly determined, in that it followed directly from earlier stances adopted by the party, but also profoundly uncertain, for it required the reaffirmation of those decisions and, more specifically, of New Labour's leadership. Blair had to prevail and he did, but there was much unhappiness in the ranks.

Blair's personal role in all this was perhaps the easiest thing to explain. He had clearly developed a taste for foreign policy during his first term as prime minister and had begun to evolve a distinctive outlook and style. After the election of June 2001 he had not only replaced Cook as Foreign Secretary but also taken steps to enhance the role of Number 10 in formulating and carrying out policy in the international arena.[70] And the emerging confrontation over Iraq was precisely the sort of occasion in which Blair had tended to come into his own. The sense of moral clarity, of resolution and courage, of being willing to do the right thing even if it is not popular, is vintage Blair and the opportunity for re-engaging with the 'tradition of radical reform rhetoric' offered by such occasions seems to have been irresistible.[71] Joining up with the Bush administration over Iraq was also perhaps the precondition for Blair, indeed for anyone outside the United States, exercising any real influence over the course of American policy. Blair certainly argued that point to his Cabinet colleagues. There was also the evident attraction of playing on the world stage in a role that seemed to transcend the petty considerations of domestic politics. It seems obvious that Blair found it more appealing to appear on the side of right and virtue when standing up to Saddam Hussein and to terror than to be the focus of controversy when the government decided to resist the wage claims of the nation's firemen or proposed additional fees for university students or when it was called upon to defend the merits of public–private partnerships in health care and transport. Given his history, however, it seems quite mistaken to regard Blair as merely 'Bush's poodle'. He is perhaps more accurately portrayed as 'a petty mastiff, snarling at the leash', but neither canine metaphor is especially helpful in making sense of Blair's position or in explaining why the party agreed in the end to go along.[72] Such criticisms might seem to bite, but they fail to recognise the roots and rationale of New Labour's stance and miss the essential fit between the New Labour position on Iraq and its more basic goal of creating a modern and 'modernised' Labour Party that has repositioned itself at a new and distinctive place on the political spectrum.

The New Labour project, of course, did not literally require that Blair and New Labour back Bush over Iraq, but it did make the choice much more likely. Nor did the project dictate the precise mix of new taxes, new funding and initiatives to restructure the public services that so clearly defined New Labour's domestic policies after 1997. Nevertheless, the long road that led to the emergence of New Labour had major consequences for what New Labour would do when it achieved power. Its unique past made it highly likely that New Labour in government would continue to weaken the ability of the party as an organisation to control its leaders so as to expand its freedom of manoeuvre; that it would persist in its pursuit of the confidence of business and the middle-class public by maintaining its fiscal rectitude; that it would increase public expenditure only on the condition that the public services reform, or at least promise to reform; and that it would pay higher wages to public sector workers on those same terms. All of these policies grew out of New

Labour's rejection of its past and its determination not to be controlled by its legacy, by any undue reverence for past achievements, or by the weight of the party's institutional heritage.[73] New Labour's resolve to break with what it saw as the failed policies of the past would lead also and finally to a novel inflection in its foreign policy. Labour in the past had been charged with being weak, so now it would bend every effort to appear strong. In its more radical moments Labour had proposed opting out of world markets and their consequences, so now Labour would embrace globalisation whatever its discontents. In the 1960s and 1970s the left within the party had begun to question the Atlantic Alliance and by the 1980s the party proposed actually to withdraw from NATO. Under New Labour the alliance with the United States would be reaffirmed and even embraced. Though the choice was in critical respects a restoration of previous policy and as such conformed to a long, bipartisan history, for Labour it was effectively new; and it certainly felt new and different. It was yet another rejection of the party's heritage as it had come to be embodied in the policies, practices and promises of the late 1970s and 1980s. It was that Labour Party out of which New Labour had grown and against which it took on its essential shape and meaning. Understanding that connection, and that repudiation, is the prerequisite to understanding New Labour, at home and abroad. It is an understanding shared by those who made New Labour and who continue to lead and guide it; and the strategic calculations that flow from it have been absorbed into the very fibre of the remade party and the common sense of the government. It is possible, perhaps even likely, that as New Labour's particular past – and the events and traditions against which and through which it came to be defined – fades from memory, the importance of that history will be replaced by a new set of histories and conflicts. Still, the starting point for that story will be New Labour and its already formidable record of achievement, and hence the past that it has come simultaneously to reject but also, in the very act of repudiation, to represent and to carry forward.[74]

Notes and references

1 Richard Wilson, review of Peter Riddell, *Hug Them Close: Blair, Clinton, Bush and the 'special relationship'* (London: Politico's, 2003), *Times Literary Supplement*, 17 October 2003, 13.

2 Both the speed of the decision and the attenuated process that produced it are discussed in Andrew Rawnsley, *Servants of the People* (London: Hamish Hamilton, 2000), 31–8.

3 On the background, see Jim Tomlinson, 'Economic Policy: Lessons from past Labour Governments', in Brian Brivati and Tim Bale, eds, *New Labour in power: precedents and prospects* (London: Routledge, 1997), 11–27.

4 The problem is that the rhetoric of globalisation can be as constraining as globalisation itself and can be used to rationalise particular choices by treating them as the inevitable product of global capitalism. See, for example, Colin Hay and David Marsh, *Demystifying Globalization* (New York: St Martin's, 2000); and Rorden Wilkinson, 'New Labour and the Global Economy', in David Coates and Peter Lawler, eds, *New Labour in Power* (Manchester: Manchester University Press, 2000), 136–48.

5 See Michael Moran and Elizabeth Alexander, 'The Economic Policy of New Labour', in Coates and Lawler, *New Labour in Power*, 108–21.

6 Cited in Peter Riddell, 'Blair as Prime Minister', in Anthony Seldon, ed., *The Blair Effect: The Blair Government, 1997–2001* (London: Little, Brown, 2001), 29.

7 *Financial Times*, 9 October 1997.

8 *Report of the Working Group on the Government Information Service* (London: HMSO, 1997), cited in Margaret Scammel, 'The Media and Media Management', in Seldon, ed., *The Blair Effect*, 523.

9 The estimate is from Richard Rose, *The Prime Minister in a Shrinking World* (Cambridge: Polity, 2001), cited in Dennis Kavanagh, 'New Labour, New Millenium, New Premiership', in Seldon, ed., *The Blair Effect*, 15. See Peter Riddell, 'Blair as Prime Minister', 21–42, and Rod Rhodes, 'The Civil Service', 117–38, in Seldon, ed., *The Blair Effect*.

10 There was some friction between Sir Robin Butler, the Cabinet Secretary in 1997, and the new government; more with Terry Burns, Permanent Secretary at the Treasury. From January 1998, relations were much improved with Sir Richard Wilson's appointment as Butler's replacement.

11 Philip Gould, *The Unfinished Revolution: How the Modernisers Saved the Labour Party* (London: Little, Brown, 1998), xxiii.

12 The actual document agreed by Brown and Blair, not dated but presumably drafted on 1 June 1994, was unearthed by *The Guardian* and published on 6 June 2003. It confirmed the division of labour over policy, but was silent on the supposed agreement for Brown to succeed Blair as leader. That might also have been agreed, of course, but it was not written down in this particular fax drafted by Mandelson.

13 Peter Hennessy, *The Prime Minister: The Office and its Holders since 1945* (London: Allen Lane, 2000), 477; Brown/Blair note.

14 Martin Kettle, 'We can have only one Prime Minister – and we've got two', *The Guardian*, 15 May 2003. More generally, see James Naughtie, *The Rivals: The Intimate Story of a Political Marriage* (London: Fourth Estate, 2001).

15 The quote has been attributed variously to Blair or to a close aide, probably Jonathan Powell, but in either case it captures an aspiration entirely consistent with New Labour's plans for managing both the party and the government. See Hennessy, *Prime Minister*, 478. There has been much discussion of the implications of this concentration of power at the top. See, among others, Michael Foley, *The British Presidency: Tony Blair and the Politics of Publics of Public Leadership* (Manchester: Manchester University Press, 2000); Foley, *John Major, Tony Blair and a Conflict of Leadership: Collision Course* (Manchester: Manchester University Press, 2002); and, for a more sceptical view, Richard Heffernan, 'Prime Minsterial Predominance? Core Executive Politics in the UK,' *British Journal of Politics and International Relations*, V, 3 (2003), 347–72.

16 *The Independent*, 20 July 1998.

17 *The Independent*, 20 July 1998; *Financial Times*, 18 December 1998; *Public Services for the Future*, Cm. 4181 (London: HMSO, December 1998).

18 David Richard and Martin Smith, 'New Labour, the Constitution and Reforming the State', in Steve Ludlam and Martin Smith, eds, *New Labour in Government* (London: Macmillan, 2001), 151.

19 These were preceded by Richard Wilson's unpublished report in 1998. See Hennessy, *Prime Minister*, 491, who sensibly argues that under Wilson's influence a compromise was struck between the new government and its Napoleonic aspirations and the traditional approach of the civil service. For background and context, see Vernon Bogdanor, ed., *The British Constitution in the Twentieth Century* (Oxford: Oxford University Press, 2003).

20 See David Marquand, 'The Blair paradox', *Prospect*, 30 (1998), 19–24.

21 Quoted in Hennessy, *Prime Minister*, 512.

22 Peter Mandelson, 'Introduction', to *The Blair Revolution Revisited* (London: Politico's, 2002), xii–xv.

23 Raymond Plant, 'Blair and Ideology,' in Seldon, ed., *The Blair Effect*, 563. The concept and rhetoric of community apparently remains attractive to David Blunkett and might well be resurrected as a theme in the manifesto with which Labour will fight for a third term. See *The Guardian*, 11 June 2003.

24 See Geoff Mulgan and Charles Leadbeater, *Mistakeholding: Whatever Happened to Labour's Big Idea?* (London: Demos, 1996).

25 John Rentoul, *Tony Blair: Prime Minister* (London: Little, Brown, 2001), 431–5; Douglas Jaenicke, 'New Labour and the Clinton Presidency', in Coates and Lawler, *New Labour in Power*, 35–6. Olaf Palme, the Swedish socialist, used the concept in a comparable manner as early as 1982, and there were no doubt still earlier uses. On Palme, see Giles Radice, *Labour's Path to Power: The New Revisionism* (London: Macmillan, 1989), 9.

26 Jill Lovecy, 'New Labour and the "Left that is left" in Western Europe', in Coates and Lawler, *New Labour in Power*, 50.

27 Blair and Schröder, *Europe: The Third Way/Die Neue Mitte* (London: Labour Party and Social Democratic Party, June 1999). The French socialist leader Lionel Jospin never bought it, of course, but then he also never bought into New Labour's insight about modern campaigning and media management and for that he would paid a very steep price in 2002. See the roughly simultaneously published summer 2002 issues of the *Political Quarterly* and *Esprit* for a detailed set of comparisons.

28 The literature on the Third Way is now quite extensive. Key texts are Tony Blair, *The Third Way: New Politics for the New Century*, Fabian Pamphlet 588 (London: Fabian Society, September 1998); and Anthony Giddens, *The Third Way: The Renewal of Social Democracy* (Cambridge: Polity, 1998). See also Giddens, *The Third Way and Its Critics* (Cambridge: Polity, 2000). See also Gidden's essay, 'Brave New World: The New Context of Politics', in David Miliband, ed., *Reinventing the Left* (Cambridge: Polity, 1994), 21–38, for an essay that anticipates many of the themes in the Third Way discussion but uses quite a different language and remains much less accessible.

29 Neil Kinnock, *The Future of Socialism* (London: Fabian Society, 1985), Fabian Tract 509. For Kinnock the third way was 'democratic socialism', as 'distinct from the stale vanguardism of the ultraleft and from the atavistic and timid premise of social democracy'. This was not quite what later usages were meant to convey. For a broader discussion, see Tudor Jones, *Remaking the Labour Party: From Gaitskell to Blair* (London: Routledge, 1996). For a useful overview of the debate, see Stephen Driver and Luke Martel, *Blair's Britain* (Cambridge: Polity, 2002), chapters 3–5.

30 Blair, *The Third Way*, 3–4.

31 See Alan Finlayson, *Making Sense of New Labour* (London: Lawrence & Wishart, 2003), chapter 4 on the sociological determinism of this variation of the Third Way argument.

32 Blair, *The Third Way*, 20.

33 Blair, speech at The Hague, 20 January 1998, quoted in Ben Clift, 'New Labour's Third Way and European Social Democracy', in Ludlam and Smith, *New Labour in Government*, 61.

34 Giddens, *The Third Way*, 62; Blair, *The Third Way*, 9.

35 Giddens, 'Introduction', in Giddens, ed., *The Global Third Way Debate* (Cambridge: Polity, 2001), 6.

36 See Ed Balls, 'Open macroeconomics in an open economy', *Scottish Journal of Political Economy*, XLIII, 2 (1998).

37 On the 'active welfare state', see Gøsta Esping-Andersen et al., *Why We Need a New Welfare State* (New York: Oxford University Press, 2002). An earlier version of this appeared as an EU Report in 2000 and was excerpted in Giddens, *The Global Third Way Debate*, 134–56. See also Charles Sabel and Jonathan Zeitlin, 'Active Welfare, Experimental Governance, Pragmatic Constitutionalism: The New Transformation of Europe', paper prepared for the international conference on 'The Modernisation of the European Social Model and EU Policies and Instruments', Ioannina, Greece, May 2003.

38 See Stuart White, 'Interpreting the Third Way: Not one road, but many', *Renewal*, VI, 2 (1998); and 'The Ambiguities of the Third Way', in White, ed., *New Labour: The Progressive Future?* (London: Palgrave, 2001), 10–11.

39 *Financial Times*, 18 December 1998.

40 Rawnsley, *Servants of the People*, viii.

41 Giddens, 'Introduction', 2.

42 David Purdy, 'New Labour and Welfare Reform', in Coates and Lawler, *New Labour in Power*, 181–94; Claire Annesley, 'New Labour and Welfare', in Ludlam and Smith, *New Labour in Government*, 202–18.

43 *Financial Times*, 16 July 1998.

44 Seumas Milne put the case for the TUC and public-sector workers, who claimed that their pay had fallen behind the private sector by 16 per cent since 1982, in *The Guardian*, 15 July 1998.

45 *Financial Times*, 15 July 1998.

46 Philip Stephens, 'The Treasury under Labour', in Seldon, ed., *The Blair Effect*, 205.

47 *Financial Times*, 16 July 2002.

48 See Esping-Andersen, 'Equality and Work in the Post-industrial Life-cycle', in Milband, ed., *Revinventing the Left*, 167–86; and, for a broader and more extended treatment, *Why We Need a New Welfare State*.

49 Polly Toynbee, 'The Brownite dream could turn into a real nightmare', *The Guardian*, 23 July 2003.

50 In the TGWU, for example, Tony Woodley defeated the New Labour candidate Jack Dromey; Derek Simpson beat the pro-Blair candidate in Amicus; and Kevin Curran of GMB and Dave Prentis of Unison were also well to the left of the government. See Andrew Murray, 'Critical mass', *The Guardian*, 2 June 2003; and Murray, *A New Labour Nightmare: The Return of the Awkward Squad* (London: Verso, 2003).

51 Rawnsley, *Servants of the People*, 60–2.

52 For a thorough airing of these and other scandals, see Nick Cohen, *Pretty Straight Guys* (London: Faber & Faber, 2003).

53 The key studies are Pippa Norris, ed., *Britain Votes 2001* (Oxford: Oxford University Press, 2002); Anthony King, ed., *Britain at the Polls, 2001* (London: Chatham House, 2002); and David Butler and Dennis Kavanagh, *The British General Election of 2001* (London: Palgrave, 2002).

54 See Mark Franklin, *Voter Turnout: Solving the Puzzle of Electoral Participation* (Cambridge: Cambridge University Press, 2004), for a strongly argued case to the effect that the key to varying levels of participation is the experience of successive cohorts as they first acquire the right to vote and then develop electoral habits and allegiances.

55 The most thorough accounts of New Labour foreign policy, before and after 9/11, are Riddell, *Hug Them Close*; and John Kampfner, *Blair's Wars* (London: Free Press, 2003). See also Richard Little and Mark Wickham-Jones, eds, *New Labour's Foreign Policy: a New Moral Crusade?* (Manchester: Manchester University Press, 2000) and Philip Stevens, *Tony Blair: The Making of a World Leader* (London: Viking, 2004). On the detailed conduct of the war in Iraq, see Peter Stothard, *Thirty Days: Tony Blair and the Test of History* (London: HarperCollins, 2003).

56 Jonathan Schneer, *Labour's Conscience: the Labour left, 1945–51* (Boston: Unwin Hyman, 1988). There were antecedents before 1945, of course, but the war against fascism had drastically transformed the poles of debate and rendered earlier positions less relevant.

57 Lawrence Freedman, 'Defence', in Seldon, ed., *The Blair Effect*, 290–1.

58 Matthew Parris, *The Times*, 6 July 1993, reprinted in *Look Behind You: Sketches and Follies from the Commons* (London: Robson, 1993), 211–12.

59 Blair, *Third Way*, 18.

60 John Kampfner, *Robin Cook* (London: Victor Gollancz, 1998), 41–3; Edward Pearce, *Hummingbirds and Hyenas* (London: Faber & Faber, 1985), 138.

61 Edward Pearce, *The Senate of Lilliput* (London: Faber & Faber, 1983), 129.

62 See Kampfner, *Robin Cook*, 141–6.

63 *Strategic Defence Review*, Cm. 3999 (London: HMSO, July 1998).

64 Cook in *New Statesman*, 6 March 1998, cited in Kampfner, *Robin Cook*, 210–11.

65 Blair, 3 May 1999, quoted in Rawnsley, *Servants of the People*, 276.

66 Rentoul, *Tony Blair*, 423, 509–32; Rawnsley, *Servants of the People*, 257–90.

67 Tony Blair, speech to the Chicago Economic Club, 22 April 1999, excerpted in Andrew Chadwick and Richard Heffernan, eds., *The New Labour Reader* (Cambridge: Polity, 2003), 263–7. On the background, see Kampfner, *Blair's Wars*, 50–3. The ideas for the speech came primarily from Professor Lawrence Freedman of King's College London. The Foreign Office were taken by surprise and unhappy over it.

68 See Andrew Rawnsley, 'The plotters have lost the plot', *The Observer*, 20 July 2003; and Toynbee, 'The Brownite dream', *The Guardian*, 23 July 2003 on the manoeuvring against Blair and on Brown's behalf in the post-war debate over Iraq.

69 Ironically, it appears that the phrase was introduced into discussions of NATO's evolving mission by the German defence minister, Volker Ruhe, who on 7 June 1995 proposed that future military actions might not require unanimous consent from all member states and instead be based on a 'coalition of the willing'. See *Financial Times*, 8 June 1995. Two years later Sir Brian Urqhuart, with long experience at the UN, lamented the fact that the failure of UN peacekeeping missions had led to growing support for the notion of ad hoc 'coalitions of the willing', typically organised around the United States, even within the UN and its bureaucracy (M2 Presswire, 16 September 1997). Roughly a year later the *New York Times* opined that such coalitions were dangerous if they involved only NATO members and should include nations from the region where intervention might occur (*New York Times*, 7 December 1998).

70 The appointment of David Manning to the staff at Number 10 was the critical move. See Kampfner, *Blair's Wars*, 92–4. Again, the Foreign Office were unhappy.

71 See Ross McKibbin, 'Why did he risk it?', *London Review of Books*, 3 April 2003, who sees Blair's aggressive foreign policy as a kind of compensation for the difficulties faced in New Labour's efforts in domestic policy.

72 The formulation is from Tariq Ali, 'Re-colonizing Iraq', *New Left Review*, 2nd Series, 21 (May–June 2003), 10.

73 Blair would reassert these themes again and again. For example, even when faced with intense criticism over the recent war in Iraq and over the reshuffle of June 2003, and with attention still focused on the previous week's decision to defer a referendum on the euro, he returned to the very same and by now achingly familiar arguments in his restatement of policy to the Fabian Society on 17 June 2003. Thus he warned again that 'If we fail to reform public services, then one day the right will come back and demolish the very ethos

on which they are built . . .', and presumably also destroy them institutionally and financially. See Blair, 'The next progressive steps for Britain', speech to the Fabian Society, 17 June 2003, Labour Party.

74 The Cabinet reshuffle of June 2003 prompted speculation about the shortage of Blairites and implicitly suggested that the experiences which shaped New Labour might be becoming a less compelling force. But the changes in the organisation and rhetoric of the party and the achievements of several years of successful government – and of re-election – had by that time already established a tradition that would of necessity continue to shape the evolution of Labour for a long time. Rather more dangerous than the shortage of Blairites was the growing number of ex-ministers for whom party discipline meant very little and for whom the temptation to rebel and embarrass the government might be irresistible. That was surely part of the reason why the rebellion over 'top-up fees' in January 2004 came so close to succeeding. On both of these issues, see Andrew Rawnsley, 'President Blair? Haha', *Observer*, 15 June 2003; and 'Tony Blair's coalition is coming unstuck', *Observer*, 29 June 2003.

Postscript:
Bournemouth 2003

The tensions between the Labour Party's past and its New Labour present were rehearsed yet again in an unusually tense confrontation at the annual conference held at Bournemouth at the end of September 2003. The meeting was held in the aftermath of the Iraq war, with the report of the Hutton Inquiry on the death of David Kelly still looming. The party chose once more to put its difficulties and differences on vivid public display. The outcome of that meeting would demonstrate with some precision the balance between old and new, between Blair and Brown, between the leadership and party members, between the unions and the party, and between promise and results after the longest period of Labour government in history. The government, Blair especially, were sharply challenged, but nevertheless emerged from the conference far stronger and more self-confident than they had dared to hope as, in what was said to be 'a fatalistic mood, Downing Street . . . [had begun] bracing itself for a procession of denouncements and defeats' at the party's annual gathering.[1]

What made the challenge so powerful was the coming together of discontent over the war in Iraq and anger over government policy towards the public sector. The leaders of the major unions were the most persistent critics: they wanted a greater share of the increased government investment in public services to go to their members and, more important, they strongly opposed New Labour's apparent obsession with 'reform'. To speak continually about reform, they suggested, implied that the public sector was basically broken and in need of fixing; and that those who worked in the public sector were obstacles rather than allies in the effort to deliver better service to clients and citizens. The unions' sense of grievance was undoubtedly magnified by the accession to power of new leaders in four of the biggest trade unions – Unison, Amicus, TGWU and GMB. They were an 'awkward squad' in more ways than one:

their dealings with government were strained and awkward – angry on the surface, quick to denounce but all the while ready to deal; their relationship with their members was new and untested and so at least tentative; and they would prove awkward allies for other critics of Blair and the government. The unions would largely determine the agenda of the conference and insist on votes that, it was assumed, would embarrass the government. But their cause seemed to many to be backward-looking and largely defensive, their presentations displayed the same retro look, and they did not help themselves by deciding to establish a new Labour Representation Committee to recall the party to its roots.[2] The name referred to the Labour Party in its earliest incarnation, when it was literally a party founded to defend the trade union interest and nothing else. It was not the banner under which to launch an initiative with a genuine vision of the future.

In the build-up to the conference the unions' discontent seemed to have fused with frustration over the war, and the combination appeared quite dangerous to the leadership. Even if the choice to go to war in Iraq was logically consistent with New Labour's record in foreign policy and with its outlook and practice in other spheres, it was nevertheless a shock to see where that logic had led. The effect was to turn doubters into critics and to revive somewhat the fortunes of the left within the party. The resignations of Cook and Short, whatever the timing, brought them back into a de facto alliance with the left of the party and lent new credibility to the by now familiar charges about New Labour having sold its soul. The two ex-ministers, along with Michael Meacher, were all over the conference fringe, fêted by their former opponents, happy at the renewed attention and eager to lead what appeared for a time to be a broad and growing opposition. In the weeks leading up to conference their influence had been magnified still further by the ongoing testimony to the Hutton Inquiry into the death of David Kelly. The unusually open hearings became a major media event with consequences that went well beyond the question of who was responsible for Kelly's apparent suicide.[3] In the contest between the government and the BBC, the government seemed to come off surprisingly well. Alastair Campbell performed effectively before the committee and defused much of the criticism surrounding his attack on the BBC, while Andrew Gilligan fared poorly. Supervisors conceded that his reporting and note-taking had been sloppy and it became clear that, if the government had 'sexed up' the intelligence on weapons of mass destruction, Gilligan had 'sexed up' what Kelly had told him. The BBC were also put on the defensive by another of its reporters, who claimed to have been pressured to toe the Corporation's line on the matter, and by its executives' admission that they had risen to Gilligan's defence and counter-attacked against Campbell without first determining whether Campbell's complaints had a basis.

As the inquiry drew to a close, it seemed likely that its final verdict would be mixed, judicious and no bombshell. There was as yet no 'smoking gun' implicating Blair or even Campbell in anything especially sordid or improper. Nevertheless, the continued airing of the argument about whether the government had massaged the truth over Iraq had a clearly corrosive effect on its standing with the public. The end of the summer opinion polls showed that trust in Blair and in the government had been seriously diminished. The documents, emails and diaries made public through the inquiry contained few surprises for journalists and politicians familiar with the compromises, fudges and rivalries inherent in politics, but to ordinary citizens the revelations conveyed a sense that at the heart of government were people just as flawed, petty and fallible as anywhere else. Again, the effect was to erode the deference normally accorded British political leaders and the willingness to give the government the benefit of the doubt. Blair was particularly vulnerable on this account, for he had clearly made use of his impressive powers of persuasion and of the public's willingness to listen to him to allay fears and win support for the war in Iraq. Even if the inquiry was in the end likely to absolve Blair and Campbell and the rest of government of any serious responsibility in the death of David Kelly, it had political consequences nonetheless. The difficulties that continued to plague the occupation in Iraq, the failure to locate weapons of mass destruction and the daily exposures of the messy details of life at the political centre together meant that over the course of the investigation criticism steadily mounted. As conference approached, the critics of the war seemed to be winning the argument about the reasons for fighting it and it appeared that they held the moral high ground as well. The desire for peace, the commitment to international law and institutions, and respect for truth were now joined and on the same side. Blair and the government were not, or so it was widely believed.

New Labour was embattled on other fronts as well. Ten days before conference the party lost a by-election at Brent East to the Liberal Democrats. A few days prior to that an impressive roster of Labour intellectuals launched 'Compass', an organisation aimed at rejuvenating the New Labour project by articulating a new 'vision for the democratic left'.[4] The Compass statement was mainly the product of the directors of a cluster of left-leaning think tanks – the Fabian Society, Demos, the Institute of Public Policy Research, and Catalyst – and the editors of two left-wing journals – *Renewal* and *Progress* – and its publication a sign that dissent over the direction of the government was becoming more widespread and respectable even among its academic friends. At roughly the same moment the *London Review of Books* carried two pieces by distinguished historians – Ross McKibbin and Peter Clarke – calling for Blair to resign in favour of Robin Cook or Gordon Brown.[5] On the eve of conference a MORI/*Financial Times* poll revealed that half the voters wanted Blair to resign. The very next day *The Observer* reported that in a poll of Labour Party members over 40 per cent believed the Prime Minister should resign; and the paper's political editor claimed that 'The Prime Minister faces a complete breakdown in his relations with large sections of the Labour Party.'[6] Fantasies of a world after Blair were obviously gripping the minds of ordinarily very cautious commentators, and it appears that even Gordon Brown, the very embodiment of political caution, was infected and tempted. Brown's claim was advanced with special force by Stephen Frears's television drama, *The Deal*, broadcast on Channel Four on 28 September, the first night of conference, and shown earlier that day just outside the conference hall.[7] The point was hardly subtle: Blair had made a deal with Brown to get to the top, Brown kept to his end of the bargain, and Blair was refusing to live up to his. Wasn't it time, so many began to think, for the deal to be truly consummated and for Brown to replace Blair?

As delegates and observers gathered in Bournemouth, expectations ran high that the opposition might well spill over the normal boundaries of conference disputes and become a genuine contest over the direction and leadership of the party. It did not happen. On the contrary, the Blair

leadership survived conference and emerged from it in a stronger position than it had been in before it began. It lost votes over its proposals for
reshaping the health service, though by less than expected; and the
unions forced and won votes on pensions and manufacturing and
employment rights that were meant to put pressure on the government.
But on the whole the government's positions received surprisingly strong
support from the conference floor. Blair's speech was rated a major
success. He was resolute and insistent in defence of the government's
policies on Iraq and on crime, public service reform and taxation, and he
proudly proclaimed that he had 'no reverse gear'. But Blair was also
modest, engaging, self-effacing and respectful of his critics. The sense
that his position was under threat was quickly dissipated, and by the end
of conference at least some journalists were visibly disappointed that
there was no blood on the floor. It would, at the least, have been a more
exciting story.

Why did the challenge to Blair fail to materialise? What, if anything,
caused his critics to back off or reconsider? A major factor was the lack
of a viable alternative around whom or which to rally. For a moment,
especially when he gave his rousing speech on the Monday of the conference, it seemed that Gordon Brown was perhaps making a bid to replace
Blair and might serve as a rallying point for opposition. Certainly his
speech was meant to put distance between him and Blair. Brown men-
tioned 'Labour' more than 50 times, 'New Labour' but once. He called
for support for Blair in reconstructing Iraq, but offered no endorsement
of the decision to go to war. Brown's peroration – 'best when we are
boldest . . . , best when we are Labour' – was both an echo and a rebuke to
Blair who first hit on the formulation but would never have said that the
party was best when it was Labour. Whether Brown was offering himself
as a candidate for the leadership then and there, or merely staking a claim
to the future, was impossible to determine with confidence, but the
distinction was less important than the basic message.

But Brown did not actually go so far as to provoke a contest with Blair.
Part of the reason was that it was technically not on the agenda and the
procedural obstacles enormous; part of the reason was that Brown chose
not to go that route because he knew it would be a boon to the party's
opponents; and partly it did not happen because Blair's fiercest critics
understood that on the issues they cared most about Brown was simply

not with them. Even as he spoke to the hearts of conference delegates in Bournemouth, Brown reiterated his commitment to the restructuring of public services to which trade union leaders were so opposed: 'requiring reform before resources' was how Brown framed it in his speech. And this was not new. It had been Brown and the Treasury who had set the controversial performance targets in health, education and transport and had made meeting them a condition of increased expenditure; and it was they who insisted that wages in the public sector be held down in order to guarantee that more spending led to more services. Brown's rhetoric might be more traditional, his instincts and appeal more tribal, but what was known about his policies and his record did not differ enough from Blair's to inspire a rebellion on his behalf.

Opponents of the government also lacked unity. Before conference there was a visible coming together of the left within the parliamentary party and the 'awkward squad' of trade unionists. But the incipient coalition lacked not only a leader but also a programme. Unions leaders did voice criticisms of the war in Iraq, but as an afterthought, while those opposed to the war did not feel passionately about the unions' agenda. The divergence was evident at the very beginning of conference, when union block votes determined what issues would be debated as emergency resolutions, and Iraq was not one of them.[8] The leadership did allow a debate on Iraq in the context of its overall strategy on defence and foreign policy, but there was no opportunity to vote against the decision to go to war. Nor was there much effort by the unions to evolve an alternative other than simply to oppose government plans for reform of the public services. In consequence, the opposition to Blair was fragmented and largely uncoordinated and so bound to falter. It did so very quickly, in fact, as early in the conference the government's critics all backed away from the notion of changing leaders. Cook and Short claimed they had no such plans, Roy Hattersley ridiculed the idea, and Tony Benn disavowed it.

The reluctance or inability to take on Blair was also a reflection of the fact that party members at large did not really want this. Despite the poll cited just before conference, delegates from constituency parties – who cast half the votes in conference but made up considerably more than half of those on the floor – largely supported Blair.[9] The strongest evidence came when votes were taken on health policy. The NEC's composite resolution laying out the government's health care strategy was defeated, but the results indicated a sharp split between the unions and the members, or at least delegates, from local parties. Party members voted almost 2–1 with the government; unions even more strongly against. The net result was a margin against of roughly 10 per cent, but it had been secured by the exercise of that most controversial franchise, the trade union block vote, which still counted for half the total votes at conference. The effect was to reduce the impact of the defeat and to accentuate the separateness of the trade union interest and the trade union perspective within the party. It also led to renewed debate about the wisdom of the block vote and of the need for public funding of political parties, which would have the effect of breaking the Labour Party's financial dependency upon trade union largesse. Conference delegates were also clearly more supportive of the government's policy in Iraq than had been anticipated. During the debate on defence policy the case for regime change in Iraq met with as much support, at least judged by attendance and applause, as the case against it.

It would be naive to assume that support for the government's position was entirely spontaneous. The response had been worked on assiduously, planned in detail and argued for steadily in the run-up to conference and during the meeting itself. The leadership understood it was under siege and developed a strategy to deal with the problem. What is important in the context, however, is the nature of that strategy and what its implementation meant for the evolution of New Labour. Blair and his allies were given lots of advice prior to conference. Three arguments were made repeatedly. The first was that the government's record was extremely solid and that it should be defended more openly. New Labour's policies had in fact redistributed wealth to the poor and done much to reduce child poverty in particular; they had massively increased spending on health, education and transport; taxes had been raised to fund all this; and there were solid accomplishments on foreign affairs as well – increased foreign aid, debt relief for developing countries and successful interventions in Kosovo and Sierra Leone. Afghanistan and Iraq were obviously more controversial, but the record overall was not hard to defend if only the government chose to do so. But New Labour, it was argued, had chosen to make progress by stealth and to communicate with spin. A more forthright defence, not new rhetoric or new ideas, was therefore what was needed.

The second argument was about ideology: Labour required a more compelling vision of its long-term goals and aspirations and it needed desperately to explain it first to itself and then to voters. That vision should presumably be based on values like community, fairness, social justice and, it was assumed, should offer a more radical critique of existing society and its failings. It might well entail a rhetorical shift towards the left and a restatement of Labour's distinctive identity as the party of progress. This was essentially the argument put forward in the Compass statement produced by Labour-oriented think-tanks just before conference and it was not unlike the 'radical and popular vision' with which Robin Cook would end his book, *Point of Departure*, published just after conference.[10] It was a modernising creed, but a more thorough and radical variation more openly proclaimed.[11] The third batch of advice came from the left and from certain trade union leaders and that was to change course dramatically, reverse the process of modernisation, pull out of Iraq, break with the United States, begin raising taxes and cease all talk of reforming the public services. This was not advice the government and the Blair leadership were likely to heed, and they did not.

It would seem, though, that the leadership listened carefully to its more friendly critics and crafted its strategy in a manner designed to be responsive to calls for a more open defence of its record and for a larger dose of ideology. It was at the same moment, however, more aggressive about its distinctly New Labour outlook and policies. A sure sign that it was paying attention was the appointment of two of the drafters of the Compass statement – Matthew Taylor of the IPPR and Mike Jacobs of the Fabians – to positions in government even before the group went public. Taylor was to work for Number 10 and take responsibility for shaping the manifesto for the next election; Jacobs went to work for Brown. A similar message was sent out informally by spokespeople from Number 10 in the week before conference and it was reinforced by closely coordinated and carefully placed statements from New Labour stalwarts. Just two days before conference, for example, former ministers Alan Milburn and Stephen Byers published nearly identical pieces outlining the emerging message. Byers announced that New Labour was confronting its 'most difficult phase', the phase of 'renewal in office', and he explicitly ruled out turning back to the past.[12] To meet the present test, Milburn argued, the party and the government needed to renew their sense of mission by becoming both 'more Labour and more New Labour'.[13]

Still more transparent signals were sent by the iconography and rhetoric deployed at conference. The walls in and around the meeting were plastered with posters listing in precise detail Labour's achievements in government and they were portrayed in unabashedly progressive fashion. Equally significant was the falling away of the 'new' in the party's efforts to advertise itself. Logos and letterheads proclaiming 'New Labour' were still there, but much less prominent than signs and slogans announcing simply 'Labour'. The phrase 'the third way' was scarcely heard at all. Gordon Brown's stirring speech contributed, intentionally or not, to delivering much the same message: he defended Labour as economically competent but also as determinedly progressive and committed to social justice, the reduction of poverty, the creation of jobs, and improvements in benefits and social services. New Labour had clearly decided that it could reconnect, if not with 'old Labour', at least with 'Labour' and with the party's tradition of reforming zeal.

This move back towards the party's historic identity was coupled, however, with quite forceful restatements of the government's stance towards public services and in terms that grounded its position in values dear to the party. Charles Clarke, the Education Secretary, was very active on the fringe defending the government's choices on education. He was extremely effective in arguing that the biggest gains for children, especially poor and working-class children, would come through investment in pre-school or primary school programmes; that substantial advances could also be made by increasing funding on secondary education and training; and that expanding access to higher education was essential but should be paid for in part by those who would benefit directly from it. University top-up fees were in this view both just and appropriate. Whether he convinced sceptics was not clear, but what was evident was a readiness to engage in the debate and to do so on traditional Labour grounds of social justice and equity as well as on more 'New Labour' grounds of efficiency. John Reid produced an even more fulsome defence of the government's priorities and preferences on health care. He drew a pointed contrast between the government's willingness to invest huge sums in building hospitals, in buying equipment, and in training and hiring staff to repair the damage done by 18 years of Tory neglect and under-investment, and the unions' self-interested defence of existing structures. The unions, he argued, were interested in defending systems and structures and producer interests; the government wanted to relieve pain, reduce waiting times and improve care. The attack was slightly demagogic, but effective, and it was loudly applauded by delegates who were clearly not convinced that the unions' fierce resistance to reform and, in particular, to proposals for foundation hospitals, was entirely reasonable or disinterested.[14]

Clarke and Reid were ubiquitous at conference. So, too, were Patricia Hewitt and Peter Mandelson, who spoke repeatedly at fringe meetings. The same four had been at the very centre of the modernising project when it was first begun under Neil Kinnock. It was fitting that they should be there alongside Blair – and Brown, too, if at a distance – for its mid-course correction and renewal. Would the repositioning take? Would it work, within the party and with the mass of voters outside? Was Blair the person to oversee it? Was it plausible to make the seemingly contradictory claim to be now both 'more Labour and more New Labour'? New Labour had been at its core a repudiation of old Labour. As Bryan Gould reflected in 1998, 'New Labour is not Labour renewed. It is Labour rejected. Renounced . . . New Labour is, and is meant to be, Not Labour.'[15] How could the two now be reconciled? Was it in fact possible to combine traditional commitments to social-democratic values and policies with an equal resolve to a macroeconomic strategy and to fiscal policies reassuring to business *and* reforms aimed at increasing flexibility and offering greater choice within essential public services? Was it possible, as Brown claimed in his speech, for Britain under New Labour to avoid choosing between an American model that privileged the market and a European model that prized social stability over economic growth, and to become not a 'bridge' between the United States and Europe, but a 'beacon', a viable model of its own, a genuine 'third way'? Was it reasonable to imagine that a centre-left party such a Labour could inspire enduring loyalty from its core supporters while tacking so consistently to the centre?

New Labour was betting that these seemingly divergent goals could be combined and that they were the party that could do it successfully. It was a bold wager and a bold move. The chances of achieving lasting success for any ambitious political project must always be rated low, but

New Labour's bid had three distinct advantages that ought to tilt the odds at least slightly in its direction. First, New Labour was the invention of a uniquely talented generation who had tasted defeat in their formative years and who were determined to do whatever was necessary to avoid it in future. Second, the attempt to reconnect New Labour with Labour, to merge the traditions, was made possible because of the previous rout of what had been 'old' Labour and the dramatic transformation of the party's culture, its institutions and its programme. It was perhaps now safe, in this post-socialist and post-labourist era, to bring together what had previously and necessarily been opposed. And most important, New Labour could make a compelling case that what it was trying to achieve – a more just and equitable society with a more robust sense of community that nevertheless provided greater opportunity, choice, flexibility and economic dynamism – was the right prescription for the society that Britain had become. Whether that case would prevail, and New Labour's wager pay off, would become clear only over time. The key test would be whether the 'project' would endure after Blair ceased to lead the party, and even then it might not be evident right away. But the contest over Labour's identity, its past and its future, would be worth watching, for the outcome would be of truly historical importance.

Notes and references

1 *The Guardian*, 25 September 2003.

2 *The Independent*, 25 September 2003; *The Guardian*, 3 October 2003.

3 On this context, see James Fenton, 'Blair in trouble', *New York Review of Books*, 23 October 2003. In the end the Hutton Report would largely exonerate the government and direct its criticisms primarily at the BBC. See the *Report of the Inquiry into the Circumstances Surrounding the Death of Dr. David Kelly C.M.G.*, by Lord Hutton, 28 January 2004.

4 Patrick Wintour, 'Labour's thinktanks in revolt', *The Guardian*, 15 September 2003; Tom Bentley and Sue Goss, assisted by Neal Lawson, 'Labour is drifting in a sea of pessimism; it needs help', *The Guardian*, 15 September 2003; the group's 'manifesto', *Compass: A Vision for the Democratic Left*, is available online at www.compassonline.org.uk. The appeal was strikingly similar to the Manifesto of the 15 MPs who proclaimed themselves New Wave Labour on 24 November 2003. See *The Guardian*, 24 November 2003, and the website: http://newwavelabour.co.uk.

5 Ross McKibbin, 'How to put the politics back into Labour', *London Review of Books*, 7 August 2003; Peter Clarke, 'Peter Clarke explains why he once supported Blair and now believes he should go', *London Review of Books*, 11 September 2003.

6 Peter Kellner, 'What Labour's members really think', *The Observer*, 28 September 2003; Kamal Ahmed, 'Party ready to turn on PM', *The Observer*, 28 September 2003.

7 The production was widely acclaimed. But was it entirely accidental that while the Brown character was strong, thoughtful and utterly dependable, the actor chosen to play Blair – the young phenomenon Michael Sheen – was at the very same moment appearing as the devilish Lucian, the leader of the werewolves, in the film *Underworld*?

8 The issues were the health service, pensions, employment rights and manufacturing.

9 The transformation in the politics of local parties seems to have been the result of changing political beliefs, of the changing composition of the party and, most important, of the decreasing attachment of party members to trade unions. Thus Seyd and Whiteley find very few significant differences in the demography of 'old Labour' party members who joined before Blair became leader and 'New Labour' members who joined after, although New Labour members were slightly more middle class and slightly better educated. However, they also report a very significant decline in party members who were also in trade unions. In 1990 those who belonged to trade unions outnumbered those who did not by 64 per cent–36 per cent; by 1997 the proportions had been reversed: 66 per cent were not in trade unions, only 34 per cent were. See Patrick Seyd and Paul Whiteley, *New Labour's Grass Roots: The Transformation of the Labour Party Membership* (New York: Palgrave, 2002), 35–44; see also Whiteley and Seyd, *High-Intensity Participation: The Dynamics of Party Activism in Britain* (Ann Arbor: University of Michigan Press, 2002), chapter 5. The support Blair has enjoyed from Labour Party members has been reluctantly acknowledged by even his fiercest critics. See, for example, Susan Watkins, 'A Weightless Hegemony: New Labour's Role in the Neoliberal Order, *New Left Review*, n.s., #25 (January/February, 2004), 32.

10 Robin Cook, *Point of Departure* (London: Simon & Schuster, 2003); see also Cook, 'Labour must look beyond the Pebbledash People', *The Guardian*, 20 October 2003; and Martin Kettle, 'Cookites and Blairites must now make common cause', *The Guardian*, 21 October 2003. Among other recommendations Cook had argued for a return to notions and policies of 'stakeholding'.

11 Mandelson had clearly heard arguments of this sort before and was not impressed. He remarked at conference that 'Reasserting ideology and values on its own is frankly not sufficient, especially when this means a tired regurgitation of the themes and clichés from a 1980s editorial drawn from *Marxism Today*' (*The Guardian*, 22 October 2003). Nevertheless, Mandelson had been taking part in weekly strategy sessions with Blair and Philip Gould prior to the conference and so was very much involved in developing a response that in fact went some way towards meeting the call for more vision, ideology and values.

12 Stephen Byers, 'We must follow the example of Mrs Thatcher', *The Independent*, 26 September 2003.

13 Alan Milburn, 'Shift the political geography to the left', *The Guardian*, 26 September 2003.

14 The details of the government's proposals for reforming health care were complex and their likely impact extremely hard to measure. The effect was that the debate was often oversimplified to an unusual degree, with the two sides typically talking past one another. Defenders of the government argued, for example, that the proposals for foundation hospitals had already been so modified as they went forward that the unions' initial objections were fully met. Critics nevertheless continued to warn of the creation of a 'two-tier' system that would make inequality even more firmly entrenched. The outcome of government policy over the long term will presumably resolve the argument, but it will take time. For a surprisingly optimistic assessment, see Polly Toynbee, 'Market forces are going to kill off private health care', *The Guardian*, 22 October 2003. See also the earlier, provisional assessment by Anna Coote, of the King's Fund, who concluded that 'Overall, it appears that the Government is travelling in the right direction – that is, towards a more robustly funded NHS, improved standards of health and social care, more patient-centred services and a system that is trying to reduce inequalities' (*The Observer*, 14 April 2002).

15 *New Statesman*, 29 January 1998.

Appendix: Results of British General Elections, 1945–2001

	Percentage of popular vote						Seats in House of Commons					
	Turnout	Con.	Lab.	Lib.[1]	Nat.[2]	Other	Con.	Lab.	Lib.	Nat.	Other	Government majority
1945	72.7	39.8	48.3	9.1	0.2	2.5	213	393	12	0	22	146
1950	84.0	43.5	46.1	9.1	0.1	1.2	299	315	9	0	2	5
1951	82.5	48.0	48.8	2.5	0.1	0.6	321	295	6	0	3	17
1955	76.7	49.7	46.4	2.7	0.2	0.9	345	277	6	0	2	60
1959	78.8	49.4	43.8	5.9	0.4	0.6	365	258	6	0	1	100
1964	77.1	43.1	44.1	11.2	0.5	0.8	304	317	9	0	0	4
1966	75.8	41.9	47.9	8.2	0.7	0.9	253	363	12	0	2	96
1970	72.0	46.4	43.0	7.5	1.3	1.8	330	288	6	1	5	30
Feb 1974	78.7	37.8	37.1	19.3	2.6	3.2	297	301	14	9	14	−34[3]
Oct 1974	72.8	35.8	39.2	18.3	3.5	3.2	277	319	13	14	12	3
1979	76.0	43.9	37.0	13.8	2.0	3.3	339	269	11	4	12	43
1983	72.7	42.4	27.6	25.4	1.5	3.1	397	209	23	4	17	144
1987	75.3	42.3	30.8	22.6	1.7	2.6	376	229	22	6	17	102
1992	77.7	41.9	34.4	17.8	2.3	3.5	336	271	20	7	17	21
1997	71.4	30.7	43.2	16.8	2.6	6.7	165	419	46	10	19	179
2001	59.4	31.7	40.7	18.3	2.5	6.8	166	413	52	9	19	167

[1] Liberal Party 1945–79; Liberal/Social Democrat Alliance 1983–87; Liberal Democrat Party 1992–2001.

[2] Combined vote of Scottish National Party (SNP) and Welsh National Party (Plaid Cymru).

[3] Period of minority government, February–October 1974.

Index

The Index includes the Introduction; Chapters 1–11; and the Notes and References at the ends of the chapters. Page references in **bold** indicate a defintion or an explanation. Filing order is word-by-word; numbers are arrange in ascending order at the beginnings of sequences.